Perspectives from *Historical Archaeology*

Revealing Landscapes

Compiled by
Christopher C. Fennell

No. 5

SOCIETY *for*
HISTORICAL
ARCHAEOLOGY

Compiled by: Christopher C. Fennell

Contact Information:
Christopher C. Fennell
Department of Anthropology
University of Illinois at Urbana-Champaigne
109 Davenport Hall, MC-148
607 S. Mathews Ave.
Urbana, IL 61801

Cover: John William O'Brien, *Old Man Grey, 1 1/2 miles south of Plainfield on Road to Alton*, 1852. Watercolor on paper. Collection of the Illinois State Museum / Gift of the Dorothy Drennan Estate.

Perspectives from Historical Archaeology is a reader series providing collected articles from the journal of the Society for Historical Archaeology (SHA). Published since 1967, <u>Historical Archaeology</u> is the oldest North American scholarly publication on the archaeology of sites and materials from the historic past, and one of the world's premier publications on this subject. Each volume in the *Perspectives* series is developed on either a subject or regional basis by a compiler, who selects the articles for inclusion and their order. The compilers also provide an introduction that presents an overview of the substantive work on that topic. *Perspectives* volumes offer non-archaeologists a convenient source for important publications on a subject or a region; an excellent resource for students interested in developing a specialization in a specific topic or area; as well as a convenient reference for archaeologists with an interest in the material.

The *Perspectives* series is managed by the SHA's Journal Editor and Co-Publications Editor and is published through the SHA's Print-On-Demand Press. Individuals interested in compiling a volume for publication through this series are encouraged to contact the Series Editors:

J. W. Joseph, PhD, RPA
Journal Editor, SHA
New South Associates, Inc.
6150 East Ponce de Leon Avenue
Stone Mountain, GA 30083
jwjoseph@newsouthassoc.com

Annalies Corbin, PhD
Co-Publications Editor, SHA
The PAST Foundation
1929 Kenny Road, Suite 200
Columbus, OH 43210
annalies@pastfoundation.org

Formed in 1967, the SHA is the largest scholarly group concerned with the archaeology of the modern world (A.D. 1400-present). The main focus of the society is the era since the beginning of European exploration. SHA promotes scholarly research and the dissemination of knowledge concerning historical archaeology. The society is specifically concerned with the identification, excavation, interpretation, and conservation of sites and materials on land and underwater. Geographically the society emphasizes the New World, but also includes European exploration and settlement in Africa, Asia, and Oceania. To learn more about the SHA and historical archaeology, visit www.sha.org.

Contents

Christopher C. Fennell

Carved, Inscribed, and Resurgent: Cultural and Natural Terrains as Analytic Challenges

ABSTRACT

This introduction provides a summary of trends in landscape archaeology over the past several decades, outlines ongoing debates in theories, research questions, and interpretative frameworks, and provides an overview of the selected readings included in this volume.

Landscapes work to slow and fix time (Jackson 1984:8). Within the frame of human perception and analytic capacities, we are fascinated by a contest of three dimensions with a fourth. We try to freeze time by etching maps, excavating through strata, and creating contour models with laser pulses from airplanes. What, then, is time, one might ask. It is the conceptual gloss we offer to stand for the concourse of natural forces and human agency writ in movement upon the earth. As this somewhat ethereal opening indicates, the subjects of landscape analysis and landscape archaeology are highly diverse and often challenge us with prosaic inquiries.

Overview of a Diverse Analytic Domain

Landscape archeology addresses the complex issues of the ways that people have consciously and unconsciously shaped the land around them. Human populations have engaged in a variety of processes in organizing space or altering the landscape around them for a variety of purposes, including subsistence, economic, social, political, and religious undertakings. People often perceive, protect, and shape the land in the course of symbolic processes engaging with their sense of place, memory, history, legends, and the boundaries of realms sacred and profane. Archaeology provides invaluable tools for examining such processes, and we can provide morphological and environmental data on past landscapes that are typically unavailable from other sources.

Landscape analysis thus involves the use of archaeological, documentary, and oral history evidence to study and interpret the ways past peoples shaped their landscapes through the deployment of cultural and social practices. In turn, analysis focuses on the ways in which people were influenced, motivated, or constrained by their natural surroundings. Such a focus on landscapes, rather than a more limited concentration on sites and their relationships with one another, gained significant momentum within archaeology in the late 20th century. The archaeological evidence utilized in landscape studies ranges across a continuum of methods including the uses of satellite and aerial imagery, ground penetrating prospection technologies, ground surface surveys, stratigraphic excavations, topographic modeling, geomorphology assessments, macrofloral and microfloral studies, and paleoethnobotany analysis.

How do we define landscape? Carole Crumley and William Marquardt (1990) emphasized that this domain is defined by both socio-cultural and natural processes. They observed that social changes were often fueled by systemic contradictions, contested resources, structural tensions, and resulting resolutions of those dynamics over time. Key locations in the natural environment often tend to become centers of gravity in cultural activities, whether they are bodies of water, promontories, or remarkable outcroppings of rock. Radiating out from such myriad nodes of significance, one can analyze a diverse set of relationships: hierarchies and the clinal spread of influence; heterarchies with modal or mosaic distributions; and centers, semi-peripheries, and peripheral localities. Similarly, James Deetz (1990) proposed a focus on landscapes as the "total terrestrial context" of cultural activities. Studies in landscape archaeology have thus included those strongly influenced by natural science methods, other methods to analyze the cultural shaping of terrains, and yet others that examine the ways particular cultures have been influenced by their surrounding topographies.

Within the realm of archaeological classifications, Robert Dunnell (1992) challenged researchers to abandon an overemphasis on "sites" spread across a countryside. By emphasizing attempted designations of sites, archaeologists tend to neglect the data presented in the spaces filling the topography between those areas of concentration. Dunnell (1992) proposed that archaeologists reconceptualize space as three dimensions possessing continuous and varying distributions of artifacts shaped by human agency. Within this definition, low-density spaces are as equally interesting as are areas of high artifact clustering. Most critically, an over-simplistic approach of site definitions leads to an open license for construction developers to carve up the terrain between such points in the landscape.

Instilling human meanings into layers of the countryside, Barbara Bender (1998) and like-minded analysts speak of landscapes as cultural "palimpsests" and the embodiment of "sedimented pasts." Terrains reveal evidence of past cognitive investments and shifting modes of cultural identities. Such spaces also represent "taskscapes," as emphasized by Timothy Ingold (1993), which consisted of the ways in which areas were perceived and utilized by past actors. Research questions initially focused on terrestrial subjects have similarly been expanded to address the relationship of particular landscapes with celestial orientations, skyscapes, and related aquatic domains (Corbin 1998; Patterson 2008:79). Archaeologists will also benefit from understanding the interdisciplinary works of landscape analysts and cultural geographers, such as Denis E. Cosgrove (1984), W. G. Hoskins (1977), John B. Jackson (1984, 1994), D. W. Meinig (1979), Amos Rapoport (1969, 1990), Carl Sauer (1963), and Yi-Fu Tuan (1977). Studies of the cultural "production of space" and cognition of landscapes by social theorists provide additional resources for interpretation (e.g., de Certeau 1984; Lefebvre 1991).

A number of studies have attempted to assess the ways in which past people took cognizance of their surrounding terrain. For example, Dell Upton (1985) analyzed the likely ways in which plantation landscapes were perceived by European-American owners and enslaved African-American laborers. White planters often defined their landscapes with concepts of status presentation, vistas, and perceptions of measured space, cardinal ordering, and hierarchical surveillance. Enslaved African-American laborers likely experienced those same cultural landscapes based on landmarks of oppression and relative promises of freedom. Rather than move through a space defined by standardized cardinal direction and measurement, African Americans perceived relative degrees of malevolent surveillance. The importance of north, south, east, and west were dwarfed by the importance of blocked view-sheds within the built environment, and by spaces in surrounding woods where free domains could be experienced even for short periods.

Building on Upton's work, Rebecca Ginsburg (2007, 2010) analyzed the ways in which African Americans sought to navigate the dangers of the plantation and to escape slavery. Enslaved laborers attempted to maintain a "secret and disguised world, as compared to the planter landscape of display and vistas" (2007:37). They moved across terrains by working from the known to the unknown, using their past abilities to carve out a modicum of free movement within the plantation as encouragement that they could similarly navigate greater spaces of escape.

Questions of how social actors perceived and shaped their landscapes were addressed by Christopher Tilley (1994) in his study entitled *A Phenomenology of Landscape*. Tilley presents a theoretical framework for investigating cultural landscapes that spans multiple scales and offers great promise for deployment by other analysts. He proposes that analysts move in ascending analytic scales through somatic, perceptual, existential, architectural, and cognitive spaces (Tilley 1994:7-34). Somatic space consists of sensory experiences and bodily movements – such as the close spaces we habituate and navigate almost in the dark. Perceptual spaces are egocentric in character, inhabited by individual memories and personal spatial encounters. Existential space embraces group dynamics and individual experiences based on group socialization and shared meaning systems. This is a primary measure of cultural landscapes, and includes natural landscape features imbued with social mythologies and meanings. Architectural space addresses the conscious creation and definition of the built environment and erection of boundaries and the containment of spaces. Cognitive space represents an analyst's perspective, reconnaissance, and study of these varied scales as they pertained to a past people (Tilley 1994). Yet, Tilley chose not to systematically employ this framework in the case studies presented in his book, and this approach, although highly promising, has yet to find concerted adoption within the field.

One can imagine the traverse of these scales by

a single social actor in many settings. In teaching landscape analysis and archaeology, I illustrate this span of scales to my students with an interview of a Buddhist monk in Werner Herzog's (2003) documentary film entitled *Wheel of Time*. Young monks make a pilgrimage on foot to Bhod Gaya, a village in India where Buddha is believed to have attained enlightenment. Monks often make this pilgrimage over two years of walking and prostrating themselves in prayer with every other step. Thousands of miles of landscape are crossed, following a cultural trajectory from home monastery to Bhod Gaya, with the intervening space known with an intimacy of the body stretched across the ground every other stride. Interviewing a young monk who has completed such a journey, Herzog (2003) notes a scar on his forehead, the result of touching his brow to the ground over a million times. This is a social actor who has experienced landscapes through somatic, perceptual, and existential investments, and finally in the architectural configurations of Bhod Gaya at his destination. Many analogues for historical archaeology studies can be considered, from an escaping laborer fleeing bondage, to a farmer engaged with his productive domain, from hearth to field to market.

Tilley (1994:21-22) also provides a very useful summary of a continuum of analytic approaches to landscape analysis. In such a schema of contrasts, an approach consistent with the natural sciences and Enlightenment epistemology places emphasis on economic and subsistence concerns. An approach consistent with a humanistic or non-western epistemology instead places emphasis on the meanings with which populations view the landscape. At one end of a spectrum one can imagine approaches dominated by western Enlightenment epistemologies that emphasize landscape as: (i) open and subject to standardized measurements; (ii) desanctified in character; (iii) shaped by concerns of control, surveillance, and partitioning; (iv) an economic domain that is useful within human action; (v) marked by architectural forms that resemble natural forms; (vi) serving as a backdrop to actions; and (vii) providing a stage for actions in time as a linear, measurable progression. In contrast, a non-western concept of cultural landscapes could emphasize terrains as: (i) shaped by different densities of meaning and experience; (ii) sanctified; (iii) characterized by

sensuousness, ritualized engagement, and anthropomorphic associations; (iv) cosmological in import and useful to think with; (v) marked by architectural forms that embody natural phenomena; (vi) serving as a sedimented, ritual domain; and (vii) presenting a spatial matrix for cyclical time (Tilley 1994:20-21; see Anschuetz et al. 2001).

The methodologies for evaluating meaning-laden landscapes and non-western epistemologies can be challenging, however. For example, John Barrett and Ilhong Ko (2009:284) criticize Tilley for relying, through an "unwarranted optimism," on his own intuitions in formulating proposed spatial correlations in his case studies of potential location and view-shed associations in the prehistoric landscapes of Wales and England. Such a phenomenological analysis of past actors' perceptions and intentions in landscape engagement is often criticized as naïve in its methods and for producing interpretations that are very difficult to test and validate (Barrett and Ko 2009; Darvill 2008:67-68; Lekson 1996:889-90). Applications of such phenomenological frameworks may prove more promising in historical archaeology, however, due to the greater body of different data sets available for historic-period studies.

A variety of analytic frameworks have also been refined within natural science approaches to landscape. Geomorphology studies and Michael Schiffer's examination of formation processes provide detailed accounts of how natural phenomena shape and transform terrains (e.g., Goldberg and Macphail 2006; Rapp and Hill 1998; Schiffer 1987). "Systems ecology" looks to large geographic and temporal scales, employs assumptions of homeostasis and environmental equilibria, and asks when carrying capacities limit and motivate societies in different scenarios. The "new ecology" takes a more focused approach, examining smaller-scale terrains and time periods, while pursuing hypotheses of irregular and contingent disturbances that can contribute to biodiversity and cultural specialization. In turn, "historical ecology" looks for an interdependence of natural constraints and cultural agencies and explanations based on multivariate causality (Anschuetz et al. 2001:166-67; Balée 1998; Erickson 1999; Lansing and Kremer 1993; Whitehead 1998; Zimmerer 1994).

Cultural landscapes in historical archaeology often entail erasures and elements of heritage no longer visible on the ground surface. For example, Paul Mullins (2004) has worked in uncovering the heritage of African-American neighborhoods that were erased and transformed by a university in Indianapolis into a "barren urban cityscape" of parking lots and asphalt. Through community engagement this project provides the city residents who were once associated with that neighborhood with at least a "symbolic proprietorship of spaces that today bear no visible traces of African-American heritage" (Mullins 2004:63-64). Similar initiatives employ "participatory mapping" in which Geographic Information Systems computer applications and Global Positioning Satellite receivers enable community members to generate cognitive maps that record their oral histories and perceptions related to each location (e.g., Archibald 1999; Sletto 2009).

Studies and surveys of landscapes have also flourished within the context of cultural resource management (CRM) projects in the United States and United Kingdom. The expansion of landscape archaeology has been paralleled in time by promulgation of laws and regulations requiring archaeological surveys of the terrains to be impacted by large-scale developments. The late 20th century similarly witnessed construction development projects of increasingly large scale. Many new CRM projects examined large topographic spaces while using increasingly sophisticated survey and remote sensing technologies to achieve cost efficiencies (David and Thomas 2008:33-34).

The studies presented in Parts II through V of this book are drawn from the pages of the *Historical Archaeology* journal and attest to the remarkable diversity of subjects and methods encompassed by landscape archaeology. Part II presents articles on the theme of methods and cartographies of analysis, while Part III shifts to studies focused on the ways terrains have been shaped by economics, class, and social identities. Part IV turns to analysis of the ways in which landscapes have been configured by concerns of geometry, ideology, and surveillance. Part V concludes with a number of studies addressing the impacts of racism and inequality on geographic contours.

Methods and Cartographies of Analysis

The articles in Part II address basic methodological challenges and available sources for analyzing past landscapes. William Adams (1990:93) opens this discussion in chapter 2 with a focus on rural topographies and the interplay of cultural and natural domains: "The fence built across a prairie farm becomes a new habitat for plants and animals as trees and shrubs grow from seeds left in bird droppings. The built environment has become a natural one." He outlines the ways in which farmstead sites should be analyzed in the context of the history of surrounding terrains.

Adams' article provides a concise overview of the myriad documentary resources analysts can examine in conjunction with oral histories and archaeological data. Some past texts provide historic-period prescriptions of ideals for the spatial shaping of rural landscapes. Those intended plans were most often ignored in the actual activities of rural families and their enterprises. Other historic-period documents of value to analysts include: books and journals on farm management and design; farm day books recording challenges of terrain and climate; early photographs; maps and atlases; artists' sketches and paintings; aerial photography; early topographic maps by the U.S. Geological Survey; federal surveyors' diaries of pedestrian surveys from the early 19th century; early soil surveys; and the diaries, journals, and correspondence of people absorbed with the contours and events of the surrounding countryside (Adams 1990). Remnants of past landscape investments can also provide visible markers on the ground today, as concentrations of lilacs or day lilies reveal the buried sites of by-gone houses scattered across a backcountry hollow (Adams 1990; Martin 1984).

Chapter 3 presents an overview of field methods for understanding landscape changes of relatively smaller scales. Documentary evidence often provides useful data on garden designs and construction techniques, and the ways in which past site occupants perceived the terrain surrounding them. Archaeological data from soil core probes, linear trench and transect unit excavations, and remote sensing provide data that can be compared and contrasted with documentary records and oral history accounts. Detailed measurements of elevation contours of cultural features also prove very useful in interpreting and analyzing a landscape shaped by human agency. Conrad Goodwin, Anne Yentsch and their colleagues (1995) bring all of these methods and sources to bear in investigating the 18th century Morven plantation in Princeton, New Jersey.

In chapter 4, James Schoenwetter and John Hohmann (1997) demonstrate how a combination of biological, historical, and archaeological data best accounts for changes over time in the landscape called Las Vegas, Nevada. This early Spanish name, translated as "wet meadows," was applied to the area with some reservation in the early 19th century. This label became largely incongruous for that landscape by the early 20th century (1997:41-42). A combination of palynological, macrobotanical, faunal, archaeological, and geological evidence produced an integrated analysis of changing landscape use and topographic conditions over time. A processual-oriented analysis finds that the landscape was less shaped by reactions and adaptations to ecological changes and was instead impacted primarily by the strategic land uses of human agents pursuing socio-economic gains (1997:55-56).

LouAnn Wurst (2007) examines detailed drawings of farmstead spaces, which were published in numerous county atlases in the late 19th century, in chapter 5. Such cartographic publications included renderings of particular farms, with depictions of the overall spatial layouts, main houses, and secondary buildings. Are these informative documents, or were they typically idealized or otherwise inaccurate portrayals? Wurst compares intensive archaeological investigations with corresponding farmstead drawings. She finds the depictions more accurate in portraying the buildings than in reporting on the distribution and character of topographic features across the surrounding landscape (Wurst 2007).

Annalies Corbin (1998) shifts our attention to riverine contours and related cartographic resources in chapter 6. A critical analysis of historic-period maps of the Missouri River's trajectories, channels, and shifting basins can help produce a predictive model for locating and investigating numerous 19th century shipwrecks. In turn, data derived from such maps can be compared and contrasted with evidence from archives of aerial photographs of the same areas (Corbin 1998).

"More than mere illustrations, maps are simultaneously a document, artifact, and metaphor in controlling the politics of knowledge through representation" (Smith 2007:82). In chapter 7, Angèle Smith uses survey maps of Ireland, created by the British military just before the devastating potato famines of the 1840s, to analyze the layers of representation and elision in these documentary sources. In turn, she observes, archaeologists must be aware of the ways in which their own data maps serve to legitimate or contest past and present claims of knowledge and dominion (Smith 2007).

Chapter 8 presents the methods of mapping landscape components with Global Positioning Satellite (GPS) receivers and representing those recorded terrains through Geographic Information System (GIS) computer applications. Steven Smith and his colleagues (2003) used these techniques to investigate the "once-bloody landscape" of Civil War earthworks spread across the lowcountry counties of South Carolina. The strategic choices made in placement of batteries and earthworks were explicated through GIS analysis of surrounding topographic conditions of the mid-19th century. Comparative layering of archaeological and documentary evidence in GIS applications allowed the researchers to identify such past conditions and terrain contours. Those past landscape exigencies are invisible in today's heavily modified topography of drained wetlands and expanded roadway systems (Smith et al. 2003:28-29).

We take a closer look at methods for GIS applications in chapter 9. Edward González-Tennant (2009) describes steps for recording GPS location data and integrating that information with documentary evidence and archaeological site investigations. Moreover, he then formulates new ways to present such diverse data sets to public audiences through GIS applications and the techniques of integrated displays that those computer systems facilitate (González-Tennant 2009).

Terrains Shaped by Economics, Class, and Social Identities

Part III of this book turns to studies of the myriad ways in which landscapes have been shaped by the dynamics of economics, class, and social group identities. In chapter 10, James Delle (1999) presents a study of socio-economic class structures reflected in spatial hierarchies within three coffee plantations in Jamaica. Among other changes over time, class hierarchies during the period of slavery resulted in terrain molded by investments in cash-crop agriculture. In a post-emancipation period following 1834, those agricultural impacts dissipated dramatically, as the African Jamaican population refused to "develop into a rural proletariat" (1999:143). At a closer scale of examination, coffee plantations during slavery were topographies shaped by hierarchies of owners, overseers, and enslaved laborers, and spaces divided into cash crop fields, small provisioning gardens, and a spectrum of production and residential domains. Surveillance and control in this period were also evident through an analysis of "site vectors" and view sheds from the vantage points of planters and overseers across the space of labor production (1999:151-53).

Gender dynamics intersect class structures and the built environment in Deborah Rotman and Michael Nassaney's (1997) study of Plainwell, Michigan in chapter 11. Observing that "there is no single scale of analysis for the study of cultural landscapes because social relations are reproduced at multiple spatial scales," the authors examine the terrain of a homelot and its successive occupations (1997:43). Approaching their study as the investigation of a late 19th century "urban farmstead," they work to deconstruct simplistic urban/rural dichotomies in the analysis of cultural landscapes. Examining the spatial components of successive occupations in this farmstead over time, Rotman and Nassaney (1997:53) found that "lower socioeconomic status lends itself to increased dependence upon women for household production, which in turn results in higher status for women." This study contributes to a growing literature on such intersections, which have focused variously on the "embodiment of sex and gender in landscape forms, differentiating landscape space by gender-linked activities, physically marking landscapes with gender-related images and monuments, and constituting gendered aspects of cosmology and history in the landscape" (Ashmore 2006:211).

Paul Shackel (2004) shifts our focus to industrial landscapes in chapter 12. Early American industries, such as textile works in Lowell, Massachusetts, included planned landscapes in nonurban areas to implement strategies of production efficiency and surveillance of work and residential districts (2004:47). Others, such as the Federal armory at Harpers Ferry, left domestic domains unregulated, resulting in a more organic and eclectic evolution of the townscape. Examining a number of such case studies, Shackel (2004:53) counsels that "[d]esignating industrial places as a prominent part of our past should also be about remembering people and their struggles."

Kenneth Lewis (1999) studies the divergent development of lowcountry and backcountry colonial landscapes in South Carolina in chapter 13. His analysis provides excellent examples of the interplay of topography, natural resources, economic development, and commodity chains. The increase of regional transport and economic infrastructure in backcountry regions in the early colonial period of the 18th century created a "second nature" of features in the cultural landscape that shaped later patterns of movement and settlement. A focus on rice production in coastal, lowcountry plantations, in contrast, created a more static transport and settlement pattern that persisted throughout the colonial period (Lewis 1999).

Margaret Purser and Noelle Shaver (2008) turn our attention, in chapter 14, to dynamics in frontier settlements of the western United States in the late 19th century. Frederick Jackson Turner (1893) proposed a "frontier hypothesis" that emphasized the unique, unplanned, and contingent character of western frontier zones as crucibles for social and political innovation. Later analysts, such as John Reps (1981) and William Cronon (1991), challenged Turner's hypothesis and marshaled evidence of extensive use of urban planning in past development of the western frontier areas.

Plat maps of speculative town designs, along with topographic maps, deeds, tax ledgers, and insurance records, provide valuable data for archaeologists researching such western frontier settings. Contrasts between idealized designs and the actually constructed development of these cultural landscapes provide valuable insights into past social and economic dynamics. Purser and Shaver (2008) examine two case studies of urban planning and actual topographic changes in the Sacramento River region of

California during the 19th century. In doing so, they struggle with analysis at the scale of the community and from the perspective of a larger, regional domain of economic networks in which that localized space was enmeshed.

Christopher Clement (1997) analyzes intersite plantation patterns on Tobago in the Lesser Antilles islands in chapter 15. Examining impacts of aquatic resources, he finds fresh water accessibility shaped the placement of sugar plantations focused on rum production, while all plantations were anchored close to coastal water transport arteries. Considering aeolian resources as well, Clement finds that mills to grind sugar were more easily powered by reliable trade winds than water courses. A view-shed analysis of estate houses, sugar factories, and villages for enslaved laborers produced an interesting insight. Estate houses were placed on rises to take advantage of wind cooling and ventilation, but were primarily situated for intervisibility to other estate houses or populated towns nearby. Rather than each estate house emphasizing visibility and surveillance of its own associated sugar factory and laborers, intervisibility very likely served to enhance a sense of social solidarity among the planter class members themselves (Clement 1997).

Configuring Landscapes of Geometry, Ideology and Surveillance

Part IV of the book includes case studies of the ways in which particular ideologies of difference and solidarity impacted a spectrum of terrains spanning planned gardens, plantations, industrial districts, cityscapes, and related concepts of nationhood. Mark Leone and his colleagues (2005) open this series in chapter 16 with a study of the expressive power of garden designs in colonial plantations. They analyze the manipulations of visual perspective in William Paca's 18th-century plantation on Wye Island, Maryland. Prominent vistas within Baroque garden plans accentuated a consciousness of social surveillance and order (Leone et al. 2005). In other research projects, analysts such as Leone and Grey Gundaker have examined the ways in which African Americans shaped gardens, yards, and cemeteries to reflect their cultural heritage and cosmological

beliefs (e.g., Gundaker 1993, 1998; Gundaker and McWillie 2005; Ruppel et al. 2003).

In chapter 17, Henry Miller (1988) examines the history of St. Mary's City, established in Maryland's Chesapeake basin in the 17th century. Previously perceived as an unplanned, haphazard development, archaeological and historical analysis demonstrated that St. Mary's City was established in accordance with a Baroque urban plan of prominent building locations and related cityscape alignments. While Annapolis also employed a Baroque plan of prominent nodes and alignments expressing power relationships, Mark Leone and Silas Hurry (1998) examine a panoptic landscape of Baltimore's urban design in chapter 18.

Michael Given (2005) studies colonial and capitalist landscape configurations over time on the island of Cyprus in chapter 19. Using strategies similar to British colonial administration, early 20th-century mining operations shaped and defined large terrains through a process of imposed names, contrived maps, surveillance, and control of resources. Overseers' houses were accordingly placed along ridge tops within such territories, positioned "topographically and symbolically above those of the workers" (2005:54).

Turning to the commemorative treatments of battlefields and military cemeteries, Brooke Blades (2003) examines the impact of nationalist ideologies on cultural investments in such landscapes in chapter 20. Examining a spectrum of historical, memorial, and modern topographies, she analyzes the interplay of concepts of regional and national identities, moments of violent sacrifice and destruction, and the tangible facets of associated terrains. A number of battlefield and military cemetery sites across Europe have received notably diverse treatment as a result of these social dynamics.

Tracy Ireland (2003) focuses in chapter 21 on the ways in which concepts of landscape have impacted Australian national identity and archaeological practice. An early paradigm of *terra nullius* provided a means for Europeans to perceive the continent as uninhabited and undeveloped by human societies. Later concepts of the landscape as a hostile challenger of Australians' fortitude and as an unpredictable feminine domain similarly fueled ideas of national identity in the 19th and 20th centuries. Cultural heritage management and archaeological practice in Australia have also been influenced by perceptions of landscapes as domains of nature, rather than as historically and culturally constructed.

Geographies of Racism and Inequality

Part V of this text presents studies examining the contours of racism written upon varied topographies. Charles Orser, Jr. (2006) opens this discussion in chapter 22 by examining how territorial divisions and demarcations served to teach social orders and hierarchies to subjugated populations in Ireland. He examines that ways in which landscapes are employed as "symbolic capital" which "represents a situation of dominance whereby the dominators have shifted their power from overt coercion and the threat of physical violence to symbolic manipulation" (2006:29). Racial ideologies and colonial strategies deployed against the Irish became manifest in hierarchical configurations of the countryside. Colonial strategies have frequently entailed the displacing of indigenous people from their landscape and the concomitant renaming of those spaces within a new system of categories (e.g., Harris 2002).

In chapter 23, I present a study of the racially integrated town of New Philadelphia, established in 1836 in western Illinois (Fennell 2010). Founded by a former slave within a region torn by racial strife, the spatial integration of European Americans and African Americans in the houses and businesses of this town were counterpoised against impacts of separation. Schooling of the town's children and care of the deceased in nearby graveyards were activities marked by segregation. The most profound impact of racism on the town's history, however, may have been the development of a new railroad and the route it traversed across the surrounding countryside.

Jamie Brandon and James Davidson (2005) chart changes from the antebellum to late 19th century in the racial interactions enveloping a substantial lumber mill in the Ozark region of Arkansas. Changes in the segregated and hierarchical divisions of this Ozark "hollow" encompassing Van Winkle's Mill are examined over the span of a century in chapter 24. The authors provide a comparative analysis of the ordered terrain of this "capitalist enterprise" with

that of agricultural plantations (2005:121).

Turning to urban settings in the late 19th and early 20th centuries, Eric Larsen (2003) provides a case study of Annapolis, Maryland in chapter 25. He analyzes the intersections of social group identities with racism and the segregation of urban landscapes in the era of "Jim Crow" discrimination. Larsen finds evidence of a process of landscape segregation that resulted in consequences both planned and unintended. Segregation served variously to facilitate, reinforce, and alter social group identities over time, and "was always an unfinished product" (2003:120).

Scales, Variables, and Perceptions

As this diversity of studies indicates, landscape analysis entails the intellectual challenge of moving interpretive frameworks across multiple temporal and spatial scales. Understanding the changes in particular terrains over time will also typically require an analyst to grapple with a plurality of environmental and cultural variables that impacted past conditions and conduct. As Yi-Fu Tuan (1979:97) observed:

> Landscape, as a distinct concept sanctioned by past usage, is a fusion of disparate perspectives. We have seen . . . how it can be both a domain and a scene, both a vertical view and a side view, both functional and moral-aesthetic. To see landscape properly, different sets of data must be conjoined through an imaginative effort.

Studies in historical archaeology will continue to provide valuable opportunities to expand and refine these methods of investigation.

REFERENCES

ADAMS, WILLIAM H.
   1990   Landscape Archaeology, Landscape History, and the American Farmstead. *Historical Archaeology* 24(4): 92-101.

ANSCHUETZ, KURT F., RICHARD H. WILSHUSEN, AND CHERIE L. SCHEICK
   2001   An Archaeology of Landscapes: Perspectives and Directions. *Journal of Archaeological Research* 9(2): 157-211.

ARCHIBALD, ROBERT R.
1999　*A Place to Remember: Using History to Build Community*. Alta Mira, Walnut Creek, CA.

ASHMORE, WENDY
2006　Gender and Landscapes. In *Handbook of Gender in Archaeology*, Sarah M. Nelson, editor, pp. 199-218. AltaMira, Lanham, MD.

BALÉE, WILLIAM
1998　Historical Ecology: Premises and Postulates. In *Advances in Historical Ecology*, William Balée, editor, pp. 13-29. Columbia University Press, New York, NY.

BARRETT, JOHN C., AND ILHONG KO
2009　A Phenomenology of Landscape. *Journal of Social Archaeology* 9(3): 275-294.

BENDER, BARBARA
1998　*Stonehenge, Making Space*. Berg, Oxford, UK.

BLADES, BROOKE S.
2003　European Military Sites as Ideological Landscapes. *Historical Archaeology* 37(3): 46-54.

BRANDON, JAMIE C., AND JAMES M. DAVIDSON
2005　The Landscape of Van Winkle's Mill: Identity, Myth, and Modernity in the Ozark Upland South. *Historical Archaeology* 39(3): 113-131.

CLEMENT, CHRISTOPHER O.
1997　Settlement Patterning on the British Caribbean Island of Tobago. *Historical Archaeology* 31(2): 93-106.

CORBIN, ANNALIES
1998　Shifting Sand and Muddy Waters: Historic Cartography and River Migration as Factors in Locating Steamboat Wrecks on the Far Upper Missouri River. *Historical Archaeology* 32(4): 86-94.

COSGROVE, DENIS E.
1984　*Social Formation and Symbolic Landscape*. University of Wisconsin Press, Madison, WI.

CRONON, WILLIAM
1991　*Nature's Metropolis: Chicago and the Great West*. W. W. Norton, New York, NY.

CRUMLEY, CAROLE, AND WILLIAM H. MARQUARDT
1990　Landscape: A Unifying Concept in Regional Analysis. In *Interpreting Space: GIS and Archaeology*, Kathleen Allen, Stanton Green, and Ezra Zubrow, editors, pp. 73-79. Taylor and Francis, London, UK.

DARVILL, TIMOTHY
2008　Pathways to a Panoramic Past: A Brief History of Landscape Archaeology in Europe. In *Handbook of Landscape Archaeology*, Bruno David and Julian Thomas, editors, pp. 60-76. Left Coast Press, Walnut Creek, CA.

DAVID, BRUNO, AND JULIAN THOMAS
2008　Landscape Archaeology: Introduction. In *Handbook of Landscape Archaeology*, Bruno David and Julian Thomas, editors, pp. 27-43. Left Coast Press, Walnut Creek, CA.

DE CERTEAU, MICHEL
1984　*The Practice of Everyday Life*. University of California Press, Berkeley, CA.

DEETZ, JAMES
1990　Landscapes as Cultural Statements. In *Earth Patterns: Essays in Landscape Archaeology*, William M. Kelso and Rachel Most, editors, pp. 1-4. University Press of Virginia, Charlottesville, VA.

DELLE, JAMES A.
1999　The Landscapes of Class Negotiation on Coffee Plantations in the Blue Mountains of Jamaica, 1790-1850. *Historical Archaeology* 33(1): 136-158.

DUNNELL, ROBERT C.
1992　The Notion Site. In *Space, Time, and Archaeological Landscapes*, Jacqueline Rossignol and LuAnn Wandsnider, editors, pp. 21-41. Plenum Press, New York, NY.

ERICKSON, CLARK L.
1999　Neo-environmental Determinism and Agrarian "Collapse." *Antiquity* 73: 634-642.

FENNELL, CHRISTOPHER C.
2010　Damaging Detours: Routes, Racism, and New Philadelphia. *Historical Archaeology* 44(1): 138-154.

GINSBURG, REBECCA
2007　Freedom and the Slave Landscape. *Landscape Journal* 26(1): 36-44.
2010　Escaping through a Black Landscape. In *Cabin, Quarter, Plantation: Architecture and Landscapes of North American Slavery*, Clifton Ellis and Rebecca Ginsburg, editors, pp. 51-66. Yale University Press, New Haven, CT.

GIVEN, MICHAEL
2005　Mining Landscapes and Colonial Rule in Early-Twentieth-Century Cyprus. *Historical Archaeology* 39(3): 49-60.

GOLDBERG, PAUL, AND RICHARD I. MACPHAIL
2006 *Practical and Theoretical Geoarchaeology*. Blackwell, Malden, MA.

GOODWIN, CONRAD M., KAREN B. METHENY, JUDSON M. KRATZER, AND ANNE YENTSCH
1995 Recovering the Lost Landscapes of the Stockton Gardens at Morven, Princeton, New Jersey. *Historical Archaeology* 29(1): 35-61.

GONZÁLEZ-TENNANT, EDWARD
2009 Using Geodatabases to Generate "Living Documents" for Archaeology: A Case Study from the Otago Goldfields, New Zealand. *Historical Archaeology* 43(3): 20-37.

GUNDAKER, GREY
1993 Tradition and Innovation in African-American Yards. *African Art* (April 1993) 26(2): 58-71, 94-96.
1998 *Signs of Diaspora, Diaspora of Signs: Literacies, Creolization, and Vernacular Practices in African America*. Oxford University Press, New York, NY.

GUNDAKER, GREY, AND JUDITH MCWILLIE (EDITORS)
2005 *No Space Hidden: The Spirit of African American Yard Work*. University of Tennessee Press, Knoxville, TN.

HARRIS, COLE
2002 *Making Native Space – Colonialism, Resistance, and Reserves in British Columbia*. University of British Columbia Press, Vancouver, BC.

HERZOG, WERNER
2003 *Wheel of Time*. Werner Herzog GmbH, Munich.

HOSKINS, W. G.
1977 *The Making of the English Landscape*. Hodder & Stoughron, London, UK.

INGOLD, TIMOTHY
1993 The Temporality of Landscape. *World Archaeology* 25(2): 152-74.

IRELAND, TRACY
2003 "The Absence of Ghosts": Landscape and Identity in the Archaeology of Australia's Settler Culture. *Historical Archaeology* 37(1): 56-72.

JACKSON, JOHN B.
1984 *Discovering the Vernacular Landscape*. Yale University Press, New Haven, CT.
1994 *A Sense of Place, A Sense of Time*. Yale University Press, New Haven, CT.

LANSING, J. STEPHEN, AND JAMES N. KREMER
1993 Emergent Properties of Balinese Water Temple Networks: Coadaptation on a Rugged Fitness Landscape. *American Anthropologist* 95: 97-114.

LARSEN, ERIC L.
2003 Integrating Segregated Urban Landscapes of the Late-Nineteenth and Early-Twentieth Centuries. *Historical Archaeology* 37(3): 111-123.

LEFEBVRE, HENRI
1991 *The Production of Space*. Donald Nicholson-Smith, trans. Blackwell, Oxford, UK.

LEKSON, STEPHEN H.
1996 Landscape in Ruins: Archaeological Approaches to Built and Unbuilt Environments. *Current Anthropology* 37(3): 886-892.

LEONE, MARK P., JAMES M. HARMON AND JESSICA NEUWIRTH
2005 Perspective and Surveillance in Eighteenth-Century Maryland Gardens, Including William Paca's Garden on Wye Island. *Historical Archaeology* 39(4): 138-158.

LEONE, MARK P., AND SILAS D. HURRY
1998 Seeing: The Power of Town Planning in the Chesapeake. *Historical Archaeology* 32(4): 34-62.

LEWIS, KENNETH E.
1999 The Metropolis and the Backcountry: The Making of a Colonial Landscape on the South Carolina Frontier. *Historical Archaeology* 33(3): 3-13.

MARTIN, CHARLES E.
1984 *Hollybush: Folk Building and Social Change in an Appalachian Community*. University of Tennessee Press, Knoxville, TN.

MEINIG, D. W.
1979 The Beholding Eye: Ten Versions of the Same Scene. In *The Interpretation of Ordinary Landscapes: Geographical Essays*, D. W. Meinig, editor, pp. 33-48. Oxford University Press, New York, NY.

MILLER, HENRY M.
1988 Baroque Cities in the Wilderness: Archaeology and Urban Development in Colonial Chesapeake. *Historical Archaeology* 22(2): 57-73.

MULLINS, PAUL R.
2004 African-American Heritage in a Multicultural Community: An Archaeology of Race, Culture and Consumption. In *Places in Mind: Public Archaeology as Applied Anthropology*, Paul A Shackel and Erve J. Chambers, editors, pp. 57-70. Routledge, London, UK.

ORSER, CHARLES E., JR.

2006 Symbolic Violence and Landscape Pedagogy: An Illustration from the Irish Countryside. *Historical Archaeology* 40(2): 28-44.

PATTERSON, THOMAS C.

2008 The History of Landscape Archaeology in the Americas. In *Handbook of Landscape Archaeology*, Bruno David and Julian Thomas, editors, pp. 77-84. Left Coast Press, Walnut Creek, CA.

PURSER, MARGARET, AND NOELLE SHAVER

2008 Plats and Place: The Transformation of 19th Century Speculation Townsites on the Sacramento River. *Historical Archaeology* 42(1): 26-46.

RAPOPORT, AMOS

1969 *House Form and Culture.* Prentice Hall, Englewood Cliffs, NJ.

1990 *The Meaning of the Built Environment: A Nonverbal Communication Approach.* University of Arizona Press, Tucson, AZ.

RAPP, GEORGE, JR., AND CHRISTOPHER L. HILL

1998 *Geoarchaeology: The Earth Science Approach to Archaeological Interpretation.* Yale University Press, New Haven, CT.

REPS, JOHN

1981 *The Forgotten Frontier: Urban Planning in the American West before 1890.* University of Missouri Press, Columbia, MO.

ROTMAN, DEBORAH L., AND MICHAEL S. NASSANEY

1997 Class, Gender, and the Built Environment: Deriving Social Relations from Cultural Landscapes in Southwest Michigan. *Historical Archaeology* 31(2): 42-62.

RUPPEL, TIMOTHY, JESSICA NEUWIRTH, MARK P. LEONE, AND GLADYS-MARIE FRY

2003 Hidden in View: African Spiritual Spaces in North American Landscapes. *Antiquity* 77: 321-335.

SAUER, CARL O.

1963 *Land and Life: A Selection from the Writings of Carl Ortwin Sauer.* University of California Press, Berkeley, CA.

SCHIFFER, MICHAEL B.

1987 *Formation Processes of the Archaeological Record.* University of Utah Press, Salt Lake City, UT.

SCHOENWETTER, JAMES, AND JOHN W. HOHMANN

1997 Landuse Reconstruction at the Founding Settlement of Las Vegas, Nevada. *Historical Archaeology* 31(4): 41-58.

SHACKEL, PAUL A.

2004 Labor's Heritage: Remembering the American Industrial Landscape. *Historical Archaeology* 38(4): 44-58.

SLETTO, BJORN I.

2009 "We Drew What We Imagined": Participatory Mapping, Performance, and the Arts of Landscape Making. *Current Anthropology* 50(4): 443-466.

SMITH, ANGÈLE

2007 Mapped Landscapes: The Politics of Metaphor, Knowledge, and Representation on Nineteenth-Century Irish Ordnance Survey Maps. *Historical Archaeology* 44(1): 81-91.

SMITH, STEVEN D., CHRISTOPHER O. CLEMENT, AND STEPHEN R. WISE

2003 GPS, GIS and the Civil War Battlefield Landscape: A South Carolina Low Country Example. *Historical Archaeology* 37(3): 14-30.

TILLEY, CHRISTOPHER

1994 *A Phenomenology of Landscape: Places, Paths and Monuments.* Berg, Oxford, UK.

TUAN, YI-FU

1977 *Space and Place: The Perspective of Experience.* University of Minnesota Press, Minneapolis, MN.

1979 Though and Landscape: The Eye and the Mind's Eye. In *The Interpretation of Ordinary Landscapes: Geographical Essays*, D. W. Meinig, editor, pp. 89-102. Oxford University Press, New York, NY.

TURNER, FREDERICK J.

1893 The Significance of the Frontier in American History. *Report of the American Historical Association* 1893: 199-227.

UPTON, DELL

1985 White and Black Landscapes in Eighteenth-century Virginia. *Places* 2(2): 59-72.

WHITEHEAD, NEIL

1998 Ecological History and Historical Ecology: Diachronic Modeling vs. Historical Explanation. In *Advances in Historical Ecology*, William Balée, editor, pp. 43-66. Columbia University Press, New York, NY.

WURST, LOUANN

2007 Fixing Farms: Pondering Farm Scenes from the Vanity Press. *Historical Archaeology* 41(1): 69-80.

ZIMMERER, KARL S.

1994 Human Geography and the "New Ecology": The Prospect and Promise of Integration. *Annals of the Association of American Geographers* 84(1): 108-125.

WILLIAM HAMPTON ADAMS

Landscape Archaeology, Landscape History, and the American Farmstead

Rural Archaeology

The term "rural archaeology" is suggested here as a means of organizing several related approaches in the study of human history. Just as urban archaeology contributes to the understanding of the development of urban areas, rural archaeology makes possible the integration of understanding about rural sites. Urban archaeologists might consider rural sites to be nonurban, but it is really the other way around, for farms preceded cities in antiquity, as well as in American history.

Rural archaeology is defined here as the study of sites which can only occur within a rural context—exploitative and extractive sites like those associated with farming, timbering, and mining. The mere location in a rural setting does not mean that a site lies within the topic of rural archaeology, since ghost towns, forts, and other kinds of sites do not reflect a specifically rural phenomenon. While distinct from urban archaeology, rural archaeology shares some processes in common, like central places and transportation networks. A rural center or node can become an urban setting eventually, and so rural researchers must be familiar with urbanization as a process. Similarly, if archaeologists view frontiers in a dynamic sense, rather than as an edge phenomenon, then the rural area is the frontier for the city/urban landscape. The rural frontier ebbs and flows with soil exhaustion, clear cutting of forests, rise and fall of demand for products, access to national markets, and family life cycles. The rural landscape is the battleground between humans and nature where only temporary victories exist. People clear a forest, plant crops, exhaust the soil, die, the forest returns—only to be cut again in a few generations, and the process

begins anew. As long as equilibrium is maintained, the landscape is rural, but if humans win a tactical victory in one area it becomes a town or city, and the ground so polluted as to make nature's task impossible without considerable time. Rural archaeology is, in part, landscape archaeology or landscape history.

Landscape Archaeology

Landscape archaeology could also be called settlement archaeology, but landscape history is perhaps a better term. Settlement archaeology is familiar to most archaeologists as a movement within the discipline to put archaeological sites within a geographic and environmental context. The word "settlement" in the name, however, has subtilely affected the direction which this area of study has followed, for it focuses upon settlements, meaning villages and dwellings therein, rather than the landscapes upon which those settlements were built. When the landscape is addressed at all, usually only fixed variables like soils, slope factors, distance to water, or other resources are the subject of analysis.

Archaeologists would have a better understanding of rural sites by focusing on landscape *history*. Because archaeology began as a study of urban sites and monuments, the concept of the archaeological site has been that of the house lot, containing the house, yard, and outbuildings. Such a definition is appropriate only in an urban setting, if even then. Using a systems approach, that kind of site is but one small subsystem of the urban system. The system is what archaeologists should be trying to understand, not the subsystem of the house lot.

Some scholars refer to the *built environment* as being separate from a *natural environment*. While this dichotomy is useful for some purposes, it is nevertheless artificial. The built environment, of course, is never really separate from the natural one, but many human cultures like to think that they are above nature, not part of it. Humans build houses, ditches, and fences, and nature tears them down, rots them away, and covers them over. A better viewpoint would use the *affected environment* and the *unaffected environment*. The forest woodlot on a farm provides an example of the affected environment (L. Allen 1888:323–329). From the woodlot has come firewood and fence posts, squirrels for the pot, poke for the salads, and nuts for the Christmas stockings. While the forested woodlot may appear to be "natural" it is no longer unaffected by humans. Certain species of trees have been selected and cut for special purposes, for example, hawthorn cut for fence posts. In addition, when farmers clear adjacent land for planting, the forest is bordered by an ecotone not previously present, with the wildlife biomass increased in potential, as deer and rabbits, for example, find food in the fields and shelter in the forest. Similarly, a forest stream may be natural and unaffected, but once it flows into tilled fields or pastures, it is no longer either natural or unaffected, due to the actions of soil erosion, cattle, and other factors. The fence built across a prairie farm becomes a new habitat for plants and animals as trees and shrubs grow from seeds left in bird droppings. The built environment has become a natural one.

A new definition of what composes a site in a rural setting therefore must be proposed. While this reformulation may cause headaches for cultural resource managers, the rural site is the property owned or controlled by an individual or family. A site is more than just the house, yard, and outbuildings. Thus, a 640-acre farm comprises a site. The farm is a higher-order subsystem, containing many other subsystems. It must be studied in its entirety, not in pieces. Such a site includes affected and unaffected environments. All areas used by a farm family to produce a crop or to produce energy would be included whether the land was owned or leased.

This definition of a rural site was espoused by landscape architects in the 1970s as "open space that is vital for maintaining the traditional man-land relationship of our historic small towns, farmsteads, battlefields, ghost towns, agricultural areas, cemeteries, mines, trails, and camps" (Tishler 1976:54). The survey form William H. Tishler (1976:55) used to study farmsteads included virtually all the variables an historical ar-

chaeologist would choose: "The farmstead survey form . . . contained a matrix for classifying landscape characteristics including topography, vegetation and surface water features for four zones making up the farmstead setting: the vicinity of the buildings, the immediate area around the buildings, the site edges within visual proximity, and the landscape extending around the site."

The landscape history of a farm would detail the history of its land acquisition and usage, and the following questions might be asked: When were forests cleared? When and why were roads and fences built? What tillage practices were used? What crop rotation was used? Once exterior energy sources were captured, what was the effect on the woodlot and on the pasture? Were horses, mules, and oxen kept on the farm after powered farm machinery was used? Was the woodlot cleared for crops, once oil and coal became available for heating and cooking? How does diversification of land use vary through time? What crops were planted? When were orchards planted? Were they replanted after the trees reached maturity?

Boundary Maintenance

According to S. Edwards Todd (1860:57), "If there is any one thing more than another which is a source of constant anxiety and unremitting care to the farmer, it is the erection of suitable fences for enclosing his own grounds for the purpose of excluding lawless intruders, or keeping his own animals within proper bounds." Fences form a practical barrier to keep farm animals restricted to certain portions of the land. But fences also serve legal and symbolic purposes as well. Fences provide boundaries to mark the extent of one's landholdings. The ways the fences are constructed reflect the aspired-to permanence of the holdings. John B. Jackson (1969:33) has argued that fencing animals out of certain areas created a cognitive difference among farmers and ranchers which was distinct from those who fenced animals into an area: "Spaces for containment are therefore apt to grow larger in the course of time, while spaces for exclusion are apt to remain the same or become fragmented.'' In other words, the landholdings of people who fenced animals in created a situation whereby the holdings could grow.

Fencing laws varied from county to county. Farm animals were either fenced out of gardens or were fenced into pastures. Until the mid-19th century, fences were built around crops and gardens to keep animals out. Few subjects raised a more spirited debate than that over fencing, for farmers wanted herds fenced in, while herders wanted the crops fenced. Farmers were told to char their fence posts, to backfill the hole with rocks, ashes, charcoal, or lime to increase their durability, and to use particular kinds of timber: ''The best timber for posts, in the order of its durability, is red cedar, yellow locust, black walnut, white oak, and chestnut'' (Allen 1888:314). The importance of fencing to farmers can be seen in the amount of space devoted to fences in farming manuals. Todd (1860) spent 170 of 459 pages on fences and hedges in his book, *The Young Farmer's Manual*. Excellent discussions of the kinds of fences used (Noble 1984: 118–133) and of the role of fences in American agriculture are available elsewhere (L. Allen 1888: 313–323; Leechman 1953; Hart and Mather 1954, 1957; Zelinsky 1959; Jackson 1969).

Farm Layout

Central place theory is directly applicable to the landscape history of a farm, since the farm's layout is in part a reflection of energy flow and economy of motion. As Todd (1860:28) wrote, ''Convenience would dictate that the buildings should be located as near the middle of the farm as is practicable.'' The higher human energy expenditures are located closest to the house whenever possible, while less intensive activities occur farther away. Thus, on the most efficient farms, the large pastures would be located furthest from the house, because little energy is invested in it on a daily basis. Although a central location had been advocated for many decades, traditional locations next to roads continued to be selected well into this century:

Such arrangement [of farm buildings] as we find in certain parts of the country is obviously the result of tradition rather than of intelligent study of the matter. . . . The house is commonly placed next to the road, the barn 100 feet away from it in almost any direction, and the other buildings fall into any space which happens to be open at the time of their making (Waugh 1914:145–146).

Lewis Allen (1842:116) suggested another advantage to being located away from the roads: The family would be less distracted by gossip and busybodyness, and more inclined toward productive tasks. In a later book, Allen (1888:333) stated the house ''ought to occupy a position easily accessible to the other buildings and fields, and yet be within convenient distance of the highway.'' Isaac Phillips Roberts (1907:82–83) argued against a central location because the work in the distant fields ''forms but a small part of the farmer's activities,'' and farm families should be closer to the road so that they were closer to their community. He argued against being directly adjacent to the road, however; instead, it was best to locate the house back 100 or 200 feet from the road.

According to Todd (1860:28), ''Americans almost universally will erect buildings along the highway, even when such a location would place them entirely on one side of their farm.'' One of the major distinctions between the farmsteads of the Upland and the Lowland South is that those in the uplands are usually located on the main road (Newton 1974). Might the Upland pattern have resulted from a more conservative, traditional system, while the Lowland pattern reflects more widespread adoption of progressive farming ideas? The Upland South is generally regarded as more conservative than the Lowland South, at least in terms of adopting change (Newton 1974). Researchers in areas settled by Southerners during the great westward migrations of the 19th century should consider where the farmers originated. While areas like southern Indiana would not generally be regarded as part of the Upland South, the settlement patterns there are largely those of the upland, because this region's settlers were mostly highlanders from the Carolinas into Tennessee and down the Ohio River.

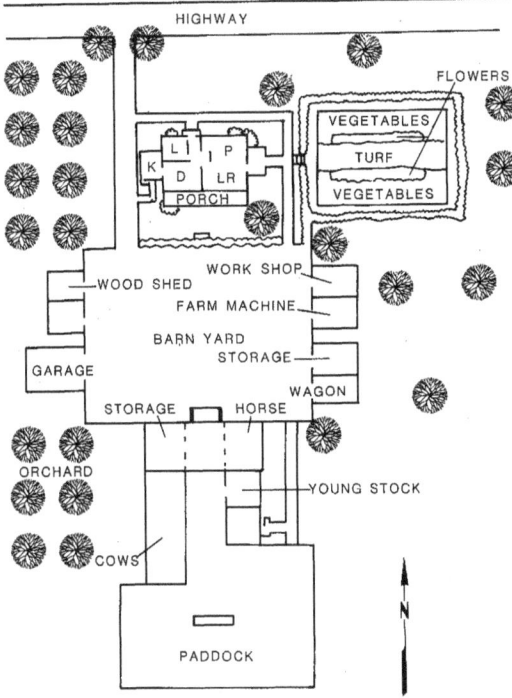

FIGURE 9-1. The ideal farmstead envisioned by Waugh (1914).

In an attempt to remedy many of the deficiencies in farm organization, Frank Waugh (1914) wrote a book in which he described the need for central locations and an administrative center for each farm (Figure 9-1):

> Now, when a man has found a farm and has got possession of a suitable tract, conveniently and compactly located, his next problem is to plan that whole area so that it may be most effectively and economically administered. The first thing to be done is to fix an administrative center. In plain English this usually means the location of the farmhouse and farm building. There are a good many farms now, and ought to be more in the future, on which the business will be conducted from a central office, leaving the dwelling house to seek a detached location. It is plain that the administrative center of the farm should be placed as nearly as possible at the geographical center. The location of buildings at one side or extreme corner of the farm is a very common and expensive fault. It is important, of course, that the buildings be located conveniently to the public road; and in case the public road touches only one side of the farm,

this may justify an eccentric location. The practical question is whether there will be more coming and going between the buildings and the various parts of the farm, or between the buildings and the village corners and the railroad station (Waugh 1914:142–143).

Waugh (1914:143) also offered a scorecard to assess the importance of locational factors:

Administrative convenience (central location) 30%
Public convenience (outlet to village and railroad) 20%
Water supply 15%
Drainage 10%
Protection from winds 10%
Outlook 15%
TOTAL 100%

The progressive agricultural movement produced many journals and books which provided models for farmers to follow and presented the ideal expressed by scientific agriculturalists. Historical archaeologists can investigate how far that *ideal* was adopted by American farmers and became *real*. One historian, Sally McMurry (1988), has begun this broad investigation by examining published house plans for farmhouses and comparing those with houses actually built.

Farmhouses

The spatial arrangements of farm buildings in relation to terrain, roads, and streams is evolutionary, dynamic, changing, yet paradoxically also fossilized. The location of the house and many outbuildings will reflect the prevailing attitudes for the period of construction, as interpreted by the builder and affected by traditional values and ideas, and so that aspect is fossilized. Yet, over time, the farmstead changed to meet new needs. While a set of rules could be established within regional chronologies, these vernacular buildings, after all, were built by people who, as individuals, held their own ideas on what they wanted. Easily seen examples from an urban context would be the pre-fabricated houses placed side-by-side in many post-World War II subdivisions. Although manufactured to be the same, the components were assembled slightly differently by the owners during construction. And, of course, in the ensuing years these were modified further.

In the 1830s, several events occurred making

farm buildings easier to build and making greater variation of architecture feasible. About 1832, house plans for farmhouses began to appear in agricultural publications, reflecting a growing progressive movement in American agriculture (McMurry 1988:5). In 1832 George Snow built the first balloon-framed structure in Chicago, a warehouse, due to a shortage of good timbers (P. Sprague 1981). Augustine Deodat Taylor has also been credited as having built the first balloon-framed building in Chicago in 1833 (Condit 1960: 22). In either case, within a decade frame construction dominated in the western United States. This change in construction was made possible by the availability of inexpensive, machine-made nails. Early machine-cut and headed nails appeared around 1815 and were made until the late 1830s, when they were replaced by fully machine-made nails (Nelson 1968:7–8). Thus, by the mid-1830s, farmers had access to the knowledge and to the technology to build more efficient and less expensive homes and work buildings. Even in 1860, however, one writer felt obligated somewhat to defend this relatively new technique as being as sturdy as framed buildings (Todd 1860:57).

The rural and urban domicile began to evolve along much different lines:

> At mid-century, farmhouse plans, some designed by women, featured efficiency for greater productivity, placed children's nurseries close to the kitchen, and designated rooms for farm 'helps.' This contrasted with the emerging ideal in urban literature of the home as an asylum, where the emphasis was on women furnishing but not planning their houses, where children's spaces were prominent, kitchens were isolated or hidden, and home and work were sharply differentiated (McMurry 1988:5).

The farmhouse reflected other changes in social values and labor. With increased specialization toward cash crops or products, men assumed many of the chores commonly viewed as women's work: "The ideal of the farmhouse as a unified workplace began to erode, and there were noticeable shifts in the arrangements of rooms" (McMurry 1988:6). With increased emphasis on adolescent development in the 1880–1900 period and with smaller families, separate bedrooms for each child became the ideal, if not the norm (McMurry 1988: 6, 177–208). By making their rooms more enjoy-

able, farm families may have been trying to keep their children from moving to better opportunities elsewhere. Kitchens had faced the women's work areas until the 1880s, when they began to face the roadway. This change reflected the changing role of the farm wife from farm market production to family care: "After about 1855, the ideal of the 'profitable farm wife' gave way to another image—that of a worker whose primary tasks more often consisted of services to the family—child nurture, cooking, sewing, cleaning—rather than participating in the farm's production for market" (McMurry 1988:88). Until the mid-19th century, rooms in rural houses were integrated, but by the end of the century the rooms had become segregated by sex and by age.

Progressive farmers may have been better educated than their neighbors, at the least they had to be able to read. While their farms may have quickly reflected the ideals then in vogue in agricultural journals like the American Agriculturalist, American Farmer, or Prairie Farmer, and their ideals viewed as crackpot by their neighbors, many of the progressive ideas would filter through them into the traditional farming system. In any case, someone was reading the 250,000 copies of journals in circulation in 1860 (McMurry 1988:4). The progressive movement in American agriculture was an effort to use concepts of efficiency with the expressed purpose being the emergence of a more capitalist rural economy, in contrast to farming oriented more toward subsistence. With increased mechanization in the 1850s, men's work was made easier, but relatively little was done for women to make their work easier (McMurry 1988:90–91).

Division of labor on the basis of sex has long been observed on the farm, but the distinctions must be tempered by the real world demands farming placed on small families. The work needed to be done, often within a short time frame, and under such circumstances the concepts of men's work and women's work became only academic. With the death of one's spouse a frequent occurrence and rural populations low, a widow or widower always had to do things on the farm which would have been done by their spouse. Women's work traditionally included gardening, food processing,

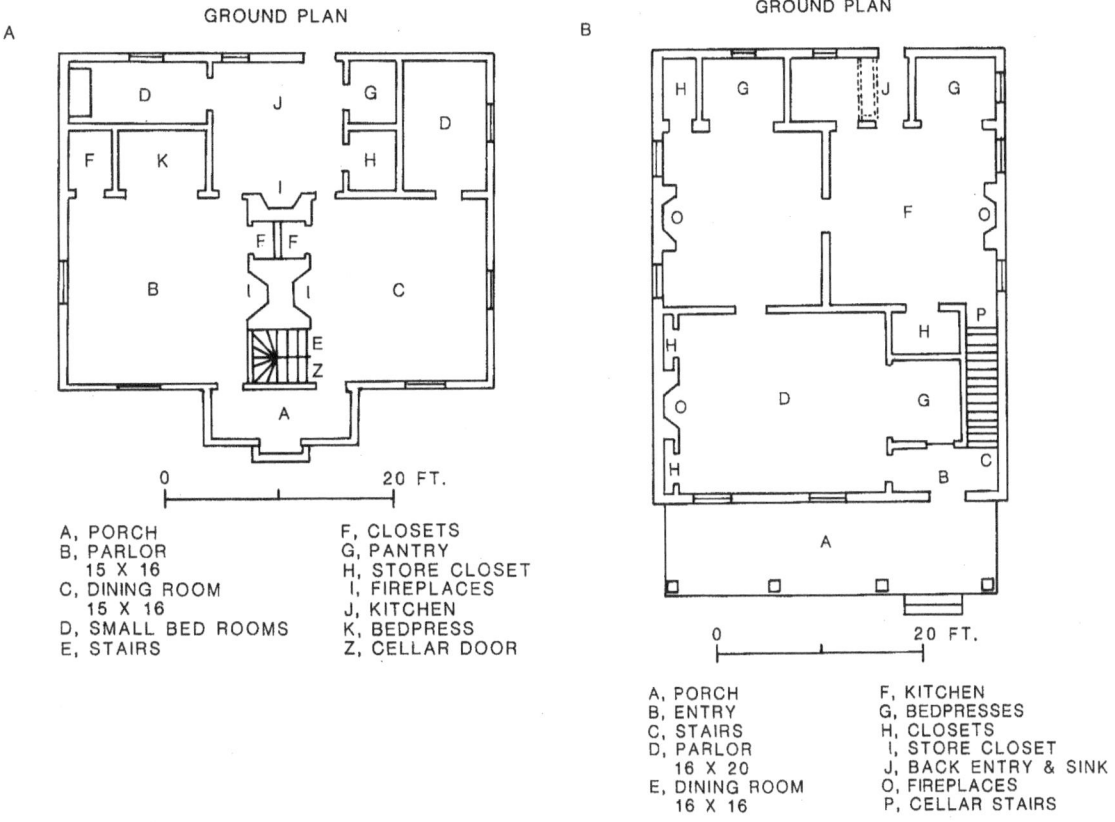

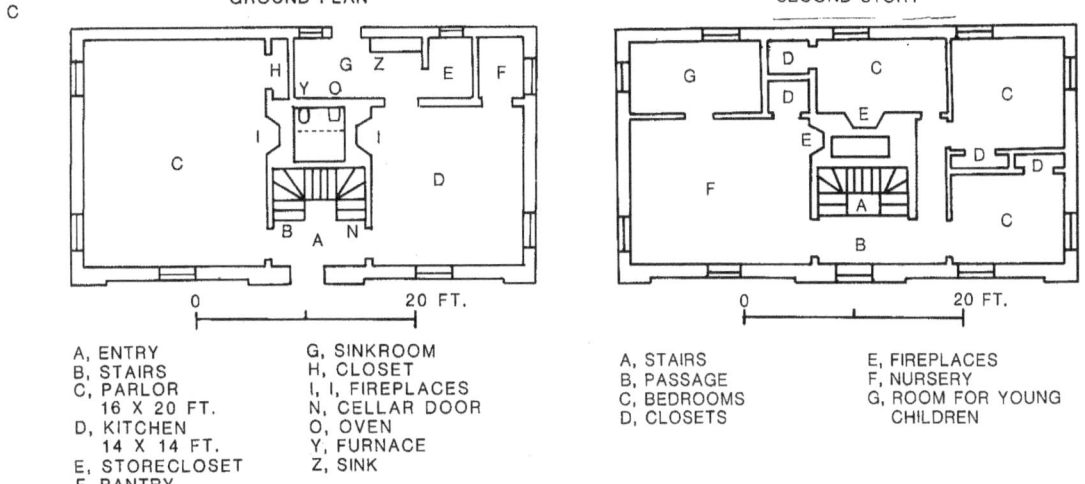

GROUND PLAN   A

A, PORCH   F, CLOSETS
B, PARLOR   G, PANTRY
   15 X 16   H, STORE CLOSET
C, DINING ROOM   I, FIREPLACES
   15 X 16   J, KITCHEN
D, SMALL BED ROOMS   K, BEDPRESS
E, STAIRS   Z, CELLAR DOOR

GROUND PLAN   B

A, PORCH   F, KITCHEN
B, ENTRY   G, BEDPRESSES
C, STAIRS   H, CLOSETS
D, PARLOR   I, STORE CLOSET
   16 X 20   J, BACK ENTRY & SINK
E, DINING ROOM   O, FIREPLACES
   16 X 16   P, CELLAR STAIRS

GROUND PLAN   C

A, ENTRY   G, SINKROOM
B, STAIRS   H, CLOSET
C, PARLOR   I, I, FIREPLACES
   16 X 20 FT.   N, CELLAR DOOR
D, KITCHEN   O, OVEN
   14 X 14 FT.   Y, FURNACE
E, STORECLOSET   Z, SINK
F, PANTRY

SECOND STORY

A, STAIRS   E, FIREPLACES
B, PASSAGE   F, NURSERY
C, BEDROOMS   G, ROOM FOR YOUNG
D, CLOSETS   CHILDREN

FIGURE 9–2. Three house plans by Beecher (1845:262, 266, 267): *a*, house with bedpress in parlor; *b*, house with three bedpresses and no bedrooms; *c*, house with front kitchen.

making clothing and household necessities like soap, doing the laundry, raising poultry, and seeing to the dairying. Men's work included obtaining firewood from the woodlot, plowing, planting, harvesting, and stock tending. Farm daybooks of actual activities reveal that women did many more of the men's tasks than has been commonly realized (McMurry 1988:61). By 1857, as raising chickens and pigs for market became more profitable, men began to take over what was heretofore generally regarded as women's work (McMurry 1988:95).

From the mid-1850s onward, farmhouse plans began to separate the house into public and private areas. The public areas of porch, front door, and sitting room or parlor contrasted with the private areas of kitchen and bedrooms. The isolation of the kitchen was practical, but equally important; it symbolized the growing divergence between farm men and farm women. The kitchen had changed from being a family gathering area to a female bastion. Eating areas were set aside elsewhere in the house, resulting in smaller kitchens—a change of from 240 sq. ft. in the 1840s to 187 sq. ft. in the 1890s—based upon farmer-designers' plans (McMurry 1988:108–114). The *Treatise on Domestic Economy* states:

> There is no point of domestic economy, which more seriously involves the health and daily comfort of American women, than the proper construction of houses. There are five particulars, to which attention should be given, in building a house; namely, economy of labor, economy of money, economy of health, economy of comfort, and good taste (Beecher 1845:258).

Beecher (1845:259) thus argued in favor of economy of labor for the homemaker by not separating the woman's activity areas: "If it be possible, the nursery, sitting-parlor, and kitchen, ought always to be on the same floor." She offered six house plans to show her ideas of domestic economy; these are of interest here in that they provide a woman's perspective on the ideal, to contrast with what was actually built. In each, the main entranceway does not enter directly into a room to avoid winter drafts. To save space, the parlor makes use of a bedpress at one end and thus doubles as the master bedroom (Figure 9–2a), while in another design bedrooms are eliminated entirely by using bedpresses in the kitchen, dining room, and parlor (Figure 9–2b). In the third design, the kitchen is moved from the rear to the front of the house (Figure 9–2c).

Catharine Beecher and Harriet Beecher Stowe (1869:26) provided only one floor plan, but from the aspect of efficiency, it is most interesting because it used a tiny kitchen (9 × 9 ft.) located midway between two large (16 × 25 ft.) sitting rooms. By using a movable screen, these large rooms could be divided into smaller rooms as needed. Beecher and Stowe also devoted 18 pages to earth-closets. (Unlike water-plumbed toilets, earth-closets use dry earth and a bucket). This influential book would have found its way into many farms. The impact of Beecher and Stowe's ideas on farm architecture remains to be studied.

Advice on building farmhouses and outbuildings, and on farming in general, was available from a variety of sources: Foster and Carter (1922) provided detailed plans for farm buildings; Roberts (1907) provided excellent information on architecture and construction of farm buildings; Reed (1883) provided plans and elevations for a variety of farm cottages, along with estimates of costs for materials; and Downing (1852) provided considerable information on materials, interiors, including floor plans and elevations for everything from small farm cottages to country estate houses, as well as outbuildings and even drawings of furniture. Other sources which would be worth examining include H. Allen (1881), L. Allen (1842), Cleaveland (1856), Downing (1967 [1842]), and Waring (1880). From some standpoints the plans and elevations reflect more of what architects hoped would be adopted instead of what actually was built. For instance, Figure 9–3 provides an example of an idealized workingman's house. Nevertheless, these books were widely read and would have influenced builders. The degree of influence should be of interest to researchers, for it will show relative conservatism which may be manifest in other, more subtle ways.

Archaeologists should bear in mind that structures did not necessarily stay put. Farmhouses, barns, and other outbuildings were moved when

Perspectives from *Historical Archaeology*

WORKINGMAN'S MODEL COTTAGE

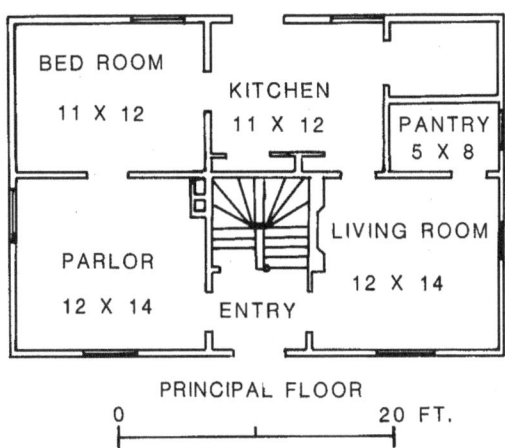

BED ROOM
11 X 12

KITCHEN
11 X 12

PANTRY
5 X 8

PARLOR
12 X 14

ENTRY

LIVING ROOM
12 X 14

PRINCIPAL FLOOR

0   20 FT.

FIGURE 9–3. A workingman's house as envisioned by Downing (1852:94).

the need arose. Todd (1860:48–49) mentioned that he had moved a large barn about 150 feet in a day with one horse and four helpers, and that in the city even more was being done: "The art of moving buildings of all kinds has been so perfected, that in most of our large cities there are those who possess sufficient skill and machinery to move with safety, not only the heaviest wooden buildings, but those that are built of brick, and which are computed to weigh *three hundred tons*" (emphasis in original).

Studying Landscape History

The landscape history of a specific farm will usually be very difficult to establish thoroughly, although several approaches can be useful. With the advent of popular photography in the 1890s, the visual record of rural settings became more widespread, but even before this occurrence, sketches, paintings, and early photographs are sometimes available. In each of the latter, however, researchers must bear in mind that an artist was at work creating an image, and often that was a romantic one. One famous photograph of Windsor Castle shows it sitting high above a river with forested banks; the original negative for that photograph shows shacks and other eyesores located along the riverbank which the photographer removed during printing. A study comparing contemporary photographs with the sketches of houses and farms which appeared in commercial county histories—in which the farmer or city dweller paid for a biography to be included and paid extra for photographs and sketches—might yield interesting information. Aerial photographs are another source of information on landscape history which should not be overlooked. Some of the best quality aerial views—and often the most useful for archaeological purposes because they generally predate deep plowing—are ones taken in the 1930s. In mountains or hilly terrain with some scenic beauty, which would attract photographers, one can obtain time-series oblique photographs which rival aerial photographs in their utility.

Other important sources for landscape history can be found in public records. The starting point in the western United States is the surveyor's notes from the Government Land Office which platted each township into sections. While the quality of the notes varies (and some were faked), these provide important descriptions of the natural vegetation and topography, as well as any early settle-ment. County atlases were often prepared by the tax assessor or others showing the ownership of land parcels; as these change hands through time one can sometimes glean information about individual fields. Early soil surveys show buildings and roads as well as soils; by correlating building location to soil type and slope one can predict the locations of older roads, houses, and outbuildings. In the Bay Springs, Mississippi, area, 76% of the buildings shown on the 1937 soil maps were located on upland soil types with a slope gradient of 7% or more (Adams et al. 1981:68–70). Similarly, older editions of USGS topographic maps show buildings which may no longer be standing. Probated wills, newspaper advertisements, court cases, and other public documents also can be expected to yield information on a farmstead's landscape history. The best source would be from the farm family itself, through its day books, diaries, letters, and oral testimony, although the preservation of these data vary.

The physical examination of the landscape, though, is of primary importance. By mapping extant roads and fences and searching for traces of earlier ones, one can prepare a map of potential fields and pastures. The observant person can find those traces by carefully examining the landscape for erosional and vegetational differences. For example, at Waverly Plantation one can follow an old road or fenceline through the woods by noting the cedar trees which had grown along the edge of an old field (Adams 1980). Henry David Thoreau found old house sites at Walden Pond by spotting lilacs in the woods:

Now only a dent in the earth marks the site of these dwellings, with buried cellar stones, and strawberries, raspberries, thimble-berries, hazel-bushes, and sumacks growing in the sunny sward there; some pitch pine or gnarled oak occupies what was the chimney nook, and a sweet scented black birch, perhaps, waves where the door stone was. Still grows the vivacious lilac a generation after the door and lintel and the sill are gone, unfolding its sweet-scented flowers each spring, to be plucked by the musing traveller; planted and tended once by children's hands, in front yard plots,—now standing by wall-sides in retired pastures, and giving place to new-rising forests: —the last of that stirp sole survivor of that family. Little did the dusky children think that the puny slip with its two eyes only, which they stick in the ground in the shadow of the house and daily watered, would root itself in the rear that shaded it, and grown man's garden and orchard, and tell their story faintly to the lone wanderer a half-century after they had grown up and died,—blossoming as fair, and smelling as sweet as in that first spring (Thoreau 1958:196).

To understand the farm's landscape history requires the wise use of documents coupled with a careful survey using Thoreau's powers of observation.

Conclusions

The historical archaeology of a farmstead site must place that site within the context of the farm as a whole, not just the house and yard. The farm was a system with many subsystems. While the farmstead itself is an important subsystem, it is only one part. By examining the farm within the context of landscape history, a better understanding of the relationship between the domicile and the land will be created. Because the farm had to respond to a variety of outside forces and ideas, it is a microcosm of those changes in broader society. The placement of structures in relation to one another and to the outside world reflects the degree of conservatism and innovation for the farmer. By examining the acceptance by farmers of the progressive agriculture movement, modern researchers can establish their relative conservatism, and by comparing conservatism and progressive farmers' successes and failures may reach a better understanding of this process.

REFERENCES

ADAMS, WILLIAM H. (EDITOR)
1980   Waverly Plantation: Ethnoarchaeology of a Tenant Farming Community. Heritage Conservation and Recreation Service, Atlanta, Georgia.

ADAMS, WILLIAM H. STEPHEN D. SMITH, DAVID F. BARTON, TIMOTHY B. RIORDAN, AND STEPHEN POYSER
1981   Bay Springs Mill: Historical Archaeology of a Rural Mississippi Cotton Milling Community. National Technical Information Service, Washington, D.C.

ALLEN, HORACE L.
1881   The American Farm and Home Cyclopedia. Davis and Curtis, Indianapolis.

ALLEN, LEWIS FALLEY
1888   Farm Buildings. American Agriculturalist 1. New York.

BEECHER, CATHERINE E.
1845   A Treatise on Domestic Economy for the Use of Young Ladies at Home and School. Harper and Brothers, New York.

BEECHER, CATHERINE E. AND HARRIET BEECHER STOWE
1869   The American Woman's Home. J.B. Ford, New York.

CLEAVELAND, HENRY
1856   Village and Farm Cottages. Appleton, New York.

CONDIT, CARL W.
1960   American Building Art: The Nineteenth Century. Oxford University Press, New York.

DOWNING, ANDREW JACKSON
1852   The Architecture of Country Homes. D. Appleton, New York.

FOSTER, W. A. AND DEANE G. CARTER
1922   Farm Buildings. John Wiley and Sons, New York.

HART, JOHN FRASER AND EUGENE COTTON MATHER
1954   Fences and Farms. Geographical Review 44Z:201-223.
1957   The American Fence. Landscape 6(3):4-9.

JACKSON, JOHN B.
1969   A New Kind of Space. Landscape 18:33-35.

LEECHMAN, DOUGLAS
1953   Good Fences Make Good Neighbors. Canadian Geographical Journal.

MCMURRY, SALLY
1988   Families and Farmhouses in Nineteenth Century America: Vernacular Design and Social Change. Oxford University Press, New York.

NEWTON, MILTON B., JR.
1974   Cultural Preadaptation and the Upland South. In Man and Cultural Heritage: Papers in Honor of Fred B. Kniffen, edited by H. J. Walker and W. G. Hagg. Geoscience and Man 5:143-154.

NOBLE, ALLEN G.
1984   Wood, Brick and Stone: The North American Settlement Landscape, Vol. 2 Barns and Farm Structures. University of Massachusetts Press, Amherst,

REED, S. B.
    1833   Cottage Houses for Village and Country Homes, Together with Complete Plans and Specifications. Orange Judd, New York.

ROBERTS, ISAAC PHILLIPS
    1907   The Farmstead: The Making of the Rural Home and Lay-out of the Farm. Macmillan, New York.

SPRAGUE, RODERICK
    1981   A Functional Classification for Artifacts from 19th and 20th Century Historical Sites. North American Archaeologist 2:251-261.

THOREAU, HENRY DAVID
    1958   Walden, Or Life in the Woods. Harper and Row, New York.

TISHLER, WILLIAM H.
    1976   Survey and Inventory Procedures for Historic and Cultural Features in Rural Areas. Echoes of History 6:54-54.

TODD, S. EDWARDS
    1860   The Young Farmer's Manual. The American News Company, New York.

WARING, GEORGE E.
    1880   Farmer's and Mechanics Manual. E. B. Treat, New York.

WAUGH, FRANK
    1914   Rural Improvement. Orange Judd, New York.

ZELINSKY, WILBUR
    1959   Walls and Fences. Landscapes 8:14-20.

CONRAD McCALL GOODWIN
KAREN BESCHERER METHENY
JUDSON M. KRATZER
ANNE YENTSCH

Recovering the Lost Landscapes of the Stockton Gardens at Morven, Princeton, New Jersey

ABSTRACT

A variety of field techniques for the recovery of buried landscapes has been successfully and unsuccessfully used in the Midatlantic. Using examples from Morven, the utility of several are surveyed here. Of particular service was the practice of recording elevations as feet (ft.) above-sea-level readings; it permitted planned variations in garden contours (i.e., terraces, falls, sunken groves, drainage grading) to be observed across wide areas of the site. The system of measurement used in the 18th century, based on Renaissance surveying techniques, and knowledge of its use in designing gardens, enables modern archaeologists to predict where key elements of older landscapes may be found below ground. Other methods discussed include the use of the split spoon auger, the steel T-probe, post hole digger, backhoe trenching, checkerboard excavation, and areal excavation. While none is particularly unique or innovative, using them in combination provides the archaeologist with powerful tools for interpretation of buried historic landscapes.

Morven: The House and Gardens

In 1783, when Annis Stockton decided to advertise Morven for rent after her husband Richard's death, the house was home to five children aged 10 to 20. Its surrounding yard held a carriage house, a granary, an ice-house, a wagon house, and *two* ornamental gardens (*New York Gazette* 1785). At this time both gardens were in disorder and in need of repair (Sheridan and Murrin 1985:17). In 1987, when a landscape study of Morven began, no one knew for certain whether or not the early gardens were simple, ornate, designed for pleasure, or essential units of a productive working farm. Since no documents clearly and precisely told of the gardens' design, and since preservation and restoration of the house and its grounds obviously required knowledge of their prior form, contents, and use, the New Jersey State Museum hired an archaeological team consisting of an historical archaeologist, Dr. Anne Yentsch; an ethnobotanist, Dr. Naomi F. Miller; and a phytolitharian, Dr. Dolores Piperno, to provide information on the evolution of the gardens. A primary concern was whether or not enough of the original garden remained below ground to warrant its restoration.

Morven is one of New Jersey's most historic homes (Figure 1) because of its construction and subsequent use by individuals prominent in Princeton's, New Jersey's, and the nation's history. Richard and Annis Stockton built the house and gardens in the 1760s; Richard became one of New Jersey's signers of the Declaration of Independence, and the Stocktons hosted several leaders of the Revolution at Morven—George Washington, for example, was a close friend. The home, which became one of Princeton's architectural landmarks, remained for nearly 175 years in the Stockton family, many of whom became prominent in their own right (Yentsch et al. 1987:1–3). For example, Commodore Robert Field Stockton, who owned and occupied the house between 1837 and 1866, led the Pacific Squadron during the Mexican War (1846–1848) and for a very short period afterwards acted as Governor of California; he also earned another place in U.S. naval history by promoting the single propeller and iron-clad ships (Yamin 1989:3). Between 1928 and 1945, Robert Wood Johnson, of Johnson & Johnson, rented Morven from family descendants. Next, it was occupied by New Jersey Governor Walter Edge and his family. In 1953, Morven was acquired by the State of New Jersey as the Governor's Mansion and remained so until the early 1980s (Yentsch et al. 1987:1–3). It is the aforementioned associations with famous personages that give Morven its historical significance and is one reason why, in 1986, the house became a satellite museum of the New Jersey State Museum in Trenton. Between 1987 and 1989, it was open to the public as a "museum in the making," and exhibited the process of historic preservation

FIGURE 1. The House at Morven. (Photo by J. Crilley; courtesy of New Jersey State Museum.)

in action. Closed from January of 1990 to July of 1992, the house and archaeology exhibit are now reopened to the public once more.

Theoretical Considerations

The archaeological research incorporated into the public interpretation programs of 1987, 1988, and 1989 addressed the symbolic uses—past and present—of the American landscape while displaying the process of recovering an earlier landscape (e.g., Yamin 1988; Yentsch 1988c). During the time the excavation units represented in profile in Figure 2 were open, for example, guides at Morven would point out the remnants of the 18th-century walkway and suggest that Richard Stockton may have paced upon its stones while making up his mind to sign the Declaration of Independence:

The depth of the walkway, buried beneath his grandson's more elaborate walk, denotes the passage of time [through] the visibility of the walk; the visitors' very presence simultaneously bridges time, projecting the event forward until it partakes of the present. There is no gainsaying the presence of the walk; its existence is as sharply defined as a signature on an 18th-century document (Yamin and Yentsch 1989:7).

We also brought the perspective of anthropological history to the study. With the help of James Deetz, the archaeological team created for the project an analytical framework to depict how each subsequent generation reformed the original landscape in ways that could reveal the sequential series of the then prevalent societal attitudes toward the past, toward family and home, toward the roles—monetary and symbolic—of a family farm. Reflected in these changing attitudes are a series of culturally construed—and hence mutable—world views in which the landscape provided a material, symbolic dimension framing daily life. This mate-

Perspectives from *Historical Archaeology*

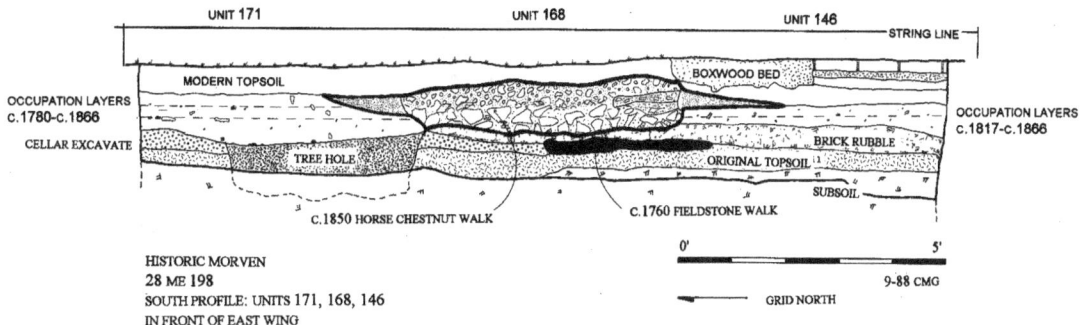

FIGURE 2. Profile of ca. 1850 Horse Chestnut Walk and earlier features off the East Wing (from Yentsch et al. 1987).

rial dimension is read as a series of buried features, surviving natural elements, and preserved plant remains that allow the archaeological delineation of the evolving garden form.

Broadly speaking there are, in archaeology as in anthropology and history, two groups of scholars: the fact seekers who hone their craft to obtain new facts, and the macrotheorists who hone more abstract models. One historian described them as either truffle hunters or parachutists: "The first group grub about with their noses in the dirt, searching for some minute and precious fact . . . the second float down from the clouds, surveying the whole panorama of the countryside, but from too great a height to see anything in detail very clearly" (Stone 1981:8). Ivor Noël Hume realized 40 years ago that archaeology is tied to craft. This is not something much discussed among historical archaeologists, for discussions of techniques do not arouse the same intellectual passion as macrotheory. He searched for garden facts in Williamsburg (Noël Hume 1974) with a field crew who might be said to have apprenticed with him; he taught them to truffle-hunt. These archaeologists then went out and searched for 17th-century houses and 18th-century gardens in the Chesapeake. Overviews are given in Martin (1991) or Kelso (1992). In retrospect, Noël Hume nudged Chesapeake archaeologists to consider the myriad of minute details that combine to form the social landscape. As landscape archaeologists whose research areas stretch from Maine to the West Indies and Virginia to

Hawaii, we too have become avid truffle hunters because it is the method that best enables the recovery of a buried field, barn yard, working or pleasure garden wherever it is located.

The techniques used at Morven are ones that have been refined and polished for more detailed search and recovery on landscape studies of 18th- and early 19th-century gardens at Old Economy Village (De Cunzo et al. 1990, [1994]), Wye Island (Bescherer and Yentsch 1989; Goodwin and Kratzer 1989a), Grumblethorpe (Bescherer, Goodwin et al. 1990), Belmont (Yentsch and Kratzer 1991), Cliveden (Yentsch 1992a), the Highlands (Bescherer, Kratzer et al. 1990), Tulip Hill (Yentsch and Kratzer [1994]), in the town gardens of Annapolis (Yentsch 1984, 1986, 1988a, 1989, 1990a; Paca-Steele and Wright 1987; Shackel 1987; Goodwin and Kratzer 1989b), on plantations in the Carolinas (Yentsch and Kratzer [1994]), and on. The methodologies employed for the collection and analysis of Morven botanical data—an existing plant inventory, dendrochronology, soil and pollen studies, and examination of phytoliths— were reported previously (Yentsch et al. 1987; Miller and Yentsch 1988; Yentsch 1990b; Miller et al. 1990). Here, the concern is with field techniques that, with one important exception, are applicable cross-culturally. The exception—discussed in more detail below—is the employment of a field strategy that incorporates and makes use of folk models, or native views, of the landscape.

In all cases, the data are ordered within an anthropological framework organized according to the sequence of households that lived at each site. Close attention is paid to the relation between events in the family life cycle and clusters of activities observable in the archaeological record (cf. Beaudry 1984, 1988; Brown 1987; Yentsch 1988b, [1994]). Households are defined as composed of the people, not necessarily related by kinship ties, who occupy any given domestic site and who share in the daily activities associated with the sphere of household production (cf. Goodwin et al. 1992; Pulsipher 1993a, 1993b). The domestic site includes the house, adjacent outbuildings, and the external space associated with them. The daily tasks are those associated with social sustenance—eating, sleeping, resting, leisure—and reproduction of the family unit, together with the economic activities needed to sustain it. This broad definition permits the contrast between the household and family, and further comparison with the community and its system of politico-jural relationships, rights, and obligations (e.g., Yentsch [1994]). This approach reflects concern for understanding the social interaction of past people and its role in the formation of the archaeological record; concern with the social logic of space; and knowledge of the past culture in which a garden was situated.

In studies of garden landscapes, historical archaeologists use documents to create contexts of use and of thought, to give names, sometimes faces, and even life records to the men and women who created the gardens (Figures 3, 4). Situating the social actors of past times firmly within the ethnographic context of their own eras and cultures, and using this framework to provide firmly grounded ethnographic analogy, reveals the logic organizing a community. Knowing the logic by which a past culture operated provides a basis for projections about what their members were likely to do in a given situation. This information is of great utility in deciding where to dig, how deep to go, and what to expect. It is part and parcel of a landscape archaeologist's craft.

At Morven, the research team searched continuously for a model of 18th-century spatial logic in documents and in the ground that would provide data not only to help interpret garden features as

FIGURE 3. Annis Boudinot Stockton. (Courtesy of New Jersey State Museum.)

they were revealed, but also to allow for predictions regarding the appearance and meaning of the whole of Morven's past landscape. As is revealed in the course of this presentation, in this effort the archaeologists were successful.

Methods of Testing and Excavation

Hole, Flannery, and Neely (1969:24) observed that "digging down into the unknown" is a romantic and exciting concept, but constitutes clumsy and poorly-planned archaeology. At Morven, even as the first public tours stressed unknowns, modern means for previewing sites were used. These included remote sensing; mechanical stripping; trenching; the excavation of intermittent

FIGURE 4. Commodore Robert Fields Stockton. (Courtesy of New Jersey State Museum.)

partially traced some modern pipe and wire lines and suggested a buried path northeast of the house, the overall results of the remote sensing were disappointing in that the depths of features were misidentified and several large features that one would have expected to be detected—i.e., a 10-×-20-ft. expanse of cobble-paved forecourt, a 200-ft. garden path, a buried foundation—were not:

> As can happen with geophysical surveys, this one found some unexpected features [mostly unknown drain pipes] but did not detect expected features. The cause . . . is not known, possibly remnants are too small, too scattered, or too much masked by other things (Bevan 1987:5).

Bevan (1987:4–5) also indicates that a communications antenna for the Princeton municipal building on an adjacent parcel seemed to cause strong interference to the radar in some cases, varying thickness of asphalt in the parking lot seemed to cause noise in some cases, and extensive landscape alterations on the north side of the house may account for the lack of detection of the 18th-century tree-lined walk. The depth of the buried foundation at 9 ft. below grade may simply have been too great for the equipment used, especially when the intervening "noise" from demolition and landscape alteration are considered.

Exploratory Probes

Before discussing the field methods—trenching and large area excavation—that were of the most use in recovering information on the gardens, a brief discussion of other field techniques is in order. Critical to these is the fact that the built landscape in an 18th-century garden is not composed of artifact-rich deposits such as those that fill privies and wells, but is more often an artifact-poor imprint made by features the dimensions of which may be less than 6 in. across, consisting of individual plantings such as those illustrated in Figure 5, or 100 ft. in width or length, such as a terrace or a garden walk. To bring an entire garden down to the level of the 19th century at a reasonable pace, record it, and then strip down to the 18th century is laborious, expensive, and takes time not usually allowed in restoration schedules or by the enthusi-

5-×-5-ft. units along, in this case north–south, transects; a sampling plan of excavation units patterned like a checkerboard; and various types of probes and/or windows into the soil. Each met with varying degrees of success.

Remote Sensing

After determining the soil at Morven suitable for radar work through an electrical resistivity test, Geosight of Pitman, New Jersey, employed ground-penetrating radar using both a 180 MHz and a 315 MHz antenna, a proton magnetometer, and an electromagnetic induction meter as tools to locate and define buried landscape features on the property (Bevan 1987). Although the instruments

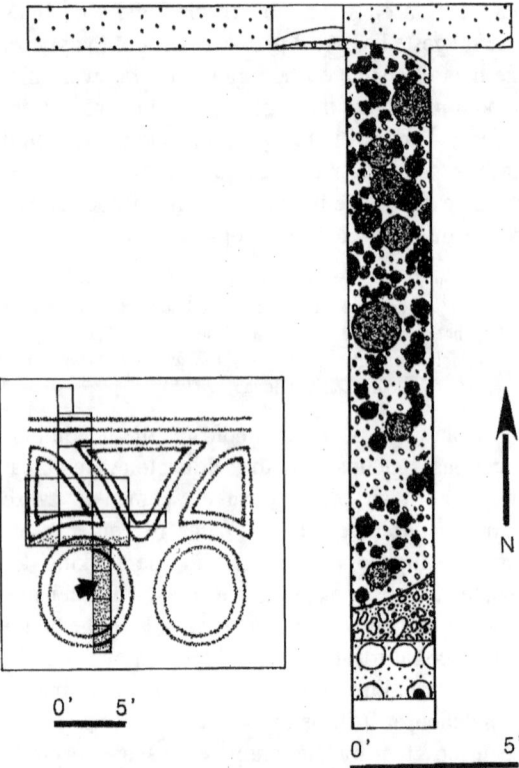

FIGURE 5. Plan view of garden beds showing clusters of individual plantings at Grumblethorpe. (Redrawn by Julie Hunter Abbazzia from field drawings in Bescherer, Goodwin et al. 1990.)

The first, and least destructive, type was to sample the lower layers with a split-spoon auger. Although it did not produce results that could be used to construct stratigraphic sections with precise elevations, this tool gave the team a qualitative feel for what lay ahead; it provided data on sediment content, consistency, and sometimes artifacts that aided in making decisions on excavation strategy. The split-spoon was used frequently and was always helpful.

Second, the team also used a steel T-probe to locate buried brick paths and to trace building walls, but this tool was not as useful as had been hoped at Morven, where brick rubble and fieldstone were abundant across the entire site. Still, the probe enabled the researchers to locate large sections of a brick-paved mid-19th-century walkway and work area leading to an ice-house, and to trace a fieldstone-lined carriage way extending from the 1760s forecourt toward Stockton Street (Figure 6).

Third, a post-hole digger was used to test the depth of deep fill layers. The fill sequences required to make a terraced garden into one single level expanse of yard can be so deep that the impression gained by excavation is similar to that of digging through subsoil—an impression further intensified because terrace fill is often derived from excavation of a new cellar or cellar extension.

Patterned placement of large cores, shovel test pits, or auger holes as a sampling strategy are sometimes used as a testing procedure to locate structures, features, or landscape changes. Yentsch (1992, pers. comm.) reports that at Reynolds Tavern (Annapolis, Maryland) in 1982 auger holes were used in a test pattern spaced 10–15 ft. apart, but the placement was too far apart to extrapolate and obtain meaningful sections; artifact recovery was too sparse to firmly date soil layers. More recently, similar results were obtained from a 50-ft. pattern of shovel test pits laid out in transects across the Cliveden landscape (Lewis 1991; Yentsch 1992a). Deagan (1981), however, used this technique successfully at St. Augustine as did Rubertone (Rubertone and Gallagher 1981) in Providence to locate and define both horizontal and vertical depositional patterns in urban situations.

At Morven, the cores from the post-hole digger

astic private donors who fund much of the garden restoration in the United States. Further, the Morven grounds were located inside a small town; its perimeters were hidden on land that has been developed as adjacent Stockton lands were divided and sold. Unlike many Chesapeake gardens—e.g., Colonial Williamsburg (Noël Hume 1974), Carter's Grove, Kingsmill (Kelso 1984b), Monticello (Kelso 1984a, 1990), Bacons Castle (Luccketti 1990), see also Kelso and Most (1990)—at Morven there is very little plow zone that can be safely removed by machine, a situation characteristic of many Midatlantic gardens. To excavate large areas expeditiously, therefore, requires a system that allows one part of the excavation to move downward prior to the rest. At Morven four types of exploratory probes were used for this purpose.

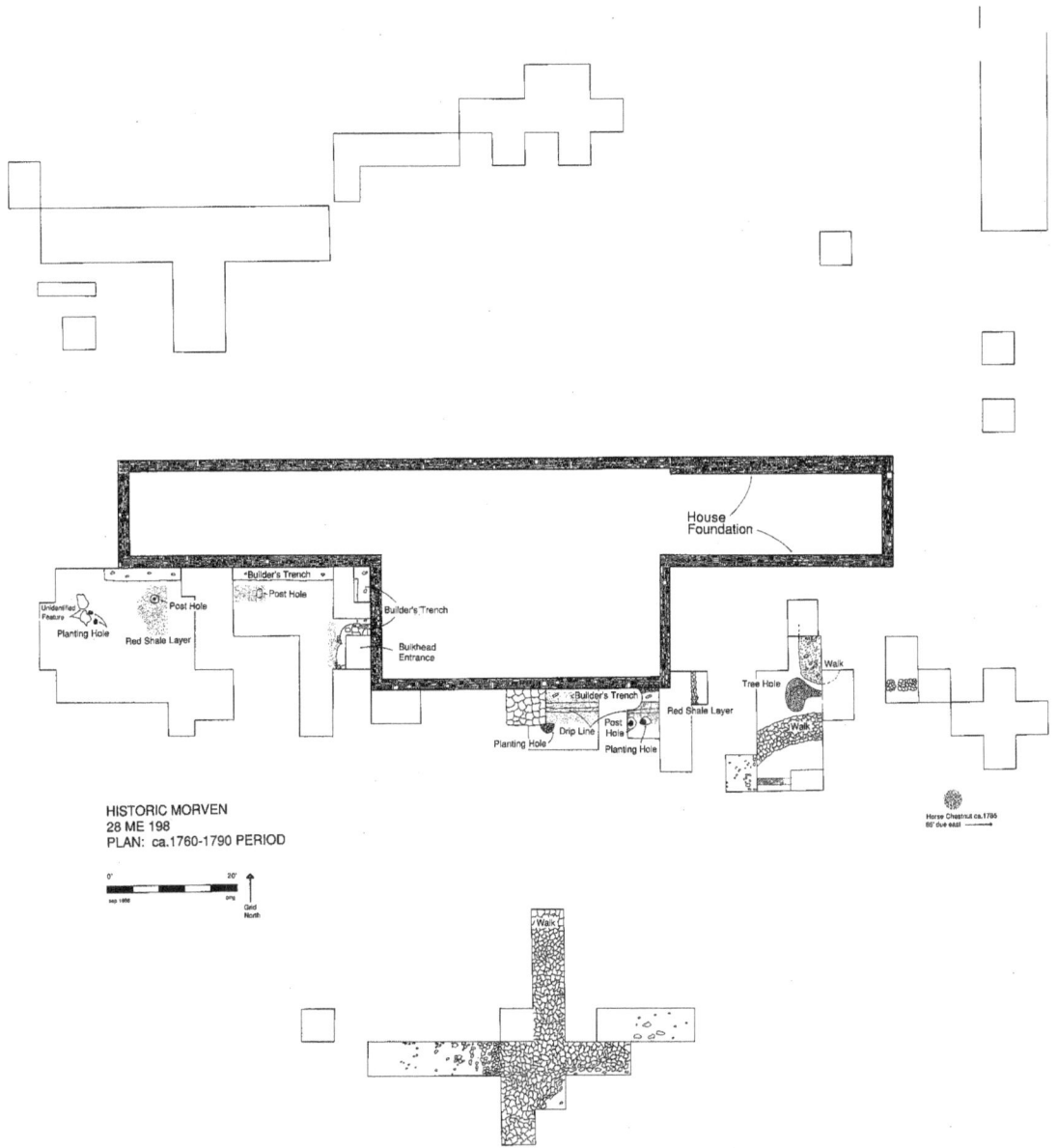

FIGURE 6. Plan view of 18th-century garden features at Morven, including the cobble-paved lower forecourt in the south yard which extended towards Stockton Street (from Yentsch et al. 1987).

were useful as one means of evaluating fill deposits (see section on terraces, below) while small auger cores were used routinely in a variety of ways to preview and assess work in progress. The digger was not used often, but used judiciously it was informative and saved labor. The reasons why the technique was useful in one archaeological context and not as useful in another are still unclear. It seems likely that the type of information sought is pivotal. Landscape archaeologists need data on features that are broadly spread on the ground but whose boundaries are often less distinct than those of a well or privy pit. They choose not to search for artifact "hot spots" because they obtain their best data from in situ features and soil layers. Overall, difficulties noted by McManamon (1981, 1984) and Elia (1987), as well as the work at Morven and the authors' ongoing research at other sites, is a convincing argument that auger cores are not a dependable way to define garden landscapes. If they are used, however, auger techniques should always be employed by working outward from a known point or feature on the past landscape, and not in sampling (cf. Elia 1987).

Fourth and finally, the Morven team sometimes excavated one unit—the standard excavation unit at Morven was a 5-ft. square—in a given block of units down to subsoil rather than proceeding stratum-by-stratum across the entire block. This was done to provide a larger-scale view of sediment stratigraphy, possible features, and artifact content in the particular area selected. On occasion, this method was employed to meet the Museum's need for a good, illustrative photographic record or a provocative on-site "unit exhibit," as well as to provide data for the archaeologists. In addition, excavation of some areas at Morven, especially at doors and paths, was delayed because of their practical utility in the overall public interpretation program.

Larger-Scale Sampling Procedures

To recover information both on the broad landscape forms such as terraces and paths and on structural elements or smaller garden features like beds, the Morven archaeologists used three different strategies: checkerboard excavation, backhoe trenching, and areal excavation. Each of these methods had strengths and weaknesses, but having the option to alter excavation method as the field situation warranted and when considered with the practical issues of time, budget, and public access and interpretive programs proved most useful for the archaeology program.

The first strategy, which made use of an excavation plan in which alternate units were dug in a checkerboard pattern, proved moderately useful at Morven, especially for defining small-scale features, but it was not as valuable in the preparation of yard-wide profiles. Braidwood and Howe (1960) noted that underlying strata at sites can pitch and toss in unanticipated ways; it often seemed at Morven that they did so precisely in those units which, in terms of the checkerboard sampling pattern, fell within the not-to-be-excavated sequence of units.

The second, trenching, is a technique used successfully again and again at Morven as well as at gardens in the Philadelphia region (Bescherer, Kratzer et al. 1990; Bescherer, Goodwin et al. 1990; Yentsch et al. 1990; Yentsch and Kratzer 1991). It also was useful at the Calvert site in Annapolis in understanding grading and filling episodes across the site (Yentsch 1989), and more recently at the Kalaupapa farmstead site on Molokai, Hawaii, in understanding both sediment formation and sweet potato cultivation techniques (Goodwin 1994). Trenching proved particularly effective as a means to establish variations in earlier surface grades or the presence of terraces.

At Morven the initial trench plans were designed to obtain a long north–south profile across the entire yard by means of a 5-ft.-wide backhoe trench (Figure 7). Because crucial sensitive features were often located close to buildings, the excavation of the mechanically dug trenches arbitrarily stopped 75–100 ft. from the house, and hand excavation took its place. Data on the 18th-century garden appeared first in the profile of Trench 3, which revealed a terrace fall. The archaeologists also observed the edge of a wide set of fieldstone steps that provided passage from the main terrace to a lower garden in Trench 3. Continuation of the terrace fall line to the west was found in Trench 4, to the east. Conversely, no evidence of terracing was revealed in the profile of Trench 6. Thus, the first season's trenching located one corner of the garden, but without further information on other boundaries, the garden's formal design remained elusive.

When time and budget permit, areal excavation, the third approach, can be the preferred strategy if

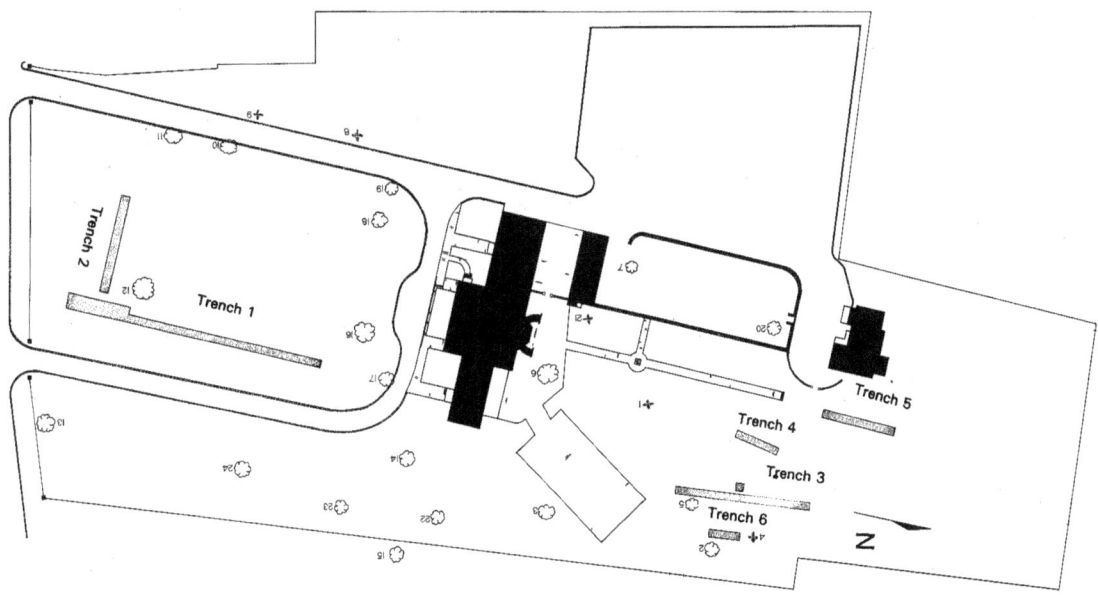

FIGURE 7. 1987 trench and site plan (from Yentsch et al. 1987).

one wishes to obtain the maximum information possible. At Morven, as stated earlier, it was not feasible nor necessarily desirable to excavate the entire property. This procedure, therefore, was employed only in particularly sensitive sections of the site, especially in areas adjacent to the main house and outbuilding and in other areas where the aforementioned methods had revealed principal garden features or multiple changes in the landscape. As demonstrated below, information derived from this method has proved crucial not only in understanding the buildings, and their alterations, on the property, but also in learning about how the principal elements of the sequential gardens related to those buildings to form the different landscapes.

Field methods designed for testing and excavation of buried landscapes, however, are not the only paths to information for discerning gardens of the past. The landscape archaeologist must have some idea of what kinds of elements past inhabitants had in their gardens, how they were constructed, and why the people chose particular features and placed them in a distinctive arrangement. Historical documents and previous archaeological studies can provide insight.

Terraced Gardens and Horizontal Planes

Among European horticulturists garden terraces were a favored means of preventing soil erosion or rainwater runoff, and providing level garden beds (e.g., Nourse 1988[1700]; D'Argenville 1988 [1712]; Spence 1988[1751]). As landscape archaeology is carried out in other geographic locales and the depth of knowledge increases, practitioners still are discovering that terracing was a technique used in virtually all periods in many different regions including China, Africa, South America, and the Near East (e.g., Spencer and Hale 1961; Kirch 1985; Denevan et al. 1987:215–236; Miller and Gleason [1994]). During the Italian Renaissance, people realized that the dimensions used in a set of terraces could be manipulated in one of two ways to achieve different visual results, and hence their boundaries and fall lines became important elements in creating rural vistas (Wölfflin 1966 [1888]). With cultural artifice, by manipulating the exterior boundaries of a terrace to angle outward or inward, 18th-century designers could and did intentionally bring the focal point of their garden closer or make it seem more distant even as they masked the extent of the optical illusion with natural plantings (Leone 1988; Weber et al. 1990: Figures 9.6, 9.7). They also worked with two garden views in mind: (1) that of the outsider looking into the garden, i.e., the public vista; and (2) that of the insider looking out toward society, i.e., the private vista (Yentsch [1994]:chap. 6). With respect to the former, terraces also gave an appearance of unity to the disparate vegetation and planting beds that formed the garden; they provided the architecture. With respect to the latter, terraces and their illusions allowed planters to appropriate visually more land than they actually owned (Hunt and Willis 1988).

At Morven, terraces, and their planting beds, were studied by visualizing a garden as a series of flat horizontal planes, relatively shallow, that articulate in one way or another with each other (cf. Leone and Potter 1988). The construct of a horizontal plane is a relatively simple one; it is a living surface like many of the soil layers that archaeologists see. The horizontal plane, however, is one that was created as a level surface extending over a broad area, often 150 ft. or more, as a foundation for a garden. As such, it is unlike other archaeologically defined soil layers. The horizontal plane has finite boundaries that were artificially imposed on the earth. Within its confines, as within the walls of a house, a villa, or fortified city, spatial relationships were created by smaller, distinctive units of garden space. When a garden had outlived its usefulness, when fashions changed, or when a garden was damaged by natural or human-made cataclysms—hurricanes, winter gales, fire, or war—residents often rebuilt anew on the older surface. They usually began by adding new soil. Thus, a garden's surface—like Near Eastern tells and Florida shell mounds—rose over time. In this, the building and subsequent evolution of early gardens contrasts sharply with modern construction, which usually begins by digging deep and cutting away the soil for subterranean garages, deep cellar and basement foundations, destroying elements of the land no longer wanted.

In an 18th-century terraced garden, the horizontal planes contain the parterres and are linked by terrace falls, by garden walks that follow major

FIGURE 8. The mid-18th-century garden layout at Sabin Hall Plantation, near Warsaw, Virginia. (Photo by C. M. Goodwin.)

axes, and by exterior boundaries—fences, hedgerows, or lines of trees—that encompass the garden as a single unit, binding together the different terraces, and providing verticality. They provide passage through the garden, contain it, create different social spaces within it, and provide varying access to these social spaces and their related vistas. Establishing the boundaries of a garden and the passageways through it is of major importance in understanding the spatial relationships created in a garden's design.

Garden boundaries and passageways vary in terms of their archaeological visibility. At the William Paca Garden in Annapolis, the 18th-century boundaries were provided by thick brick walls, and, once located archaeologically, variations in the depths of their baselines delineated the terrace fall lines (Little 1967–1968; Leone 1984, 1987). See also maps in Paca (1983), or her illustration in Yentsch et al. (1987). At the later Paca Garden on Wye Island, the boundaries were provided by more naturalistic elements, by land contours, and by the meeting of sky and land (Bescherer and Yentsch 1989). Because the site underwent no major alteration in the 19th century, the boundaries are still clearly visible today, as they are at some southern plantations (Figure 8). At Morven; at Grumblethorpe and Cliveden—both in the Germantown sector of Philadelphia; and at Belmont—in Philadelphia, overlooking the Schuylkill River, the garden boundaries were also provided by walkways and terraces, but major episodes of landscape change effectively covered and hid them. Construction material—local field stone and limestone, or, in later gardens, gravel, ash, and charcoal—and microstratigraphy, created because the construction materials required periodic replenishment of walks, gave them less archaeological visibility than the sturdy brick features of Chesapeake gardens.

The recovery of a buried landscape is further complicated by the custom of hauling in soil to build up or level ground surfaces. This practice has been observed in many New England yards (Deetz 1977; Moran et al. 1982; Reinke and Paynter 1984; Beaudry 1986). The same situation exists at most Philadelphia and Annapolis gardens. Occasionally the fill may be as deep as 9 ft., e.g., the William Paca Garden in Annapolis (Little 1967–1968), but it is normally less on a household lot, although it often reaches impressive depths when analysts look at city landscapes as entities in themselves (Yentsch 1992b). Its presence is one reason why Deetz (1977:15) cautioned that, in contrast to prehistoric sites, at historic sites, ''it is not uncommon to encounter soil that seems disturbed but is in fact a deposit of sterile fill that might be three feet thick or more.''

Sources for 19th-century fill were often rural fields outside cities, and hence the fill could contain sterile subsoil; the anomalous, artificial profiles it creates, however, are not always visible in small, shallow, or single excavation units. Although an analogous layer of clean, sterile fill from the 18th century was present at Morven, created from an on-site displacement of soil during the construction of the first cellar, the deepest fill sequences were also those associated with the 19th century. These, as elsewhere, speak of the 19th-century practice of using fill to enrich and build up town lots (Praetzellis and Praetzellis 1992:80), or to hide unsightly and out-of-fashion activity areas. As noted earlier, use of a post-hole digger or large auger in such deposits permits excavators to probe deeper to verify that the base of cultural deposition has actually been reached.

Considering the practice of artificially raising the contours of the land from the perspective of the Grumblethorpe garden, Bescherer, Goodwin, Kratzer, and Yentsch (1990) suggest such earth-moving may have been prompted by the ungainly encroachment of urban development into a naturally beautiful ''prospect.'' In some cases, 19th-century lot division had cut and divided the 18th-century terraces themselves and, in other cases, it had simply inserted visual distractions, i.e., new house lots with homes, barns, and outbuildings, into the rural vista. In isolated, rural areas or on steep hillsides—such as the upper banks of the James River in Virginia, where lots suitable for building could not be created easily between a house and its major vista—terraces seem to have been preserved more often than on town or city lots. At Morven, Grumblethorpe, and possibly Cliveden, the process of filling the terraces can be correlated with episodes of lot division and subsequent house construction.

Recording Garden Planes: The Use of ASL Elevations

It is ironic that archaeologists working on 18th-century terraced gardens are working with cultural spaces that were intentionally arranged to deceive the viewer's eye, for at every turn spatial relationships in the modern world also are visually deceptive. This is particularly true when it comes to the depth at which features seem to appear in a garden. Often there may be little visual indication of variation in depth when one views a set of features in a series of units. Simply put, they look as if they lie at equivalent depths. Perceiving little variation, it is hard for field workers to recognize the critical separation that distinguishes one early level from another if the soil strata are not easily distinguished on the basis of color or texture. The process is further complicated in a garden landscape by the constant mixing of soil layers in a gardener's yearly preparation for planting inside the garden beds. Furthermore, because the horizontal planes used in the past were relatively shallow (3–8 in.),

FIGURE 9. Photograph of the commodore's wall. (Photo by A. E. Yentsch.)

features within them may have less focus than when they cut deeply into subsoil.

The Morven team corrected for this possibility by using a recording system that notes elevations in feet (ft.) above-sea-level (ASL) rather than as ft. below-datum. In this case, the ASL readings were calculated as soon as they were taken rather than left for later in the day, week, or year. On the large Morven site where more than one datum point was used, this technique was particularly advantageous as it enabled the archaeologists to know immediately, as they excavated a feature or level, precisely what its depth was relative to similar features or levels located elsewhere. This knowledge often suggested stratigraphic relationships not immediately apparent, and expedited timely testing and tracing of linkages between garden features. It also helped the team to build images of a site at different points in time and did not leave this task exclusively in the director's hands.

At Morven, a comparison of strata and depths between two sets of units was difficult because of the distance between them (approximately 100 ft.) and an intervening brick wall (Figure 9). Excavation in one unit revealed a pair of stone slabs, a narrow stone pathway, and a fill sequence covering a large oval fieldstone platform. Excavation in the other revealed a set of stone steps. While the field team was not exactly sure of the relationship—in terms of the overall garden design—between these

features, the elevation comparison placed the top of the eastern steps at 213.48 ft. ASL, the bottom of the steps at 211.78 ft. ASL, the top of the stone slabs (west) at 213.46 ft. ASL, and the surface of the fieldstone floor at 211.67 ft. ASL. The base of the western steps, found 30 ft. further west, was 211.7 ft. ASL. Midway between the two sets of terrace steps lay either a fieldstone ramp or still another set of fieldstone steps. Their top elevation is 213.8 ft. ASL. Even though this area is not yet fully excavated, the comparative readings have unquestionably located two temporal horizontal planes, each extending in a band 10 ft. wide on an east–west line across the site, 160–165 ft. or 10 perches—a perch, also known as a rod or pole, is a unit of measurement 16.5 ft. in length and constitutes a major division of Gunter's chain (66 ft.) used in 18th-century surveying (Brinker 1969: 14)—distant from the house. These in turn are connected by a fieldstone walk, at the slightly higher elevation of 214.8 ft. ASL, that extends east–west the full 10 perches marking the northern edge of the major terrace (see Figure 12 in the section on perches, below).

Meanwhile work near the house revealed a third 18th-century plane at a depth range of 215.5 ft. ASL that extends no more than 30 ft. north of the original building. There is also a fourth level, on the west side of the site outside the garden, but its precise depth is undetermined, although it is probably at 211 ft. ASL if not lower (ca. 209 ft. ASL) and perhaps held, in addition to the working gardens, outbuildings associated with the family farm. Finally, immediately in front of the house, which was set on a rise, there is a fifth or upper level that formed a small terrace, 32 × 48 ft. (2 × 3 perches), leading out and gently dropping off to the fieldstone forecourt in the south yard, the surface of which is at 216 ft. ASL.

These 18th-century horizontal planes—in contrast to the deep, vertical mass produced by a well shaft, privy hole, or building foundation—are the remains of level yard surfaces created by garden landscaping. In one sense, they are occupation layers and in another they are not. They are not a result of people scattering household refuse across a yard, a process by which a midden gradually

Perspectives from *Historical Archaeology*

forms. Richard and Annis Stockton intentionally created the level surfaces of the garden in a series of short-term, intensive land manipulations, and their design incorporated a moderate slope that drained the garden away from the house. Because of the rapid deposition of the soil, the artifact densities in the strata are unusually low. The planes result, in some cases, from carving away the hillside, and in others, from building it up. It is in this sense that the activities of the Stockton family accord well with a statement made in an article in *Common Sense* in 1739:

> Every Man Now be his fortune what it will, is to be *doing something at his place,* as the fashionable Phrase is; and you hardly meet with any Body, who, after the first Compliments, does not inform you that he is *in Mortar* and *moving of Earth;* the modest terms for Building and Gardening (quoted in Hunt and Willis 1988:25).

Note that most of the garden strata at Morven are relatively thin, although they are, in some cases, covered now with as much as 3–4 ft. of fill. Raising the level of the yard and creating new surfaces, or planes, began in the late 18th century during the occupation of Richard Stockton's eldest son. Although the "Duke," as he was known, left the lower terrace fall lines intact, he gave a more fashionable appearance to his new home, built ca. 1795 on the foundation of the first house, by following "Capability" Brown's work and sweeping the lawn straight up to the walls of his home (Hunt and Willis 1988:31), eliminating the upper terraces and their decorative embellishments. Commodore Stockton, the Duke's son, did not make Morven his primary home until it was altered once more in the 1840s, at which time he further raised and leveled areas of the yard. The horizontal plane associated with the commodore's yard is close to the surface, and varies only slightly, 216.3–216.5 ft. ASL near the house, sloping to 215 ft. ASL further into the yard.

In the same way that archaeologists study layers of successive deposits in old cities, knowledge of relationships among and between the various successive horizontal planes tells how a garden evolved over time and how its present-day contour lines developed. When landscape archaeologists look at vertical relationships—soil strata in a profile, for example—they see a sequence of landscape features. But vertical views provide only a fragmentary view of a garden, not its design. A bird's-eye view is required to see a garden's design. When features can be seen within a horizontal frame or plan view that includes the garden's boundaries, its relationships to buildings on site, and its articulation with the wider environment, then and only then does the overall design at any one point in time appear. Delineating the design is critical because it tells of garden aesthetics and reveals how social space was divided and used. These elements, in turn, express the way a garden symbolically and pragmatically fit into the social, economic, and religious life of a household or, in the case of Old Economy Village, a community (De Cunzo et al. 1990).

Since gardens are normally adjacent to houses, the size and shape of the property, or lot, and the size and way a house is placed on a lot influences the garden's location and spatial layout. Little houses in urban locations normally do not have gigantic gardens, while large homes on larger lots might be expected to have sizable and elaborate gardens. One problem at Morven was that no one knew the proportions of the original house or whether it was actually the structure standing at Morven today, albeit in modified form (Figure 1). Thus aspects of the design and placement of the original house could not be used in the planning phases for the first field season. But once it was established that there was an 18th-century terraced garden contiguous to the present mansion, archaeological attention shifted to the house itself to determine the relationships between the two and thereby push recovery of the garden further.

The House in the Garden

Because a house holds central importance in a garden landscape, because it normally is built prior to the garden, and because artifact deposition close to a house is more concentrated, a house is an excellent place to begin to date different occupation layers across its surrounding grounds. Because doorways provided exit and entry points to different sectors of a pleasure garden or working yards, they are logical starting points for excavation. The archaeologist simply reads the stratigraphic sequence at this access point and moves outward from it across the grounds, although this is not always simple to do. Doorways are areas of a site that normally have extremely complex stratigraphy; numerous features for paths and walkways converge upon them, and door stoops or stairs must be rebuilt or repaired with each change in yard level. Still, beginning at doorways and working outward has helped determine the excavation strategy at three garden sites—Belmont, Cliveden, and Morven—and in each case it has enabled the archaeologists to locate 18th-century yard surfaces with sufficient certainty that, using ASL measurements for similar strata in other sectors of the garden, the contours of the earliest surfaces could be traced.

At the main south or front doorway of Morven, facing Stockton Street, at least five sequences of change were apparent. Initially there was a small fieldstone door stoop opening onto a level terrace that led, in turn, to a fieldstone forecourt which, in turn, either abutted (initially) Stockton Street, its route has since changed, or led to a long tree-lined carriage drive to Stockton Street (Figure 6). In this, the site layout was much like the landscape plan for Tryon Palace in New Bern, North Carolina (Figure 10). From the eastern and western side yards, fieldstone walks must have led to the terrace, and possibly to shallow sets of fieldstone steps like those 50 ft. off the house in the north yard. The west walk would have directed foot traffic from the terrace above the forecourt to the kitchen wing and the kitchen gardens; the east walk led to a small, formal garden off the office quarters in the East Wing, and then wended its way further east to the town of Princeton, passing through the outlying gardens and orchards as it did so. Whereas the west walk disappeared as the orientation of the buildings altered, the east walk was renewed as a formal landscape element in the 19th century (cf. Figures 6, 11).

During the Revolutionary War the British occupied Morven and, from some of the recovered artifacts, the soldiers seem to have tossed household

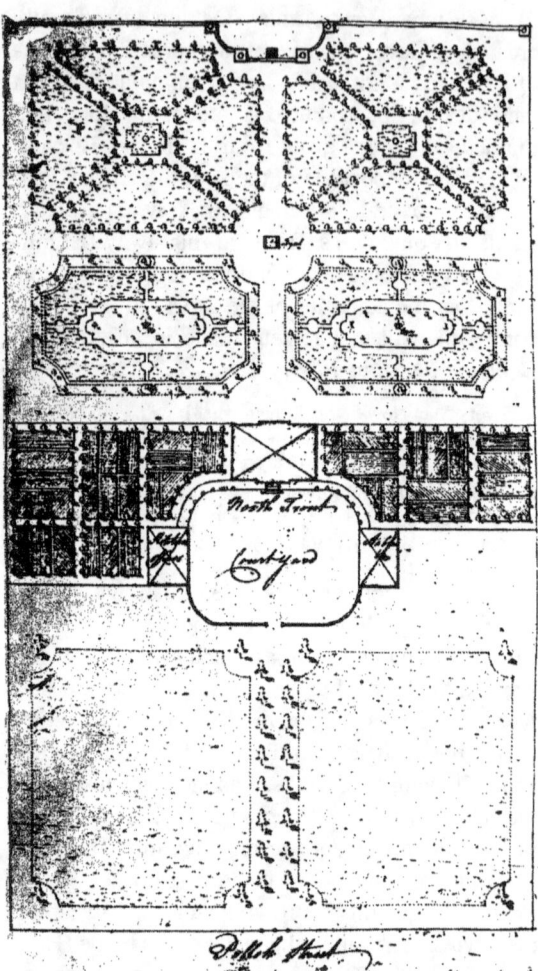

FIGURE 10. Plan of Tryon Palace (from the Papers of Francisco de Miranda; courtesy of Academia Nacional de la Historia, Biblioteca Nacional, Caracas, Venezuela; courtesy of Tryon Palace, New Bern, North Carolina).

trash across the front terrace when, during one occupation, they reportedly "sacked and pillaged" the house (Bill 1978:42). Shortly after the war, the terrace was renewed and a larger fieldstone door stoop installed. The new terrace level covered the older red shale "apron" close to the house. This work may have coincided with the very brief co-occupation of the site by Annis Stockton's brother, Elias Boudinot, then President of Congress who, while living at his widowed sister's home, presided

Perspectives from *Historical Archaeology*

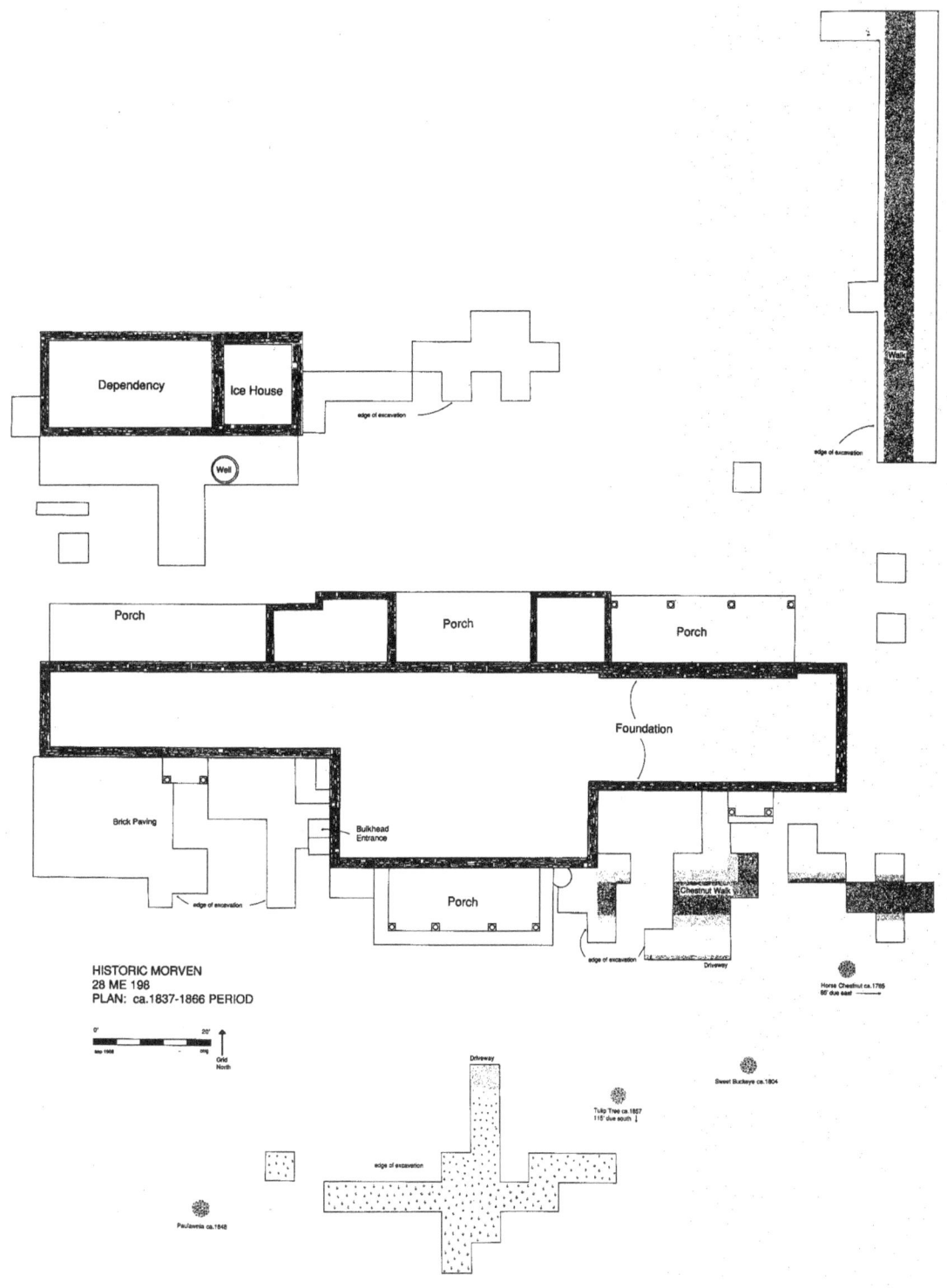

FIGURE 11. Plan view of 19th-century garden features at Morven (from Yentsch et al. 1987).

over the 1783 session convened in Princeton (Sheridan and Murrin 1985:16–17).

A front porch was the third change. It was probably in place before Richard and Annis Stockton's son, the Duke, had his men dismantle the house in the 1790s. Ceramics from the earliest deposits here included pre-1790 sherds of creamware and white salt glaze and hand-painted pearlware fragments that are dated no later than 1785; in addition, there is no accumulation of household or architectural debris beneath the porch floor from the ca. 1795–1820 period. The new house, built upon the foundations of the old, no longer had a doorway in the eastern gable end of the central block; it may or may not have substituted a new front porch for the first porch. After its construction, the lawn surface off the East Wing was also raised and the first fieldstone walk was covered. What other changes may have been made in the 1790s are not known, but all indications are that the primary entry to the house and yard continued to come due north from Stockton Street. The front porch was renovated ca. 1820 (Albee 1990) when other repairs were made after a fire.

The next era of change to the doorways appears ca. 1850 when Commodore Robert Field Stockton rebuilt Morven. He enlarged and raised the rooflines in both wings, renovated the main block, installed a bath addition—purportedly the first interior, private bath in Princeton—and built a separate servants' quarters (Greiff 1989; Albee 1990), thereby creating new activity areas in house and yard. These, in turn, necessitated new and/or differently marked entrance ways. Those in the north yard and off the kitchen wing were surrounded by large brick-paved areas that clearly demarcated the servants' passageways to and from the household work areas.

Although his father may have done so, it was probably the commodore who covered the original 18th-century lane to Stockton Street. The commodore also installed a substantial U-shaped drive using a limestone base identical to that beneath his Horse Chestnut Walk. He also built a small artificial rise, or hillock, on the south side of the drive immediately in front of the house, and atop the old forecourt, possibly to provide privacy since it

would have prevented Princetonians walking or driving down Stockton Street from seeing the visitors who exited and entered the carriages that wheeled up to his landing stage opposite the porch. The commodore's new drive also had a western north–south extension that ran behind the kitchen wing towards the stable or carriage house and other working areas of the farm, but the primary entrance for the working horses and wagons became a second drive, built only of dirt and rough stone, that entered the property from Bayard Lane and traversed the length of the 18th-century lower third terrace. Archaeological evidence for this drive was discovered in 1987.

The profile drawing in Figure 2 clearly depicts the build-up of the landscape off the East Wing and shows the sequence from the original occupation to the present-day brick walk and boxwood hedge, seen in the upper right corner. At its very base is a 2–3-in. stratum, 215.5 ft. ASL, that was the original ground surface prior to construction of the ca. 1760 house. Within 6–8 in. of the surface, at 216.29 ft. ASL, is the surface of the Commodore's 19th-century Horse Chestnut Walk, which was made of finely crushed gravel, with mica chip inclusions for sparkle, also shown in Figure 2. A trench through the walk exposed its sub-base of recycled, cut stone, and the adjacent decorative border—indicated by the presence of two linear features containing a high concentration of crushed red shale—inserted into the brown loam of his father's lawn. Apparent below the sub-base are several occupational levels and a critical architecturally-related layer—the sandy sterile yellow soil, or cellar excavate, laid down when the cellar was dug ca. 1760. The lowest section of stone is a ca. 1760 walkway of fieldstone. Note here that the walk is not directly aligned with the one above, but rather curves gently to the left where it eventually links up with the terrace and/or fieldstone forecourt (Figure 6).

The convergence of paths oriented towards the main south entrance to Morven, and their articulation with one another, particularly off the East Wing, is a dramatic illustration of stratigraphic complexity, but it also enabled the team to grasp the relationships between the different architectural phases of the house and the sequences of garden levels that the crew located in the north and south yards. The original ground surface is a clear marker that allows one to see where the Stocktons carved away the hilltop and where they built it up using an almost sterile soil, obtained on site and probably recycled from the destroyed sectors that had been carved away.

Near the house, the base of the level formed by the cellar excavate lies immediately above the original ground surface and immediately adjacent to walls of the main block. In turn, it is sealed by a layer of red Brunswick shale (Figure 6). The red shale is badly degraded, and it is impossible to know whether it once formed a dry-laid paved apron around the house or an apron of crudely crushed stone. Adjacent to the main south door, the apron is covered by a thin surface accumulation which contained white salt-glazed stoneware plate rims, creamware, and small sherds of China-glazed pearlware—the latter type is found at Revolutionary sites in New Jersey (Miller 1987; Seidel 1990). This assemblage provides very tight dating for the red shale and hence for the main house. Using artifact manufacturing dates—after ca. 1755 for the molded stoneware plates and before ca. 1785 for the Oriental motif pearlware, and taking into account known historical events, the construction of the cellar foundation can be narrowed to a time range of ca. 1758, Richard Stockton's wedding date, and ca. 1775, the start of the Revolutionary War.

The present standing structure contains no building materials made prior to ca. 1795. Had it been necessary to depend on this evidence alone, the architectural historians would have assigned a later date to the occupation of the site than they now do. Successive deposits of original ground surface, cellar excavate, red shale, and surface build-up extending directly to the builder's trench and/or to the house itself, however, are evidence that the present structure is a rebuilding that utilizes an earlier foundation. In this process, the archaeologists worked in close collaboration with Blaine Cliver and Peggy Albee of the National Park Service who, faced with the anomaly of a ca. 1795 building and a ca. 1760 foundation, found addi-

tional places inside the East and West Wings where walls could be cut through and tested for evidence of an earlier building sequence. The evidence in the East Wing, for example, indicates that its north wall predates the construction of the east wall of the main block and also indicates a one and one-half story wing rather than the present two stories. These data have been of critical importance in discovering the basic outline of the ca. 1760 gardens because 18th-century gardens served as embellishments to the main dwelling house owned by a family and their design often drew upon the dimensions of a mansion's front and side walls to form the primary unit in the network of rectangles used in its garden design (Paca-Steele and Wright 1987).

Eighteenth-Century Spatial Logic

The design principles illustrated in the 1760s Stockton gardens are based on Euclidean geometry, which has quite different presuppositions from those of the 1990s about what objects can exist and in what relation. In other words, the grammar its use creates is unlike a modern aesthetic. The grammar, however, was incorporated and embedded in the folk models 18th-century people used in house and garden design. When considering a site in terms of the way geometric principles were used to orient or place specific features in it, the archaeologist also is using either the same or a very similar system of logic as the people who created the garden. Using 18th-century spatial models as a guide to the site was another technique employed by the archaeologists at Morven. It was highly successful, but there was a need first to obtain enough individual pieces of the landscape to identify the spatial model that Richard Stockton used before it became an effective predictive tool.

Perches in the Garden

One element in the cultural logic of the 18th century was the way in which people surveyed land and measured property. They did this using a

system of perches, a sub-unit of the Gunther surveyor's chain. Perches formed the blocks of spatial
dimensions that Richard Stockton used in building
his ca. 1760 home. For example, the west or
kitchen wing is 16.5 ft. wide (1 perch); the main
house is 2 perches wide, and its length is 3 perches.
A reasonable inference would be that the original
East Wing was also 1 perch wide.

In Paca-Steele and Wright's (1987) study of the
William Paca Garden in Annapolis, Maryland, the
authors demonstrate how the proportions that comprise the main block of the house are extended out
into the landscape. At Morven, the research team
found that the south terrace between the front door
and the fieldstone forecourt drew its dimensions
from the house—i.e., it is 3 perches wide and 2
perches deep, based on changes in elevation—and
repeated, in the garden, the imprint of the first
Stockton home. In fact, the geometric grid at Morven, as in William Paca's Annapolis garden, determined the placement of features such as the terrace fall lines; garden outbuildings—an ice-house,
a garden house, a grotto; walkways; and other decorative elements.

Understanding and being able to use the geometric grammar adapted by 18th-century men and
women for the design of their gardens brought
about the greatest breakthrough we had in understanding the garden's design. It was accompanied
by the decision to consider the main block and both
wings as the essential units comprising the exterior
facade, or public view of the house—a facade that
had to be framed by the garden's boundaries if the
garden was to have both unity and symmetry. It
was an intuitive decision based on the premise that
the main block and the extant West Wing by themselves were asymmetrical and provided an unbal-
anced visual backdrop for the garden given the
existence of the northeast fieldstone steps and the
placement of the northwest corner of the garden.

The garden midpoint was located in 1989 by
combining the length of the original West Wing, as
defined in Albee (1990) and Greiff (1991); the
length of the hypothesized East Wing—as established by the length of an anomalous extra-wide
cellar wall incorporated into the 1850 cellar foundation, i.e., the reused sector of an earlier wall;

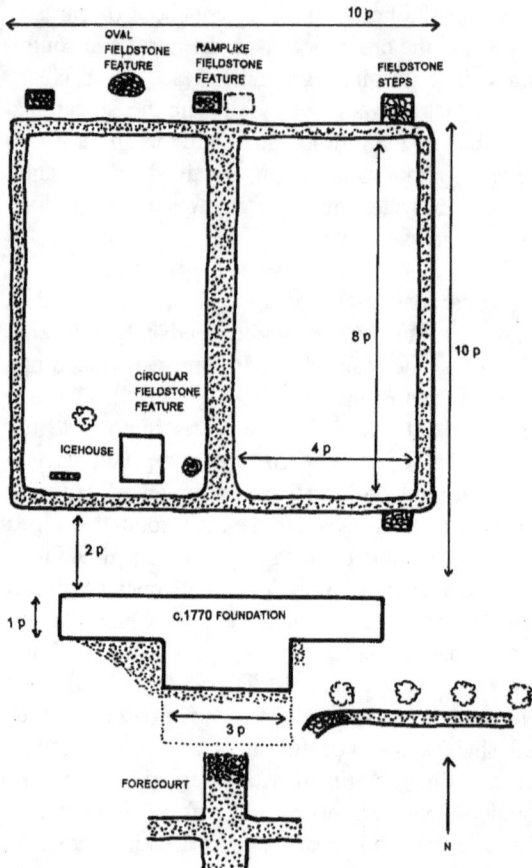

FIGURE 12. The garden plan at Morven with the dimensions in perches, e.g., 10 p = 10 perches. (Redrawn by C.
M. Goodwin based on drawing by Jon Snyder Yentsch
1990.)

and the length of the foundation wall (ca. 1755–
1775) for the original main block and dividing
their total length in half. The imaginary grid that
was then laid outward over the site from this midpoint was composed of 16.5-ft. units or a series of
square perches (Figure 12). The midpoint drawn
from the dimensions of the walls is off-center from
the present north door in the main block because
the original West Wing was longer than the East
Wing. The placement of the present north door is
not actually relevant, for the present building was
constructed ca. 1795, or 30–35 years after the garden, and utilized only the foundation of the earlier

home; it did not repeat its design. Clearly the Duke, who altered the gardens, too, shortly after he built the new house, felt no need to repeat the layout of his parents' ca. 1760 doors and windows in his own new home.

The assumption that the garden was symmetrical and that the eastern 18th-century north–south fieldstone walk was a major boundary provided garden dimensions of 166 ft.[2] (10 perches). Using this as a model, an east–west trench was placed where it would intersect the walkway on the western side of the site, parallel to the eastern 18th-century north–south walk. Here, immediately beneath 19th-century planting beds, Feature 327, a fieldstone walk exhibiting lesser workmanship and cruder stone than its eastern counterpart, was found; it is also slightly lower in elevation than its eastern counterpart. This western walk lay on the less formal side of the garden toward the working gardens and working buildings, as determined, in part, by the function of the West Wing as a kitchen unit—a use easily demonstrated by the number and type of artifacts recovered from the soil strata in its immediate environs; it had also been cut away somewhat during the construction of the later planting beds. For these reasons, the variation in the elevation, composition, and quality of the western walk, compared to the eastern one, was not considered significant in terms of defining the garden's original dimensions. Symmetry in 18th-century Princeton only approximated the golden rule.

Locating Additional Garden Features

Since locating one segment of a walk does not establish its length, further mechanical trenching was done in the fall of 1989 to confirm the full extent of Feature 327 and to search for the northwestern corner of the garden. The mechanically dug trenches were highly successful, although the northwestern corner was found to have been substantially disturbed by the burial and later removal of large oil tanks. Additional trenches were also dug to determine the extent of a large, oval fieldstone feature at the base of the second terrace fall line exactly 33 ft. west of the central axis. Another

trench was placed to see if a similar feature was located 33 ft. east of the central axis. The results of this trenching indicate that a feature does exist in this location, but further work is required to identify its form and function. Thus, the garden exhibits symmetry, although it is not a "pure" or exact symmetry.

A series of excavation units was also placed along the central axis and its accompanying walkway—a walkway created of a decomposed white limestone material. Two of these units revealed linear garden beds that lay parallel to the center walk. Adjacent to the walk on its western border a spiral, circular fieldstone pad was found which might have once supported a post (Rudy Favretti 1989, pers. comm.; photos in Yentsch 1990b or Metheny et al. [1994]). While it is unlikely that this circular feature existed by itself, its counterparts were not located before the Morven project ended.

Three additional trenches unearthed a number of horticultural tools, flowerpots, and additional garden features. Most importantly, they uncovered a shallow set of steps at the first terrace's gentle fall line located 3 perches north of the house. These steps provide the southeast corner of the main parterre, and they step down to another east–west walkway that leads across the garden, repeating the rectangular motif also present in the south yard. This walkway, like its counterpart in the south yard, may have extended further east or west. Like the spiral feature above, it too was located shortly before the project closed; thus, its full dimensions are not yet known.

Conclusion

In the 1760s, Richard and Annis Stockton designed a garden that used the axes provided by the original main house and its wings as integral elements in its design. Their use of geometric principles was derived from a widely-used cultural tradition practiced in England and its colonies. Once the original dimensions of the Stockton home were defined and recognized, the archaeological team was able to pinpoint specific areas in the garden where major features might be located. Knowledge

TABLE 1

MORVEN ASL ELEVATIONS OF 18TH-CENTURY NORTH YARD LANDSCAPE ELEMENTS

Feature Location	Feature No.	Feature Description	ASL Elevation (Ft.)
Garden features close to house by East Wing	263	Set of N–S and E–W fieldstone walks	215.5
	298	Limestone scatter (continuation of walk?)	215.3
	329	Limestone walk (abuts East Wing)	215.5
Garden features close to center block of house	009	Well (stone lining)	215.6
	025	Ice house fieldstone foundation	215.2
	035	Ice House door stoop (fieldstone)	215.5
	038	Fieldstone/flagstone walk or wall	215.5
	134(L)	Original topsoil on north center side of house	214.8
	134(L)	Original topsoil in courtyard area	215.0
	264	Planting bed associated with Feature 263	215.4
	278	Tree hole off center block	214.6
	327	Western N–S walk across terrace (by parking lot)	213.4
	334	Fieldstone foundation walk east of ice house	215.3
	342	Red shale (disintegrating paving stone?)	215.3
Garden features in center section of the first major terrace	012	Stone steps (east) at top	213.5
	024	Flat stones—Unit 34	215.1
	024	Garden bed east of east N–S walkway—Unit 34	215.0
	170(L)	18th-century garden topsoil—west sector	214.1
	286(A)	Center N–S walkway across terrace in perch 3	214.8
	286(B)	Center N–S walkway across terrace in perch 5	215.4
	328	Narrow garden bed abutting center N–S walkway	214.8
	335	Tree hole or garden outbuilding(?)	214.8
	338	Eastern N–S walkway across terrace	214.9
Garden features associated with the fall line of the first major terrace	002	Northern E–W walkway across terrace by Feature 12	214.8
	012	Stone steps (east) at base	211.8
	225	Stone slabs on upper terrace (in west)	213.5
	231	Possible fieldstone walk on lower terrace	211.7
	283	Northern E–W walkway (mid-level) across terrace	214.3
	286(C)	Center N–S walkway across terrace near Feature 303	214.5
	303	Stone steps (center) at top	213.8
	303	Stone steps (center) at base	211.7
	338	Eastern N–S walkway across terrace near Feature 12	214.8

of the below-surface depths of the different horizontal planes (Tables 1, 2) told the team how deep to expect to dig before finding the features. The ethnohistorical or contextual knowledge of the way public space and private space, work areas, and pleasure gardens were intermingled in the 18th century also served as a guide to the site.

Accepting that one essential element of all social action is the potential for change, and that change both defines and responds to world view, what can archaeology reveal of the evolving Morven landscape and the way in which it reflects attitudes towards society? To use but one example, in the mid-19th century, Commodore Robert Stockton dramatically changed the appearance of his house, as described earlier, and also altered the spatial organization of Morven's gardens to impose visible and distinctive divisions between private family space and staff or work space (Yamin 1988, 1991). He built a high brick wall (Figure 9) to

TABLE 2
MORVEN ASL ELEVATIONS[a] OF 18TH-CENTURY SOUTH YARD LANDSCAPE ELEMENTS

Feature Location	Feature No.	Feature Description	ASL Elevation (ft.)
Garden features close to center	059	Second fieldstone front door stoop	217.7
block or aligned with it	070	Refuse deposit by front door	217.1
	078	Fieldstone forecourt on lower terrace	216.6
Garden features close to house by	194	Brick rubble off East Wing	215.8
East Wing	195	East–West fieldstone walk	215.5
	214	Limestone walk to East Wing (north)	215.8
	218	Shale (walk?) parallel to house (center block east wall)	215.1
Garden features by West Wing	141	Cobble apron abutting brick paving	216.3
	341	Red shale apron (disintegrating paving stone?)	216.5

[a]July 1989

separate the pleasure garden—embodied in the landscape as an informal natural setting of trees, lawn, and unobtrusive gravel walks—from the working garden, its related staff buildings, and the stable area with its Arabian race horses, chickens, ducks, Alderney bull, and milk cows.

The wall was but one of many changes the Commodore made, but with its construction the yard became organized asymmetrically, in terms of its public facade, with respect to the axes provided by the original main block and its wings. The asymmetrical organization was less important, if it assumed any visual importance at all, than the separation between family and staff, between the ornamental garden with its semitropical lemon trees and the farm gardens with their vegetables and marketable Irish potatoes, turnips, wheat, and clover. The garden vista provided private pleasure; the once public—i.e., community—view was no longer open. What is seen in Commodore Stockton's use of space at Morven is a distinct change from the past as it was encoded in the built landscape—an attitude characteristic of many educated Americans of his era and encoded in the philosophy, promoted by Emerson, of self-reliance and individualism (Bellah 1979; Yamin 1989).

At the same time not all elements of the old order were erased; persisting components—including a few horse chestnut trees and certain renewed garden walks—provided for constancy in the garden landscape and enabled later generations to look out upon their lands and believe that they were seeing what their ancestors saw and experienced even as their own lives altered and diverged further from 18th-century tradition.

This essay has presented a discussion of the various tools and techniques the archaeological research team utilized to reveal the Stockton gardens at Morven. Remote sensing, while locating some features, proved disappointing at this site, and we suggest that archaeologists learn as much as possible about local conditions that may cause interference—such as nearby communication antennas or the extent of prior landscape alteration as derived from oral histories and documents—before placing great reliance on such results.

As an everyday tool for peering below the surface prior to excavation, the split-spoon auger was invaluable for the Morven project. The steel T-probe helped define some of the stone features and the post-hole digger, used as a large auger, provided data on fill episodes and composition but was not very useful in delineating large horizontal features. Trenching, checkerboard excavation, and areal excavation each had their usefulness in aiding in the location, definition, and interpretation of garden features.

The field methods were used in combination with information about perspectives and vistas for gardens in 18th-century landscapes. Using elevation measurements in ft. above-sea-level (ASL) permitted the researchers to associate separate, sometimes hidden, garden elements, especially terraces, paths, and related features, as contemporary with each other. An essential element in the interpretative process was the knowledge that often in the 18th century builders designed and constructed house and garden as a unified whole using models of spatial logic presented in their literature and then adapted to their specific location. The first researches at Morven, both documentary and archaeological, elicited the data to discern the model used on the property. With all this composite knowledge from the disparate sources, the research team then was able to predict, locate, and define not only the original dimensions and age of the house but also the ordered landscape in which it was placed.

As stated early in this presentation, the archaeological tools and methods used in the field at Morven are not, in and of themselves, particularly unique or innovative. When used in combination, however, and coupled with knowledge gained from the other sources, they give the archaeologist great flexibility in building the necessary blocks of knowledge for the interpretation of the site. We have presented the story here in the hope that the experiences at Morven will aid others in their studies of gardens elsewhere.

ACKNOWLEDGMENTS

Primary funding for the Morven Project was provided by the New Jersey State Museum. Additional work on the use of geometric principle in garden design was done in 1991–1992 with funding from the James Marston Fitch Charitable Trust. Morven's strong public interpretation program built on that designed for Annapolis; we thank our colleagues Rebecca Yamin, Parker B. Potter, Jr., and Mark P. Leone for their help with this. Morven's field excavation strategy also grew out of work done earlier in Annapolis at Reynolds Tavern and the Calvert site. Its application to the Morven site was managed in 1987 by Gary Norman, who was also field director at the Calvert site in 1984, in 1988 by Conrad M. Goodwin, and in 1989 by Judson M. Kratzer. Fieldwork at the Morven site was carried out by volunteers, museum interns, a paid professional staff, and students enrolled in two field schools sponsored by Mercer Community College in 1988 and 1989. Alvin Felzenberg, Robin Austin, Suzanne C. Crilley, Marie Murawski, and their staffs employed at Morven did a yeoman's service in terms of on-site assistance to the project. Other individuals at the New Jersey State Museum were also of great help, as were two historians, Constance Greiff and Wanda Gunning, whose knowledge of Princeton history, the Stockton family, and the architectural heritage of Morven was shared unstintingly with the archaeologists.

The architectural survey by the North Atlantic Office of the National Park Service formerly at Charlestown (they have moved to Lowell), Massachusetts, under the direction of Blaine Cliver and Peggy A. Albee, provided critical structural details for the archaeological project. As their role in the Morven project came to its natural conclusion (Albee 1990), their colleagues in the Mid-Atlantic Office in Philadelphia stepped in to help, specifically Bertram Herbert, Katherine H. Stevenson, and William Bolger, with advice on how to preserve the site during the 1990 closure of the project. Finally, we would like to acknowledge the encouragement and support of Dr. John L. Cotter, Professor Emeritus at the University of Pennsylvania, who suggested that the withdrawal of state funds for a formal and final report might preclude widespread knowledge of the work that was done at the Morven site. In October 1990, he urged us to submit an article to Historical Archaeology where, as the primary journal within the discipline, information on this project would be available to generations of future historical archaeologists, some of whom might be asked in the next 50–100 years to reopen the site. If he had not made this suggestion, this paper would not have been written, and we thank him for it.

REFERENCES

ALBEE, PEGGY A.
1990   Historic Structures Report for Morven. Report pre-

pared by North Atlantic Regional Office, National Park Service, Lowell, Massachusetts. Submitted to New Jersey State Museum, Trenton.

BEAUDRY, MARY C.
1984 Archaeology and the Historical Household. *Man in the Northeast* 28:27–38.
1986 The Archaeology of Historical Land Use in Massachusetts. *Historical Archaeology* 20(2):38–46.
1988 Comments on the Historical Archaeology of North American Households. Paper presented at the Annual Meeting of the Society for Historical Archaeology Conference on Historical and Underwater Archaeology, Reno, Nevada.

BELLAH, ROBERT N.
1979 New Religious Consciousness and the Crisis in Modernity. In *Interpretive Social Science: A Reader,* edited by Paul Rabinow and William M. Sullivan, pp. 341–364. University of California Press, Berkeley.

BESCHERER, KAREN, CONRAD M. GOODWIN, JUDSON M. KRATZER, AND ANNE YENTSCH
1990 The Gardens at Grumblethorpe, Germantown, Pennsylvania. *Landscape Archaeology Report* No. 2. Prepared by Morven Research Group in Landscape Archaeology, Princeton, New Jersey. Submitted to Philadelphia Society for the Preservation of Landmarks, Philadelphia, Pennsylvania.

BESCHERER, KAREN, JUDSON M. KRATZER, AND CONRAD M. GOODWIN
1990 The Highlands Gardens, Fort Washington, Pennsylvania: 1989 Archaeological Explorations. *Landscape Archaeology Report* No. 3. Prepared by Morven Research Group in Landscape Archaeology, Princeton, New Jersey. Submitted to Highlands Historical Society, Fort Washington, Pennsylvania.

BESCHERER, KAREN, AND ANNE YENTSCH
1989 Initial Archaeological Testing at Wye Hall, Wye Island, Maryland. *Landscape Archaeology Report* No. 1. Prepared by Morven Research Group in Landscape Archaeology, Princeton, New Jersey. Submitted to Historic Annapolis, Inc., Annapolis, Maryland.

BEVAN, BRUCE
1987 A Geophysical Survey at Morven. Report prepared by Geosight, Pitman, New Jersey. Submitted to New Jersey State Museum, Trenton.

BILL, ALFRED HOYT
1978 *A House Called Morven: Its Role in American History.* Revised edition. Princeton University Press, Princeton, New Jersey.

BRAIDWOOD, ROBERT J., AND BRUCE HOWE
1960 Prehistoric Investigations in Iraqi Kurdistan. *Studies in Ancient Oriental Civilization* No. 31. University of Chicago Press, Chicago.

BRINKER, RUSSELL C.
1969 *Elementary Surveying.* Fifth edition. International Textbook, New York.

BROWN, MARLEY R. III
1987 *Among Weighty Friends: The Archaeology and Social History of the Jacob Mott Family, Portsmouth, Rhode Island, 1640–1800.* Ph.D. dissertation, Department of Anthropology, Brown University, Providence, Rhode Island. University Microfilms, Ann Arbor, Michigan.

D'ARGENVILLE, A. J. DÉZALLIER
1988 *The Theory and Practice of Gardening.* Excerpt of 1712 publication. In *The Genius of the Place: The English Landscape Garden, 1620–1720,* edited by John Dixon Hunt and Peter Willis, pp. 125–131. MIT Press, Cambridge, Massachusetts.

DEAGAN, KATHLEEN
1981 Downtown Survey: The Discovery of 16th-Century St. Augustine in an Urban Area. *American Antiquity* 46(3):626–634.

DE CUNZO, LU ANN
1990 The Harmony Society Garden at Old Economy Village: A Report on Preliminary Historical and Archaeological Investigations. Report with contributions by Conrad M. Goodwin, Naomi F. Miller, Dolores Piperno, Andropogon Associates, Ltd., and Jennifer Goodman. Prepared by CLIO Group, Inc., Philadelphia, Pennsylvania. Submitted to Pennsylvania Historical and Museum Commission, Harrisburg, Pennsylvania.

DE CUNZO, LU ANN, THERESE O'MALLEY, MICHAEL J. LEWIS, GEORGE E. THOMAS, AND CHRISTA WILMANNS-WELLS
[1994] Father Rapp's Garden at Economy: Harmony Society Culture in Microcosm. In *Landscape Archaeology: Studies in Reading and Interpreting the Historical Landscape,* edited by Rebecca Yamin and Karen Bescherer Metheny, in preparation.

DEETZ, JAMES
1977 *In Small Things Forgotten: The Archaeology of Early American Life.* Anchor Press/Doubleday, New York.

DENEVAN, WILLIAM M., KENT MATHEWSON, AND GREGORY KNAPP
1987 Pre-Hispanic Agricultural Fields in the Andean Region. *BAR International Series* 359 (i). Oxford, England.

ELIA, RICARDO J.
1987 Needle-in-a-Haystack Archaeology: The Use of Soil Cores to Discover Archaeological Sites. Paper presented at the Annual Meeting of the Northeast Anthropological Association, Amherst, Massachusetts.

GOODWIN, CONRAD "MAC," WITH CONRAD ERKELENS AND
CARLA FAVREAU
   1994   *A Kalaupapa Sweet Potato Farm—Report on Ar-
          chaeological Data Recovery Operations, Kalaupapa
          Airport Improvement Project, Kalaupapa, Molokai,
          Hawaii,* Vol. 1. Prepared by International Archaeo-
          logical Research Institute, Inc., Honolulu. Submitted
          to Edward K. Noda and Associates, Inc., Honolulu.

GOODWIN, CONRAD M., AND JUDSON M. KRATZER
   1989a A Survey and Map of the Late Eighteenth Century
          William Paca Garden at Wye Island. Report prepared
          by authors. Submitted to Historic Annapolis, Inc.,
          Annapolis, Maryland.
   1989b A Survey and Map of Bordley-Randall. Report pre-
          pared by authors. Submitted to Historic Annapolis,
          Inc., Annapolis, Maryland.

GOODWIN, CONRAD "MAC," MICHAEL PIETRUSEWSKY,
MICHELE TOOMAY DOUGLAS, AND RONA MICHI IKEHARA
   1992   The Burials from the Marin Tower Property—Pre-
          liminary Report. Prepared by International Archaeo-
          logical Research Institute, Inc., Honolulu. Submitted
          to Office of Housing and Community Development,
          City and County of Honolulu; and to family descen-
          dants of Don Francisco De Paula Marin.

GREIFF, CONSTANCE M.
   1989   Morven: A Documentary History. Two volumes.
          Heritage Studies, Hopewell, New Jersey, and New
          Jersey State Museum, Trenton.
   1991   Views of Morven. *Princeton History* 10:5–41.

HOLE, FRANK, KENT V. FLANNERY, AND JAMES A. NEELY
   1969   Prehistory and Human Ecology on the Deh Luran
          Plain. *Memoirs of the University of Michigan Mu-
          seum of Anthropology* No. 1. University of Michigan,
          Ann Arbor.

HUNT, JOHN DIXON, AND PETER WILLIS
   1988   *The Genius of the Place: The English Landscape
          Garden, 1620–1820.* MIT Press, Cambridge, Massa-
          chusetts.

KELSO, WILLIAM M.
   1984a Landscape Archaeology: A Key to Virginia's Culti-
          vated Past. In *British and American Gardens in the
          Eighteenth Century,* edited by Robert P. Maccubbin
          and Peter Martin, pp. 159–169. Colonial Williams-
          burg Foundation, Williamsburg, Virginia.
   1984b *Kingsmill Plantations, 1619–1800: Archaeology of
          Country Life in Colonial Virginia.* Academic Press,
          New York.
   1990   Landscape Archaeology at Thomas Jefferson's Mon-
          ticello. In *Earth Patterns: Essays in Landscape Ar-
          chaeology,* edited by William M. Kelso and Rachel
          Most, pp. 7–22. University Press of Virginia, Char-
          lottesville.
   1992   Big Things Remembered: Anglo-Virginian Houses,
          Armorial Devices, and the Impact of Common

Sense. In *The Art and Mystery of Historical Archaeology: Essays in Honor of James Deetz,* edited by
Anne Elizabeth Yentsch and Mary C. Beaudry, pp.
127–145. CRC Press, Boca Raton, Florida.

KELSO, WILLIAM M., AND RACHEL MOST (EDITORS)
   1990   *Earth Patterns: Essays in Landscape Archaeology.*
          University Press of Virginia, Charlottesville.

KIRCH, PATRICK VINTON
   1985   *Feathered Gods and Fishhooks: An Introduction to
          Hawaiian Archaeology and Prehistory.* University of
          Hawaii Press, Honolulu.

LEONE, MARK P.
   1984   Interpreting Ideology in Historical Archaeology: Us-
          ing the Rules of Perspective in the William Paca
          Garden, Annapolis, Maryland. In *Ideology, Power,
          and Prehistory,* edited by Daniel Miller and Chris-
          topher Tilley, pp. 25–35. Cambridge University
          Press, Cambridge.
   1987   Rule by Ostentation: The Relationship between
          Space and Sight in Eighteenth Century Landscape
          Architecture in the Chesapeake Region of Maryland.
          In *Method and Theory for Activity Area Research,*
          edited by Susan Kent, pp. 604–633. Columbia Uni-
          versity Press, New York.
   1988   The Georgian Order as the Order of Merchant Cap-
          italism in Annapolis, Maryland. In *The Recovery of
          Meaning: Historical Archaeology in the Eastern
          United States,* edited by Mark P. Leone and Parker B.
          Potter, Jr., pp. 235–261. Smithsonian Institution
          Press, Washington, D.C.

LEONE, MARK P., AND PARKER B. POTTER, JR.
   1988   Introduction: Issues in Historical Archaeology. In
          *The Recovery of Meaning: Historical Archaeology in
          the Eastern United States,* edited by Mark P. Leone
          and Parker B. Potter, Jr., pp. 1–22. Smithsonian In-
          stitution Press, Washington, D.C.

LEWIS, LYNNE
   1991   The Cliveden Survey of August 1991. Report on file,
          National Trust Archaeological Laboratory, Montpe-
          lier, Montpelier Station, Virginia.

LITTLE, J. GLENN II
   1967– Archaeological Research on Paca Garden, 8 Novem-
   1968   ber 1967, 24 May 1968. Letters on file, William Paca
          Garden Visitors' Center, Annapolis, Maryland.

LUCCKETTI, NICHOLAS
   1990   Archaeological Excavations at Bacon's Castle, Surry
          County, Virginia. In *Earth Patterns: Essays in Land-
          scape Archaeology,* edited by William M. Kelso and
          Rachel Most, pp. 23–42. University of Virginia
          Press, Charlottesville.

MARTIN, PETER
   1991   *The Pleasure Gardens of Virginia: From Jamestown
          to Jefferson.* Princeton University Press, Princeton,
          New Jersey.

McManamon, Francis P.

1981 Probability Sampling and Archaeological Survey in the Northeast: An Estimation Approach. In *Foundations of Northeast Archaeology,* edited by Dean R. Snow, pp. 195–227. Academic Press, New York.

1984 Discovering Sites Unseen. *Advances in Archaeological Methods and Theory* 7:223–292. Michael B. Schiffer, editor. Serial publication series. Academic Press, New York.

Metheny, Karen Bescherer, Judson Kratzer, Anne Yentsch, and Conrad M. Goodwin

[1994] Methodology in Landscape Archaeology: Research Strategies in a Historic New Jersey Garden. In *Landscape Archaeology: Studies in Reading and Interpreting the Historical Landscape,* edited by Rebecca Yamin and Karen Bescherer Metheny, in preparation.

Miller, George

1987 Origins of Josiah Wedgwood's "Pearlware." *Northeast Historical Archaeology* 18:83–95.

Miller, Naomi F., and Kathryn L. Gleason (editors)

[1994] *The Archaeology of Garden and Field.* University of Pennsylvania Press, Philadelphia, in press.

Miller, Naomi F., and Anne Yentsch (editors)

1988 Morven Interim Report No. 2: Archaeobotanical Results from the 1987 Excavation at Morven, Princeton, New Jersey. Report on file, New Jersey State Museum, Trenton.

Miller, Naomi F., Anne Yentsch, Dolores Piperno, and Barbara Paca

1990 Two Centuries of Landscape Change at Morven, Princeton, New Jersey. In *Earth Patterns: Essays in Landscape Archaeology,* edited by William M. Kelso and Rachel Most, pp. 257–275. University Press of Virginia, Charlottesville.

Moran, Geoffrey P., Edward F. Zimmer, and Anne E. Yentsch

1982 Archaeological Investigations at the Narbonne House, Salem Maritime National Historic Site, Salem, Massachusetts. *Cultural Resources Management Study* No. 6. Division of Cultural Resources, North Atlantic Regional Office, National Park Service, Boston, Massachusetts.

New York Gazette

1785 Advertisement. *New York Gazette,* 8 February 1785.

Noël Hume, Audrey

1974 Archaeology and the Colonial Gardener. *Colonial Williamsburg Archaeological Series* No. 7. Colonial Williamsburg Foundation, Williamsburg, Virginia.

Nourse, Timothy

1988 *Campania Foelix: or A Discourse of the Benefits and Improvements of Husbandry.* Excerpt of 1700 publi-cation. In *The Genius of the Place: The English Landscape Garden, 1620–1720,* edited by John Dixon Hunt and Peter Willis, pp. 100–105. MIT Press, Cambridge, Massachusetts.

Paca, Barbara

1983 The William Paca Garden Surveyed and Mapped. Report on file, William Paca Garden, Historic Annapolis, Inc., Annapolis, Maryland.

Paca-Steele, Barbara, and St. Clair Wright

1987 The Mathematics of an Eighteenth-Century Wilderness Garden. *Journal of Garden History* 6(4):299–320.

Praetzellis, Adrian, and Mary Praetzellis

1992 Faces and Facades: Victorian Ideology in Early Sacramento. In *The Art and Mystery of Historical Archaeology: Essays in Honor of James Deetz,* edited by Anne Elizabeth Yentsch and Mary C. Beaudry, pp. 75–99. CRC Press, Boca Raton, Florida.

Pulsipher, Lydia Mihelic

1993a Changing Roles in the Life Cycles of Women in Traditional West Indian Houseyards. In *Women and Change in the Caribbean,* edited by Janet Momsen, pp. 50–64. Ian Randall, Kingston; Indiana University Press, Bloomington and Indianapolis; James Currey, London.

1993b 'He Won't Let She Stretch She Foot': Gender Relations in Traditional West Indian Houseyards. In *Full Circles: Geographies of Women over the Life Course,* edited by Cindi Katz and Janice Monk, pp. 107–121. Routledge, London and New York.

Reinke, Marguerite, and Robert Paynter

1984 Archaeological Excavation of the Surroundings of the E. H. Williams House, Deerfield, Massachusetts. Report on file, University of Massachusetts Archaeological Services, Amherst.

Rubertone, Patricia E., and Joan Gallagher

1981 Archaeological Site Examination: A Case Study in Urban Archaeology—Roger Williams National Memorial. *Cultural Resource Management Study* No. 4. Division of Cultural Resources, North Atlantic Regional Office, National Park Service, Boston, Massachusetts.

Seidel, John L.

1990 "China Glaze" Wares on Sites from the American Revolution: Pearlware before Wedgwood? *Historical Archaeology* 24(1):82–95.

Shackel, Paul A.

1987 The Garden at the Carroll House, Annapolis, Maryland. In *Perspectives on an 18th-Century Garden,* edited by Parker B. Potter, Jr. Pamphlet for Tourists at the Carroll Gardens for the 250th Anniversary of the Birth of Charles Carroll of Carrollton. Pamphlet on file, Historic Annapolis, Inc., Annapolis, Maryland.

SHERIDAN, EUGENE R., AND JOHN M. MURRIN (EDITORS)
1985   *Congress at Princeton: Being the Letters of Charles Thomson to Hannah Thomson, June–October 1783.* Princeton University Press, Princeton, New Jersey.

SPENCE, JOSEPH
1988   Letter (on gardening) to the Rev. Mr. Wheeler. Reprint of 1751 letter. In *The Genius of the Place: The English Landscape Garden, 1620–1720,* edited by John Dixon Hunt and Peter Willis, pp. 268–272. MIT Press, Cambridge, Massachusetts.

SPENCER, J. E., AND G. A. HALE
1961   The Origin, Nature and Distribution of Agricultural Terracing. *Pacific Viewpoint* 2:1–40.

STONE, LAWRENCE
1981   *The Past and the Present.* Routledge and Kegan Paul, Boston, Massachusetts.

WEBER, CARMEN A., ELIZABETH ANDERSON COMER, LOUISE E. AKERSON, AND GARY NORMAN
1990   Mount Clare: An Interdisciplinary Approach to the Restoration of a Georgian Landscape. In *Earth Patterns: Essays in Landscape Archaeology,* edited by William M. Kelso and Rachel Most, pp. 135–152. University Press of Virginia, Charlottesville.

WÖLFFLIN, HEINRICH
1966   *Renaissance and Baroque,* translated by Kathrin Simon, with an introduction by Peter Murray. Reprint of 1888 edition. Cornell University Press, Ithaca, New York.

YAMIN, REBECCA
1988   To Restore or Not to Restore: Morven's Interpretive Question. Paper presented at the Annual Meeting of the Council for Northeast Historical Archaeology, Québec, Canada.
1989   The Public and Private Mr. Stockton: Morven's Commodore. *New Jersey Folklore Society Review* 10(2–3):3–16.
1991   Letter from Princeton: A Journey Through Time. *Archaeology* 44(2):46–49.

YAMIN, REBECCA, AND ANNE E. YENTSCH
1989   Interpretation in the Ethnographic Present: Morven, Princeton, New Jersey. Paper presented at the Annual Meeting of the Society for Historical Archaeology Conference on Historical and Underwater Archaeology, Baltimore, Maryland.

YENTSCH, ANNE ELIZABETH
1984   Contrary to Nature: The Calvert Orangery as a Symbol of Power for a Patrician Household in Annapolis, Maryland. Paper presented at the 45th Conference on Early American History, "The Colonial Experience: Eighteenth Century Maryland," Baltimore, Maryland.
1986   The Earlier Posthole Buildings at the Calvert Site. *Calvert Interim Report* No. 1. Report on file, Historic Annapolis, Inc., Annapolis, Maryland.
1988a   Report on the Preliminary Testing of the Bordley-Randall Site in Annapolis, Maryland. Report on file, Historic Annapolis, Inc., Annapolis, Maryland.
1988b   Legends, Houses, Families, and Myths: Relationships Between Material Culture and American Ideology. In *Documentary Archaeology in the New World,* edited by Mary C. Beaudry, pp. 5–19. Cambridge University Press, Cambridge.
1988c   Finding Earlier Gardens and Sharing Morven's Landscape Archaeology with the Public: 1988 Summary and Recommendations. Report on file, New Jersey State Museum, Trenton.
1989   The Use of Land and Space on Lot 83, Annapolis, Maryland: An Interpretive Analysis of Symbolic Form and Space. In New Perspectives on Maryland Archaeology, edited by Richard J. Dent and Barbara J. Little. *Maryland Archaeology* 26:1–2. Archaeological Society of Maryland, Annapolis.
1990a   The Calvert Orangery in Annapolis, Maryland: A Horticultural Symbol of Power and Prestige in an Early 18th-Century Community. In *Earth Patterns: Essays in Landscape Archaeology,* edited by William M. Kelso and Rachel Most, pp. 169–187. University Press of Virginia, Charlottesville.
1990b   Historic Morven: The Archaeological Reappearance of an 18th-Century Princeton Garden. *Expedition* 32(2):14–23.
1992a   A Landscape Research Plan for the National Trust Property of Cliveden on Germantown Avenue in the Germantown Suburb of Philadelphia, Pennsylvania. Report prepared by the author. Submitted to Martin Jay Rosenblum, R.A., and Associates, Philadelphia, Pennsylvania. On file, Cliveden, Germantown, Pennsylvania.
1992b   Working with Fill in San Francisco. In Tar Flat, Rincon Hill, and the Shore of Mission Bay: Archaeological Research Design and Treatment Plan for SF–480 Terminal Separation Rebuild, Vol. 2, edited by Mary Praetzellis and Adrian Praetzellis, pp. 4/103–4/120. Report prepared by Cultural Resources Facility, Anthropological Studies Center, Sonoma State University, Rohnert Park, California. Submitted to California Department of Transportation, San Francisco.
[1994] *Yesterday's People: The 18th-Century Chesapeake World of the Calvert Family and Their Slaves.* Cambridge University Press, Cambridge, in press.

YENTSCH, ANNE, AND JUDSON KRATZER
1991   An Archaeological Strategy for the Recovery of the 18th-Century Gardens at Belmont in Fairmount Park,

Philadelphia. Report prepared by the authors. Submitted to Martin Jay Rosenblum, R.A., and Associates, Philadelphia, Pennsylvania.

[1994] Potting Round Pleasure Gardens: Techniques for Excavating and Analyzing Buried Eighteenth-Century Landscapes. In *The Archaeology of Garden and Field*, edited by Naomi F. Miller and Kathryn L. Gleason. University of Pennsylvania Press, Philadelphia, in press.

YENTSCH, ANNE, JUDSON KRATZER, AND KAREN BESCHERER
1990   Management Summary of the 1989 Field Season at a National Historic Landmark: Morven in Princeton, New Jersey. Report on file, New Jersey State Museum, Trenton.

YENTSCH, ANNE E., NAOMI F. MILLER, BARBARA PACA, AND DOLORES PIPERNO
1987   Archaeologically Defining the Earlier Garden Landscapes at Morven: Preliminary Results. *Northeast Historical Archaeology* 16:1–29.

CONRAD MCCALL GOODWIN
DEPARTMENT OF ANTHROPOLOGY
UNIVERSITY OF TENNESSEE
KNOXVILLE, TENNESSEE 37996 AND
INTERNATIONAL ARCHAEOLOGICAL RESEARCH INSTITUTE, INC.
HONOLULU, HAWAII 96826

KAREN BESCHERER METHENY
DEPARTMENT OF ARCHAEOLOGY
BOSTON UNIVERSITY
765 COMMONWEALTH AVENUE
BOSTON, MASSACHUSETTS 02215

JUDSON M. KRATZER
ANNE YENTSCH
DEPARTMENT OF HISTORY
ARMSTRONG STATE COLLEGE
SAVANNAH, GEORGIA 31419

JAMES SCHOENWETTER
JOHN W. HOHMANN

Landuse Reconstruction at the Founding Settlement of Las Vegas, Nevada

ABSTRACT

Integration of artifactual, architectural, historical, geoarchaeological, faunal, macrobotanical, and palynological evidence provides the grounds for a model of the landuse history of Las Vegas, Nevada, from the second quarter of the 19th century until 1905. The integrated model reinforces and elaborates upon landuse changes noted in the historic record, but adds details to support a processual, explanatory, analysis that is not well-evidenced by available documentation. From this perspective, the landuse history of Las Vegas appears always to have been more significantly influenced by socioeconomic factors than ecological conditions—a reality that continues to the present day.

Introduction

In this article, our goal is to identify and interpret the interrelationships of a number of landuse indicators recovered from the Old Mormon Fort site at Old Las Vegas Mormon Fort State Historic Park. Though structured by the landuse history documented for the site, our analysis uses an integrative approach (Luff and Rowley-Conwy 1994) in which no single information source fully supports our landuse reconstruction independently. Our results serve to illustrate the value of integrating types of information which are often ignored in historic archaeology. More importantly, we have sought to apply principles of processual analysis to explain the interrelationships of relevant historical, archaeological, biological, and geological information. We believe the outcome is sensitive to both the particulars of Las Vegas Creek's paleoecology and the broad outlines of a half-century of Western American socioeconomic history.

We realize that our reconstruction of landuse history is directly evidenced by a relatively small fraction of the site's artifactual and nonartifactual records and a narrow array of historically documented information. Thus, it is more appropriate to speak of it as a testable model than a finding. We are also very much aware of two factors that strongly influence the character of this paper. First, we recognize that this paper is an inappropriate place to present the details of historical, archaeological, geological, faunal, macrobotanical, and palynological data. So those details must remain unstated even though the information is only available in a source (Hohmann 1996) that is not widely circulated. Second, this is not an appropriate place to review the distinctive theory (Schoenwetter 1996:259–261) and method (Schoenwetter 1990) we have employed to interpret palynological records from the site. We are thus sensitive to the fact that scholars without access to our earlier work may hold that the lines of reasoning that underlie our model are vague, and they will find it difficult to assess either the model or the conclusions we have drawn from it. We have attempted, therefore, to design the paper less as an argument in support of our model of landuse history than as an illustration of the ways information has been integrated to achieve it. Following a brief review of the project's history, we shall present the view of landuse changes between 1830 and 1905 that is supported by documentary evidence. We then explore the contributions that other forms of information have made to our reconstruction, and follow this with our integrated model. The subsequent section presents our processual explanation of events, and we end the paper with a summary statement that places the sequence of landuse changes in cultural context.

Today, the landscape of Las Vegas is wholly inconsistent with the English translation of its Spanish name, "The (Wet) Meadows." Whether illuminated and carefully engineered to appeal to gamblers and tourists, or manicured to suit the sensibilities of its large resident population, or reduced to widely-spaced shrubs and herbs hardy enough to survive half a year of oppressive heat and aridity, Las Vegas looks as if it could never have supported the sorts of rich bosque and grassland its name implies. Since the landuse changes identified by our model were responsible for conversion of a lush desert oasis to the overgrazed desert habitat that existed at the Las Vegas townsite when development began in 1905, one imagines that the meadowland must have been subject to ecological changes produced through groundwater depletion, the ravages of terrible livestock mismanagement, or both. Viewed in processual perspective, however, from the vantage of information only integration of biological, archaeological, and historical research can provide, we find that a more complex explanation is appropriate.

Project History

In 1991, Nevada Division of State Parks (NSP) acquired a 3.1-acre parcel upon which the first historic settlement at Las Vegas, a fort constructed by Mormon missionaries, was located. Working in conjunction with a large number of local, statewide, and national organizations, NSP established a small park complex within this parcel for the protection and interpretation of the architectural remains of that, and subsequent, occupations. Following a number of more specialized studies (Elston and McLane 1993; Hatzenbuehler and Lowe 1993; Hohmann and Irish 1994; Hohmann et al. 1994; Hohmann et al. 1995), NSP contracted an expanded program of historic documentation research and a corresponding program of archaeological subsurface testing (Hohmann and Ryden 1994; Hohmann 1994, 1995, 1996). Ultimately, hundreds of historic documents ranging from Mormon journals and diaries to property inventories were studied in detail (Hohmann, Hatzenbuehler, et al. 1996). The archaeological test revealed a wide range of architecture foundations and other features (Hohmann 1996:161–197) and produced numerous prehistoric (Seymour 1996; Irwin 1996) and historic artifacts for study. Analysis of the latter (Hohmann, Davis, et al. 1996) allowed definition of specific space and time parameters for the architectural features and stratigraphic compo-

nents of the site complex. It also provided temporal control for the faunal, macrobotanical, and palynological studies of changes in resource use and ecosystem conditions related to successive occupations of the locale (Lawrence 1996; Bohrer 1996; Schoenwetter 1996).

While this paper has evolved from the work contracted by NSP, it is distinct from it in both spirit and execution. The work and conclusions of Hohmann (1996) were meant to meet the informational and managerial needs necessary for development of the Old Las Vegas Mormon Fort Historic Park. Here, work is focused on scholarly appreciation of landuse change events and their cultural implications.

The Site's Documented Landuse History

Between 1830 and 1831, New Mexico traders George C. Young and William Wolfskill established the all-season trade route linking Santa Fe and Spanish California that would become known as the "Old Spanish Trail." It passed by the Old Mormon Fort locale where a spring-fed creek provided the only water for a stretch of over 53 mi. along the trail. Euroamerican frontierspeople knew of the Las Vegas valley as early as the 1840s. John C. Frémont's (1845) record of a stop at Las Vegas in his 1843–1844 journals notes his surprise that the Spanish place-name suggested a wetter environment than he observed.

About 1847 the "Mormon Road" connecting Salt Lake City to California and Santa Fe was joined to the trail near the site. Acquired by the United States in 1848 following the War with Mexico, southern Nevada became a corridor for immigrants and gold seekers on their way to California. In 1851, Amasa Lyman stopped to explore the area while leading the original group of 500 mormon settlers to San Bernadino. His journal noted the potential of "The Vegus" to support a mill and an agricultural settlement of "at least 50 inhabitants." In June 1855, a party of 32 Mormon missionaries began construction of an adobe fort on the north bank of Las Vegas Creek.

The missionaries were charged with (1) developing the site's agricultural potential, (2) working with and teaching the Native Americans about Christ, (3) serving as a way station linking Mormon settlements between southern Utah and southern California, and (4) protecting and keeping open the trails which allowed year-round travel and trade. An 1855 sketch map (Figure 1) shows the fort was planned to face the northern edge of a 2.5-mi. long, 0.5-mi. wide, expanse of grass south of the creek, watered by channels which branched to the south. Near the creek's southeastern branch was a small area of "Tooly" (tule) grass, identifying that part of the meadow as, at least seasonally, marshy ground.

The mission's highest priority was to establish agricultural fields, lay in a crop, and harvest it before winter. To this end, they immediately began excavation of an irrigation ditch that diverted water from Las Vegas Creek near what would become the southeast corner of the fort.

Primary and secondary irrigation ditches watered garden plots of one-quarter acre per person east of the fort and five-acre farm plots (2.5 acres per person) on the valley floor. While agriculture was always the primary industry of the Las Vegas mission, the discovery of lead ore in the Potosi mountains in April 1856 led President Brigham Young to dispatch additional missionaries to mine and smelt this strategic resource. Social and political conflicts between those committed to the mission's original and its subsequent objectives led to the fort's total abandonment by December 1857.

In February of 1858, Amasa Lyman, responding to Brigham Young's call to return to Utah to defend the Church against a possible threat from the U.S. Army, led the last Mormon missionaries out of San Bernardino. Lyman stopped at the fort, rebuilt its small furnace, and began mining and smelting lead. These operations were not maintained, however, as the fort was aban-

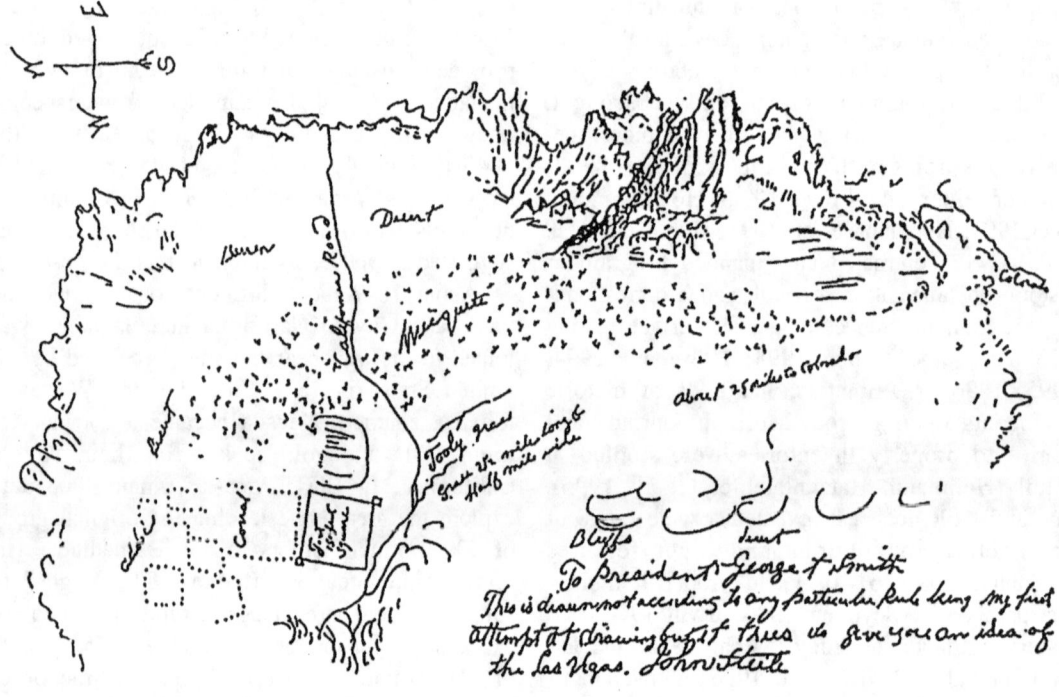

FIGURE 1. John Steele's 1855 sketch map of the planned layout of the Las Vegas Fort and Mormon Mission.

Perspectives from *Historical Archaeology*

doned by the time T. S. Kenderdine passed along the Mormon Trail in the spring of that year. In June of 1858, Brother Benjamin Hulse and a small group of Mormon farmers managed to plant over 40 acres of corn and wheat in the old Mormon fields. Loss and theft of the vast majority of the harvest by "hostile mountain Indians" resulted in abandonment of their temporary encampment at the fort on 26 September 1858.

Throughout 1859, numerous travelers and wagon trains on the Spanish Trail used the shelter and water available at the ruins of the fort. In August of 1860, a California prospecting party found silver deposits worth mining at the old Potosi Lode. This group reopened the mine in early December, attracting other prospectors to the area. The population increase created demands for fresh vegetables, fruit, and grains that prompted a resumption of farming along Las Vegas Creek. Albert Knapp, an original Mormon settler, returned to the fort early in 1860 to begin ranching and farming. Surplus produce and meat was sold to the miners.

The Potosi silver boom began to subside substantially by late 1861. Correspondingly, most small farms established in the valley during the spring of 1861 failed by early 1862. One marked exception was Albert Knapp's Las Vegas Fort ranch and farm. The reduced market for the 1862 crop caused Albert to move to California, however, leaving his brother William in charge. William Knapp had opened a dry goods store across the creek from the fort by the time he inherited the ranch from his brother late in 1864. Shortly thereafter, Octavius Decatur Gass came to Las Vegas from California to reconnoiter the area's possibilities.

O. D. Gass bought William Knapp's ranch in 1865 and began extensive cattle operations while he continued farming and maintaining the general store. His store served passing wagon trains and stage lines and his ranch provided supplies of meat, grain, vegetables, and fruit to nearby mining communities and military posts. During his occupation of the site (1865–1881), Gass became

the principal landowner in the Las Vegas valley, and he ultimately owned all of the springs contributing to Las Vegas Creek. In August 1879, Gass borrowed $5,000 in gold from a fellow rancher, Archibald Stewart, of Bristol, Nevada. The one-year promissory note was secured by a mortgage on the 640-acre Las Vegas Ranch and the adjacent 140-acre Spring Ranch. Gass failed to repay the loan within the year, and on 2 August 1880 Archibald Stewart acquired those properties, although Gass and his family did not leave the site until early June of 1881.

Stewart sold a third interest in the Las Vegas Ranch to H. G. (George) Haggerty in 1881. Within a month, Haggerty had moved to the ranch and begun upgrading its buildings. He reopened the store across the creek and that year harvested over 600 gallons of wine and "about a ton of raisins" from the grapevines planted by its Mormon settlers. For reasons which remain unclear, Haggerty sold his interest in the ranch back to Stewart in early 1882. By April 1882, Stewart, his wife Helen, and their three children had moved onto Las Vegas Ranch.

The ranch continued to grow as both a farm and cattle spread. In the summer of 1884, however, Archibald Stewart was killed in a gunfight at neighboring Kiel Ranch. Helen Stewart put the ranch up for sale but could find no buyers and remained to work the property she had inherited. From 1886 through 1902, Mrs. Stewart and her family maintained the ranch, a store, and a bar. Documents from the mid- to late1880s identify the Stewart Ranch as a stopover for local pioneers and regional travelers who wanted "a taste of the finer things in life." In 1893, the U.S. Postal Service reopened a branch at the ranch (spelled "Los Vegas"; it was 1903 before the name was changed to "Las Vegas"). By April 1901, Mrs. Stewart's holdings included a large cattle herd, 557 peach trees, 114 apple trees, over 1,560 grapevines, 40 acres of redtop hay, over 6.5 acres of wheat, and 2.5 acres of sweet potatoes. Las Vegas Ranch had become one of the economic cornerstones of southern Nevada and, indeed, the entire state.

In the early summer of 1902, Helen J. Stewart sold 1,836 acres of her ranch to the San Pedro, Los Angeles, and Salt Lake (SP, LA, & SL) Railroad, under the supervision of Montana's Senator William A. Clark. A complete inventory of all springs and water rights, acreage, stock, crops, ranch buildings, ranch equipment, and nonpersonal ranch property was prepared as a condition of the $55,000 sale. According to the inventory, Helen Stewart's holdings included over 2,000 fenced acres of irrigated crops, of which 450 acres were held by deed.

Walter Bracken, the railroad's representative, lived and worked at the ranch while a substantial portion of the property south of the ranch was surveyed, subdivided, and subsequently sold at auction as townsite lots on 15 May 1905. That auction is today considered the "official" founding of the City of Las Vegas. Subsequent to its use as housing for railroad employees, in 1905, Harry R. Beale began conversion of the Stewart Ranch house and immediately surrounding property to a restaurant and resort for residents of the valley. For the next 50 years this would be its principal use.

Other Relevant Information

Other relevant information includes geology, architecture, artifacts, and faunal, macrobotanical, and palynological data. These are considered in greater detail below.

Geology and Stratigraphy

Las Vegas Creek valley is a large, broad basin surrounded by the Spring, Pintwater, Desert, Sheep, Las Vegas (Sunrise), River, and McCollough mountain ranges. The sediments of the basin floor are principally clay and silt deposits produced through vigorous Late Wisconsin spring discharge episodes (Quade and Pratt 1989; Quade et al. 1995). The artesian springs that sup-

port the permanent flow of Las Vegas Creek are located some 2.5 mi. west of the site (Figure 2). Along Las Vegas Creek, the escarpment of the terrace that supports the spring once lay roughly 150 m to the west of the escarpment of the terrace upon which the site is located. The primary irrigation ditch excavated by Mormon settlers carried water from Las Vegas Creek north along the escarpment of the site terrace to fields cleared from a mesquite bosque on the valley floor.

Sometime before human occupation began, Las Vegas Creek incised a channel into the clays and silts of the site terrace. The channel was infilled by a silt which also forms an overbank deposit extending roughly 10 m north of the south wall of the fort. The organically rich, thick, A horizon of the Paradise Silt Loam soil (Speck 1985), which formed on the surface of the overbank deposit, extended north from Las Vegas Creek to

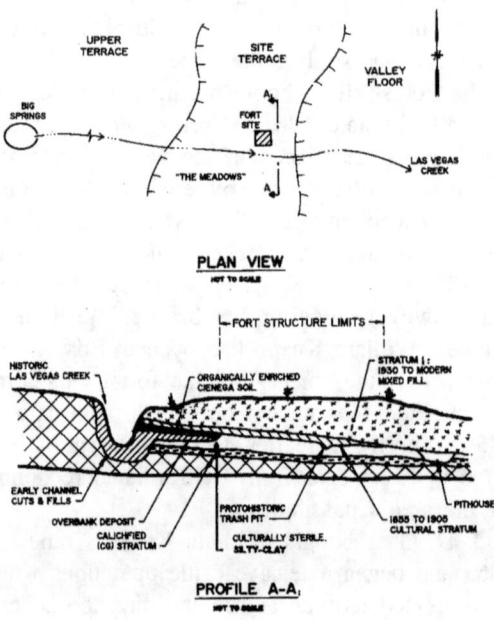

FIGURE 2. *Top*, schematic plan of the course of the upper reaches of Las Vegas Creek; *bottom*, generalized stratigraphic profile at Old Las Vegas Mormon Fort State Historic Park.

Perspectives from *Historical Archaeology*

the vicinity of the south wall of the Old Mormon Fort. It demarcates the extent of direct influence of the stream on local vegetation at the time of Mormon occupation.

During the years of Mormon- and Ranching-period occupations, excavations were made through these soils, and cultural features and occupation debris—archaeological trash deposits— were placed upon their surfaces. Superimposed upon these natural and cultural deposits are two others, designated Stratum 1 and Site Stratum I. Stratum 1 is a dark, grayish-brown silt loam that appears to be the product of several grading or leveling episodes. It includes cultural materials dating between 1930 and 1950, and a mixture of the site's older natural and cultural deposits. Site Stratum I, which overlies all the others, is a modern cultural deposit of mechanically deposited exotic backfill.

Architectural Remains

Excavations revealed portions of most of the architectural elements of the Old Mormon Fort, as expected. They also identified a probable protohistoric Native American habitation structure and a group of Native American trash-filled pits that flotation studies (Bohrer 1996) identify as products of Mormon missionizing efforts. Exposure of other architectural features produced evidence of the blacksmith shop, reuse of the fort's northwest bastion during Gass's occupation, and the remodeling of Gass's L-shaped residence to the T-shaped structure that subsequently served as headquarters for the Stewart Ranch.

Material Culture

Excavations yielded a collection of 9,309 historic artifacts incorporating items of glass, metal—mostly nails and cartridges—pottery, and shell, glass, celluloid, and plastic buttons. Their analysis was primarily geared towards identifying potential chronological markers to assist calendric dating of associated architectural features, strati-

graphic units, and biological samples. In combination, historic documents analysis and the artifact assemblage analysis defined eight principal historic periods represented at the site. These are (1) a Pre-Mormon period, (2) the Mormon period (1855–1857), (3) the 1858 to 1865 period, (4) the Gass Ranch period (1865–1881), (5) the Early Stewart Ranch period (1881–1884), (6) the Middle Stewart Ranch period (1884–1900), (7) the Late Stewart Ranch period (1900–1902), and (8) the Railroad period.

Faunal Remains

Lawrence's (1996) faunal analysis was directed towards other research questions, so we have reorganized her raw data to identify differences in faunal exploitation that might evidence landuse activities. Table 1 records the percentage of bone specimens of each taxon associated with datable features and/or artifact assemblages. Since the minimum number of individuals (MNI) recovered from any given feature or excavation unit was not established in Lawrence's study, the tabulated values only provide a rough index of the faunas of each horizon. Also, since the majority of specimens from most horizons were identified only as "mammal," much of the data potentially relevant to landuse assessment has been obscured.

We suspect that though other animals are undoubtedly represented, the "small mammal" remains category mainly reflects the presence of dogs, while larger mammal remains mostly represent cattle, both cow and calf. Significantly higher frequencies for these taxa are associated with evidence of the Gass Ranch occupation. The most unusual record, however, is presented by the fauna associated with archaeological evidence of the Stewart Ranch occupation. This is the only fauna that includes rabbit remains, and it incorporates about twice as many taxa as are represented in the faunas of the other horizons. Mrs. Stewart employed local Native Americans of both sexes at her ranch; the distinctive char-

TABLE 1

FAUNAL REMAINS FROM THE OLD MORMON FORT SITE

Fauna	Period			
	Stewart Ranch (1881–1902)	Gass Ranch (1865–1881)	Mormon	Pre-Mormon
Gopher	0.4	1.9	0.4	---
Rodentia	3.5	---	---	0.6
Small Mammal	1.4	3.8	1.3	0.6
Medium Mammal	4.6	---	---	1.9
Med–Large Mammal	4.6	21.2	1.6	3.9
Large Mammal	5.3	1.9	2.5	0.6
Mammal	33.3	61.5	84.9	79.8
Cattle	---	---	1.3	---
Pig	0.4	---	---	---
Lagomorph	0.4	---	---	---
Cottontail	3.5	---	---	---
Eggshell	20.0	---	0.4	---
Small Bird	7.3	---	1.3	1.3
Bird	1.4	3.8	5.0	8.4
Large Bird	---	1.9	---	---
Chicken	3.2	3.8	0.8	1.3
Turkey	0.4	---	---	---
Duck	0.4	---	0.4	---
Unknown	9.8	---	---	0.6
Total	285	52	238	154

acter of the faunal record of this occupation may be a function of their dietary practices.

Macrobotanical Remains

Nine of the 21 flotation samples that have been analyzed were associated with Native American features or cultural materials, while an additional nine samples were associated with Mormon-period features. Flotation samples associated with Native American archaeology typically contain seed concentrations reflecting significant reliance on two introduced, fig and tomato, and one native plant, ground cherry. Grape, raspberry, pickleweed, and charred saltbush seeds are also common. Fig and tomato seeds occur in fewer samples, and in lesser quantities, associated with Mormon-period artifacts; indeed, only ground cherry and charred saltbush seeds are commonly observed. The similarities suggest Native American adoption of Mormon food plants when they were camped in the vicinity, and the contrasts probably reflect food preparation and waste disposal habits more than differences in plant use.

Palynological Remains

The pollen records of the samples collected at the site have been organized by a method specifically designed to allow analysis of the ecosystem history of historic-period archaeological sites (Schoenwetter 1990). This method has the additional potential to suggest interpretations of landuse changes. Although theoretical differences also distinguish this method from those used in traditional pollen analysis, the way palynological data is displayed is notably distinctive. Instead of the traditional pollen diagram, information is arrayed in either graphic or tabular forms that average the pollen statistics of groups, or populations, of samples of the same antiquity.

The types of palynological data used in the landuse analysis (Table 2; Figure 3) are: (1) average relative pollen frequency values (percentages) that have been calculated on pollen sums which exclude observations of two locally overrepresented taxa, chenoam (Chenopodiineae) and pellitory (*Parietaria*); (2) average values of the ratio of the overrepresented pollen types to the pollen sums; and (3) average pollen concentration per cubic centimeter of deposit.

For reasons explored in detail previously (Schoenwetter 1996:264–271, 278–279), pollen frequency values for cattail (*Typha* sp.), willow (*Salix* sp.), and cottonwood (*Populus* sp.) are interpreted, respectively, as monitors of the amount of water available to support plant and animal life in the bed of Las Vegas Creek, on the creek bank, and on the creek's floodplain. The combined pollen frequency values for desert composites, Ambrosieae and Tubuliflorae, are taken as monitors of conditions favoring plants and animals adapted to the desert habitat. Changes in the relative ratio values for chenoam pollen are interpreted as indices of the intensity of local disturbance. Ratio values of pellitory pollen are taken as a monitor of water quality. Pollen of the trees and shrubs of the canyon and slope habitat—pine (*Pinus* sp.), oak (*Quercus* sp.), sagebrush (*Artemisia* sp.), and Mormon tea (*Ephedra* sp.)—was transported to the site from a relatively long distance, so the pollen concentration values for these taxa would be expected to be essentially stable throughout the half century considered here. Major fluctuations in their values are taken as monitors of factors affecting pollen production and, therefore, as indices of each taxon's vitality. Given the short periods of such fluctuations, interpretations of human impact are more probable than interpretations in terms of climatic or vegetation pattern change.

An Integrated Model of Landuse Changes

Landuse changes for each of the eight principal historic periods represented at the site are treated below.

Pre-Mormon Landuse

Construction of the south wall of the fort took place on the surface of the A horizon of the Paradise Silt Loam in the southern district of the

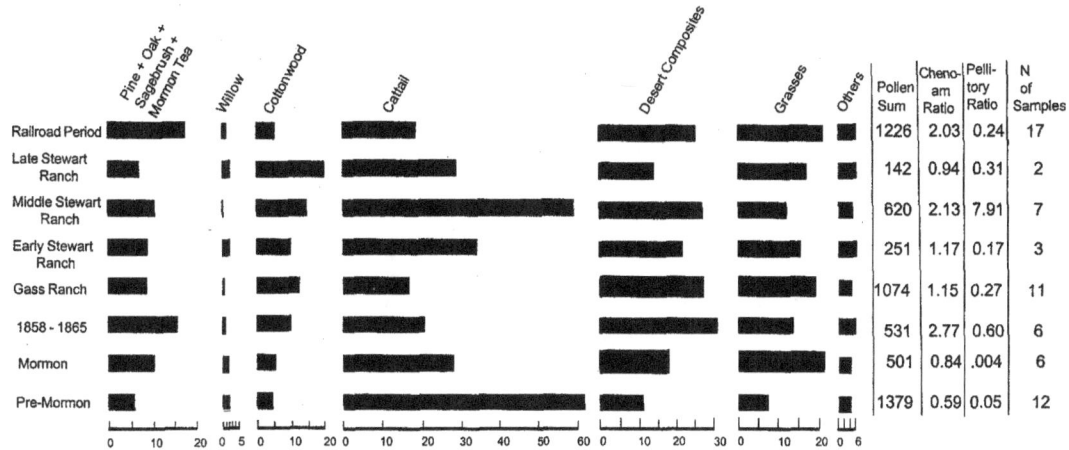

FIGURE 3. Average relative pollen frequencies (percentages of the pollen sum) and average ratios to the pollen sum (locally overrepresented taxa) for samples of different occupation horizons. Samples dated by direct association with datable material culture.

TABLE 2

AVERAGE POLLEN CONCENTRATION VALUES FOR POLLEN GROUPS OF THE OCCUPATION HORIZONS

Period																
					Pollen Concentration Values										
	Pine	Oak	Sagebrush	Mormon Tea	Willow	Cottonwood	Cattail	Grass	Low Spine	High Spine	Chenoam	Pellitory	N	Total	
Railroad	178	59	416	---	89	238	950	861	891	238	8,580	1,009	465	27,612	
Late Stewart Ranch	174	29	29	155	193	1,179	1,904	1,063	933	553	5,653	1,739	1,388	93,891	
Mid-Stewart Ranch	116	77	193	77	39	714	1,486	618	772	540	10,326	38,314	2,772	160,514	
Early Stewart Ranch	131	253	262	87	297	900	3,243	1,512	1,285	787	10,969	1,600	2,508	241,136	
Grass Ranch	325	142	183	244	122	1,362	3,254	2,115	1,485	1,362	12,447	2,969	1,308	159,616	
1858–1865	82	82	226	50	50	314	742	428	704	245	8,722	13	1,788	56,216	
Mormon	329	362	436	41	304	659	3,529	2,526	1,547	592	9,518	543	2,565	253,211	
Pre-Mormon	297	157	245	26	376	372	8,122	591	769	168	4,432	9	2,353	143,848	

Perspectives from *Historical Archaeology*

site. The pollen samples collected from this surface, however, segregate into two pollen groups. Since one pollen group is associated with Mormon-period architecture, the other is presumably older. Both the highly organic soil (Figure 2) and the local overrepresentation of cattail pollen (Figure 3) documents the presence of standing water—probably a marsh which became a seasonally open pool—when the earlier pollen group was deposited. The protohistoric Native American structure was located near but north of the floodplain margin. If it was occupied when the Pre-Mormon-period pollen records were deposited, the camp would have had immediate access to water, and would not have been too distant from both a very productive mesquite harvesting district and hunting grounds for birds and mammals that watered at the creek and occupied the meadow. This reconstruction is consistent with ethnographic accounts (e.g., Euler 1966; Schroth 1987) of preferred Southern Paiute summer encampment areas. It is also consistent with the name given the site by Spanish-speaking traders.

By the time Frémont camped at the site in 1841, the marsh no longer existed. By 1853, Las Vegas Creek was confined to two deep but narrow channels, flanked by willow and vines on the site's terrace, with extensive meadow to the south and on the lower terrace to the southeast, and mesquite bosque where the creek flowed across the valley floor. Travelers on the Old Spanish Trail certainly took advantage of its water and grazing potential but, like the Native American residents, occupied the site only through temporary encampments.

Mormon Landuse

The reduced average cattail pollen frequency for the group of pollen samples associated with archaeological evidence of Mormon occupation suggests the volume of water in the creek had declined since the Pre-Mormon, presumably protohistoric, occupation. We strongly suspect this was the result of water diversion into the Mormon irrigation ditch. A slight increase in the chenoam ratio suggests more local disturbance of the site, but the pollen record otherwise offers no evidence of the fort's construction or the agricultural activities that the historic record documents as the prominent features of Mormon landuse. The flotation and faunal records for this period, however, illustrate the significance of agricultural production to both the Native American and the Mormon populations that occupied the site. The increases in pine, oak, sagebrush, and Mormon tea pollen concentration values in this period (Table 2) are most likely an indirect effect of increased human activity at the margins of the valley.

1858 to 1865 Landuse

Local landuse changes documented by the historic record focus on the abandonment and debilitation of the fort; its reoccupation as a residence and corral by the Knapp brothers, redevelopment of the Mormon garden, vineyard, and fields; and the establishment of a store across Las Vegas Creek from Old Mormon Fort. The archaeological record attests Knapp's blacksmith shop, where mining equipment was probably repaired as often as traveler's horses were reshod. Property ownership documents show patenting of plots of land on both sides of Las Vegas Creek upstream of Knapp's lands. Beyond the site, historic accounts allow us to recognize that mining reached its maximal intensity during this period.

Although it is a very short interval of time, pollen records of this date can be recognized by their associations with Civil War-period artifacts. On average, a further reduction in the cattail pollen frequency suggests exploitation of the waters of Las Vegas Creek was intensified, and a significant rise in the desert composites pollen frequency value indicates enhancement of that habitat. An extraordinary decline in pollen production by the trees and shrubs of the slope and canyon habitats at the valley margins (Table 2) may index the impact of human harvests for smelter fuel or the effects of smelter smoke on pollen production in that area.

The reconstruction that emerges from integration of the archaeological, palynological, and historic information is of a time when landuse patterns were responsive to the demands of a larger, more diverse, community than had existed earlier. Basically, the Mormon objective of economic self-sufficiency gave way to one motivated by the cash profit created by satisfying the needs of populations of miners and travelers. Knapp's establishment of a blacksmith shop and store were the most obvious signs of this change, but the documentary and palynological records provide clues that the Knapp brothers were not the only ones responding to this by-product of the silver boom. By patenting plots of land along the creek, a number of individuals seem to have established rights to divert some of its flow into small-scale irrigation systems that watered desert plots. Only the Knapps seem to have been able to make a go of it, though, and most of their competitors were "out of business" when O. D. Gass and his partners purchased the fort.

Gass Ranch Landuse

Historic records document Gass's success at farming; for example he doubled the amount of harvested irrigated acreage between 1871 and 1880. He also systematically purchased the lands and water rights along Las Vegas Creek as farm failures made them available. His 1878 purchase of the 120-acre Spring Ranch finally gave him virtually sole control of all the water of Las Vegas Creek. His principal source of wealth, however, was livestock production. He herded more than 400 head of cattle, and butchered a bull or a cow twice weekly to satisfy local demand. The faunal record independently suggests ranching took precedence over farming, since the frequency of bone attributable to domestic fauna increased substantially on this horizon. As Gass prospered, however, both mining and small-scale farming in the valley declined. Gass's store continued to satisfy local needs, but the primary markets for his beeves were the soldiery stationed at Camp Eldorado, workers at the Potosi mine, and mining communities northwest of the Las Vegas valley.

Average pollen concentration values increased for the flora of the canyon and slope habitat in the group of samples dated to the Gass Ranch occupation, concurrent with a reduction in sagebrush pollen concentration. Alternatively, average frequency values for the pollen types that monitor water quantity (cattail) and desert enhancement (desert composites) both decrease in this period, while both relative frequency and pollen concentration values for grass (Poaceae) pollen increase. Increased pollen production by the floras of the valley margins seems likely to have been a response to the cessation of intensive mining and prospecting activities in those areas. The landuse reconstruction, however, must accommodate evidence of a reduction in the quantity of water in Las Vegas Creek and the evidence for enhancement of one or more ecological niches favored by grasses, during the period in which upstream agricultural production was in decline. Gass's intensification of irrigated agriculture no doubt accounts for much of the quantitative loss, but cannot explain the other features of the palynological record. We believe, however, they are linked to the reduced sagebrush pollen concentration value and suggest a landuse scenario that is not documented in the historic record.

As we reconstruct the situation, Gass was the first of the district's residents with both the initial capital and the enterprise to take advantage of more than one of the valley's resources. Those who preceded him had hoped to profit from either its agricultural potential or its mineral wealth. Gass diversified his interests, identifying secure markets his activities could serve as a hostler, a merchant, a farmer, and a rancher. In the latter capacity, we believe he recognized the extraordinary potential of the open desert range. Like Hell, all it needed was a bit of water. We believe his systematic purchase of failed farms along Las Vegas Creek was not principally intended to provide more water for the irrigated acreage of his farming operations. The creek watered cattle, but we think Gass's real objective was control of the small-scale irrigation systems that had been abandoned during the silver boom bust of 1862. These systems could be developed into stock tanks to water cattle feeding on the open range at strategic desert locations. The banks of the canals extended floodplain habitat conditions, appropriate for invasion by grasses, into the desert.

When he was able to purchase the Spring Ranch in 1878, Gass had total control of the only water available to livestock that grazed the central part of the Las Vegas basin. Springs at the margins of the valley, however, could also water herds. We think the effect of those herds on the sagebrush habitat is reflected in the pollen record, and that by the time Gass lost the ranch to Stewart there were a number of competing ranching operations in the area.

Early Stewart Ranch Landuse

Pollen records we can attribute to the early years of Stewart Ranch operations (ca. 1881–1883) suggest much the same landuse pattern as Gass had employed. An increase in the quantity of water reaching the Old Mormon Fort site, however, suggests less was diverted to upstream stock tanks and more was used to irrigate orchard and croplands and to support grazing in the meadow in the immediate area of the ranch headquarters. The pellitory pollen ratio evidence of an increase in water quality at this time suggests that livestock production was actually decreased. The historic record supports this landuse reconstruction. Paher (1971) notes that agricultural production, especially grapes for wine and raisins, was increased in 1881 and 1882, while livestock production was decreased.

Mid-Stewart Ranch Landuse

Local range disputes and increased cattle rustling created conditions for an alternative use of

the land by the mid-1880s. Historic records document intensification of both livestock and crop production at the Stewart Ranch, but photographs suggest both operations were developed close to ranch headquarters. In 1883, Mrs. Stewart purchased an additional 1,100 acres, which included roughly half the meadowland south of her Old Mormon Fort property and about one-third of the irrigated area developed from the Mormon fields to the northeast. Added to the 780 acres situated along the length of Las Vegas Creek that had been transferred by Gass, she now owned all the land directly influenced by that water. This allowed her sole use of an additional 1,500 acres of irrigated cropland and approximately 600 additional acres of meadowland. Control of all the water of Las Vegas Creek meant that no one else could irrigate cropland acreage or water cattle grazing on meadow adjacent to her property.

Mrs. Stewart, like Gass and other ranchers before and since, used more land for livestock production than she owned. Gass extended the watering potential of Las Vegas Creek into open range by diversion ditches that carried it out to desert stock tanks. Gass's strategy could not remain effective, however, if aggressive competitors challenged his unique access to that water. Following her husband's violent demise, Mrs. Stewart devised a strategy that could effectively ward off competition and support her herd closer to her ranch headquarters—and so discourage rustling, though it used both grazing and water resources more intensively and required the purchase of more property. Her purchases allowed her to restrict access to the watering potential of Las Vegas Creek, and thus reduce competition for the grazing potential of the lands adjacent to those she owned.

The pollen record expression of this situation is manifested by: (1) evidence of an increase in the quantity of water reaching the environs of the site as upstream desert stock tanks were abandoned, (2) a doubling of the chenoam ratio as local disturbance increased, and (3) increased use of the meadow habitat reflected as a decrease in grass pollen and an increase in the desert composites pollen frequency values. Now that her cattle were concentrated near the ranch headquarters, however, the quality of water arriving at the fort location was drastically affected. The pellitory pollen ratio monitor of that ecosystem condition increased logarithmically at this time.

Late Stewart Ranch and Railroad Landuse

Documentary evidence suggests Mrs. Stewart continued to execute the strategy implemented earlier, but stabilized the size of her cattle herd to conserve her meadowland resource and expanded production on the irrigated land under her control. She prospered financially and socially as a result. The palynological record of this period, however, yields insight into the ecological side-effects of these activities.

The effects of wise management of the meadowland close to ranch headquarters is observable as a positive change in the pollen concentrations of grass, willow and cottonwood pollen. Though the relative frequency value for desert composites pollen was reduced, the pollen concentration value for desert composite pollen types and Mormon tea increased, suggesting an increase in pollen production and vitality of plants of the desert habitat. Taken as a whole, the pollen record suggests enrichment of the meadowland pasture Mrs. Stewart owned but coincident expansion of the desert habitat that lay beyond the southern border of her land. The principal reason seems suggested by the dramatic decline in the cattail pollen relative frequency value, which we interpret as a reduction in the quantity of water available for support of the meadow habitat. This change, like the parallel change observed between the Pre-Mormon and Early Mormon horizons, can be accounted for as a product of the diversion of water that previously supported meadow to the support of cultivated plants via development of the irrigation system.

Both the reductions in oak and sagebrush pollen concentrations and major increases in the chenoam pollen concentration value can be interpreted as indices of overgrazing on lands beyond the boundaries of Las Vegas Ranch. This interpretation explicates the ecological conditions existing at the site of the modern settlement of Las Vegas when townsite development began in 1905. Though it lay within the area mapped as meadowland in 1855, diversion of the creek's water to support episodes of intensified agricultural production, plus a 20-year history of intensive use of the meadow resource close to the Stewart Ranch headquarters for beef production, drew off water that had sustained the southern margin of the meadow prior to Mormon settlement. By the turn of the century, the townsite district had become overgrazed desert land unsuitable for rural use.

Beginning in 1900, Mrs. Stewart reduced her cattle holdings to prepare for sale of her property. Once acquired by the SP, LA, & SL Railroad, some of the Stewart property was platted as the townsite which became modern Las Vegas. In 1905, when lots were put up for sale, Montana's Senator William A. Clark, the railroad's principal shareholder, assured a water supply for both the town and the railroad by piping water from Las Vegas Creek south from its upstream source to the townsite and north from a point near the Stewart Ranch headquarters building to the railroad station site. These landuse changes are represented in the pollen record by declines in the indices of water pollution and water quantity and an increase in the chenoam pollen ratio, which monitors land disturbance.

Processual Analysis of the Landuse History Model

Landuse in the period prior to Mormon settlement reflected the sorts of ways the valley's resources could be exploited by small, mobile, groups of Native Americans or Euroamerican travelers. The stated objectives of the Mormon mission brought a wholly new perspective, as well as a new landuse ethic. The land was now to be used to support both a permanent settlement and a proselytizing effort. Food production was essential to both. The political significance of control over the transportation routes that converged near the site was not lost upon the Mormons, of course. After all, the building they constructed was a fort. Obviously, though, the economic significance of the valley's resources were now assessed in relation to quite different social and political parameters and seen through the screen of religious motivations.

Discovery of metallic ores in the mountains marginal to the Las Vegas valley changed its strategic and economic potential in at least two ways. First, it placed new priorities on the mission's functions, which led to social conflict and abandonment of Old Mormon Fort; second, it shifted the economic focus from self-sufficient agriculture to resource exploitation for fiscal profit. Prospectors and the miners who localized at strikes and successful mines sought the quick wealth they could extract from the earth; those who controlled food production along Las Vegas Creek sought the quick wealth they could extract from the prospectors and miners.

Most farmers failed late in 1862 as the silver boom collapsed and the demand for the small surpluses they could produce on raw desert land declined. Alfred Knapp, however, commanded property with unusual advantages. Though upstream farmers reduced the amount of water he could use, he controlled sufficient cleared and arable land to generate enough surplus to exploit economies of scale. When insufficient market for the crops he produced in 1863 provoked his departure, his brother William survived through management of the store constructed south of the creek. Less than a year after inheriting them, however, he sold all holdings to O. D. Gass.

Gass's economic behavior was also motivated by fiscal profit, but he introduced a new strategy. He deliberately organized the work and production of his farming, livestock, blacksmithing, and merchandizing operations to satisfy three specific, secure markets: mining communities, military outposts, and travelers along the wagon roads that passed through his holdings. This strategy was effective, but we believe Gass recognized the

long-term profit to be made by developing his herd, and that his systematic accumulation of water rights along Las Vegas Creek as they became available was intended to fulfill that objective. By 1878, when he purchased the Spring Ranch, he controlled all of the only source of water in the central Las Vegas valley. The water he could divert to stock tanks allowed his cattle access to much of the desert vegetation beyond Las Vegas Creek's floodplain and meadowland.

Gass's strategy was unable to withstand competitive pressure, however. As other entrepreneurs enlarged their herds, his lowland stock tanks became natural focal points for rustling and conflict. We were originally surprised that Gass had defaulted on so small a loan secured by the entirety of his holdings. Given his age, and the character of the rough and ready socioeconomic context of ranching in his day, we now view his action as a strategic retreat. Archibald Stewart, apparently, believed the continued success of Gass's strategy required only ambition, threats, and belligerence. His death by gunshot on the porch of a neighboring ranch was never satisfactorily investigated. As Paher (1971:57) writes, "Not much sympathy was expressed for Stewart, and many believed he was an overbearing man who got his just desserts."

Mrs. Stewart, as inheritor of Las Vegas Ranch, was unable to sell it off and realized she required an economic strategy that minimized competitive relations with other ranchers, yet offered opportunity for expansion of her assets. By relinquishing the open desert range north and south of Las Vegas Creek, confining her cattle to her own property and adjacent meadowlands south of her ranch headquarters, she maintained her herd within defensible borders—albeit at the cost of more intensive landuse. She simultaneously developed and expanded her irrigable cropland and played the role of gracious hostess to travelers and locals using the Mormon Road and Old Spanish Trail.

Sale of Mrs. Stewart's holdings to the railroad ushered in an era of economic changes and changes in landuse practice. As the foci of local economic activity became the townsite established a mile south of the Old Mormon Fort site—on now-overgrazed desert land—and the site of the railroad terminal, the bulk of the artesian springs water that fed Las Vegas Creek was diverted to those locations.

Summary

The landuse history of the founding settlement of Las Vegas mirrors the economic history of Western America. In both prehistoric and protohistoric times, landuse was regular though intermittent. The exceptional character of locally available resources was appreciated and exploited, but the priorities of visitor populations were focused on conditions and opportunities that existed elsewhere. Prior to the area's historic uses, Native Americans oriented their seasonal movements to the rhythm of the pinyon and oak harvests at higher elevations, when surpluses allowed larger gatherings and broader social intercourse. Early historic traders and travelers were oriented towards further destinations. As a result, the oasis at Las Vegas was culturally marginalized. It was simply a convenient and relatively comfortable place to halt a journey that began and ended elsewhere.

Landuse during the Mormon Mission period, short-lived as it was, exemplified the same motives and cultural ideals that brought contemporary pioneers to Oregon, southern California, and the Arizona Territory: their intention was creation of self-sufficient frontier communities with potential to "civilize" the wild landscape and its wild inhabitants. Those willing to labor to enact these ideals, however, could not effectively coexist with those who flooded the West with the landuse ethic consistent with prospecting and mining. The new ethic sought exploitation of those qualities of a landscape which promised rapid achievement of wealth and power. In many places, it was ore deposits; at Las Vegas, it was the travelers and miners who needed the meat and produce that development of Las Vegas Creek's waters could provide. As elsewhere in the American West, some individuals found ways to survive the bust that followed the boom.

For the 20 years that followed the Civil War, O. D. Gass prospered as a result of an economic strategy that centered on personal control of the only water supply adequate for large-scale meat and produce production and personal control of secure markets for those commodities. As competitors—who were prepared to back their demands through bravado, brute strength, and lawless action—came to claim shares of both, however, that strategy proved ineffective. Archibald Stewart's violent death was sufficient proof that a new set of socioeconomic conditions existed. It was those conditions Stewart's widow had to adapt to in order to succeed.

Her solution was to explore both a new ethic and a new strategy. Her objective was neither wealth nor power, but survival and elevation of social position. Carefully planned investment allowed her to concentrate the entirety of the supply of her principle resource, water, within the bounds of properties she owned outright or could protect from intrusion. She used less land more intensively than Gass, but was thus able to distance herself from competition with her neighbors and avoid even opportunity for conflict. She was probably fully aware that her strategy also exploited contemporary cultural expectations for a widow responsible for her children's upbringing.

By the end of the 19th century, then, at least in this little corner of the whole, the ideals of those who sought to civilize the Western frontier 50 and 60 years before had finally begun to be fulfilled. Not as they had expected, of course. One doubts travelers of the 1840s would credit a prophesy that neither Native Americans, antelope, nor buffalo would exist along the Old Spanish Trail 50 years hence. Or that changes in the ways the landscape at the Las Vegas Oasis would be utilized over the course of that 50 years would mirror a broader sequence of changing socioeconomic conditions as the history of the American West evolved.

Though we are aware of the perspective exemplified in the work edited by Crumley (1995), our archaeological training and prior experience originally led us to expect that a processual analysis of landuse changes at the Old Mormon Fort site and environs would find them to have been adaptations to changes in the ecology of the local district. Adaptations, for example, to changes in the water table or adaptations to ways in which the open range and meadowlands were affected by introduced livestock. We believe, however, this expectation has not been fulfilled. Rather, in the words of M. Van Buren (1996:338), landuse changes at the Old Mormon Fort locale are "better understood as strategic decisions in the context of contemporary socioeconomic conditions, not ecological adaptations rooted in cultural tradition." At various times, strategic decisions prioritized religiously and idealistically motivated interests; they exploited the opportunities for quick riches offered by boomtown settlements; they shrewdly identified the profit in supplying the demands of specific markets; and they successfully identified a secure means of withdrawing from the competitive pressures of the early days of business ranching. Sometimes they were reactions to the demands of population growth, and sometimes they were proactions based on accurate predictions of a foreseeable future. Las Vegas was not ineptly named, nor is the present state of its landscape simply a product of mismanagement or exploitation by greedy and uncaring developers. The ways the land is used today are effectively controlled by the same factors that controlled its use even into the prehistoric past. Landuse at Las Vegas has always been a matter of strategic response to the prioritized interests of its occupants and the character of socioeconomic conditions existing within, but created beyond, the margins of the Las Vegas valley.

ACKNOWLEDGMENTS

We wish to express our appreciation to Phares Woods and Laura Eissmann of Nevada Division of State Parks for supporting these investigations and their comments and suggestions regarding earlier research results. Also, we thank Vorsilla Bohrer, Donald Hardesty, Lonnie Pippin, and an anonymous reviewer for comments and suggestions made on an earlier version of this article. We take responsibility for any misinterpretations of their ideas and comments, and for the character of errors we have made.

REFERENCES

BOHRER, VORSILA L.
1996   The Plant Remains from the Old Las Vegas Mormon Fort State Historic Park, Clark County, Nevada. In The Old Las Vegas Mormon Fort: The Founding of a Desert Community in Clark County, Nevada, edited by John W. Hohmann. *Studies in Western Archaeology* 4:H1–H18. Louis Berger & Associates, Phoenix, AZ.

CRUMLEY, CAROLE L. (EDITOR)
1995   *Historical Ecology: Cultural Knowledge and Changing Landscapes.* School of American Research Press, Santa Fe, NM.

ELSTON, ROBERT G., AND ALVIN R. McLANE
1993   *Old Las Vegas Mormon Fort: Historical and Archaeological Perspectives.* Manuscript on file, Intermountain Research, Silver City, NM.

EULER, ROBERT C.
1966   Southern Paiute Ethnohistory. *University of Utah Anthropological Papers* 78. Salt Lake City, UT.

FRÉMONT, JOHN C.
1845   *Report of the Exploring Expedition to the Rocky Mountains in the Year 1842, and to Oregon and North California in the Years 1845–44.* 28th Congress, second session, House of Representatives Document 166. Blair and Rives, Washington, DC.

HATZENBUEHLER, LYNN E., AND JAMES C. LOWE
1993   Monitoring Report for Overburden Removal, Old Las Vegas Mormon Fort, Las Vegas Nevada. Report submitted to State of Nevada Parks Department, Las Vegas.

HOHMANN, JOHN W.
1994   A Research Design and Scope of Work for Phase II Archaeological Testing at the Old Las Vegas Mormon Fort State Historic Park, Las Vegas, Clark County, Nevada. *Cultural Resource Group Research Report* 23. Louis Berger & Associates, Las Vegas, NV.
1995   The Founding of Las Vegas Nevada: Phase II Archaeological Investigations at the Old Las Vegas Mormon Fort State Historic Park, Clark County, Nevada. *Cultural Resource Group Research Report* 24. Louis Berger & Associates, Las Vegas, NV.

HOHMANN, JOHN W. (EDITOR)
1996 The Old Las Vegas Mormon Fort: The Founding of a Desert Community in Clark County, Nevada. *Studies in Western Archaeology* 4. Louis Berger & Associates, Phoenix, AZ.

HOHMANN, JOHN W., MARGARET "PEG" DAVIS, DONALD C. IRWIN, JAMES C. LOWE, AND MICHAEL REID
1996 Historic Materials Analysis. In The Old Las Vegas Mormon Fort: The Founding of a Desert Community in Clark County, Nevada, edited by John W. Hohmann. *Studies in Western Archaeology* 4:221–257. Louis Berger & Associates, Phoenix, AZ.

HOHMANN, JOHN W., MARGARET "PEG" DAVIS, AND JOEL D. IRISH
1995 The Reliability of Three Remote Sensing Techniques Used at the Old Las Vegas Mormon Fort State Historic Park. Paper presented at the 60th Annual Meeting of the Society for American Archaeology, Minneapolis, MN.

HOHMANN, JOHN W., LYNN HATZENBUEHLER, AND PHARES WOODS
1996 A History of the Old Las Vegas Mormon Fort and Its Surrounding Environments. In The Old Las Vegas Mormon Fort: The Founding of a Desert Community in Clark County, Nevada, edited by John W. Hohmann. *Studies in Western Archaeology* 4:17–96. Louis Berger & Associates, Phoenix, AZ.

HOHMANN, JOHN W., AND JOEL D. IRISH
1994 Additional Remote Sensing Studies Conducted at the Old Las Vegas Mormon Fort State Historic Park, Las Vegas, Clark County, Nevada. *Cultural Resource Group Research Report* 18. Las Vegas, NV.

HOHMANN, JOHN W., JOEL D. IRISH, AND MARGARET "PEG" DAVIS
1994 Recent Investigations at the Old Las Vegas Mormon Fort, Nevada. Paper presented at the 67th Annual Pecos Conference, Mesa Verde National Park, CO.

HOHMANN, JOHN W., AND DON W. RYDEN
1994 A Proposal to Conduct Historic Research and Phase II Archaeological Testing at the Old Las Vegas Mormon Fort State Historic Park, Clark County, Nevada. Joint *Berger/Ryden Technical Report* 5. Las Vegas, NV.

IRWIN, DONALD C.
1996 Lithic Analysis. In The Old Las Vegas Mormon Fort: The Founding of a Desert Community in Clark County, Nevada, edited by John W. Hohmann. *Studies in Western Archaeology* 4:17–96. Louis Berger & Associates, Phoenix, AZ.

LAWRENCE, PAMELA
1996 Faunal Analysis. In The Old Las Vegas Mormon Fort: The Founding of a Desert Community in Clark County, Nevada, edited by John W. Hohmann. *Studies in Western Archaeology* 4:247–257. Louis Berger & Associates, Phoenix, AZ.

LUFF, ROSEMARY, AND P. ROWLEY-CONWY (EDITORS)
1994 *Whither Environmental Archaeology?* Oxbow, Oxford, UK.

PAHER, STANLEY W.
1971 *Las Vegas, As It Began—As It Grew.* Nevada Publications, Las Vegas, NV.

QUADE, JAY, MARTIN D. MIFFLIN, WILLIAM L. PRATT, WILLIAM McCOY, AND LLOYD BURKLE
1995 Fossil Spring Deposits in the Southern Great Basin and Their Implications for Changes in Water Table Levels Near Yucca Mountain, Nevada, During Quaternary Time. *Geological Society of America Bulletin* 107(2):213–230.

QUADE, JAY, AND WILLIAM L. PRATT
1989 Late Wisconsin Groundwater Discharge Environments of the Southern Indian Springs Valley, Southern Nevada. *Quaternary Research* 31:351–370.

SCHOENWETTER, JAMES
1990 A Method for the Application of Pollen Analysis in Landscape Archaeology. In *Earth Patterns: Essays in Landscape Archaeology*, edited by William M. Kelso and Rachel Most, pp. 277–296. Charlottesville University Press, Charlottesville, VA.
1996 Archaeological Palynology at the Old Las Vegas Mormon Fort State Park: The Pilot Study. In The Old Las Vegas Mormon Fort: The Founding of a Desert Community in Clark County, Nevada, edited by John W. Hohmann. *Studies in Western Archaeology* 4:247–257. Louis Berger & Associates, Phoenix, AZ.

SCHROTH, ADELLA
1987 The Use of Mesquite in the Great Basin. In Papers on the Archaeology of the Mohave Desert, edited by Mark Q. Sutton. *Coyote Press Archives of California Prehistory* 10:53–78. Salinas, CA.

SEYMOUR, GREGORY R.
1996 Native American Ceramics from the Old Las Vegas Fort. In The Old Las Vegas Mormon Fort: The Founding of a Desert Community in Clark County, Nevada, edited by John W. Hohmann. *Studies in Western Archaeology* 4:247–257. Louis Berger & Associates, Phoenix, AZ.

SPECK, ROBERT L.

  1985 *Soil Survey of the Las Vegas Valley Area Part of Clark County, Nevada.* United States Department of Agriculture Soil Conservation Service., Washington, DC.

VAN BUREN, M.

  1996 Rethinking the Vertical Archipelago. *American Anthropologist* 98(2):338–351.

JAMES SCHOENWETTER
DEPARTMENT OF ANTHROPOLOGY
ARIZONA STATE UNIVERSITY
TEMPE, AZ 85287

JOHN W. HOHMANN
CULTURAL RESOURCE GROUP
LOUIS BERGER & ASSOCIATES, INC.
LAS VEGAS, NV 89119

LouAnn Wurst

Fixing Farms: Pondering Farm Scenes from the Vanity Press

ABSTRACT

Historical archaeologists are familiar with the illustrated farm views found in late-19th-century local history publications. Analysis of the farm views from the town of Hector in Schuyler County, New York, shows that they do not simply represent the wealthiest farmers or earliest settlers, but they do seem to cluster in family groups of fairly prosperous families representing the second generation of the area's second wave of settlement. The drawings are accurately rendered in terms of the house and the spatial layout of the farms, but topographical features are generally more mythic. This indicates that the buildings were meant to be recognized from the drawings, probably by people who already knew them. The family relationships connect these separate, individual drawings into nodes within a larger community network.

Introduction

The farm views found in late-19th-century local history publications have an obvious utility since viewers intuitively recognize that these illustrations accurately portray a farm's size, configuration, and layout. Scholars have rarely used these sources systematically and have little understanding of how or why they were created. An in-depth analysis of these farm views may provide a greater understanding of both these sources and rural social life during the second half of the 19th century. Farm illustrations found in the *History of Schuyler County, New York,* originally published in 1879 (Everts and Ensign), are examined with a focus primarily on those farms located in the Town of Hector. Through a long-term archaeological research project in Hector, two of the farms portrayed have been intensively excavated. Three issues are considered: (1) what is known about the farmers who had these illustrations and portraits commissioned; (2) what do the illustrations show; and (3) what is their accuracy? An examination of the context within which these texts were created could reveal the roles played and implications of these farm views.

The Vanity Press

The 1879 history of Schuyler County (Everts and Ensign 1879), and countless other local histories like it from across the nation, was part of the "county history school of historiography" that became very popular after the Centennial Celebration of 1876 (Malin 1955:598). These publications have been called the "vanity press," alluding to their aggrandizing function or "subscription histories," referring to their method of distribution. These publications were sold only by subscription, and door-to-door canvassers attempted to sell the book as well as space for "artistic views of the farm" (Carson 1958:78).

People had to pay to be included in these volumes, and it could cost participants an enormous amount of money. Brief biographies cost about 2.5 to 5 cents per word, selecting a spot for a farm scene could cost $36, while portraits cost up to $100 (Carson 1958:78; Daniels 1987:18). These costs clearly prohibited many individuals from participating. Since average daily wages for common laborers were $1 per day at that time, a brief biography or farm scene could easily cost a significant portion of a laborer's yearly earnings. These publications are obviously biased to include those who could afford the cost.

Historians have seldom discussed these publications, although a few statements can be found. Sarah Burns (1989:51) suggests, "these histories illustrate farmers' strivings toward middle-class status and its attendant symbols." Others have emphasized how the vanity press focused on those who had laid down roots and legitimated the successful long-time residents or prosperous farmers (Faragher 1986:229; Bushman 1992: 382). Ted Daniels (1987:20) claims that the atlases are not necessarily maps of reality but, rather, advertisements of the resident's vision of a prosperous, good life. Bernard Herman (1987: 236) argues that inclusion in these histories was rooted in the desire and ability of individuals to fix themselves in time as well as place. While sketchy, this background does provide some expectations for the Schuyler County sample—that it portrays the wealthiest farmers, long-time residents or early settlers, or progressive farmers striving towards some vague ideal of middle-class standing.

The people of Schuyler County participated in this general movement to record history. On 23 December 1875 the editor of the *Watkin's Express*, the largest local newspaper, claimed that "it seems proper that the local celebrations of the Fourth of July, 1876, which will be held throughout the land, should be made to contribute to a permanent historical memorial of the Centennial Celebration." The editor recommended that historians be appointed for each town, and that historical addresses be prepared to trace the history of each community. A short series of historical articles ran in the *Watkin's Express* throughout 1876, indicating that several communities had followed his advice.

The editor of the *Watkin's Express* also embraced Everts and Ensign's publication of the history of Schuyler County. On 25 July 1878 the newspaper contained an article titled "The New Proposed History of Schuyler County." After describing the organization and contents of the proposed volume, the editor argued that "to do this successfully and satisfactorily, the prompt and earnest cooperation of our people is indispensably necessary, which will enable the historians to properly discharge their arduous labors." County residents who had historical information were exhorted to have it ready "and thereby contribute to the fullness and perfection of a large, beautifully printed, richly bound, and splendidly illustrated work, of which all interested and concerned may justly feel proud." On 26 December 1878, the editor of the *Watkin's Express* reported that the history "is now being delivered to subscribers in this county, and is giving universal satisfaction," further noting that at the $10 subscription price, "it is one of the cheapest works ever issued from the American press." The *Watkin's Express* makes no further note of this book; no advertisements for the sale of the history or for agents to distribute the history occur in the local papers, indicating that the publishers developed their own mechanisms to hire agents to collect subscriptions; sell space for farm views, portraits, and biographies; and distribute the final volume.

The Farms

The *History of Schuyler County, New York* (Everts and Ensign 1879) contains portraits and farm views representing all eight of the county's townships. All of the illustrations of farms and residences included in this volume were drawn by L. H. Everts of Philadelphia, a situation that mediates any potential for variability introduced by different artists. The book contains 74 illustrations that are evenly divided between farms or residences and portraits. They are not evenly distributed throughout the county (Table 1). The villages of Watkins and Havana have significantly higher percentages of portraits than any of the rural towns and among the lowest values for farm views and residences. Aside from this, the most dramatic pattern in this data is that the town of Hector is represented by more than half of all of the farm views, a pattern that certainly seems significant compared to the incidence of farm views from the other towns. The town of Catherine has the next highest

TABLE 1
FARM VIEWS AND PORTRAITS:
SCHUYLER COUNTY TOWNS AND VILLAGES

	Farm views/ Residences		Portraits	
	No.	%	No.	%
Rural Towns				
Catherine	4	10.8	5	13.5
Cayuta	1	2.7	0	0
Dix	3	8.1	2	5.4
Hector	23	62.1	6	16.2
Montour	1	2.7	1	2.7
Orange	1	2.7	1	2.7
Reading	3	8.1	0	0
Tyrone	0	0	2	5.4
Villages				
Watkins	1	2.7	9	24.3
Havana	0	0	11	29.7
Totals	37	99.9	37	99.9

percentage (10.8%), followed by Reading and Dix (8.1%). Keep in mind that the 1875 census enumerated 505 farms for the entire town of Hector, meaning that less then 5% of the farms in the town are represented by illustrations in the history of Schuyler County.

The concentration of farm views in Hector appears unusual. Some of the factors that may explain this pattern are town size, population density, and the distribution of wealth. It is true that in 1875 Hector had the largest acreage, encompassing 61,280 acres, and the highest population with 4,970 residents. It also had the largest number of houses and the highest percentage based on total house value. This indicates that Hector contained relatively more expensive houses compared to the rest of the towns in the county (Table 2). These percentages are not commensurate with and do not seem to relate to the percentage of farm views however. In terms of size, Hector is followed by Orange and Tyrone, both of which have the lowest percentage of farm views. If inclusion in the vanity press were simply a factor of size, population density, or wealth, more farm views would be expected from the towns of Dix, Montour, and Orange, since their percentages of land, population, and number of dwellings are all consistently higher than their percentage of farm views. The decision to be included in

this vanity press publication does not seem to be simply based on sample size.

The concentration of farm views in Hector may simply correlate with the location of the best farmland (and thus wealthy farms) in Schuyler County. Again, this simply does not appear to be the case. Absolute value of farmland is difficult to assess and is beyond the scope of this paper, but some sense of this can be gleaned from land assessment maps made during the early-20th century (Darrah 1942), which show the distribution of Schuyler County land divided into five land classes. Land classes I and II are characterized as marginal or submarginal for agricultural production, while land classes III through V represent the most productive (and thus best) farmland. The grouped percentages of the total number of acres falling to these good and bad agricultural lands do not seem to conform in any obvious way to the percentage of farm views (Table 3). For example, the towns of Dix, Hector, Montour, Reading, and Tyrone have the highest percentages of land in classes III through V, and yet the incidence of farm views for these towns ranges from the highest to the lowest, touching on all points in between.

A more in-depth examination of the farms from Hector may provide more clues as to the nature of these visual artifacts. Information on 22 of the 23 farms represented in the Hector

TABLE 2
SCHUYLER COUNTY TOWNS:
FARM VIEWS, ACRES, POPULATION, DWELLINGS, AND HOUSE VALUE

Town	Farm views[1]	Acres %	Population %[2]	Dwellings %[2]	House value %[2]
Catherine	10.8	9.3	8.2	8.6	8.2
Cayuta	2.7	6.4	3.5	3.8	3.4
Dix	8.1	10.5	22.3	20.5	9.5
Hector	62.1	31.6	26.3	27.1	27.1
Montour	2.7	5.8	9.9	9.4	18.0
Orange	2.7	16.2	10.3	10.8	7.1
Reading	8.1	8.3	9.1	8.6	13.7
Tyrone	0	12.0	10.4	11.2	12.9
Totals	97.2	100.1	100.0	100.0	99.9

[1] Percentages of total number based on Schuyler County totals, excluding villages.

[2] Based on 1875 New York State census.

TABLE 3
PERCENTAGE OF TOTAL TOWN LAND REPRESENTING COMBINED LAND CLASSES,
EXCLUDING RESIDENTIAL AREA

Town	Farm views %	Farm classes I, II	Farm classes III, IV, V	Total
Catherine	10.8	60	36	96
Cayuta	2.7	80	15	95
Dix	8.1	33	61	94
Hector	62.1	42	57	99
Montour	2.7	30	56	86
Orange	2.7	69	31	100
Reading	8.1	32	66	98
Tyrone	0	38	60	98

Note: Data from Darrah 1942.

sample was collected from the 1875 New York State agricultural schedule of the census. As per expectations, the illustrated farm sample does appear to represent wealthier farmers. Table 4 shows the average values for farm, farm buildings, livestock, machines and tools, and gross sales compared to a larger sample collected for Hector (Ridarsky 2003). The farms that have been illustrated do have significantly higher numbers, particularly in terms of farm value, farm buildings, and machinery and tool values. The livestock and gross sales values are not as starkly different from the larger sample as might be expected.

These numbers can be misleading since there are three farms with excessively high values, ranging between $16,000 and $25,000, that are skewing the mean. When these three farms are removed, the remaining farms have a mean farm value of $5,411, a figure that is not starkly different from the $3,910 mean of the larger sample, especially given the gross sample size differences. This pattern alludes to the fact that these families may have had other motivations to have their farms illustrated than to simply display wealth.

Examining the locations of these farms within Hector adds another dimension. Twenty of the 23 farms in Hector were correlated to the 1874 atlas of Schuyler County (Beach 1874). Figure 1 shows that these farms were not evenly distributed through the town. While there are a few outliers, many of these farms cluster near modern Route 79. It follows the course of the old Catskill Turnpike, one of the original roads through the area that locally linked Ithaca to Watkin's Glen. This route continued as an important transportation corridor, and rail lines were added in the 19th century.

Within the general linear trajectory, there are smaller clusters of farm views, perhaps indicating that neighbors or family relations played a role in the decision to have farm views included in the history. Indeed, several of these clusters do represent related families. Some of these relations are obvious, such as brothers Martin and Charles Keep, and father and son John and A. O. Coddington. Several other families were related through marriage.

TABLE 4
AVERAGE VALUES
FROM THE 1875 NEW YORK STATE CENSUS

	Hector census sample (n=215)	Farm illustrations sample (n=22)
Farm value	$3,910	$7,605
Farm buildings	$514	$964
Livestock	$545	$787
Machine/tools	$177	$238
Gross sales	$546	$745

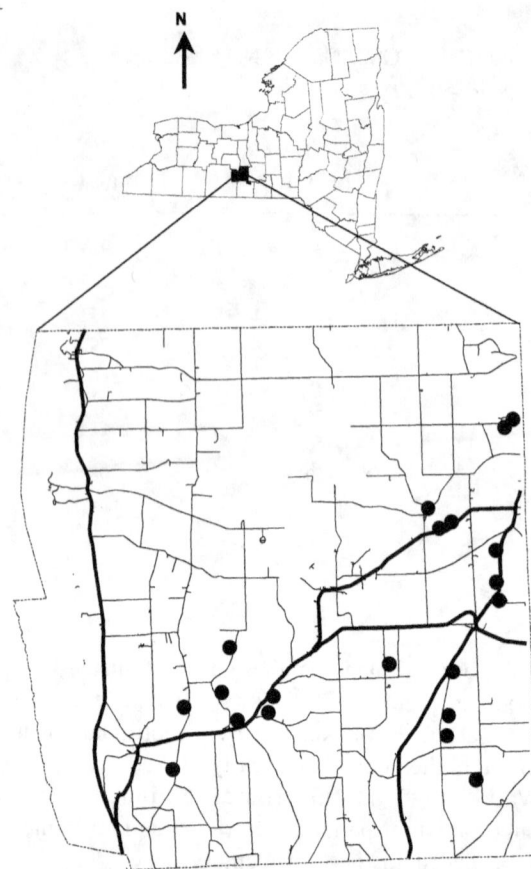

FIGURE 1. Location of illustrated farms in Hector. (Drawing by author.)

For example, Elnathan Wixom was married to Mordecai Carman's sister, and both Martin Keep and Chester Benson married sisters. Other information suggests there may be additional relations that cursory research did not reveal. For example, the 1875 agricultural schedule lists the farms of Minor T. Jones and Albert Proper right next to each other, with Samuel Warren across the street; the Darling and Hazlett farms were also next to each other. Since they all had farm views drawn, it is possible that either they were related or that peer pressure may have been involved in the decision-making process. These family relations may also explain a few of the lower-than-expected farm values. For example, Charles Keep had a farm value of $5,000, while his brother Martin's farm was only valued at $1,500. While Mordecai Carman's farm was not modest at $7,800, it

seems measly next to his brother-in-law's farm valued at $24,300.

While this "kin selection" seems to account for some of the illustrations, it does not explain them all. Daniel Lee's farm was located off the main thoroughfare and was not included in any of the spatial clusters. Research also clarifies that Lee did not have any other relatives in the Hector area. Lee registered title to this land in 1819 and was one of the first occupants in that vicinity. Lee's father, Jepther, served in the Revolutionary War, and his son Daniel acquired this land as part of the Military Tract "wages" paid to these veterans. It is interesting that Daniel Lee died in 1878, prior to this book's 1879 publication (Figure 2). The other portraits that accompany the illustration depict his daughter's father-in-law and his son, neither of whom lived in the house at the time of Lee's death. The Lee farm was not particularly wealthy, nor did the owners have a large and extended family in the area. The decision to have Lee's farm illustrated appears to have been motivated by somewhat different factors. It is necessary to look more deeply at who these men actually were.

One of the most consistent patterns in this data relates to the age of these men at the time the Schuyler County history was published. With the exception of Lee who had died the previous year and Minor T. Jones who operated his father's farm, all of the remaining farm illustrations represent elderly farmers. Excluding the outliers, their average age was 63. These families were not necessarily the earliest settlers of the town. In fact, for those families for whom information is available, they mostly appear to be the second generation of a second wave of migration into the area. Martin Keep and Chester Benson both married daughters of Phineas Bennett who moved to the area in 1828. Martin and Charles Keep's father moved to Schuyler County in 1832. William Fish's father moved to the area in 1821 (Everts and Ensign 1976: 140). Several of the families did move to the area a bit earlier. Elnathan Wixom's grandfather and John M. Coddington both settled in 1807 (Everts and Ensign 1976:133), and Albert Proper's father settled in 1810 (Everts and Ensign 1976:134). Even so, only Erastus Wickham seems to be descended from an early settler; his father, William, is recognized as the

Perspectives from *Historical Archaeology*

FIGURE 2. Lee Farm. (Everts and Ensign 1879.)

first settler in the town, having moved there in 1790 (Everts and Ensign 1976:116). In general, the farm illustrations do not seem to represent the earliest settlers as perhaps expected.

There is one other aspect of the farm illustration sample that bears mentioning. Two farms are labeled with a female's name. One farm view is labeled "Residence of Mrs. J. E. Darling" and includes the portraits of Mrs. Darling and Thomas Darling. Mrs. Darling is listed in the 1875 census without a spouse, and it is likely that Thomas was her son. The second of these illustrations is less clear. It designates the farm as the "Residence of Mrs. Grace P. Culver," and yet her husband Enos is pictured. The farm is listed under Enos's name in the 1875 agricultural schedule (Figure 3), but it is not clear if that reflects the census collector's expectations or the actual ownership of the farm. The illustration suggests that Grace owned

the farm and its visual statement proclaims that ownership very publicly.

The Illustrations

This background information on the general location, context, and circumstances of the farm families who purchased farm views provides a setting to begin examining the motifs rendered in the actual illustrations. Common elements in these illustrations include buildings, animals, people, fences, roads, and carriages or other means of transport. Each of these elements will be discussed in turn.

Most of the farm illustrations focus on the entire farmstead. Only three illustrations concentrate solely on the house and yard. These include the village houses of Spencer Wheeler and Dr. Fish, both in the hamlet of Burdett, as well as the illustration of Grace Culver's farm

(Figure 3). While the Culver lithograph focuses on the house, the barns are shown in an inset. In terms of house style, the vast majority of the houses are Greek Revival in style. Of the remainder, three are Italian Villa and two are Gothic Revival. For the most part, the dates during which these styles were popular is consistent with the settlement dates for these families.

In addition to the house, these illustrations include barns and other farm buildings. The number of buildings represented for the farm views varies from 4 to 14, with an average of 8 barns and outbuildings depicted. No simple correlation seems to exist between the number of buildings shown and the value of farm buildings as listed in the 1875 census. While Wixom's farm, drawn with 14 outbuildings also has the highest farm building value at $4,500, Erastus Wickham's illustration (Figure 4) shows 9 buildings with a farm building value of only $150.

All but five of the illustrations include farm animals. Cows, horses, and sheep are the most commonly shown animals. Like the farm buildings, there seems to be no simple relationship between the number and kinds of animals depicted and the value of livestock or enumeration of animals from the 1875 census. Mrs. Culver's farm view (Figure 3) contains no animals at all, and yet that farm had the second highest livestock value, based on an inventory of 12 cows, 5 horses, 6 pigs, and 37 sheep. On the other hand, James Hazlett's farm illustration shows the largest number of animals, with 9 cows, 22 sheep, and 2 horses, while the census lists their livestock value at the low end with $348, and their schedule lists no cows, sheep, or horses for this farm.

Human figures are included in 21 of the illustrations. Based on their attire, most can be identified by sex, and age can be determined by size. Males are shown most often, represented in 17 illustrations, while females are shown in 13, and only 7 include children. Overall, people are shown doing very little in

FIGURE 3. Culver Farm. (Everts and Ensign 1879.)

Perspectives from *Historical Archaeology*

FIGURE 4. Wickham Farm. (Everts and Ensign 1879.)

the way of activity. This is more generally true of the females who are universally depicted sitting or standing on the front porch, walk, or yard (Figure 2); only one is shown in a field carrying a bucket, presumably for picking berries. In eight instances, children are shown standing on the porch or yard, two are shown standing or walking through a field, and one is shown on a tree swing (Figure 4). Of the males represented, five are shown standing or sitting on the porch or in the yard, six are depicted in the vicinity of a vehicle, six are shown standing or walking in fields, generally associated with animals, and two are shown cutting hay or wheat with horse-drawn equipment. While certainly men are shown as more active in these illustrations than women or children, the overall impression is not one of movement or productive activity.

One other striking aspect of these farm illustrations is the inclusion of much fencing of various kinds. Several of the house yards are enclosed with formal iron fences, while others have picket or plank fences. Plank fences surround most of the barnyards, and even distant fields are bordered by plank, split rail, and even stump fences. These farms are indeed neatly contained.

Even though many of these farm views are perceived from distant fields to incorporate most of the farm layout, every single one shows a roadway, and in several cases, more than one road is included. Obviously, every one of these farms was located on a road, so this pattern is not that surprising. What is interesting is that all but one of these illustrations show some form of vehicular traffic on the road. Most of the illustrations have at least one carriage, while two of the farm scenes show three different carriages or wagons. While this may simply be an artistic convention to render the function of the road, this artistic element also accomplishes several different things. It conveys both movement and connection. Each of these farms is rendered in isolation, neatly bounded by various kinds of fences. The passing carriages reaffirm that they are linked to other places that are not included in the illustrations. These passing carriages have come from some place and are traveling to a different place outside of the view. Another intriguing element is that these passing conveyances provide an additional audience to these illustrations. In essence, the viewers gaze at the illustration and see that the occupants of the carriages are doing the same thing; each farm view thus has an additional built-in audience.

How Accurate Are the Farm Views?

The final question to be addressed is just how accurate are these farm illustrations. More than half of the houses still exist, showing that the representations of the dwellings are uncannily accurate. In some cases, the houses have been drastically altered, but it was still clear that the right one had been located. One of the clearest examples is Chester Benson's house (Figures 5, 6), but they all clearly resemble their illustrations, making it obvious that the actual houses were accurately pictured. The precision of these illustrations is implied by the inclusion of the artist himself. In two of the farm views, the artist has drawn himself into the picture, standing in the road and talking, presumably, to the farmer. This suggests that the drawings were made in consultation with the farmers themselves, and that they include what the farmers wanted to show. Chester Benson's farm view (Figure 5) even includes the artist sitting in the foreground actually drawing the illustration at which the viewer is gazing.

Two of the farms illustrated in this publication are currently located within the Finger Lakes National Forest and have been extensively excavated as part of the State University of New York at Brockport archaeological field school. Work at the Daniel Lee and Erastus Wickham farms show that these illustrations were amazingly accurate in terms of the spatial layout and location of barns and other outbuildings. The size and configuration of the features documented in the field make it as obvious as the standing houses that the illustrations are actual renderings of these farms. The Lee farm illustration (Figure 2) shows the cellar entrance on the southeast corner of the house, and this is precisely were it is located. All of the other structures visible conform to documented archaeological features. The Wickham farm illustration (Figure 4) shows nine buildings, and most of them were identified in the same spatial configuration in which they were depicted. While working in the field, the author referred to the drawing so often that one

FIGURE 5. Benson Farm. (Everts and Ensign 1879.)

student laminated a copy and fixed it to a string to wear for ready reference.

Even though the buildings and spatial arrangements appear accurate, other aspects of these illustrations are more imprecise. This is most clear in terms of the topography and landscape features, where much more "artistic license" came into play. The Wickham farm view (Figure 4) shows cows grazing peacefully in a field across the road from the house. In reality, the ground surface plummets dramatically into a steep ravine beginning at the edge of the road. It would be impossible for cows to graze here unless they wore crampons. Perhaps some of the fences delineating the landscape may have been figments of the artist's or farmer's imaginations as well. While the research design did not include documenting fencing, Gerald Carson (1958:78) mentions how the illustrator made changes that the client would like, such as putting in "a picket fence in front instead of

showing the rails that were actually there, 'as you would be doing that soon anyway.'"

It is also important to recognize that the illustrations do not accurately represent these farms' productive activities. Many of the farm views include cows, horses, and sheep, and, indeed, these animals all represent important aspects of agricultural production. Many equally important productive activities, however, are not included. Only three of the illustrations show orchards; yet all but one of these farms had apples, with an average of 91 trees. Dried apples and other orchard products were significant cash crops in this area (Ridarsky 2003). Only one illustration showed pigs, and that was James Hazlett's farm, which was one of only two that did not list any pigs in the agricultural schedule. The illustrated farms had an average of four pigs, and produced an average of about 900 pounds of pork. Only Albert Proper's illustration included poultry, and yet fowl were ubiquitous on these farms.

FIGURE 6. Contemporary view of Benson Farm. (Photograph by author.)

The average annual sales of poultry and eggs for these farms was almost $26, not a paltry amount. Although in fairness, agricultural production does not seem to be the point of these illustrations. As discussed above, few of the people are represented performing much if any kind of labor. Only two illustrations show distant figures cutting grain, and only three include farm wagons, with or without occupants.

Conclusions

This discussion of the vanity press farm illustrations has led in several different directions. Just what is it that can be said about such a small and diverse sample? The ideas expressed by the small sample of historians who have discussed these sources, in addition to common sense notions, could lead to the expectation that the illustrations represent the largest and wealthiest farms in the area or that the farms belong to the area's first settlers. First, as was obvious simply from their values, the illustrated farms are not a representative cross-section of every farm in Hector. The illustrated farms mainly cluster along the route of the old Catskill Turnpike, which represents one of the earliest transportation corridors through the area as well as the location of some the best farmland in the area. While some of these farms are clearly among those with the highest values, they are not all what would be considered the most prosperous farms in the town. In effect, wealth does not seem to be the most important criteria for inclusion.

Neither can the farm illustrations be explained as celebrating the first settlers or pioneers of Hector. Most of the household heads were elderly when the illustrations were published, but they can consistently be characterized as the second generation of the area's settlers. This pattern is not contradictory to ideas that emphasize how the vanity press focused on those who had laid down roots and legitimated the successful long-time residents or the desire and ability of these farmers to fix themselves in time as well as place (Faragher 1986:229;

Herman 1987:236; Bushman 1992:382). Many of the illustrations show farms of related family groups, suggesting that they were not simply motivated by the individualizing goals that might be recognized in Burns's (1989:51) suggestion that "these histories illustrate farmers' strivings toward middle-class status and its attendant symbols."

The fact that the drawings are rendered so accurately in terms of the house and the spatial layout of the farms and that the topographical features are generally more mythic indicates that the buildings were meant to be recognized from the drawings, probably by people that already knew them. The family relationships, as well as the emphasis on carriages on the roads, connect these separate, individual drawings into nodes within a larger community network. Herman argued that the goal of these illustrations was to fix these farms in both space and time. The illustrations also fixed these farm families into the larger relations of community in which they existed. It is easy to forget that when these books were published, the intended audience would already know these people and would easily be able to identify their farms. The linearity of text and individual drawings presents them today as discrete entities, with the farms as islands rendered on separate pieces of paper. This interpretation seems evident since today's viewers are not intimately acquainted with these people or the area. The book's subscribers, who already knew the spatial and familial connections hidden behind the drawings, would probably not have read them that way.

References

BEACH, N.
1874 *Atlas of Schuyler County.* Pomeroy, Whitman and Company, Philadelphia, PA.

BURNS, SARAH
1989 *Pastoral Inventions: Rural Life in Nineteenth-Century American Art and Culture.* Temple University Press, Philadelphia, PA.

BUSHMAN, RICHARD L.
1992 *The Refinement of America: Persons, Houses, Cities.* Alfred A. Knopf, New York, NY.

CARSON, GERALD
1958 "Get the Prospect Seated ... And Keep Talking." *American Heritage* 9(5):38–80.

DANIELS, TED
1987 Advertisements for American Selves: Nineteenth-Century Pennsylvania County Atlases. *Landscape* 29(3):17–23.

DARRAH, LAWRENCE B.
1942 *An Economic Study of Land Utilization in Schuyler County, New York.* Cornell University, Agriculture Experiment Station, Ithaca, NY.

EVERTS AND ENSIGN (EDITORS)
1879 *History of Schuyler County, New York.* Reprinted in 1976 by W.E. Morrison & Co, Ovid, NY.

FARAGHER, JOHN MACK
1986 *Sugar Creek: Life on the Illinois Prairie.* Yale University Press, New Haven, CT.

HERMAN, BERNARD L.
1987 *Architecture and Rural Life in Central Delaware, 1700–1900.* University of Tennessee Press, Knoxville, TN.

MALIN, JAMES
1955 The "Vanity Histories." *Kansas Historical Quarterly* 21(4):598–643.

NEW YORK STATE
1875 Agricultural Schedule of the 1875 Census. Manuscript, Schuyler County Clerk's Office, Watkin's Glen, NY.

RIDARSKY, CHRISTINE
2003 "Keep up Good Courage": Submarginal Hill Farming in Upstate New York, 1850–1880. Master's thesis, Department of History, SUNY, College at Brockport, NY.

WATKIN'S EXPRESS
1875 Local History. *Watkin's Express*, 23 December. Watkins Glen, New York.
1878 The New Proposed History of Schuyler County. *Watkin's Express*, 25 July. Watkins Glenn, New York
1878 The New History of Tioga, Chemung, Tompkins, and Schuyler. *Watkin's Express*, 26 December. Watkins Glenn, New York.

LOUANN WURST
SUNY, COLLEGE AT BROCKPORT
DEPARTMENT OF ANTHROPOLOGY
BROCKPORT, NY 14559

ANNALIES CORBIN

Shifting Sand and Muddy Water: Historic Cartography and River Migration as Factors in Locating Steamboat Wrecks on the Far Upper Missouri River

ABSTRACT

Steamboating on the Missouri River began in 1819 and, by 1860 Fort Benton, Montana Territory was established as the world's innermost port. Between 1819 and the mid-1920s more than 1,000 vessels were lost and subsequently forgotten on the Missouri River. Missouri River migration is investigated as a primary factor in predicting, locating, and assessing inland river wreck sites today. The study examines three historic river surveys conducted in 1867, 1874, and from 1892 to 1897, plus modern aerial photography for clues suggesting the location of steamboat wreck sites and information useful in predicting site conditions and site formation processes prior to archaeological disturbance.

Introduction

The opening of the upper Missouri River region made possible such developments as the upper river fur trade, military operations, mining in the Rockies, and settlement in the various Plains regions along the river. Steamboating on the Missouri River began in May 1819 when the 98 ton (89,000 kg) *Independence* ascended 250 mi. (400 km) from St. Louis to Chariton, Missouri. In 1832, the American Fur Company's steamboat, the *Yellow Stone,* ascended as far as Fort Union at the mouth of the Yellowstone River (Jackson 1985; Corbin 1995). Almost three decades later, in 1860, the American Fur Company's *Chippewa* reached Fort Benton, the effective head of steamboat navigation on the Missouri, and offloaded 250 tons (227 t) of cargo. This trip set a new distance record in the history of steamboat navigation, as the *Chippewa* journeyed 2,285 mi. (3,675 km) above the mouth of the river, and established Fort Benton as the steamboat capital of the upper northwest region.

Steamboat traffic at Fort Benton quickly became commonplace, and with the discovery of gold in Montana in 1862, traffic along the upper Missouri River increased dramatically, as miners, speculators, and suppliers flocked to the Fort Benton area (Corbin 1996). Between the years of 1861 and 1885 steamboats delivered well over 100,000 tons (90,700 t) of freight to the Fort Benton levee. Although often overlooked by scholar's preoccupation with the fur trade, military activity, and the coming of the railroad, the steamboat era was one of the fundamental building blocks in the history of Montana and the upper Missouri River region.

Fortunately for archaeologists and historians alike, not all of the steamboats that plied the upper Missouri and Yellowstone rivers survived the journey. Current research indicates that there are a minimum of 37 historic wrecks, including steamboats, barges, ferries, and early motor vessels, located along the Missouri and Yellowstone rivers in Montana (Figure 1) with more than an estimated 1,000 wrecks along the Missouri down river from Montana. Few, if any, of these sites have been properly verified, recorded, or investigated, although these historic archaeological resources offer a variety of opportunities for interpreting steamboat traffic on the Nation's interior rivers (Corbin and Karsmizki 1997).

Missouri River migration is investigated as a primary factor in predicting, locating, and poten-

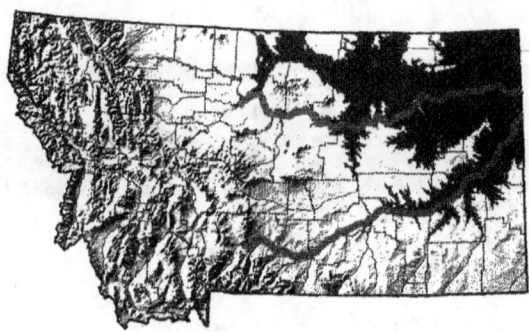

FIGURE 1. The Missouri-Yellowstone River drainage area in Montana (by the author).

Perspectives from *Historical Archaeology*

tially assessing inland river wreck sites. Through careful utilization and examination of historic maps, documents, survey reports, and aerial photographs, changes in the course of the river over the past 138 years are clearly visible. Understanding changes in river migration through historic cartography is essential for accurately predicting wreck sites today. Historic maps provide the most important "first step" in developing a model for predicting inland river wreck sites. This work examines three historic survey projects, focusing on the manner and accuracy in which the surveys were conducted and asks if a predictive model for locating potential wreck sites is possible based a comprehensive examination of Missouri River migration. More importantly, will an appreciation of river migration help archaeologists determine aspects of the natural site formation processes before the site is investigated and subsequently disturbed?

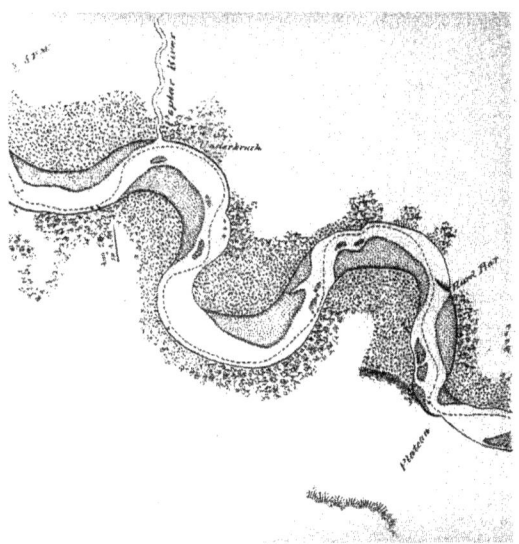

FIGURE 2. 1867 *Sketch of the Missouri River from the Mouth of the Platte to Fort Benton Montana*, map showing Hard Bar bend, the river channel, tributary streams, and landscape vegetation (National Archives 1867).

Three Historic Upper Missouri River Surveys—Post 1860

Fortunately, the importance of the far upper Missouri River in the fur trade, the mining industry, and in the development of the United States military in the West spurred relatively consistent surveys of both the Missouri River and its tributary systems. These surveys were undertaken both during and after the steamboat era. The three most important surveys of the Missouri River drainage, pertinent to this study, were conducted in 1867, 1874, and from 1892 to 1897 (National Archives 1867, 1874, 1892-1897).

In 1867, Col. John M. Macomb of the United States Army authorized the first comprehensive survey of the far upper Missouri River, since Lewis and Clark, that included the Montana region. The field survey was conducted by Bvt. Major C. W. Howell, Captain in the Corps of Engineers. The "Sketch of the Missouri River from the Mouth of the Platte to Fort Benton" (Figure 2), provides the first detailed view of the river and the landscape through which it passed during the mid-19th century. The area was surveyed from the pilot house of the steamer *Minor*

and the map was compiled with the aid of several Missouri River boat captains and pilots.

The "sketch" provides critical information on the riverbed including the course of the deepest channel, the location of snags and obstructions, and the placement of sand bars in relationship to the bends and curves of the river. Interestingly the survey also notes the location of the "Wreck of the *Trover* [1867]." This notation is both critical and curious. Present research suggests that by 1867, when the survey took place, a minimum of three steamboats had already sunk within the Montana section of the survey (Corbin and Karsmizki 1997). This raises the question of why the wreck of the *Trover* was the only wreck noted on the Montana area survey maps. Although Howell does not mention in his field notes that the wreck was visible from the surface, perhaps the wreck was still recent enough to be a considerable navigational hazard at the time of the survey and therefore was included on the survey maps. Documentary evidence suggests that wrecks prior to the 1867 survey were quickly absorbed into the environment.

The 1867 survey map also has several other important cartographic attributes. The maps name and illustrate the locations of tributary streams and creeks, note vegetation in great detail, and mark the locations of bluffs and other land forms adjacent to the river (National Archives 1867). But how can we better understand and therefore better utilize the information from these maps? The answers lie in the original field notes taken during the survey. Fortunately, Major Howell was a diligent note-taker.

Howell's notes provide information concerning the nature of the survey and how the survey was conducted. His original field notes document the landscape, the turbulence of the river, and the frequency of snags and steamboat wrecks. Most importantly, he details the river's influence on both the cultural and natural environment. Two vital pieces of information are provided. First, Howell noted the presence of wrecked steamboats (some wrecks were noted on the maps while others were only mentioned in the report but were not noted on the maps) in both the upper and lower river and their impact on the river environment.

As might be expected from the character of the river a great number of wrecks lie sunken . . . but the majority of them at present are not in the way and pilots are familiar with their positions. Many of them have been partially removed by the underwriters, leaving but the hulls and wheels, so the labor of cleaning them out of the channel has been greatly simplified. . . . (Howell 1868).

Second, Major Howell provided clues concerning the manner in which wreck sites are formed and are subsequently protected or destroyed by the natural environment:

The sand of which these bars are formed is of the nature of quicksand. Iron, stone or other materials too heavy to be moved by the current sink below the surface of the sand in a few seconds . . . This characteristic of the bottom makes it simply necessary for a boat when working through a bar, to push ahead with its spars and keep in position so that the current may wash under and around it (Howell 1868).

This same action, used in freeing a vessel from a sand bar, takes place when a vessel is snagged and sinks. The river quickly absorbs the obstruc-

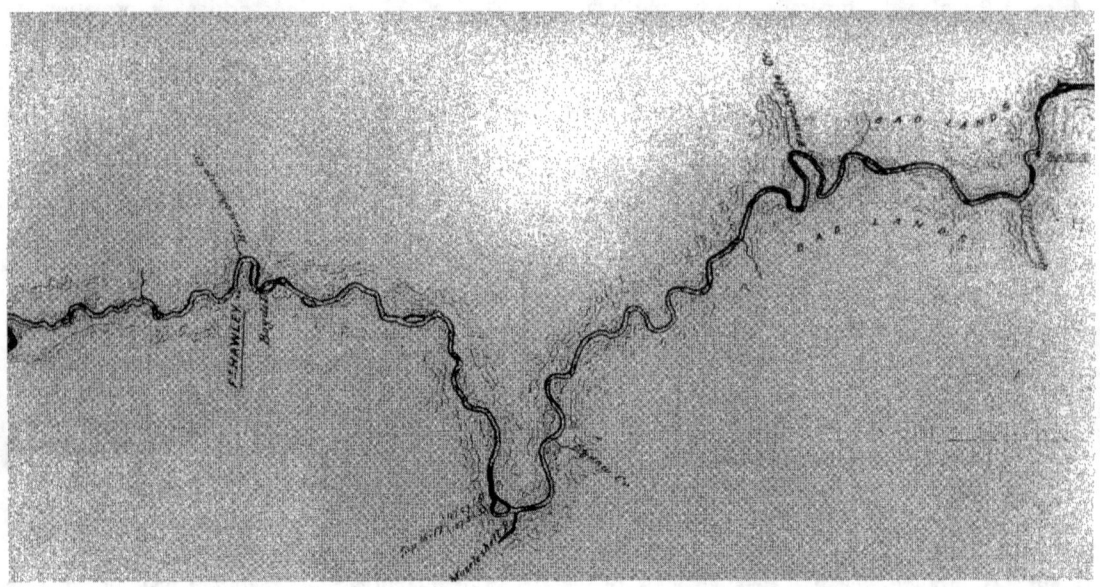

FIGURE 3. 1874 *Missouri River Boat Survey*, map showing the river channel, tributary creeks, land forms, and adjacent military posts (National Archives 1874).

Perspectives from *Historical Archaeology*

tion, while simultaneously shifting around, under, and over it, forming an island around the wreck or simply shifting the current away from the obstruction entirely.

> Every bend of the river gives more or less emphatic evidence of this cutting action of the river at peculiarly susceptible points, shifting in a few weeks from 2 to 3 hundred yards into the bottom lands, and frequently cutting through the necks of bends[,] chang[ing] the whole channel for miles on either side . . . (Howell 1868).

By closely examining Howell's field notes we gain information vital for predicting site conditions, formation processes, and the potential for natural disturbance after the site was initially formed.

The second survey with its corresponding set of maps is the "Missouri River Boat Survey" (Figure 3), completed in 1874 by William J. Twinning of the United States Engineers Office and Lt. F. V. Greene, Chief Astronomer of the Engineers Office. Unfortunately this survey did not produce maps as detailed as the 1867 survey. The survey plots the course of the river and includes some information on channel composition, including depth, the prevalence of sandbars, and the names and locations of islands. No wreck locations are noted and few of the river bends are named. The names and locations of most of the larger tributary streams and creeks are present and river side military posts are also included. The overall topography is not as detailed as the previous survey, but the basic locations of bluffs and ridge lines are present. Noting the general land forms that are present proves crucial in evaluating the accuracy of this survey compared with modern topography. Further research revealed problems with the positional accuracy of the mapping. Twinning wrote, "I have compared the latitude with those of Captain Raynolds [1859/60 report and maps], and find no essential differences—the longitudes are however quite different in many places" (National Archives 1860; Raynolds 1860; Twinning 1875). Twinning's survey was a preparatory survey to

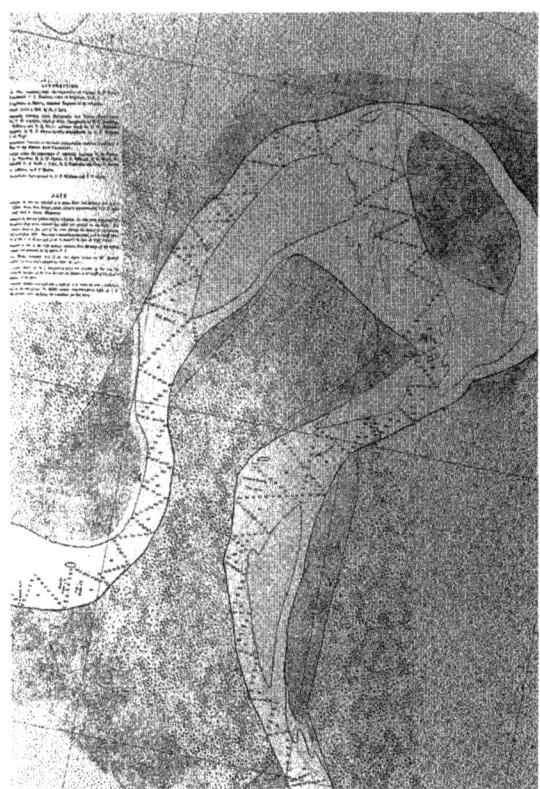

FIGURE 4. 1892-1897, *Missouri River Commission Map of the Missouri River from its Mouth to Three Forks, Montana*, 1:7,200. Hard Bar bend, location of the 1883 wreck of the steamboat *Big Horn* (National Archives 1892-1897).

be used in the logistical planning for the next big survey effort.

The Missouri River Commission's 1878-1895 survey (National Archives 1892-1897) which produced, "the Map of the Missouri River from its Mouth to Three Forks, Montana," is by far one of the most comprehensive historic surveys of the Missouri River. Most of the survey was conducted by Captains C. F. Powell and H. F. Hodges of the Corps of Engineers, with additional survey work in Montana conducted by Captain Hiram M. Chittenden of the Corps of Engineers.

Initially, two sets of maps were produced from the Missouri River Commission Survey. One set is large scale, 1:7,200, and a second set is a scale of 1:63,360. Although the two map sets cover the same geographical area, they provide slightly different information. For example, the larger set (Figure 4) provides river depths and soundings, bottom configuration, details of island composition, and vegetation of the land closely associated with the river channel. The smaller set (Figure 5) provides information about details further from the river bed and includes cultural information often left off the larger scale maps. Individual maps detail the location and depth of the river channel, and often illustrate areas with a high concentration of snags and other obstructions to navigation such as rapids and sandbars. Besides detailing the river channel, the survey also notes the surrounding natural landscape such as bluffs, tributary rivers, and canyons. Most notably, the Missouri River Commission maps illustrate the largest number of cultural features in the landscape. The names and locations of towns, individual homesteads, cemeteries, railroad lines and beds, and schools are often present on these maps. In addition, the cultural effects of long-term steamboating are present in the landscape and noted on the maps, with information such as river locations named for steamboats, steamboat pilots, and notable occurrences involving steamboat disasters. Although 19 wrecks had been reported by 1892 in the Montana area, the locations of only 3 wrecks are noted within the Montana section of the maps: the "wreck of the *Amelia Poe*" (1868), the "Wreck of the *Red Cloud*" (1882), and the "Wreck of the *Big Horn*" (1883) (Corbin and Karsmizki 1997).

The landscape and cultural information available on the 1892-1897 maps are an invaluable aid in predicting the location of wrecks in modern topography. Frequently, wreck locations are

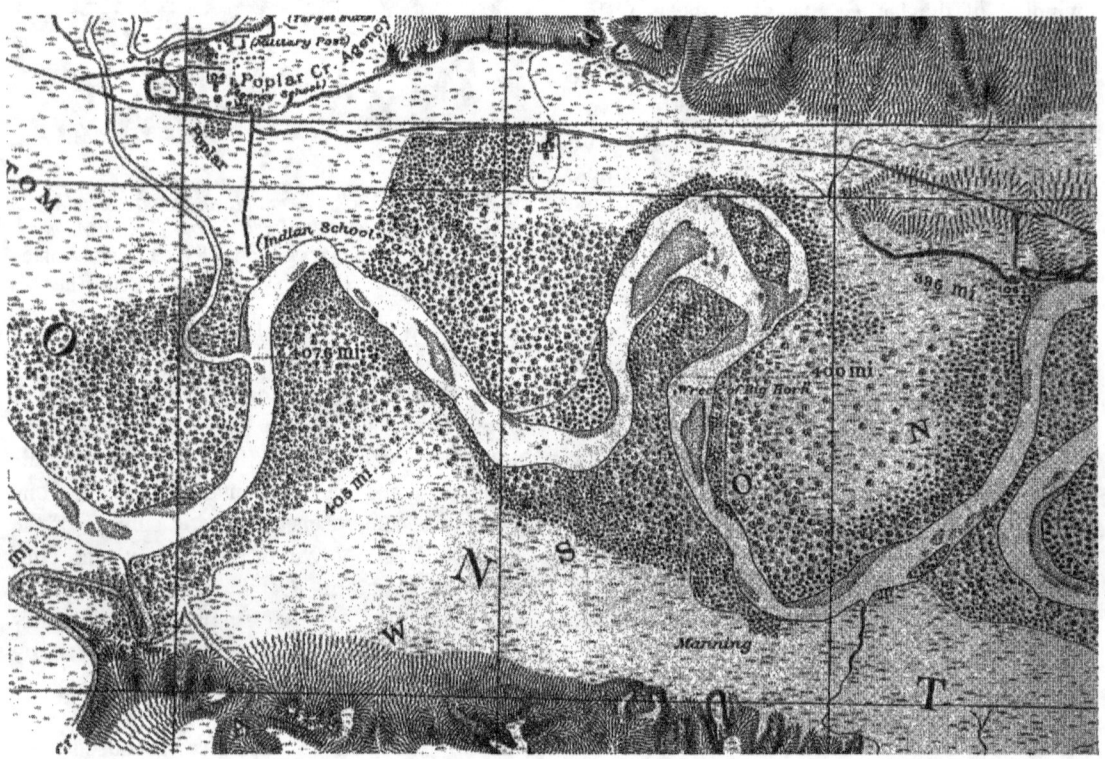

FIGURE 5. 1892-1897 Missouri River Commission *Map of the Missouri River from its Mouth to Three Forks, Montana,* 1:63,000. Hard Bar bend, location of the 1883 wreck of the steamboat *Big Horn,* note at this scale the wreck location is noted on the map (National Archives 1892-1897).

Perspectives from *Historical Archaeology*

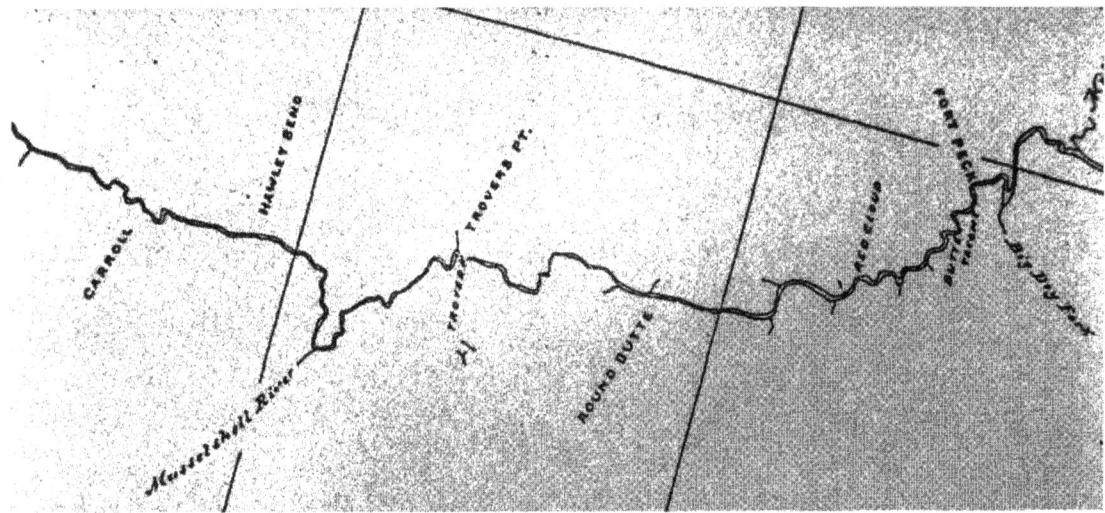

FIGURE 6. 1897 Chittenden map showing location of steamboat wrecks in Montana noted during the Missouri River Commission survey (Chittenden 1897).

noted by the use of a point or head of land, a bend in the river, or a proximity to a rural community. Often the only references to these places, frequently long forgotten, are on the historic survey maps. These historic place names become crucial when trying to relocate reported wreck sites today.

In addition to the original two sets of maps, Chittenden (1897) also produced a list of steamboat wrecks on the Missouri River and an accompanying map (Figure 6) derived from the Missouri River Commission survey. Chittenden's map only includes 47% of the Montana wrecks reported by 1897. His map, although sparse in landscape information, is the most complete mapping of Montana wrecks available in the historical map sources (Corbin and Karsmizki 1997).

Historic maps also provide significant data regarding stability and/or change at specific river locations over time, and thus provide an opportunity to evaluate site conditions prior to intrusive investigation. This is illustrated by examining the same point on the river on all three survey maps (Figure 7). An examination of the now familiar wreck of the *Trover* demonstrates that

the bend in the river where the boat sank becomes known as Trover Point by 1897. In examining the three maps, both the bend adjacent to the wreck and the shape of the point of land associated with the wreck changed through time. This shifting of the river is further illustrated by examining the 1882 wreck of the steamboat *Red Cloud*. When comparing visible river migration between the 1897 Missouri River Commission Map's site of the wreck of the *Red Cloud* and Chart 18 of the 1934 Fort Peck Reservoir survey (United States Engineers Office 1934), it is clear that the river channel moved south, away from the wreck of the *Red Cloud* (Figure 8). This is consistent with a *Helena Independent* (1920) news article in which Elmer Werner, a Montana local, claims to have found the wreck of the *Red Cloud* in an island formed as a result of the river meandering around the wreck. The 1934 survey shows that the island was absorbed into the surrounding landscape as a result of river migration (Corbin 1996; Corbin and Karsmizki 1997), thus verifying Howell's 1868 description concerning the formation of steamboat wrecks sites on the Missouri River.

River Migration in Aerial Photographs

The phenomenon of river migration is further illustrated by examining aerial photographs. Aerial photographs of "Hard Bar Bend" (Figure 9), location of the 1883 wreck of the *Big Horn*

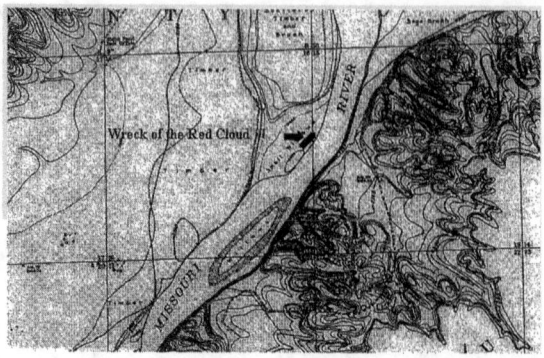

FIGURE 8. Chart 18 of the 1934 Fort Peck Reservoir Survey (U. S. Engineers Office 1934) with the wreck of the *Red Cloud* superimposed on it from an overlay of the 1892-1895 Missouri River Commission map (National Archives 1892-1897).

(Figure 10), document the changes in river bends, the formation and/or absorption of islands and sandbars, and the rate of erosion on the river landscape. Like changes that were noted in the 19th century maps, this particular bend of the river is still undergoing notable reconfiguration in the 20th century. In the 1956 photograph, the modern river (just south of the historic bend) splits around a large island in the south half of the photo. By 1991 this same island has been absorbed by the riverbank and now appears as a river scar much like the bend of the 1890s. Just as the 19th century Missouri River shifted continually to absorb or destroy cultural sites in the past, the same process is still observable today.

Conclusion

Investigating historic surveys and cartography is extremely important for understanding river migration of the upper Missouri River. This study has raised and subsequently answered several important questions concerning the use of historic cartography in evaluating the potential for locating archaeological sites. In 1979 Raymond Wood argued three important points:

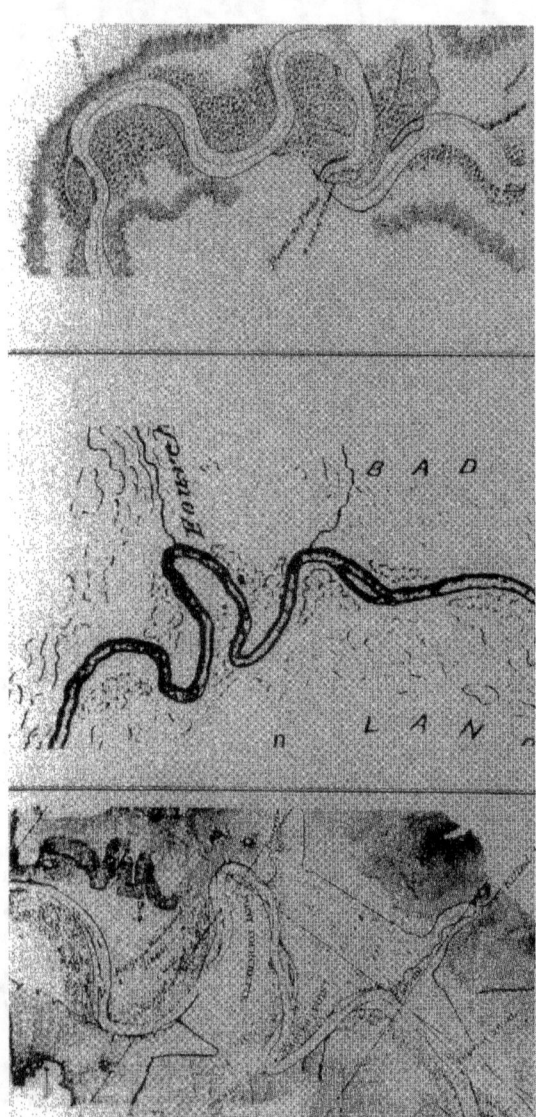

FIGURE 7. "Trover Point," site of the 1867 wreck of the steamboat *Trover* in all three upper Missouri River surveys; upper 1867, center 1874, lower 1897 (National Archives 1867, 1874, 1892-1897).

Perspectives from *Historical Archaeology*

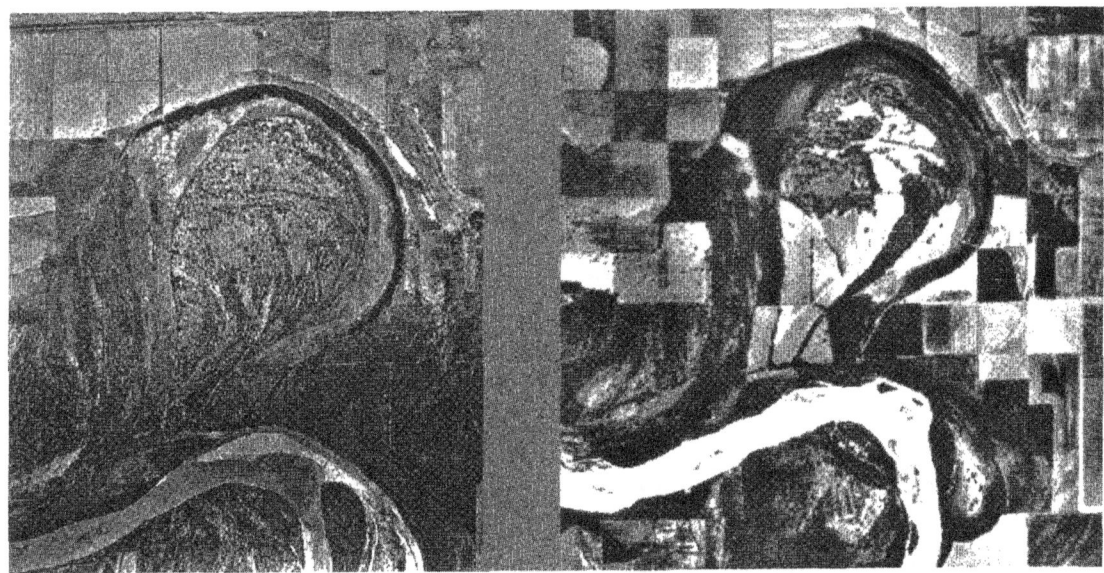

FIGURE 9. 1956 (left) and 1991 (right) aerial photographs of "Hard Bar bend" area, location of the 1883 wreck of the *Big Horn*, on the Missouri River. Note the 1890s river channel scar north of the twentieth century river scars (National Archives 1956, 1991).

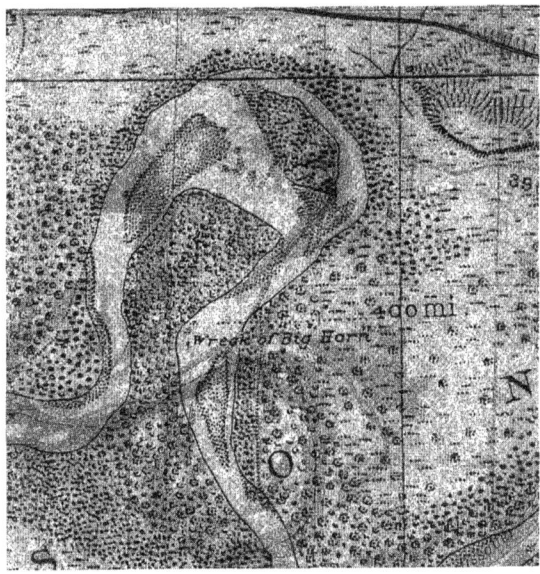

FIGURE 10. Predicted location of the 1883 wreck of the steamboat *Big Horn* in an old river scar just north of the present channel (by the author).

Maps are an important part of the interpretive program for any historic site. (1) First, because "maps are a precise index of geographical knowledge." . . . (2) Maps also preserve a variety of data relating to the locations of nearby features of importance to the mapmaker or his audience. . . . (3) Finally, maps preserve data on local ecology, information which is difficult [if not] impossible to reconstruct from written sources, but which is necessary in understanding the environmental setting of a site (Wood 1979).

Wood's arguments hold true for this study as well. Without a comprehensive cartographic evaluation of the migration of the Missouri River, it would be impossible to put together a predictive model for relocating lost steamboat sites along a volatile and unpredictable front. The Missouri River is one of the most historically turbulent rivers in the United States. Today, we often brace ourselves against the river leaving its banks during high flood years. We must not forget that long before modern dikes and levees, the river literally "ran wild," constantly altering its coarse at will. Understanding the meandering patterns of the Missouri and other river systems should be the basis of a well-informed archaeological investigation in any river basin and is, therefore, worthy of close scrutiny.

ACKNOWLEDGMENTS

The author thanks the University of Idaho's Honorable John Calhoun Smith Memorial Fund, Sons and Daughters of Pioneer Rivermen, which administers the J. Mack Gamble Fund, and the Museum of the Rockies for contributing funding for this research.

REFERENCES

CHITTENDEN, HIRAM M.
1897 List of Steamboat Wrecks on the Missouri River from the Beginning of Steamboat Navigation to the Present Time. *Annual Report of the Chief of Engineers, U. S. Army,* Serial Set 3631-3636. Washington.

CORBIN, ANNALIES
1995 Material Culture of Nineteenth Century Steamboat Passengers on the *Bertrand* and *Arabia.* Unpublished Masters thesis, Department of History, Program in Maritime History and Nautical Archaeology, East Carolina University, Greenville, NC.
1996 I. G. Baker & Co.'s Steamboat *Red Cloud*: Rediscovering a Forgotten Piece of Upper Missouri River History. Manuscript, University of Idaho, Department of History, Moscow, ID.

CORBIN, ANNALIES, AND KENNETH W. KARSMIZKI
1997 Steamboats in Montana: Wrecks of the Far Upper Missouri-Yellowstone River Drainage Area, Phase I—The Search for Historical Evidence. *Underwater Archaeology* 1997:61-68.

HELENA INDEPENDENT
1920 Location of Old River Steamer is Found in Jordan. *Helena Independent*, 8 June, p. 12. Helena, MT.

HOWELL, CHARLES W.
1868 Letter to General A. A. Humphreys from Colonel J. H. Macomb forwarding the Report of the Upper Missouri River conducted by Major C. W. Howell, in nine parts, January 14, 1868. Records of the Office of the Chief of Engineers, Correspondence of the Office Division, Entry 25, Letters Received, 1865-1870, Box 17-18, No. 641, Record Group 77, National Archives, Washington.

JACKSON, DONALD
1985 *Voyages of the Steamboat Yellow Stone.* Norman: University of Oklahoma Press.

KJORNESS, ANNALIES CORBIN
1995 See Corbin, Annalies

NATIONAL ARCHIVES
1860 Map of the Yellowstone and Missouri Rivers, U. S. War Department, Topographical Engineers. WDMC, 20, Record Group 77, National Archives, Washington.
1867 Sketch of the Missouri River from the Mouth of the Platte to Fort Benton, U. S. Corps of Engineers. Q137, Record Group 77, National Archives, Washington.
1874 Missouri River Boat Survey, U. S. Corps of Engineers. Q271, Record Group 77, National Archives, Washington.
1892- Map of the Missouri River from its Mouth to Three
1897 Forks, Montana, in Eighty-four Sheets and Nine Index Sheets, Missouri River Commission. Civil Works Map File, 930 Portfolio Map, Record Group 77, National Archives, Washington.
1956 Aerial Photograph, Missouri River, Montana-ZV-3R-154. National Archives, Washington.
1991 Aerial Photograph, Missouri River, Montana-NAPP-3703014. National Archives, Washington.

RAYNOLDS, W. F.
1860 Topography and Hydrography of the Rocky Mountains and the Missouri River. Manuscript Q 106-1, Subgroup b, Headquarters Map File, U. S. War Department, Record Group 77, National Archives, Washington..

TWINNING, WILLIAM J.
1875 Letter from Captain W. J. Twinning to the Northern Boundary Commission, 1 December. Records of the Office of the Chief of Engineers, Correspondence of the General Record Division, Entry 52, Letters Received, 1871-1886, Box 20, No. 2998, Record Group 77, National Archives, Washington.

UNITED STATES ENGINEERS OFFICE
1934 *Fort Peck Reservoir*, Chart 18. U. S. Engineer Office, Missouri River Division, Kansas City, MO.

WOOD, W. RAYMOND
1979 Notes on the Historical Cartography of the Vicinity of Fort Union, North Dakota. Manuscript, National Parks Service, Midwest Archeological Center, Lincoln, NE.

ANNALIES CORBIN
DEPARTMENT OF HISTORY
(HISTORICAL ARCHAEOLOGY)
UNIVERSITY OF IDAHO
Moscow, ID 83844-3175

Angèle Smith

Mapped Landscapes: The Politics of Metaphor, Knowledge, and Representation on Nineteenth-Century Irish Ordnance Survey Maps

ABSTRACT

Historical archaeologists routinely use historical maps in their interpretations of the past. Nineteenth-century Ordnance Survey maps of Ireland illustrate that maps are simultaneously document, artifact, and metaphor. These colonial maps, which shape understanding of the sociohistorical period, are used as "snapshot" documents of the past to complement the archaeological record. Maps as documents control the knowledge of the landscape and so are often used as a metaphor of that control and power. Historical maps serve better with the recognition that they, too, are artifacts. As visual representations of landscapes, thinking about maps as artifacts highlights maps as the sites of contestation and negotiation, visually representing the social relations of power and the contesting of different understandings of landscapes.

Maps: Document, Metaphor, Artifact

Historical cartographer John Harley (1990) asserts that maps have rhetorically claimed objectivity. They offer, as scientific fact, a depiction of the world in a two-dimensional form. Harley (1990:3–4) argues that historians make little use of historical maps:

> The usual perception of the nature of maps is that they are a mirror, a graphic representation, of some aspect of the real world. The definitions set out in various dictionaries and glossaries of cartography confirm this view. Within the constraints of survey techniques, the skill of the cartographer, and the code of conventional signs, the role of a map is to present a factual statement about geographic reality. Although cartographers write about the art as well as the science of mapmaking, science has overshadowed the competition between the two. The corollary is that when historians assess maps, their interpretation is molded by this idea of what maps are supposed to be. In our own Western culture, at least since the Enlightenment, cartography has been defined

as a factual science. The premise is that a map should offer a transparent window on the world.

It is important to recognize that visual (as well as linguistic) representations are culturally determined. Although the modern Western world tends to take as legitimate and true that which is seen, there is nothing "natural" or "instinctive" about the sense of sight (Porteous 1990). Seeing is not objective, rational, or universal but, rather, is culturally determined. Mapping is based on what is culturally visible. Denis Wood (1992) suggests that maps construct the world rather than reproduce it. That is not quite correct either, for there are partial truths encoded in maps—the truth of the mapmaker—since maps are the visual representations of the culturally perceived world of the cartographer.

How does this affect the ways archaeologists understand maps? Maps play a central role in the production of archaeologies. Archaeologists make and use maps to verify knowledge. The site map, the distribution map, the plan drawing, all illustrate and document interpretations and confirm control over the spatial context of the archaeology. These maps validate "the authoritative truth" of the archaeologists, endorsing their conviction that there is a single correct way of knowing the past that has been guaranteed as a right of the archaeologist. Archaeologists regularly produce maps of their findings; distribution and site maps accompany most published works. Do archaeologists recognize that the making of such maps is in itself culturally determined and a partial truth? The *making* of archaeological maps has not often been problematized, questioned, or critiqued.

With some notable exceptions (especially Seasholes 1988), the same is also true of how historic maps have at times been used in the construction of archaeological knowledge. Historic maps often accompany scholarly texts as the visual representation of the "truth"—the "evidence" of the archaeological interpretations. Maps are sometimes regarded as unquestionable data, as facts of the truth that have been "found" in the course of the archaeological search and discovery (Upton 1992). Significantly, maps have rarely been the *focus* of the archaeological research itself.

In recent years, some archaeologists (as well as some historians and historical geographers) have focused critical attention on the historic map as documentation of colonial control. These authors (Hamer 1989; Monmonier 1991; Kain and Baigent 1992; Pickles 1992; Wood 1992; Delle 1998; Smith 1998; Binnema 2001) have drawn attention to the map as a symbol of power, as documentary evidence of that power in controlling the visual representation of space and landscape. This literature is important for initiating a critical analysis of the taken-for-granted nature of maps as actual and real representations of the world and to challenge this unconscious acceptance. Maps are thus regarded as tools of the state and of the powerful, as a means to dominate and control the (most often colonial) landscape. This view takes a top-down approach wherein maps are regarded as the all-powerful and absolute control of landscape knowledge. Not surprisingly, out of this critical analysis of maps comes the use map as a metaphor, representing power, control, and domination. In other words, from the analysis of maps as documents, it is reasonable to read maps in the larger context as the embodiment of power and control, writing out the voices of others. The visual representation of the controlled landscape becomes a metaphor or symbol for the control itself. Use of this metaphor of the map is recognized in much feminist and postmodern geographies, such as those by Liz Bondi (1990), Patricia Price-Chalita (1994) and Edward Soja and Barbara Hooper (1993).

The top-down approach to understanding maps is challenged as is the use of maps in historical archaeology as mere visual representations that accurately represent "the authoritative truth" of the past. Neither is the map a document that depicts a solely colonial view and hence, control over the landscape. Maps are much more complex representations; they are documents and metaphors. By regarding them simultaneously as artifacts in which multiple perspectives are encoded, historical archaeologists can explore the process of negotiation of power and control over the representation. In this way, the metaphor of maps as power can be redefined and broadened to include resistance and political action of those without access to power.

The use of maps in historical archaeology as the visual representation of both the physical and social landscapes is discussed here. The archaeological investigation focuses on the process of mapmaking and the map itself—specifically, 19th-century Ordnance Survey (OS) maps of Ireland, produced by British soldier-surveyors just a few years before the devastating Potato Famine forever changed the face of the Irish countryside. These detailed maps of Ireland have been used to interpret the historical landscape as well as to visually illustrate those interpretations. More than mere illustrations, maps are simultaneously document, artifact, and metaphor in controlling the politics of knowledge through representation.

Nineteenth-Century Ireland

Ireland in the 19th century was under British colonial rule, as it had been for almost 700 years. Long after the initial colonization of Ireland by the British in the late-12th century and long after the period of the expansive plantation schemes (through the 1500 and 1600s), Ireland in the early 1800s was ruled both in parliament and, to a large extent, in the local countryside, by an Anglo-Protestant class closely connected economically, politically, and socially with neighboring Britain. This class, often called the "Ascendancy," comprised the urban elite of Dublin and London. The Ascendancy, composed of many absentee landholders of large estates in the country, was influential in the Irish Parliament. These were not the only landlords. In the early 1820s, a number of the "absentees" sold their lands to a Catholic middle class that oftentimes lived beyond their means and so, like their Anglo-Protestant counterparts, raked exorbitant rents from the farmer tenants (McMahon 1996).

The contrast between the landed gentry class and the local Irish population was startling. In 1800, the population of Ireland was estimated at 5 million. By the census of 1841, that number had rapidly increased to a recorded population of approximately 8.2 million, making Ireland one of the most densely populated countries in Europe (Campbell 1995:14). The local population was also one of the poorest in Europe with 3 million at poverty level, according to the Poor Inquiry of 1832. The local tenant farmers and cotters lived in small settlements rented from the landlords' agents. Many more landless laborers occupied small plots of land to grow a year's crop of potatoes. Often the poorest were forced into higher and rockier, less fertile areas. Isaac Weld's (1832) *Statistical Survey of Roscommon* recounts the extremity of the poverty:

> The hovels which the poor people were building as I passed, solely by their own efforts, were of the most abject description; their walls were formed, in several instances, by the backs of fences; the floors sunk in the ditches; the height scarcely enough for a man to stand upright; poles not thicker than a broomstick for couples; a few pieces of grass sods the only covering; and these extending only partially over the thing called a roof; the elderly people miserably clothed; the children all but naked.

Generally, the local Irish population as a whole was dependent on the cheap and nutritious mono-cropped potato. Although Irish peasants did not own land, the traditional method of subdividing their occupancy rights meant that they were eking out a living on ever-smaller plots of land. The plight of the local tenant farmer was made more tenuous as grain prices fell after the Napoleonic Wars ended in 1815 and a shift occurred from tillage to grazing. While tillage farming is labor intensive, grazing is not, and some landlords sought to clear their estates of the smallholders in order to restructure the landholdings into larger, more open pastures (Kissane 1995). Tensions between the locals and their landlords were at a breaking point in the early years of the 1800s, in part due to the population crowding, increased rents, and the threat of agricultural and infrastructure improvements that would clear local tenants off the land. The proliferation of rural protest societies such as the Whiteboys and the Ribbonmen was evidence of unrest as members stole about the countryside in acts of subversion and at times violence against the middlemen and landlords.

Consequently, Parliament was pressured to revise the valuation of rents and taxes. A survey of the country's bogs in the early years of the 19th century sought to address the economic needs of the overpopulated countryside with the goal to reclaim "wastelands" (Andrews 1975). This survey did not speak to the tax issues, nor did it address the inadequacies of the outdated land-value assessment upon which the county tax was based. This was further complicated by the land-tenure system in which local farmers did not own but leased land from landholders. In many cases between tenant and landlord were two or more intermediaries. The system was not regularized and was often abused, leaving the largest burden of the tax to the poorest.

As a result, the Ordnance Survey of Ireland was initiated in 1825 and carried out by three survey corps of Royal Engineers and Royal Sappers and Miners of the British army. This mapping project recorded the entire country at the scale of six map inches for every mile on the ground, while it standardized and anglicized the representation of the Irish landscape. In doing so, the survey regularized (and legalized) a new relationship between tenant and landlord. At the same time, it served the British colonial interests in knowing and controlling the landscape, the people and their daily life, as well as their past.

The 19th-century OS maps of Ireland illustrate how maps can be understood as simultaneously document, metaphor, and artifact. These maps are documents in two ways: first, they represent the colonial control over the landscape and its people; second, these maps have been used uncritically as the single authoritative truth of that colonial control. As such, these colonial maps, produced by the British to facilitate governing Ireland at the local level, are clear metaphors for top-down unmitigated power and control. The process of mapping, however, is influenced by more than simply the colonial view, and even that view is not a homogeneous perspective. Mapping incorporates many perspectives, including that of the local Irish tenant farmer. By examining the maps as artifacts of the process of contestation and negotiation, a new metaphor for maps may be inscribed.

Map as Document

The OS maps of Ireland were a detailed depiction of the Irish landscape and its people. Not only was the physical topography mapped at a scale of exacting closeness but so too was the social topography of the landscape. Where and how people lived, how their field systems were organized, and how they moved through the countryside were depicted on the map document. This mapping project was intended to control the knowledge of the landscape in order to better administrate and collect taxes and rents. At the same time, the maps also allowed for better knowledge of and control over the local population, regularizing and legalizing the local tenant farmers' relations with the landlord class.

Since the Irish Parliament was composed of the small, elite Anglo-Irish class of large landholders, it is not surprising that their interests were well represented in the OS maps. These landholders (along with the number of middle-class Catholic landholders) made up a small percentage of the population but owned most of the Irish countryside. Their estates, built in the 18th and early-19th centuries, were the new symbols of colonial rule. With increased economic expansion, increased population, and increased pressures on the land resources, landlords became more assertive, both politically and economically (Whelan 1997). The economic and political self-confidence of the landed class flourished, fed by increased tenant rents that allowed the gentry to focus attention on aggrandizing their estate homes within tree-lined landscaped grounds. Rapid house, estate, and village building as well as new agricultural and infrastructural development resulted in dramatic changes to the landscape. The older ethos of imposing British rule through military and plantation schemes gave way to an ethos of "order, progress, and rationality" that was symbolized in the landlord's estate.

As a symbol of this control and ownership of land, the gentry had private surveys of their own properties carried out. A permanent profession of land surveyors was established to meet the increased demand for estate mapping (Reeves-Smyth 1983). Names like Bernard Scalé and Thomas Sherrard were well-known to the gentry class: "A landowner seeing a neighbor's Scalé atlas (and such treasures must often have been displayed in the library or drawing room) would surely want one for himself, thus opening up another channel of cartographic influence in addition to those already traced" (Andrews 1985:170). In its mapping work, the Ordnance Survey used the maps of Scalé and Sherrard, along with those of Richard Brassington and Clarges Greene as references for a true and accurate depiction of the landscape, although it was more "accurate" of the landlord's perspective than of the local Irish perspective.

Once the Ordnance Survey mapping began, all other independent mapping projects, like the estate mapping, were forbidden, in order that there might be standardization in the official representation of the landscape. Despite this, the earlier estate maps of the landlords became the authoritative documents assumed to depict the "true" landscape. Such features as place names and boundaries, as well as the location, size, and value of the tenantry's settlements, were often copied directly from or "verified" by the earlier estate maps. A new map was required to document and legalize a changed relationship between tenant and landlord, but a new map might also serve to reinforce the control the landlords held over the local landscape, both on the ground and on the map documents. The control inscribed on the maps was not just over the land but also over the process of documentation—the survey and mapping process itself—that created the visual representation of the landscape. The map was a powerful tool that represented and documented control and authority on many levels. It is not surprising then that landlords often displayed maps in the library or drawing room of their estate homes. Maps were valued as works of art that only the elite could afford. Perhaps more importantly, maps were valued for their scientific accuracy in visually representing and thus legitimizing the landlord's claim to land. The "authority" of mapping science meant that the map was a trophy of the landlord's status.

Historians and historical archaeologists recognize the use of earlier maps as authoritative documents in the 19th century, but they can (and ought) also reflect on the use of maps in their own research today. Not only are maps understood as documents of the colonial control over the landscape and its people, but also these documents have been used as "proof" of a single authoritative truth of colonial control. The uncritical use of these maps as documents of control legitimizes and reifies an unchallenged domination of colonial powers over the local. In the disciplines of history and archaeology, OS maps have been used as documents to authoritatively illustrate what the 19th-century landscape looked like, as if the map were a "snapshot" record of the past (Aalen et al. 1997; McDonald 1997). Shortly after the first maps were completed, the Irish landscape underwent tremendous changes. Almost four million people, approximately half the population, either died or emigrated because of the Potato Famine (1845–1851) (Morash 1995). It is assumed that pre-famine Ireland is "preserved" in the maps, and these maps are often uncritically used by famine historians and in famine archaeology to re-create that time. This is clearly problematic, given that maps tell just part of the story about the complex relations of the social landscape of 19th-century Ireland. At the same time, it is understandable that the concept of "maps" has been used as a metaphor of power, control, and domination.

Map as Metaphor of Power

"Space is fundamental in any exercise of power." In this often-quoted statement, Michel Foucault (1984:252) declares that knowledge and power are often socially constructed in spatial terms. All social relations and inter- actions have a spatial element, and since all social relations are social relations of power, spatial relations and power relations are closely interrelated (Wolf 1999). Henri Lefebvre (1991) and Edward Soja (1989) have argued that spatial relations are both the product of and the pro- ducer of social relations. The power differences that exist in social relations are reflected in the spatial enactment of that power differential, at the same time the spatial patterning of social interactions help to create or reinforce the unequal access to social power.

It is not surprising that social relations of power, both dominant and marginal to that power, are often constructed and represented as positional difference. Places of difference are metaphorically linked with social differ- ence. Spatial language clearly represents power differentials in a variety of ways. People lack- ing access and power may be expressed in an abstract or unnamed manner as people denied space, displaced, or placeless. Spatial language is also used to represent the relational and explicitly the oppositionality of social relations, using the relation to other spaces in such meta- phors as margin/center, periphery/core, or inside/ outside. The spatial metaphor of power differ- ence may also be well defined in terms of (and control over) spatial concepts, such as the body, borderland, or home (Price-Chalita 1994).

As the visual representations of space and, more importantly, the control over that space, maps become a powerful metaphor for the dominant social relations of power. Traditionally, they are regarded as transparent "truth," scientifi- cally controlling the knowledge of the landscape and its people. The map is a "meta-narrative" in the sense that it claims universal understanding and truth, while masking the fact that it rep- resents only a single authoritative version of the truth. Maps have been used to exclude by constructing certain kinds of spatial knowledge while silencing others. This is the top-down per- spective of "map as document"—unquestioned, unproblematized, accepted as representing true- ness. The local people do not need to map their landscape; they know the stories, the people, and the heritage that make it meaningful. They are intimately familiar with moving through the landscape. Maps are made by outsiders for outsiders, so that they can know, occupy, and have control over the landscape. This is clearly illustrated in the 19th-century colonial OS maps of Ireland, made by the British for administering British rule and collecting rents and taxes.

The documentary evidence of colonial power found on these maps is not the whole picture of the Irish countryside. Were there alternative ways to perceive, use, and understand the local landscape? Were these alternative views depicted on the map? Was the OS map merely a fabrica- tion of the colonial mapmaker?

These questions call attention to larger issues in historical archaeology. While long accepted, the discussion concerning the role of documen- tary versus archaeological evidence needs revisit- ing when speaking of the use of maps. Whether one excavates first and uses the documentary record to identify the archaeological finds (with the assumption that the documentary record is the truth) or whether one begins with a history based on the documentary record in order to provide context and then excavates to fill in gaps or add detail does not matter; neither of these two meth- ods is fully adequate. It is generally accepted that these two sets of data (documents and archaeol- ogy) should be regarded as independent of each other. The inconsistencies or ambiguities that exist between the two sources of information should expand and deepen interpretations.

Henry Glassie (1972:29) states, "a method- ological limitation to *print* [document] binds the scholar to studying only the handful of people who were literate" [emphasis added]. That handful of people is of interest precisely because they were the ones who were recording and producing the landscape maps. Mark Leone and Parker Potter, Jr., (1988) have cautioned that in the past those who produced documents and those who used the material culture were not producing their independent data sets in the same context. In other words, these authors would suggest that in 19th-century Ireland the mapmakers, as document producers, and the local Irish, as producers of archaeological material culture, were independent of each other and acted in separate social contexts. This study asserts that the mapmakers *did* interact with the local population in the Irish landscape. The two worlds of the mapmaker and the local Irish farmer collided in the making of the map and in the map itself. The difference between the landscape and the representation of that landscape in the maps is the site of contestation and negotiation that was taking place through the colonial act of mapping.

In the case study of 19th-century Ireland, the differences between the finished map document and the landscape need to be explored, as do the interaction and negotiation between the mapmakers and those who lived in the local landscape. Seldom have scholars considered the act of creating a map as a process that can be examined archaeologically. Similarly, few have archaeologically examined maps as artifacts in themselves. Research is better served if maps are recognized as artifacts for understanding the sociohistorical relations of power (Deetz 1977a, 1977b) that have helped to shape both the landscape and the map as its visual representation.

Map as Artifact

Some archaeologists insist that a map is not an artifact, unless it is discussed in terms of the kind of paper that it was printed on or the type of ink that was used to draw it. These details as well as the measurements of the map sheets and the binding on the volume of maps could easily be described. Is there, however, something more important to be gained in recognizing the map as an artifact? If artifacts are the product of human manufacture, then the map as artifact allows the map to be seen as a product

of the surveyors' perceptions of the landscape as well as the surveyors' interactions with the local community, the landed gentry class, and the Ordnance Survey supervisors in the Dublin offices. The map-artifact embodies the negotiations of power and control over the representation of the landscape.

Each ordnance surveyor signed his name to the field notebooks that he was responsible for, thereby authorizing what was recorded on the maps. Col. Thomas Colby (1825), the superintendent of the Irish survey, wrote explicit survey guidelines (*The Instructions for the Interior Survey of Ireland*) that were meant to standardize the procedure in the field as well as the look of the final map product. These instructions set the guidelines for measuring boundaries, recording of place name orthography, and the depiction of landscape content. The majority of the instructions were concerned with the labor organization of the survey and the various means for checking mathematical accuracy. Orthography, too, was given close attention in Colby's instructions. The superintendent demanded that each officer keep a record of the local spelling and all variations of place names and write "a short description of the place and any remarkable circumstances relating to it" (Colby 1825, article 35). The nature of the content of the maps was to include "everything attached to the ground" (article 65). Colby addressed this in article 1: "The interior survey of Ireland is to be performed on a scale of six inches to one English mile; and the plans are to be drawn with all the accuracy and minuteness of detail which that scale admits." The scale determined what level of detail was required to "fill the map space." Not only the political boundaries of the barony, parish, and town land but also field fence lines were depicted. Occupied and unoccupied houses and buildings were each distinguished on the map. Even the type of script used in labeling indicated the category (and significance) of what was being named.

Colby's instruction with respect to the representation of archaeology, specifically "mounds, forts, and tombs," was related to place names and the "short description of the place and any remarkable circumstances relating to it" and because "mounds, forts and tombs" could be used as trigonometric stations. His interest in the archaeological landscape was practical as it served the surveyors in the process of mapping. For his own part, Colby was less inclined to include antiquities as features of inquiry on the maps. In a letter dated 10 November 1842 to his wife, Colby admitted his dislike of such "ornamental or insubstantial knowledge" as ancient monuments (Close 1969:94).

While the surveying instructions were comprehensive, it should not be assumed that all instructions were followed to the letter. The surveyors, after all, were in the field making daily decisions about what was or was not identified and recorded, and it is not surprising that these guidelines were not always rigorously followed. For example, in the study area of Carrowkeel-Lough Arrow in County Sligo, the hilltop place names such as "Glan East," "Gull's Finger Stone," "Crockanaw," and "Crocklosky" were not recorded on the final maps. The upland topography was generally poorly mapped and appears on the maps as blank open spaces, leaving plenty room for place names (Figure 1, showing the lack of upland detail and no hilltop name on the left side of the map). Likewise, the almost 5,000-year-old megalithic tombs of this area, situated at the summit of each hilltop, were also not recorded. These large stone burial mounds are very visible on the landscape. In some cases, the surveyors even erected their trigonometric stations on top of the cairns, but even then the cairns did not make it onto the map (Figure 1, showing none of the 14 cairns on the hilltop on the left side of the map). These examples suggest that the lower ranking field surveyors had a role in negotiating how the local landscape was visually represented on the maps.

While surveyors were carrying out their work, they were locally stationed, either at barracks in nearby towns, lodged at public houses or in camps erected in the countryside they were mapping. The official *Progress Reports* (Ordnance Survey of Ireland 1836a) indicate that

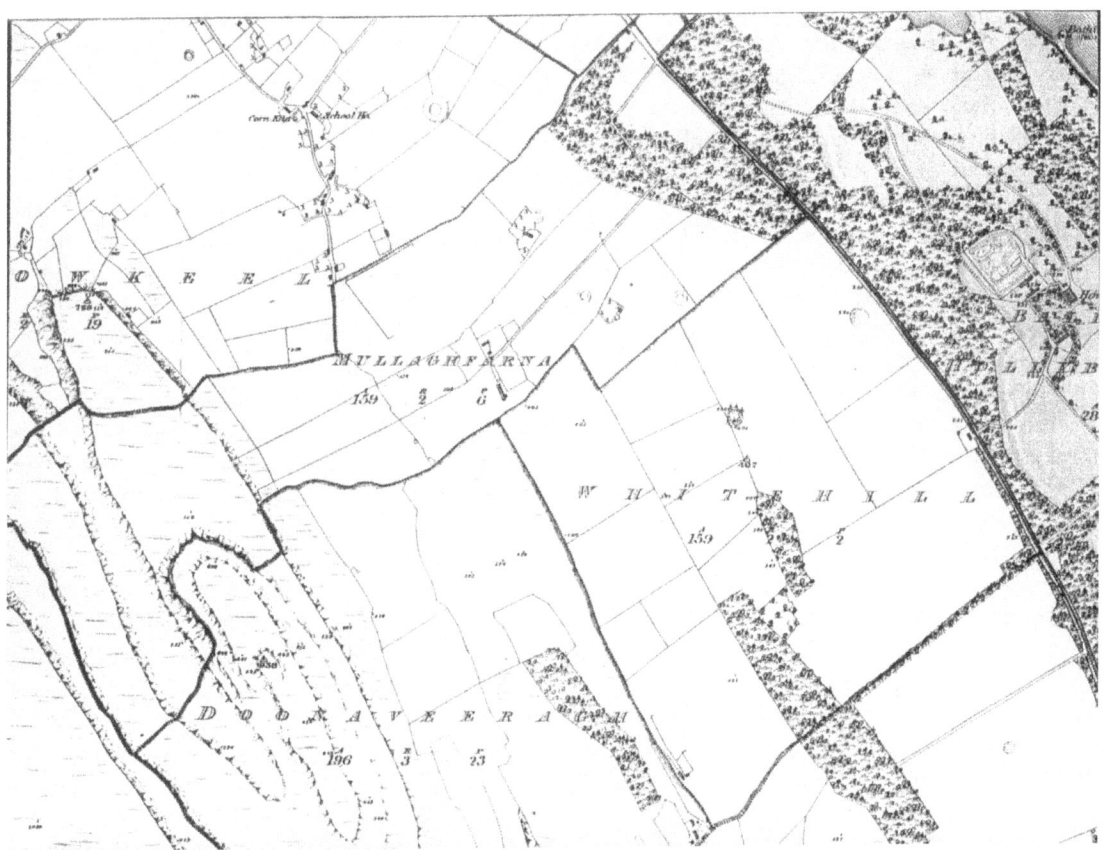

FIGURE 1. 1837 Ordnance Survey map of the Carrowkeel-Lough area of southern County Sligo. (Ordnance Survey Ireland permit no. 7891. © Ordnance Survey Ireland and Government of Ireland.)

two field divisions under Lt. Edward Dunford (with 1 second lieutenant, 3 corporals, and 29 privates) and Lt. Robert Boteler (with 1 second lieutenant, 11 corporals, and 22 privates) entered the study area of Carrowkeel-Lough Arrow on 15 March 1836 and began plotting, leveling, and drawing the land. The area map was ready for publication five months later at the end of August. The surveyors would have been conspicuous in the local setting—the community population would be well aware of their presence as would the local landlords whose lands were being surveyed. The Ordnance Survey letters (Ordnance Survey of Ireland 1836c, 1837b) indicate many instances in which the head of the field party supervisors visited the local landlords as a gesture of recognition of their authority in the area. These supervisors would also verify the place names and boundaries with the landlord himself and, importantly, with his earlier estate maps. The surveyors used these early maps to depict the estate lands in such exacting detail that one might even be able to count the trees that lined the manicured grounds. The designs and patterns of the formal estate gardens were depicted, the houses named, and the whole estate shaded grey on the otherwise black and white map, thus highlighting its significance in and control over the landscape (Figure 1, showing the detail of the "tree'd" and highlighted landscape of the Hollybrook estate on the right side of the map). The field surveyors were clearly influenced by landlord authority, and this is reproduced in the map.

Interactions with the local Irish inhabitants also influenced the surveyors. Brian Friel's play *Translations* (1981) brings alive the dynamics of local life at this time and provides a glimpse of what the social interactions between the locals and surveyors might have been like. Set in a small rural village of County Donegal, this play that enacts the personal and cultural effects of the interaction between the local residents of the town and the Ordnance Survey surveyors ends in tragedy and foreshadows a turbulent future. Friel also presents an image of the local Irish engaged in resistance: first, in the suspicious disappearance of Lt. Yolland and, second, in arson at the surveyors' encampment.

While the study found no evidence of violent resistance against the intervention of the Ordnance Survey in the Carrowkeel-Lough Arrow area, there is evidence in the Ordnance Survey Correspondences (Ordnance Survey of Ireland 1836b) that tension between the members of the survey and the local inhabitants was real. One such example is found in a letter from Captain Waters, dated 28 February 1836, reporting that robbers had broken into the field surveyors' lodgings, taken their bayonets, and had torn and ruined survey field books. Another incident was reported of bayonets being stolen from the lodgings of Private Frazer on 8 August 1836 by persons disguised in women's clothes (a trademark associated with the Irish agrarian secret societies). Ordnance Survey guidelines also described how to deal with locals who were caught defacing boundary marks or tampering with trigonometric stations, suggesting that this too must have been a problem. A real sense of resistance and struggle existed over the mapping project, and that contestation was mediated and negotiated in the maps themselves.

Far from being completely removed from the process of mapping, local civilians were hired to help with manual labor as well as guide the surveyors through the local landscape. In field books, the surveyors recorded their daily measurements taken from newly built hilltop trigonometric stations. They also recorded the place names often provided by the civilian worker or the local farmer. Through these interactions, the surveyors learned the stories of saints and fairies and of Irish families long since dispossessed of their homelands. While not identified by name, the "local inhabitant" was often listed in the place name books of the surveyors (Ordnance Survey of Ireland 1837a) as the source of local place names. (Of note, the landlord also was sometimes listed by name and, more often, local clergymen were named as verifying the local information.) Back in Dublin, official orthographers would validate the place name information (and spelling) that would appear on the final map. Nevertheless, the local inhabitant played a role in controlling what the surveyor learned and what was recorded on the map, deciding what names and stories were not told and what access through the landscape was denied. The map-artifact was a site for competing knowledges of the landscape.

By critically examining maps as artifacts of contestation and negotiation, as a process of the complex social interactions that took place in the local landscape, rather than as documents of the overarching colonial control of that landscape, a very different metaphor of maps emerges.

Politics of Mapping: Metaphor, Knowledge, and Representation

While maps do indeed act as metaphors for control and are powerful documents, they are also artifacts. As artifacts—the visual representation of landscapes, people, and their histories—maps are the sites of relations and negotiations between those with the power to construct the images and those with power to contest them. These are the relations of power among the local Irish farmers, Anglo-Protestant landlords, soldier-surveyors in the field, and superiors back in Dublin who supervise and instruct the mapping process. These power relations are acted out on the local landscape and on the mapped landscape. The map is also a vehicle for resistance. The metaphor of the map representing dominant and exclusive control and power must be redefined. The new metaphor of the map artifact is one of resistance, competing voices, inclusion, and political action.

This more complex metaphor of the social relations of power on the local landscape, challenging the all-pervasive nature of colonial control, is clearly exemplified in the 19th-century Ordnance Survey maps of Ireland. Archaeologists must be aware of how maps are used and interpreted as representations of the landscape: do researchers rely on the "authority" of existing historic maps, taking for granted the colonial view as the single true perspective? Furthermore, archaeologists must also be aware of their own role as mapmakers. In the production of archaeological interpretation, surveys and excavations depend on maps to illustrate and document the archaeologist's control over the spatial context.

Archaeologists must take care to evaluate their own work and research and how it is represented. Does archaeology create documents, recording archaeological space as static, controlled by archaeological knowledge? In the process, are archaeologists creating authoritative "truth" in their maps that silences other understandings, other knowledges and thus controls the social relations of power? Alternatively, are archaeologists attempting to create maps as artifacts

that are sites of interactions and negotiations of different knowledges and representations of the mapped landscape? Maps are complex representations. By regarding them as documents and metaphors of power and, simultaneously, as artifacts and metaphors of the process of negotiation of power and control over the representation, researchers can more completely understand the politics of metaphor, knowledge, and representation of the mapped landscape.

References

AALEN, FRED H. A., KEVIN WHELAN, AND MATTHEW STOUT (EDITORS)
    1997 *Atlas of the Irish Rural Landscape.* Cork University Press, Cork, Ireland.

ANDREWS, JOHN H.
    1975 *A Paper Landscape: The Ordnance Survey in Nineteenth-Century Ireland.* Oxford University Press, Oxford, England.
    1985 *Plantation Acres: An Historical Study of the Irish Land Surveyor and His Maps.* Ulster Historical Foundation, Omagh, Co. Tyrone, Ireland.

BINNEMA, THEODORE
    2001 How Does a Map Mean? Old Swan's Map of 1801 and the Blackfoot World. In *From Rupert's Land to Canada*, Theodore Binnema, Gerhard Ens, and Rod MacLeod, editors, pp. 201–224. University of Alberta Press, Edmonton, Canada.

BONDI, LIZ
    1990 Feminism, Postmodernism, and Geography: Space for Women? *Antipode* 22(2):156–167.

CAMPBELL, STEPHEN J.
    1995 *The Great Irish Famine.* The Famine Museum, Strokestown, Ireland.

CLOSE, CHARLES
    1969 *The Early Years of the Ordnance Survey.* Augustus M. Kelley, New York, NY.

COLBY, THOMAS
    1825 *Instructions for the Interior Survey of Ireland, 1825.* Ordnance Survey of Ireland, Phoenix Park, Dublin.

DEETZ, JAMES
    1977a *In Small Things Forgotten: The Archaeology of Early American Life.* Anchor Books, Garden City, NY.
    1977b Material Culture and Archaeology: What's the Difference? In *Historical Archaeology and the Importance of Material Things,* Leland Ferguson, editor, pp. 9–12. The Society for Historical Archaeology, *Special Publications Series,* No. 2, Tucson, AZ.

DELLE, JAMES
  1998   *An Archaeology of Social Space*. Plenum Press, New York, NY.

FOUCAULT, MICHEL
  1984   Space, Knowledge, and Power. In *The Foucault Reader*, P. Paul Rabinow, editor, pp. 239–256. Pantheon, New York, NY.

FRIEL, BRIAN
  1981   *Translations*. Faber and Faber, London, England.

GLASSIE, HENRY
  1972   Eighteenth-Century Cultural Process in Delaware Valley Folk Building. *Winterthur Portfolio* 7: 29–57.

HAMER, MARY
  1989   Putting Ireland on the Map. *Textual Practice* 3(2): 84–201.

HARLEY, JOHN B.
  1990   Text and Contexts in the Interpretation of Early Maps. In *From Sea Charts to Satellite Images: Interpreting North American History through Maps*, David Buisseret, editor, pp. 3–15. University of Chicago Press, Chicago, IL.

KAIN, ROGER, AND ELIZABETH BAIGENT
  1992   *The Cadastral Map in the Service of the State: A History of Property Mapping*. University of Chicago Press, Chicago, IL.

KISSANE, NOEL
  1995   *The Irish Famine: A Documentary History*. National Library of Ireland, Dublin.

LEFEBVRE, HENRI
  1991   *The Production of Space*. Basil Blackwell, Oxford, England.

LEONE, MARK P., AND PARKER B. POTTER, JR.
  1988   Introduction: Issues in Historical Archaeology. In *The Recovery of Meaning: Historical Archaeology in the Eastern United States*, Mark P. Leone and Parker B. Potter, Jr., editors, pp. 1–22. Smithsonian Institution Press, Washington, DC.

MCDONALD, THERESA
  1997   *Achill Island*. I.A.S. Publications, Tullamore, Co. Offaly, Ireland.

MCMAHON, SEAN
  1996   *A Short History of Ireland*. Mercier Press, Dublin, Ireland.

MONMONIER, MARK
  1991   *How to Lie with Maps*. University of Chicago Press, Chicago, IL.

MORASH, CHRISTOPHER
  1995   *Writing the Irish Famine*. Oxford University Press, Oxford, England.

ORDNANCE SURVEY OF IRELAND
  1836a *Monthly Progress Reports*, District B, 1836, OS 1/12. National Archives of Ireland, Dublin.
  1836b Ordnance Survey Correspondences. April 1833–Nov. 1836. OS 2/14, Vol. II F, 4532-7068. National Archives of Ireland, Dublin.
  1836c Ordnance Survey Letters, Co. Roscommon, Vol. 3. National Archives of Ireland, Dublin.
  1837a Field Namebooks, Co. Sligo. National Archives of Ireland, Dublin.
  1837b Ordnance Survey Letters, Carrowmore Parish, Co. Sligo. National Archives of Ireland, Dublin.

PICKLES, JOHN
  1992   Texts, Hermeneutics, and Propaganda Maps. In *Writing Worlds: Discourse, Text, and Metaphor in the Representation of Landscape*, Trevor Barnes and James Duncan, editors, pp. 193–230. Routledge, London, England.

PORTEOUS, J. DOUGLAS
  1990   *Landscapes of the Mind: Worlds of Sense and Metaphor*. University of Toronto Press, Toronto, Canada.

PRICE-CHALITA, PATRICIA
  1994   Spatial Metaphor and the Politics of Empowerment: Mapping a Place for Feminism and Postmodernism in Geography. *Antipode: A Radical Journal of Geography* 26(3):236–253.

REEVES-SMYTH, TERENCE
  1983   Landscapes in Paper: Cartographic Sources for Irish Archaeology. In *Landscape Archaeology*, Terence Reeves-Smyth and Fred Hammond, editors, pp. 119–177. BAR British Series 116, Oxford, England.

SEASHOLES, NANCY S.
  1988   On the Use of Historical Maps. In *Documentary Archaeology in the New World*, Mary C. Beaudry, editor, pp. 92–118. Cambridge University Press, Cambridge, England.

SMITH, ANGÈLE
  1998   Landscapes of Power: The Archaeology of Nineteenth-Century Irish Ordnance Survey Maps. *Archaeological Dialogues* 5(1):69–84.

SOJA, EDWARD
  1989   *Postmodern Geographies*. Verso, London, England.

SOJA, EDWARD, AND BARBARA HOOPER
  1993   The Spaces That Difference Makes. In *Place and the Politics of Identity*, Michael Keith and Steve Pile, editors, pp. 183–205. Routledge, London, England.

UPTON, DELL
  1992   The City as Material Culture. In *The Art and Mystery of Historical Archaeology: Essays in Honor of James Deetz*, Anne E. Yentsch and Mary C. Beaudry, editors, pp. 51–74. CRC Press, Boca Raton, FL.

WELD, ISAAC
　　1832　*Statistical Survey of Co. Roscommon, Ireland. Grand Jury Survey.* R. Gaisberry Publisher, Dublin, Ireland.

WHELAN, KEVIN
　　1997　The Modern Landscape: From Plantation to Present. In *Atlas of the Irish Rural Landscape*, Fred H. A. Aalen, Kevin Whelan, and Matthew Stout, pp. 67–103. Cork University Press, Cork, Ireland.

WOLF, ERIC
　　1999　*Envisioning Power: Ideologies of Dominance and Crisis.* University of California Press, Berkeley.

WOOD, DENIS
　　1992　*Power of Maps.* The Guilford Press, New York, NY.

ANGÈLE SMITH
DEPARTMENT OF ANTHROPOLOGY
UNIVERSITY OF NORTHERN BRITISH COLUMBIA
3333 UNIVERSITY WAY
PRINCE GEORGE, BC V2N 4Z9
CANADA

Steven D. Smith
Christopher Ohm Clement
Stephen R. Wise

GPS, GIS and the Civil War Battlefield Landscape: A South Carolina Low Country Example

ABSTRACT

The results of Global Positioning System (GPS) mapping and Geographic Information System (GIS) analysis of Civil War earthworks in Beaufort and Jasper counties, South Carolina, are presented. Most earthworks were part of a defensive system built by Confederate forces over the course of the war to protect the Charleston to Savannah railroad, which itself was part of a vital supply line allowing rapid transport of men and materiel throughout the Confederacy. For most of the war, Union forces were deployed at Port Royal Sound less than 40 km from the railroad. The Confederates met this threat through fixed defenses at strategic locations combined with rapid movement of troops by rail. This strategy and these tactics are understandable within the geographic context provided by GPS/GIS technology and a military context provided by a detailed campaign history.

Introduction

In May 1861 the new Confederate states initiated efforts to defend the South Carolina coast and interior lines of supply from Union invasion by the construction of defensive positions at strategic locations between Charleston and Savannah. Critical to the movement of troops and supplies was the railroad between these two southern ports (Robinson 1950). In November of that year, Union forces arrived at Port Royal Sound, South Carolina, and gained a solid beachhead on Hilton Head Island. Unable to dislodge the Union from Port Royal Sound, the Confederates fell back and began fortifying the numerous inlets and approaches vulnerable to potential Union thrusts against their vital rail lifeline. From spring 1862 until early 1865, the Union Army attempted to cut the railroad, the most serious effort being the move against the rail stop at Grahamville, South Carolina. On 30 November 1864, only two miles short of their goal, the Union forces were stopped at the Battle of Honey Hill, suffering heavy casualties. The Confederates successfully protected the railroad until General William T. Sherman captured Savannah. The loss of Savannah and the threat of Sherman's army moving north into South Carolina finally caused the Confederates to abandon the railroad's defense.

Three years of Union maneuvering and Confederate response resulted in numerous batteries and long lines of infantry trenches scattered across the landscape of South Carolina's Jasper and Beaufort counties. Today, evidence of this struggle is largely gone, due to postwar land modification, road creation and widening, wetlands draining, and increased population. These landscape changes have largely obliterated the geographical context of the lines, making it difficult to understand their strategic significance. While there are some remarkably well-preserved batteries, forts, and lines, their historical meaning and purpose is obscure to all but the most ardent students of the Civil War in South Carolina. Tourists hurrying to recreational areas like Beaufort, Hilton Head, and Hunting Island, South Carolina, may occasionally wonder about those little mounds and ditches just off the highway, but most will speed past never knowing they are crossing a once-bloody landscape.

This article presents the results of a first step towards rediscovering and preserving the remaining monuments of the low-country struggle by mapping their locations and major features using Global Positioning System (GPS) technology (Clement et al. 2000). The work was performed by the South Carolina Institute of Archaeology and Anthropology and funded by the National Park Service's American Battlefield Protection Program. The project had two mutually supporting goals: (1) gather sufficient GPS data to produce Geographic Information System (GIS) maps of the Honey Hill battlefield and 16 other batteries associated with the defense of the Savannah to Charleston Railroad (Table 1), and (2) provide enough historical and archaeological data to interpret their histories. The generation of GIS maps of the lines and batteries, combined with a detailed historic context in the form of a campaign history, provided South Carolina resource managers with the data necessary for understanding the significance of these sites and developing a multiple National Register Nomination. At the same time, researchers were able to provide a

TABLE 1
BATTERIES AND LINES MAPPED

Name	Site Number	Type of Site
Frampton House	38JA1017	battery remnant
Frampton Creek	38JA255	earthworks, lines
Pocotaligo/Castle Hill Complex	38BU1859	lines, batteries
Pocotaligo	38BU1862, 38BU1863	batteries
Pocotaligo West	38JA256	lunette
Brewton	38BU1861	battery
Tomotley	38BU1860	battery
River Road	38BU1864	battery, line
Combahee Fort	38BU1217	redoubt
Mackey (Mackay) Point	38JA254	lines, redoubt, salient
Pages Point	38BU1857, 38BU1858	battery
Bees Creek	38JA249	lunette
Euhaw Church	38JA248	lines
Dawsons Bluff	38JA250	redoubts
Boyds Landing/Boyds Neck	38JA251, 38JA253	lines with salients, lunette
Honey Hill	38JA1008	lines
Delta Plantation	38JA169, 38JA252	lines, fortified camp

better understanding of the batteries and lines in relation to the two adversaries' strategies and tactics. With this first step accomplished, it is hoped that protection measures can be taken and programs developed with the goal of interpreting the low country's Civil War past for both tourists and natives alike.

The Project Area

The project area consisted of the counties of Beaufort and Jasper, South Carolina (Figure 1). Beaufort County is almost exclusively in the Coastal Zone, while much of Jasper is in the Outer Coastal Plain. The Outer Coastal Plain is characteristically flat and slopes very gradually to sea level; it contains most of the batteries and lines mapped for this project. It was formed as a result of millions of years of sea-level fluctuations, beginning in the Miocene Epoch, 18 million years ago. The latest series of sea level rises and falls occurred during the Pleistocene as a result of the forming and melting of the glaciers. Most of the topography seen today was shaped by the action of the seas smoothing the landscape. The result was a series of gentle terraces from the Coastal Zone to the Inner Coastal Plain that are not readily apparent to most people except geologists and geographers. About 50% of the area has elevations less than 42 ft. (Kovacik and Winberry 1987:18–22).

The Coastal Zone, much more complex and diverse than the Outer Coastal Plain, is the interface between the ocean and the mainland, and the waterways are affected by tides. In the project area, the Coastal Zone is full of barrier islands, tidal inlets, interior waterways, bays, river mouths, and backwater swamps. From Cape Romaine just south of the Santee River, south into Georgia, barrier islands and erosional remnant islands make up the sea island

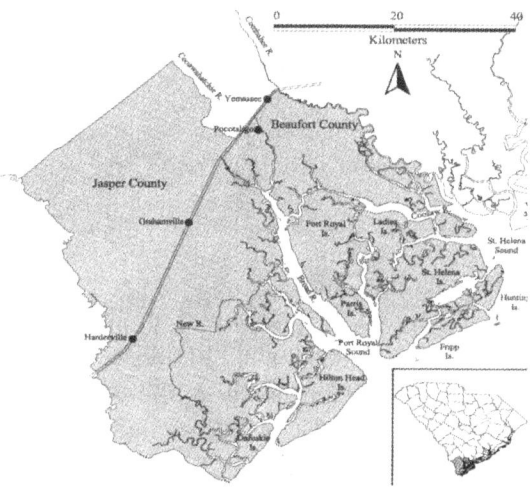

FIGURE 1. Beaufort and Jasper Counties, South Carolina (South Carolina Department of Natural Resources).

complex. Erosional remnants are so classified because they were once part of the mainland; barrier islands, on the other hand, are active, changing sand dunes, held together by vegetation and subject to the winds and tides (Kovacik and Winberry 1987: 23–26). Nineteen percent of the Coastal Zone is flooded daily or occasionally by tidal flow.

Two major rivers drain the project area. The Coosawhatchie River empties into the Broad River, a tidal river that opens to become Port Royal Sound. The Combahee River, north of the Coosawhatchie empties into St. Helena Sound. Between the two sounds, Whale Branch and the Coosaw River join to cut off a complex of remnant islands. This complex includes the larger islands of Port Royal, St. Helena, Parris, and Ladies, the barrier islands of Fripp and Hunting, and many other smaller islands mixed between. A smaller river called the New, south of the Coosawhatchie, drains the narrow land between the Coosawhatchie-Broad rivers and the Savannah River.

The rivers, islands, and interior waterways of the Coastal Zone in the project area created obstacles to the construction of the Charleston and Savannah Railroad around the Jasper County-Beaufort County border. As a result, although they were laid entirely within the Outer Coastal Plain where only the Coosawhatchie and Combahee Rivers formed major impediments, the tracks in this area closely follow the interface between the two geographic provinces. Unlike in other areas, then, the Charleston and Savannah Railroad at the border of Jasper and Beaufort counties was accessible by water, a fact that was readily apparent to the Union Army occupying the islands around Port Royal Sound. It was these factors that dictated the Confederate defensive strategies and tactics in the project area.

Methods

The field effort consisted of identifying and mapping batteries located previously by regional Civil War avocational and professional historians. One very active avocational historian had been attempting to research and locate all the batteries in the region for several years and knew the landowners either by name or personal acquaintance. He was quite interested in sharing his knowledge and became the project's lead liaison between the numerous landowners and the project team.

GPS data were collected using a Trimble® Pro-XR data logger with real-time differential correction. The data were also corrected in the laboratory during post-processing and were then edited. The National Park Service's Civil War batteries data dictionary, developed and tested by the American Battlefield Protection Program (ABPP), was adopted to capture and record field data. The ABPP's data dictionary has separate fields for such attributes as width and height of parapets, gun emplacements, ramps, and embrasures.

Post-processing consisted of downloading the data into Pathfinder Office® software on a Windows® NT-operated computer. The files were downloaded each evening and checked. In the laboratory, positions were differentially corrected using base station files obtained on the World Wide Web from the closest public base station. Most of the data were edited in the laboratory using Pathfinder Office® software once fieldwork was completed. Editing consisted of smoothing lines created by individual positions recorded by the data logger. The data dictionary and field notes assisted this process. Once the data were edited, they were transferred into ArcView® for generating battery location and feature maps.

Simultaneously with the field effort, an historical context was researched and written by the project historian. It focused on the military campaign in the region, with emphasis on the various military features that were constructed as a result of Confederate defensive and Union offensive efforts. This history, presented below, is admittedly lengthy, detailed, and complex, but it is, after all, the military context within which the lines and batteries were created. It represents one of the primary contributors to the locations of the lines and batteries on the landscape. Past archaeological examinations of military landscapes have sometimes oversimplified the historical events that created them. This can make a battlefield appear as a static set piece rather than the scene of a highly dynamic, fluid series of events, each event influenced by human personality, physical limitation, and emotion as well as by the lay of the land. The goal was to attempt to understand and interpret a complex remnant landscape. To do so, it is necessary to illuminate both the cultural and geographical nature of that landscape with equal fervor.

Historical Background

With the completion of a bridge over the Savannah River in spring 1861, the Savannah to Charleston Railroad was to be the region's principal transportation and commercial link to the rest of the South and the nation. Long before the completion date, small railroad stops and communities were established along the route in anticipation of becoming interior distribution centers for goods going to and coming from Port Royal's harbor. Though there were no docking facilities in the region, small vessels could reach the railroad by navigating the Broad and Pocotaligo rivers to a location where goods could be transferred for a short hop to the railroad and then throughout the South (Wise 2000:12). But war was at hand.

As early as May 1861, the Confederate commander in South Carolina, General Pierre G. T. Beauregard, undertook an examination of the coast to plan its defense. The expedition resulted in construction of the first of what would be many earthen fortifications stretching from Charleston to the Savannah River. These first works were placed at the mouth of navigable inlets. Their purpose was to deny enemy vessels access to the inland sounds and waterways (Wise 2000:13; *Official Records of the Union and Confederate Navies in the War of the Rebellion* [*ORN*] 1901[I]:167–168, 178). With so many possible access routes, the coastal landscape soon became dotted with small forts. The batteries were positioned and designed by General Beauregard and constructed under the direction of state and Confederate engineers. Labor was accomplished by slave gangs requisitioned from neighboring plantations (Freeman [1]:607–608, 613–615; *War of the Rebellion: Official Records of the Union and Confederate Armies* [*ORA*] 1899–1901 [VI]:38).

Construction of the defenses actually fell to Brigadier General Roswell Sabine Ripley, who took over the command of South Carolina in August 1861. Ripley and his commander at Port Royal, Brigadier General Thomas Drayton, believed the fortifications could resist naval attacks, keeping the enemy from capturing the sea islands and reaching the Charleston and Savannah Railroad. Ripley's confidence stemmed from the outdated military theory that one gun on land was worth 10 on board a ship and that land-based gunners, using larger guns than could be mounted on a ship, could take their time and sight-in on the slow moving, sail-powered warships. This theory was soon proved to be disastrously wrong when on 7 November 1861, Union steam power shattered the Confederacy's forward coastal defenses in the Battle of Port Royal (Viele 1885:329–340; Rowland et al. 1996:451–455). Ripley had the sad duty of reporting the defeat to the new commander of the Department of South Carolina, Georgia, and East Florida, General Robert E. Lee, who arrived at Coosawhatchie, South Carolina, on the evening of the battle.

Lee assembled the remnants of Ripley's defeated command along the headwaters of the Broad River and immediately prepared for an enemy attack inland. He saw that the South did not have enough men or cannon to defend every inlet, so he turned to a new defensive scheme, predicated on mobility, to defend the region and the railroad. He drew on his father's theories on coastal defense, an army report written in 1826 by Major Joseph G. Totten, and Colonel Ambrosio Gonzales's proposed coastal defense, which used "flying batteries" that could be rushed to any threatened coastal region. Lee adopted these strategies and added the element of rail transportation (Freeman 1951 [1]:613–614). Critically, Lee did not want to fight the enemy from fixed fortifications. He wanted to meet and defeat his adversaries in the field. So he planned his strategy around the use of fixed positions that would serve as bases from which he could launch counterattacks, using troops assembled and concentrated via the railroad (Wise 2000: 16). Savannah and Charleston were to be the anchors in his new defense line. While these bulwarks were strengthened, Lee concentrated his efforts on fortifying the headwaters of the Broad River and key points between the Savannah and Combahee rivers. Reinforcements allowed Lee to improve his defenses. Works were started at Red Bank on the New River, at Pages Point, at Port Royal Ferry on the Coosaw River, and at Tar Bluff on the Combahee. Besides the batteries, Lee ordered additional obstructions and torpedoes in the region's rivers and creeks (*ORA* [VI]:85–87; *ORN* [XII]:500–506).

On 8 December 1861 Union troops made their first of many uninspired attempts against the Confederates, coming ashore at Cunningham

Point near Hall's Island at the mouth of the Coosawhatchie, Tullifinny, and Pocotaligo rivers. Lee immediately rushed troops from nearby Pages Point and Garden's Corners, but the Federals withdrew before any engagement occurred (*ORA* [VI]:329–331, 338). By Christmas 1861, Lee's command was growing in numbers, and he began establishing positions closer to waterways patrolled by Federal warships. These forward positions proved tempting to the Union, and on 1 January 1862 an amphibious expedition led by Brigadier General Isaac Stevens and supported by gunships swept over the Confederate works at Port Royal Ferry, driving off the defenders and destroying the fortifications. This affair chastised Lee and reminded him of the dangers of exposing his men and equipment in battles against the enemy's warships and amphibious mobility. The exposed positions were abandoned (Wise 2000: 19). Though Lee hoped his command could protect the railroad, Lee prepared an alternate rail route through Augusta, Georgia, and, at the same time, ordered Major George W. Rains to locate fortifications upstream on the Savannah River to guard Augusta.

Lee directed the most concentrated effort in the region of the entire war. Mid-February 1862 saw the first of a long, slow, continual drain of men and materiel from the region. Because of disasters in the western theater, the Confederate War Department had to send reinforcements from Lee's command to Tennessee. Soon some 4,000 men were on their way to Mississippi. Lee was not pleased with the prospect of defending his department with a weakened force, but he would soon have new, more challenging problems to face. In March, Jefferson Davis requested Lee's presence in Richmond, Virginia. By the time Lee left his Coosawhatchie Headquarters, he had established a strong force ready to react to any enemy movement, despite the manpower drain (Freeman 1951 [1]:627–630, [2]:1–8).

Major General John C. Pemberton assumed Lee's South Carolina command on 4 March 1862. Pemberton was forced to deal with the same tactical problems that had so harried Lee, but he also faced a more aggressive enemy and a continuing drain of men and materiel. By spring 1862, the Federals, so long dormant on their sea island beachhead, began to stir. Union forces first tested Pemberton's preparations in mid-March, embarking from Seabrook on Hilton

Head for a reconnaissance into the May River. On 20 March, proceeding in barges, the Northerners landed at Bluffton and drove off some Confederate cavalry. The Union forces left soon afterward, but the reaction displayed how the Southern defensive scheme worked. Cavalry pickets reported the presence of the enemy. While they skirmished with the attackers, word was relayed to the district and department headquarters. Troops from the surrounding military districts moved forward to meet the enemy, while others were rushed by rail to man the fortifications guarding Grahamville and Coosawhatchie. This dress rehearsal proved the strategy successful as did another on 1 April 1862 at Pages Point (Wise 2000:23). But nine days later, Pemberton received orders from Lee to send six of his regiments to Beauregard in Tennessee. From this point on, where once regiments stood, there would be only companies (*ORA* [VI]:428, 432, 433–443).

On 29 May 1862 Union Brigadier General Isaac I. Stevens organized a reconnaissance in force to probe the Confederate defenses guarding the railroad near Pocotaligo Station. His force crossed over to the mainland at Port Royal Ferry and moved toward Pocotaligo. Driving in enemy pickets, the Federals marched through Gardens Corner and along Sheldon Church Road until they were stopped by dismounted cavalry at a causeway crossing Screven's canal. Here the Southerners fought a protracted skirmish until they were driven back to a position some 400 yd. past the town of Pocotaligo. Reaching the town, the Union troops learned that Confederate reinforcements were arriving and decided against pushing on to the railroad. Again they withdrew. The attack convinced Pemberton to keep more troops near Pocatalico. Meanwhile, Lee siphoned more troops from Pemberton's command, telling him that the hot and sickly summer months would stop all enemy movements in the Beaufort area (*ORA* [XIV]:20–27, 505, 539, 584–586; Robinson 1950:16–21).

In August 1862 Beauregard was reassigned to command the Department of South Carolina, Georgia, and East Florida, but he did little to supplement Colonel William S. Walker, now in charge of the Beaufort District. In October Walker wrote Beauregard pointing out that he had no heavy artillery and only 2,000 troops to man defenses designed for 10,000 men. Later

Perspectives from *Historical Archaeology*

in the month Beauregard sent aides to meet with Walker who reported back on the colonel's defensive plan. As a portion of this report demonstrates, the defense of the railroad was like attempting to plug a leaky dike. There were simply too many avenues of approach:

> Should the enemy attempt to force their way to the railroad at Pocotaligo he [Walker] calculated to hold them in check in rear of Screven's rice fields ... . Should they attempt to advance to the bridge across the Combahee River at Salkehatchie by the road parallel to the river and another small road known as Seller's road, he would then hold them in check at the junction of the two roads near the bridge ... . In case of a landing being made at Huguenin's, on Broad River, he would hold them in check at the causeway and bridge across Bee's Creek, on the old mail road, at the junction of the Euhaw and Grahamville roads ... . Should they land at Bluffton, he has selected a position at New River Bridge, on the old mail road, where he has an embrasure battery to protect the bridge. If they land at Red Bluff, ... he has selected a position near New River, where he has two small works erected (*ORA* [XIV]:640–641).

The report convinced Beauregard to dispatch some reinforcements. Walker consolidated these forces around Pocotaligo, Grahamville, and Hardeeville. He did not have long to wait. Less than a week after filing his report, Federal troops again moved against Pocotaligo. On the night of 21 October, under the protection of a Naval Squadron, a Union force of 4,500 men sailed up the Broad River. The next morning, a division of 4,200 men under Brigadier General John M. Brannan landed at Mackey Neck, between the Pocotaligo and Coosawhatchie rivers, and marched toward Pocotaligo. At the same time, a much smaller force of about 300 infantrymen and engineers ascended the Coosawhatchie River with orders to break the railroad near Coosawhatchie (Wise 2000:27). Walker distributed his forces between the two threatened points and called for help from Savannah and Charleston. Walker directed a guard of artillery with some sharpshooters and two companies of cavalry to meet Brannan's Division as it advanced along Mackey Point Road. Although Brannan's men made steady progress against Walker's rolling defense, overrunning the fixed batteries in front of them, the Federals were eventually stopped by a combination of Confederate reinforcements and the Pocotaligo River. The Federals again withdrew. But the weaker prong of the Federal

attack had made its way along the Coosawhatchie and delivered an effective fire into a passing Confederate troop train. The course of this battle hints that the Confederate defensive works, so long labored over, may not have been very effective in stopping a determined enemy. With so few troops to man them, these fortifications were becoming essentially useless. Still, even undermanned and undefendable, they delayed the enemy long enough for Walker to respond to the threat.

For the rest of the year, newly promoted Brigadier General Walker had an effective force ranging from about 2,300 to 3,000 men with more than half being cavalry. Reductions continued and by the end of May 1863, the Third District numbered 527 infantry, 1,463 cavalry, and 596 artillerymen. With the hot months coming on again, the district's heavy artillery was removed from the fortifications and their garrisons pulled back to healthy areas away from the marshy low lands (*ORA* [XIV]:290–308, 983, 945, 962–963). Through most of the spring and summer, the Federals left the Confederates in the Beaufort District alone as a result of a renewed effort against Charleston.

Finally, in December 1863 the Confederate high command began to take a greater interest in the Third District. To assist Walker, Beauregard sent Major General Jeremy Gilmer, Chief Engineer of the Confederacy and Beauregard's acting second-in-command, to inspect the area. During his tour, Gilmer suggested a number of improvements, including the combining of the Third District with the District of Georgia. Beauregard concurred, and on 24 December Gilmer was given temporary command of the combined district. Gilmer went to work improving positions and roads. On the last day of 1863, Walker's command, supplemented by men from the Savannah defenses, numbered about 4,100 effectives. Their distribution still centered around the district's three main depots of Pocotaligo, Grahamville, and Hardeeville (*ORA* [XXVIII] Pt. II:506, 568, 577, 578, 601).

Through the first half of 1864 and into the fall, there was little action in the Beaufort District. The Federals launched a campaign from Jacksonville, Florida, against Tallahassee. Confederate units were rushed south from Georgia and South Carolina, and the Union drive was stopped at Olustee. During the campaign, Walker with a reduced command was left in South Carolina. He harassed the enemy forces around Port Royal by firing rockets and beating drums in an attempt to prevent Union reinforcement of the Florida campaign (Wise 2000:39).

Gilmer and Walker ultimately had more to do with the development of fortifications within the Third District than any of the previous district or department commanders. Whereas Lee initially used fortifications as a delaying measure, he did not intend to use them to stop the enemy. Gilmer and Walker, however, had to deal with a greatly reduced command, and this called for fortifications to stop the enemy before it reached the railroad. Walker designed a more-fixed defensive scheme in which cavalry units armed with rifles and batteries of field artillery were used to slow down enemy attacks at fortified choke points but could still utilize the rail system to bring in infantry units (Wise 2000:40).

Over the summer, troops were further reduced, and the withering Department of the South was reorganized for the final act of the war. Beauregard was replaced by Lieutenant General William J. Hardee as commander of the department. Hardee arrived in Charleston on 5 October 1864. Hardee made the best of a deteriorating situation. But as work crews were sent out to repair the rail line and strengthen fortifications throughout the area, other events were occurring that forced the Confederates to make major alterations in their defensive plans.

On 16 November 1864 Sherman led an army of 65,000 effectives out of Atlanta on a march toward Savannah. Before leaving Atlanta, Sherman requested that the War Department send orders to the Union commander of the Department of the South, Major General John G. Foster, to break the railroad around Pocotaligo during or near the first week of December. The attack could trap the Confederates in Savannah, or it could make the Southerners spread their meager forces even thinner as they attempted to fend off attacks from the east and west. Foster organized a field division under the command of Brigadier General John T. Hatch. The division was under strength and more than half of the regiments were composed of black soldiers led by white officers.

The Federals planned to sail the 5,500-man division from its rendezvous off Hilton Head to Boyds Landing on the southern shore of the Broad River. Once ashore, they planned to march through Grahamville and on to the railroad junction at Gopher Hill. Delayed by fog, faulty maps, poor guides, and Confederate skirmishers, the Federals lost the entire day of 29 November in landing and then marching and countermarching. Finally, on the morning of 30 November 1864 the lead Union brigade located the correct road and made camp for the night, planning to continue the drive toward Gopher Hill the next morning. Their confusion, however, had given the Confederates time to react (Wise 2000:43–45).

Though greatly diminished in numbers, the Confederates followed their prearranged defensive scheme. District commander Colonel Charles Colcock of the Third South Carolina Cavalry covered the Savannah River crossings with over half his regiment in case Sherman should try to cross the river north of Savannah and move cross country to Port Royal. This left the Confederates only a battalion of cavalry (about 250 men) and five artillery companies under Major John Jenkins to guard the railroad between the Savannah and Combahee rivers. Still, Jenkins and his men did their job. They spotted the Federal vessels when they entered Boyds Creek and sent word of the enemy advance to the Confederate forces at Grahamville, Savannah, and Charleston. Jenkins split his command between the defenses that guarded the approaches to Coosawhatchie and Grahamville while his cavalrymen skirmished with the Federals. Hardee, the Confederate department commander, was unable to weaken the garrison in Savannah but ordered Major General Samuel Jones in Charleston to send units to Jenkins's relief. Jones was too far away, so General Gustavas W. Smith's 3,200-man Georgia militia was deployed as soon as they arrived from Macon. When the sleepy militiamen reached Savannah at 2:00 A.M. on 30 November, Hardee ordered them on into South Carolina.

Meanwhile, Jenkins and his cavalry were ordered to Honey Hill, where fortifications had been built back in 1861. There his men cleared off the brush that had grown up around a redoubt and dug additional trench lines on either side of the battery. This small work was part of a defense line of detached works covering the two widely spaced roads leading from the northeast and east to Grahamville and the railroad. In front of the earthwork ran a marsky creek that the main road crossed on a wooden causeway. The bridge had been partially dismantled, and the area in front of the redoubt was cleared of trees and undergrowth, providing an open field of fire.

At dawn on 30 November, the Federals broke camp. Soon Hatch's command stretched from the Grahamville Road back to Boyd's Landing on the Broad River. Once some reinforcements came up, Hatch began his final advance about 8:00 A.M. Delayed by Confederate artillery and cavalry, the Federals did not reach the Confederate defense lines until the Georgia militia arrived and took position in the main works overlooking the road. At 11:00 A.M. the lead Northern brigade, some 3,000 men, reached the partially dismantled bridge. To their front at Honey Hill, at least 2,000 Confederates were waiting in fixed works with their cannon positioned to sweep the roadway with deadly canister. The Federals deployed for battle. Two artillery pieces were placed on the road to duel with the Confederate guns. In the first attempt to dislodge the Confederates, the Union officers sent the 35th United States Colored Troops to charge up the road. Under heavy fire, the black regiment was stopped.

The Federals then moved to test the Confederate flanks. Shortly after midday, elements of the second brigade under Colonel Alfred Hartwell arrived. Orders were passed to Hartwell to charge up the road while the rest of the command moved on the Confederate flanks. Hartwell placed five companies of the 55th Massachusetts in a double column and led the black soldiers forward. The men crossed the bridge and charged the hill. Hartwell went down with a severe wound and within five minutes the attack was repulsed. Of the 150 men who went forward, 100 were killed or wounded.

Though their attack against the Confederate center had been turned back, the Federals continued to press the Confederate flanks. But Confederate reinforcements from Charleston arrived and Union General Hatch abandoned the attack. Once again, the Confederates' mobile defensive strategy worked, at the heart of which was the use of the railroad they were attempting to protect. The fight cost the Northerners more than 700 casualties of the 3,000 men engaged, while the Confederates lost about 150 men from their force of approximately 2,300 men. The battle of Honey Hill proved to be a last hurrah for the Confederates. Although successful in defending the railroad from the coast, they could not stop the march of Sherman in their rear.

The Southerners did not pursue after defeating the Federal forces at Honey Hill but allowed them to fall back to a defensive position near their initial landing area at Boyd's Neck. Constructing fortifications, the Federals stayed in this position for five days before they began shifting men by boat to Gregorie's Neck, a peninsula between the Coosawhatchie and Tullifinny rivers for another strike at the railroad. To meet any new attacks, the Confederates reorganized their defenses, brought in reinforcements, and gave command to Jones.

Early on the morning of 6 December, the Federal forces came ashore in two separate landings on Gregorie's Neck. Once ashore, the Federals moved inland. To stop the attack, Jones ordered the Confederates at Coosawhatchie to counterattack in force, but the entire Confederate front collapsed. For once, the Federals pressed on, seized the roadway, and then, running out of ammunition, stopped and entrenched at an area known as Tullifinny crossroads (Wise 2000: 46–47). Jones was outraged by the failure and counterattacked the next day. The movement started well, but support troops failed to materialize. Without support, Jones called off the attack, and his men retired to their fortifications at Coosawhatchie, the Tullifinny trestle, and along the railroad. The two sides began an artillery duel, the Union attempting to disrupt rail traffic between Charleston and Savannah by using long-range siege guns to fire on enemy positions at Dawsons Landing and at the trestle over the Coosawhatchie River (*ORA* [XLVIV]: 438–448; Robinson 1950:54–57). As the two sides dueled, on 10 December artillery fire was heard by Hatch's men in the direction of Savannah. Sherman had reached the sea.

Under pressure from Sherman and Hatch, the Confederates abandoned Savannah and moved their forces into South Carolina. Not only was Savannah evacuated but so, too, was the Beaufort District. The men guarding Hardeeville, Grahamville, Coosawhatchie, and Pocotaligo joined their comrades in retreating across the Combahee. While the retreat was in progress, Beauregard once again became the new overall commander of the Confederate district. With dwindling forces, he attempted to rush reinforcements from the shattered Army of Tennessee to South Carolina. Time was running out for the Confederates, but slowly. Nearly a month passed as the Union Army remained in their works, while Sherman refitted his troops in Savannah in preparation for the final drive into South Carolina.

Finally on 15 January 1865, Sherman put his forces in motion. High water delayed his advance, but eventually the Federals drove the fragments of the Confederate forces before them as they pushed into the old Beaufort District from Savannah. The Confederate defenses fell. Sherman spent the next few days inspecting the evacuated Confederate works around Pocotaligo. He was surprised that they had been abandoned without a fight. He later wrote,

> All the country between Beaufort and Pocotaligo was easily defended by a small force; and why the enemy had allowed us to make a lodgement at Pocotaligo so easily I did not understand, unless it resulted from fear or ignorance ... . It was to me manifest that the soldiers and people of the South entertained an undue fear of our western men, and, like children, they had invented such ghostlike stories of our prowess in Georgia, that they were scared by their own inventions (Sherman 1892 [2]:240–243, 252–257).

More likely, there were just too few men to occupy the batteries, and, as had been proven time and again against a determined foe, the isolated batteries were easily overcome.

Strategic Analysis

Behind any successful campaign runs an effective system of supply and logistics. By holding onto the Charleston and Savannah railroad and protecting the land side of Savannah and Charleston from attack, the Confederates were able to keep open lines of communications and support that assisted them in maintaining their war effort. For a little over three years, the Southern defenders, manning an earthen defense line that stretched from the Edisto to the Savannah River, successfully guarded the vital railroad against Union invaders.

As detailed in the historic context, the Confederate defensive strategy for the protection of the Charleston to Savannah Railroad evolved as the war beyond southern coastal South Carolina intensified. Started by General Ripley, the earthworks were initially established to stop

further incursions after the fall of Port Royal Sound. General Lee took these fortifications and designed them into a line of departure from which his troops could sally forth to counterattack the advancing enemy. This offensively oriented defensive strategy required a few fixed positions in combination with large numbers of defenders for punch and counterpunch. After Lee was transferred to Virginia, General Pemberton briefly retained Lee's concept of launching massive counterattacks against an invading enemy, but as troop strength was reduced, a new strategy had to be developed.

Though Pemberton began the development of a more fixed defense line, it was General Walker who was responsible for the construction of additional earthworks and the defensive strategy that went with them. Walker's entrenchments were not all built at once. They evolved over time as Walker added new fortifications as a result of continued depletion of his forces. His dedicated work resulted in a series of batteries and forts that effectively covered all potential attack routes against the railroad. Still, even in this weakened posture, the Confederates attempted to maintain a somewhat fluid defense, using interior lines of supply and maneuver. Walker also developed an overall strategic plan that made use of the very thing he was guarding. The mobility provided by the railroad gave Walker the ability to shift his troops to any point threatened by the enemy. Though only attacked twice, Walker was able to counter the Federal advances by utilizing his fortifications and the railroad. Later in the war, General Gilmer added his expertise to the region's defenses. Gilmer was especially sensitive to the area along the New and Savannah rivers. Under his direction, new works were built in this region. Walker's command was tied to the District of Georgia, but Gilmer's input was minimal when compared to Walker's accomplishments.

In late 1864, after Walker and Gilmer left the department, their lines were tested by renewed Federal attacks. To meet the strikes, the Confederates continued to use their fortifications and the railroad. At the same time, they added numerous field works and trench lines to the existing entrenchments. They stopped the Federals at both Honey Hill and Tullifinny. During the extended operations, the Northerners added their own entrenchments that created a far-ranging and complex labyrinth of earthworks throughout the low country.

Any explanation of Confederate success must be tempered with the reality that the Union's grand Atlantic Coastal strategy was focused from the beginning on the establishment and protection of a base for the South Atlantic Blockading Squadron. Only later in the war was the army tasked with the capture of Charleston, South Carolina, and Savannah, Georgia. Cutting the link between them was never a high priority of the department commanders or the War Department. Port Royal Sound was not captured to cut the railroad link but, rather, as a base for blockaders and a defensible enclave that might serve as a staging area for campaigns against Charleston and Savannah. As with the Southern forces, events beyond South Carolina caused a continual weakening of Union forces in the region as the war progressed. Serious threats against the railroad were not mounted until late in 1864, when the siege of Charleston had stagnated and Sherman was on the march through Georgia. Thus the Confederates successfully defended the railroad from the sea throughout the war by applying two basic principals of warfare, mass and economy of force. By using interior lines of communication and supply, Confederate strategists were able to mass their meager forces rapidly and efficiently at the point of Union attack while maintaining an economy of force in areas not threatened. The Confederates also made excellent use of the local topography to maintain this economy of force.

Tactical Analysis

The events in Beaufort and Jasper County from 1861 to 1865 reflect an evolving Confederate defensive strategy and tactical intent. The surviving earthworks in the study area offer a static picture of this evolution but one that is clearly illustrated through accurate mapping of earthwork locations, extent, character, and orientation. When combined with a context highlighting the geographic and military situation characterized by the defense, by a limited number of troops, of a long, linear feature (the railroad), and with numerous but identifiable approaches available to a highly mobile opposing force, the widely scattered Confederate defenses become part of a larger picture that is both clear and comprehensible.

Figure 2 depicts that portion of the study area where the Charleston to Savannah Railroad crosses both the Combahee River and the Coosawhatchie River. Roads, the railroad, and wetlands on Figure 2 are derived from modern GIS data maintained at the South Carolina Department of Natural Resources. Only those roads

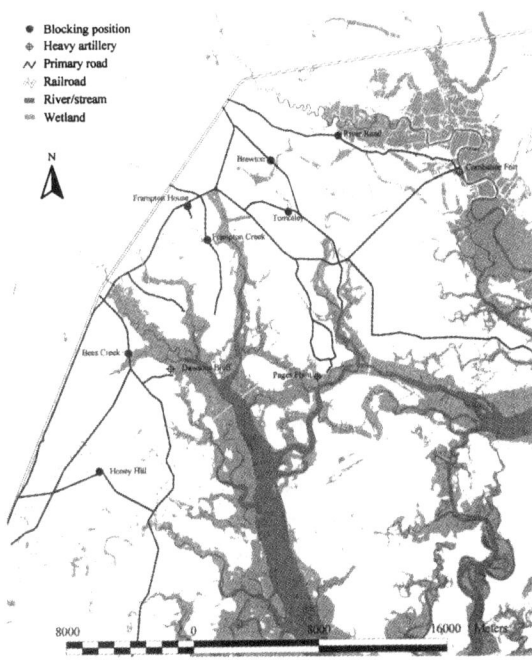

FIGURE 2. Confederate defensive positions in the Combahee River and Coosawhatchie River area (South Carolina Department of Natural Resources).

that occur on Robert Mills's (1825) map of the Beaufort district and on early topographic maps (United States Geological Survey 1918a, 1918b; United States Army Corps of Engineers 1943) are depicted. Though navigation up either river to the railroad was difficult, Union forces could most closely approach the tracks using the rivers or Whale Branch as transportation routes. The Confederates countered this possibility by siting heavy artillery where it could bring fire on Union gunboats and troop ships advancing upriver. Combahee Fort on the Combahee, Pages Point on Whale Branch, and Dawsons Bluff on the Coosawhatchie, all command long reaches of their respective target watercourses, maximizing the time that Union forces could be brought under fire. But to truly disrupt Confederate supplies, the railroad tracks needed to be torn up for a considerable length. It took troops to accomplish this task. Troop landings could only be effected at locations characterized by the juxtaposition of deep, navigable channels and dry ground. On Figure 2, such locations are suggested by areas where the darkly shaded rivers and streams abut unshaded portions of the map.

The juxtaposition of deep water and high ground was also the most advantageous location for plantations, which had to ship their crops to the market via waterways (South and Hartley 1980). The early overland transportation system developed largely within the plantation road system that led to river landings, so by the Civil War, many of the main roads accessed, either directly or indirectly, potential Union landing zones. The Confederate defenders were well aware of this but could not easily deny the enemy troops their landing zones in the face of accompanying gunboats. The tactic adopted by the Confederates was to establish blocking positions along the main roads leading from potential landing zones to the railroad. In siting these positions, the Confederates took advantage of the natural terrain features where possible by keeping low, swampy land to their immediate front and, thereby, limiting the ability of Union commanders to maneuver in the face of the enemy. The locations of works at Brewton, Frampton Creek, and Bees Creek (Figure 2) are clear examples.

These basic principles are clearly illustrated in the Battle of Honey Hill. When Union troops effected a landing in force at Boyds Landing on Boyds Creek, the Confederates rushed troops to their blocking position at Honey Hill (Figure 3 [Parapet widths in this and subsequent figures are not to scale]). This position sits atop a 25 ft. (7 m) escarpment overlooking a small, intermittent stream (Figure 4). Both geographic features limited Union maneuverability. The Honey Hill position was also strengthened, both during and after the battle. The works visible today at the southern end of the Confederate lines, where the blocking position was initially established, are much more massive than the other blocking positions located by the project. They are not complex, however, testament to the rapidity with which they were thrown up. During the course of the battle, as more Confederate troops

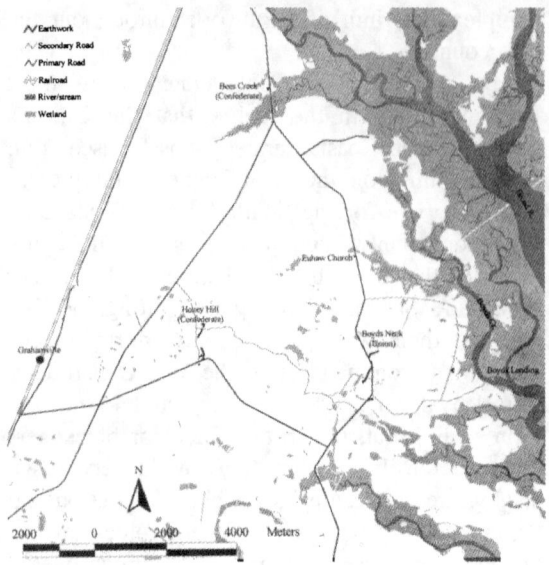

FIGURE 3. Confederate and Union earthworks at the Honey Hill battlefield (South Carolina Department of Natural Resources).

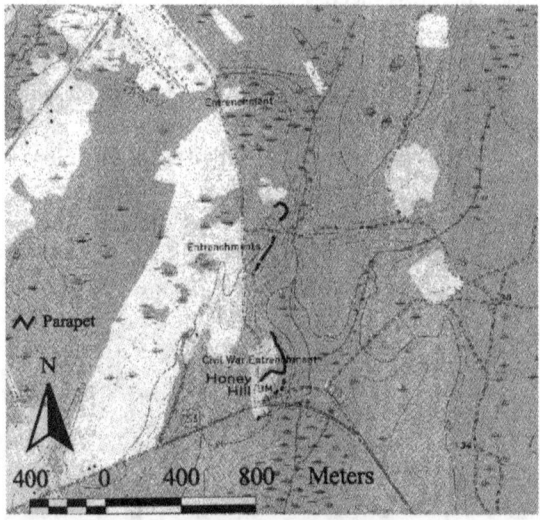

FIGURE 4. Confederate earthworks at Honey Hill overlaid on United States Geological Survey Quadrangle (USGS 1961).

became available, the lines were extended from the strong point on the main road, northward to cover an adjacent secondary road that would have allowed Union forces to flank the main works. Though these improvements have been greatly disturbed by continued land use, this extension

Perspectives from *Historical Archaeology*

consists mainly of a line of infantry trenches and terminates in a second strong point where the secondary road crosses the line. A USGS topographic map shows additional earthworks further to the north (USGS 1961), but these could not be relocated. In any event, faced with a well-entrenched foe and repulsed in their efforts to storm the Honey Hill works, the Union forces retreated to Boyds Neck where they established a defensive perimeter before reorienting their attack towards landings at Gregories Neck.

Principles of Fortification

To better understand the extant remnants of Civil War earthworks in their historical context, we must reconstruct the past landscape and consider the military tactics of the times. The earthworks in the project area were not randomly placed nor constructed. Of all human behaviors, the art of war is perhaps the most ordered—fortification is but one clear example. The science of fortification advanced somewhat during the course of the war, but in reality the changes were merely refinements and local adaptations of the formal fortification practices established long before. The basic foundations of military engineering had been laid by Sebastien LePrestre de Vauban back in the early-18th century (de Vauban 1740). De Vauban's manual for siege craft and fortification became the bible for both the construction and reduction of 18th-century European fortifications. Largely due to very little change in the technology of warfare during this period, it remained the basic text into the early-19th century.

For Civil War engineers, many of whom were trained at West Point, several manuals appeared before or during the war to supplement and update the basics laid down by de Vauban. Foremost among many titles were D. H. Mahan's *A Treatise on Field Fortifications* (1836), and J. C. Duane's *Manual for Engineer Troops* (1864). There were others; however, according to Francis Lord, these two volumes were in "general use" (Lord 1960:41). Duane's section on the "Construction of Batteries" in his engineering book closely imitates Mahan's work, so a closer look at Mahan is sufficient.

Generally, the fortifications seen during this project were what Mahan called *redans, lunettes*, and *redoubts*. Redans are simply earthworks consisting of two faces (parapets) forming a point toward the enemy and an open rear called the gorge. According to Mahan, redans were used to defend an important position or point located behind it and could be constructed quickly with no great expertise needed. Lunettes are simply redans with an additional flanking face on each end of the primary face but still with an open gorge. Redoubts were closed fortifications and could come in many shapes, the simplest being a triangle or square. Mahan defines a battery as a collection of several guns, and (probably for that reason) by the time of the Civil War *battery* had come to be a generic term for just about any small fortification—redan or lunette. Duane, for instance, defines a battery as "any position prepared for the reception of artillery in such a matter as to cover the pieces and cannoneers from enemy fire" (Duane 1864:241).

While command may be an art, a glance at Mahan will quickly confirm that fortification was a science. Mahan goes into great detail regarding the construction of fortifications, even to the point of suggesting the number of men, their positions, and the distance a man could, on average, throw a shovel of dirt—two shovelers to one pick man, spaced 4.5 to 6 ft. apart, throwing dirt about 6 ft. To build a fortification like a redan, the first task was to find the best location. This part was indeed art based on experience but adhering to basic principles. For instance, the position should be located on ground higher than the surrounding landscape if at all possible. Allowing the enemy to get above you and fire down on your position is in violation of the basic military principle of controlling the high ground. Also the land in front of the position should have few dead zones or areas where the enemy could crawl into to escape fire from the battery. The ground in front of a position was often prepared by filling in low areas when time permitted in order that the defenders have good sweeping fields of fire. Mahan also suggested that positions be chosen to avoid giving the enemy flanking cover, such as woods, which would allow the enemy to close or surround the position rather than attack its front.

Once the position was chosen, the exact location of the centerline or crest of the battery was marked on the ground using a pick. At 20-ft. intervals along this line, another line of stakes was placed perpendicular to the line drawn by the pick. On these stakes were placed wood or string to indicate to the laborer the profile of the battery. The basic profile consisted of (from front to rear) a ditch, berm, parapet, and on the interior perhaps ramps or platforms for the guns. The laborers (note the use of laborer rather than soldier, many of these batteries were built by slave labor) then stood in the area where the ditch was to be dug and began picking and throwing dirt to the area where the parapet would be created. Another laborer worked to ram the loose dirt down to form the parapet. Mahan suggested that the average man in average soils could dig about 6 cu. yd. per day. In order to be effective in stopping an enemy advance, the ditch had to be not less than 6 ft. in depth (1.8 m), and not less than 20-ft. wide (6.1 m) or out from the parapet (Mahan 1836:22). The parapet, too, had to be a certain height to be effective. It should not be less than 5 ft. high. In practice, 8-ft. height (2.4 m) was the suggested standard, and Mahan noted that it was impractical for laborers with pick and shovel only to construct a parapet greater than 12 ft. The thickness of the parapet is proscribed by the height of the parapet, the enemy face or scarp of which needs to be about 60° or better. Experiments with various caliber cannon balls and musket shot showed that, for instance, a 18-lb. cannon ball,

fired at a range of 110 yd. could penetrate 6 ft. 6 in. into a compacted earthen embankment. A smoothbore musket ball penetrated about 10 in. at 60 yd. (Mahan 1861:19). As a general rule for all ranges, the parapet had to be about 3 to 4 ft. thick to be musket-proof or about 9 to 12 ft. thick (2.7 to 3.6 m) to stop a 12-lb. cannon ball (Wright 1982:20).

How do the batteries we recorded compare with these ideals? In terms of general shape, the isolated batteries we mapped do not fit the ideal Mahan redan, a triangular shaped, two-faced structure with open gorge, the angle formed by the two parapet faces at 60°. Many of our batteries were more crescent-shaped or rounded structures with wide fronts facing the enemy. Erosion and time may have rounded some of these works from their original shape—the sharp-angled shape of the classic redan. These wide fronts would have allowed more guns within the battery. Brewton (Figure 5) is an example, as are the second and third batteries at Fort Pocotaligo/Castle Hill, the River Road battery, and the Tomotley battery. The Tomotley battery has a single flanking face like an incomplete lunette.

Very well defined lunettes are seen at Boyd's Landing (Figure 6), built by the Union Army, and at Pocotaligo North. Combahee Fort, Mackey

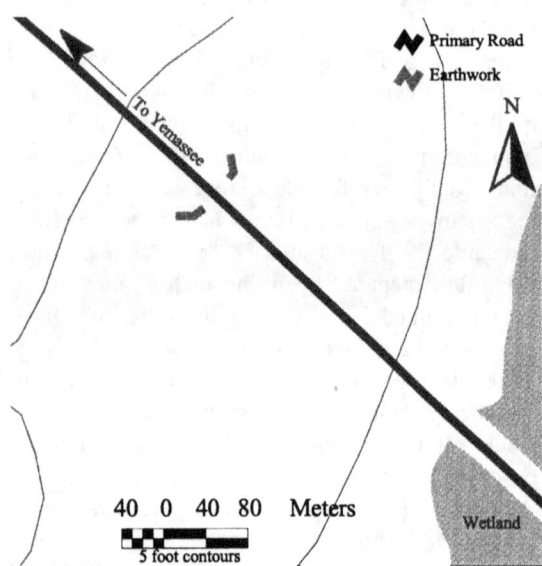

FIGURE 5. Brewton earthwork (South Carolina Department of Natural Resources).

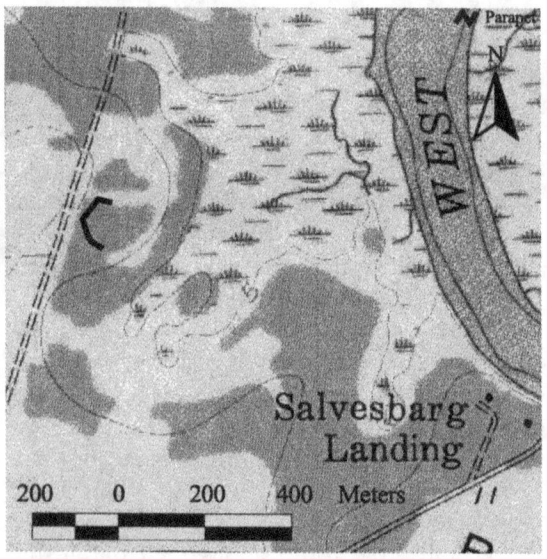

FIGURE 6. Boyds Landing earthwork (USGS 1962).

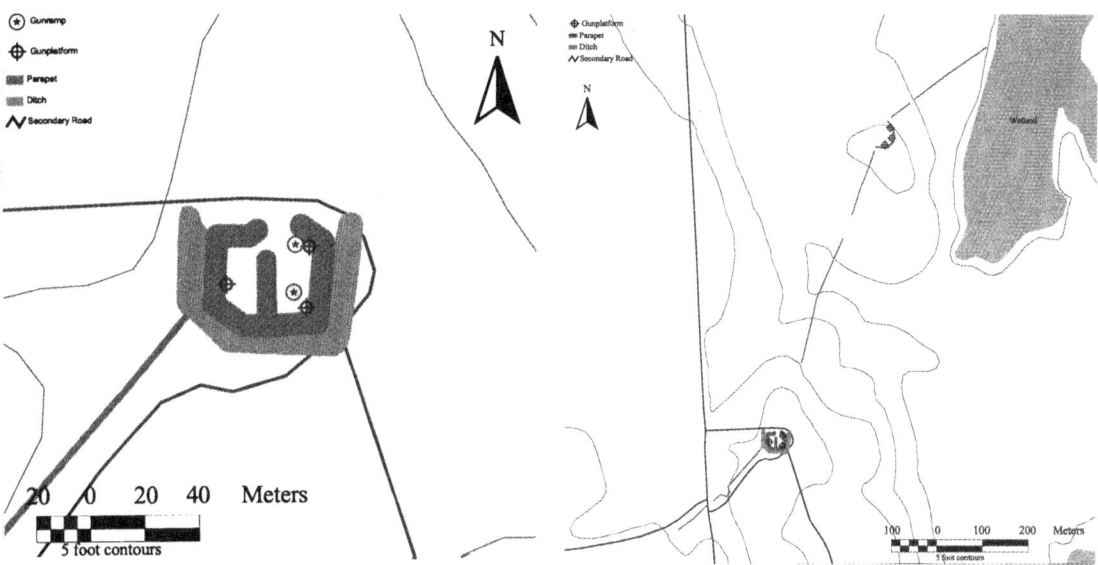

FIGURE 7. Mackey Point main battery earthwork (South Carolina Department of Natural Resources).

FIGURE 8. Overview of Mackey Point earthworks (South Carolina Department of Natural Resources).

Point main battery (Figure 7), and Dawsons Bluff are well-preserved examples of redoubts. The Mackey Point complex is especially interesting as, like Honey Hill, it provides a good example of a variety of fortifications and their use in defending a wide front (Figure 8). From its northern anchor along the edge of a wetland, an infantry trench line runs west-southwest to a large salient consisting of a rounded lunette. The infantry line then continues south-southeast to the main battery (the line interrupted by modern farm development). This main battery, a well-preserved redoubt with a central traverse, anchors the line, which from there turns again southwest and then gradually west. Along this final stretch is a salient shaped like a classic redan. Within a stretch of some 500 m, the three most common fortifications are exhibited, linked by an infantry trench.

Two fortifications stand out as unusual (at least as far as the batteries in this region go): the fortifications found at Honey Hill and at Delta Plantation. The Honey Hill works have already been discussed. Hardy's Camp on Delta Plantation is an enclosed camp covering some 12 acres (Figure 9). The parapet of this fortification is unique in its condition in that the parapet along the highway retains its original parallelogram-like shape with flat crest and sharp angles along the scarp, both front and rear. It is an impressive

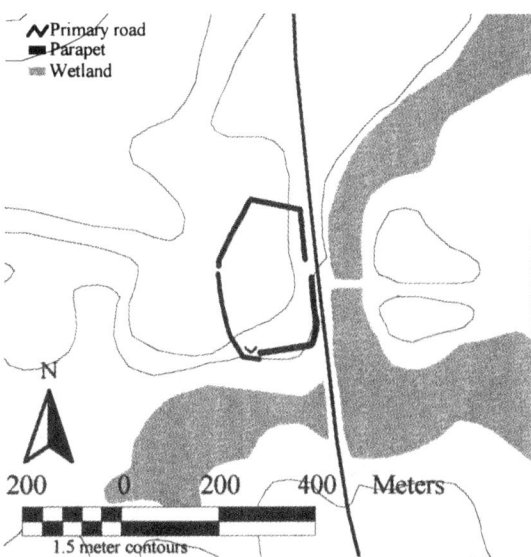

FIGURE 9. Delta Plantation (Hardy's Camp) earthwork (South Carolina Department of Natural Resources).

fortification but seems tactically unnecessary and overbuilt. It does show, however, that the designers were clearly following Mahan's engineering manual.

Following Mahan's manual or not, the parapets of many of the batteries, where they are in good shape, appear to be overbuilt for defense against mere field cannon. Some of this is due to postwar erosion, causing the base of these batteries to widen. It is also possibly the result of experience with the increased velocity of Civil War ordinance over that of the 1830s. For instance, the second battery at Fort Pocotaligo/Castle Hill was 3 m high and 7 m wide at the base, likewise Hardy's Camp parapet was some 9 m wide, much more than necessary it would seem. Some redoubts along the river, like that at Dawsons bluff, Combahee Fort, and Page's Point were equally massive, though that would be expected to be the case as they might be attacked by heavy naval ordinance. Overall, it would appear that both the Confederate and Union armies adopted the basic principles of Mahan's and Duane's manuals but made necessary changes according to the needs of the tactical and practical situation.

Use of GPS and GIS in Reconstructing the Battlefield Landscape

What we see today across the interior Beaufort-Jasper County landscape is the end result of both a dynamic Confederate defensive strategy over an extended time period and short-term, intense efforts by the Union Army. Additionally, the defensive works of the Confederates were strengthened by expedient efforts when an attack was imminent. The Honey Hill battleground is

a clear example. Sorting out the purpose of a fragmentary isolated battery today, all that exists of much more extensive works during the war, is very difficult. Adding to the confusion are inadequate and missing records. However, the greatest problem in understanding these complex and fragmentary positions is postwar landscape modification, particularly to the road network, combined with natural erosion of the works. In the field it was not always obvious why the location of a battery or position had been chosen. However, in looking at early-20th-century topographic maps, prepared before many wetlands had been drained and roads modified, their strategic locations made greater sense. This is an important, albeit basic, lesson that military sites archaeologists need to remember. Figure 10 depicts the works at Bees Creek. To the right, the works are overlain on an early 15-ft. quadrangle (United States Geological Survey [USGS] 1918a), while to the left the background is provided by a modern quadrangle (USGS 1988). Comparison of the two suggests that as late as 1918, the Bees Creek works were surrounded on all sides by low swampy ground, but by 1988 draining and filling had converted the landform into a small peninsula, approachable from the rear.

A second problem results from the scattered nature of the earthworks. Tying them together into a cogent interpretation was only possible

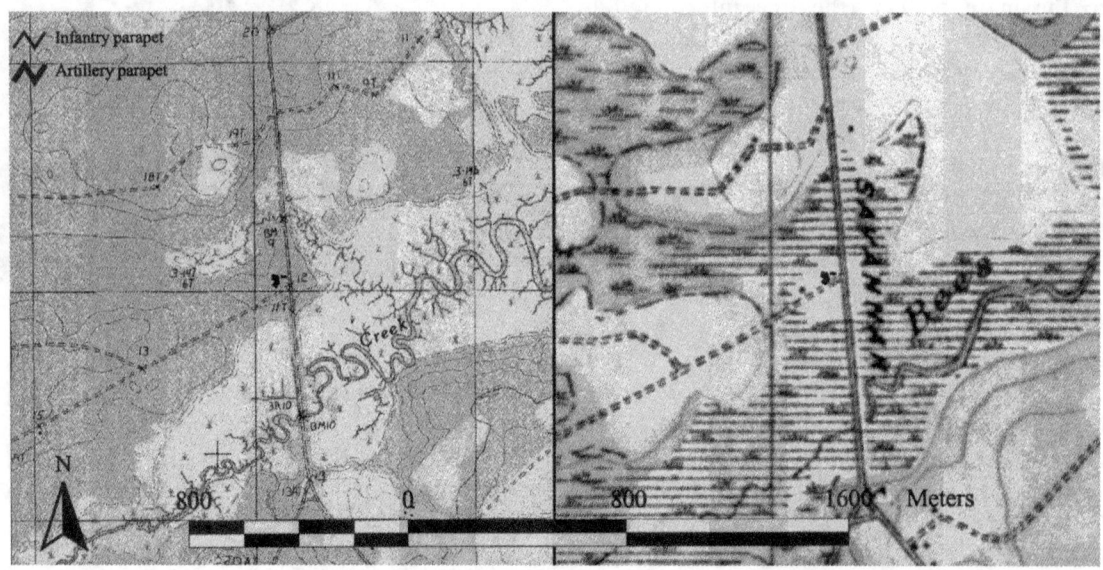

FIGURE 10. Setting of Bees Creek earthworks in 1918 and 1988 (USGS 1918a; 1988).

after detailed maps had been created and the historic context closely examined. In large part, it is the scattered and discontiguous character of the Beaufort-Jasper lines that has affected the public's interpretation. Earlier in this paper, it was stated that while these lines are known, for the most part they are viewed in isolation. Only within the larger picture provided by maps and context do their meaning and importance on both a tactical and strategic level become clear. A case in point is the lines at Euhaw Church (Figure 3). In the field, these were assumed to be Confederate lines and mapped as of "ditch in front" construction, meaning that the ditch from which the earth forming the parapet was taken faced the enemy. This seems counterintuitive because placing the ditch *behind* the parapet provides additional protection for sheltering troops. Only when the entire project area was mapped did it become apparent that the Euhaw Church lines are probably not of Confederate construction at all. Rather, more likely, they were built by Union troops in support of their main defensive works at Boyds Neck in the aftermath of the Battle of Honey Hill. In this context, both the position of the ditch as well as the location of the lines in relation to the small stream to the north make sense. The purpose of the lines at Euhaw Church was not to defend against Union attacks from the south but from Confederate counterattacks from the north.

The project clearly demonstrated that using GPS/GIS technology for mapping a complex system of batteries, forts, and lines is highly time effective and efficient. For fine-grained data recording of a single battery, a modern total-station may provide greater accuracy at a smaller recordation interval. GPS technology is (currently) very weak in the collection of topographic data for generating contour maps. However, it is unprecedented in its ability to collect locational data for earthworks and their larger features such as parapets, ramps, traverses, and embrasures. For planning and management purposes in the course of preservation, GPS technology provides the optimal method of collecting a large amount of data quickly.

Downloading the data into a GIS system and analyzing this data in conjunction with the historical record provides a useful method of battlefield analysis. This method is extremely simple and can be used universally at battlefields nationwide.

In understanding the campaign in the defense of the Charleston to Savannah Railroad, the GIS system allowed researchers to sort through the numerous but scattered and fragmentary earthworks seen on the ground and to make sense of their strategic purpose and tactical design. For this project, then, the use of GPS and GIS technology has allowed archaeologists see more clearly, not only through the fog of war but also through the fog of time caused by human and natural landscape modifications.

ACKNOWLEDGMENTS

For this project we received tremendous support from a number of organizations and people across the nation. Foremost, our thanks go to the staff of the American Battlefield Protection Program and the Cultural Resources GIS Program, both of the National Park Service, Washington, DC. At the American Battlefield Protection Program, we thank Tonya Gossett and Ginger Carter. At the Cultural Resources GIS Program, we thank David Lowe, James Stein, Bonnie Burns, Kathleen Madigan, and Deirdre McCarthy. Our local contact and field assistant was William Olendorf, Jr., local historian, former chairman of the Jasper County Historic Preservation Board and a 1997 recipient of the Award for Preservation from the South Carolina Department of Historic Preservation. With the exception of the GPS data generated by this project, GIS data were retrieved via the Web from the South Carolina Department of Natural Resources. We thank them for their commitment to making this valuable data available. Finally, we thank our reviewers for making this paper better, though errors and omissions remain ours, and Paul Shackel for the invitation to contribute.

REFERENCES

CLEMENT, CHRISTOPHER OHM, STEPHEN R. WISE, STEVEN D. SMITH, AND RAMONA M. GRUNDEN
    2000 Mapping the Defense of the Charleston to Savannah Railroad: Civil War Earthworks in Beaufort and Jasper Counties, South Carolina. Report to the National Park Service, American Battlefields Protection Program, from the South Carolina Institute of Archaeology and Anthropology, University of South Carolina, Columbia.

DE VAUBAN, SEBASTIEN LEPRESTRE
    1740 *A Manual of Siegecraft and Fortification.* Translated by and with an introduction by George A. Rothrock. Reprinted in 1968 by University of Michigan Press, Ann Arbor.

DUANE, J. C.
    1864 *Manual for Engineer Troops.* D. Van Nostrand Co., New York, NY.

FREEMAN, DOUGLAS SOUTHALL
1951 *R. E. Lee.* 2 volumes. Charles Scribner's Sons, New York, NY.

KOVACIK, CHARLES F., AND JOHN J. WINBERRRY
1987 *South Carolina, A Geography.* Westview Press, Boulder, CO.

LORD, FRANCIS A.
1960 *They Fought for the Union: A Complete Reference Work on the Federal Fighting Man.* Bonanza Books, New York, NY.

MAHAN, D. H.
1836 *A Treatise on Field Fortifications,* 3rd edition in 1861 by John Wiley and Sons, New York, NY.

MILLS, ROBERT
1825 "Beaufort District" in *Mill's Atlas of South Carolina.* Reprinted in 1965 by Robert Pearce Wilkins and John D. Keels, Jr., Columbia, SC.

OFFICIAL RECORDS OF THE UNION AND CONFEDERATE ARMIES (ORA)
1899–1901 War of the Rebellion: *Official Records of the Union and Confederate Armies.* Series I, 128 volumes, Government Printing Office, Washington, DC.

OFFICIAL RECORDS OF THE UNION AND CONFEDERATE NAVIES (ORN)
1901 Official Records of the Union and Confederate Navies in the War of the Rebellion. Series I, 32 volumes, Government Printing Office, Washington, DC.

ROBINSON, JOSEPH M.
1950 The Defense of the Charleston and Savannah Railroad 1861–1865. Master's thesis, Department of History, University of South Carolina, Columbia.

ROWLAND, LAWRENCE S., ALEXANDER MOORE, AND GEORGE ROGERS, JR.
1996 *The History of Beaufort County, South Carolina: Volume 1, 1514–1861.* University of South Carolina Press, Columbia.

SHERMAN, WILLIAM TECUMSEH
1892 *Memoirs of Gen. W. T. Sherman.* Vol. 2. Charles L. Webster & Co., New York, NY.

SOUTH, STANLEY, AND MICHAEL HARTLEY
1980 Deep Water and High Ground: Seventeenth Century Lowcountry Settlement. *Research Manuscript Series* 166, Institute of Archaeology and Anthropology, Columbia, SC.

UNITED STATES ARMY CORPS OF ENGINEERS
1943 Okatie Quadrangle (1:62,500). War Department, Corps of Engineers, U.S. Army.

UNITED STATES GEOLOGICAL SURVEY (USGS)
1918a *South Carolina, Yemassee Quadrangle* (1:62,500). U.S. Dept. of the Interior, Geological Survey, Washington, DC.
1918b *South Carolina, Green Pond Quadrangle* (1:62,500). U.S. Dept. of the Interior, Geological Survey, Washington, DC.
1961 *Ridgeland Quadrangle, South Carolina, 7.5 Minute Series (Topographic)* (Photorevised 1979). U.S. Dept. of the Interior, Geological Survey, Washington, DC.
1962 *Laurel Bay Quadrangle, South Carolina, 7.5 Minute Series (Topographic).* U.S. Dept. of the Interior, Geological Survey, Washington, DC.
1988 *Coosawhatchie Quadrangle, South Carolina, 7.5 Minute Series (Topographic)* (Provisional Edition). U.S. Dept. of the Interior, Geological Survey, Washington, DC.

VIELE, EGBERT L.
1885 The Port Royal Expedition 1861: The First Union Victory of the Civil War. *Magazine of American History,* XIV:329–340.

WISE, STEPHEN R.
2000 Port Royal Civil War Fortifications. In *Mapping the Defense of the Charleston to Savannah Railroad: Civil War Earthworks in Beaufort and Jasper Counties, South Carolina.* Report to the National Park Service, American Battlefields Protection Program, from Christopher Ohm Clement, Stephen R. Wise, Steven D. Smith, and Ramona M. Grunden, South Carolina Institute of Archaeology and Anthropology, University of South Carolina, Columbia.

WRIGHT, DAVID RUSSELL
1982 Civil War Field Fortifications: An Analysis of Theory and Practical Application. Master's thesis, Department of History, Middle Tennessee State University, Murfreesboro.

STEVEN D. SMITH
SOUTH CAROLINA INSTITUTE OF ARCHAEOLOGY AND ANTHROPOLOGY
UNIVERSITY OF SOUTH CAROLINA
1321 PENDLETON ST.
COLUMBIA, SC 29208

CHRISTOPHER OHM CLEMENT
SOUTH CAROLINA INSTITUTE OF ARCHAEOLOGY AND ANTHROPOLOGY
UNIVERSITY OF SOUTH CAROLINA
1321 PENDLETON ST.
COLUMBIA, SC 29208

STEPHEN R. WISE
PARRIS ISLAND MUSEUM
712 DUKE ST.
BEAUFORT, SC 29902

Edward González-Tennant

Using Geodatabases to Generate "Living Documents" for Archaeology: A Case Study from the Otago Goldfields, New Zealand

ABSTRACT

Geographic Information Systems (GIS) are still growing in relation to historical archaeology, and the related literature contains little on the actual methods for structuring such data. The author draws on fieldwork at four sites in the Otago Region of New Zealand to present a sample data model as well as various uses for GIS in historical archaeology—from initial data collection to public presentation. Methodology developed here was used to map surface remains with GPS at four gold mining sites. Because unforeseen problems can arise when transitioning field data into digital formats, the process developed as part of the author's work to translate, organize, and disseminate data is presented in clear steps. The benefits for public consumption of archaeological material is discussed as well as the potential for GIS to address simple phenemonelogical questions about past decisions in regards to site placement.

Introduction

The combination of increasingly accurate global positioning system (GPS) receivers and improvements in the intuitiveness of geographical information systems (GIS) software provides historical archaeologists with a unique means for both conducting research and, particularly, presenting information to the public. The benefits of combining these technologies include the rapid recording and dissemination of accurate data, creation of publicly accessible and user-friendly presentations, and assisting with future research. Setting up and using GPS units to collect accurate and precise data requires specific but by no means complex planning to achieve solid returns and to insure continued usability. Unfortunately for beginning and intermediate users of GIS, the archaeological literature that deals with creating GIS rarely features usable training models. This regrettable circumstance forces new users of GIS to create their own models. Such situations, as many project leaders can attest, often create future problems for projects that require time-intensive solutions.

Role of GIS in Archaeology

Maps are perhaps one of the most fundamental tools of archaeology. These two-dimensional representations of the world often divulge complex patterns and relationships, from early distribution maps of flake scatters to international networks of villages and forts (Williams 1992). The introduction of GIS into the archaeologist's toolkit means complex, contextual geographical relationships can be more readily quantified than in the past; GIS facilitates the rapid integration and analysis of spatial information. Advances in both data-acquisition techniques (such as the introduction of GPS) and computational power mean that work, which took weeks to complete just one generation ago, can be completed in a matter of hours today.

Mark Aldenderfer (1992) divides the uses of GIS into three classes, and this classification system remains an effective way to discuss the archaeological uses of GIS. The first class calls upon GIS to be used for its traditional purpose, mainly to create maps, becoming "little more than a two-dimensional (2D) cartographic presentation tool" (Kvamme 1999:164). Initially, many archaeologists predicted that GIS would eventually stagnate and do little more than reproduce the uses of CAD programs (Lock 1993:1). GIS software includes, however, a number of sophisticated features not available in CAD. The ability to link with database management systems allows the user to access information from a visual interface rather than a text-driven one (Chartrand et al. 1993; Miller 1995, 1996). GIS structures allow for the incorporation of ancillary data (Romano and Tolba 1995) and can display continuous data (rainfall patterns, artifact densities, annual temperatures, etc.) in relation to a spatially defined area (Biswell et al. 1995).

Aldenderfer's second class begins to draw upon these more advanced uses of GIS to complete complex analysis, rarely undertaken. Examples of this type include the predictive modeling of archaeological sites (Allen 1996; Hasenstab 1996), which involves bringing together large amounts of data, such as slope and soil type, and examining the relationships that exist among known sites and these resources. Kenneth Kvamme (1999:169) compares the uses of chi-squares and GIS to make this point: if 70% of sites are located on a slope of 20%, this is still not significant if 70% of the overall areas are situated on a slope of 20%. The time required to calculate this by hand (with a calculator and terrain maps, for example) is high, but GIS software can make such computations rapidly, which allows archaeologists to develop more sophisticated statistical and geographical models.

The third class of GIS uses defined by Aldenderfer looks at new and unique methods of analysis. These techniques include two wholly new concepts, both born out of GIS developments. The first is termed cost surface analysis (CSA) and assigns weights to individual physical locations. Looking at slope, for example, steep slopes might be assigned a high weight in the uphill direction because they involve more energy to traverse. Numerous CSA datasets (re-created vegetation maps, terrain, prehistoric waterways) were used to predict possible pathways of the first Americans (Steele et al. 1996). This technique was termed "optimum corridor analysis" (Madry and Rakos 1996). The second new technique is termed viewshed analysis and has become one of the most common analytical uses of GIS in archaeological studies of landscape. Viewshed analysis has been used to address the social statements associated with assigned meanings of visible locations (Gaffney and van Leusen 1995; Lock and Harris 1996). It has also been used to examine the placement of barrows near Stonehenge, where David Wheatley (1996) found that intervisibility was statistically significant, suggesting a conscious decision was made to place sites within the landscape in a manner that would make them visible from other, similar, sites.

Peter Fisher (1999) uses a different scheme to classify GIS uses. His approach stresses using the material produced by GIS as a means of classification. The first use Fisher terms "inventory." This corresponds with Aldenderfer's first class of GIS: continuing to do what archaeologists have commonly done in the past. Fisher (1999:8) is a proponent of using GIS for map making, stating that this ability "should be regarded as a strengthening of the survey method." He believes that using GIS to record and map archaeological resources on the landscape, without any analysis, is still a valid use of the technology and should not be ignored or treated as useless. The second use outlined by Fisher focuses on spatial analysis and corresponds closely with the second and third classes outlined by Aldenderfer. Spatial analysis has been explored above, but Fisher offers an additional important insight through the work of Scott Madry and Carol Crumley (1990), which looked at the visible areas from a series of hill forts in the south of France to verify that each fort was located in view of nearby roads. Fisher (1999:8) termed this study—completed without the use of statistical proofs—as a "contextual study." The third use outlined by Fisher is for publication, referring to the use of GIS for publishing the results of archaeological data. Unique ways of presenting data are possible by employing a visual GIS interface. For example, a site plan in GIS format, accessed through a GIS interface (such as ArcReader), can contain links to text, graphics, statistics, and other elements—allowing an author to share a large amount of information with interested parties in a highly efficient manner and allowing a researcher to select information for viewing according to specific needs.

Unfortunately, while many historical archaeologists recognize the potential benefits of GIS, one of the greatest difficulties faced in the use of new technology is the lack of educational materials that speak directly to the archaeological discipline. In relation to GIS, a number of resources have sought to remedy this situation since 1990 (Allen et al. 1990; Lock and Stancic 1995; Aldenderfer and Maschner 1996; Maschner 1996; Johnson and North 1997; Lock 2000; Westcott and Brandon 2000; Wheatley and Gillings 2002; Conolly and Lake 2006). Generally, these authors center on various forms of analysis (viewshed analysis, least cost pathway analysis, etc.) and do not discuss actual schemes used to organize the data itself. The prevailing attitude of these authors in relation to sample database designs is summed up in the recent volume, where James Conolly and Mark Lake (2006:33) state, "It is not our intention to discuss ... the appropriate structure of a spatial database for managing the archaeological record, as these decisions are most appropriately made by government bodies and the archaeologists charged with the tasks of recording and managing the archaeological resource." The unfortunate result of this approach is an absence of model organizational schemes available for archaeologists engaged in data translation and organization. To help fill this literature gap, the methodology used for GIS mapping at four Otago goldfields sites is described, from regional history and site descriptions through to public presentation of data.

Industrial History of Otago

The four sites selected for GIS mapping are all located in the Otago region of New Zealand's South Island (Figure 1). Gold was discovered in the region in May 1861, sparking a rush that affected all of Australasia (Salmon 1963:11). The initial rushes lasted less than two years. During this time, the Otago city of Dunedin, temporarily New Zealand's most prosperous town, was briefly considered as a candidate for the capital of the country and became home to the Bank of New Zealand (Bristow 1994:9). The gold rushes were directly responsible for development of roads and infrastructure throughout the Otago region, including a stagecoach, well-maintained roads, and power generators. By 1865, however, the number of gold miners had already dropped from the high mark of 10,000 in 1864 and to 6,000 by 1867 (Ritchie 1986:17–20). In the late 1860s and early 1870s, a majority of the miners left for the west coast (Pyke 1962:90–92) where the gold rush was less intense but longer lived.

The Otago goldfields also featured a significant Chinese population. The fear that Otago's gold rush days were over following the 1865 exodus to the west paved the way for an invitation to Chinese miners later that same year. This development was generally greeted with condemnation by European miners. The owners of flagging businesses and provincial leaders believed, however, that the invitation might alleviate poor gold returns and sagging economies. The first Chinese arrived in 1866,

initially from Australia and then later directly from China after the provincial treasurer guaranteed protection (Ritchie 1986:14–15). The population of Chinese miners grew almost as quickly as did the European, although never reaching quite the same numbers.

There were five major goldfields in Otago (Figure 2). The first was Gabriel's Gully, where, according to contemporary sources, 150 miners had arrived by July 1861. This number swelled to an estimated 6,000 miners by year's end (Salmon 1963:57). The next field was Waitahuna, where nearly 4,000 men were working by the end of 1861 (New Zealand House of Representatives 1861:3). The Carrick, Old Man, and Dunstan ranges, considered a single field, were discovered as miners spread into the interior of Otago. Maori Jack discovered the Arrow and Shotover rivers in 1862 (Pyke 1962:84–85), a particularly profitable field (Pyke 1962:88; Salmon 1963:87). The Mount Ida field was discovered in May 1863, where a small number of miners initially worked in relative secrecy for several months (New Zealand House of Representatives 1863:6), but 2,000 miners soon arrived to work the area (Salmon 1963:97).

Individual Site Histories

The author investigated four sites as part of this project (Figure 3). The fist site, Nenthorn, was home to one of Otago's last gold rushes and saw rapid rise and fall (Figure 4). First surveyed and inhabited in 1889, it was completely abandoned less than five years later. The possibility of a new gold mining town this late in the history of Otago gold mining brought many settlers to the area, and Nenthorn was even prosperous enough to have its own newspaper (Thompson 1949).

A brief archaeological survey of the site was undertaken in 1984 (Jacomb and Easdale 1984), centering on identification of historic features found on an aerial photograph, with sites selectively visited if they appeared threatened by pastoral development of the area. The information collected for the author's project resulted in the recording of nearly 20 structures and several dozen features, none of which had been accurately mapped previously. The information collected by the author at this site was shared with the Institute of Geological

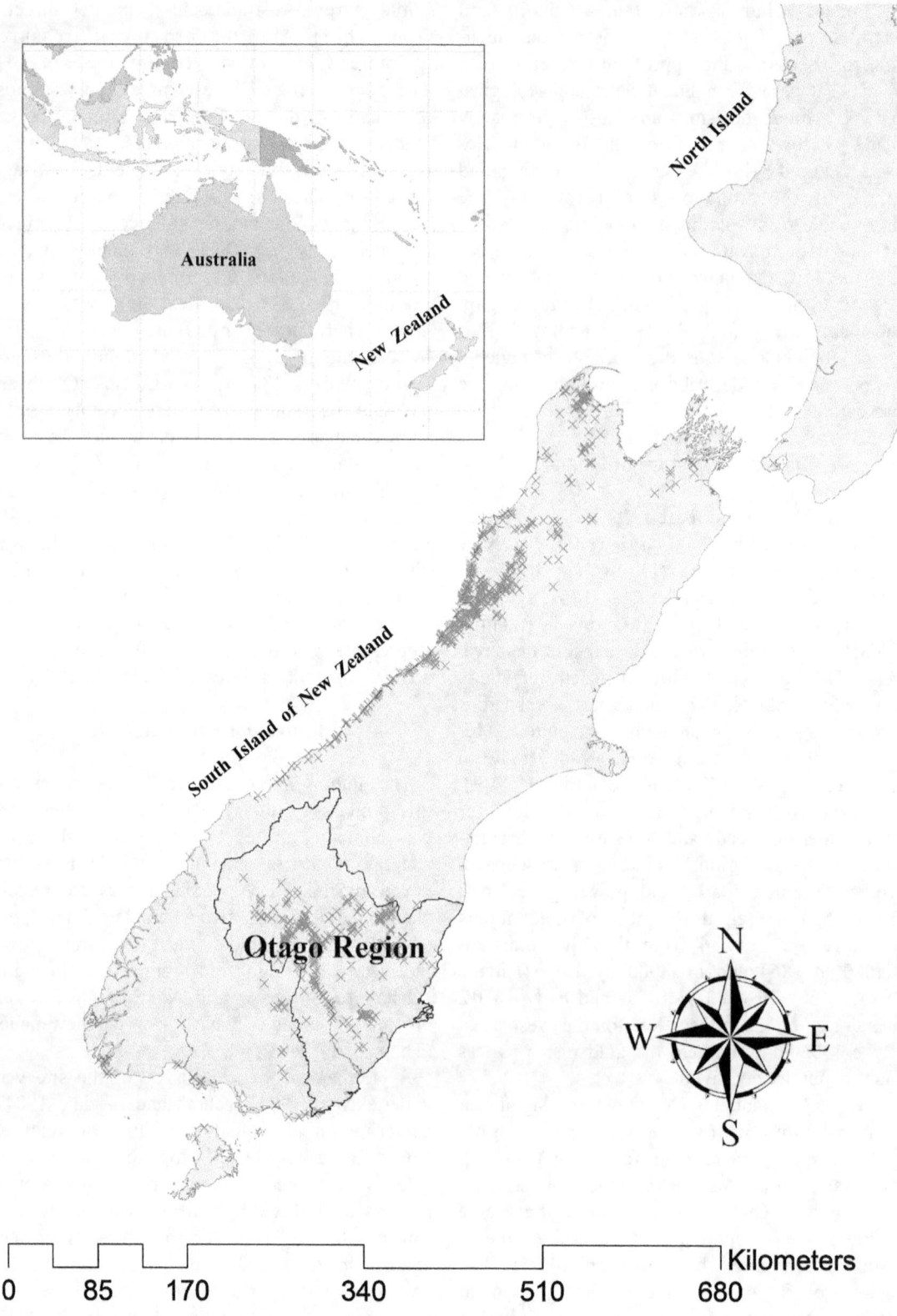

FIGURE 1. Otago region in New Zealand. (Map by author, 2004.)

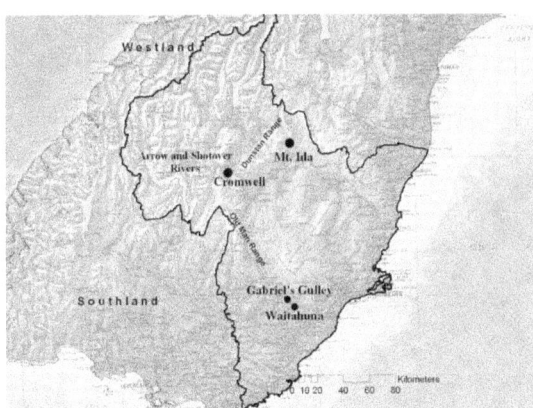

FIGURE 2. Gold mining areas and sites mentioned in text. (Map by author, 2004.)

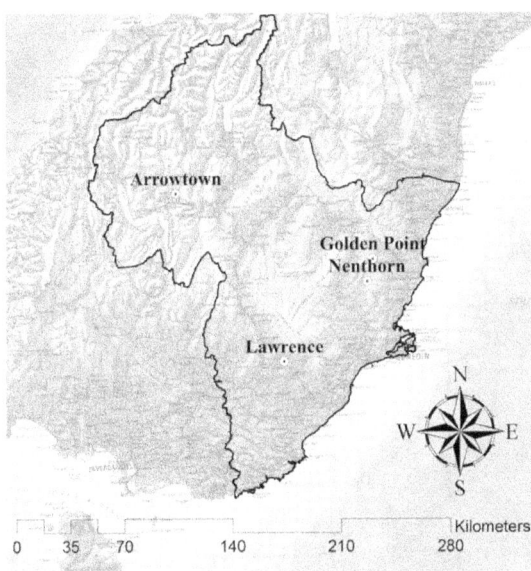

FIGURE 3. Location of sites investigated by author. (Map by author, 2004.)

and Nuclear Sciences in Dunedin to help protect heritage resources during future mineral prospecting operations (Tennant and Bristow 2004:208–209).

The second site investigated, formed in 1866, was the Lawrence Chinese Camp. This camp served as the gateway for miners, Chinese and non-Chinese, heading for the goldfields in western Otago (Figure 5). This was a prosperous settlement with three restaurants and probably more than one gambling establishment. Historic photographs show many distinctively Chinese buildings, such as a Joss House (Figure 6), Chinese stores, and gambling houses. Prior to

the addition of rudimentary water facilities in 1882 by the Tuapeka County Council, it can be assumed that wells were dug and water boiled, "a factor which was recognized to have kept down the disease rate of the camps" as well as the "Cantonese preference, almost a fetish, for having their food as fresh as possible" (Ng 1993:251). A multiseason fieldwork project at the Lawrence Chinese camp is underway as of this writing. These investigations are the result of cooperative efforts between James Ng of Dunedin, the New Zealand Department of Conservation and Historic Places Trust, and the Anthropology Department at the University of Otago. The author's GIS mapping of this site was undertaken as part of the preparation for the excavation.

The Golden Point Historic District reserve currently consists of approximately 1 sq km of protected land managed by the Department of Conservation and is home to the third case study (Figure 7). The hills and mountains surrounding the site are home to New Zealand's largest mining operation, the Macraes Mining Project (currently known as Gold and Resource Developments N.L.). Procurement of gold began here with the arrival of Chinese miners in 1869, and initially consisted of small-scale alluvial gold extraction. Hard-rock mining began soon after, with the building of the first ore-crushing complex in the early 1870s. Hard-rock mining continued well into the 20th century, when scheelite became the primary ore sought at Golden Point, for use in the construction of munitions casings for WWI (Williams 1974:55). The area contained five different hard-rock mining operations; one still operable stamping battery is curated by the New Zealand Department of Conservation. GIS mapping was undertaken by the author at the Historic Reserve to assist the New Zealand Department of Conservation with monitoring the onsite heritage resources.

The fourth site is located along the Arrow River where gold was discovered in 1862 (Figure 8). The first Chinese miners arrived here in 1866, and in 1870 a row of 20 huts was recorded in the Arrowtown Chinese settlement. Local anti-Chinese sentiment and the availability of vacant Crown land probably influenced the Chinese to settle outside of Arrowtown proper. The Arrowtown Chinese settlement is one of about 10 Chinese camps or settlements that

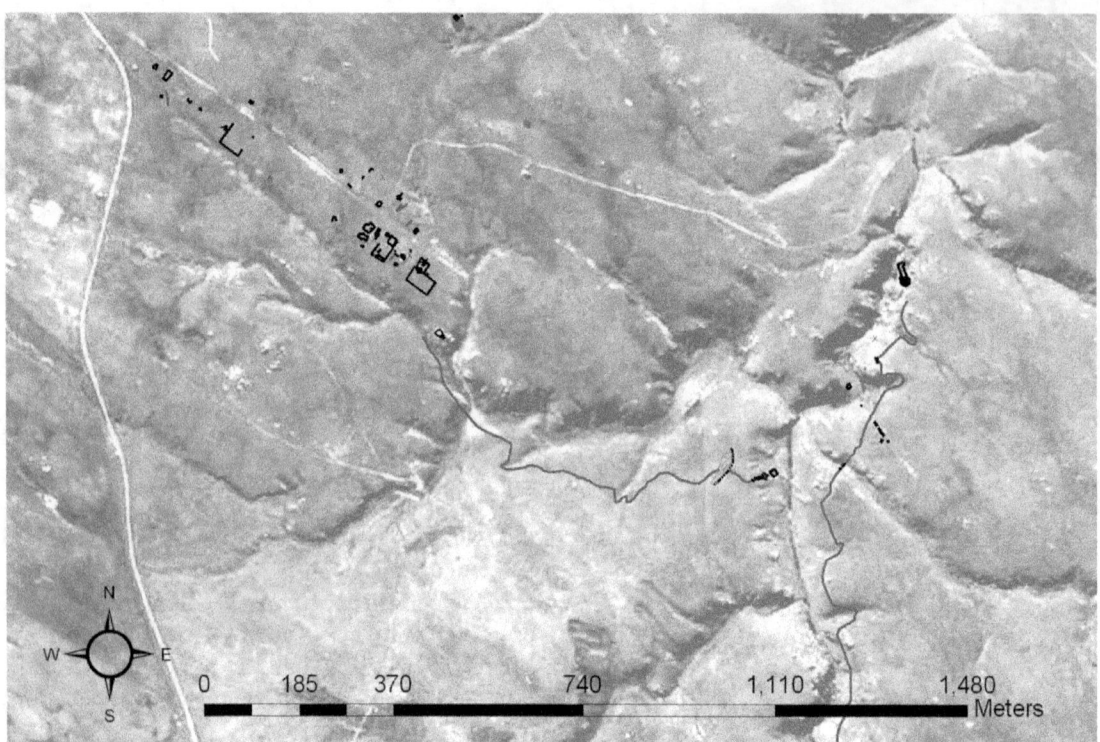

FIGURE 4. Nenthorn, showing surface and water features. (Map by author, 2004.)

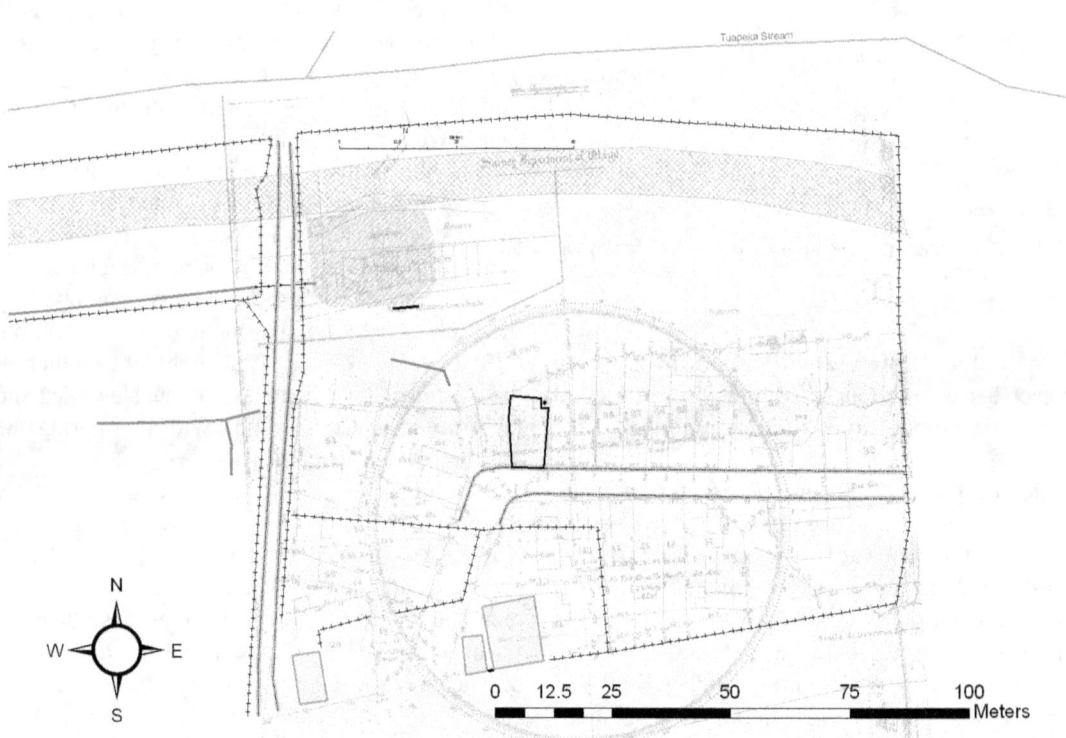

FIGURE 5. Lawrence, showing surface and water features and 1882 historic survey. (Map by author, 2004.)

FIGURE 6. Joss house at Lawrence Chinese camp, ca. 1890. (Alexander Turnbull Library, New Zealand.)

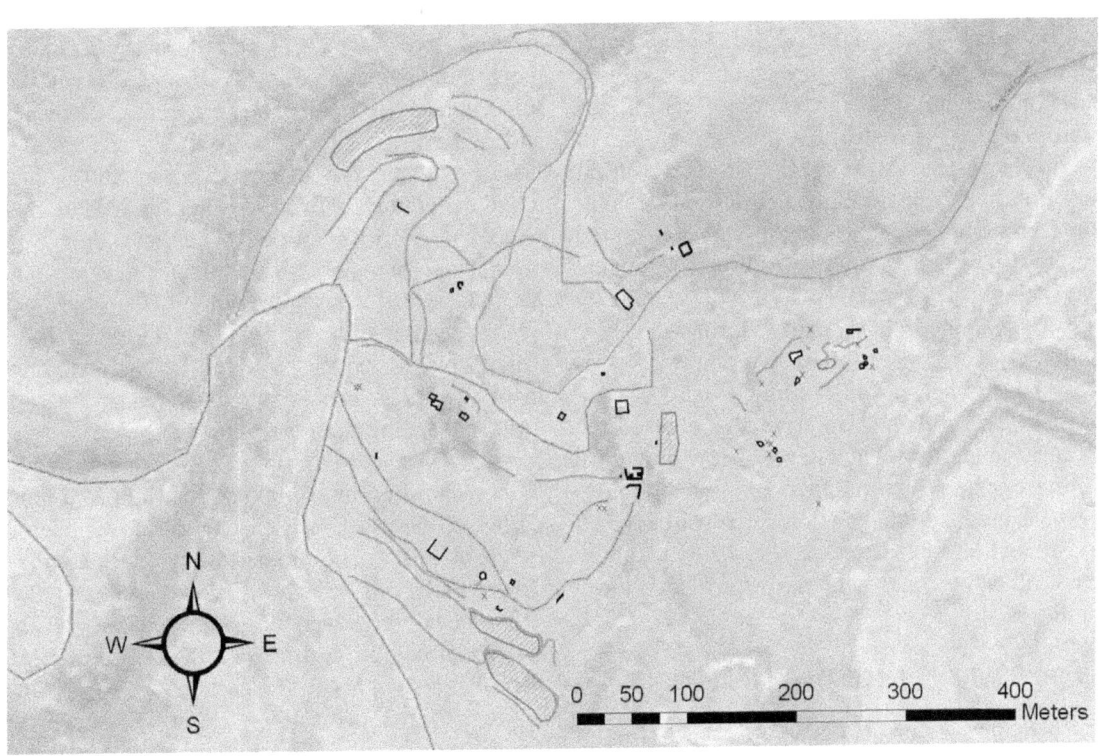

FIGURE 7. Golden Point, showing surface and water features. (Map by author, 2004.)

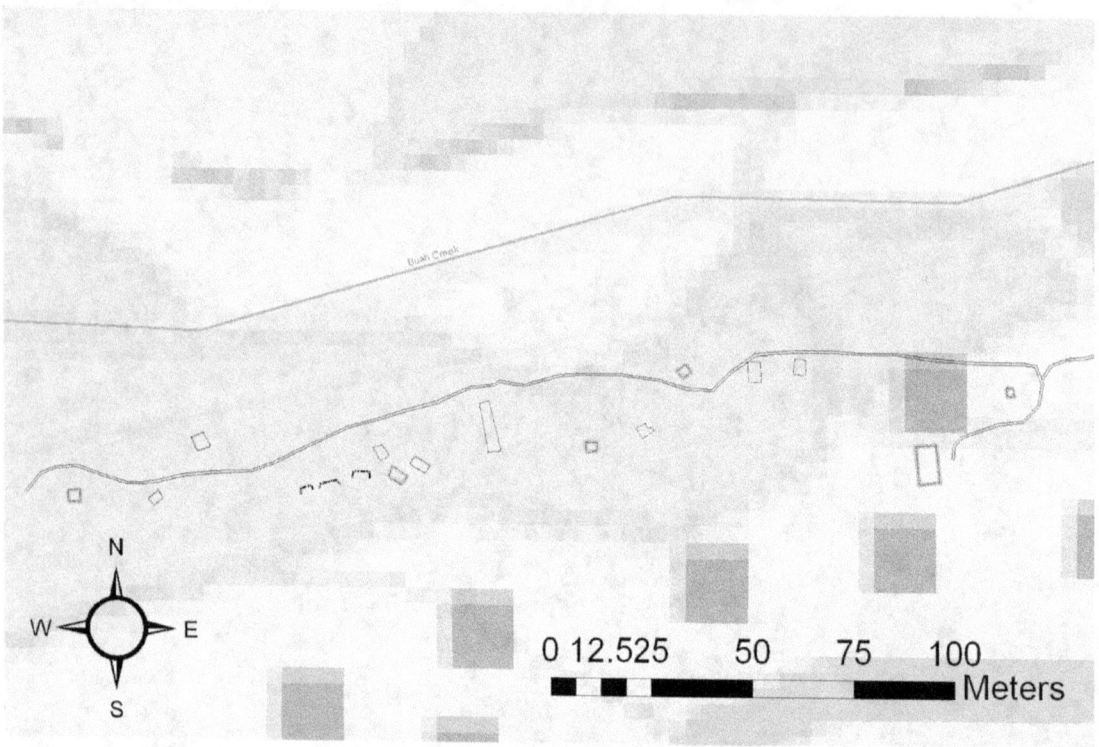

FIGURE 8. Arrowtown with topographic underlay. (Map by author, 2004.)

developed adjacent to Otago goldfields towns and is part of the Otago Goldfields Park, which contains 21 sites throughout the region, each site highlighting an aspect of goldfields history. The Arrowtown Chinese settlement is the only all-Chinese site in Otago that has not been substantially obscured by later development. The settlement was excavated in the 1980s and partially restored. Following the national government's 2002 public apology for the treatment of Chinese during the 19th and early-20th centuries, restoration work was again undertaken in 2003, using monies granted to help preserve and interpret aspects of the Chinese experience in Otago. The Arrowtown Chinese camp was mapped by the author to provide base information for the construction of a virtual tour site aimed at site visitors <http://www.little-yeti.com/nzarch/arrowtown/arrowtown.html>.

Fieldwork in the Otago Goldfields

The majority of fieldwork consisted of mapping surface features with GPS receivers. The unit used for recording measurements was the Trimble GeoExplorer CE XT, which has replaced more cumbersome units (such as the Trimble Pro-XR backpack units used by Smith, Clement, and Wise [2003] to map Civil War battlefield features) since it was introduced in 2002. The main difference between earlier units and the GeoExplorer is accuracy. The new unit can provide measurements to sub-meter accuracy in the field prior to postprocessing, which improves overall accuracy to approximately 25 cm or less. This increased accuracy allowed for the recording of fine features such as structure foundations and artifact mapping across the four sites.

As a test for measuring GPS accuracy, readings from the same staked position (one for each site) were taken each day during fieldwork to check the "drift" in accuracy of the units. These daily positions were compared, and the differences were used to gauge accuracy. This test confirmed an accuracy (or level of error) of approximately 25 cm for each site.

Including a preproject planning stage for the initiation of GPS surveys is a vital step in ensuring data integrity. In order to gain the greatest return from a GPS survey, the use of an almanac file is necessary. Almanac files, which are automatically collected by Trimble GPS units, record the positions of each satellite for the following month, allowing the user to create a timetable (also known as a plan) of excellent, good, and poor satellite service. Almanac files must be updated every 30 days to account for a GPS satellite's drift.

GPS units come with a built-in ability to predict the amount of error present from moment to moment. This capacity is referred to as dilution of precision (DOP), which measures the amount of error (uncertainty) at the moment GPS measurements are recorded. There are two main types of DOP values: the horizontal dilution of precision (HDOP) and the position dilution of precision (PDOP). HDOP gauges accuracy in two dimensions (horizontally) and relates to the x, y coordinate measurements. The more common

PDOP gauges accuracy in three dimensions, and relates to x, y, z coordinate measurements. As a rule, the lower the PDOP, the more accurate the measurement, and a PDOP of 4 or less is ideal. The large spikes at 13:00 and 17:00 hours in Figure 9 demonstrate PDOP values that are too high for accurate recording. A more complete review of practical GPS field methods can be found in *Global Positioning Systems (GPS) in the Field: A Practical Guide to the Theory and Application of GPS Technologies* (Tennant and Rescot 2005).

The newer models of GPS units allow for real-time comparison of collected measurements with a map function. The experienced GPS user will make heavy use of this utility to guarantee that the collected data closely conform to the features mapped. As with many new technologies, ultimately the best way to develop expertise in GPS use is simple practice.

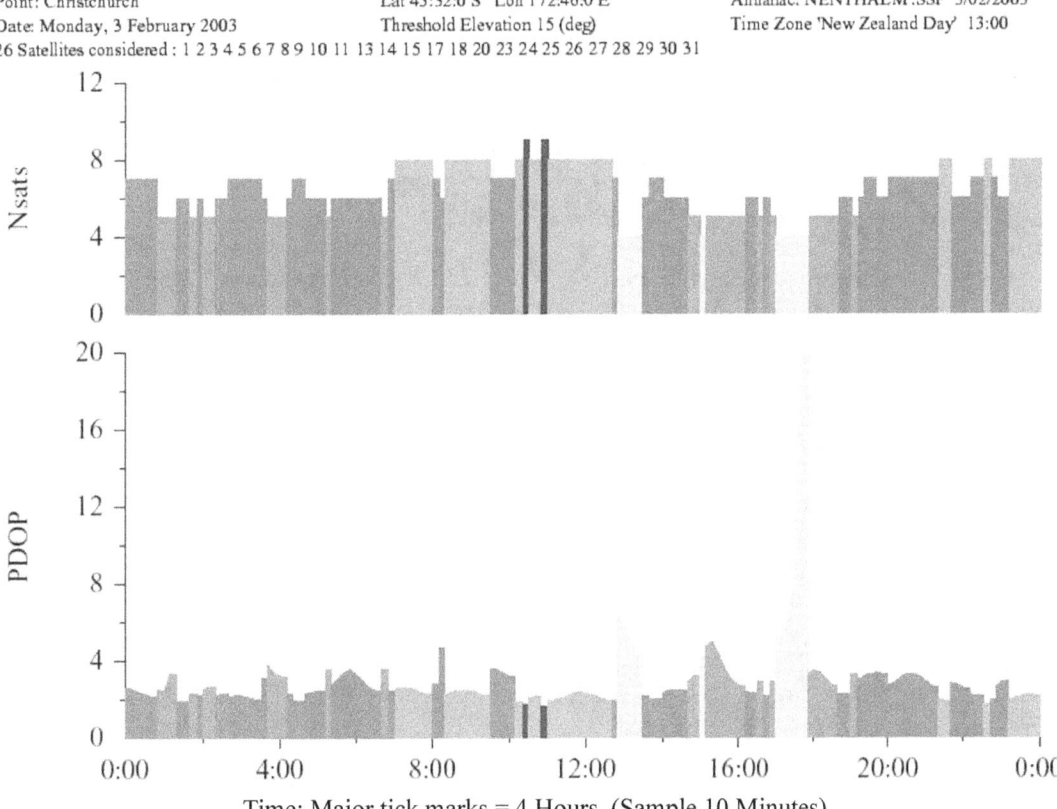

FIGURE 9. Sample plan from Nenthorn survey. (Graph by author, 2004.)

Data Processing

The ArcGIS suite of programs developed by the ESRI firm was the fundamental tool used for GPS data compilation in the Otago fieldwork. ArcGIS, as opposed to a CAD program, was used to manipulate the data for two important reasons: first, to develop a document that could assist and coexist with future archaeological research in Otago; second, to explore applications of ArcGIS that extend beyond simple map making.

Importing GPS data into ArcGIS is convenient for a number of reasons. The Trimble GeoExplorer units were designed to work with Trimble's Pathfinder Office software. The GPS receivers can be connected to a computer via a serial or USB cable, and the program then transfers the files, which contain mapping vector data already in point, line, and polygon shapes. This allows data collected with Trimble GPS receivers to be quickly integrated into ArcGIS documents. There are two possible approaches to organizing this data, which exist as "shapefiles" or "feature classes" within ArcGIS. The first approach is to create a series of individual shapefiles that correspond to the different features the user wishes to represent. In the case of archaeology, this approach can create a bewildering number of shapefiles and system files. For example, the creation of artifact files in GIS with this method requires at least three shapefiles representing points, lines, and polygons. Since each shapefile actually consists of several system files (anywhere from 3 to 12, depending on the type of file), this means that 3 shapefiles may require up to 36 different system files. It is not difficult to imagine an archaeological database achieving truly epic numbers of system files, especially for a large project. A GIS program accessing several dozen individual shapefiles (literally hundreds of system files) requires significant system resources.

The second approach is to structure data in ArcGIS through a geodatabase, as was done with the work at Otago. This format option was introduced by ESRI in the ArcGIS 8.1 release in 2000 and was subsequently improved with ArcGIS 9.0 (2004) and 9.1 (2005). Using the geodatabase structure has numerous advantages. An immediate benefit is the much lower number of system files created. A GIS accessing a few dozen separate shapefiles is, in actuality, accessing several hundred system files simultaneously. This action creates an enormous drag on system resources and results in unsteady performance, even crashing some computers (the author's included). The geodatabase, instead, is one system file, and the GIS software, no matter what is asked of it, only has to access this one file, freeing up system resources.

Tim Ormsby and colleagues (2001) outline three further advantages to using a geodatabase. These advantages deal with the structure of GIS data. As already mentioned, vector data (points, lines, and polygons) are stored in shapefiles, otherwise known as feature classes and defined as "a group of points, lines, or polygons representing similar" geographically related objects (Ormsby et al. 2001:351). A geodatabase allows for the creation of feature datasets. The creation of a feature dataset enables coordinated relationships between feature classes instead of using individual shapefiles. If a feature class representing artifact points is moved, the subsequent artifact polygon and line feature classes are also moved, ensuring their continued relationship.

Another advantage of the geodatabase structure is that it allows for the creation of domains. A domain assigns valid values or ranges for the attribute table that forms part of the information contained within a feature class. This feature reduces errors in data entry by eliminating invalid entries and reducing data-entry time through the creation of a series of drop-down menus. The construction of a geodatabase also has advantages for future research, specifically work that uses GPS receivers. The structure of a geodatabase, with its domain settings in place, mirrors the data dictionary structure used in GPS units. Data collected with a GPS unit records data, using a data dictionary derived from the geodatabase, in a format that is immediately translatable into a usable GIS file. These GIS files can be quickly incorporated into the geodatabase for updating purposes, fulfilling the requirement that an information system remain updatable.

The actual formatting of a geodatabase is, in reality, not very complicated. The possible structural elements number less than a dozen. The most basic element is the feature class or shapefile. Vector data (points, lines, and polygons) have attribute tables as part of their basic structure. At the same fundamental level are raster feature classes, which consist of continuous data such as aerial photographs, scanned images, or continuous elevation data. Feature classes are grouped together to form feature datasets. Datasets can hold an unlimited number of feature classes.

Domains are set up in the properties of the geodatabase itself (Figure 10). They involve setting limits on possible inputs in the attribute tables of the feature classes (shapefiles). In essence, domains create drop-down menus in these tables that, as noted above, help decrease data entry error. Relationship classes connect fields in one feature-class attribute table to fields in another feature-class attribute table. One possible use of this would be an address table that is used for feature classes that contain different types of features at one address, such as polygons representing houses, points representing telephone poles, lines representing underground pipes, and so forth. A major benefit of using relationship classes is the time saved by eliminating the need to enter repetitive data in multiple feature classes.

As the feature classes created from the Otago goldfields field data were prepared, examples of data structuring from three additional sources were examined in order to decide what type of data to attach to the GIS files. The first example was from New Zealand: *Archaeological Site Recording in New Zealand* (New Zealand Archaeological Association 1999). The other two examples were American: *Arkansas Archaeological Survey's Automated Management of Archeological Site Data in Arkansas* (Hilliard and Riggs 2000) and the Florida Department of State Division of Historical Resources' *Smart-*

Form II information system. This comparison was undertaken to provide an idea of standard types of data routinely attached to archaeological data within database and GIS projects.

A series of data fields was then constructed within each feature dataset using common attributes from the comparisons above. Six datasets were created, each containing a number of feature classes:

Arch-Tools	Information about archaeological organization of the work
Boundaries	Simple polygons labeled to outline work areas in the study
Structures	Information about standing or ruined structures, past or present
Artifacts	Information about individual artifacts or scatters of artifacts
Environment	Characteristics of the physical environment (natural or manmade)
Transportation	Information about transportation facilities, past or present

This data structure should not be construed as a call for standardizing structures according to these criteria. This organization is offered simply as a starting point for the archaeologist new to GIS (Figure 11). Basic attribute tables will often require additional data fields as work progresses. Additionally, some sites may have features that do not neatly fit into defined divisions such as artifact, structures, environment, and transportation. The basic concept of creating feature classes under broader feature datasets, however, allows users to create a "clean" dataset that can be added to in a timely and efficient manner.

Use of GIS Data at the Otago Goldfields

The simplest use of the data generated and organized as part of this project was the creation of site inventories for each of the four sites. The most practical way to access these data is through a series of paper maps or a visual interface. ESRI has eliminated the need to purchase the ArcMap program if a user is only interested in looking at, searching through,

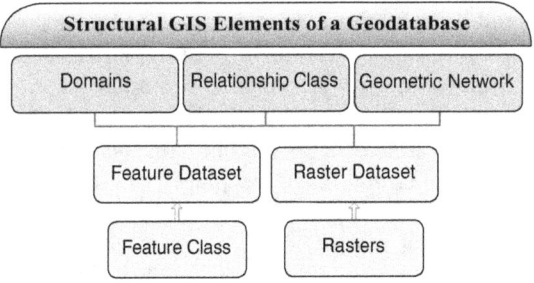

FIGURE 10. Diagram of geodatabase elements discussed in the text. (Drawing by author.)

Flowchart of Data Processing

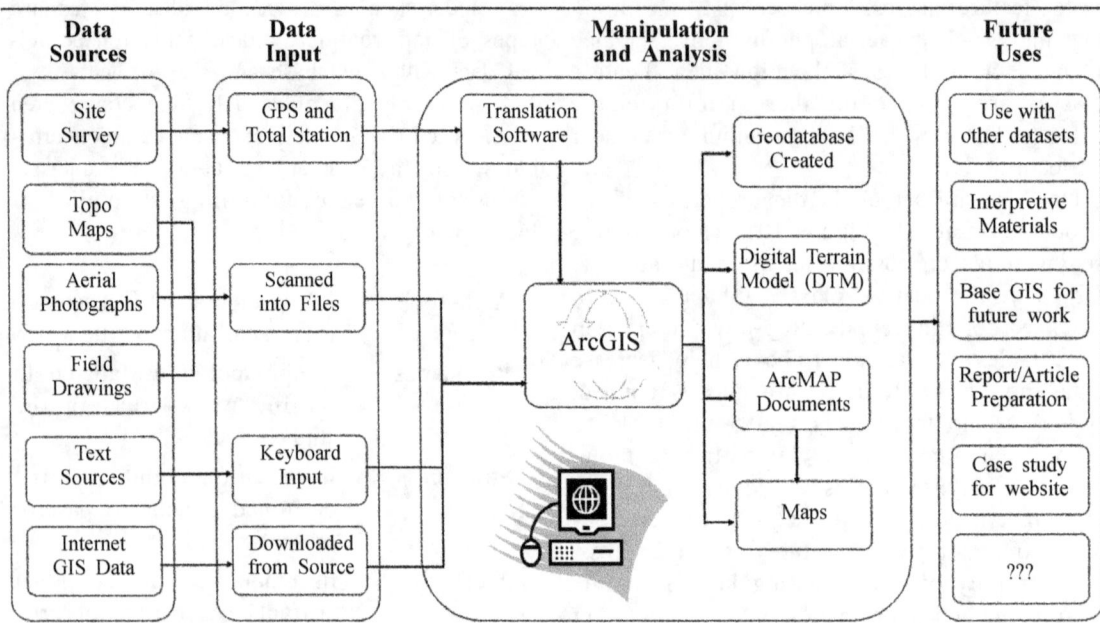

FIGURE 11. Flowchart of data processing. (Drawing by author.)

and printing maps of GIS data. The free ArcReader program is available for download from the ESRI website and can be used to view published map documents created by ArcMap. This enables anyone with a computer to view GIS data free.

On a more analytical level, a study of viewsheds at the Nenthorn site provides a case study of the type of analysis possible once basic data are appropriately organized. The sites of Nenthorn and Golden Point both featured hardrock mining operations and their associated stamping batteries, which are often incredibly noisy when in operation. The late Peter Bristow of the New Zealand Department of Conservation believed that sound may have guided the placement of structures in relation to these loud machines. The possibility that the natural landscape may have been used by the workers in order to shield them from the noises of these mills was considered during GIS analysis; the base hypothesis in this specific case was that locations that provided geographical buffers from noise might have been intentionally sought out by local residents.

The town of Nenthorn was situated above and away from the stamp mills. The placement of stamp mills is partially one of economics, in response to factors such as the availability of water, location of mine entrances, and suitable land features for construction. Figure 12 shows the location of the two stamp mills and the town. The town is on a portion of land with a gentle slope. While other areas that are closer to the stamp mills offer the same kind of geography, the town and individual huts were not placed there. Figure 13 shows two other possible locations with a similar amount of gentle sloping areas, but no remains currently exist there.

Finally, phenomenological approaches are rare in historical archaeology, and the inability to reproduce phenomenological methods is one reason why. However, using GIS to compute soundscapes is one potentially reproducible method, something increasingly addressed in phenomenology (Hamilton and Whitehouse 2006). Using the viewshed to compute soundscapes from the two mills (Figures 14, 15) provided at least one possible reason why no habitation structures were placed in the other two possible locations. Figures 14 and 15 show how a line of sight from the stamp mills includes portions of the other possible habitation areas. Soundscapes do not directly correspond to lines of sight, but the viewshed analysis does

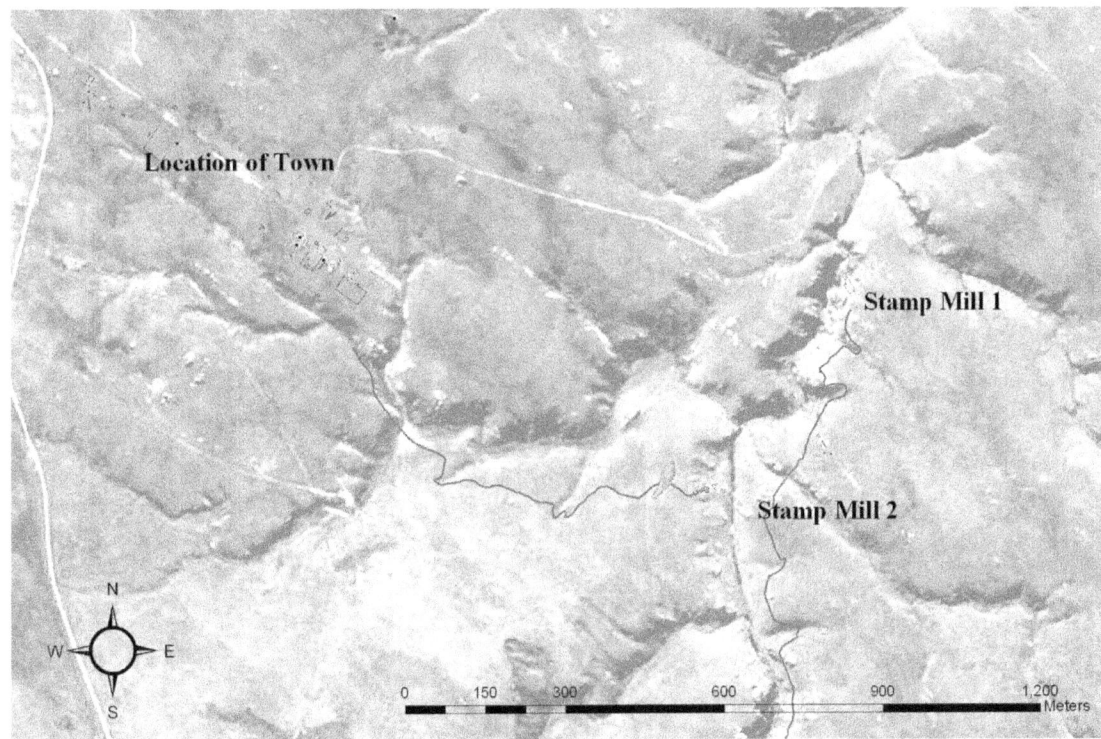

FIGURE 12. Location of stamp mills and Nenthorn township. (Map by author, 2004.)

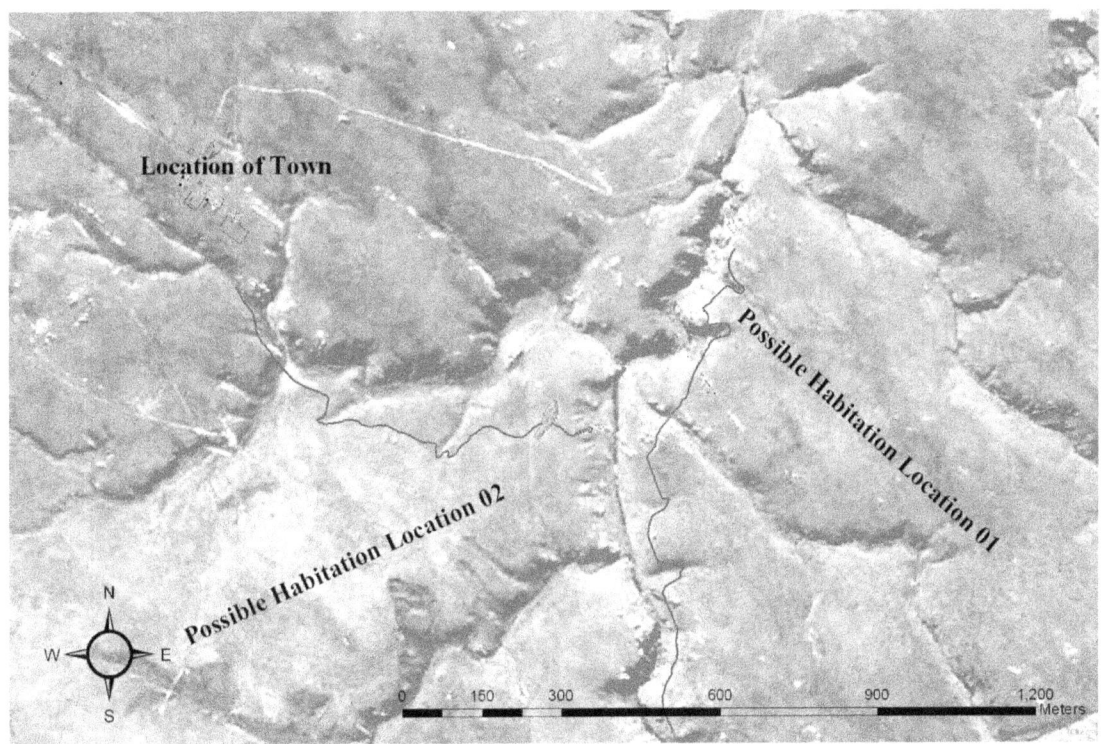

FIGURE 13. Possible habitation locations at Nenthorn. (Map by author, 2004.)

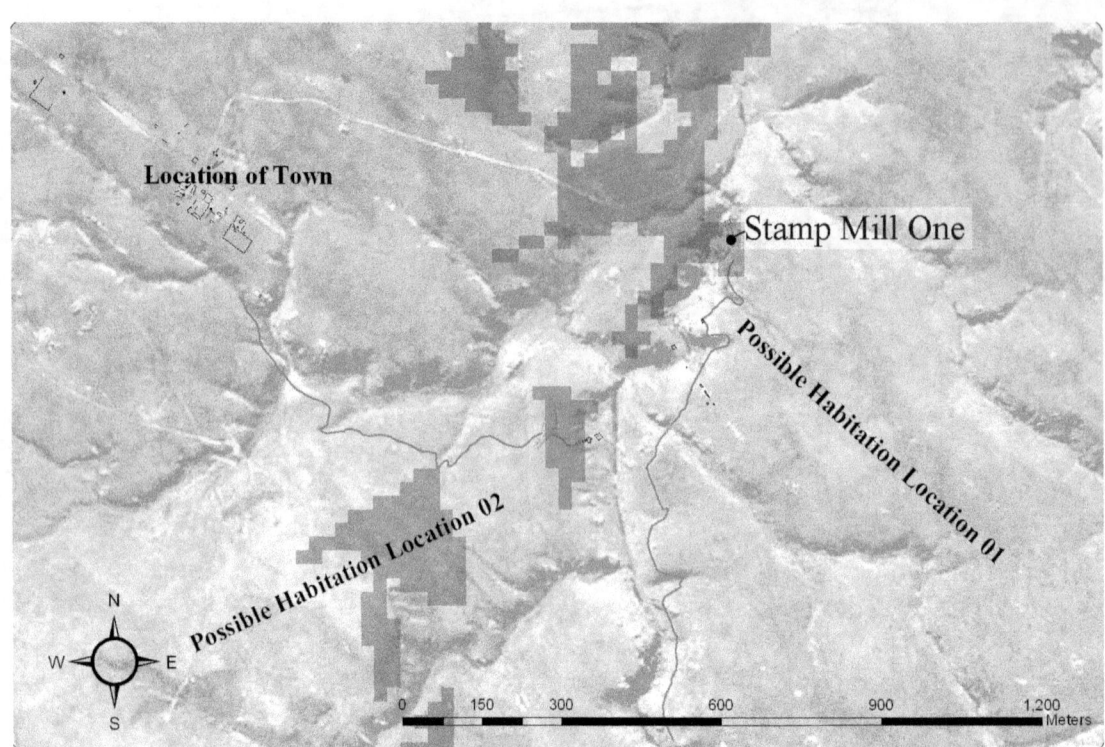

FIGURE 14. Viewshed from stamp mill one. (Map by author, 2004.)

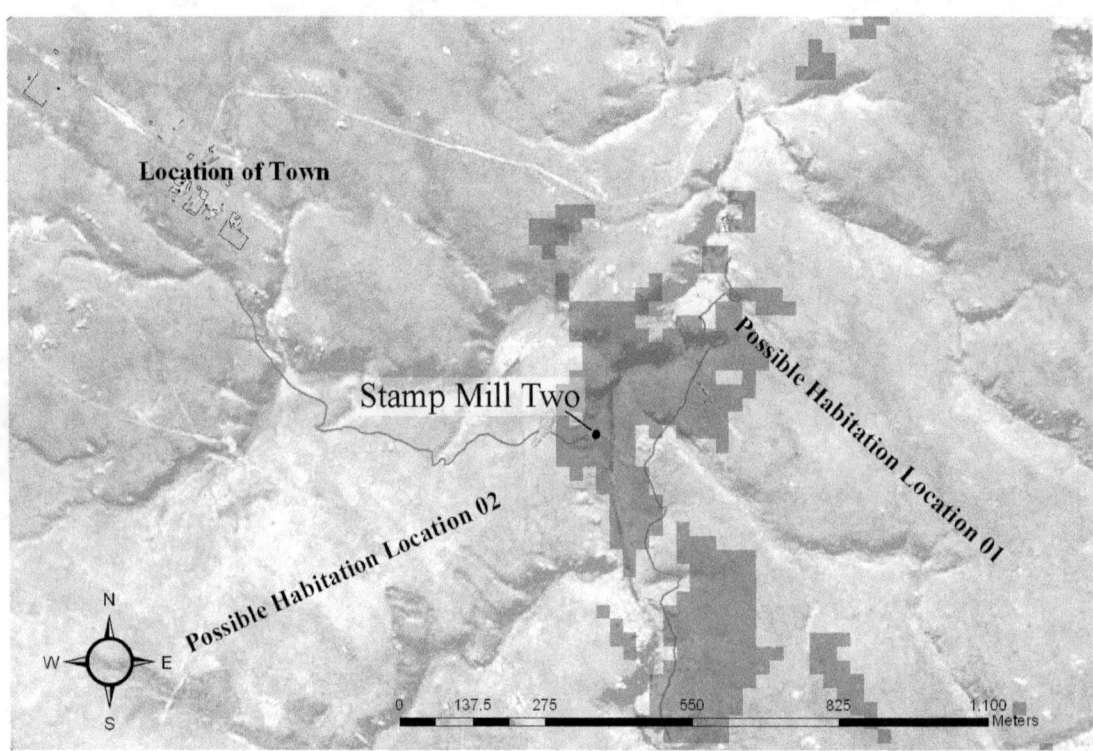

FIGURE 15. Viewshed from stamp mill two. (Map by author, 2004.)

confirm that sound might have been a determining factor in discouraging the placement of huts in these areas. While the placement of the town itself was possibly the result of other factors, there is no other apparent reason why miners would not have placed their own huts closer to their work sites.

Data Dissemination

As important as GIS analysis is to the archaeologist, it also provides an excellent tool for the public interpretation and dissemination of data, but the sharing of data is not limited to fellow professionals. Many archaeologists have walked the thin line between attracting the public to experience heritage areas while, at the same time, discouraging private citizens from going out and digging the sites themselves (Lerner and Hoffman 2000:231). The tension between involving the public and protecting sites is increasing, especially in places where tourism has become a major industry. One of the main methods for successfully navigating this type of situation is to control the amount and type of archaeological data released to the public. The use of GIS for storing archaeological data makes control of that data much more efficient (Wheatley and Gillings 2002:217).

Using the GPS data gathered, two forms of public presentation were designed for the Otago goldfields research. Archaeological maps were created using ArcMap. In addition, a website was created to host virtual tours of each site <http://www.little-yeti.com/nzarch>. These virtual tours include brief histories of the sites and hyperlinks to historic and modern photographs. This format allows users to navigate plan views of each site, with hyperlinks to pop-up windows of images, creating an interactive, self-guided virtual tour. Readers are encouraged to visit the web page to see the final outcome of the step-by-step GIS methodology previously described.

The use of web statistics software also allows website owners to monitor visitors to their sites on a page-by-page basis, thereby assessing how widely and efficiently data is disseminated. The statistics for a 12-month period demonstrate the effectiveness of using the Internet to disseminate this type of information to the public. The author's site uses AWStats software <http://awstats.sourceforge.net/> to monitor the number of visitor to the website and duration of the visit. While there is no way to determine how many hits are repeat visitors, the figures demonstrate that the Otago goldfields website was visited on nearly 25,000 separate occasions. Many of the visits each month come from search engines, and individuals may not remain at the site for a long period. Regardless, the web statistics still suggest that a large number of individuals have accessed the site over a 12-month period (Table 1).

Conclusion

Many archaeologists are familiar enough with the basics of GIS and GPS to appreciate the benefits that these technologies can bring to their research, but literature that guides the archaeologist in how to best organize GIS data for archaeological research was lacking. The use of GPS and GIS to map intrasite features is growing, mainly because as the prices of these units continue to drop, their accuracy improves dramatically, and the related software becomes increasingly intuitive. The uses of these technologies are becoming widely acknowledged, and increasing numbers of researchers are exploring their uses, demonstrated by the spread of courses at the undergraduate and graduate at

TABLE 1
MONTHLY VISITORS (NOV. 2005–OCT. 2006):
ARCHAEOLOGY AND TECHNOLOGY
ON THE OTAGO GOLDFIELDS
<HTTP://WWW.LITTLE-YETI.COM/NZARCH>

Month/Year	No. Visitors
Nov. 2005	2,161
Dec. 2005	2,646
Jan. 2006	1,963
Feb. 2006	1,782
Mar. 2006	2,130
Apr. 2006	2,602
May 2006	2,175
Jun. 2006	2,999
Jul. 2006	1,597
Aug. 2006	1,767
Sep. 2006	3,018
Oct. 2006	3,045
Total	**24,840**

universities around the world. Use of the steps and methodological approaches outlined in this paper will greatly improve data collection, ease data handling, and create documentation strategies that can benefit both present and future research. This tight control and quick manipulation of spatial data inside a GIS is well suited for heritage management purposes. The use of 3-D site reconstructions on the Internet as a reputable vehicle for publication is a recent development. The acceptance of this medium is growing, evidence that many archaeologists want to share their work with each other and the lay public in a direct and immediate manner.

Acknowledgments

The Fulbright Scholarship funded this project for Study Abroad at the University of Arkansas. Peter Bristow at the New Zealand Department of Conservation was a constant source of inspiration and practical advice. I am eternally grateful for his guidance. While his unexpected passing in December 2004 was a source of great sadness and sorrow, his dedication and passion for archaeology will not be forgotten. The web version of the author's thesis on the growing use of GPS and GIS in archaeology is at <www.little-yeti.com/nzarch>. A website that provides practical information about using ArcGIS for archaeology, including a series of tutorials, is at <http://gis.little-yeti.com>.

References

ALDENDERFER, MARK
    1992 The State of the Art: GIS and Anthropological Research. *Anthropology Newsletter* 33(5):14.

ALDENDERFER, MARK, AND HERBERT D. G. MASCHNER
    1996 *Anthropology, Space, and Geographic Information Systems*. Spatial Information Series. Oxford University Press, New York, NY.

ALLEN, KATHLEEN M. S.
    1996 Iroquoian Landscapes: People, Environments, and the GIS Context. In *New Methods, Old Problems: Geographic Information Systems in Modern Archaeological Research*, Herbert D. G. Maschner, editor, pp. 198–222. Occasional Paper No. 23. Southern Illinois University Center for Archaeological Investigations, Carbondale.

ALLEN, KATHLEEN M. S., STANTON W. GREEN, AND EZRA B. W. ZUBROW (EDITORS)
    1990 *Interpreting Space: GIS and Archaeology, Applications of Geographic Information Systems*. Taylor and Francis, London, England, UK.

BISWELL, S., L. CROPPER, J. EVANS, V. GAFFNEY, AND P. LEACH
    1995 GIS and Excavation: A Cautionary Tale from Shepton Mallet, Somerset, England. In *Archaeology and Geographical Information Systems: A European Perspective*, Gary Lock and Zoran Stancic, editors, pp. 269–286. Taylor and Francis, London, England, UK.

BRISTOW, PETER
    1994 Archaeology and Ethnicity of the Remote Otago Goldfields. Master's thesis, Department of Anthropology, University of Otago, Dunedin, New Zealand.

CHARTRAND, JEFFREY, JULIAN RICHARDS, AND BLAISE VYNER
    1993 Bridging the Urban-Rural Gap: GIS and the York Environs Project. In *Computing the Past: Computer Applications and Quantitative Methods in Archaeology, CAA92*, Jens Andresen, Torsten Madsen, and Irwin Scollar, editors, pp. 159–166. Aarhus University Press, Aarhus, Denmark.

CONOLLY, JAMES, AND MARK LAKE
    2006 *Geographical Information Systems in Archaeology*. University Press, Cambridge, England, UK.

FISHER, PETER F.
    1999 Geographical Information Systems: Today and Tomorrow? In *Geographical Information Systems and Landscape Archaeology*, Mark Gillings, David Mattingly, and Jan van Dalen, editors, pp. 5–12. Oxbow Books, Oxford, England, UK.

GAFFNEY, V., AND P. M VAN LEUSEN
    1995 Postscript: GIS, Environmental Determinism, and Archaeology. In *Archaeology and Geographical Information Systems: A European Perspective*, Gary Lock and Zoran Stancic, editors, pp. 367–382. Taylor and Francis, London, England, UK.

HAMILTON, SUE, AND RUTH WHITEHOUSE
    2005 Phenomenology in Practice: Towards a Methodology for a 'Subjective' Approach. *European Journal of Archaeology* 9(1):31–71.

HASENSTAB, ROBERT J.
    1996 Settlement as Adaptation: Variability in Iroquois Village Site Selection as Inferred through GIS. In *New Methods, Old Problems: Geographic Information Systems in Modern Archaeological Research*, Herbert D. G. Maschner, editor, pp. 223–241. Occasional Paper No. 23. Southern Illinois University Center for Archaeological Investigations, Carbondale.

HILLIARD, JERRY E., AND JOHN RIGGS
  2000 *AMASDA Site Recording Manual*. Technical Paper
        No. 1. Arkansas Archeological Survey, Fayetteville,
        AR.

JACOMB, CHRIS, AND SCOTT EASDALE
  1984 Nenthorn Interim Report. Manuscript, Department
        of Lands and Survey, Dunedin, New Zealand.

JOHNSON, IAN, AND M. NORTH (EDITORS)
  1997 *Archaeological Applications of GIS: Proceedings of
        Colloquium II, UISPP XIIIth Congress, Forli, Italy,
        September 1996*. Archaeological Methods Series, No.
        5. Sydney University, Sydney, Australia.

KVAMME, KENNETH L.
  1999 Recent Direction and Development in Geographical
        Information Systems. *Journal of Archaeological
        Research* 7(2):153–202.

LERNER, SHEREEN, AND TERESA HOFFMAN
  2000 Bringing Archaeology to the Public: Programs in the
        Southwestern United States. In *Cultural Resource
        Management in Contemporary Society: Perspectives
        on Managing and Presenting the Past*, Francis P.
        McManamon and Alf Hatton, editors, pp. 231–246.
        Routledge, New York, NY.

LOCK, GARY R.
  1993 GIS or CAD: What's in a Name? *Archaeological
        Computing Newsletter* 37:1–2.
  2000 *Beyond the Map: Archaeology and Spatial
        Technologies*, North Atlantic Treaty Organization,
        Science Series A: Life Sciences. IOS Press,
        Amsterdam, Netherlands.

LOCK, GARY R., AND T. M. HARRIS
  1996 Danebury Revisited: An English Iron Age Hillfort
        in a Digital Landscape. In *Anthropology, Space, and
        Geographic Information Systems*, Mark Aldenderfer
        and Herbert D. G. Maschner, editors, pp. 214–240.
        Oxford University Press, New York, NY.

LOCK, GARY R., AND ZORAN STANCIC
  1995 *Archaeology and Geographical Information Systems:
        A European Perspective*. Taylor and Francis, London,
        England, UK.

MADRY, SCOTT L. H., AND CAROLE L. CRUMLEY
  1990 An Application of Remote Sensing and GIS in a
        Regional Archaeological Settlement Pattern Analysis:
        The Arroux River Valley, Burgundy, France. In
        Interpreting Space: GIS and Archaeology, Kathleen
        M. S. Allen, Stanton W. Green, and Ezra B. W.
        Zubrow, editors, pp. 364–80. Taylor and Francis,
        Bristol, PA.

MADRY, S. L. H., AND L. RAKOS
  1996 Line-of-Sight and Cost-Surface Techniques for
        Regional Research in the Arroux River Valley. In *New
        Methods, Old Problems: Geographic Information
        Systems in Modern Archaeological Research*, Herbert
        D. G. Maschner, editor, pp. 103–126. Occasional
        Paper No. 23. Southern Illinois University Center
        for Archaeological Investigations, Carbondale.

MASCHNER, HERBERT D. G. (EDITOR)
  1996 *New Methods, Old Problems: Geographic
        Information Systems in Modern Archaeological
        Research*. Occasional Paper No. 23. Southern Illinois
        University Center for Archaeological Investigations,
        Carbondale.

MILLER, A. PAUL
  1995 How to Look Good and Influence People: Thoughts
        on the Design and Interpretation of an Archaeological
        GIS. In *Archaeology and Geographical Information
        Systems: A European Perspective*, Gary Lock and
        Zoran Stancic, editors, pp. 319–334. Taylor and
        Francis, London, England, UK.
  1996 Digging Deep: GIS in the City. In *Interfacing the Past:
        Computer Applications and Quantitative Methods in
        Archaeology, CAA95*, Hans Kamermans and Kelly
        Fennema, editors, vol. 2, pp. 369–376. Analecta
        Praehistorica Leidensia, No. 28. University of Leiden,
        Leiden, Netherlands.

NEW ZEALAND ARCHAEOLOGICAL ASSOCIATION
  1999 *Archaeological Site Recording in New Zealand*.
        Monograph No. 23. New Zealand Archaeological
        Association, Department of Conservation, Wel-
        lington, New Zealand.

NEW ZEALAND HOUSE OF REPRESENTATIVES
  1861 Goldfields Warden's Reports, Section D. In *Appen-
        dices to the Journal of the House of Representatives*.
        Department of Justice, Wellington, New Zealand.
  1863 Goldfields Warden's Reports, Section D. In *Appen-
        dices to the Journal of the House of Representatives*.
        Department of Justice, Wellington, New Zealand.

NG, JAMES
  1993 *Windows on a Chinese Past*, vol. 1. Otago Heritage
        Books, Dunedin, New Zealand.

ORMSBY, TIM, EILEEN NAPOLEN, ROBERT BURKE, CAROLYN
GROESSL, AND LAURA FEASTER
  2001 *Getting to Know ArcGIS Desktop: Basic of ArcView®,
        ArcEditor™, and ArcInfo™*. ESRI, Redlands, CA.

PYKE, VINCENT
  1962 *History of the Early Gold Discoveries in Otago*. Otago
        Daily Times and Witness Newspapers Company,
        Dunedin, New Zealand.

RITCHIE, NEVILLE A.
  1986 Archaeology and History of the Chinese in Southern
        New Zealand during the Nineteenth Century: A Study
        of Acculturation, Adaptation, and Change. Doctoral
        dissertation, University of Otago, Dunedin, New
        Zealand.

ROMANO, DAVID G., AND OSAMA TOLBA
  1995 Remote Sensing, GIS, and Electronic Surveying:
        Reconstructing the City Plan and Landscape of Roman
        Corinth. In *Computer Applications and Quantitative*

Methods in Archaeology, 1994, J. Huggett and N. Ryan, editors, pp. 163–174. BAR International Series, No. 600. Tempus Reparatum, Oxford, England, UK.

SALMON, J. H. M.
1963 *A History of Gold-Mining in New Zealand.* R. E. Owen, Wellington, New Zealand.

SMITH, STEVEN D., CHRISTOPHER OHM CLEMENT, AND STEPHEN R. WISE
2003 GPS, GIS, and the Civil War Battlefield Landscape: A South Carolina Low Country Example. *Historical Archaeology* 37(3):14–30.

STEELE, J., T. J. SLUCKIN, D. R. DENHOLM, AND C. S. GAMBLE
1996 Simulating Hunter-Gatherer Colonization of the Americas. In *Interfacing the Past: Computer Applications and Quantitative Methods in Archaeology, CAA95,* Hans Kamermans and Kelly Fennema, editors, vol. 2, pp. 223–227. Analecta Praehistorica Leidensia, No. 28. University of Leiden, Leiden, Netherlands.

TENNANT, EDWARD W., AND PETER BRISTOW
2004 Mapping Nenthorn: Taking Advantage of Emerging GPS and GIS Technologies. *Archaeology in New Zealand* 47(3):203–214.

TENNANT, EDWARD W., AND ROBERT A. RESCOT
2005 *Global Positioning Systems (GPS) in the Field: A Practical Guide to the Theory and Application of GPS Technologies.* U.S. Department of Transportation, Eastern Roads Division, Sterling, VA.

THOMPSON, HELEN M.
1949 *East of the Rock and Pillar: A History of the Strath Taiere and MacRaes Districts.* Otago Centennial Historical Publications, Dunedin, New Zealand.

WESTCOTT, KONNIE L., AND R. JOE BRANDON
2000 *Practical Applications of GIS for Archaeologists: A Predictive Modeling Kit.* Taylor and Francis, London, England, UK.

WHEATLEY, DAVID
1996 Between the Lines: The Role of GIS-Based Predictive Modelling in the Interpretation of Extensive Survey Data. In *Interfacing the Past: Computer Applications and Quantitative Methods in Archaeology, CAA95,* Hans Kamermans and Kelly Fennema, editors, vol. 2, pp. 275–292. Analecta Praehistorica Leidensia, No. 28. University of Leiden, Leiden, Netherlands.

WHEATLEY, DAVID, AND MARK GILLINGS
2002 *Spatial Technology and Archaeology: The Archaeological Applications of GIS.* Taylor and Francis, London, England, UK.

WILLIAMS, GORDON J.
1974 *Economic Geology of New Zealand.* Monograph Series, No. 4. Australasian Institute of Mining and Metallurgy, Carlton, Australia.

WILLIAMS, JACK
1992 The Archaeology of Underdevelopment and the Military Frontier of Northern New Spain. *Historical Archaeology* 26(1):7–21.

EDWARD GONZÁLEZ-TENNANT
DEPARTMENT OF ANTHROPOLOGY
UNIVERSITY OF OTAGO
DUNEDIN, NEW ZEALAND

JAMES A. DELLE

The Landscapes of Class Negotiation on Coffee Plantations in the Blue Mountains of Jamaica: 1790-1850

ABSTRACT

Analyzing the material elements of class negotiation should be a focus of historical archaeology. One of the most promising forms of material culture with which to conduct such analysis is landscape. To examine how landscapes shaped the negotiation of class relations in 19th century Jamaica, the material remains of three coffee plantations—Sherwood Forest, Clydesdale, and Chesterfield—are described and analyzed. The archaeological analysis of the landscapes of 19th century class negotiation can shed light on the historical development of capitalist social processes, many of which still impact the negotiation of class relations today.

> —Free negroes are found to act differently from other free men; not because they differ from others in character, but because their circumstances are different; and just in proportion as they are brought within the reach of those motives by which Europeans are governed, will their conduct resemble that of the natives of Europe (Henry George Grey to the Deputation of the Standing Committee of West India Planters, 1833).

Introduction

In recent years historical archaeologists have begun to seriously consider how material culture functions in the negotiation of the social relations of production. While such endeavors have traditionally focused on the various ways in which capitalist society has historically been stratified through the construction of hierarchies of "status" or "ethnicity" (Otto 1977; Schuyler 1980) only a few historical archaeologists have, to date, risked the challenging task of analyzing the material processes through which class relations are constructed and negotiated (Paynter and McGuire 1991; Wurst 1991; Scott 1994; Hood 1996; Johnson 1996; Mullins 1996; Orser 1996;

Shackel 1996). Given that class is one of the most important organizing structures of capitalist society and that most historical archaeologists study material culture produced and consumed within the capitalist system, it would seem to follow that historical archaeologists are logically situated to analyze the relationships that exist between material culture and the dynamics of class negotiation.

The analysis of class relations remains rare in historical archaeology, however. This may in part be related to the general difficulty archaeologists still have in interpreting dynamic social phenomena from the static archaeological record. Class relations are such dynamic phenomena; although class relations are constructed with material culture, it is the negotiation of the social relations expressed by such material culture, and not the material culture itself, that defines social class. An added barrier to class analysis results from the typical research design which tends to focus on individual sites or even subareas within sites. Interpretations are made on sites in isolation, not in relation to other sites. Such an approach limits what can be said about class dynamics. To convincingly interpret class dynamics from the material record, historical archaeologists must reach beyond traditional methodologies which more often than not fetishize portable artifacts from isolated sites. While quantification and classification of portable artifacts recovered from excavations may reveal the kinds of possessions typical (or atypical) of members of specific social classes, it remains difficult to interpret anything meaningful about the relationships negotiated between members of different classes from such exercises. Class exists within these relationships; a class is only truly meaningful in relation to other classes and to the political economy which shaped them. While such social relations can be interpreted through the analysis of many types of historical material culture, landscapes may be among the most fruitful avenues of research as they materially serve as the arenas in which people negotiate class relations. It thus follows that the emerging specialization of land-

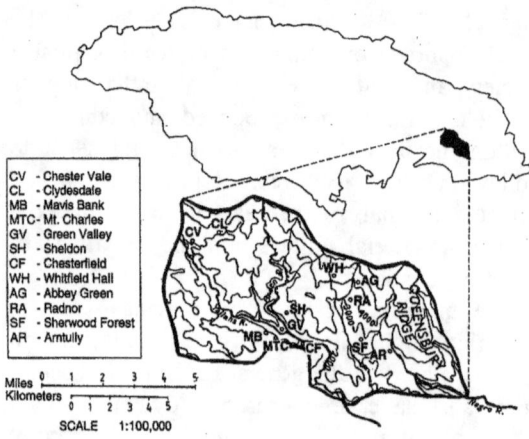

Figure 1. Location of Yallahs River drainage and plantations mentioned in the text.

the first half of the 19th century in the upper Yallahs River drainage, located in the Blue Mountains of eastern Jamaica (Figure 1). The Yallahs region incorporates the uplands of two historic parishes: St. David's and Port Royal. This analysis of the negotiation of class in this region will: 1) suggest how landscape archaeology can inform class analysis; 2) describe the class structure of the case study; 3) discuss how land and labor relations were incorporated into the negotiation of this class structure; and 4) analyze how coffee plantation landscapes specifically influenced the negotiation of class relations.

Landscape Archaeology and the Study of Class Relations

Although a relatively new moniker, landscape archaeology has recently emerged from several intellectual traditions which have had a long and profound impact on the practice of historical archaeology, notably settlement pattern analysis and vernacular architecture studies, and should in fact be considered an extension of these types of spatial analysis. While many recent landscape and spatial studies in archaeology have been explicitly designed to inform preservationists on the accurate reconstruction of isolated spaces, particularly gardens (Beaudry 1996), several have demonstrated how landscapes impact the negotiation of class relations on a variety of scales. For example, Robert Paynter (1980, 1981, 1982, 1983, 1985) has demonstrated how regional settlement patterns can be analyzed to interpret change within class structure. In his examination of rural western Massachusetts, Paynter has argued that by controlling access to the flow of surplus and by concentrating surplus at entrepôts, regional elite classes created a spatial system that supported the maintenance of class-based inequality. Although not explicitly concerned with class dynamics, Ken Lewis (Lewis 1984, 1985) has similarly used a settlement pattern study to suggest how spatial analysis can inform the analysis of the dynamic processes of Euroamerican colonialism. Lewis emphasized that colonial expan-

scape archaeology provides one means by which archaeologists can shed light on the historical negotiation of class relations.

The ultimate goal of this work is to demonstrate through a case study how landscapes influence the material negotiation of class relations in capitalist society. As a work of landscape archaeology, this article is based on two premises: 1) that material culture plays a significant role in the negotiation of social relations; and 2) that landscape is a form of material culture. Added to this second premise is the idea that landscapes are constructed of various spatial elements, some of which, like buildings, are empirically observable in the archaeological record, while other spatial elements, like land tenure systems, are best interpreted from cartographic and documentary records. To be most successful, an archaeology of historic landscapes should incorporate analyses of all three data sources: material, documentary, and cartographic. This essay attempts to do just that in considering how the organization of coffee plantation landscapes in pre- and post-emancipation Jamaica influenced and directed the negotiation of class relations.

To this end, this paper analyzes class relations as they were negotiated on coffee plantations in

sion on the South Carolina frontier was dependent on a hierarchically arranged system of frontier towns and settlements. He argued for the use of a diachronic model as he hypothesized that economic changes, and thus shifts in class relations, will precipitate changes in spatial forms (Lewis 1984:1-7, 17-27, 107-113).

In examining the spatial dynamics of class relations at a more refined scale, a number of historical archaeologists have focused their analysis on specific villages, towns, or cities. For example, Ed Hood's examination of landscapes in Deerfield, Massachusetts (Hood and Reinke 1989; Hood 1995, 1996) demonstrates how an elite class intentionally manipulated the town landscape in the attempt to create a false impression of past landscapes. This sanitized vision of Deerfield's past served primarily to reinforce the ideology of early 20th-century capitalism by creating a landscape which reflected modern inequality. By suggesting that such landscapes were ancient, 20th-century elites served to justify their class position by projecting its presence into the tangible past.

A major contribution to spatial analysis in historical archaeology has emerged from Mark Leone's long-term archaeology project in Annapolis, Maryland. Leone has argued that in the late 18th century, the so-called Georgian elites manipulated their landscapes to reflect their control over both the natural and social orders, including the class structure (Leone 1984, 1988).

This line of argument has been thoughtfully taken up by Elizabeth Kryder-Reid in her study of the Annapolis garden site known as St. Mary's. She demonstrated that the ability to control the space of the 18th-century garden served to reflect the control of knowledge as well as space; gardens thus served as powerful media "of the colonial elite to communicate and negotiate their social identity," i.e. their class position (Kryder-Reid 1994:132). Paul Shackel (1994) has demonstrated that the baroque city plan of St. Mary's City, Maryland's first capital, was designed specifically to bolster the class status of the administrative elite. When the capital was

transferred from St. Mary's to Annapolis in 1694, this new city was designed so that the Anglican Church and the State House stood on the city's two highest points, visible from any location thus constantly reinforcing the authority of both church and state (Shackel 1994:88). The control of space evident in the town plan and architecture of these two capital cities reinforced social and economic hierarchies constructed on social divisions based not only on class, but on race and religion.

Randy McGuire has examined town and community landscapes to analyze the changing ideology of capitalism in late 19th- and early 20th-century Broome County, New York (McGuire 1988, 1991; Wurst 1991). The differences in the industrial landscapes constructed by the industrialists Jonas Kilmer and George F. Johnson demonstrate transformations in how class relations were materially negotiated through the manipulation of the social landscape. McGuire documents how in the late 19th-century Kilmer constructed his factories and mansion in such a way as to exude power, physically demonstrating the social gulf between himself and the working class. In contrast, and in reaction to two generations of labor unrest, Johnson constructed an industrial landscape that overtly minimized social distance; in building his house in the same style as that of his workers, Johnson sought to obscure class differences by manifesting a sliding scale of relative equality. By constructing an industrial welfare system through which company profits were used to subsidize the construction of parks, hospitals, and other public monuments, Johnson attempted to construct an ideology which emphasized the mutual interests shared by employers and employees and create an illusion of equality between classes (McGuire 1991). Similar material expressions of the changing ideology of capitalism can be read in the mortuary architecture, design, and layout of the cemeteries of Broome County (McGuire 1988; Wurst 1991). Similar questions concerning the relationship between urban industrial landscapes and the negotiation of class relations have been addressed by Steve

Mrozowski and Mary Beaudry in the their long-term study of the Boott Mills industrial complex in Lowell, Massachusetts (Beaudry 1989; Mrozowski and Beaudry 1990; Beaudry, Cook, and Mrozowski 1991; Mrozowski 1991; Mrozowski et al 1996).

Vernacular architecture studies have contributed a great deal to the historical archaeology of landscapes. For example, Dell Upton has demonstrated that the most evident material expression of class relations on 18th-century Chesapeake tobacco plantations are the spatial relationships between the landscapes of the planters and those of the enslaved (Upton 1988). Chesapeake tobacco plantations were generally isolated and self-contained communities, likened to a village, with the planter's house serving as a "town hall" or center of power (Upton 1988:362). To reinforce this authority, planters' houses were physically elevated above other buildings, on a hill for instance, and were segregated from the surrounding countryside by systems of terraces and fences (Upton 1988:362). Plantation houses were thus intentionally constructed to dominate the landscape just as the planters dominated the class structure.

The methodologies of landscape archaeology have also been applied in the examination of how class is negotiated through plantation landscapes (Orser 1988; Armstrong and Kelly 1990; Hudgins 1990; Kelso 1990; Luccketti 1990; Delle 1994; McKee 1996; Pogue 1996). For example, Chuck Orser has demonstrated how landscapes impacted the negotiation of post-emancipation class relations at Millwood, a South Carolina cotton plantation (Orser and Nekola 1985; Orser 1988a, 1991). The owner of Millwood Plantation, James Edward Calhoun, was a well connected member of the southern elite. With the defeat of the Confederacy, planters like Calhoun reorganized the system of labor exploitation and class relations on their plantations. To this end, several new strategies of labor extraction were established, including farm wage labor and systems of time and crop sharing (Orser 1988:45-51). This restructuring of class relations following emancipation resulted in the restructuring of plantation landscapes. Unlike antebellum plantation settlements which put a premium on direct surveillance of the laborers, post bellum plantation settlements tended to be dispersed; each farmer, whether renter or sharecropper, lived with his or her family near the fields they tended. Significantly, where sharecroppers made up the bulk of the plantation tenants, the settlement form more closely resembled antebellum forms in that barns, sheds and other outbuildings were located near the planter's house, providing the planter class with the capability to directly supervise the sharecroppers (Orser 1988:92).

Studies like Orser's demonstrate how historical archaeologists can interpret the role landscapes play in the negotiation of class relations in a plantation context in which, despite the end of slavery, the elite classes manipulated the landscape to implement and reinforce a class structure in which they remained in control of land and production. Jamaica's Yallahs drainage provides an interesting context in which to examine how plantation landscapes shaped the development of class relations in the Caribbean. It is necessary first to characterize the region's class structure as it existed in the 19th century, and then to analyze the role landscapes played in the negotiation of class relationships.

The Class Structure of Coffee Plantations in the Yallahs Region: 1790-1850

In the 19th century Jamaica's political economy was defined by the production and export of agricultural products; the class structure on the island was thus largely defined by access to the agricultural means of production, particularly land. Members of the agrarian elite class in Jamaica referred to themselves as "planters." The planters were not a homogenous group free from internal division. This ruling segment of society included not only the members of the landed oligarchy, but also those employed as estate staff, and other members of Jamaican society involved in the commodities trade and service industries required to maintain it, including merchants, attorneys, and financiers (Pares 1950; Checkland 1957; Lobdell 1972; Davis 1975; Butler 1995; Stinchcombe 1995). The members of the planter classes most closely associated with the production of agricultural commodities were subdivided by social ranking, particularly as that ranking applied to an individual's relationship to the means of production. Heuristically, the planters can be divided into three overlapping classes. The most powerful, which can truly be called the "planter class," was comprised of proprietors who held legal title to estates as well as attorneys or factors who managed the financial affairs of absentee or deceased proprietors. The overseers who ran the daily operation of the estates and their assistants (often called "bookkeepers") can be characterized as an "agrarian middle class." The final group, the "professional middle class," included artisans, merchants, doctors, and other professionals, most of whom lived in the urban centers and some of whom owned plantations (Roughley 1823; Sheridan 1974). As can be seen from this rough outline, class membership was fluid. Members of the professional class could become proprietors of large estates; the occasional overseer ascended to the planter class through the acquisition of land, Hall (1989) presenting a notorious example.

Throughout Jamaica's history, most manual work has been performed by African slaves and their descendants. Until slavery was abolished in 1834 members of this class were not free to sell their labor power in an open market, but were dehumanized and considered commodities, valued by their potential to provide labor power to commercial agricultural estates. Between 1834 and 1838 most able-bodied workers were required to remain on the estates which had previously enslaved them as "apprentices," a transitional social category created by Parliament. The apprenticeship system was designed to teach former slaves the conditions of wage labor; while they were required to work for a certain number of hours each week for the estates, apprentices were free to sell their labor power at other times. In Jamaica this condition was abolished in 1838 and the laborers were nominally free to sell their labor power to the highest bidder.

A key element in the negotiation of this class structure was the planter class's ability to establish and maintain control of surplus production. This involved many social processes, including creating a particularly violent form of racism expressed through cruel dehumanization, physical abuse, and denigration. The planter class sought to exert control over access to land as part of their larger intention to dictate the nature of the social relations of production. It is self-evident that the planter class claimed the legal right to most surplus production under slavery by claiming ownership of the labor power of enslaved workers and most of the commodities they produced. The negotiation of post-emancipation labor relations was an entirely different matter. With the end of slavery the planter class claimed to recognize the former slaves as "free" laborers, yet strove to the best of their ability to limit that freedom by controlling the wages and terms of work. In the decades following the end of slavery, the planter class attempted to reassert their monopoly control over land as a means of production in the attempt to create a landless rural proletarian peasantry alienated from the means of production and thus dependent on wage labor for subsistence (Holt 1992, Butler 1995).

Just as the planter class was divided by an internal hierarchy which separated large proprietors from small, planters from merchants, and proprietors from overseers, the enslaved class was segmented by an internal division of labor which served as the template for the post-emancipation class structure. The nature of this pre-emancipation division of labor on Yallahs region coffee plantations can be interpreted from two sources: *The Coffee Planter of St. Domingo* (1798), an instructive treatise written for Jamaican planters by the Haitian émigré P. J. Laborie, and a surviving day book for Radnor plantation (1822-1826) which, among other things, lists the tasks performed by specific members of the plantation work force.

Laborie provided Jamaican coffee planters with a model for the division of labor to be established among the enslaved population of a working coffee plantation. In Laborie's model the economic roles slaves played in the coffee plantation economy were defined by a clearly articulated division of labor based on the type of labor expected to be performed. Laborie suggested that coffee plantations should have a class structure composed of artisans (which he calls "artificers"), skilled laborers (e.g. coffee-men, midwives, doctresses), various supervisors ("drivers"), and an unskilled labor force, which he calls "the gang in general." According to Laborie, the artisan group, many of whom were highly skilled laborers, should include carpenters, tilers, masons, and saddlers He explicitly listed the duties expected from each of these workers (Laborie 1798:164).

Laborie suggested that the unskilled labor force be divided into at least three work gangs One gang was to be assigned the specialized task of pruning. Another gang, responsible for lighter work such as weeding and gathering coffee, was to be composed of young adolescents between the ages of 12 and 16, while the bulk of the heavy work was to be done by the third group, the great gang. Once elevated into this group, adolescents would be considered adults; significantly, Laborie suggested that this status be affirmed by giving them houses, provision grounds, utensils, and two hens (Laborie 1798:175).

The Radnor plantation book indicates that the division of labor proposed by Laborie in the late 18th century was actualized by the 1820s. The journal indicates that Radnor field workers were organized into three gangs. The first gang was composed of 85 workers, of whom three were drivers. The second gang consisted of 23 people, including a driver and a cook. The third gang was composed 22 workers, again including a driver and a cook. As recommended by Laborie, the vast majority of skilled positions on Radnor were occupied by men: seven carpenters, one doctor, a boatswain, three masons, a saddler and five sawyers. According to the plantation book, there were only three specialized occupations on Radnor open to women, all characterized by Marietta Morrissey (1989) as "semi-skilled": midwife, nurse, and cook.

The immediate post-emancipation era in the Yallahs region was characterized by dissent over wages and what was then termed the planters' rights to "continuous labor." Underlying the strife between planters and workers in the immediate post-emancipation period was a new logic within the capitalist world order based on the concept of free trade. In 1846, the British Parliament passed the Sugar Duties Act, which lifted protective duties on produce imported from the colonies into Britain. This legislation was intended to stimulate production in the newer British Colonies in the East Indies and the Indian Ocean, particularly Ceylon and Mauritius. The passage of the act reflected the newly dominant ideology of Free Trade which dictated that unimpeded market forces should determine economic relations. The result for the Jamaican planter class was devastating. Without protective duties Jamaican planters could not produce crops cheaply enough to compete with Mauritius sugar and Ceylon coffee, which was being produced with cheap contract labor from the Indian subcontinent; nor could the Jamaican planters compete with producers in Cuba and Brazil, who utilized slave labor into the 1880s (Holt 1992:117). In response to their crisis the planters attempted to minimize the costs of production by keeping wages low and hiring laborers only when needed. It was the hope of the planters not only to create an army of surplus labor by making the people dependent on wages, but to remain in control of the terms by which those wages were paid and when people could work.

One strategy that the planters used in their attempt to control post-emancipation labor was wage capping. Within the various parishes local planter cartels colluded to establish standard wage rates by creating what they called "scales of labor." Due to the reticence and sometimes violent resistance of the Jamaican workers to accept low wages, however, solidarity between the planters quickly broke down, as the laborers forced planters into a wage bidding war to secure sufficient labor to harvest the crops. The planters encouraged the immigration of new labor pools to break the solidarity of the laboring class. In 1840, Governor Metcalfe of Jamaica appointed immigration agents in North America, Great Britain and elsewhere. These agents met with little success, however, as neither the black populations of the United States and Canada nor the laboring classes of Britain or Ireland showed much interest in emigrating to Jamaica (Holt 1992:197).

In 1841 the planter class introduced indentured African labor to Jamaica. It was thought that the introduction of contract labor would serve the planters well, as such laborers would not be at liberty to leave the estates to which they were attached, nor would they have the right to negotiate for higher wages. At this same point in time the British imperial government was attempting to stem the illicit slave trade, which still operated despite being outlawed by both the American and British governments earlier in the century. As part of the strategy to end the illicit slave trade, British warships seized slavers in the eastern Atlantic and repatriated the captive Africans to Sierra Leone. Knowing that many of these people were being deposited hundreds or thousands of miles from their homes, immigration agents sought to recruit indentured laborers from their numbers. Between 1834 and 1865, Green (1976:284) estimates that approximately 10,000 laborers were recruited to Jamaica from this population. This immigration policy met with public and official resistance, however, as many felt that the policy of recruiting Africans to work under coercive conditions in the West Indies was too reminiscent of slavery. In reaction to the limited success of recruiting African indentured labor, the planter class began recruiting indentured laborers from India in 1844. This scheme, too, met with only limited success; the number of Indian laborers transported to Jamaica probably was less than 10,000 (Green 1976:284). In all, it has been estimated that between 1834 and 1865, no more than 25,000 indentured laborers

were recruited to Jamaica, at an expense of £231,488 (Green 1976:284; Holt 1992:202).

The impetus to import indentured laborers into Jamaica was not merely to keep wages low, but to stimulate the development of an agrarian proletariat. Since many emancipated laborers were raising their own food on available vacant land, the laborers were not completely dependent on wages. Furthermore, the planters wanted the freedom to hire workers only during those times when they needed them most. Nevertheless, it was difficult for some planters to find workers even at high wages. The planter class thus sought to coerce the development of a proletarian work force dependent upon wages. In December of 1842, for example, the Jamaica Assembly enacted a series of taxes on imports, targeting those goods that were most commonly consumed by the laboring classes. Holt (1992:204) reveals, for example, that while no tax was levied on expensive manufactured goods, duties on imported salt beef and pork—staples of the laboring classes—rose by 40%.

The post-emancipation attempts by the planter class to manipulate labor relations affected Yallahs coffee plantations in several ways. For example, an analysis of crop accounts for ten plantations traced from the beginning of the century through the 1860s revealed that only four of them reported crops after 1839 (Delle 1996). This suggests that from the planters perspective, coffee production entered a crisis stage following emancipation, as it became increasingly difficult for the planters to control labor. This is reflected in a sworn statement by William George Lowe before a special committee of the Jamaica Assembly appointed in 1847. Lowe, who owned several coffee properties in the Blue Mountains, reported difficulty in obtaining labor to cultivate his estates. When asked about the condition of his properties Lowe reported "[my] property, Green Hill, in St. George's, I have been obliged to abandon for want of labour. When the coffee was ripe on the trees, I was unable to find labourers to gather it in. In 1833 there were 52 labourers attached to the property; more than two-thirds of them have purchased or leased lands, and become independent settlers; the other property, Violet Bank, I continue to cultivate, but not now to advantage" (Parliamentary Papers [PP] 1848, 23/3:163).

During the same set of hearings concerning the condition of sugar and coffee cultivation in Jamaica, Hugh Fraser Leslie reported that in 1847 he was in possession of several coffee plantations in the Yallahs region as well as a sugar estate. He reported that while there were 1,268 workers attached to his plantations during slavery, by 1847, fewer than 400 workers remained in his employ (PP 1848, 23/3:167). Leslie complained that he had a difficult time organizing and controlling labor on these estates, hampering his efforts at efficient estate management:

> From the indisposition of the people to work during the Christmas holidays, a great sacrifice of property takes place from the loss of coffee, which falls to the ground from want of hands to pick it during a period of two or three weeks, when no wages, however extravagant, can obtain their labour, this too being the period when the ripening of the coffee is the most general . . . Another difficulty is the refusal of the people to work on Fridays and Saturdays, even when the coffee is ripe on the field (PP 1848, 23/3:167)

Such overt expressions of independence on the part of the laboring class frustrated the attempts of the planters in the Yallahs region to conduct coffee cultivation as they saw fit. The post-emancipation decline in coffee production can in part be explained by the refusal of the African Jamaican population to develop into a rural proletariat dependent on wages paid for work on the estates. As early as 1839 special magistrate Henry Kent reported that Yallahs estates were experiencing difficulty in maintaining a labor force. Kent attributed the labor difficulties to a lack of available capital on the part of the planters, and the increasing economic independence of the workers. On the former development, he reported that the larger estates had more "hands than they can afford to pay at the present rate of wages. . . ." On the latter, he reported that on other properties "great difficulty is found in pro-curing labour, as the Negroes are certainly more intent in working their own grounds than cultivating the estate, finding it more profitable than any wages that could be offered them . . ." (Colonial Office [CO] 137/242/240).

Landscapes and the Means of Production in the Yallahs Drainage

Just as the economy of the Yallahs drainage in the 19th century was dominated by the production of coffee the landscape of the region was dominated by coffee plantations. To understand how class relations were negotiated on coffee plantations it is now necessary to examine how members of the various classes interacted within coffee plantation landscapes and to describe the relationships members of the various classes had with the primary means of production required for coffee.

In the pre-emancipation era the planter class established hegemonic control over the means of production through the exercise of monopoly control over the legal possession of agricultural land and the knowledge and capital required to construct coffee works. In Jamaica, this monopoly was established by the middle of the 18th century when a mere 467 people, or 2.9% of the white population, held possession of 78% of this land, each holding in excess of 1000 acres (Sheridan 1974:219). This figure seems all the more oppressive when one considers that by 1790 the enslaved population of Jamaica was approximately 211,000 people while the planter classes numbered less than 25,000. Thus approximately 0.002% of Jamaica's estimated population (here considering absentees in the equation) had economic control of over 78% of the island's productive land (Deerr 1950; Higman 1976:255). As the mills and other industrial buildings required for preparing commodities for export were generally located on the individual plantations, one can conclude that this same small minority of landowners controlled approximately the same proportion of the industrial means of production, including the knowledge, raw material, capital and/or the technology required to construct the mill machinery required for export production.

Jamaican planters usually required the enslaved population to produce their own food. Heads of enslaved households were granted access to land known as provision grounds; the food grown in provision ground gardens provided most of the nutritional requirements for the population, as well as the small amount of surplus exchanged in local markets. Prior to emancipation it was recognized by both the planters and the enslaved that these provision grounds were the de facto economic property of the enslaved; that is to say, it was the enslaved who controlled the sale and distribution of produce grown in these garden plots. The historic record for Radnor Coffee Plantation, one of the estates located in the Yallahs drainage (Figure 1), indicates that by the early 1820s a number of the enslaved workers sold produce directly to the white estate staff in exchange for cash (Delle 1996). The actual size of the allotted plots probably varied depending on the individual planter and the quality of land designated for provisions (Mintz 1960). For example, in 1790 the Jamaican plantation observer William Beckford commented that a "quarter acre . . . will be fully sufficient for the supply of a moderate family, and may enable [them] to carry some to market besides . . ."(Beckford 1790:257).

Since provision grounds were spaces occupied and utilized by the enslaved for their own use, little information on pre-emancipation provision grounds appears on period maps or plans of the Yallahs region. Nevertheless, some observations can be made from the cartographic record. A pre-emancipation estate map of Mavis Bank identifies 79 $\frac{3}{4}$ of the estate's 302 acres, approximately 26% of the estate's acreage, as "Negro Grounds and Provisions." While the boundaries of the "Negro Grounds" are clearly demarcated, no internal subdivision within the general area is rendered. This suggests that the surveyor either was not interested in the exact allocation of that land, or else did not gain access to this particu-

lar area of the plantation. It is also possible, given the use of this space, that the planters were not interested in the exact allocation of the land, but left the allocation and occupation of the land to the enslaved workers themselves. As the enslaved population of Mavis Bank in 1817 numbered 106, it can be estimated that approximately $\frac{3}{4}$ of an acre was allocated per capita; it remains impossible to say, however, just how much of the land was under cultivation at any given time.

An 1806 depiction of Radnor Plantation gives some further indication of how provision grounds fit into the internal division of material space on coffee plantations (Higman 1986, 1988). Of the estate's 689 acres, 133 acres were in "Negro grounds and provisions," while an additional 222 acres were in "woodland and Negro grounds." There were four separate areas of the plantation designated as "Negro grounds," and a fifth identified as "woodland." As was the case on Mavis Bank, most of this land was located along the periphery of the estate. On Radnor, the distance between the slave village and the provision grounds was between one-third and three-quarters of a mile. Just under one acre of provision ground and woodlot was allocated per capita in 1807 (Higman 1986).

When the British Parliament abolished slavery in 1834, the relationships both the planter and laboring classes had with land changed. The Jamaican planters attempted to create a new class structure which would maintain their hegemonic control over the island's export economy and the laborers' relationship to land. After 1838 many formerly enslaved workers entered into wage relationships with the planter class, selling their labor power to the estates in exchange for a wage. These newly freed tenant farmers were expected by the planters-turned landlords to pay rent both for the houses they occupied (which in many cases were the same houses the occupants had built for themselves while enslaved) and on the provision grounds they tilled. Land that had once been recognized as the economic property of the enslaved was redesignated as the economic property of the planters. To make use of the provision grounds, land in which ironically they were free to produce surplus while enslaved, many emancipated workers were forced into wage relationships with the planters just to be able to afford the rent on their gardens.

The planters' demand for rent often met with resentment, and was resisted by many of the newly freed laborers; the courts were crowded with cases for non-payment of rent (Holt 1992:138). When several cases were decided in favor of the workers, the planter class sought to legislate new conditions through which they could control the land. A notable example of this strategy of domination was the Summary Ejectment Law passed by the Jamaica Assembly in 1840. This law allowed the planters to eject at will people from land they occupied but which they did not hold legally, including provision grounds. The laboring class resisted such efforts by purchasing their own land or squatting on vacant land in areas remote from the centers of white settlement.

By the end of the 1840s it was clear that the planters' strategy to remain in monopoly control over the means of production was failing. For example, while in 1840 there were only 2,830 small freeholds of less than 50 acres in the island, by 1845 this number had increased almost ten-fold to 24,268, and more than doubled again to 60,000 by 1865. Simultaneously, the number of large land holdings of 1000 acres or more declined from 755 in 1850 to 503 in 1880 (Higman 1988:17; Holt 1992:268).

After the abolition of slavery, the planter class began to pay closer attention to how the laborers used their provision grounds. As some records were kept by the planter class concerning acreage tilled and rents paid by emancipated laborers it is possible to say more about the material spaces of African Jamaicans in the post-emancipation period than it is during the time of slavery. For example, a plan of Green Valley (Figure 1) plantation rendered in 1837 was drawn specifically to measure the extent of the provision grounds cultivated by the apprenticed laborers attached to the estate. According to this plan,

the only rendition of provision grounds known to exist for the Yallahs region, that part of the estate utilized for provisions was divided into 18 pieces, ranging in size from 3½ to 13½ acres. This document is all the more significant in as much as it identifies the types of foodstuffs produced on each parcel and identifies the people who worked each piece of land. The heading above the lists of names reads "[the] following are the names of those apprentices who posses grounds . . ." indicating that even from the perspective of the planters the laborers held some claim to possession, if not ownership, of their provision grounds.

The post-emancipation history of Whitfield Hall exemplifies a different course followed by the planter class in the Yallahs region (Figure 1). Crop accounts for this plantation indicate that the formerly enslaved workers and their descendants rented cottages and land from the estate. Unfortunately, the records do not indicate the size of the rented grounds or the number of renters. One can surmise, however, that the renting option was not a popular one with the laboring class. In 1842 the estate collected £36 in rent. The total amount of rent collected declined each year through 1846, when a mere £8..2..0 was collected. No record of rent collected appears in the accounts following this date, which may indicate either that the landlords abandoned the idea of trying to construct tenant farming on the estate, or else the farmers abandoned their rented lands and relocated on better terms on another estate, purchased land for themselves, or else began squatting on one of the many abandoned plantations located in the region.

The Landscapes of Class Negotiation

Historical archaeologists, particularly those involved in landscape archaeology, recognize that particular spaces influence and shape the negotiation of social relations between classes in context-specific ways (Leone 1988, 1995; Mrozowski 1990; Shackel 1994; Hood 1996). Having discussed in general terms how the class hierarchy in Jamaica was constructed socially and in the landscape, we now turn to a consideration of three specific landscapes—those of Chesterfield, Clydesdale, and Sherwood Forest plantations (Figure 1). A description of the material remains of these Yallahs coffee plantations is followed by an analysis of how these spaces mediated the negotiation of class relations in the Blue Mountains.

The Material Remains of Chesterfield, Clydesdale, and Sherwood Forest

As Jamaican coffee plantations were built in accordance to the general logic of estate production, the landscapes of Chesterfield, Clydesdale, and Sherwood Forest were segmented into task specific zones. The estate staff, including the overseers, plantation managers, and owners if they were present, inhabited an elite space dominated by the great house and its appendages, yards, and gardens. The overseer inhabited a space which mediated between the spatial dominance of the great house and the spaces of both coerced labor and the supervised domestic lives of the workers. The estates were further divided into coffee fields, industrial processing and storage areas, and provision grounds (Laborie 1798; Roughley 1823:187-188; Pulsipher and Goodwin

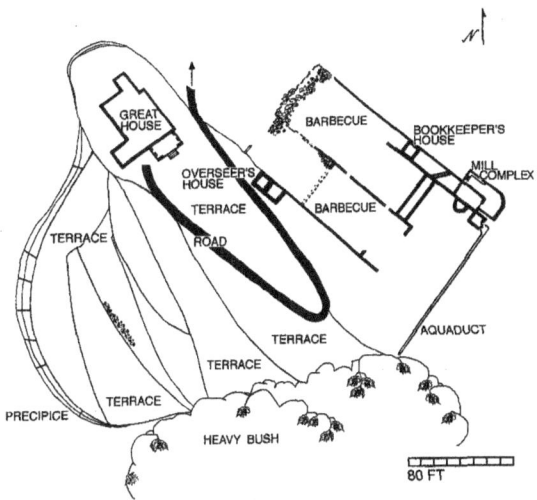

Figure 3. Site plan of Chesterfield.

1982; Higman 1988:80-81; 82; Orser 1988:85-93; Armstrong 1990; Delle 1994; Pulsipher 1994; Reeves 1997).

Coffee works minimally included a pulping mill to extract the beans from the berries, a set of drying platforms known as barbecues, and a second machine for removing a thin skin, known as parchment, from the dried beans. The process of pulping required a vast amount of water, not only to power the machinery, but also because the process of separating the beans from pulp required suspending the pulp in water and then separating the beans from the solution. Coffee works thus required holding tanks or vats and an aqueduct system to divert water from a river, stream, or spring to the coffee works (Laborie 1798; Higman 1988; Montieth 1991).

The pulping mill at Clydesdale is located within a massive two-story stone structure, which measures 26 ft. 8in. x 54 ft. 10 in. The ground floor of the structure contains the mill machinery; the pulping mill and water wheel are located on the western side of the large single room composing the ground floor. The vertical overshot water wheel was originally powered by an aqueduct which transported water from the Clyde River into the mill complex. The upper floor

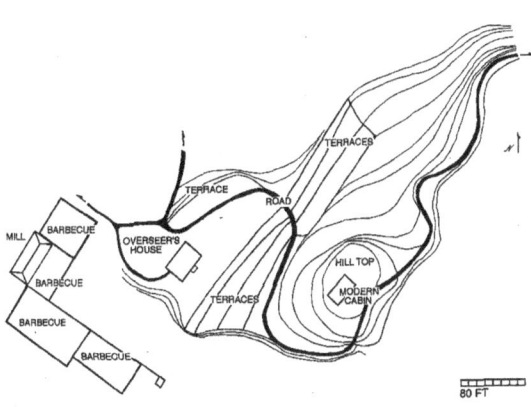

Figure 2. Site plan of Clydesdale.

contains two large rooms that may have been occupied by members of the estate staff, but given that these rooms are located within the mill building, and that they were probably never finished, it is likely that they were used as a warehouse space or coffee store. The mill is flanked to the west by a linear series of barbecues (Figure 2).

The mill complex at Chesterfield is in a poor state of preservation (Figure 3). Nothing remains of the pulping mill save a foundation. From this scanty evidence, however, several observations about the material space of the mill can be drawn. The ruins of an aqueduct indicate that water from the Fall River was diverted to power the mill and to fill the several cisterns surrounding the foundation ruin. As was the case with Clydesdale, the mill was a distinct structure, located away from the overseer's house. Unlike the Clydesdale barbecues, which were located on level ground abutting the Clyde River, a series of barbecues at Chesterfield were terraced into a hillside which overlooks the confluence of the Yallahs River and the Fall River.

The original pulping mill at Sherwood Forest differs from those at Clydesdale and Chesterfield as it was actually located within the overseer's house. The mill was housed in one room of this structure, while the overseer's domestic space

was located in the other. Like the mills at Clydesdale and Chesterfield, the pulping mill was water powered. Unlike the other two estates, however, Sherwood Forest is not situated below a river, but rather is located above the Negro River. To compensate for this, the mill complex contains a spring-fed cistern, which serves as a sort of "mill pond." During the pulping process, water from the cistern was channeled to the mill by means of a small aqueduct, which survives today, but is not functional. The barbecues at Sherwood Forest are similar to those at Chesterfield, as they are terraced into a hillside. Above the terraced barbecues is a series of smaller terraces which are currently used as a coffee nursery. It is possible that this was the original function of these terraces, as coffee plants require careful nurturing for several years before they can be transplanted into the coffee fields. It is likely that each plantation had some kind of nursery facility (Figure 4).

Although the European population on each coffee plantation was small, there was nevertheless a distinct class structure in place incorporating planter/owners, overseers, and bookkeepers. The class structure was reified by the spaces reserved for members of these distinct classes; this class-stratified space was manifested most directly in the creation of the material spaces of overseers' houses and great houses.

As was the case during the actual production of coffee, the production of plantation space was supervised by the overseer. The overseer was the de facto manager of the estate, responsible for organizing labor and supervising the production and distribution of coffee as an agricultural commodity (Stewart 1971 [1808]:129-130; Hall 1989; Walvin 1994:239). As resident managers, overseers served as intermediaries between the planter-owners and the laborers; their houses both reflected and created this relationship. To interpret the material space of this class of supervisor, we can turn to the archaeological record of the Yallahs region, which retains several examples of overseers' houses in various stages of preservation.

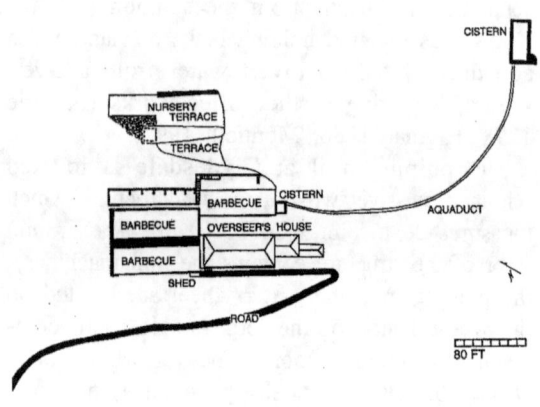

Figure 4. Site Plan of Sherwood Forest.

Perspectives from *Historical Archaeology*

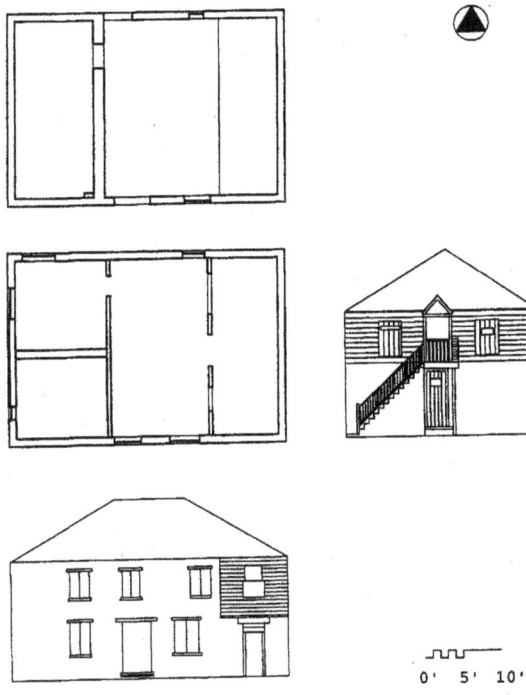

Figure 5. Architectural drawing of Clydesdale overseer's house.

Perhaps the best example of an extant overseer's house is that located on Clydesdale (Figure 5). The Clydesdale overseer's house is located within the industrial complex of the plantation. This is a two story building; however, the only access to the second story is an exterior staircase, originally constructed of wood. The upper story is finished, suggesting that this area was the domestic space of the overseer, while the lower story is not, suggesting that this area was used for either storing tools, equipment, or coffee. The upper story is divided into three rooms and originally included a second floor veranda, now sheathed in clapboards. It is likely that the largest of the three rooms served as a social area in which the overseer would entertain guests and conduct business, while the other two served as bedrooms. The veranda overlooked the coffee works, allowing the overseer to supervise the pulping and drying of coffee without having to leave the comfort of this house. The walls of this building are constructed of cut stone, and are two feet thick. Clearly, the overseer was able to isolate himself and his family with a significant physical buffer between them, the elements, and the enslaved workers. Since the exterior stairway was the only access to the domestic quarters of the upper story, once the door was bolted the overseer was in a virtually impenetrable fortress.

The overseer's house at Sherwood Forest exhibits two phases of construction, with the older section actually serving as part of the foundation for the later house. As was the case with Clydesdale, the earlier overseer's house is a relatively small structure built with massive stone walls. This structure is divided into two rooms which housed the domestic space of the overseer and the pulping mill, respectively. In this case, the overseer was in direct sensual contact with the first stage of coffee processing. The other key architectural feature of this building was a veranda, oriented toward the barbecues. From this vantage point, the overseer had the capability to continuously observe the drying beans. At Sherwood Forest, the domestic space of the overseer, at least during the first phase of the plantation's existence, was inseparable from the space of production.

Another example of an overseer's house survives at Chesterfield. This small house also exhibits two phases of construction (Figure 6). In the first phase it was a squat, two story building, with one room on each floor. The interior rooms each measure 10 x 10 ft. and the 2 ft. thick walls are made from field stone covered with lime plaster. Both this building and the plantation experienced a second phase of construction, probably beginning in 1824. During this phase of expansion, a 10 x 12 ft. room was added to the second story, atop a massive stone foundation. The walls of this new room were far more gracile than the massive field stone walls of the original. The new walls were a mere 7 in. thick, constructed with a technique which local informants described as "nag"— which is little more than a sophisticated form of wattle and daub. The wattle is a mesh of iron wire, which would be attached to studs. A type of lime mortar or concrete would be poured between the studs, forming, in effect, a seven inch thick plaster wall. The remains of the Chesterfield Great House, located nearby, demonstrate that this building, too, was constructed with the nag technique. The historic record of the plantation indicates that in 1824 the planter hired a "jobbing gang" from a nearby plantation to assist with the construction of these buildings. It seems likely that given the expense of such hired labor in the mid 1820s, the two buildings indicate a considerable investment in the improvement of elite space on Chesterfield.

As was the case at Sherwood Forest, the overseer at Chesterfield was in direct contact with production. Although the pulping mill was not located in the house, it was oriented in such a way as to allow the overseer to supervise the coffee crop as it dried on the barbecues. He was in visual contact with the mill, so that although not as intimately linked to the production process, the overseer was indeed in a position to

watch production as he saw fit, without having to leave his own domestic space.

Although it is possible that these structures were massively built out of stone to protect the overseers from hurricanes, an ecologically-based explanation for the massive construction is unsatisfactory. At least two nearby plantations, Abbey Green and Whitfield Hall, had overseers' houses built of timber. Both of these houses are still standing, and are actually in better shape than the Chesterfield house. In addition, the second phase of construction at Sherwood Forest was also a timber-framed house. It is notable that both Whitfield Hall and Sherwood Forest had smaller laboring populations than did Clydesdale or Chesterfield (Delle 1996). The fact that timber-framed buildings existed in the Yallahs region suggests that the construction of stone overseers' houses was a choice not a necessity based on ecological constraints. Massive stone walls may have been built to provide a more secure buffer between the overseers and the enslaved population on the larger estates.

In contrast to the number of standing overseers' houses in the Yallahs region, there are very few surviving great houses. For example, while the locations of the great houses for both Sherwood Forest and Whitfield Hall are known by local residents neither remains standing. It is unclear why this is the case, although it may be speculated that 1) the cost of maintaining larger houses in the post-emancipation era prohibited their reuse after the coffee industry failed or 2) since these houses were often vacant even prior to emancipation they fell to ruin more quickly than overseers' houses which would have been continuously occupied. Regardless of the cause, of the three plantations under consideration, visible ruins of a great house exist only at Chesterfield.

The great house at Chesterfield was much larger than any of the overseers' houses in the region, reflecting the class distinction between estate proprietors and their white employees. The floor plan of the great house indicates that the structure contained a 15 ft. 6 in. x 18 ft.

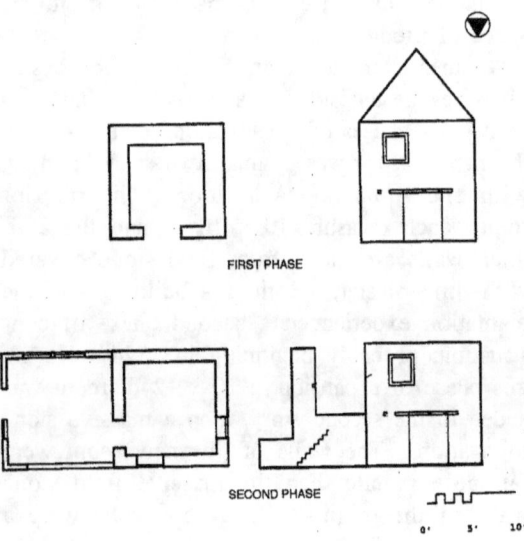

Figure 6. Architectural drawing of Chesterfield overseer's house.

hall, three chambers, and an attached kitchen with a store room. A small 4 x 9 ft. room with its own attached veranda may have served as the planter's office. Two additional rooms in the back of the house, near the kitchen, may have served as the quarters for domestic servants. This house also had a veranda, which overlooked the river valley, the industrial works, the overseer's house, and the coffee fields; the cartographic record of Chesterfield indicates that the latter were located on the opposite side of the Yallahs River.

Enslaved workers in the Yallahs region probably lived in nucleated villages clustered in areas defined by the planters as marginal to coffee production. Unlike the industrial and elite housing on the estates, the domestic houses of the workers were constructed of perishable materials, and thus were impermanent structures. In the attempt to locate the villages surface surveys of Chesterfield, Sherwood Forest, and Clydesdale were conducted in 1994. Comparing location information obtained from the historic maps to modern topographic maps and the actually existing landscapes, the locations of slave villages at Radnor and Clydesdale were identified; unfortunately the presence of modern coffee trees at the former and severe bulldozer disturbance at the latter prohibited excavation. Surface reconnaissance at Chesterfield did not reveal the location of a village. Attempts to locate this village were thwarted not only by the relative silence of surface record for the structures, but by erosion and other depositional processes which have undoubtedly removed surficial evidence of the village. Furthermore, as both Clydesdale and Sherwood Forest were under coffee cultivation during the 1992-1994 field seasons, the areas available for subsurface testing were limited.

Nevertheless, some preliminary observations can be made about the layout of slave villages based on an analysis of two cartographic representations of pre-emancipation villages. The first such representation is Barry Higman's (1986, 1988) reproduction of an 1806 plan of Radnor. In 1806 the entire slave village, a cluster of 30

buildings located in a meadow, which occupied 2.7 acres of land (Higman 1986) housed 252 people (Delle 1996). If one assumes that the plan reproduced by Higman accurately depicted the number of houses, and that the relevant slave return data accurate, then an average of 8 people occupied each structure. Regardless of the actual number of houses, if all 252 people were indeed living in the 2.7 acre meadow, the village would have been a very densely populated place indeed. It should be noted that this densely populated zone only incorporates the area encompassing the slave village. It is likely that many people spent much of their time in the provision grounds. The only other representation of a slave settlement on a coffee plantation map that can be confidently dated to the pre-emancipation period is a depiction of Clydesdale dated 1810. According to this map, 10 houses were located in a 10-acre field. In 1818 it was reported that 109 laborers were attached to the plantation. If we accept that there were 10 houses in the village, this information suggests that there were approximately 11 people per house.

Features of post-emancipation villages can be interpreted from historic estate plans of two nearby estates, Ayton and Abbey Green, rendered by the surveyor James Smith in the 1850s. These indicate the location of "Negro Houses"; in each case, the houses appear clustered together, much as they had in the pre-emancipation villages. The Abbey Green plan shows the relative location of 17 individual buildings; in January of 1839, special magistrate Henry Kent reported that there were 108 laborers residing on the estate (CO137/242/241). Assuming the accuracy of the house counts and Kent's figures, each structure on Abbey Green housed an average of about 6 people; those at Ayton between 2.1 and 3.5 people per house. These numbers are consistent with a variety of possible household membership structures, including both nuclear family and extended family structures. The maps may thus represent the number of houses and hence the household size in the post-emancipation Yallahs region.

Negotiating the Landscape

As should be clear by now, members of the various classes perceived and experienced Yallahs plantations landscapes differently. The planter class who designed the estate landscapes actively constructed plantation spaces—or more accurately, had enslaved workers create the plantation spaces according to the planters' designs—as an active part of their strategy of social control. It was within these landscapes that class relations were negotiated; as such, the planter classes designed spaces with which they could most effectively control the lives and labor of African Jamaican workers, and thus better create profits for them-

selves. Just as these landscapes of control were designed to maximize efficient production and exert subtle social controls over those forced to toil on Jamaican coffee estates, so too did these landscapes serve as arenas of resistance against these same oppressive social relations of production.

As Upton (1988, 1992), Orser (1988b), and Leone (1995) have argued, under capitalism the position of structures and the division of social space on a landscape express power and class relations. The archaeological evidence of the Yallahs plantation landscapes indicates that such power was negotiated particularly through surveillance over the plantation population both at home

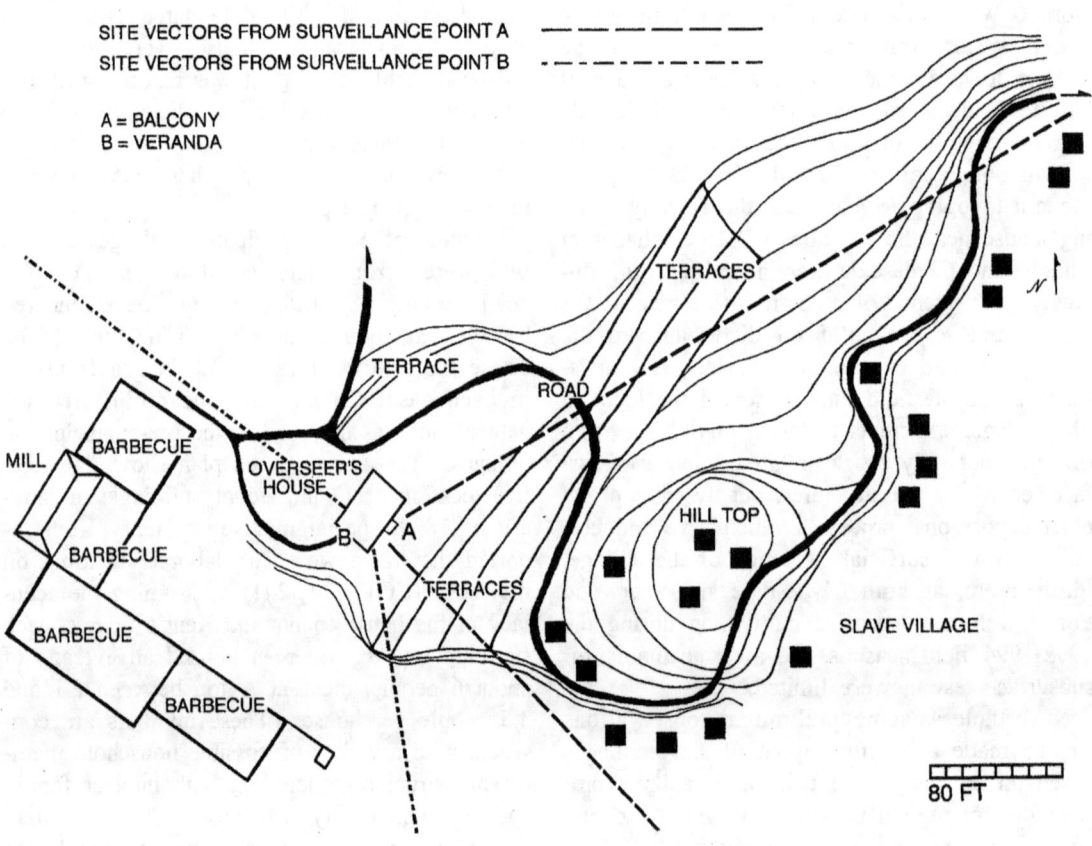

Figure 7. Composite site plan of Clydesdale

and at work; maximizing panoptic viewscapes was key to landscape design. In the Yallahs context such landscapes of surveillance are best considered at Clydesdale, given the superior preservation of the plantation's buildings and the extent of its cartographic record. Using these two data sources, it is possible to create a composite map which can usefully reconstruct the landscape of surveillance (Figure 7). The overseer's house featured two surveillance positions. The first was the entrance door to the overseer's house, which probably had a small landing at the top of a wooden stair. From this point, the overseer could monitor the slave village, which was located uphill from the house, within the viewscape of this position. The path from the village to both the coffee fields and the industrial works passed directly by this point. Thus, without leaving the material confines of his house, the overseer could survey the domestic quarters of the workers, and supervise the morning procession to work as the laborers passed below him on their way to the fields and mill.

The second surveillance point was the veranda of the overseers house. The coffee works and barbecues were located downhill and within the viewscape of this vantage point. From the comfort of his veranda the overseer could supervise the coffee works and any activity occurring on the barbecues. During those times when the overseer wanted to exert the greatest measure of control over the workers, he could practice panoptic surveillance over the population. This method of social control relied equally on the direct observation of the watcher and on creating the perception that the workers were being constantly observed, whether the overseer was watching them directly or not. By locating the overseer's house in such a way that the overseer could survey both the village and works from the veranda, or even by simply gazing out of one of the house's windows, the workers could never be entirely sure when they were being watched. The purpose behind the construction of this landscape was the construction of an internalized discipline in the work force; the logic of the panopticon dictated that the workers would cooperate if they thought there were a possibility that their behavior at any given moment was under scrutiny (Foucault 1979).

Changes in the domestic spaces of the elites, particularly the overseer's houses, reflect the changes in social relations that occurred following emancipation. For example the form of the overseer's house at Sherwood Forest changed considerably over time. The original overseer's house was constructed with 21 in. thick stone walls. A veranda provided the overseer with a southern view which encompassed the coffee drying platforms while an 18 in. thick interior wall separated the overseer's room from the pulping mill which was contained in the same building as the overseer's domestic space. Although contained within an imposing fortress-like structure, as long as he was in his room or on his veranda, the overseer could directly supervise the production of coffee. From the veranda the overseer could monitor the coffee crop as it dried, while from his room he could watch the coffee as it was pulped and channeled to the drying platforms. This spatial arrangement created an intensive capacity for surveillance over production while simultaneously and physically segregating the overseer from the work force.

The second phase of construction at the overseer's house was much more gracile, and served to remove the overseer from the direct surveillance of production. The second house was literally built on top of the first; the older house served as part of the foundation for the newer structure. This later building was timber framed, and itself experienced several phases of construction. The pulping and grinding mills remained in the building, but were now located on a lower floor, separating the overseer's domestic space somewhat from the direct activity of production. Interestingly, the veranda of the second building is oriented to the east. The viewscape from this perspective encompasses a scenic view of the valley and surrounding hills and not the barbecues. To directly see what was happening on the barbecues, the overseer would have to crane his neck as it takes more than a casual effort to supervise production from this vantage point.

This new spatial arrangement reflects the change in the relations of production which developed after emancipation. Beginning in the late 1840s, Sherwood Forest began acquiring the estates which bounded it to the east and south; the previously independent estates of Arntully and Eccleston were defined in the crop accounts of the 1850s as appendages to Sherwood Forest. The comfortable wooden structure may have developed into a post-emancipation great house from which the affairs of the several plantations were managed. In his discussion of Arntully, Higman (1988:175) notes that no great house was indicated in the 1839 plan of this Yallahs region estate; this may substantiate the hypothesis that during the 1840s at least, the affairs of Arntully may have been directed from Sherwood Forest.

Conclusion

By the middle of the 1850s, the Jamaican coffee industry was on the verge of collapse. In 1855 special magistrate Henry Kent remarked: "[i]t is difficult now to procure labour, the able bodied people having mostly left the estates" (CO 137/327/97). An unsigned dispatch from 1857 reveals that the newly developing class structure was such that the planter class could no longer control the landscapes of production: ". . . there is great difficulty experienced in carrying on cultivation; the able bodied Negroes having left the estates and idlying their time away upon their small freeholds . . ." (CO137/334/24).

A final blow to the Jamaican coffee industry was the leveling of colonial duties. In the late 1840s and 1850s the Jamaican planters could not compete with the cheaper coffee produced with the fresher soils and contract labor of Ceylon and the vast slave-labor production of Brazil. When asked by a Parliamentary committee to account for the rapid abandonment of Jamaican coffee

plantations, the coffee planter Alexander Geddes testified that "the great cause for the abandonment of the coffee plantations is the low price now obtained . . . owing to the introduction of slave and Ceylon coffee" (PP 1847-1848, 23/2:20). According to Geddes's testimony, the abandonment of coffee estates had begun immediately following the end of apprenticeship, a time when the planter class had great difficulty controlling the negotiation of class relations between themselves and the newly freed workers. It is quite evident that changes in the global economy were directly effecting changes both in class relations and the form of plantation landscapes in the Yallahs region at this time.

The class dynamics of the Yallahs region changed dramatically in the first half of the 19th century, as both the conditions of labor and land tenure, two key factors in the negotiation of class relations, were radically reconstructed with the end of slavery. It was, of course, relatively simple for the planter class to maintain its virtual monopoly over land and labor prior to the abolition of slavery, a time when the planters exerted great control over the conditions of labor, the class structure, and thus the relations of production. With emancipation, however, the planters' quest to retain control over both the means and the social relations of production became much more difficult. Even before the abolition of slavery, many of the estates that had previously been productive during the boom years of the Napoleonic wars had failed; hundreds of estates were abandoned by the planters following emancipation. As a result, there were literally hundreds of thousands of acres of land lying unoccupied when slavery was fully abolished in 1838. Following emancipation, many African-Jamaican people abandoned both the land on which they had lived and their role in the production of export crops, opting instead to carve a subsistence living on small plots in the interior, supplementing their domestic economy by producing small surpluses to be sold in local town and city markets. They were acting in such a way as to take control over the material negotiation between themselves as working people, and the landowners, who attempted to construct from their numbers a wage-earning rural proletariat.

If, as Leone and Potter (1988) argued a decade ago, historical archaeologists need to be aware of the social context in which they work, and make their analyses of the past relevant to the present, we are given no choice but to confront the issue of class. The unequal accumulation of material wealth holds a place of central importance in the structure of capitalist society; one's relative ability to accumulate that material wealth plays a large part in the negotiation of class relations. As society is increasingly fragmented into specialized markets based on a given demographic group's ability to purchase material goods, as citizens continue to be redefined as consumers, as the largest corporations continue to control more wealth than most national governments, as capitalism penetrates into the final hidden corners of Amazonia, Central Asia, and Eastern Europe, and as these phenomena increasingly define the shape of global society, we as social scientists would do well to focus our studies on the processes that resulted in the historical trajectories which created the world of the late 20th century. At the head of this list of processes is the definition and negotiation of social classes.

The landscapes of coffee plantations in eastern Jamaica were but one arena in which class relations were historically negotiated. In many ways the landscapes of these plantations were designed and lived in such a way as to maximize the planter class's ability to control the work force through technologies of surveillance. In the years following the end of slavery, these landscapes of surveillance, despite the best efforts of the planter class, became less useful in the maintenance of the severe class hierarchy imposed under the slave regime. The newly freed workers found ways to resist the planter class by creating new landscapes of their own, in which they exerted control over both meanings of and production from landscapes. It was only by the creation of oppressive government controls over

vacant land, like the Summary Ejectment Law, and the enforcement of legislation controlling the amount of surplus production which the laboring class was allowed to export, that the post-emancipation planter class was able to dictate the terms of the landscapes of class hierarchy and maintain their control over Jamaica's political economy.

The late 20th century is witnessing two not unrelated phenomena. While communication and surveillance technologies are becoming increasingly sophisticated, an ever-increasing percentage of the world's population is being incorporated into the global capitalist system, most as members of the working class. As the number of people in the working class is growing exponentially, manufacturing and financial corporations are creating new and better technologies with which to create and direct the flow of surplus wealth and to exert control over the dynamics of class negotiation. Specific forms of material culture play a central role in this process; for example internet hardware, cellular phones, and automatic surveillance cameras are increasing the ability of the wealthier classes to supervise and direct the production and distribution of goods by the working classes. Such phenomena did not spontaneously appear in a vacuum but are the result of specific and complex historical trajectories, including the creation and negotiation of coffee plantation landscapes in 19th-century Jamaica. As scholars interested in the ways that material culture mediates social relations, historical archaeologists would do well to examine how various forms of material culture, including such landscapes, influenced the shape of class relations in the recent past to better understand how and why the current class structure emerged.

ACKNOWLEDGMENTS

I would like to thank all of those who assisted me in constructing this paper. I am grateful to LouAnn Wurst and Rob Fitts for inviting me to participate in this volume; especially LouAnn who read through numerous drafts and always offered sound advice for the paper's improvement. The HA reviewers also provided helpful comments. I would also like to thank Bob Paynter, Martin Wobst, and Ben Howatt who advised me on the larger project from which this paper sprung. A number of individuals assisted my research in Jamaica, including Doug Armstrong, Matt Reeves, Dorrick Gray, Spider Walters, Dr. Charles Deichman, John Allgrove, Lance Douglas, Mike Volmar, Jim Dooley, Jackie Watson, and especially Mary Ann Levine. I am grateful for the assistance extended me by the staffs of the Jamaica National Heritage Trust, the Jamaica Forestry Department, the Jamaica Archives, and the National Library of Jamaica. This research was funded by the Wenner-Gren Foundation for Anthropological Research.

REFERENCES CITED

ARMSTRONG, DOUGLAS V.
1990 *The Old Village and the Great House: An Archaeological and Historical Examination of Drax Hall Plantation, St. Ann's Bay, Jamaica.* University of Illinois Press, Urbana.

ARMSTRONG, DOUGLAS V. AND KENNETH G. KELLY.
1990 Settlement Pattern Shifts in a Jamaican Slave Village, Seville Estate, St. Ann's Bay, Jamaica. Paper Presented at the Annual Conference on Historical and Underwater Archaeology, Tucson, AZ.

BEAUDRY, MARY C.
1989 The Lowell Boott Mills Complex and Its Housing: Material Expressions of Corporate Ideology. *Historical Archaeology* 23 (1):19-32.
1996 Why Gardens? In *Landscape Archaeology: Reading and Interpreting the American Historical Landscape*, edited by Rebecca Yamin and Karen B. Metheny, pp. 3-5. University of Tennessee Press, Knoxville.

BEAUDRY, MARY C., LAUREN COOK, AND STEPHEN A. MROZOWSKI
1991 Artifacts and Active Voices: Material Culture as Social Discourse. In *The Archaeology of Inequality*, edited by Randall H. McGuire and Robert Paynter, pp. 150-191. Basil Blackwell, Oxford.

BECKFORD, WILLIAM
1790 *A Descriptive Account of the Island of Jamaica.* T. and J. Egerton, London.

BUTLER, KATHLEEN M.
1995 *The Economics of Emancipation: Jamaica & Barbados, 1823-1843.* University of North Carolina Press, Chapel Hill.

CHECKLAND, S. G.
1957 Finance for the West Indies, 1780-1815. *Economic History Review* 10:461-469.

COLONIAL OFFICE RECORDS (CO)
1839 Colonial Office Records. Public Records Office of -1857 England, Kew.

DAVIS, DAVID BRION
1975 *The Problem of Slavery in the Age of Revolution, 1770-1823.* Cornell University Press, Ithaca, NY.

DEERR, NOEL
1950 *The History of Sugar.* Chapman and Hall, London.

DELLE, JAMES A.
1994 A Spatial Analysis of Sugar Plantations on St. Eustatius, Netherlands Antilles. In *Spatial Patterning in Historical Archaeology: Selected Studies of Settlement*, edited by Donald W. Linebaugh and Gary G. Robinson, pp. 33-62. King and Queen Press, Williamsburg, VA.
1996 *An Archaeology of Crisis: The Manipulation of Social Spaces in the Blue Mountains of Jamaica, 1790-1865.* Ph.D. dissertation, Department of Anthropology, University of Massachusetts, Amherst. University Microfilms International, Ann Arbor, MI.

FOUCAULT, MICHEL
1979 *Discipline and Punish: The Birth of the Prison.* Vintage Books, New York.

GREEN, WILLIAM
1976 *British Slave Emancipation: The Sugar Colonies and the Great Experiment, 1830-1865.* Clarendon Press, Oxford, England.

HALL, DOUGLAS
1989 *In Miserable Slavery: Thomas Thistlewood in Jamaica, 1750-86.* Macmillan, London.

HIGMAN, BARRY
1976 *Slave Population and Economy in Jamaica, 1807-1834.* Cambridge University Press, London, England.
1986 Jamaican Coffee Plantations 1780-1860: A Cartographic Analysis. *Caribbean Geography* 2:73-91.
1988 *Jamaica Surveyed: Plantation Maps and Plans of the Eighteenth and Nineteenth Centuries.* Institute of Jamaica, Kingston.

HOLT, THOMAS
1992 *The Problem of Freedom: Race, Labor, and Politics in Jamaica and Britain, 1832-1938.* Johns Hopkins University Press, Baltimore, MD.

HOOD, J. EDWARD
1995 Some Observations on Interpreting the Archaeology of a New England Village to the Public. Paper Presented at the Annual Meeting of the Society for American Archaeology, Minneapolis, MN.

1996 Social Relations and the Cultural Landscape. In *Landscape Archaeology: Reading and Interpreting the American Historical Landscape*, edited by Rebecca Yamin and Karen B. Metheny, pp. 121-146. University of Tennessee Press, Knoxville.

HOOD, J. EDWARD AND RITA REINKE.
  1989 Manipulating the Landscape: Some Evidence from Deerfield, Massachusetts. Paper Presented at the Annual Meeting of the Eastern States Archaeological Federation, East Windsor, CT.

HUDGINS, CARTER L.
  1990 Robert "King" Carter and the Landscape of Tidewater Virginia in the Eighteenth Century. In *Earth Patterns: Essays in Landscape Archaeology*, edited by William Kelso and Rachel Most, pp. 59-70. University Press of Virginia, Charlottesville.

KELSO, WILLIAM
  1990 Landscape Archaeology at Thomas Jefferson's Monticello. In *Earth Patterns: Essays in Landscape Archaeology*, edited by William Kelso and Rachel Most, pp. 7-22. University Press of Virginia, Charlottesville.

KRYDER-REID, ELIZABETH
  1994 "As Is the Gardener, So Is the Garden": The Archaeology of Landscape as Myth. In *The Historical Archaeology of the Chesapeake*, edited by Paul A. Shackel and Barbara J. Little, pp. 131-148. Smithsonian Institution Press, Washington.

LABORIE, P.J.
  1798 *The Coffee Planter of Saint Domingo*. T. Caddell and W. Davies, London.

LEONE, MARK P.
  1984 Interpreting Ideology in Historical Archaeology: The William Paca Garden in Annapolis, Maryland. In *Ideology, Power and Prehistory*, edited by Daniel Miller and Christopher Tilley, pp. 25-35. Cambridge University Press, London, England.
  1988 The Georgian Order as the Order of Merchant Capitalism in Annapolis, Maryland. In *The Recovery of Meaning: Historical Archaeology in the Eastern United States*, edited by Mark P. Leone and Parker B. Potter, Jr., pp. 219-229. Smithsonian Institution Press, Washington.
  1995 A Historical Archaeology of Capitalism. *American Anthropologist* 97(2):251-268.

LEONE, MARK P. AND PARKER B. POTTER, JR.
  1988 Introduction: Issues in Historical Archaeology. In *The Recovery of Meaning: Historical Archaeology in the Eastern United States*, edited by Mark P. Leone and

Parker B. Potter, Jr., pp. 1-20. Smithsonian Institution Press, Washington.

LEWIS, KENNETH
  1984 *The American Frontier: An Archeological Study of Settlement Pattern and Process*. Academic Press, New York.
  1985 Plantation Layout and Function in the South Carolina Lowcountry. In *The Archeology of Slavery and Plantation Life*, edited by Theresa Singleton, pp. 35-66. Academic Press, San Diego.

LOBDELL, R.
  1972 Patterns of Investment and Sources of Credit in the British West Indian Sugar Industry. *Journal of Caribbean History* 4:31-53.

LUCCKETTI, NICHOLAS
  1990 Archaeological Excavations at Bacon's Castle, Surry County, Virginia. In *Earth Patterns: Essays in Landscape Archaeology*, edited by William Kelso and Rachel Most, pp. 23-42. University Press of Virginia, Charlottesville.

MCGUIRE, RANDALL H.
  1988 Dialogues with the Dead: Ideology and the Cemetery. In *Recovery of Meaning*, edited by Mark Leone and Parker B. Potter, Jr., pp. 435-480. Smithsonian Institution Press, Washington.
  1991 Building Power in the Cultural Landscape of Broome County, New York, 1880 to 1940. In *The Archaeology of Inequality*, edited by Randall H. McGuire and Robert Paynter, pp. 102-124. Basil Blackwell, Oxford, England.

MCKEE, LARRY
  1996 The Archaeology of Rachel's Garden. In *Landscape Archaeology: Reading and Interpreting the American Historical Landscape*, edited by Rebecca Yamin and Karen B. Metheny, pp. 70-90. University of Tennessee Press, Knoxville.

MINTZ, SIDNEY AND DOUGLAS HALL
  1960 The Origins of the Jamaican Internal Marketing System. *Yale University Publications in Anthropology*. New Haven, CT.

MONTIETH, KATHLEEN
  1991 The Coffee Industry in Jamaica, 1790-1850. Master's thesis, Department of History, University of the West Indies at Mona.

MORRISSEY, MARRIETTA
  1989 *Slave Women in the New World: Gender Stratification in the Caribbean*. University of Kansas Press, Lawrence.

MROZOWSKI, STEPHEN

1991 Landscapes of Inequality. In *The Archaeology of Inequality*, edited by Randall. McGuire and Robert Paynter, pp. 79-101. Basil Blackwell, Oxford, England.

MROZOWSKI, STEPHEN A. AND MARY C. BEAUDRY

1990 Archaeology and the Landscape of Corporate Ideology. In *Earth Patterns: Essays in Landscape Archaeology*, edited by William Kelso and Rachel Most, pp. 189-208. University Press of Virginia, Charlottesville.

MROZOWSKI, STEPHEN A., GRACE H. ZIESING, AND MARY C. BEAUDRY

1996 *Living on the Boott: Historical Archaeology at the Boott Mills Boardinghouses, Lowell, Massachusetts.* University of Massachusetts Press, Amherst.

MULLINS, PAUL R.

1996 *The Contradictions of Consumption: An Archaeology of African America and Consumer Culture, 1850-1930.* Ph.D. dissertation, Department of Anthropology, University of Massachusetts, Amherst. University Microfilms International, Ann Arbor.

ORSER, CHARLES E., JR.

1988a *The Material Basis of the Postbellum Tenant Plantation: Historical Archaeology in the South Carolina Piedmont.* University of Georgia Press, Athens.

1988b Toward a Theory of Power for Historical Archaeology: Plantations and Space. In *The Recovery of Meaning*, edited by Mark Leone and Parker Potter, Jr., pp. 235-262. Smithsonian Institution Press, Washington.

1996 *A Historical Archaeology of the Modern World.* Plenum Press, New York.

ORSER, CHARLES E., JR. AND ANNETTE M. NEKOLA

1985 Plantation Settlement from Slavery to Tenancy: An Example from a Piedmont Plantation in South Carolina. In *The Archeology of Slavery and Plantation Life*, edited by Theresa Singleton, pp. 67-94. Academic Press, San Diego.

OTTO, JOHN S.

1977 Artifacts and Status Differences: A Comparison of Ceramics for Planter, Overseer, and Slave Sites on an Antebellum Plantation. In *Research Strategies in Historical Archeology*, edited by Stanley South, pp. 91-118. Academic Press, New York.

PARES, R.

1950 *A West-India Fortune.* Longmans, Green and Co., London.

PARLIAMENTARY PAPERS (PP)

1847 Parliamentary Papers. British Library, London.
-1848

PAYNTER, ROBERT

1980 *Long Distance Processes, Stratification and Settlement Pattern: An Archaeological Perspective.* Ph.D. dissertation, Department of Anthropology, University of Massachusetts, Amherst. University Microfilms International, Ann Arbor.

1981 Social Complexity in Peripheries: Problems and Models. In *Archaeological Approaches to the Study of Complexity*, edited by S. E. van der Leeuw, pp. 118-141. A. E. van Giffen Institute, Amsterdam, The Netherlands.

1982 *Models of Spatial Inequality.* Academic Press, New York.

1983 Expanding the Scope of Settlement Analysis. In *Archeological Hammers and Theories*, edited by James Moore and Arthur Keene, pp. 234-277. Academic Press, New York.

1985 Surplus Flow between Frontiers and Homelands. In *The Archeology of Frontiers and Boundaries*, edited by S. W. Green and S. M. Perlman, pp. 163-211. Academic Press, Orlando.

PAYNTER, ROBERT AND RANDALL H. MCGUIRE

1991 The Archaeology of Inequality: Material Culture, Domination and Resistance. In *The Archaeology of Inequality*, edited by Randall H. McGuire and Robert Paynter, pp. 1-27. Basil Blackwell, Oxford, England.

POGUE, DENNIS

1996 Giant in the Earth: George Washington, Landscape Designer. In *Landscape Archaeology: Reading and Interpreting the American Historical Landscape*, edited by Rebecca Yamin and Karen B. Metheny, pp. 52-69. University of Tennessee Press, Knoxville.

PULSIPHER, LYDIA

1994 The Landscapes and Ideational Roles of Caribbean Slave Gardens. In *The Archaeology of Garden and Field*, edited by Naomi Miller and Kathryn Gleason pp. 202-221. University of Pennsylvania Press, Philadelphia.

PULSIPHER, LYDIA AND CONRAD GOODWIN

1982 A Sugar and Boiling House at Galways: An Irish Sugar Plantation in Montserrat, W. I. *Post-Medieval Archaeology* 16:21-27.

REEVES, MATTHEW

1997 *"By Their Own Labor": Enslaved Africans' Survival Strategies on Two Jamaican Plantations.* PhD dissertation, Department of Anthropology, Syracuse University, Syracuse, NY. University Microfilms International, Ann Arbor, MI.

ROUGHLEY, THOMAS.

1823 *The Jamaican Planter's Guide.* Longman, Hurst, Rees, Orme and Brown, London.

SCHUYLER, ROBERT (EDITOR)
1980 *Archaeological Perspectives on Ethnicity in America: Afro-American and Asian American Culture History.* Baywood, Farmingdale, NY.

SCOTT, ELIZABETH (EDITOR)
1994 *Those of Little Note: Gender, Race, and Class in Historical Archaeology.* University of Arizona Press, Tucson.

SHACKEL, PAUL A.
1994 Town Plans and Everyday Material Culture: An Archaeology of Social Relations in Colonial Maryland's Capital Cities. In *Historical Archaeology of the Chesapeake,* edited by Paul A. Shackel and Barbara J. Little, pp. 85-100. Smithsonian Institution Press, Washington.
1996 *Culture Change and the New Technology: An Archaeology of the Early American Industrial Era.* Plenum, New York.

SHERIDAN, RICHARD B.
1974 *Sugar and Slavery: an Economic History of the British West Indies, 1623-1775.* Johns Hopkins University Press, Baltimore, MD.

STEWART, JOHN
1971 *An Account of Jamaica and its Inhabitants.* Books for Libraries Press, Freeport. Reprint of 1808 edition.

STINCHCOMBE, ARTHUR
1995 *Sugar Island Slavery in the Age of Enlightenment.* Princeton University Press, Princeton, NJ.

UPTON, DELL
1988 White and Black Landscapes in Eighteenth-Century Virginia. In *Material Life in America, 1600-1860,* edited by Robert B. St. George, pp. 357-369. Northeastern University Press, Boston, MA.
1992 The City as Material Culture. In *The Art and Mystery of Historical Archaeology,* edited by Anne Yentsch and Mary C. Beaudry, pp. 51-74. CRC Press, Boca Raton FL.

WALVIN, JAMES
1994 *Black Ivory: A History of Black Slavery.* Howard University Press, Washington.

WURST, LOUANN
1991 "Employees Must Be of Moral and Temperate Habits": Rural and Urban Elite Ideologies. In *The Archaeology of Inequality,* edited by Randall H. McGuire and Robert Paynter, pp. 125-149. Basil Blackwell, Oxford, England.

JAMES A. DELLE
DEPARTMENT OF ANTHROPOLOGY
FRANKLIN AND MARSHALL COLLEGE
LANCASTER, PA 17604

DEBORAH L. ROTMAN
MICHAEL S. NASSANEY

Class, Gender, and the Built Environment: Deriving Social Relations from Cultural Landscapes in Southwest Michigan

ABSTRACT

The houses, barns, and gardens that comprise cultural landscapes embody information about their makers because the
built environment actively serves to create, reproduce, and
transform social relations. Members of society use space
to reinforce and resist relations of power, authority, and
inequality by organizing the landscape to facilitate the
activities and movements of some individuals, while con-
currently constraining others. Historical investigations
indicate that the occupants of the village of Plainwell,
Michigan, have witnessed political, economic, and social
changes at the local, regional, and national levels since the
mid-19th century. Yet, archaeological investigation of the
Woodhams site (20AE852)—a residential homelot in
Plainwell—provides evidence for considerable continuity in
class and gender relations, despite transformations in
American society at these multiple scales of analysis.

Introduction

For more than a decade, historical archaeologists have considered cultural landscapes—the
articulation between the built environment and
the natural world—to be worthy of systematic
reconstruction, both conceptually and physically
(Leone 1984; Crumley and Marquardt 1987;
Kelso and Most 1990; Mrozowski 1991;
Patterson 1994:57–61; Paynter et al. 1994;
Nassaney and Paynter 1995; Rotman 1995;
Yamin and Metheny 1996). While initially the
domain of cultural geographers (e.g., Harvey
1973; Jackson 1984; Meinig 1979; Stilgoe 1982;
Cosgrove 1984), landscape studies have emerged
as a central concern in the field of historical
archaeology (Kelso and Most [1990]; Miller and
Gleason [1994]; and Yamin and Metheny [1996]
present a broad range of recent case studies).

Approaches to cultural landscapes are, as one
might expect, as varied as their advocates. Both
scientific and humanistic perspectives have been
useful in identifying and explaining change and
continuity in the built environment through interpretations of documentary sources and material
remains. For instance, landscape scientists represent a multidisciplinary group who tend to
emphasize the technical aspects of data collection
and analysis in their field, be it botany, pedol-
ogy, or palynology (e.g., Piperno 1988; Miller
and Gleason 1994). These specialists often provide the data upon which landscape reconstructions are based. More humanistic-oriented studies usually incorporate archaeological data with
period documents and/or oral history to derive
insights into landscapes from a "native" point of
view. Here the work of garden historians and
vernacular architectural historians immediately
comes to mind (e.g., Favretti and Favretti 1991;
Garrison 1991; Herman 1992).

The need for historically accurate landscape
reconstructions began at sites associated with
American elites where funding sources helped to
establish an "early connection between garden
archaeology and the preservation movement"
(Yentsch 1996:xxiv). The field has grown to
encompass the landscapes of people with limited
historical documentation, including "studies that
explore issues of gender, ethnicity, class, and
economic history (in everyday life) as they relate
to landscape function, alteration, and meaning"
(Yamin and Metheny 1996:xvi). Our study exemplifies this latter type of research by focusing
on nonelite people through funding support that
is not tied specifically to preservation (e.g.,
Reinke and Paynter 1984; Paynter et al. 1987;
Paynter et al. 1994; Hood 1996).

Landscapes were usually designed and created
to be seen and experienced. Accordingly, historical archaeologists often conceptualize landscapes as a medium of communication that symbolically expresses status or other social roles.
The size, shape, location, and condition of barns,
fences, gardens, and outbuildings encode messages to viewers about their makers and users.
As actively constructed features, these modifica-

tions may serve to legitimize authority (Mrozowski 1991:90), express religious ideology (Kryder-Reid 1996), or serve as political metaphors (Leone 1984).

Landscapes, and the studies on which they are based, may also vary according to their spatial scale. Trigger (1968), for example, addresses issues of scale in archaeological settlement patterns. At the macro- or regional scale, archaeologists have shown how spatial relationships became reconfigured in the Connecticut River valley of western Massachusetts as this periphery of the British world economic system developed more core-like characteristics of capital accumulation in the early 19th century (Paynter 1982). Community studies, for which there are fewer examples, may attempt to explore the meaning of spatial variation and change in the context of a village or small city (Lewis 1993; Hood 1996). The smallest or micro-scale of analysis examines the house, yard, and associated activity areas of the occupants. For nonelite groups, the archaeology of the homelot or homesite often excludes agricultural fields. Of course, elite households can be quite large, often exceeding the size of a small community in some cultural contexts. The point is that there is no single scale of analysis for the study of cultural landscapes because social relations are reproduced at multiple spatial scales.

In this study we chose to focus on the homelot to explore change and continuity in the activities and social roles associated with a succession of occupants beginning in the late 19th century. This paper serves to illustrate how recent investigations conducted under the auspices of the Southwest Michigan Historic Landscape Project can illuminate the social meaning of the built environment over the past 12 decades at a site in Plainwell, Michigan. We take a political-economic approach that views everyday cultural landscapes as a means to create, reinforce, and alter social relations. Our focus on historical landscapes represents a synthesis of scholarly interest in settlement patterns at the micro-scale and social organization associated with the development and reproduction of social stratification. By using the material world to codify social re-

lations, humans reproduce the structure of society and/or attempt to alter it. Domestic housing and associated exterior spaces are prominent arenas used for social reproduction, particularly along class and gender lines. The challenge for the landscape archaeologist is to design and operationalize a methodology for "the study of land use over time through a broad, intensive use of sources in a multidisciplinary and fully ethnographic enterprise" with a concern for both the generalities of the past and the peculiarities of the case at hand (Beaudry 1996:4).

Our interest in employing a landscape perspective in southwest Michigan began when the gardening activities of a 20th-century homeowner exposed an abandoned brick feature containing historic artifacts and we were invited to investigate it. During the course of investigations, we were forced to confront the meaning of rural and urban places; the case study shared characteristics of both but did not fit neatly into either category. Researchers have often understood rural and urban landscapes, and even lifestyles, in opposition (cf. Wurst 1993). Rural is characterized as agricultural, family-oriented, and egalitarian while urban represents the opposite—industrial, profit-motivated, and stratified. Because 19th-century properties in the region may embody aspects of both categories, any simple dichotomy is lacking. It seems more likely that rural and urban are not mutually exclusive but constitute poles of a continuum. The difficulty in distinguishing the two is particularly acute during the transition from agrarian to industrial capitalism, a process that began in 19th-century Michigan and continues to this day.

In attempting to characterize the site of our recent studies in Plainwell, Michigan, we have found some utility in the concept of "urban farmstead" (Stewart-Abernathy 1986). Yet, even this concept has limited interpretive potential for understanding changes in the organization of the built environment because landscape continuity and change may be shaped by broad social, political, and economic forces as well as the dynamics of class and gender. While researchers have often examined how the organization of space was used to reinforce and resist relationships of power, authority, and inequality (Spain 1992; Nassaney and Abel [1997]), the examination of landscapes to interpret social relations has seldom, if ever, been used in southwestern Michigan.

The purpose of this paper is to present a case study in the political economy of landscape. The case is used to evaluate the utility of the urban farmstead model as a means of mediating the difficulties associated with the rural-urban dichotomy. In addition, we underscore the idea that built environments are actively constituted to express social relations. Moreover, their materiality has a recursive quality that reinforces class and gender messages for their makers, users, and viewers. We begin by discussing some of the theoretical and methodological problems encountered in our landscape reconstruction efforts before presenting research strategies and some preliminary interpretations.

The Urban Farmstead Reconsidered

Defining "rural" and "urban" has been problematic in archaeological research (cf. Wurst [1993], [1995]). Part of the difficulty stems from the fact that many of the attributes once thought to be distinctly rural are also found in urban settings (Hahn and Prude 1985:9). Among historical archaeologists, Stewart-Abernathy (1986:6) notes that a "parallel exists between some of the activities carried out on a rural farmstead and some aspects of urban occupation."

This parallel is particularly apparent during the 19th century when agrarian life was becoming transformed for many Americans. During this period, many farm families produced agricultural goods for market exchange, crafted limited numbers of goods for consumption by farm residents, and tended to their daily needs of sanitation and trash disposal. The same was often true for urban households which lacked the services of supermarkets, wastewater systems, and garbage collectors. Thus, for Stewart-Abernathy (1986:6), the urban farmstead "represents in three dimension the result of a process through which the household in a nucleated settlement supplied many of its own needs . . . by grow(ing) some of its own food, feed(ing) and car(ing) for some of its own animals, acquir(ing) its own water through wells, dispos(ing) of its own organic and inorganic waste, and stor(ing) its own fuel for cooking and heating." This process should not be confused with suburbanization which also appeared in the 19th century. Suburbs represent the creation of residential space in proximity to a city while maintaining the rural surroundings of the country (Jackson 1985, cited in Slocum and Shern [1997:148]).

Because domestic and subsistence tasks at the urban farmstead were integrated simultaneously with a cash economy, the separation between rural and urban activities appears blurred. Moreover, "in small town America, the urban farmstead has never totally disappeared, although many of its elements have been stripped away by the extension of urban services, town ordinances, and the spread of the ideal of green lawns" (Stewart-Abernathy 1986:13).

The urban farmstead model brings into better focus some of the landscape changes observed at the Woodhams site (20AE852) in historic southwest Michigan. For example, there are five factors which can account for the abandonment of farmstead elements on the landscape (Stewart-Abernathy 1986:12–13). The first is infilling, whereby larger land holdings are divided into smaller parcels to permit the building of additional houses. Second is the development of municipal services. As public utilities such as water and sewer become available, the need for decentralized facilities (e.g., recharge basins and privies) was eliminated. The third factor is zoning. Building codes and city ordinances often prohibited chickens and other livestock on the urban farmstead to foster sanitary conditions and avoid public nuisance. Transportation improvements, the fourth factor, led to the elimination of the horse and other associated landscape features such as barns. Finally, innovations in the transportation, storage, and packaging of foods directly affected, and often replaced, food production at the property.

These factors contributed to additive, subtractive, and substitutive modifications over time, as Stewart-Abernathy (1986) predicts. Additive adjustments may include the construction of new landscape features, such as the addition of a kitchen ell or bathroom wing to the house. Subtractive adjustments lead to the removal or abandonment of landscape elements. Privies or other obsolete waste disposal systems were often abandoned and/or eliminated once they were no longer needed. Finally, the replacement of one building with another is a substitutive adjustment. Barns were sometimes replaced by garages as automobiles increased in popularity or as agricultural activities declined in importance.

In sum, the urban farmstead model is a useful heuristic device for deconstructing the rural-urban dichotomy by identifying similarities between activities carried out in both rural and urban settings during the 19th century. Landscape changes, however, are not merely adaptations to the external world (e.g., zoning ordinances, property tax policies). The organization of the built environment has active and recursive qualities designed to create, reinforce, and transform social relations. Nevertheless, social dy-

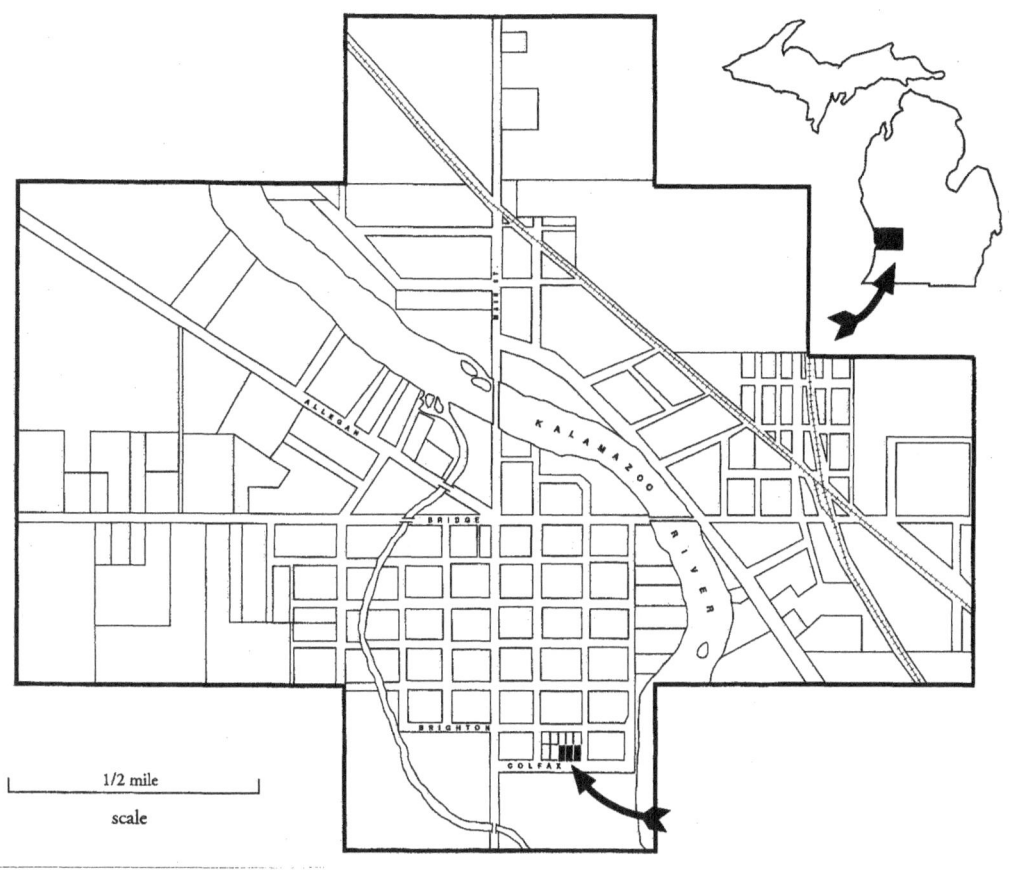

FIGURE 1. The first map of the incorporated village of Plainville, Gun Plain Township, Allegan County, Michigan (after Titus 1873).

namics are contingent upon local, regional, and national influences leading to outcomes of various forms which may be expressed in the changing organization of space at multiple scales from the homelot to the region.

Plainwell, Michigan, in Historical Context

Recent archaeological and historical investigations have been conducted at the site of an "urban farmstead" in Plainwell, Michigan, better to understand late 19th- and early 20th-century life in a small, nucleated midwestern village (Figure 1). Table 1 briefly summarizes the history of some significant events associated with the town and the homelot of our focus.

Early Euroamerican settlement in the area, first known as Gun Plain Township, began in the 1830s (Ensign 1880:218). Many of the early settlers to the region were first-generation immigrants from Britain (Ensign 1880:34), while others were restless New York and Connecticut Yankees (cf. Gray 1996). These early settlers were described as generally being of two groups, either "men with more or less capital, who erected mills and went into lumbering, or poor, who purchased 40 to 60 acres from the government" (Ensign 1880:35). These observations are supported by census data which show significant differences in the value of real estate owned by men of comparable age in Gun Plain Township in 1850 (U.S. Bureau of the Census 1850). As was frequently the case, economic conditions may have motivated migration. The wealthy may have wanted to acquire additional wealth, while those of lesser means may have sought new financial opportunities or the American dream of owning a farm. Mascia (1996:151), for example, addresses social mobility and the "agricultural ladder." Thus, disparities in wealth marked Plainwell from the outset and eventually came to represent distinct social classes.

The Township remained sparsely populated until the early 1850s when two plank toll roads were constructed that intersected at the village, then known as "the Junction" (Weir and York 1990:12). This connection linked the town to a broader network of markets which led to pro-

found economic and social changes. Commercial developments soon emerged to supply the needs of this transportation center. The construction of a mill race across a bend in the Kalamazoo River in 1856 spawned further industrial growth (Figure 1). The mill race allowed industry, notably flour and paper mills, to capitalize on the river's steep gradient. In 1869 the town was officially incorporated and by 1870 the population had reached 1035, a five-fold increase from the previous decade (Titus 1873:11; Weir and York 1990:20).

The arrival of the Lake Shore & Michigan Southern Railroad and the Grand Rapids/Indiana Line stimulated further settlement and increased industry in the area. After 1870, Plainwell experienced a significant economic boom made possible by the fast and inexpensive shipment of agricultural products and manufactured goods to outlying areas by rail (Weir and York 1990:25). In addition to improved transportation networks, other factors encouraged the settlement of southern lower Michigan. For instance, the free land offered in conjunction with the Homestead Act of 1862 was a powerful incentive for New England and Mid-Atlantic residents to push westward (Bailey and Kennedy 1983:419).

The manufacturing revolution of the post-Civil War years influenced social as well as economic dimensions of Michigan life. In addition to generating surplus capital, industrialization produced "a leisure class committed to the conspicuous consumption of their new riches . . . seen in the lavishly ornate residential architecture of the wealthy, in the opera houses built in many towns, and in the development of tourism" (Kern 1977:44). Industrialization enabled residents of Plainwell who possessed financial resources upon their arrival to accumulate additional wealth. As capital became increasingly concentrated in the hands of some individuals—such as the factory owners—class distinctions became even more marked and expressed materially. According to William Woodhams, a wealthy early settler who originally owned the homelot in this study, class differences in Plainwell were becoming exacerbated in the latter part of the 19th century. In an article for *The Plainwell Enterprise*, he wrote:

Perspectives from *Historical Archaeology*

"Not that I would claim there is less of a kindly feeling in this day of grace 1886 than forty years ago, but difference of circumstance and the greater density of mankind has had its *natural affect* of setting (members of the community) off in cliques or sets [emphasis added]" (Woodhams 1886). As a member of Plainwell's upper class in the 19th century, Woodhams likely embraced some tenets of Social Darwinism. His observation serves not only to demonstrate the growth of a wealthy elite, but also to illustrate how the elite legitimized emerging class differences by perceiving them as "natural" (e.g., Leone 1984).

Although economic conditions were favorable at the turn of the century, Michigan residents faced the ills of urbanization and industrialization such as overcrowding and the exploitation of its workers with long days and low wages, particularly for women and children. At the state level, people attempted to solve social problems through the political process. During the Progressive Era (ca. 1890–1920), for instance, the state constitution was revised and new legislation was passed to achieve social reforms and regulate industry (Kern 1977:43).

The rights and interests of women received special attention at the turn of the century. Industrialization, financial necessity, and changing ideas about women's roles in society attracted women into the work force. Women laborers "were sucked into the clanging mechanism of factory production . . . typically toil(ing) six days, earning a pittance for dreary stints of twelve or thirteen hours" (Bailey and Kennedy 1983:280). Likewise, "women's wages for skilled and unskilled labor in Michigan . . . averaged 56 percent of the pay which men received for comparable work" (Kern 1977:48). One Progressive Era legislative act (1911) terminated the power of husbands to retain the earnings of their wives. This measure gave women legal control of their own labor as a salable resource.

World Wars I and II brought women many new agricultural and industrial jobs that had previously been reserved for men. The military efforts required the cooperation of all citizens, regardless of gender, class, or race. Women were encouraged to do their part by entering industry and agriculture, spurred by such slogans as "Labor Will Win the War" and "A Woman's Place Is in the War" (Bailey and Kennedy 1983:671). Women's labor was particularly important during the second global conflict when women were called upon to participate in even the heaviest industries—building tanks, ships, and airplanes. Once the war ended, however, many women wanted to continue working and "thus touched off a revolution in the roles of women in American society" (Bailey and Kennedy 1983:799).

There have been significant changes in class and gender ideals at the local, regional, state, and national levels during the history of Plainwell; however, residents differentially participated in and were influenced by these social changes. The landscape of an urban farmstead on the village periphery, for example, exhibits significant continuity in the midst of economic and social change, as this analysis will show.

Methodology

The Italianate-style house (Figure 2) on a corner lot in Plainwell, Michigan, presents a useful case study for analysis because it possesses landscape features that provide information about the history of landuse patterns which, in turn, can be linked to social relations. Investigations began

FIGURE 2. The ca. 1879 Italianate-style house, taken ca. 1938. (Courtesy of the Gerald Brown family.)

TABLE 1
SIGNIFICANT EVENTS ASSOCIATED WITH THE WOODHAMS SITE (20AE852)

Date	Event	Information Source
1830s	First settlement in Gun Plain Township	Ensign (1880:218)
1869	Village of Plainwell incorporated	Weir and York (1990:20)
1872	William Woodhams surveyed several blocks of real estate on the southern periphery of the village of Plainwell	Abstract of Title
1878	Joseph W. Hicks purchased a three-parcel homelot in Woodhams' Third Addition	Abstract of Title
1879	House and barn built on lots 170–171 on periphery of village	Tax Assessment Rolls
1879	Hicks sold the homelot to Asael and Carrie Mapes	Abstract of Title
1883	Mapes sold the homelot to Amos Wheeler	Abstract of Title
1887	Amos Wheeler died	Abstract of Title; Probate Records
1907	Heirs of Wheeler sold the homelot to Myron and Eliza Briggs	Abstract of Title
1908	Briggs sold the homelot to Albert Thorpe	Abstract of Title
1908	Thorpe sold the homelot to Ira D. Middaugh	Abstract of Title
1908–1913	Homelot may have served as rental property	The Plainwell Enterprise (12/06/1908, 01/13/1909, 05/08/1913)
1913	Middaugh sold the homelot to Albert H. Jackson	Abstract of Title
1913–1935	Homelot may have served as rental property	The Plainwell Enterprise (07/11/1916, 10/03/1916, 04/01/1921, 05/02/1922)
1915	Municipal water arrived in Plainwell	Sandy Stamm (1994, pers. comm.)
ca. 1920	Albert H. Jackson died	Abstract of Title
1920s	Coal slag driveway covered with sand and gravel	Archaeological record
1935	Heirs of Jackson sold the homelot to Arthur Brown	Abstract of Title
late 1930s	Recharge basin was abandoned, front porch was added	Brown family (1995, pers. comm.)
1941	Arthur Brown sold the homelot to his son, Gerald Brown	Abstract of Title
1954	Kitchen wing was added to the house	Brown family (1995, pers. comm.)
Late 1950s	Bedroom wing was enlarged	Brown family (1995, pers. comm.)
1957	Gerald Brown died, widow Isabell Brown is heir	Abstract of Title; Brown family (1995, pers. comm.)
1958	Isabell Brown sold lot 169 to Gael Marvin	Abstract of Title
1958	Barn was razed and the garage built	Brown family (1995, pers. comm.)
1962	Brown sold the remaining homelot to Gracie Larson	Abstract of Title
Mid-1960s	Fireplace was added	Brown family (1995, pers. comm.)
Late 1980s	Gracie Larson died	Lyden family (1994, pers. comm.)
1990	Heirs of Larson sold the homelot to Patrick and Anita Lyden	Lyden family (1994, pers. comm.); Tax Assessment Rolls

by searching and examining five document groups as suggested by Mascia (1996:154) with varying degrees of success. These data sources include: 1) primary government and legal documents (vital records, census records, tax records, probate records, maps); 2) family or farm documents (personal diaries, farm and/or household accounts, letters, and specific materials unique to the farm); 3) newspapers and journals; 4) photographic evidence; and 5) any relevant secondary documentary sources (agricultural, town, and family histories).

Primary government and legal documents (Group 1) were the most useful resources in this study (Table 1). Tax rolls, the Abstract of Title for the property, and land deeds were consulted to identify the economic status of individual residents and the choices they made in their expenditures associated with landscape changes. Census records and tax rolls were utilized to determine occupations of residents and household sizes for each period of household occupancy. According to these documents, the residents of this property were primarily farmers, skilled

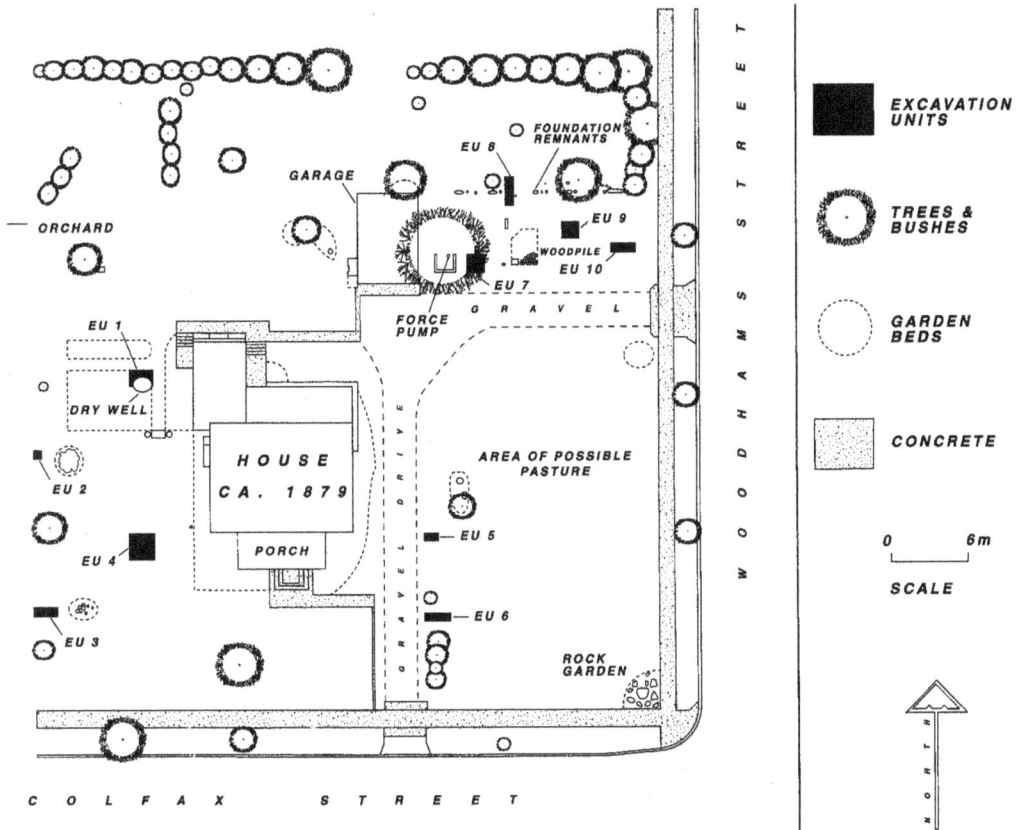

FIGURE 3. Plan view of lots 170 and 171 at the Woodhams site (20AE852) in Plainville, Michigan, showing the locations of excavation units (EU) and important landscape features.

members of the working class (e.g., pipe fitter), and lower paid professionals (e.g., teacher, social worker) with roughly equivalent incomes. Census data and tax rolls provided the most valuable details regarding economic status (Table 2). This information is lacking for some individuals due, in part, to the destruction of the 1890 federal census in a fire. Probate records were also consulted. However, these documents were only marginally useful. These records were not available for many of the landowners, perhaps because their estates were not settled in Allegan County, Michigan. A series of historic maps (Titus 1873; Kace 1895; Ogle 1913) were examined to observe the spatial organization of the village and the way in which it developed, for example, the emergence of economically homogeneous neighborhoods.

Family and farm documents (Group 2) were not available for this study. However, interviews with current and past residents provided oral accounts regarding the history of the homelot that were particularly useful in understanding periods of change and continuity in landuse, especially after the Depression.

Newspapers and journals (Group 3) provided only limited information about two property owners. Both of these individuals, Ira D. Middaugh and Albert H. Jackson, appear to have been businessmen and were involved in multiple real estate transactions between 1908 and 1935. The homelot perhaps served as a rental property during this period.

Photographic (Group 4) and architectural evidence was also obtained to identify additions to the house as well as how landscape features in the yard may have changed over time. The earliest photographs provided perspectives of the property as it appeared beginning in the 1930s. A more rigorous architectural survey could have been conducted, though we did examine the house interior and exterior with the help of Peter Schmitt, a historian at Western Michigan University with expertise in historic preservation, architecture, and local building styles.

Local and regional histories (Group 5) aided the understanding of the broader social contexts associated with the transformations that occurred in Plainwell as the area became increasingly industrial and populated. This category was supplemented by additional oral accounts regarding the social relations and economic pursuits of the site's residents.

Aside from public records, scant documentary evidence regarding specific occupants was available for the Woodhams site. The paucity of information is likely linked to the lower socioeconomic status of these individuals. The absence of written documentation about these residents in part motivated the archaeological efforts. Archaeological investigations were conducted to assist in chronological placement of landscape features and to elucidate how the organization of the landscape reproduced socioeconomic status and gender roles. While subsurface excavations were concentrated on a circular configuration of

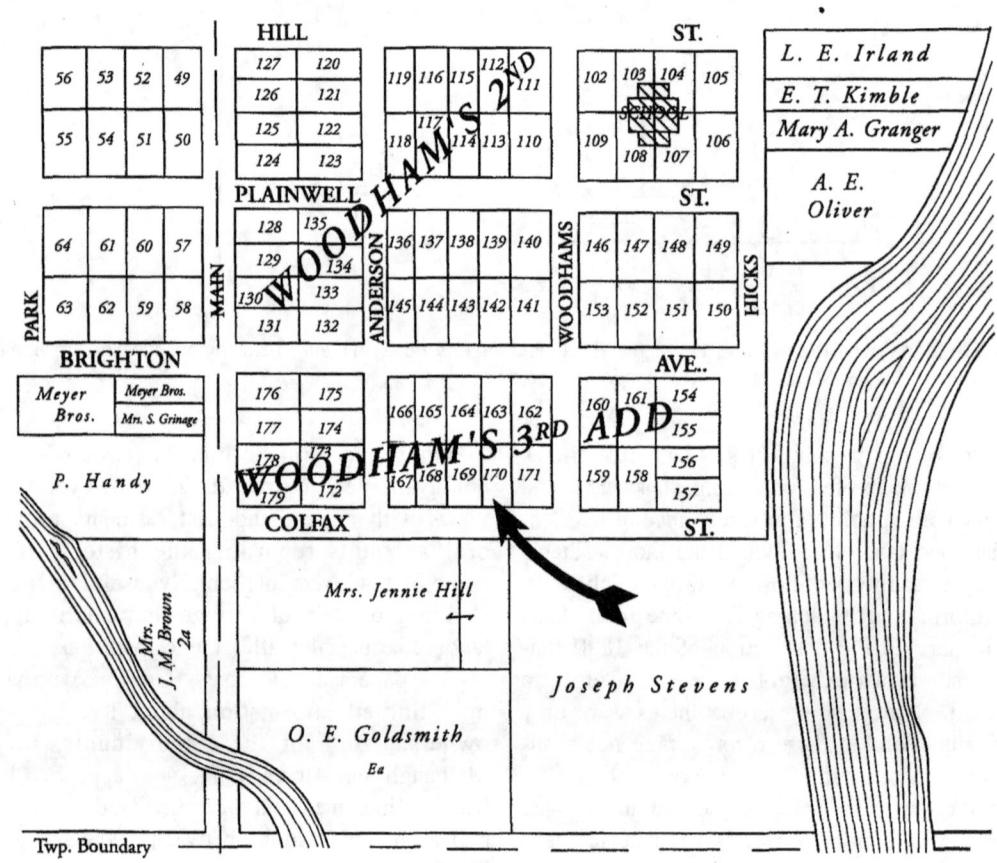

FIGURE 4. Map of Woodhams's third addition to the city of Plainwell, showing lots 169–171 (after Ogle 1913).

Perspectives from *Historical Archaeology*

bricks in the garden (excavation unit 1), the foundations of an abandoned outbuilding (excavation units 7–10), and a stone wall feature along the driveway (excavation units 5–6) (Figure 3), other material, and architectural evidence is also implicated in this analysis.

Interpreting the Material Expressions of Class and Gender: The House

In 1879 an Italianate-style home was constructed on a three-lot (169, 170, 171) parcel of land on the southern periphery of the village of Plainwell (Figures 1, 4). The house was situated within "Woodham's 3rd Addition," a portion of William H. Woodhams's farm acquired by the village for the purpose of subdivision (Ensign 1880:234). Although the house possesses the classic cube shape of the Italianate style (Figure 2), it lacked the elements which characterize an elite, single family dwelling of the late 19th century such as a fireplace, a tall floor-to-ceiling height ratio, and possibly decorative exterior brackets. These characteristic features were deemed essential by housing reformers of this era in creating a proper domestic residence. The environment that surrounded children, for example, was believed to be crucial in personality development. Housing crusaders were certain that the "morals, civilization, and refinement of the nation . . . depended on the construction of a proper domestic residence" (Clark 1988:539). If exterior brackets were initially present on the house, by the 1930s these architectural details were absent suggesting that they had been removed possibly due to deterioration. The current fireplace in the house is a relatively new addition dating to the 1960s.

Tax records, land deeds, and newspaper accounts indicate that the house was probably consistently owned and/or occupied by families of modest economic means. Former residents of the property characterized the neighborhood as being "lower-middle class" (Brown family 1995, pers. comm.). Furthermore, it appears that the house may have functioned as a rental property for nearly three decades, if not longer. According to *The Plainwell Enterprise*, the landowners

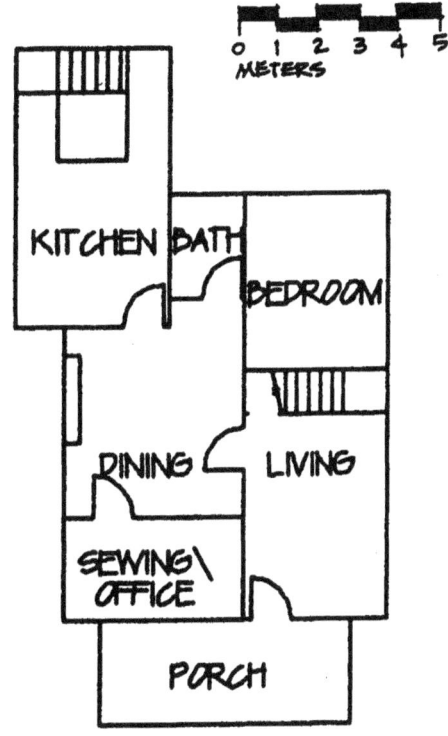

FIGURE 5. Present-day architectural plan of the Italianate house (first floor), showing room functions.

between 1908 and 1935 were involved in multiple real estate sales during this time, so the property may have been a financial investment rather than a primary residence for these individuals.

Therefore, the absence of classic Italianate features on the house in Plainwell appears to indicate that the builders of the home either did not possess the economic means necessary or the desire to create a truly proper domestic residence. Alternatively, if the house was a speculative development constructed for sale or rent, it may reflect the developer's perception of an appropriate residence for a lower income family or tenant. In any case, the emulation of some elements of the Italianate style sends a clear social message that the residents of the property were morally upright, despite their inability to project the architectural ideal.

Structural changes to the house are also of potential interest to landscape archaeologists because the interior and exterior design of dwellings are related to the size and economic status of the resident social groups (Glassie 1975; Johnson 1993; Barber 1994:75). There is no evidence of any major alterations between 1879 and the mid-1930s. In the late 1930s, a front porch was added to the house (Table 1) by the new residents (Brown family 1995, pers. comm.). The materials used for this addition imply an earlier date of construction, however. For example, the foundation of the porch is made of beveled cement blocks and the double-hung windows are three-over-one (Figure 2); such architectural features were popular construction styles prior to 1937 (ca. 1910–1920) (Peter Schmitt 1994, pers. comm.). The lumber, windows, and concrete blocks may have been recycled from another house as a means to defray the cost of building materials. Isabell Brown (1995, pers. comm.) noted that her husband made these changes to the house. New construction with old materials by a nonprofessional is consistent with choices made by homeowners of limited economic means.

There were other modifications to the house as well. A kitchen wing, dated to 1954 by a cement inscription and independently confirmed by Peter Schmitt (1994, pers. comm.), was added by the landowner. The Abstract of Title indicates that bank loans to the Browns in September 1953 ($3,000) and January 1955 ($4,100) coincide with the construction of a new kitchen and the expansion of the first floor bedroom.

Household space is a dimension of the built environment that has implications for social relations as revealed by a brief overview of spatial design (Yentsch 1991; Spain 1992;McMurry 1997). Beginning with Georgian-style architecture in the early 18th century, domestic houses were usually partitioned into separate private and public spheres, which were linked to gender but not exclusively controlled by either sex. For example, throughout the 19th century, kitchens were located at the rear of the house where women performed domestic activities, whereas the parlor was used for both masculine and public entertaining and was, therefore, placed at the front of the house (Spain 1992). However,

FIGURE 6. The late 19th-century barn at the Woodhams site, taken ca. 1950. (Courtesy of the Gerald Brown family.)

women's social gatherings, such as teas and clubs, as well as marriages and baptisms might also be held in the parlor (Nylander 1994:241). The parlor could serve as both a masculine and public space and was, therefore, a logical location for these events. Thus, women's social functions illustrate how the separation of masculine and feminine, and hence public and private, space is not always rigid and how gender roles may differ in theory and practice.

The home in Plainwell has a simplified floor plan with few specialized rooms, e.g., no parlor (Figure 5). Single-purpose, gender-specific spaces are combined with multipurpose, sexually-integrated rooms, such as the living room (Spain 1992:127). The sexual integration of many household spaces is consistent with the complementary nature of gender relations at the property, as well as the economic status of the occupants, which points to the intersection between class and gender (Stine 1992).

Women's status is inversely proportional to their role in the physical maintenance of the home (Ember 1983). Ember (1983:304) contends that "as women are more and more preoccupied in the domestic sphere, . . . men consolidate their relationships with others in the society and with those outside the society, and women's overall status declines." As a result, women have become associated with interior or private space while men are affiliated with exterior, or public, space. The separation of domestic and public domains is an important one. Rosaldo

Perspectives from *Historical Archaeology*

(1974) first argued that rigid distinctions of this nature devalued and disempowered private spheres and the women with whom they were associated.

Cross-cultural evidence has shown that the social roles of men and women are often defined in relationship not only to one another, but also in relationship to productive and reproductive activities (Brydon and Chant 1989). For example, women who work in productive activities outside of the home have a more active role in family decision making than women who do not. Boserup (1970) was pivotal in recognizing that women's status in society is linked to their productive roles. She concluded that women's status is higher when their involvement in production is greater. Defining production and reproduction, however, can be challenging; the former cannot simply be designated as remunerated work (Brydon and Chant 1989). Many activities, such as agriculture and household tasks, are not remunerated but certainly contribute to production, e.g., canning foods. Therefore, Brydon and Chant (1989:70) encourage scholars to "include subsistence production in 'work,' and recognize too, that in many cases, what is usually regarded as reproductive labor—cooking, cleaning, and child care, water and fuel collection—can have value in a productive sense."

In nonelite households, the survival of the family unit is dependent upon the labor of every member, whereas the contribution of women to production in wealthy households is less critical for economic stability. This assumption has implications for social relations. With an increase in male participation in wage labor, women often become separated from production and consequently their status declines. Spatially, this decline is reinforced by the separation of public and private domains. Socioeconomic sta-

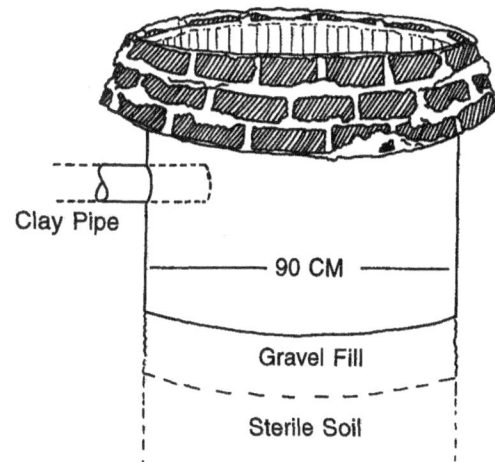

FIGURE 8. Scale drawing of the dry well exposed in excavation unit 1 at the Woodhams site.

tus and gender relations are closely linked— lower socioeconomic status lends itself to increased dependence upon women for household production, which in turn results in higher status for women. Therefore, among working class and lower paid professionals, gender roles may be hierarchical, but complementary (Brydon and Chant 1989:151–152). These social relationships are also expressed in other aspects of the landscape beyond the domestic structure.

Other Landscape Features

What might the sexual division of labor look like on an urban farmstead during the late 19th and early 20th centuries? According to Stewart-Abernathy (1992), men and teenage boys were largely responsible for the care of the hogs, mules, and horses as well as tending to the grain, hay, and firewood. Meanwhile, women and teenage girls were charged with raising the chickens, vegetables, and fruit, and performing dairying activities, such as milking cows and making butter. Oral accounts indicate that women utilized a barn at the Plainwell property to raise chickens for household consumption and limited sale to the neighbors (Brown family 1995, pers. comm.). The need for food production at the household level is consistent with the economic status of the occupants. Raising

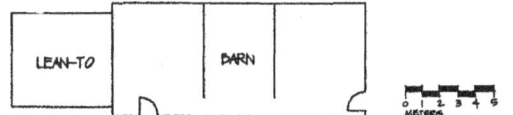

FIGURE 7. Floor plan of the late 19th-century barn based on photographic and archaeological evidence.

chickens or other livestock for food was more cost effective for the residents than purchasing eggs and poultry at a market. By contributing to the domestic economy in this way, women at the property contributed to a complementary labor arrangement and consequently had a relatively high status vis-à-vis men.

An important component of the built environment of urban farmsteads is the barn. The dry stone foundation of a barn is still visible in places at the ground surface in the northeast corner of the homelot in lot 171 (Figures 3, 6). In addition to supporting the barn, this lot may have been used to pasture a horse and possibly other animals. The barn measures 6 x 14 m (20 x 46 ft.) and is divided into three roughly equal-sized bays (Figure 7). The description of a barn first appears in the Abstract of Title in a transaction dating December 1908. The barn is probably a late 19th-century construction since its foundation is similar to that of another barn in the neighborhood which is also associated with an Italianate-style house. The structure was badly deteriorated and subsequently razed in 1958, when it was replaced by a garage (Isabell Brown 1995, pers. comm.). The broad range of artifacts associated with the foundation recovered from excavation units 7–10 include both agricultural (e.g., a glass egg used to encourage hens to roost) and domestic (e.g., canning jars, ceramics) objects that testify to the structure's variable functions (Rotman 1995:Appendix C).

Both men and women used the barn, but for different productive tasks. While the women raised chickens in the lean-to section closest to the house (Figure 7), other areas within the structure were used by men for agriculture, storage, and wood-working activities. Thus, the barn also serves to illustrate that gender-specific, as well as sexually-integrated, spaces existed beyond the walls of the domestic residence.

Gardens and orchards are other important loci of production. A rather substantial garden has existed at the Plainwell property—west of the house, near the kitchen—for more than 60 years and a small orchard occupied lot 169 until the mid-20th century (Figure 3). Like the house and barn, the garden is also a sexually-integrated

space. Although Stewart-Abernathy (1992) suggested that women took care of the vegetable gardens and fruit trees, it appears that the garden was not a wholly feminine space at this site. According to oral accounts, gardening activities at the property were undertaken primarily by men during the 1930s–1950s, though women and children assisted in the growing and processing of produce. In more recent years, the garden has become predominantly the activity of the female resident owner, but again, her husband and children are not expressly prohibited from gardening activities. It appears that the organization of the landscape exhibits a broad separation of spaces relative to the house. Whereas activities associated with animals and the public sphere occur to the east, food production and other domestic tasks took place in the more private areas west of the house (Figure 3).

An interesting landscape feature exposed in the garden area was a circular configuration of bricks that first appeared immediately below the modern ground surface in excavation unit 1 (Figures 3, 8). The exterior of this feature consisted of an expanding rim of bricks three tiers high secured with cement. The interior rim was also sealed with a thin cement coating. It appears that the hole was dug and then a layer of cement was smeared along the inside to prevent the soils from collapsing. A 4-in. clay tile pipe projects into the basin at the base of the brick casing from the direction of the house. These construction details indicate that the feature was a recharge basin or dry well that received the "gray water" generated from laundering, bathing, and washing dishes inside the kitchen. The basin would have provided a temporary catchment to facilitate water seepage into the ground.

This feature appears to be contemporaneous with the construction of the house (1879). The use of cement in the basin's manufacture is consistent with a late-19th century date of construction when cement became widely used (Peter Schmitt 1994, pers. comm.). Furthermore, the artifacts recovered from inside the feature range in age from the mid-19th century to the 1930s. These items include construction materials, such as bricks and nails, glass fruit jars and medicine bottles, assorted ceramics, butchered animal bones, and buckles, to name just a few artifact categories (Rotman 1995:Appendix C). Among the chronologically-sensitive ceramics are the types decorated with green transfer printing, flow blue transfer printing, and decalcomania (Majewski and O'Brien 1987).

Stratigraphic analysis of these artifact classes suggests that the contents of the well likely represent a secondary depositional event that took place over a relatively short period of time. Fragments of individual ceramic vessels that were later conjoined were recovered from multiple levels and fully-machined glass bottles appear in most levels. Abandoned objects that had little utility or perhaps ones belonging to earlier occupants were likely collected from another storage or disposal area on the property, such as the barn or basement, and dumped into the feature. This event appears to correspond with the shift from tenancy to owner occupation in the late 1930s.

The objects recovered from this feature support our assessment of the socioeconomic status of the site occupants during the late 19th through early 20th centuries, though their context remains problematic and a larger sample from other locations—e.g., privy, sheet midden—would strengthen this inference. The ceramics are predominantly undecorated whitewares and utilitarian ironstones that were widely available and easily accessible varieties in the period

TABLE 2
PROPERTY OWNERS AND OCCUPANTS AT THE WOODHAMS SITE, CA. 1845–PRESENT

Owner[1]	Occupation[2]	Dates of Ownership[1]	Occupancy[1,2,3]
William H. Woodhams	Farmer	ca. 1845–1872	Undeveloped (agricultural?) land
Village of Plainwell	—	1872–1878	Undeveloped land
Joseph W. Hicks	Banker	1878–1879	Occupants unknown
Asael and Carrie Mapes	RR Worker	1879–1883	Resided w/ three children
Amos & Fannie Wheeler	Laborer	1883–1887	Resided w/ two children
Clark & Mary Wheeler	unknown	1887–1898	Acquired ownership of the property following their father's death. Presumably Amos Wheeler's widow and children remained at the property.
Mary Wheeler	unknown	1898–1907	Clark sold his interest in the property to his sister, Mary. Presumably, Mary resided at the property. May have sold the property when she married or mother died.
Myron & Eliza Briggs	unknown	1907–1908	Unknown if the Briggs had children or resided at the property.
Albert & Lillie Thorpe	unknown	1908–1908	Unknown if the Thorpes had children or resided at the property.
Ira D. Middaugh	Businessman?	1908–1913	Homelot was rental property. Occupants unknown.
Albert H. Jackson	Businessman?	1913–1935	Homelot was rental property. Occupants unknown.
Arthur & Alta Brown	Laborer	1935–194_	Homelot was occupied by the Brown's son, Gerald, his wife, and three children.
Gerald & Isabell Brown	Pipefitter	1941–1957	Resided with three children.
Isabell Brown	Keeps house	1957–1962	Children are grown at the time of their father's death. Mrs. Brown resides alone.
Gracie Larsen	Keeps house	1962–1990	Resided alone until her death in the late 1980s.
Patrick & Anita Lyden	Teacher/Social Worker	1990–present	Reside with two children.

[1] Abstract of Title
[2] U.S. Bureau of Census records
[3] Oral accounts and tax assessments

(Miller 1980). Undecorated ceramics occur twice as frequently as the more expensive transfer printed types. At this point we are uncertain about how the occupants of the house were using their disposable income during the late 19th and early 20th centuries. In some cases, tenancy in southwest Michigan was as much a choice as an economic necessity (John Houdek 1997, pers. comm.). Since the occupants placed little emphasis on expressing their status by making modifications to a landscape that they did not own, they may have chosen to participate in and embrace consumer culture at a level that would seemingly belie their status as tenants. Further work is needed to explore how the artifactual remains of the pre-1940 period inform about class and gender relations at the site.

The timing of the depositional event, combined with oral accounts, suggests that the recharge basin continued in use until the late 1930s, more than two decades after the arrival of municipal services, i.e., city sewer and water, into the more affluent neighborhoods. The persistence of this landscape feature within a nucleated settlement indicates that this property was among the last in the community to be connected to centralized waste water disposal, further evidence of the socioeconomic status of the site occupants.

Archaeological investigation also exposed a row of cobbles along the eastern edge of the driveway in excavation units 5 and 6 (Figure 3). These cobbles were carefully arranged in a single layer to delineate the edge of a previous driveway surface. At approximately 25 cm below the current ground surface, there is a 4-cm-thick layer of coal slag and ashes which feathers out beneath the cobblestones. Above this slag is another driveway surface of sand and coarse gravel. During the late 19th and early 20th centuries, the driveway was covered with coal slag that could have been produced in large quantities by a coal burning stove within the house. Photographic evidence from the 1930s indicates that the clinker surface was covered over with gravel and sand—other relatively inexpensive and easily accessible materials. Today, gravel driveways predominate in this neighborhood; most home owners choose not to allocate their limited resources to crushed stone, asphalt, or some other costly surface treatment. More elaborate brick or asphalt drives serve as conspicuous displays of wealth primarily in the more expensive West Bridge Street area, located one-half mile to the northwest. Italianate-style homes in this elite neighborhood also possess the elements—height, ornamentation, and fireplace—once deemed necessary for a proper domestic residence.

When this analysis is extended into the present, it is interesting to note how the past constrains current activities. It is often too difficult or too costly to make major changes to the landscape and, therefore, landowners "are more likely to tinker with the homelot than to radically alter it" (Paynter et al. 1987:10). This was clearly demonstrated when the current landowners brought in several truckloads of gravel to refurbish the existing driveway.

The material evidence at this residential homelot suggests that the house was consistently owned and/or occupied by working-class or lower paid professional families. While the residents associated with various occupations, such as pipe fitter vs. teacher, may have held different values, each household made only modest alterations to the landscape and used inexpensive or recycled materials for these changes. Tenants in particular were unlikely to expend any of their disposable wealth on the physical appearance of the property (Mascia 1996). The presence of the barn indicates that families also engaged in subsistence pursuits to meet their dietary needs, an interpretation collaborated by oral accounts. The continuity seen at the homelot not only expresses the economic standing of the residents but also signals stability in the social roles of men and women.

The sharing of landscape spaces associated with the house, barn, and garden is an expression of the complementary nature of gender relations at the property and is consistent with nonelite production needs. Even the location of a force pump—in proximity to both male and female spaces—suggests egalitarian-like relationships between men and women (Figure 3). Borish (1995:90) further treats the importance of a convenient source of water for women's farm work.

Persistence of Rural Elements on the Urban Landscape

Although the homelot in Plainwell is located in a nucleated village, it was also the site of many "rural" activities making it amenable to analysis using the urban farmstead model developed by Stewart-Abernathy (1986:6). By the 1930s and possibly beginning as early as 1879, the residents of the property grew their own vegetables in a garden and fruit in a small orchard. They raised chickens for meat as well as for eggs, and likely kept a horse on site for transportation purposes. A deep well was driven for a force pump when the house was built to provide water for both human and animal consumption. Likewise, organic and inorganic waste was disposed of via composting and dumping along the Kalamazoo River a block and a half to the east (Figure 4). Moreover, all of these activities occurred concurrent with wage labor outside the home.

Changes in the landscape and the persistence of rural activities on the urban farmstead can result from both internal and external stimuli of a social, political, and economic nature. One of the factors that can account for abandonment of farmstead elements on the urban landscape is infilling, although class and gender relations are also implicated (e.g., infilling seldom occurred in elite neighborhoods). Woodham's sale of the original homelots (169, 170, and 171) in his second and third addition was itself the result of subdivision (Figure 4). Further subdivision occurred in 1959 when the lot (169) which supported the orchard was sold. The decision to sell this lot is more complicated than the simple desire to permit the building of additional homes in the neighborhood. Isabell Brown (1995, pers. comm.) sold this parcel on 26 June 1959, a year and a half after her husband died, "because she no longer needed all that land." The land requirements for the site occupants had changed dramatically since the late 1930s; children had grown to adulthood and moved out on their own

and the landowner became a widow. As families go through life cycles, their needs change. Additionally, as a widow, Isabell Brown had more control over decision-making, although her financial security may have decreased.

Although it is not known for certain precisely what her personal circumstances entailed, there were likely financial motivations for selling lot 169. As an older woman and a pipe fitter's widow, she may have needed to sell part of the homelot to generate additional income. Whatever the reason, this decision was clearly more than a matter of neighborhood development. Rather, it was linked to social and, perhaps, economic issues. Class and gender considerations, such as her status as a widow of modest income, were not without influence. A widower may have chosen to retain all of the property at the time of his wife's death, particularly if he had been the primary wage earner in the household and his financial status had remained relatively secure.

The development of municipal services can also account for the abandonment of rural elements on an urban farmstead, though it may not account for their persistence. For example, the arrival of city water and/or sewer to some residents of Plainwell around 1915 (Table 1) apparently did not result in the immediate abandonment of landscape features throughout the community. The force water pump located near the barn continued to be used as an outdoor source of drinking water into the 1960s, long after city water became available (Brown family 1995, pers. comm.).

The abandonment of farmstead elements can also be attributed to zoning. For instance, the Browns kept chickens at the property for poultry and egg production until the early 1940s. Decisions surrounding animal maintenance may have been related only marginally to compliance with local ordinances, given the depressed economic conditions of the 1930s which exacerbated the financial situation of lower income families. Poultry products would have served as a valuable dietary supplement, if not staple, during this period, whereas it may have been unnecessary for the family to maintain chickens by the end of the Depression. Similarly, livestock ordinances may have been suspended during this time of economic crisis, only to be enforced again after the crisis had passed.

Transportation improvements of the 20th century also resulted in the elimination of the horse and associated structures—e.g., barn, corn crib, grain storage—and contributed to other architectural changes (Stewart-Abernathy 1986). Again, it is important to note that these responses did not necessarily occur immediately. For example, horses were not kept at the property after 1935, yet the barn at the Plainwell property was standing until 1958 when it was finally razed due to deterioration (Brown family 1995, pers. comm.). For many years, the barn functioned primarily as a garage and storage facility, which again betrays the family's economic standing during this period. Only after the demolition of the barn was a new garage built to replace it.

The last factor to which landscape changes on an urban farmstead can be attributed concerns innovations in food technology, including improvements in the transportation, storage, and packaging of food goods that directly affect, and often replace, food production on an urban farmstead (Stewart-Abernathy 1986). Although this is a logical supposition, it is not consistent with the observations at the Plainwell property. Numerous canning jars that were recovered archaeologically indicate that food preservation was important during the late 19th and early 20th centuries and, according to local accounts, a rather significant garden has been maintained west of the house outside the kitchen for the remainder of the occupation.

The decision to maintain a garden often informs about more than merely food production. There are social, political, and economic considerations for creating landscape features such as vegetable gardens. Admittedly, the economic standing of the families who resided at the property makes it logical to infer that they sought to supplement their diet. Yet, there may be additional reasons for planting a garden. During the World Wars, for example, the United States was responsible for producing enough food to feed not only American citizens, but the citizens of

allied countries as well. Patriots planted "Victory Gardens" in backyards and vacant lots to aid in this effort (Bailey and Kennedy 1983:672, 798). Gardeners may also be motivated by still other factors. Individuals may enjoy gardening as a hobby or as part of a broader ecological movement which advocates home-grown, healthy, organic vegetables. Stewart-Abernathy (1986:14) noted that rural elements persist even into the late 20th century at a homelot, "with its carport and driveway, dog house, barbeque grill, and garden of tomatoes and herbs." A vegetable garden can be a locus of food production, yet it can also communicate important social messages by indicating economic hardship, signifying the patriotism of the family and its dedication to a larger political cause, or demonstrating the personal responsibility of the homeowner. Thus, gardens and other landscape modifications must be interpreted within a historical context to understand their meanings for their creators and potential observers.

Conclusions

In our attempt to interpret the heterogeneous landscape of a homelot in Plainwell, Michigan, we have found utility in the urban farmstead model as an effective means of mediating the difficulties associated with the rural-urban dichotomy. However, the urban farmstead concept has only limited value for explaining some changes in the organization of the built environment. Landscape changes are more than merely physical adaptations to the external world. Rather, they are symbolic elements that are shaped by social dynamics at multiple scales.

Alterations to the homelot in Plainwell were not simply responses to the process of infilling, the development of municipal services, zoning restrictions, transportation improvements, or advancements in food technology. For instance, lot 169 was not sold to facilitate neighborhood development, but to accommodate financial and social changes within the family. Likewise, the barn remained in use long after horses and other animals were no longer kept at the property. Furthermore, a garden has contributed to the dietary needs of the family for most of the 20th century despite innovations in the transportation, storage, and packaging of food.

Periods of landscape modification at the homelot, as well as periods of stasis, also express the socioeconomic status of the individuals who resided there. Although the house emulates some of the attributes of the Italianate style, such as the classic cube shape, other traits—elaborate ornamentation, tall floor-to-ceiling height, and a fireplace—are clearly lacking, which distinguishes the house from more ostentatious Italianate-style constructions in the elite part of town. Subsequent changes to the house and its surrounding landscape are consistent with working-class or lower paid professional household incomes; the porch was added with recycled materials, a new kitchen was built by the landowner, and the driveway was covered with the readily available and inexpensive supply of coal slag or gravel.

The spatial organization of the built environment also reflects the consistent nature of gender relations at the property. Single gendered spaces are rare on the landscape and in the house, and it is unlikely that the household occupants upheld the ideal gender separations espoused and practiced by elite members of the community (Spain 1992). The barn, a traditionally male designated space, was also shared by women who contributed to the domestic economy by raising chickens for poultry and eggs. Although men and women both used this outbuilding, they performed different tasks in separate spatial arenas, which argues against a completely isomorphic use of space. Likewise, the garden, a typically female space, has been shared by both men and women working to meet the dietary needs of the family. Even the house, with its simplified floor plan and sexually-integrated spaces, reflects the complementary nature of gender relations.

The landscape approach advocated in this paper clearly has potential application beyond the Plainwell homelot chosen for this analysis. Comparative studies of similar landscapes within the community, which vary by class, location, or domestic history, will enrich and help to contextualize the preliminary interpretations presented here. Likewise, sites in other towns, regions, and states can illuminate the ways in which class and gender relations are expressed in the built environment in specific historical and geographical settings (Paynter et al. 1987, 1994; Nassaney 1997). Continuing investigations under the auspices of the Southwest Michigan Historic Landscape Project will seek to elucidate how the seemingly static and opaque facades of American life can be penetrated by a critical eye to expose the connection between human action and its material product and precedents.

ACKNOWLEDGMENTS

This project could not have been conducted without the help of many supportive individuals. Patrick and Anita Lyden, Isabell Brown, Barbara Benedict, and Sue Hutchinson provided access to the Plainwell property and shared their understanding of the site's history. Many volunteers assisted in the archaeological and historical investigations including Michelle Akers, Allen Burt, Eric Drake, Nicole Hitzeman, Gordon Jones, Ann Kroll, Richie Laton, Diana Lynn, Christine McMillan, Taylor Michaels, Kendra Pyle, Bill Sauck, Dan Sayers, Joe Suida, Melissa Drake, and John Weaver. Sandy Stamm's knowledge of local and regional history is also appreciated. SHA Associate Editor Bill Turnbaugh and four anonymous reviewers provided constructive criticism on an earlier draft of this paper. This research was conducted under the auspices of the Southwest Michigan Historic Landscape Project and supported by a Western Michigan University Research Fellowship administered by Drs. Donald Thompson and Eileen Evans, Office of the Vice President for Research, Western Michigan University. We thank Pamela Rups of Instructional Technology Services and Randy Case of Architecture & Design for their assistance in producing the graphics that accompany the text.

REFERENCES

BAILEY, THOMAS A., AND DAVID M. KENNEDY
  1983 *The American Pageant: A History of the Republic.* Seventh edition. D. C. Heath, Lexington, MA.

BARBER, RUSSELL J.
  1994 *Doing Historical Archaeology: Exercises Using Documentary, Oral, and Material Evidence.* Prentice Hall, Englewood Cliffs, NJ.

BEAUDRY, MARY C.
1996 Why Gardens? *In Landscape Archaeology: Reading and Interpreting the American Historical Landscape,* edited by R. Yamin and K. B. Metheny, pp. 3–5. University of Tennessee Press, Knoxville.

BORISH, LINDA
1995 "Another Domestic Beast of Burden": New England Farm Women's Work and Well-Being in the 19th Century. *Journal of American Culture* 18(3):83–100.

BOSERUP, ESTER
1970 *Women's Roles in Economic Development.* George Allen and Unwin, London.

BRYDON, LYNNE, AND SYLVIA CHANT
1989 *Women in the Third World: Gender Issues in Rural and Urban Areas.* Rutgers University Press, New Brunswick, NJ.

CLARK, CLIFFORD E., JR.
1988 Domestic Architecture as an Index to Social History: The Romantic Revival and the Cult of Domesticity in America, 1840–1870. In Material Life in America, 1600–1860, edited by R. B. St. George, pp. 535–549. Northeastern University Press, Boston, MA.

COSGROVE, DENIS E.
1984 *Social Formation and Symbolic Landscape.* Barnes and Noble, Totowa, NJ.

CRUMLEY, CAROLE L., AND WILLIAM H. MARQUARDT (EDITORS)
1987 *Regional Dynamics: Burundian Landscapes in Historical Perspective.* Academic Press, San Diego, CA.

EMBER, CAROL
1983 The Relative Decline in Women's Contribution to Agriculture with Intensification. *American Anthropologist* 85:285–305.

ENSIGN, D.W., AND COMPANY
1880 *History of Allegan and Barry Counties, Michigan and Biographical Sketches of Their Prominent Men and Pioneers.* J. B. Lippincott, Philadelphia, PA.

FAVRETTI, RUDY, AND JOY FAVRETTI
1991 *Landscapes and Gardens for Historic Buildings: A Handbook for Reproducing and Creating Authentic Landscape Settings.* Second edition, revised. American Association for State and Local History, Nashville, TN.

GARRISON, J. RITCHIE
1991 *Landscape and Material Life in Franklin County, Massachusetts, 1770–1860.* University of Tennessee Press, Knoxville.

GLASSIE, HENRY
1975 *Folk Housing in Middle Virginia.* University of Tennessee Press, Knoxville.

GRAY, SUSAN E.
1996 *The Yankee West: Community Life on the Michigan Frontier.* University of North Carolina Press, Chapel Hill.

HAHN, STEVEN, AND JONATHAN PRUDE (EDITORS)
1985 *The Countryside in the Age of Capitalist Transformation: Essays in the Social History of Rural America.* University of North Carolina Press, Chapel Hill.

HARVEY, DAVID
1973 *Social Justice and the City.* John Hopkins University Press, Baltimore, MD.

HERMAN, BERNARD
1992 *The Stolen House.* University Press of Virginia, Charlottesville.

HOOD, J. EDWARD
1996 Social Relations and the Cultural Landscape. *In Landscape Archaeology: Reading and Interpreting the American Historical Landscape,* edited by R. Yamin and K. B. Metheny, pp. 121–146. University of Tennessee Press, Knoxville.

JACKSON, JOHN BRINCKERHOFF
1984 *Discovering the Vernacular Landscape.* Yale University Press, New Haven, CT.

JACKSON, K.
1985 *The Crabgrass Frontier: The Suburbanization of the United States.* Oxford University Press, New York, NY.

JOHNSON, MATTHEW
1993 *Housing Culture: Traditional Architecture in an English Landscape.* Smithsonian Institution Press, Washington, DC.

KACE PUBLISHING
1895 *Illustrated Atlas of Allegan County, Michigan.* Kace Publishing, Racine, WI.

KELSO, WILLIAM M., AND RACHEL MOST (EDITORS)
1990 *Earth Patterns: Essays in Landscape Archaeology.* University Press of Virginia, Charlottesville.

KERN, JOHN
1977 *A Short History of Michigan.* Michigan History Division, Michigan Department of State, Lansing.

KRYDER-REID, ELIZABETH
1996 The Construction of Sanctity: Landscape and Ritual in

a Religious Community. *In Landscape Archaeology: Reading and Interpreting the American Historical Landscape,* edited by R. Yamin and K. B. Metheny, pp. 228–248. University of Tennessee Press, Knoxville.

LEONE, MARK
    1984   Interpreting Ideology in Historical Archaeology: Using the Rules of Perspective in the William Paca Garden in Annapolis, Maryland. *In Ideology, Power, and Prehistory,* edited by D. Miller and C. Tilley, pp. 25–35. Cambridge University Press, Cambridge, UK.

LEWIS, PIERCE
    1993   Common Landscapes as Historic Documents. *In History from Things: Essays on Material Culture,* edited by S. Lubar and W. D. Kingery, pp. 115–139. Smithsonian Institution Press, Washington, DC.

MAJEWSKI, T., AND M. J. O'BRIEN
    1987   The Use and Misuse of Nineteenth-Century English and American Ceramics in Archaeological Analysis. *Advances in Archaeological Method and Theory* 11:97–209. M. B. Schiffer, editor. Academic Press, San Diego, CA.

MASCIA, SARA F.
    1996   "One of the Best Farms in Essex County": The Changing Domestic Landscape of a Tenant Who Became an Owner. *In Landscape Archaeology: Reading and Interpreting the American Historical Landscape,* edited by R. Yamin and K. B. Metheny, pp. 147–174. University of Tennessee Press, Knoxville.

MCMURRY, SALLY
    1997   *Families and Farmhouses in Nineteenth-Century America: Vernacular Design and Social Change.* University of Tennessee Press, Knoxville.

MEINIG, D. W. (EDITOR)
    1979   *The Interpretation of Ordinary Landscapes: Geographical Essays.* Oxford University Press, New York, NY.

MILLER, GEORGE L.
    1980   Classification and Economic Scaling of 19th-Century Ceramics. *Historical Archaeology* 14:1–40.

MILLER, NAOMI F., AND KATHRYN L. GLEASON (EDITORS)
    1994   *The Archaeology of Garden and Field.* University of Pennsylvania Press, Philadelphia.

MROZOWSKI, STEVEN
    1991   Landscapes of Inequality. *In Archaeology of Inequality,* edited by R. McGuire and R. Paynter, pp. 79–101. Basil Blackwell, Oxford, UK.

NASSANEY, MICHAEL S.
    1997   The Southwest Michigan Historic Landscape Project: Guiding Principles and Preliminary Results. Paper presented at the Annual Meeting of the Michigan Academy of Science, Arts, and Letters, Grand Rapids.

NASSANEY, MICHAEL S., AND MARJORIE R. ABEL
    [1997]   Urban Spaces, Labor Organization, and Social Control: Lessons from New England's Nineteenth Century Cutlery Industry. Manuscript submitted for review to *Current Anthropology.*

NASSANEY, MICHAEL S., AND ROBERT PAYNTER
    1995   Spatiality and Social Relations. Paper presented in the symposium "Social Space, Social Engineering, and Social Control in Nineteenth-Century America," P. Demers and J. Voss, organizers, at the Annual Meeting of The Society for Historical Archaeology Conference on Historical and Underwater Archaeology, Washington, DC.

NYLANDER, JANE C.
    1994   *Our Own Snug Fireside: Images of the New England Home, 1760–1860.* Yale University Press, New Haven, CT.

OGLE, GEORGE A., & COMPANY
    1913   *Standard Atlas of Allegan County, Michigan,* compiled by George A. Ogle. George A. Ogle, Chicago, IL.

PATTERSON, THOMAS C.
    1994   *The Theory and Practice of Archaeology: A Workbook.* Second edition. Prentice Hall, Englewood Cliffs, NJ.

PAYNTER, ROBERT
    1982   *Models of Spatial Inequality: Settlement Patterns in Historical Archaeology.* Academic Press, NY.

PAYNTER, ROBERT, SUSAN HAUTANIEMI, AND NANCY MULLER
    1994   The Landscapes of the W. E. B. Du Bois Boyhood Homesite: An Agenda for an Archaeology of the Color Line. *In Race,* edited by S. Gregory and R. Sanjek, pp. 285–318. Rutgers University Press, New Brunswick, NJ.

PAYNTER, ROBERT, RITA REINKE, J. RITCHIE GARRISON, EDWARD HOOD, AMELIA MILLER, AND SUSAN MCGOWAN
    1987   Vernacular Landscapes in Western Massachusetts. Paper presented at the Annual Meeting of The Society for Historical Archaeology Conference on Historical and Underwater Archaeology, Savannah, GA.

PIPERNO, DOLORES R.
    1988   *Phytolith Analysis: An Archaeological and Geological Perspective.* Academic Press, San Diego, CA.

REINKE, RITA, AND ROBERT PAYNTER
    1984   *Archaeological Excavation of the Surroundings of the
           E. H. Williams House, Deerfield, Massachusetts.*
           University of Massachusetts Archaeological Services,
           Amherst, MA.

ROSALDO, MICHELLE
    1974   Women, Culture, and Society: A Theoretical
           Overview. In *Women, Culture, and Society,* edited by
           M. Z. Rosaldo and L. Lamphere, pp. 67–88. Stanford
           University Press, Palo Alto, CA.

ROTMAN, DEBORAH L.
    1995   Class and Gender in Southwestern Michigan:
           Interpreting Historical Landscapes. Unpublished M.A.
           thesis, Department of Anthropology, Western
           Michigan University, Kalamazoo.

SLOCUM, ANN C., AND LOIS C. SHERN
    1997   The Historical Development of the American Lawn
           Ideal and a New Perspective. *Michigan Academician*
           29:145–158.

SPAIN, DAPHNE
    1992   *Gendered Spaces.* University of North Carolina Press,
           Chapel Hill.

STEWART-ABERNATHY, LESLIE
    1986   Urban Farmstead: Household Responsibilities in the
           City. *Historical Archaeology* 20(2):5–15.
    1992   Industrial Goods in the Service of Tradition:
           Consumption and Cognition on an Ozark Farmstead
           Before the Great War. In *The Art and Mystery of
           Historical Archaeology: Essays in Honor of James
           Deetz,* edited by A. E. Yentsch and M. E. Beaudry, pp.
           101–126. CRC Press, Boca Raton, FL.

STILGOE, JOHN R.
    1982   *Common Landscape of America, 1580 to 1845.* Yale
           University Press, New Haven, CT.

STINE, LINDA FRANCE
    1992   Social Differentiation Down on the Farm. *In Exploring
           Gender Through Archaeology: Selected Papers from
           the 1991 Boone Conference,* edited by C. P. Claassen,
           pp. 103–109. Prehistory Press, Madison, WI.

TITUS, C. O.
    1873   *Atlas of Allegan County, Michigan.*   C. O. Titus,
           Philadelphia, PA.

TRIGGER, BRUCE G.
    1968   The Determinants of Settlement Patterns. In *Settlement

Archaeology, edited by K. C. Chang, pp. 53–78.
National Press, Palo Alto, CA.

UNITED STATES BUREAU OF THE CENSUS
    1850   *Population, 1850.* U.S. Department of Commerce,,
           Washington, DC.

WEIR, LYNNE B., AND MARY GRACE YORK
    1990   *Historical and Architectural Survey of Plainwell,
           Michigan.* Historic Preservation Society, Plainwell,
           MI.

WOODHAMS, WILLIAM
    1886   Untitled article. *The Plainville Enterprise,* 16 June.
           Plainville, MI.

WURST, LOUANN
    1993   Living Their Own History: Class, Agriculture, and
           Industry in a 19th-Century Rural Community.
           Unpublished Ph.D. dissertation, Department of
           Anthropology, State University of New York,
           Binghamton.
    1995   Symposium, "Rethinking Rural Contexts," organized
           for The Society for Historical Archaeology Conference
           on Historical and Underwater Archaeology,
           Washington, DC.

YAMIN, REBECCA, AND KAREN BESCHERER METHENY
(EDITORS)
    1996   *Landscape Archaeology: Reading and Interpreting
           the American Historical Landscape.* University of
           Tennessee Press, Knoxville.

YENTSCH, ANNE ELIZABETH
    1991   The Symbolic Divisions of Pottery: Sex-Related
           Attributes of English and Anglo-American Pots. In
           The Archaeology of Inequality, edited by R. McGuire
           and R. Paynter, pp. 192–230. Basil Blackwell, Oxford,
           UK.
    1996   Introduction: Close Attention to Place—Landscape
           Studies by Historical Archaeologists. *In Landscape
           Archaeology: Reading and Interpreting the American
           Historical Landscape,* edited by R. Yamin and K. B.
           Metheny, pp. xxiii–xlii. University of Tennessee
           Press, Knoxville.

DEBORAH L. ROTMAN
MICHAEL S. NASSANEY
DEPARTMENT OF ANTHROPOLOGY
WESTERN MICHIGAN UNIVERSITY
KALAMAZOO, MI 49008-3899

Paul A. Shackel

Labor's Heritage: Remembering the American Industrial Landscape

ABSTRACT

Archaeology at industrial sites provides some of the greatest opportunities to tell the story of the impact of industrialization on workers and their communities. Archaeologists working on industrial sites have a long tradition of interpreting technology and industrial landscapes while issues related to labor are overlooked or glossed over. Other historical archaeologists have laid the groundwork for understanding labor relations and daily life in industrial contexts. An overview of the current state of industrial archaeology is provided, and a renewed call for addressing an archaeology of labor is issued. Work performed at industrial sites needs to address issues related to labor. The draft National Historic Landmark study by the National Park Service on labor archaeology serves as a good framework to deal with these ideas. Additional avenues of inquiry are also explored.

Introduction

Where history, archaeology, and memory meet at industrial sites is where we find the excitement of labor archaeology as well as some of the troubling aspects of how nations and communities use their past. Industrial archaeologists have a long tradition of documenting the engineering feats of the industrial age. Understanding what is studied, remembered, and interpreted at these industrial sites can show us who we are as a community and a nation. There are often inconsistencies between the official and unofficial memories of labor and capital. The memory of industry and its representation on the American landscape is like the memory of all significant events in history. There are winners and losers. In a time when American and international corporations continue to undermine the American workforce by weakening unions and extending the average workweek, we as a society need to think about labor issues and remember the long, arduous struggle of workers to secure a 40-hour workweek and other conces-

sions from capital that many take for granted today. Understanding labor as a component of industrial archaeology provides us the tool necessary to revisit the history of industrial sites, and it gives us a mechanism to think about labor in the past, present, and future. In the following, I provide a review and a plan for how archaeologists working in industrial contexts can create a more inclusive interpretation of the past by addressing issues related to laborers and their families.

Labor's Heritage

While many federally funded museums in the United States extol the glories of economic and social progress as a result of industry, some working class members view the preservation of old buildings and ruins as an attempt to save a degrading phase of human history. Robert Vogel once noted, "The dirt, noise, bad smell, hard labor and other forms of exploitation associated with these kinds of places make preservation [of industrial sites] ludicrous. 'Preserve a steel mill?' people say, 'It killed my father. Who wants to preserve that?'" (quoted in Lowenthal 1985:403). While I am not advocating the destruction or the neglect of industrial buildings, it is important to recognize individual dissenting views on the true effects of industrialization. T. E. Leary (1979: 182) suggested more than two decades ago that the restoration of 19th-century factories could be useful for interpreting and understanding work conditions that people faced several generations ago. Telling the story of labor's struggle can make the preservation of industrial complexes more acceptable to a greater portion of the working class community. Industrial archaeology has the potential to be an educational tool that provides "a sort of Rosetta Stone to decipher the language peculiar to industrial tombs" (Leary 1979:182).

Industrial archaeology can lead to a better understanding of life and work in an industrial capitalist system. While industrial archaeologists have made strides to tell the story of labor and the impact on daily life, the discipline still has a long way to go to meet Leary's expectations.

Since 1987 the America's Industrial Heritage Project, now called the Southwestern Pennsylvania Heritage Preservation Commission, began a long-term project inventorying surviving historic engineering works and industrial resources in the region. The Historic American Buildings Survey (HABS) and the Historic American Engineering Record (HAER), both part of the National Park Service, helped to record significant industrial sites in southwest Pennsylvania. The emphasis has been the recording of industrial engineering feats, the mission of HAER, while creating several important social histories. However, many of these engineering studies do not go beyond particularistic and functional inquiries, a state of the field that Leary (1979) and later George Teague (1987) cautioned us about.

There are some noteworthy museums that do describe the daily lives of workers, such as the Eckley Miners Village in Pennsylvania. The village is located near Hazleton, once the center of 19th-century anthracite mining. In 1971, a group of businessmen organized the Anthracite Historical Site Museum, Inc., and purchased the village of Eckley, with 200 residents still in the village. They deeded the land over to the state in order to create the country's only mining town museum. Today, fewer than 20 people reside in Eckley. The town has been preserved, and the museum interprets the daily living experience of mining families. Exhibits discuss the hardships of life in a mining community, such as impoverishment, illness, accidents, death, and labor discontent (Wesolowsky 1996). However, these frank discussions in public museums that highlight the workers' experiences do not dominate many of the discussions of industrial heritage on the American landscape.

There are few communities that celebrate labor while muting the voice of capital. Another community that does is the postindustrial city of Lawrence, Massachusetts. The official memory of Lawrence is presented in the Lawrence Heritage State Park, situated in the midst of the city's decaying industrial core. The museum is located in a restored boardinghouse with two floors of exhibit space devoted almost entirely to labor issues and the Bread and Roses Strike of 1912. The strike, led by young women and followed by immigrants of 30 different nationalities, closed most of the Northeast region's mills in an attempt to acquire better wages and

improved work conditions. Even though the strike stimulated broader appeals for better working conditions by labor throughout the Northeast, the strike failed. Workers went back to their jobs without acquiring any concessions. Today, there are mixed reactions to remembering this strike. Some citizens believe the story should be told, while others want to forget the days of exploitation (Green 2000:57–60). "How beautiful it is to sweetly forget the clubbings of 1912, the jailings of 1919, and the clubbings again of 1931," noted one former factory worker (quoted in Green 2000:60). The city remembers this labor tradition through a museum that provides a memory of labor strife. Lawrence suffered like many other northeastern industrial cities as textile mills fled the region during the 1920s in search of cheaper, unorganized labor in the southern United States. These former textile centers lost significant capital. It was not until the 1970s that some northern industrial cities were able to retool and begin revitalization. Lawrence remains one of the poorest cities in Massachusetts, suffering from the loss of its major economic base. While the official history of the United States has a long tradition of emphasizing and glorifying industry and capitalism, Lawrence is an example of a place that remembers the struggle of labor.

The city of Lowell, Massachusetts, embraces its industrial past. Statues have been placed around the town to celebrate the efforts of industrial workers. At Lowell National Historical Park many of the exhibits present a history that includes the story of both labor and capital. One exhibit extols the material benefits of industry, but the exhibit also explains labor strife. Visitors are invited to walk through the mill with earplugs while more than 100 machines operate simultaneously. The experience is enough to make one realize the strain on the mill girls and later immigrants as they labored 10 hours per day.

The above are examples of how some stories of industry and labor are represented on the American landscape and have been made part of the national public memory. While labor and capital compete for the official memory of the past, a large proportion of the industrial archaeology performed in the United States and Great Britain has been about understanding the industrial process, often at the expense of labor.

The Story of Labor's Heritage

There are many who have gone to great lengths to document and popularize the technological side of industrial archaeology (Hudson 1971, 1978, 1979; Weitzman 1980). Other works in the United States have charted new ways to understand the development of industrial technologies (Kumar 1992; Caplinger 1997; Harshberger 2002; Miller 2003) and industrial archaeology techniques (Gordon and Malone 1994; Kemp 1996; Palmer and Neaverson 1998). A major part of industrial archaeology has explained phenomena related to technological development, the economy of industry, and the industrial revolution (Trinder 1983; Stratton and Trinder 2000; Gordon 2001). Some industrial archaeologists believe that the study of industry's physical remains and landscapes is what distinguishes industrial archaeology from other disciplines (Minchinton 1983; Clark 1987). In many of these cases, either labor is not mentioned, or it serves as a secondary thought when discussing industrial technology and landscapes at these sites (Heite 1993; Pletka 1993; Howe 1994; Butler 1999). One prominent British industrial archaeologist wrote:

> ... patterns of government, religious allegiance, domestic and foreign policy, patterns of trade (although perhaps not of consumer spending)—are better arrived at by other means. Familiarity with, or even interest in, all aspects of working life in the industrial period is not essential for the industrial archaeologist so long as he [sic] recognizes their existence and is prepared to ask for advice from other specialists whose interest they are (Palmer 1990:282).

This tradition is also prominent in the United States and is reflected in *IA: The Journal of the Society for Industrial Archeology*. The articles in it are more about industry and technology than issues related to labor (Gordon 1988; Malone 1988; Holley 2001). Some of the more recent articles do acknowledge the important role workers once played at these sites, although the authors do not explore labor issues in detail (Landon et al. 2001; Wermiel 2001). Many of the studies mentioned above are good examples of industrial archaeology that focus on machines, machine products, physical layout, and power systems, but in most cases they do not address labor issues in any significant way.

I believe archaeologists working in industrial contexts need to make labor a significant part of their studies, as many historians and anthropologists have done (Gutman 1976; Wallace 1978; Brody 1979, 1980, 1993; Montgomery 1979). Historical and anthropological perspectives on labor help to define issues related to the impact of changing technology on workers and their families. These transformations in industry not only affected work, but they also impacted domestic life and health conditions. Labor historian David Brody (1989) has also encouraged scholars to look more closely at issues related to politics and power. At the recent plenary session for the annual meeting of The Society for Historical Archaeology, there was a call for archaeologists to include social history (Martin 2003) and labor (Shackel 2003b) when examining industrial sites. Others have also made the inclusion of labor and daily life a part of their archaeology (Beaudry and Mrozowski 1989; Brashler 1991; Wegars 1991; Workman et al. 1994; Shackel 1996, 2000b; Costello 1998; Trinder and Cox 2000; Van Bueren 2002).

A. Bernard Knapp (1998:2) writes about the importance of recognizing that technology in an industrial context must also consider labor and try to understand how people could negotiate social, political, and economic relationships. Acknowledging this type of relationship allows for few generalities. Each community and region has its own distinct history, and archaeology can play a powerful role in exploring these differences while also celebrating a common labor history. An important document that provides a good starting point for understanding labor's heritage is the *Labor Archaeology National Historic Landmark Theme Study*, a draft report being developed by National Park Service (Solury 1999). This document provides a brief overview of work cultures in the United States from the colonial period until recent times. The study examines the experiences of workers and addresses issues like ethnic histories, labor mobility, community studies, worker experiences, women and minority studies, and political behavior. The study provides archaeological case studies of sites that are on the National Register of Historic Places and explores issues of labor archaeology at industrial sites. Once completed, the study will help elevate the importance of labor archaeology on the national level.

Housing and Communities

The rise of American industry during the late-18th and early-19th centuries was one of the most significant issues that faced the United States as a new nation. Capitalists intentionally located factories in nonurban areas because they thought they could avoid the ills of European industrial cities that were plagued with diseases, pollution, and unemployment (Marx 1964; Kasson 1979; Prude 1983:31–41; Shelton 1986:28ff). For this reason, many companies provided housing for their workers, a tradition that began in England with Arkwright's new industrial establishments at Cromford in 1771 (Burnett 1978:12; Lowe 1982). Many industrialists believed that the control of space was as important as the control of time. Therefore, while factory owners controlled workers for 10 to 12 or more hours a day in the factory or the mines, they also controlled portions of workers' domestic lives by creating regulations in town plans and housing.

Archaeological work at Lowell, Massachusetts, best summarized by Stephen Mrozowski, Grace Ziesing, and Mary Beaudry (1996), showed the effects of changing boardinghouse policies established by industrialists for a new workforce of mill girls in the first half of the 19th century. At Lowell and at other northeastern industrial cotton mill sites, women from the countryside were brought into the labor force because they were perceived as cheap and idle hands (Dublin 1979). These industrial communities contained rows of boardinghouses with standardized facades that mimicked factory architecture. The boardinghouses were always in close proximity to the factory. The interior of the boardinghouses created an atmosphere of egalitarianism as all of the rooms were of the same size. This was but one component of a strategy by corporations to exert their control to create a compliant workforce (Dublin 1979; Hareven 1982). Archaeology shows that by the end of the 19th century, the paternal philosophy for operating the boardinghouses, whereby owners influenced and to some extent controlled the domestic lives of the mill girls, had disappeared. Poor sanitation and health conditions and the degradation of the surrounding environment became the norm for northeastern industrial towns, including Lowell (Mrozowski et al. 1996).

Not all industries operated in this fashion (Shackel and Winter 1994). In the case of the United States Armory at Harpers Ferry, the federal government did not initiate any form of corporate paternalism in the early-19th century, and this lack of paternalism eventually came to haunt those who tried to manage labor in the gun factory (Smith 1977). For instance, in the early-19th century, workers built their own houses, almost anywhere in town, as long as it was outside of the industrial complex. One worker built his house in the middle of a little traveled street. Generally, workers and their families could express their own personal identity within the confines of their own homes. Each domestic site excavated shows very different house floor plans, and armory workers used a variety of construction materials. The domestic landscape of Harpers Ferry appeared eclectic, unlike the standardized boardinghouses found in the Northeast. Each armory worker family had very different ceramic forms and types (Lucas 1994; Lucas and Shackel 1994; Shackel 2000b).

The armory workers defied any attempt to unify them as a workforce and resisted the industrial process much longer than their counterparts in Springfield, Massachusetts. Supervisors made it difficult for northerners who tried to introduce new mechanized processes. The armory superintendent gave very little support to John Hall, a gun maker from Maine working in Harpers Ferry, as he perfected the process of interchangeable parts. The archaeological record shows that armorers practiced their craft in a piecework system at home until about 1841 when the military took over control of the facility and made all workers abide by a standard work discipline found in industries throughout the country. After 1841 armory work was no longer performed in a domestic context (Shackel 1996, 1999a, 1999b).

By the end of the 1840s, the Ordnance Department took control of the management of the facility's operations. Engineers imposed a grid pattern over the town, dismantling those houses that were inconveniently placed and did not follow the new plan, like the house built in a roadway. The federal government also supported a major rebuilding of the factories. The early armory managers built factory buildings on an as-needed basis, thus creating an inefficient production line. The Ordnance Department replaced the old buildings with new structures that closely followed an orderly line of production, while skilled workers became wage laborers. Both work and home spaces were reorganized in order to create a more efficient and compliant workforce (Shackel 1996).

While the federal government at Harpers Ferry chose not to implement any form of paternalist control such as was commonly found at other industrial complexes in the northeast in the first half of the 19th century, other private industrialists in the Harpers Ferry area did recognize the value of controlling workers' space and time at work and at home. An archaeological example can be found at Virginius Island, a small industrial community adjacent to Harpers Ferry. The community began as a small industrial complex with more than a dozen small crafts and industries owned by various individuals. Entrepreneurs placed their small industrial complexes at strategic points on the landscape to access waterpower, and they did not follow a development plan. One local newspaper called it a "little Pittsburgh" (Palus 2000).

By the 1850s Abraham Herr owned most of the island. Unlike the previous owners, he subscribed to the model of paternalistic oversight. Controlling workers' living space by standardizing the built environment appears to have been part of Herr's ideal for an industrial community. Herr constructed a row house for his workers that consisted of a standardized façade, much like the row houses found in northeastern industrial communities. Archaeology shows that each house had a standardized floor plan on at least the first floor. Herr built his family's dwelling on the other side of the railroad tracks from his mill and the workers' housing, keeping both places within close eyesight of the owner (Palus 2000).

Other archaeologists have examined the relationship between the built environment, town plans, and paternalistic oversight. In the American Southwest, many of the company mining towns and large labor encampments from the late-19th century usually followed a grid pattern that reflected order and rationality, while the smaller towns formed in linear strips along roadways. Such strategies allowed owners to easily account for their workforce. Donald Hardesty's work in the American West provides

considerable attention to the composition of settlements and households. He shows that hierarchy and power are explicit in town layouts (Hardesty 1988:13–14,88; 1998).

Working Conditions at Labor Sites

Factory owners often characterized unproductive workers as unreliable, careless, or lazy. Many interpret this behavior as a deliberate attempt to resist the dominance of a machine-based system of production that left operatives with little room for personal autonomy or craft pride (Prude 1983; Scott 1990). While craftsmen often owned their own means of production and were likely to treat them with care, factory workers had little loyalty to the machines that someone else owned. "Some workers abused their machinery to show that they had little traditional pride in or attachment to their machines or to the products they made" (Zonderman 1992: 48). Workers broke machinery through various acts of sabotage in an effort to reassert the primacy of human beings over machines (Paynter 1989; Paynter and McGuire 1991).

Goods were sometimes stolen even though operatives knew that they could be fired if caught. Yet pilfering was seen by operatives as a way to "even the score" and compensate for low wages. "If they were denied what they saw as the full value of their labor, they would find a way to get what they thought was due them" (Zonderman 1992:196). Operatives were also rumored to have taken revenge by setting fires to factories. While they might have lost their jobs, they could have easily found another one at another factory in a neighboring town. In one instance, suspicious fires occurred at the Springfield Armory in 1842, when the armory management was shifted from civilian to military control. Neither the armorers nor the surrounding community helped to extinguish the fires (Zonderman 1992:196).

Factory workers' search for freedom and their expression of grievances against entrepreneurs were expressed from the outset of industrialization by quitting and moving to other jobs, rather than staying and fighting for change to alleviate the boredom, tedium, and low wages of factory labor. In some ways, the workers' transient state undermined their stability and strength as they lacked the cohesiveness for social and labor change. This does not mean that protests were nonexistent. They did occur, but often they were less collective and less overt than strikes. The earliest organized strike occurred in the early 1820s. By the 1830s and 1840s, regional labor organizations became more powerful in the Northeast. The number of strikes increased dramatically thereafter (Dublin 1977, 1979; Foner 1977; Vogel 1977; Prude 1983; Stansell 1986; Zonderman 1992:197–203). The shift from craft to industry continued into the early-20th century (Fonse-Wolf 1996). When workers were not powerful enough to organize a strike, they protested by work slowdowns, working on their own projects in the factory, and theft (Scott 1990; Bruno 1998:5,11–19).

Finding labor discontent in the archaeological record often means providing a thorough contextual analysis of the labor conditions. One example is the archaeological excavation performed by Michael Nassaney and Marjorie Abel (1993) at the John Russell Cutlery Company in the Connecticut River Valley. Their study shows how discontented workers challenged the existing power structure found in the workplace. Archaeologists found a large quantity of artifacts related to interchangeable manufacturing along the riverbank near the former cutting room and trip hammer shop. These objects tended to be inferior or imperfectly manufactured parts. While it would be easy to conclude that these artifacts form a typical industrial waste pile, the archaeologists looked at the larger context of 19th-century industrial labor relations in which discontented workers often broke machinery, tools, or products. Nassaney and Abel proposed that the abundance of imperfectly manufactured parts might represent a form of defiance against the implementation of the new industrial work system. Their work shows that by understanding context, knowing that discontent existed when manufacturing shifted to the new industrial system that alienated the work process, new interpretations can be developed related to labor and working conditions at industrial sites.

The study of labor protest camps such as the Ludlow Tent Colony Site in Colorado serves as another good example of how archaeologists may explore issues related to labor concerns and living conditions for workers and their families. The Colorado coal strike ignited a yearlong cycle of violence beginning in 1913 and culminated when the militia charged the tent colony and set fire to the tents, killing 2 women and 11 children. A guerilla-style war ensued for 10 days, and the miners attacked militia encampments, mine guards, and coalmines. The United Mine Workers of America (UMWA) ran out of funds to support the workers, and the strike was soon over. The workers received few concessions for their struggle. Through the archaeology of the tent colony, the Ludlow cooperative is exploring questions about the formation of temporary communities, protest labor movements, and government and military intervention. More important, the archaeology at Ludlow, which is supported by the UMWA, raises the visibility of this bloody episode in labor relations. It is helping make this incident part of the broader public memory (Walker 2000; Ludlow Collective 2001; McGuire and Reckner 2002; Wood 2002).

Another study related to labor unrest focuses on the bottling works associated with the Harpers Ferry brewery. While monitoring some of the stabilization and rehabilitation of the building, archaeologists found more than 100 empty beer bottles stashed behind the wall lathing in the former bottling room. They also discovered more than 1,000 beer bottles in the basement of the bottling works' elevator shaft, most of them broken after falling more than two stories (Shackel 2000a:104–113). In the 19th century, the typical brewery worker labored about 14 hours a day, 6 days per week, and on Sunday for about half this time. By 1910 brewery unions had successfully fought for a 10-hour workday. Workers were exposed to radical temperature shifts and breathed air contaminated with carbonic acid and sulfuric acid. Diseases like tuberculosis were common. Brewery-related accidents were almost 30% higher than in other industrial trades because of the higher speeds of machinery (Hull-Walksi and Walski 1994). The archaeological evidence suggests that workers drank the owners' profits and concealed their subversive behavior by disposing of the otherwise reusable bottles in walls and by dropping others down the elevator shaft. Fires at the brewery in 1897, 1906, and 1909 coincided with times of labor unrest in the brewery industry, highlighting the link between labor strife and acts of sabotage. Brewing unions eventually made major strides to improve the conditions of the workers (Shackel 2000a:104–113).

In another case study, Jed Levin (1985) compared the archaeological remains of the Telco Block and Supply Company site in New York City and the Supply Mill site in Billerica, Massachusetts (from Schuyler and Mills 1976). He noted that while entrepreneurs increasingly enforced an industrial discipline in the late-19th and early-20th centuries, there was a clear pattern of alcohol use by workers on the job site. Skilled workers often resisted the transition to industrial worker. The use of alcohol at these sites may have been a form of resisting work discipline.

Other Directions for a Labor Archaeology

Race

The questions related to labor archaeology are numerous, and they need to be made part of the national public memory. I have mentioned only a few case studies, but there are many issues that a labor archaeology can and should also address. For instance, the relationship between race and industry presents a unique opportunity for those interested in labor archaeology (Dew 1994; Shackel and Larsen 2000; Shackel 2001). Industrial slave labor is understudied and this topic has the potential to reveal not only the inequalities found between labor and capital, but it can also highlight the injustices found in race relations in an industrial context.

Ann Denkler's (2001:31–32) research on race in the Shenandoah Valley shows the importance of the iron industry in relationship to an agricultural community. In particular, the Catherine Furnace and the Shenandoah Iron Works, both dating to 1836, employed enslaved and freed blacks in the furnaces along with whites. Today, the tourist literature remembers the furnaces as important because they supported the Confederacy. Iron was shipped to Richmond and Harpers Ferry. No sources in the historical society mention the laborers at the site, nor do they recognize that African Americans, freed or enslaved, participated in the industry.

Race and labor relations also become an interesting part of the post-emancipation era story. After the Civil War, northern industrialists had a chance to hire and train a newly freed workforce.

Instead, industrialists turned to a new generation of European immigrants, thus shutting out African Americans in many northern industries and keeping many tied to tenant farming in the South (Horton 2000).

From the 1890s, northern industries began their large-scale flight to the South in search of cheaper unorganized labor (Carlton 1982). But before this transition could happen, a shift in the official memory of the Civil War was necessary. Until the 1890s the struggle for emancipation served as one of the official memories of the Civil War. But after the death of Frederick Douglass and the beginning of the Jim Crow era, the emancipationist view of the war lost out to a reconciliationists' memory. Reconciliation developed between white northerners and white southerners, making African Americans and the issues of slavery and the rights of full citizenship for blacks no longer part of the Civil War story (Shackel 2003a).

Many white southerners experienced a difficult transition into industrial capitalism. They found themselves in an increasingly individualistic and competitive society, and they suffered through the economic recessions of the 1880s and the depression of the 1890s. The move to revitalize a Confederate heritage helped southerners cope with defeat and the imposition of the new industrial order in the South (McConnell 1992:213). Whites worked in the new southern industries and African Americans remained disenfranchised. An industrial archaeology in the postbellum South as well as the North needs to understand the local and regional contexts for labor, and it must look at the issue of race.

The archaeology of Buxton, Iowa, performed in the early 1980s, examines the material remains of a predominantly black coal-mining town. The place thrived as an interracial town that was mainly inhabited by African Americans in the first quarter of the 20th century. The minority of the population consisted of European-derived nationalities. One newspaper called it "the Negro Athens of the north" (quoted in Gradwohl and Osborn 1984: 192). Archaeologists demonstrated through the material remains that the residents were part of the regional, national, and international trade networks. The spatial layout is a reflection of power and separations. The superintendents' residences stood on an isolated scenic hilltop across a valley and overlooking the main part of town (Gradwohl and Osborn 1984:192).

While African Americans were disenfranchised from industrial labor in the South, other ethnic groups had to fight prejudices too. For instance, while there was a large migration of Chinese workers to America during the California Gold Rush in the 1850s, they became unwelcome competition for employment by the early 1870s. Embracing Social Darwinism, many Anglos considered the Chinese to be less than human; anthropologists placed them on the lower end of the evolutionary scale. Chinese immigrants had few legal rights and could be legally discriminated against. By 1882, the United States legally barred people of Chinese descent from migrating to the United States (Chan 1991; Choy 1995; Salyer 1995).

The National Register nomination, Chinese Mining Camp Archaeological Site – Idaho (Elliott 1994), provides evidence of Chinese workers keeping strong material and cultural ties to their heritage at the work site and on the domestic front while they faced severe discrimination. The government prohibited Chinese workers in the Warren Mining District until 1869, and only after 1870 were they allowed to lease mining operations, although they could not purchase any land. Between 1870 and 1910, five separate Chinese companies mined in the Warren District. Archaeologists found the remains of canvas and repair tools, indicating that workers constructed impermanent homes in a distinctive Chinese style. Their assemblage contained imported Asian goods such as kitchen utensils and opium bottles, and the workers built Chinese-style garden terraces. Their mining techniques and tools were also different from those of the European Americans. The archaeological record shows that the workers at this mining camp retained their strong Chinese heritage on the domestic front (Striker and Sprague 1993).

Environment, Health, and Industry

Labor archaeology should examine the health conditions at industrial sites and towns. For instance, many mining sites endangered the health and life of workers. Work sites were often unstable, machinery often malfunctioned, pollution and harmful fumes contaminated the air, and workers often put in exhaustive work hours. These are all variables that led to accidents, chronic illnesses, and deaths. Industrialists were known for their efforts to accelerate machinery; the result was increased fatigue and an increased rate of injuries for workers (Schivelbusch 1986). Until about the mid-20th century, industrialists paid little attention to the impact that factories had on the surrounding environment until workers, scientists, and environmentalists brought these issues to the forefront of the American conscience.

One well-known example of the impact of environmental stress and pollution on the health of a working community comes from Donora, a town along the Monongahela River in Pennsylvania. Incorporated in 1901, the town contained coke ovens, coal stoves, zinc furnaces, metal works, and steel mills. The shrieking mill whistles guided the daily routines of its citizens (Davis 2002b:6). Fumes from the town's industrial plants became part of the everyday environment. The landscape stood mostly barren of vegetation because of these poisonous gasses (Davis 2002a:B9). Oral accounts attest to the extreme pollution as women reminisced about washing their curtains every week: by the time the women washed all of the windows in a house, the first one was dirty again. It was common to see elderly people in town with oxygen tanks. One person remarked, "Well, we used to say, 'That's not coal dust, that's gold dust.' As long as the mills were working, the town was in business. That's what kept your Zadde and your father employed. Nobody was going to ask if it made a few people ill. People had to eat" (Davis 2002b:8). Donora's death rate was significantly higher than that of the surrounding nonindustrial towns.

Donora became infamous on 26 October 1948 when massive blinding smog covered the town. A temperature inversion over the entire Monongahela Valley trapped the smoke and fumes of the steel mills and zinc furnace. The fumes became so thick that traffic stopped along its roads because drivers could not see in front of them. The noxious poisons killed 24 people in 24 hours. The steelworkers' union sponsored an investigative study into the sudden deaths of the workers and townspeople of Donora. Only partial and preliminary reports exist. The scanty information shows that those who died had 12 to 25 times the normal level of fluoride in their blood, a clear case of fluoride poisoning. While the investigative team never produced a final report, and the source of poison was never officially identified, the incident at Donora made the country more aware of the impact of air pollution on human health (Davis 2002b:15–25).

In a study of human osteological remains, comparing medieval urban and early industrial sites in England, Mary Lewis (2002) shows the devastating impact of industrialization on children. Children from industrial towns showed a higher rate of mortality, retarded growth, higher levels of stress, and a greater prevalence of metabolic and infectious diseases. Children from an industrial town were also more than an inch shorter than those from a contemporary urban trading town. While differences in urban and rural populations did exist in the past, Lewis (2002) argues that industrialization had the greatest impact on children's health.

Archaeology can be an important tool to examine working and living conditions at industrial towns. Archeologists have demonstrated the effectiveness of using soil samples from the area in and around factories and dwellings to search for toxins to examine general health conditions. Privy samples at workplaces may reveal the presence of parasites and other toxins, indications of poor health and resistance to paternalism (Reinhard et al. 1986; Beaudry et al. 1991; Reinhard 1994). Pollen and macrofloral samples may also supply some indication of the changing landscape and its relationship to changing ideals related to industrialization (Mrozowski et al. 1989; Cummings 1994; Rovner 1994). Exploring general sanitation landscape features (Ford 1994) and identifying the presence of medicinal and alcohol bottles may provide clues regarding workers' general health (Bond 1989; Larsen 1994). The impact of industrial pollution has had a devastating impact on human populations. It is important that these issues are made part of the story of industry and labor.

Conclusion

When we look at the historical American industrial landscape, we often see renovated buildings and stabilized ruins that tell the story of our early industrial prowess. These structures are often interpreted as a reminder of industry and stand mute when it comes to telling the story of labor practices. In 1878, Abraham J. Ryan wrote about a land of ruins in the postbellum South:

> A land without ruins is a land without memories, a land without memories is a land without liberty. A land that wears a laurel crown may be fair to see; but twine a few sad cypress leaves around the brow of any land, and, be that land barren, beautiless, and bleak, it becomes lovely in its consecrated cornet of sorrow, and it wins the sympathy of the heart and of history (quoted in Wilson 1980:59).

Industrial ruins may win the hearts of history, and they are a way to remember a prosperous economic past, but we also need to make sure that they are part of the memory of a labor archaeology.

Michael Shanks and Randall McGuire (1996) remind us that the act of archaeology is a form of commemoration. When we do archaeology, we create a memory of the past that is rooted in our present-day concerns. Therefore, labor archaeology can be a way to remember and unveil a history that has been buried all too long. The work at Lowell, Harpers Ferry, the Chinese Mining Camp, and mining sites in Nevada, the John Russell Cutlery factory, and Ludlow show that a labor archaeology may effectively address labor's heritage.

Politics will always impact the way we develop labor's history. For instance, during the Reagan and G. H.W. Bush administrations, Lynne Cheney, chair of the National Endowment for the Humanities, argued in her report to Congress that scholars were occupying themselves with issues related to gender, race, and class (Nash et al. 1998:103). She discouraged funding projects that encouraged a pluralistic view of the past. Cheney packed the Advisory Council with critics of multiculturalism and the committee rejected proposals if they questioned consensus history. NEH sharply curtailed any projects dealing with women, labor, racial groups, or any project that might conflict with the national collective memory (Nash at al. 1998:103). At about the same time columnist George Wills (1991:72) wrote that these scholars were "forces ... fighting against the conservation of the common culture that is the nation's social cement."

Recently, Secretary of the Interior Gail Norton rescinded the National Historic Landmark designation of the Fresno Sanitary Landfill because of the negative connotations associated with the site (Melosi 2002). The site was nominated for NHL status because it represents an important engineering innovation in the United States. The landfill developed because refuse could be buried and rendered inert and could not pose a health hazard or a nuisance. Landfills came into wide use after World War II because of the success of the Fresno Sanitary Landfill, and they became the primary disposal option for Americans for the second half of the 20th century. Unfortunately, the Fresno Sanitary Landfill did not have a liner, and hazardous substances were found in the adjacent groundwater. The site was closed in 1987, and it became a superfund site in 1989. The Fresno Sanitary Landfill operated for more than 50 years. Many historians consider it as the oldest "true" landfill in the United States (Melosi 2002:23–26). Unfortunately, the Bush administration, which has received increasing pressure from environmental groups (like the Sierra Club) for its environmental policies, does not want to be associated with a landfill or a landfill that is also known as a superfund site, despite its historical significance to American industrial technology.

There are always lessons and alternative views at many significant historic sites. They are places not only to celebrate our past but also to learn lessons about our history. If we look at industrial sites, there is always a counter memory to the importance of technological advancement. For instance, what about historic mills? Their history is about technological development and entrepreneurship, but it is also about exploitation of workers. And what about coal mining towns? Coal extraction was about technology and profit, but the process also destroyed landscapes and polluted water (Melosi 2002:34). These are all examples of the American past that we choose to remember and use to teach us about the past by making them part of our official history. I wonder, then, if a place that celebrates labor strife and workers' struggles for decent wages like Ludlow could receive NHL designation in today's political climate.

No matter the political climate, archaeologists should endeavor to make labor issues part of the official history of the United States. One way is to nominate these sites to the National Register of Historic Places and as National Historic Landmarks. We are all agents who have crucial moral and political choices to make. History is shaped by human intervention, and while tough choices and stances were made in the past, we need to confront what we study and how to remember our past. Designating industrial places as a prominent part of our past should also be about remembering people and their struggles. The question for all of us working at industrial sites is this: Will archaeologists working at industrial sites be courageous like the town of Lawrence, Massachusetts, and commemorate labor's heritage, or will we choose to celebrate capital and create an official history that glorifies technology at the expense of labor? That is the challenge, I believe, for any professional working in industrial contexts.

ACKNOWLEDGMENTS

A brief version of this article was presented at the plenary session at the 36th Annual Conference on Historical and Underwater Archaeology, Providence, Rhode Island. Several people were kind enough to share several sources, including Brett Burk, Bob Chidester, Terrance Martin, Randy McGuire, and Larry Zimmerman. Barbara Little and Matthew Palus provided valuable feedback on earlier drafts of this paper. I also appreciate the comments provided to me by the three journal reviewers: Thad Van Bueren, Adrian Praetzellis, and Karen Metheny.

REFERENCES

BEAUDRY, MARY C., LAUREN J. COOK, AND STEPHEN A. MROZOWSKI
1991 Artifacts as Active Voices: Material Culture as Social Discourse. In The Archaeology of Inequality, Randall H. McGuire and Robert Paynter, editors, pp. 150–191. Basil Blackwell, New York.

BEAUDRY, MARY C., AND STEPHEN A. MROZOWSKI
1989 The Archaeology of Work and Home Life in Lowell, Massachusetts: An Interdisciplinary Study of the Boott Cotton Mills Corporation. IA, The Journal of the Society for Industrial Archeology, 19(2):1–22.

BOND, K. H.
1989 The Medicine, Alcohol, and Soda Vessels from the Boott Mills. In Interdisciplinary Investigations of the Boott Mills, Lowell, Massachusetts, Vol. 3, The Boarding House System as a Way of Life, Mary C. Beaudry and Stephen A. Mrozowski, editors, pp. 121–140. Cultural Resources Management Study, No. 21. U.S. Department of the Interior, National Park Service. North Atlantic Regional Office, Boston, MA.

BRASHLER, JANET G.
1991   When Daddy Was a Shanty Boy: The Role of Gender in the Organization of the Logging Industry in Highland West Virginia. *Historical Archaeology,* 25(4):54–68.

BRODY, DAVID
1979   The Old Labor History and the New. *Labor History,* 20(1):111–21.
1980   Labor History in the 1980s: Toward a History of the American Worker. In *The Past before Us: Contemporary Historical Writing in the United States,* Michael Kammen, editor, pp. 252–69. Cornell University Press, Ithaca, NY.
1989   Labor History, Industrial Relations, and the Crisis of American Labor. *Industrial and Labor Relations Review,* 43(1):5–18.
1993   *In Labor's Cause: Main Themes on the History of the American Worker.* Oxford University Press, New York.

BRUNO, ROBERT
1998   Working, Playing, and Fighting for Control: Steelworkers and Shopfloor Identity. *Labor Studies Journal,* 28 (Spring):3–30.

BURNETT, JOHN
1978   *A Social History of Housing 1815–1970.* Davis and Charles, London, England.

BUTLER, WILLIAM B.
1999   The Grand Lake Lodge Sawmill, Rocky Mountain National Park, Grand County, Colorado. *Southwest Lore,* 65(1):9–42.

CAPLINGER, MICHAEL
1997   *Bridges over Time: A Technological Context for the Baltimore and Ohio Railroad Main Stem at Harpers Ferry, West Virginia.* Institute for the History of Technology and Industrial Archaeology, Morgantown, WV.

CARLTON, DAVID L.
1982   *Mill and Town in South Carolina, 1880–1920.* Louisiana State University Press, Baton Rouge.

CHAN, SUCHENG (EDITOR)
1991   *Entry Denied: Exclusion and the Chinese Community in America, 1882–1943.* Temple University Press, Philadelphia, PA.

CHOY, PHILIP P.
1995   *Coming Man: 19th-Century American Perceptions of the Chinese.* University of Washington Press, Seattle.

CLARK, C. M.
1987   Trouble at T'Mill: Industrial Archaeology in the 1980s. *Antiquity,* 61(232):169–179.

COSTELLO, JULIA G.
1998   Bread Fresh from the Oven: Memories of Italian Breadbaking in the California Mother Lode. *Historical Archaeology,* 32(1):66–73.

CUMMINGS, LINDA SCOTT
1994   Diet and Prehistoric Landscape during the Nineteenth- and Early-Twentieth Centuries at Harpers Ferry, West Virginia: A View from the Old Master Armorer's Complex. *Historical Archaeology,* 28(4):94–105.

DAVIS, DEVRA LEE
2002a   The Heavy Air of Donora, Pa. *The Chronicle Review: The Chronicle of Higher Education,* Section 2:B7–B12.
2002b   *When Smoke Ran Like Water: Tales of Environmental Deception and the Battle against Pollution.* Basic Books, New York.

DENKLER, ANN
2001   Sustaining Identity, Recapturing Heritage: Exploring Issues of Public History, Tourism, and Race in a Southern Rural Town. Doctoral dissertation, American Studies, University of Maryland.

DEW, CHARLES B.
1994   *Bonds of Iron: Master and Slave at Buffalo Forge.* W.W. Norton and Co., New York.

DUBLIN, THOMAS
1977   "Women, Work, and Protest in the Early Lowell Mills; 'The Oppressing Hand of Avarice Would Enslave Us.'" In *Class, Sex, and the Women Worker,* Milton Cantor and Bruce Ware, editors, pp. 43–63. Greenwood Press, Westport, CT.
1979   *Women at Work: The Transformation of Work and Community in Lowell, Massachusetts, 1826–1860.* Columbia University Press, New York.

ELLIOTT, JOHN H.
1994   Chinese Mining Camp Archaeological Site, Warren Mining District 01IH1961. National Register Nomination. U.S. Department of the Interior, National Park Service, Washington, DC.

FONER, PHILIP S. (EDITOR)
1977   *The Factory Girls.* University of Illinois Press, Urbana.

FONSE-WOLF, KEN
1996   From Craft to Industrial Unionism in the Window-Glass Industry: Clarksburg, West Virginia, 1900–1937. *Labor History,* 37(1):28–49.

FORD, BENJAMIN
1994   The Health and Sanitation of Postbellum Harpers Ferry. *Historical Archaeology,* 28(4):49–61.

GORDON, ROBERT B.
1988   Material Evidence of the Manufacturing Methods Used in "Armory Practice." *IA, The Journal of the Society for Industrial Archeology,* 14(1):23–36.
2001   *A Landscape Transformed: The Iron Making District of Salisbury, Connecticut.* Oxford University Press, New York.

GORDON, ROBERT B., AND PATRICK M. MALONE
  1994 *The Texture of Industry: An Archaeological View of the Industrialization of North America.* Oxford University Press, New York.

GRADWOHL, DAVID M., AND NANCY M. OSBORN
  1984 *Exploring Buried Buxton: Archaeology of an Abandoned Iowa Coal Mining Town with a Large Black Population.* The Iowa State University Press, Ames.

GREEN, JAMES
  2000 *Taking History to Heart: The Power of the Past in Building Social Movements.* University of Massachusetts Press, Amherst.

GUTMAN, HERBERT
  1976 *Work, Culture, and Society in Industrializing America: Essays in American Working Class and Social History.* Alfred Knopf, New York.

HARDESTY, DONALD
  1988 The Archaeology of Mining and Miners: A View from the Silver State. The Society for Historical Archaeology, *Special Publication Series,* No. 6. California, PA.
  1998 Power and the Industrial Mining Community in the American West. In *Social Approaches to an Industrial Past: The Archaeology and Anthropology of Mining,* A. Bernard Knapp, Vincent C. Pigott, and Eugenia W. Herbert, editors, pp. 81–96. Routledge, London.

HAREVEN, TAMARA T.
  1982 *Family Tie and Industrial Time: The Relationship between the Family and Work in a New England Industrial Community.* Cambridge University Press, New York.

HARSHBERGER, P.
  2002 Brooklyn: Review of the 31st Annual Conference. *Society for Industrial Archeology Newsletter,* 31(3–4): 1–2, 4–5, 7–10.

HEITE, EDWARD F.
  1993 Can Sizes and Waste at the Lebanon Cannery Site: Unscrewing the Inscrutable. *Archaeological Society of Delaware Bulletin,* 30:43–48.

HOLLEY, I. B., JR.
  2001 Steamrollers: Those Majestic Machines. *IA, The Journal of the Society for Industrial Archeology,* 27(2):37–48.

HORTON, JAMES
  2000 Freedom Fighters: African Americans, Slavery, and the Coming Age of the Civil War. Paper presented at the National Park Service Symposium on Strengthening Interpretation of the Civil War Era. Ford's Theater National Historic Site, Washington, DC, May 9.

HOWE, DENIS E.
  1994 Industrial Archaeology: A Survey of Research in New Hampshire. *New Hampshire Archeologist,* 33–34(1): 105–113.

HUDSON, KENNETH
  1971 *A Guide to the Industrial Archaeology of Europe.* Fairleigh Dickinson University Press, Madison, NJ.
  1978 *Food, Clothes, and Shelter: Twentieth-Century Industrial Archaeology.* J. Baker, London.
  1979 *World Industrial Archaeology.* Cambridge University Press, New York.

HULL-WALSKI, DEBORAH A., AND FRANK WALSKI
  1994 There's Trouble a-Brewin,: The Brewing and Bottling Industries at Harpers Ferry, West Virginia. *Historical Archaeology,* 28(4):106–121.

KASSON, JOHN F.
  1979 *Civilizing the Machine: Technology and Republican Values in America, 1776–1900.* Penguin Books, New York.

KEMP, EMORY L.
  1996 *Industrial Archaeology: Techniques.* Krieger Publishing Co., Malabar, FL.

KNAPP, A. BERNARD
  1998 Introduction. In *Social Approaches to an Industrial Past: The Archaeology and Anthropology of Mining,* A. Bernard Knapp, Vincent C. Pigott, and Eugenia W. Herbert, editors, pp. 1–23. Routledge, London.

KUMAR, PRADEEP
  1992 *A Structural Analysis of Patented Bollman Suspension Trusses.* Institute for the History of Technology and Industrial Archaeology, Morgantown, WV.

LANDON, DAVID, PATRICK MARTIN, ANDREW SEWELL, PAUL WHITE, TIMOTHY TUMBERG, AND JASON MENARD
  2001 "…A Monument to Misguided Enterprise": The Carp River Bloomery Iron Forge. *IA, The Journal of the Society for Industrial Archeology,* 27(2):5–22.

LARSEN, ERIC
  1994 A Boardinghouse Madonna: Beyond the Aesthetics of a Portrait Created through Medicine Bottles. *Historical Archaeology,* 28(4):68–79.

LEARY, T. E.
  1979 Industrial Archeology and Industrial Ecology. *Radical History Review,* 21:171–182.

LEWIS, MARY E.
  2002 Impact of Industrialization: Comparative Study of Child Health in Four Sites from Medieval and Postmedieval England (A.D. 850–1859). *American Journal of Physical Anthropology,* 119(3):211–223.

LEVIN, JED
  1985 Drinking on the Job: How Effective Was Capitalist Work Discipline? *American Archaeology,* 5(3):195–201.

LOWE, JEREMY
  1982 Housing as a Source for Industrial History: A Case Study of Blaenafon, A Welsh Ironworks Settlement, from 1788 to c.1845. *IA, The Journal of the Society for Industrial Archeology,* 8(1):13–36.

LOWENTHAL, DAVID
    1985   *The Past Is a Foreign Country.* Cambridge University Press, Cambridge, MA.

LUCAS, MICHAEL
    1994   An Armory Worker's Life: Glimpses of Industrial Life. In An Archeology of an Armory Worker's Household: Park Building 48, Harpers Ferry National Historical Park, Paul A. Shackel, editor, pp. 5.1–5.40. *Occasional Report*, No. 12, U.S. Department of the Interior, National Park Service, Washington, DC.

LUCAS, MICHAEL, AND PAUL A. SHACKEL
    1994   Changing Social and Material Routine in Nineteenth-Century Harpers Ferry. *Historical Archaeology,* 28(4): 27–36.

LUDLOW COLLECTIVE
    2001   Archaeology of the Colorado Coal Field War, 1913–1914. In *Archaeologies of the Contemporary Past*, V. Buchli and G. Lucas, editors, pp. 94–107. Routledge Press, London.

MALONE, PATRICK M.
    1988   Little Kinks and Devices at Springfield Armory, 1892–1918. *IA, The Journal of the Society for Industrial Archeology,* 14(1):59–76.

MARTIN, PATRICK E.
    2003   The Archaeology of Industrialization. Paper presented at the 36th Annual Conference on Historical and Underwater Archaeology, Providence, RI.

MARX, LEO
    1964   *The Machine in the Garden: Technology and the Pastoral Ideal in America.* Oxford University Press, New York.

MCCONNELL, STUART
    1992   *Glorious Contentment: The Grand Army of the Republic, 1865–1900.* The University of North Carolina Press, Chapel Hill.

MCGUIRE, RANDALL H., AND PAUL RECKNER
    2002   The Unromantic West: Labor, Capital, and Struggle. *Historical Archaeology,* 36(3):44–58.

MELOSI, MARTIN V.
    2002   National Historic Landmarks: Controversies and Definitions. The Fresno Sanitary Landfill in an American Cultural Context. *Public Historian,* 24(3): 17–35.

MILLER, CAROL POH
    2003   Study Tour Takes a Close-Up Look at Sweden's Industrial Heritage. *Society for Industrial Archeology Newsletter,* 31(1):1–8,17.

MINCHINTON, WALTER
    1983   World Industrial Archaeology: A Survey. *World Archaeology,* 15(2):125–136.

MONTGOMERY, DAVID
    1979   *Worker's Control in America: Studies in the History of Work, Technology, and Labor Struggle.* Cambridge University Press, New York.

MROZOWSKI, STEPHEN A., GRACE H. ZEISING, AND MARY C. BEAUDRY
    1996   *Living on the Boott: Historical Archaeology at the Boott Mills Boardinghouses, Lowell, Massachusetts.* University of Massachusetts Press, Amherst.

MROZOWSKI, S. A., E. L. BELL, M. C. BEAUDRY, D. B. LANDON, AND G. K. KELSO
    1989   Living on the Boott: Health and Well Being in a Boardinghouse Population. *World Archaeology,* 21(2):298–319.

NASH, GARY B., CHARLOTTE CRABTREE, AND ROSS E. DUNN
    1998   *History on Trial: Culture Wars and the Teaching of the Past.* Knopf, New York.

NASSANEY, MICHAEL S., AND MARJORIE R. ABEL
    1993   The Political and Social Contexts of Cutlery Production in the Connecticut Valley. *Dialectical Anthropology,* 18(3–4):247–289.

PALMER, MARILYN
    1990   Industrial Archaeology: A Thematic or a Period Discipline? *Antiquity,* 64(243):275–282.

PALMER, MARILYN, AND PETER NEAVERSON
    1998   *Industrial Archaeology: Principles and Practice.* Routledge, New York.

PALUS, MATTHEW
    2000   *"They Worked Regular": Archaeology of the Virginius Island Mill Community, Package 123 in Harpers Ferry National Historical Park, Harpers Ferry, West Virginia.* U.S. Department of the Interior, National Park Service, Harpers Ferry National Historical Park, Harpers Ferry, WV.

PAYNTER, ROBERT
    1989   The Archaeology of Equality and Inequality. *Annual Review of Anthropology,* 18:369–99.

PAYNTER, ROBERT, AND RANDALL H. MCGUIRE
    1991   The Archaeology of Inequality: Material Culture, Domination, and Resistance. In *The Archaeology of Inequality*, McGuire and Paynter, editors, pp. 1–27. Basil Blackwell, Cambridge, MA.

PLETKA, KARYN L.
    1993   Industrial Archaeology at the Robinson-Herring Sawmill Site, Greenbush, Wisconsin. *Michigan Archaeologist,* 39(1):1–35.

PRUDE, JONATHAN
    1983   *The Coming of Industrial Order: Town and Factory Life in Rural Massachusetts, 1810–1860.* Cambridge University Press, New York.

REINHARD, K. J.
  1994 Sanitation and Parasitism of Postbellum Harpers Ferry. *Historical Archaeology,* 28(4):63–67.

REINHARD, K. J., S. A. MROZOWSKI, AND K. A. ORLOSKI
  1986 Privies, Pollen, Parasites, and Seeds: A Biological Nexus in Historical Archaeology. *MASCA Journal,* 4(1):31–36.

ROVNER, IRWIN
  1994 Floral History by the Back Door: A Test of Phytolith Analysis in Residential Yards at Harpers Ferry. *Historical Archaeology,* 28(4):37–48.

SALYER, LUCY E.
  1995 *Laws Harsh as Tigers: Chinese Immigrants and the Shaping of Modern Immigration Law.* University of North Carolina Press, Chapel Hill.

SCHIVELBUSCH, WOLFGANG
  1986 *The Railway Journey: The Industrialization of Time and Space in the Nineteenth Century.* University of California Press, Berkeley.

SCHUYLER, ROBERT L., AND CHRISTOPHER MILLS
  1976 The Supply Mill on Content Brook in Massachusetts. *Journal of Field Archaeology,* 3(1):61–95.

SCOTT, JAMES
  1990 *Hidden Transcripts: Domination and the Arts of Resistance.* Yale University Press, New Haven, CT.

SHACKEL, PAUL A.
  1996 *Culture Change and the New Technology: An Archaeology of the Early American Industrial Era.* Plenum Press, New York.
  1999a Public Memory and the Rebuilding the Nineteenth-Century Industrial Landscape at Harpers Ferry. *Quarterly Bulletin: Archeological Society of Virginia,* 54(3):138–144.
  1999b Town Planning and Nineteenth-Century Industrial Life in Harpers Ferry. In The Archaeology of 19th-Century Virginia, Theodore R. Reinhart and John H. Sprinkle, Jr., editors, pp. 341–364. Council of Virginia Archaeologists, *Special Publication,* No. 36 of the Archeological Society of Virginia.
  2000a *Archaeology and Created Memory: Public History in a National Park.* Klewer Academic/Plenum Publishing Corp., New York.
  2000b Craft to Wage Labor: Agency and Resistance in American Historical Archaeology. In *Agency Theory in Archaeology,* John Robb and Marcia-Anne Dobres, editors, pp. 232–246. Routledge Press, London.
  2001 Public Memory and the Search for Power in American Historical Archaeology. *American Anthropologist,* 102(3):1–16.
  2003a *Memory in Black and White: Race, Commemoration, and the Post-Bellum Landscape.* AltaMira Press, Walnut Creek, CA.
  2003b Remembering the American Industrial Landscape. Paper presented at the 36th Annual Conference on Historical and Underwater Archaeology, Providence, RI.

SHACKEL, PAUL A., AND DAVID L. LARSEN
  2000 Labor, Racism, and the Built Environment in Early Industrial Harpers Ferry. In *Lines That Divide: Historical Archaeologies of Race, Class, and Gender,* James Delle, Robert Paynter, and Stephen Mrozowski, editors, pp. 22–39. University of Tennessee Press, Knoxville.

SHACKEL, PAUL A., AND SUSAN E. WINTER (EDITORS)
  1994 An Archaeology of Harpers Ferry's Commercial and Residential District. *Historical Archaeology,* 28(4).

SHANKS, MICHAEL, AND RANDALL H. MCGUIRE
  1996 The Craft of Archaeology. *American Antiquity,* 61(1996):75–88.

SHELTON, CYNTHIA
  1986 *The Mills of Manayunk: Industrialization and Social Conflict in the Philadelphia Region, 1787–1837.* The Johns Hopkins University Press, Baltimore, MD.

SMITH, MERRITT ROE
  1977 *Harpers Ferry Armory and the New Technology: The Challenge of Change.* Cornell University Press, Ithaca, NY.

SOLURY, THERESA E.
  1999 The Labor History Theme Study: Archaeology Component. Draft version manuscript. National Register of Historic Places, National Park Service, Washington, DC.

STANSELL, CHRISTINE
  1986 *City of Women: Sex and Class in New York, 1789–1860.* Alfred A. Knopf, New York.

STRATTON, MICHAEL, AND BARRIE TRINDER
  2000 *Twentieth-Century Industrial Archaeology.* E&FN Spon, London.

STRIKER, MICHAEL, AND RODERICK SPRAGUE
  1993 Excavations at the Warren Chinese Mining Camp Site, 1989–1992. Report to the Forest Supervisor's Office, Payette National Forest, McCall, ID.

TEAGUE, GEORGE
  1987 The Archaeology of Industry in North America. Doctoral dissertation, Department of Anthropology, University of Arizona.

TRINDER, BARRIE
  1983 New Course in Industrial Archaeology. *World Archaeology,* 15(2):218–223.

TRINDER, B., AND N. COX (EDITORS)
  2000 *Miners and Mariners of the Severn Gorge: Probate Inventories for Benthall, Broseley, Little Wenlock, and Madeley, 1660–1764.* Phillimore & Co., Ltd., Chichester, W. Sussex, England.

VAN BUEREN, THAD M. (EDITOR)
  2002 Communities Defined by Work: Life in Western Work Camps. *Historical Archaeology,* 36(3).

VOGEL, LISE
1977 Hearts to Feel and Tongues to Speak: New England Mill Women in the Early-Nineteenth Century. In *Class, Sex, and the Woman Worker*, Milton Cantor and Bruce Ware, editors, pp. 64–82. Greenwood Press, Westport, CT.

WALKER, MARK
2000 Labor History at the Ground Level: Colorado Coalfield War Archaeology Project. *Labor's Heritage*, 11(1): 58–75.

WALLACE, ANTHONY F. C.
1978 *Rockdale: The Growth of an American Village in the Early Industrial Revolution*. Alfred Knopf, New York.

WEGARS, PRISCILLA
1991 Who's Been Workin' on the Railroad? An Examination of the Construction, Distribution, and Ethnic Origins of Domes Rock Ovens on Railroad Related Sites. *Historical Archaeology*, 25(2):37–60.

WEITZMAN, DAVID L.
1980 *Traces of the Past: A Field Guide to Industrial Archaeology*. Scribner, NY.

WERMIEL, SARA E.
2001 America's 19th-Century British-Style Fireproof Factories. *IA, Journal of the Society for Industrial Archeology*, 27(2): 23–36.

WESOLOWSKY, TONY
1996 A Jewel in the Crown of Old King Coal: Eckley Miners' Village. *Pennsylvania Heritage Magazine*, 22(1). <http://www.phmc.state.pa.us/ppet/eckley/> 17 July 2003.

WILLS, GEORGE F.
1991 The Politicization of Higher Education. *Newsweek*, 22 April:72.

WILSON, CHARLES REAGAN
1980 *Baptized by Blood: The Religion of the Lost Cause, 1865–1920*. University of Georgia Press, Athens.

WOOD, MARGARET
2002 Fighting for Our Homes: An Archaeology of Women's Domestic Labor and Social Change in a Working Class, Coal Mining Community, 1900–1930. Doctoral dissertation, Department of Anthropology, Syracuse University.

WORKMAN, MICHAEL E., PAUL SALSTROM, AND PHILIP W. ROSS
1994 *Northern West Virginia Coal Fields: Historical Context*. Institute for the History of Technology and Industrial Archaeology, Morgantown, WV.

ZONDERMAN, DAVID A.
1992 *Aspirations and Anxieties: New England Workers and the Mechanized Factory System, 1815–1850*. Oxford University Press, New York.

PAUL A. SHACKEL
DEPARTMENT OF ANTHROPOLOGY
UNIVERSITY OF MARYLAND
1111 WOODS HALL
UNIVERSITY OF MARYLAND
COLLEGE PARK, MD 20742

KENNETH E. LEWIS

The Metropolis and the Backcountry: The Making of a Colonial Landscape on the South Carolina Frontier

ABSTRACT

The colonial settlement of South Carolina in the 18th century resulted in the emergence of two largely separate economies, the organization of which gave rise to distinctive frontier landscapes. The commercial rice economy of the Lowcountry was characterized by dispersed plantation production facilitated by riverine transportation. The urban functions of this largely rural landscape were centered on entrepôt of Charleston, a city whose size and material wealth reflected the region's commercial success. The Backcountry initially lacked access to the entrepôt's urban and export markets and its regional isolation fostered insular economic institutions dispersed among smaller nucleated settlements linked by overland routes. Commercial investment by Charleston interests eventually established the infrastructure of specialized production in the Backcountry and incorporated its resources in the larger export economy. The settlement system that emerged in the interior reflected these changes, but did not emulate the Lowcountry. Rather, it bore the imprint of the frontier landscape, components of which merely acquired new roles as regional nodes in South Carolina's expanding economy, the focus of which remained the older entrepôt that emerged as the South's major port in the post-frontier period.

Introduction

Over sixty years ago, historian Leila Sellers recognized that Charleston on the eve of the American Revolution was as the commercial focus of an immense interior region and occupied a central position in the overseas trade that linked Great Britain with its American colonies on the continent and the Indies. From the beginning, the city's economic position was tied to the development of its hinterland. It initial importance derived from its role as the terminus of the far-flung Indian trade as well as a hub for commerce along the coastal waterways (Sellers 1934:3-7, 25). As Charleston's hinterland expanded with the inland spread of settlement, so did its importance as a regional entrepôt. By the third quarter of the century it had become the major metropolitan center in the southern colonies as well as the center for political, religious, and social activity in South Carolina (Petty 1943:49-50; Merrens 1964:13; Rogers 1969:17-24). Charleston was inextricably tied to its hinterland, thus an examination of the city's rise as urban center cannot be divorced from its relationship with the larger region.

The dominance of Charleston was a result of the city's role in the formation of a cultural landscape that was shaped by a larger process of agricultural colonization. This process involved the region's settlement as well as its incorporation within a European world economy. Colonization occurred in the particular geographical context of South Carolina, and the resulting landscape was conditioned by a specific environment as well as colonists' perceptions of its physical characteristics and resources. The new landscape was also influenced by the manner in which colonization modified the natural geography. The development of a commercial agricultural region entailed the addition of "improvements," including settlements, fields, roads, ferries, river landings, and other alterations that transformed nature to serve human ends. These features altered the regional geography to produce a "second nature," created by its new inhabitants and containing new elements conducive to settlement (Cronon 1991:55-57). The image of this altered landscape increasingly replaced that of the "first nature" they encountered. So powerful was this image in shaping perceptions of the region that it guided the direction of its subsequent settlement. The creation of a transportation network and the establishment of central places in the initial period of settlement not only provided an infrastructure for colonization, but formed the basis upon which later immigrant farmers evaluated the value of land for commercial production.

Pattern and Process on the Frontier

The role of a second nature in directing the form of colonization is tied to the directional character of the process itself. Agricultural colonization involves the occupation of territory, accompanied by the establishment of production, the internal integration of the region through the creation of a transportation and communications system, and the eventual opening of reciprocal economic links with the homeland and other regions (Lewis 1984:19-26). These developments result in a landscape of increasing complexity, the changing form of which affects the shape of its future.

Settlements play a key role in agricultural colonization. Their functions are intimately related to the evolving structure of the process and the landscape it produces. During the period of initial colonization, a relatively simple hierarchy of settlements appears to facilitate immigration and regional integration. Consisting of an entrepôt, secondary centers called frontier towns, smaller nucleated and semi-nucleated agglomerations, and dispersed settlements, the system is an adaptation to low population density and attenuated access (Casagrande et al. 1964:312-314). There are fewer population centers in an area of colonization than in longer settled regions, thus services normally performed by many lower level settlements tend to be concentrated in those at the higher levels (Berry 1967:33-34). Many of the central functions in colonial regions are associated with the entrepôt and frontier towns, whose locations and links to other settlements also reflect their relative importance (Lewis 1984:23).

The initial colonial landscape is dynamic by nature. Increasing immigrant population density and the expansion of the agricultural production base create conditions conducive to the rise of commercial farming. If potential markets exist, the opportunity for establishing a viable export trade attracts the capital necessary to create the necessary processing and transportation infrastructure. Such a development not only alters the focus of production, but also the composition of the settlements associated with it. The incorporation of a frontier region in a national or international economy immediately enmeshes exchange in a larger context that not only increases its volume, but also its complexity. This brings about a drastic reshuffling of services in the area of colonization, with the result that many are acquired by lower level settlements while the overall proliferation of services expands in those that become central places.

The formation of a colonial economy and its subsequent absorption into one controlled by larger markets creates a landscape comprised of settlements whose composition and linkages are increasingly based on adaptations to an altered environment, a second nature. The investigation of key settlements in colonial South Carolina must be conducted in the context of such a landscape.

Landscape and Settlement in Colonial South Carolina

South Carolina's colonial landscape emerged largely in the second quarter of the 18th century. This period witnessed the consolidation of the coastal economy around the commercial production of rice and the occupation of the interior by immigrant agriculturists whose settlements opened the Backcountry to development. As the center of the trade with Native Americans and the focus of coastal trade, Charleston was a logical choice for the regional entrepôt. Possessing facilities for shipping and storage, it attracted other economic activities. Charleston was also the administrative center for the colony and the seat of its government and church offices. The function of the city was clearly shaped by its central role in the frontier region of which it was a part, and Charleston's development was tied closely to the formation of the emerging colonial landscape.

Charleston's role as a regional entrepôt was conditioned by the nature of the regional economy. Despite its possession of South Carolina's central economic, political, and ecclesiastical institutions, the city's influence extended over only a portion of the province. This situation was largely a result of the manner in which it was settled as an agricultural region. The interior was colonized later than in coastal areas where ease of access promoted commercial production. From the close of the 17th century, rice growing expanded dramatically, promoting the rise of an export economy tied closely to the fortunes of a single staple (Petty 1943:23; McCusker and Menard 1985:175-178).

Rapid entry into a commercial market allowed the Lowcountry to develop a plantation economy similar to those of Barbados and Jamaica. As in the British West Indies, agriculture was carried out on a large scale employing large numbers of slaves. It required a high initial investment of capital and managerial skill, attracting investors possessing the wherewithal to provide both. The European population of the Lowcountry contained a substantial proportion of estate owners, many of whom acquired great wealth which was displayed in their lifestyle and invested in private and public institutions (Greene 1987:201-209).

The income generated by commercial agriculture and trade enhanced the growth of the Lowcountry economy by providing the credit necessary to finance the expansion of production. In South Carolina, much of this credit was generated internally through a growing mortgage market centered in Charleston. The significant role of mortgage capital in agricultural investment strengthened the links between rural planters and lenders, merchants, and other commercial interests in the entrepôt. The expansion of credit for production thus encouraged the continued concentration of urban functions in Charleston, a process that insured its dominance as the commercial center for the province (Menard 1994:673-675).

The opening of the Backcountry began in the 1730s with the formation of a series of townships situated on region's principal river drainages (Figure 1). Created to increase South Carolina's European population and expand its area of colonization, their establishment initiated a substantial movement of population into the interior. Unlike the Lowcountry, the Backcountry

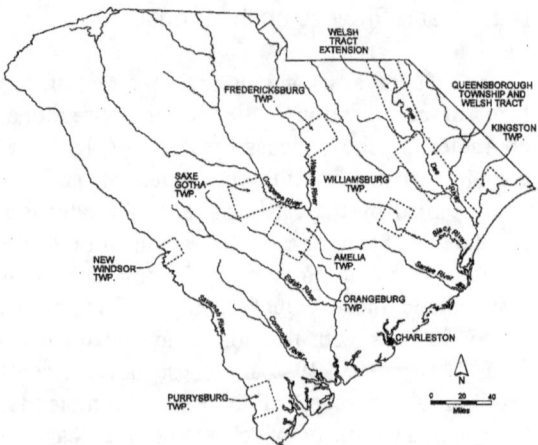

FIGURE 1. Layout of the interior townships established in South Carolina in 1731. (After Schulz 1972:14.)

offered slim possibilities for early return on investment. Consequently, the region attracted those of limited means who were willing to defer entry into commercial production. Pioneer households, occupying family farms or small plantations, usually engaged in a strategy of diversified production for a regional market within the colony. Unable to acquire the credit available to commercial producers, reinvestment took the form of improving real assets (Baldwin 1956:166-168; Nobles 1989:656-657; Kulikoff 1993:353).

The nature of small-scale production for regional markets promoted insularity from national interests and encouraged pervasive social change. The administration of such regions depended less on the imposition of outside rule than upon the creation of viable regional institutions because of their isolation. On the Backcountry frontier, formal social, political, and religious institutions were poorly developed. Here, the household served as the basic unit of both economic and social organization and its role had a marked influence on the nature of settlement in this region (Steffen 1979:94-123; Kulikoff 1993:348-349).

The bifurcated character of South Carolina's colonization led to the development of two

Perspectives from *Historical Archaeology*

economies, each of which was characterized by a distinctive pattern of settlement. Prior to the incorporation of the region within the larger commercial economy in the second half of the 18th century, these patterns produced a landscape whose components comprised the second nature that shaped South Carolina's subsequent development.

Settlement Patterning of the Frontier Period

The economies of the Lowcountry and Backcountry created settlements whose distribution and composition reflected the organization of each region. In the former, settlement locations were tied closely with the structure of production and trade. Following the riverine network of the lower Coastal Plain, most settlements were situated so as to provide access to navigable water leading to major ports such as Charleston and the smaller ports of Beaufort and Georgetown. Areas between the principal drainages appear to have been avoided because they were less accessible and were perceived as poor lands for raising cash crops. Overall, settlement became denser as proximity to coastal ports increased. The highest concentration occurred, not surprisingly, in the vicinity of Charleston (Catesby 1977:92-95; Terry 1981:7; Lewis 1984:60-64, 162-167; Kovacik and Winberry 1987:26).

The character of the Lowcountry economy is further revealed by the composition of the settlements themselves. Although rice was a bulky commodity like other grains, ease of access and the limited size of the area in which it could be grown permitted it to be shipped without the elaborate network of processing and support settlements usually associated with the commercial production of such crops (Earle and Hoffman 1976:66). Consequently, the Lowcountry did not acquire an elaborate settlement hierarchy. Most of those who lived in the region resided on dispersed plantations, where crops were produced and processed, or in the coastal ports. Small nucleated or semi-nucleated settlements grew up primarily at key transportation points where they accommodated the shipment of produce by planters to coastal ports and met the periodic economic and social needs of shippers, travelers, and local residents. Childsbury, located on the western branch of Cooper River less than 20 mi. inland from Charleston, was typical of such settlements. Despite the fact that it was situated at an important ferry crossing and river landing and played a key role as a regional transshipment center, Childsbury never contained more than a few structures (Barr 1994).

In the Backcountry the population was dispersed over much of the territory that was available, accessible, and perceived suitable for agriculture. The establishment of 11 townships scattered across the central interior from the Savannah River to the North Carolina border insured a relatively uniform occupation of the region (Meriwether 1940; Petty 1943:35-43). Limited initial access to markets and an absence of extensive outside commercial ties encouraged the development of internal trade and communications networks necessary to facilitate regional exchange. These networks were focused on small nucleated settlements that served as trading and processing centers for grain and other crops. Such settlements included Long Bluff and Cheraw Hill on the Pee Dee; Pine Tree Hill (Camden) on the Wateree; Saxe Gotha (Granby) and Ninety-Six on the Saluda drainage; and Savannah Town, on the river by the same name near present-day Augusta (Figure 2). Although early Backcountry settlements were devoted largely to economic activities, some acquired other functions as well. Pine Tree Hill, for example, was a focus of religious activity for a sizable Quaker community, many members of whom also played central roles in establishing the settlement as a social center and focus of regional trade (Gregg 1867:112, 118; Kirkland and Kennedy 1905:67-76; Meriwether 1940:170-171; Petty 1943:40-41).

Throughout the first half of the 18th century, most of the institutions that represented official authority were largely absent in the interior and their roles were taken by indigenous movements that arose at the household level. The absence of effective civil authority and a legal and administrative structure was answered by the rise of the Regulator movement, a grass-roots political movement that sought to establish and maintain order in a region increasingly beset by criminal activity (Brown 1963:13-15; Klein 1981:674-675). Similarly, ecclesiastical authority remained weak in the Backcountry. The absence of a strong state church encouraged the dominance of dissenting Protestant denominations. Unlike the larger established churches, these groups maintained a degree of flexibility by organizing rural congregations served by itinerant ministers who insured doctrinal continuity yet permitted rapid growth (Howe 1870; Bernheim 1872:88-147; Townsend 1935; Fisher 1989:703-705). Political and religious activity was thus organized at the household level and often not associated with settlements (Nobles 1989:652-653, 659).

Like their counterparts in the Lowcountry, early settlements in the Backcountry were small and functioned largely as economic centers. The economy and the transportation network that supported them were internal and based on grain production; however, these settlements were

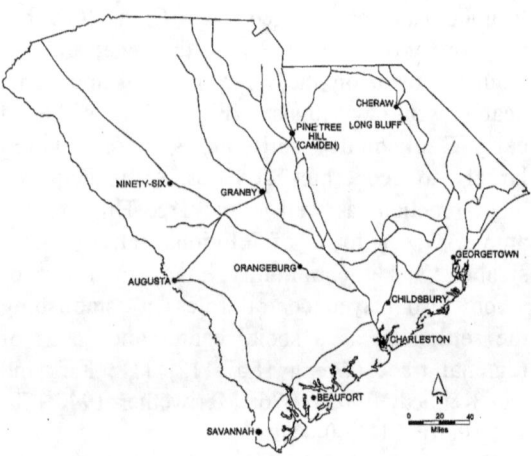

FIGURE 2. The road network of colonial South Carolina and the locations of 18th century settlements mentioned in the text. (After Petty 1943:38.)

placed centrally among the dispersed communities they served. As the nature of the regional economy changed in the second half of the century, their distribution not only facilitated the development of commercial production, but also formed the basis for an urban hierarchy unlike that found in the older rice-growing region.

The Changing Patterns of Commercial Agriculture

With the introduction of capital to establish large-scale milling in the Backcountry and the improvement of transportation to permit the efficient movement of flour and other agricultural commodities to the coastal entrepôt, production in South Carolina's interior began a transformation to meet an expanding grain market (McCusker and Menard 1985:304). The adoption of commercial production brought a dramatic change in the function of settlements in the interior. Those occupying central locations within the frontier trade and communications system attracted outside investment and acquired the complex facilities necessary to support the long-distance shipment of bulky commodities. With their larger economic functions, these settlements became nodes in a more complicated urban system developing in the Backcountry (Earle and Hoffman 1976:65-66).

As the locations of collection and processing facilities, Camden and other frontier towns became the foci of extensive agricultural hinterlands and captured the trade of smaller frontier centers. In addition, they became the sites of courts, churches, fairs, and other organized activities as formal political, social, and religious institutions were introduced into the Backcountry. Central frontier settlements grew in complexity as a result of their expanded functions. Although remaining relatively small, they served as the foci of an elaborate settlement network that would form the basis for the post-frontier agricultural economy. Camden is an outstanding example of such a transformation. A focus of regional activity in the 1750s, it expanded rapidly during the following decade following the arrival of Joseph Kershaw as the agent of a Charleston mercantile firm intent on establishing an interior business location. Within a few years he and his associates had acquired mill sites and lands, constructed stores and warehouses, and platted a town site. The settlement grew rapidly as Camden took on the role of a processing center and export market. It became the site of the district court and fair, as well as the focal point of formal religious activities. Camden's expanded economic role also attracted manufacturing and service industries and, by the 1770s, the town was home to at least three merchants, a tailor, a shoemaker, two blacksmiths, and a lawyer and contained two taverns, a bakery, an inn, a brickyard, a brewery and distillery, and a pottery factory. In two decades, Camden had not only become a settlement of substantial size, but also one of great economic complexity and social diversity (Kirkland and Kennedy 1905:12-13; Schulz 1972:19-23, 26, 29, Appendix C; Ernst and Merrens 1973:562-564; Lewis 1976:132; 1984:74-83; Thorp 1991:408).

For the most part, the late frontier Backcountry remained a sparsely settled region in which tiny settlements that had arisen with its initial regional economy found themselves taking on the activities necessary for the economic and political integration of the region. The establishment of courts at Orangeburg, Ninety-Six, and Long Bluff made these settlements foci for activity in the third quarter of the century. These, together with other older nucleated settlements at Cheraw, Granby, and Augusta, in neighboring Georgia, became important centers of trade and administration (Figure 2). In spite of the fact that all remained relatively small, their composition changed dramatically with their altered roles. All were situated at key positions in the long-distance road network and were occupied by British forces as strategic points during the Revolution. They, like Camden, had become centers in an emerging urban system. Although the Backcountry would remain a frontier until the

end of the century, its developmental infrastructure was in place before the Revolution and the second nature created by its presence shaped the region's continued evolution as a commercial agricultural region (Gregg 1867:118; Lewis 1984:79-83; Richardson 1993).

Throughout the Backcountry the effects of economic change were also evident on the household level. Not only did the opening of outside markets expand the volume of specialized agricultural production and trade, but it also replaced a regional economy with one tied more closely with international markets. The development of reliable transportation brought frontier merchants closer to sources of supply and reduced capital costs, while the appearance of well-financed entrepreneurs, such as Joseph Kershaw and his associates, provided the capital necessary both to build the infrastructure for large-scale production and underwrite the credit for business expansion (Cronon 1991:324-327). Concomitant growth in the retail and service sectors of the economy promoted the acquisition and display of wealth as an indicator of differential social standing among late frontier households, a process that dramatically affected the nature of their material culture.

Archaeological studies have revealed material evidence for such change by examining the differential appearance of high-status items, the use of which was symbolic of refinement and gentility. The sites of settlements occupied in the third quarter of the 18th century have been observed to exhibit both architectural and artifactual materials that reflect differential wealth and status on the frontier. In Camden, as elsewhere in the South Carolina Backcountry, earthfast architecture characterized structures of the initial period of colonization; however, by the 1770s it was rapidly replaced by brick construction. The buildings of Joseph Kershaw's estate there all rested on brick foundations and the "great white house" exhibited the latest stylistic elements of Georgian architecture (Lewis 1977:9-12; 37-42, 46-47; Groover 1994:46-48; Crass et al. this volume). Similarly, the use of imported ceramics expanded dramatically here after 1760. Such a pattern occurred elsewhere in the Backcountry during this period on settlements with European populations and corresponds with the increased availability of ceramics during this time (Yentsch 1991:44). The extensive use of these imported artifacts contrasts markedly with that of Colono ware, a low-fired, burnished ceramic ware manufactured by aboriginal potters or those of African descent and employed widely on plantations and many frontier settlements (Ferguson 1991:188-191; Groover 1994:50-51). Although present at Camden, the rarity of Colono ware implies that it played a minor role in households that were acquiring the wealth and opportunity to possess the symbols of gentility in daily life (Lewis 1976:138-140; Crass et al. this volume).

The addition of the frontier grain and flour trade enhanced Charleston's role as an entrepôt at a time when its economic growth had leveled off. The environmental limitations of inland swamp rice agriculture curtailed the expansion of rice production, and the trade in rice and slaves, upon which the city's economy rested, began to stagnate. With the opening of the Backcountry grain trade, however, business increased again as Charleston emerged as a major exporter of grain to the West Indies (Ramsey 1858:122; Earle and Hoffman 1976:18-19).

The growth of grain marketing in the third quarter of the 18th century also affected Charleston's role as a colonial urban center. Much of the city's earlier trade had been controlled by interests in British ports who managed the marketing, financing, and shipping of rice, an arrangement that retarded the growth of commercial institutions in the entrepôt. Beginning in the 1730s, however, the rise of an independent rice trade with southern Europe encouraged the emergence of these institutions in the colonial port. Their role was further strengthened by Charleston's subsequent growth as a regional grain market and export center, a development that increased the city's economic autonomy and enhanced its importance as an urban center (Earle and Hoffman 1976:67-68).

Rice remained South Carolina's most lucrative export, however, resident merchants never came to dominate trade to the extent that they did in northern ports. Throughout this period, British firms continued to make the entrepreneurial decisions and provide the capital and resources for much of Charleston's export trade, and their agents constituted an important element of the city's business community (McCusker and Menard 1985:186). As a result of substantial outside economic influence, Charleston failed to develop many supporting urban industries and services, such as a shipbuilding, commonly found in more autonomous colonial ports. The city's distinctive economic role also retarded the growth of its physical infrastructure. It never achieved the size of principal northern ports, such as New York, Boston, and Philadelphia, despite of the fact that it conducted a comparable volume of trade (Sellers 1934:11, 15-16; Price 1974:162).

The nature of Charleston's trade, however, enhanced its role as a major commercial center. Although much of the new trade was controlled by outside commercial interests, the wealth it generated also benefited Charleston merchants, who were heavily involved in the expansion of re-export and import trade. Their business was tied closely to the city's development as the regional credit and retail market serving a complex system of interior urban settlements (Sellers 1934:82-91; Hammond 1957:168, 170-171). A marked increase in the number of persons engaged in retail trade between the 1730s and the 1760s testified to Charleston's expanding role as the regional focus of internal commerce (Stumpf 1983:1-2; Calhoun et al. 1985:186). The foundation established by the growth and diversification of the city's economic institutions in the 18th century permitted it to remain the focus of the agricultural trade in the Lower South. As the region's principal cotton port after 1790, Charleston continued to control a vast hinterland and a substantial trade as this crop became the lower South's most lucrative export. Even after New York rose to dominate American foreign trade after the War of 1812, Charleston remained the region's most important commercial center (Albion 1939:120-121; Taylor 1951:195-197; Nettels 1962:202-204).

A Mature Colonial Landscape

By the fourth quarter of the 18th century South Carolina's economy was rapidly evolving its post-colonial form. This economy was characterized by two distinct zones of agricultural production that had evolved separately and produced distinctive settlement systems. These systems constituted a second nature that not only established a pattern for later settlement, but also encouraged and guided the direction of that growth. Lowcountry settlement patterning remained relatively static because it arose rapidly as a mature commercial agricultural region. The Backcountry, however, was settled as an agricultural frontier, and its initial regional orientation created patterning that reflected its economic and political isolation. When subsequently enmeshed in a larger commercial economy, the Backcountry's earlier settlements took on new roles, and existing transportation networks became the basis for external trade.

The form of the Backcountry landscape, characterized by central places grown from pioneer settlements, was a product of initial colonization. Improvement of existing transportation arteries reinforced older patterns of settlement as the economy of the late frontier grew in size and complexity. The frontier was a zone of transition, however, and the forces that allowed it to emergence from its regional focus continued to promote closer integration with the larger world. The expansion of commercial production would eventually bring about a shift to more efficient water transportation of bulk goods, a change that markedly altered older patterns of processing and shipment (Ramsey 1858:121; MacGill 1917:276-279). This technological shift modified the second nature of the frontier and the perception of early settlements as key landscape elements. Although many of the old frontier centers remained recognizable components on the antebel-

lum landscape of South Carolina's interior, their importance was eclipsed by settlements, such as Columbia, located more strategically in emerging canal and later railroad networks (Schulz 1972:75-77; Kovacik and Winberry 1987:92-98; Moore 1993:136-137).

The single element of South Carolina's colonial landscape that remained unchanged was its focus. From the beginning of colonization, Charleston had been the principal port of the coastal rice economy and the heart of urban activity. With the incorporation of the trade of the inland frontier, the city's domain expanded to encompass a much wider region. As the focus of a regional grain market, Charleston became the entrepôt for an extensive settlement system that restructured the old frontier and altered the nature of its own economy. Although the city's trade was still controlled largely by overseas interests, the growth of independent grain marketing expanded its role as a commercial center and retail mart for Britain's southern colonies. This change was reflected by its growth as well as in the proliferation of economic services. Both insured that the city would remain a dominant urban center into the antebellum period and a hub in the South's evolving agricultural economy.

ACKNOWLEDGMENTS

I wish to thank David C. Crass and Martha A. Zierden for their advice and comments during the preparation of this paper. Frank Krist created the graphics used to illustrate the text.

REFERENCES

ALBION, ROBERT GREENHALGH
1939 *The Rise of New York Port, 1815-1860.* Reprinted 1970. Charles Scribner's Sons, New York.

BALDWIN, ROBERT E.
1956 Patterns of Development in Newly-Settled Regions. *Manchester School of Social and Economic Studies* 24:161-179.

BARR, WILLIAM B.
1994 Ferry Crossings and Transportation Systems: Their Political, Economic, and Social Role in South Carolina's

Social Development. *Underwater Archaeology Proceedings from the Society for Historical Archaeology Conference 1994*, R. Woodward, editor, pp. 88-93. Vancouver, BC.

BERNHEIM, G. D.
1872 *History of the German Settlements and of the Lutheran Church in North and South Carolina.* Reprinted 1972. The Reprint Co., Spartanburg, SC.

BERRY, BRIAN J. L.
1967 *Geography of Market Centers and Retail Distribution.* Prentice-Hall, Englewood Cliffs, NJ.

BROWN, RICHARD MAXWELL
1963 *The South Carolina Regulators.* Belknap Press of the Harvard University Press, Cambridge, MA.

CALHOUN, JEANNE A., MARTHA A. ZIERDEN, AND ELIZABETH A. PAYSINGER
1985 The Geographic Spread of Charleston's Mercantile Community, 1732-1767. *South Carolina Historical Magazine* 86:182-220.

CASAGRANDE, JOSEPH B., STEPHEN I. THOMPSON, AND PHILIP D. YOUNG
1964 Colonization as a Research Frontier. In *Process and Pattern in Culture, Essays in Honor of Julian H. Steward*, Robert A. Manners, editor, pp. 281-325. Aldine, Chicago.

CATESBY, MARK
1977 Mark Catesby's *Natural History*, 1731-47. In *The Colonial South Carolina Scene: Contemporary Views, 1697-1774*, H. Roy Merrens, editor, pp. 87-109. University of South Carolina Press, Columbia.

CRONON, WILLIAM
1991 *Nature's Metropolis, Chicago and the Great West.* W. W. Norton, New York.

EARLE, CARVILLE, AND RONALD HOFFMAN
1976 Staple Crops and Urban Development in the Eighteenth-Century South. *Perspectives in American History* 10:7-80.

ERNST, JOSEPH A., AND H. ROY MERRENS
1973 "Camden's Turrets Pierce the Skies": The Urban Process in the Southern Colonies. *William and Mary Quarterly* 3d Ser. 30:549-574.

FERGUSON, LELAND
1991 Lowcountry Plantations, the Catawba Nation, and River Burnished Pottery. In Studies in South Carolina Archaeology: Essays in Honor of Robert L. Stephenson, Albert C. Goodyear III and Glen T. Hanson, editors,

pp. 185-191. South Carolina Institute of Anthropology and Archaeology, University of South Carolina, *Anthropological Papers* 9. Columbia.

FISCHER, DAVID HACKETT
1989 *Albion's Seed: Four British Folkways in America.* Oxford University Press, Oxford, England.

GREENE, JACK P.
1987 Colonial South Carolina and the Caribbean Connection. *South Carolina Historical Magazine* 88:192-210.

GREGG, ALEXANDER
1867 *History of the Old Cheraws.* Reprinted 1991. Southern Historical Press, Greenville, SC.

GROOVER, MARK D.
1994 Evidence for Folkways and Cultural Exchange in the Eighteenth Century South Carolina Backcountry. *Historical Archaeology* 28(1):41-64.

HAMMOND, BRAY
1957 *Banks and Politics in America: from the Revolution to the Civil War.* Princeton University Press, Princeton, NJ.

HOWE, GEORGE
1870 *History of the Presbyterian Church in South Carolina.* Duffie & Chapman, Columbia, SC.

KIRKLAND, THOMAS J., AND ROBERT M. KENNEDY
1905 *Historic Camden*, Vol. 1, *Colonial and Revolutionary.* State Printing Co., Columbia, SC.

KLEIN, RACHEL
1981 Ordering the Backcountry: The South Carolina Regulation. *William and Mary Quarterly* 3d Ser. 38:661-680.

KOVACIK, CHARLES F., AND JOHN J. WINBERRY
1987 *South Carolina: A Geography.* Westview Press, Boulder, CO.

KULIKOFF, ALLAN
1993 Households and Markets: Toward a New Synthesis of American Agrarian History. *William and Mary Quarterly* 3d Ser. 50:342-355.

LEWIS, KENNETH E.
1976 Camden: A Frontier Town in Eighteenth Century South Carolina. South Carolina Institute of Anthropology and Archaeology, University of South Carolina, *Anthropological Studies* 2. Columbia.
1977 A Functional Study of the Kershaw House Site in Camden, South Carolina. South Carolina Institute of Anthropology and Archaeology, University of South Carolina, *Research Manuscript Series* 110. Columbia.

1984 *The American Frontier, an Archeological Study of Settlement Pattern and Process.* Academic Press, Orlando, FL.

MACGILL, CAROLINE
1917 *History of Transportation in the United States before 1860.* Reprinted 1948. Peter Smith, New York.

McCUSKER, JOHN J., AND RUSSELL R. MENARD
1985 *The Economy of British America, 1607-1789.* Published for the Institute of Early American History and Culture by University of North Carolina Press, Chapel Hill.

MENARD, RUSSELL R.
1994 Financing the Lowcountry Export Boom: Capital and Growth in Early South Carolina. *William and Mary Quarterly*, 3d Ser. 51:659-676.

MERIWETHER, ROBERT L.
1940 *The Expansion of South Carolina.* Southern Publishers, Kingsport, TN.

MERRENS, H. ROY
1964 *Colonial North Carolina in the Eighteenth Century, a Historical Geography.* University of North Carolina Press, Chapel Hill.

MOORE, JOHN HAMMOND
1993 *Columbia and Richland County: A South Carolina Community, 1740-1990.* University of South Carolina Press, Columbia.

NETTELS, CURTIS P.
1962 *The Emergence of a National Economy, 1775-1815,* Vol. 2, *The Economic History of the United States.* Holt, Rinehart and Winston, New York.

NOBLES, GREGORY H.
1989 Breaking into the Backcountry: New Approaches to the Early American Frontier. *William and Mary Quarterly*, 3d Ser. 46:641-670.

PETTY, JULIAN J.
1943 *The Growth and Distribution of Population in South Carolina.* Reprinted 1973. The Reprint Co., Spartanburg, SC.

PRICE, JACOB M.
1974 Economic Function and the Growth of American Port Towns in the Eighteenth Century. *Perspectives in American History* 8:123-186.

RAMSEY, DAVID
1858 *Ramsey's History of South Carolina.* Reprinted 1960. The Reprint Co., Spartanburg, SC.

RICHARDSON, KATHERINE H.
1993 The Impact of the Township System on the Backcountry of South Carolina: From Garrison Towns to "Traditional" Towns. Paper presented at the Southern Colonial Backcountry Conference, Columbia, SC.

ROGERS, GEORGE C., JR.
1969 *Charleston in the Age of the Pinckneys.* University of Oklahoma Press, Norman.

SCHULZ, JUDITH JANE
1972 The Rise and Decline of Camden as South Carolina's Major Inland Trading Center, 1751-1829: A Historical Geographical Study. M.A. thesis, Department of Geography, University of South Carolina, Columbia.

SELLERS, LEILA
1934 *Charleston Business on the Eve of the American Revolution.* University of North Carolina Press, Chapel Hill.

STEFFEN, JEROME O.
1979 Insular vs. Cosmopolitan Frontiers: A Proposal for Comparative Frontier Studies. In *The American West: New Perspectives, New Dimensions,* Jerome O. Steffen, editor, pp. 94-123. University of Oklahoma Press, Norman.

STUMPF, STUART O.
1983 South Carolina Importers of General Merchandise, 1735-1765. *South Carolina Historical Magazine* 84:1-10.

TAYLOR, GEORGE ROGERS
1951 *The Transportation Revolution, 1815-1860,* Vol. 4, *The Economic History of the United States.* Rinehart and Co., New York.

TERRY, GEORGE D.
1981 *"Champaign Country": A Social History of an Eighteenth Century Lowcountry Parish in South Carolina, St. Johns Berkeley County.* Ph.D. dissertation, Department of History, University of South Carolina, Columbia. University Microfilms International, Ann Arbor, MI.

THORP, DANIEL B.
1991 Doing Business in the Backcountry: Retail Trade in Colonial Rowan County, North Carolina. *William and Mary Quarterly* 3d Ser. 48:387-408.

TOWNSEND, LEAH
1935 *South Carolina Baptists, 1670-1805.* Reprinted 1974. The Reprint Co., Spartanburg, SC.

Yentsch, Anne
    1991   Chesapeake Artefacts and Their Cultural Context: Pottery and the Food Domain. *Post-Medieval Archaeology* 25:25-72.

Kenneth E. Lewis
Department of Anthropology
Michigan State University
East Lansing, MI 48824-1118

Margaret Purser
Noelle Shaver

Plats and Place: The Transformation of 19th Century Speculation Townsites on the Sacramento River

ABSTRACT

Speculation townsites were integral to 19th-century California settlement and economic expansion and were often planned, formal landscapes based on explicitly urban templates. Inherently profit driven but frequently unsuccessful, many sites survived only as highly fragmentary or dependent rural entrepôts. The juxtaposition of a formal "plan" with the evolving vernacular reality of such places makes them highly significant for an understanding of 19th-century western American landscapes, both as a discrete settlement type and as a broader form of spatial organization. This speculation process defined much of the cultural landscape of the lower Sacramento River between the 1840s and World War I. Early townsite development linked settlement communities, evolving waterway infrastructure, and general land use patterns in systems that were, if not conventionally urban, emphatically cosmopolitan in nature. Two such townsites along the Sacramento illustrate very different strategies in this evolving landscape of capital manipulation, land speculation, and community formation.

Introduction

Ever since the work of John Reps in the 1970s, it has been commonplace to think that most western American settlement occurred along an inherently urban template. In his 1981 *The Forgotten Frontier: Urban Planning in the American West before 1890,* Reps laid out a theme that became known as "new western history" for the rest of that decade. Specifically, he indicted Frederick Jackson Turner's formulation of the "frontier hypothesis," with its emphasis on agrarian settlement in the West, for failing to recognize "the simple truth ... that in every section of the West, towns were in the vanguard of settlement" (Reps 1965, 1981:2). Moreover, Reps argued that the expediencies of mining booms and rushes did not necessarily override the use of plats and other conformities to the legal regulations that governed urban plan development, which the miners brought with them from the eastern United States and elsewhere around the globe, "indicating a desire for some kind of urban order, however primitive, was deeply instilled in the minds of those who flocked to the sites of new discoveries" (Reps 1981:59).

Beyond the mining camps themselves, real estate speculation focused even more intensely on the supply and trade centers that fed the mining frontiers, creating a nearly century-long speculation frenzy and a drive for urban development and expansion that Reps (1981:142–143) claims was unique to the West itself. Contemporaries like Richard Wade (1967, 1995), Gunther Barth (1975), and Judd Kahn (1979) further developed the idea of the salience of urbanism in western settlement and expansion. More recent work by people like William Cronon (1991), Patricia Nelson Limerick (1987), and William Robbins (1994:61–102,162–184) have only amplified this interpretive theme, focusing on the profound regional transformation generated by the linked processes of land speculation, urbanization, and industrialization.

What does "urban" really mean in the context of western archaeology, and how are such sites evaluated? More to the point, is there, as these authors have suggested, a substantive difference between 19th-century urban processes in the American West compared to the East? If so, how do archaeologists deal with those differences? For those working in western contexts, the quintessential representation of this urban frame of reference and aspiration is the plat map, wherein the urban conventions of an emerging legal and administrative apparatus often ran headlong into both the ambitions of individual speculators and the realities of western topography. Modern scholars have long marveled at the town lots platted halfway across San Francisco Bay or up the near-vertical slopes of some Rocky Mountain mining district. When successful, platted 19th-century speculation townsites became the urban framework of the modern West. As Reps (1981:4–5) noted, "of the thirty-one Western urbanized areas with a 1970 population of two hundred thousand or more, all but one had been founded by 1890."

Along with subsequent cartographic and property records based upon them, such as Sanborn maps and tax assessment documentation, plat maps can form the critical documentary framework for archaeological research in these western cities just as in eastern ones. Alternatively, where speculation failed, the intentions encoded in the original plat can be among the few lines of evidence available to archaeologists confronted with the ephemeral material record of the short-lived mining camp whose ore failed to meet expectations or the railroad town that died aborning when the tracks took a different route.

Where this all becomes more ambiguous, and archaeologically more challenging, is in those contexts where urban aspirations did not actually fail completely, but neither did they flower ultimately into conventional cities. These places, more accurately true towns than cities, serve as a critical vantage point from which to examine what "urban" means in the specific context of western settlement and development. The question about what counts as urban becomes particularly relevant for western archaeologists when attempting to apply National Register definitions for either "designed" or "rural historic" landscapes. A platted town, however ephemeral, is undeniably "designed." The original intention, and the speculators' only hope of lasting success, was to attain genuine urban status in a highly competitive and inherently unstable regional economy, yet much of the setting of such towns, both historically and in the present, looks at first glance to be rural by definition. They are often relatively isolated entrepôts, located in districts full of farms, ranches, and clear open spaces. Even more significantly, they often functioned originally as integral components in far-flung transportation networks that linked the distant points of western agricultural production to a few critical regional nodes of commerce. As such, they served in ways that were far less "rural" than at first they appear in the current landscape.

At the same time, even at the height of their success, the highly unstable nature of western land speculation meant these places as sites were probably always more fugitive and fragmentary than the stereotypical rural towns found in more eastern contexts. To complicate things further, there is always the question of whether some speculation townsites were, in fact, ever

really meant to attain any permanent status at all. Some clearly served much the same function as the ubiquitous false fronts of western town architecture—as commonly understood visual ciphers that invoked an urban status that was never really meant to be (Francaviglia 1991; Heath 1997).

Grappling with these issues forces archaeologists to move beyond how these sites look in the present to a re-examination of how these would-be cities worked in the larger cultural landscape of the past. In the highly unstable economic circumstances of western expansion, they functioned as critical and intensely competitive nodes of articulation between a mobile and opportunistic network of local communities, on the one hand, and increasingly diverse and far-flung markets and sources of investment capital on the other. The created settlement systems exhibit fundamental experimentations with urban form throughout the later 19th century. The term vernacular tends to be associated with more rural or agrarian contexts. In this instance, a wide-ranging vernacular experimentation with urban form in a distinctly regional economic and ecological context radically shaped a unique cultural landscape that has just begun to be recognized and explored by preservationist and resource management professionals (Alanen 2000; Francaviglia 2000:47-48; Hardesty and Little 2000:133–146).

An analysis of the landscapes of western speculation townsites takes place at two critical scales. The first is the specific context of an individual townsite, where urban templates like the ubiquitous grid plan were manipulated to maximize individual profit. In short, to sell lots, one had to file a legal plat. These towns are easily identified as named places, a mapped space that correlates reasonably well to the archaeological construct of "site." The second is the larger regional scale, where articulation between sites emerges and where, in particular, the scope of the different speculation strategies on the part of town builders becomes apparent.

In recent years, archaeologists working in both historical and prehistoric contexts have turned to the concept of cultural landscape to help resolve such issues of scale and spatial interrelatedness (Kelso and Most 1990; Yamin and Metheny 1996; Ashmore and Knapp 1999; Young 2000).

The larger issue of how to articulate the cultural-geographical concept of cultural landscape with the inherently archaeological concept of landscape archaeology is beyond the scope of this paper. But for historical archaeologists in the United States, the discipline's historical center of gravity has meant that most (although by no means all) such archaeologically relevant work has focused on contexts that are relatively more eastern in location, earlier in time, smaller in scale, and more formally planned than vernacularly or organically evolved when compared to the ones encountered in fieldwork in the 19th- and early-20th century West.

Donald Hardesty and Barbara Little (2000: 158) have identified these traits as the defining features of this later period anywhere: "complexity, blurred boundaries, and large size are typical characteristics of the archaeological remains of the modern world. They cannot be easily understood as isolated archaeological sites with clearly defined boundaries." These difficulties are often exaggerated by two basic features of western historical archaeology. First, in the context of regional cultural resource management (CRM), much of the work in the West begins and ends with extensive survey and evaluation of hundreds, and often thousands, of acres of federal or state properties. The need to recognize and make plausible evaluations of the potential significance of historical archaeological sites recorded during survey becomes a much more critical issue for many western CRM practitioners than questions related to both the scale and scope of archaeological excavation. These problems of fragmentation and large-scale phenomena tend to make site evaluation difficult, especially with regard to conventional National Register concepts like integrity, which becomes "a relative concept" in such contexts (Hardesty and Little 2000:46; Howett 2000).

Second, the relatively later date and subsequently higher level of preservation for aboveground features in the West leave historical archaeologists searching for frameworks that articulate research questions and evaluative criteria across the broadest possible range of artifact types, material culture, and potential cultural properties. In short, western historical archaeologists must deal with standing structures, linear features, traditional cultural properties, and, of course, archaeological remains in a coherent,

integrated, and publicly responsive way. All this has challenged the region's archaeologists, along with other CRM and preservation professionals, to develop both theoretical and methodological frameworks better suited to their later, larger, and often problematically categorized cultural landscapes (Francaviglia 1991; Heath 1997; Alanen 2000:112–115; Howett 2000:186–191).

The research presented here is one such attempt, drawn on a number of sources. One of the earliest is the work by Hardesty (1988: 9–12, 1991; Hardesty and Little 2000:23–25) on the archaeology of western mining camps, towns, and associated sites, and in particular his development of the concept of "feature systems" to describe spatially discrete but functionally articulated components of a settlement system. Project research, analysis, and interpretation also drew heavily on a number of regionally grounded works by cultural geographers (Groth and Bressi 1997) and vernacular architecture scholars (Carter 1997; Alanen and Melnick 2000). These studies not only helped expand the interpretive scale of the research but also provided the critical methodological breadth necessary to deal with a diverse array of material culture, from standing structures to linear features to substantive physical modifications of the landscape: levee building, channel dredging, and large-scale episodes of landfill.

The theoretical contributions of a number of "New Western" historians should be acknowledged, particularly those categorized as environmental historians (Cronon 1991; White 1991) and those interested in the relationships among western U.S. expansion, land speculation, and the global emergence of 19th-century industrial capitalism (Limerick 1987, 2000; Robbins 1994). These sources provided a critical historical framework within which to theorize about the larger economic, technological, and environmental processes that worked to influence human choices about land use and tenure in this place and time. Together with the previously referenced geographical and architectural scholars, these scholars provided the minimally adequate range of disciplinary approaches required to deal with the rich material culture that characterizes the cultural heritage of the 19th-century American West.

The two case studies that follow examine two very different landscapes created in two relatively small speculation townsites that developed along the Sacramento River in the mid- to late-19th century. The towns mapped alternative speculation strategies onto the landscape that reflected fundamentally different patterns of claiming land, allocating capital, and organizing population and economic activity. Both were components of a widely diffused but nonetheless inherently urban or, perhaps more accurately, cosmopolitan western landscape. Further, this landscape formed a critical component of the economic development of northern California during the later 19th and early 20th centuries.

The examples discussed in this paper were drawn from fieldwork and research conducted between 1995 and 2001 in the Sacramento River Delta. The Delta Waterways Project explored the creation and transformation of an inland maritime landscape in the western Sacramento River Delta from the beginning of American land speculation in the area just prior to the 1849 Gold Rush to the decade following World War I, which saw river transportation largely eclipsed by expanding railways and road systems. Following the meandering and braided channel of the Sacramento River and its tributary sloughs, these cultural landscapes, and the maritime-focused communities that created them, reached far inland from the seaport of San Francisco. The river formed the principal corridor for regional development during this period, and the communities that grew up along its banks took shape through their participation in a rapidly expanding economic context of river-based trade and market production that continued long after the initial gold boom.

The original impetus for the project grew from a 1995 field school in underwater archaeology in Steamboat Slough, directed by personnel from the Los Angeles Maritime Museum, the California Maritime Academy, the California Department of Transportation, and the San Francisco Maritime Museum, as well as Sonoma State University (SSU). The fieldwork conducted by this group focused on underwater cultural resources in Steamboat Slough and related maritime components of the adjacent landscape. The project resulted in a 1996 exhibit at the Los Angeles Maritime Museum, entitled Beyond the Gate (Purser and Shaw 1996).

Following the field school, discussions with cultural resource professionals in the California

Department of Parks and Recreation, the State Lands Commission, and the regional office of the U.S. Army Corps of Engineers identified a significant lack of recordation for historical maritime-related sites in the greater Sacramento River Delta area, then coming under increasing pressure from real estate development and flood control projects. A longer term cultural landscape project was developed that focused on recording landscape features and elements in the Montezuma Slough area of Solano County. Roughly 60 miles upstream from San Francisco and the Golden Gate and 50 miles downstream from the state capital at Sacramento, the project area lies near the center of the river-based transportation routes developed during the Gold Rush. This project was designed from the beginning to include as many methodological approaches and disciplinary perspectives as possible. A primary goal was to define critical elements of the cultural landscape of the Sacramento River channel as it developed between the years of the Gold Rush and the era that ushered in the replacement of water transport by land routes around World War I. The project was designed secondarily to provide a range of training opportunities for graduate students in heritage-related fields, to heighten awareness of these kinds of cultural resources, and to encourage their recordation and evaluation among a new generation of practitioners. Two subsequent field classes of SSU anthropology undergraduate students and one field school from the University of Utah Graduate School of Architecture, as well as a number of graduate students from the SSU master's program in CRM, provided critical labor, fieldwork, and analysis over the following five years.

The project has resulted in a preliminary survey and inventory of foreshore and maritime-related site types associated with the historical development of this small segment of the Sacramento River Delta region (Esser 1999). It also recorded site plans for a series of ranches and farms in the Bird's Landing and Collinsville areas and produced architectural drawings for a number of historical period structures. One building, the Bird and Dinkelspiel Store in Bird's Landing, was nominated successfully to the National Register of Historic Places (Storey 2000). The Montezuma project turned out to have been extremely timely, when in 1997 a significant portion of the project area was identified by the U. S. Army Corps of Engineers and the Port of Oakland, California, as the deposit zone for several thousand tons of dredged materials to be produced during a channel-clearing project undertaken at the port. Subsequent archaeological fieldwork to mitigate the impact of the project was awarded to a private-sector company (Self and Associates, 2000).

In the context of the cultural landscape study, several historical period townsites were explored and documented. Data for two of these communities are presented here: Rio Vista and Bird's Landing (Figure 1). Each began as a speculative

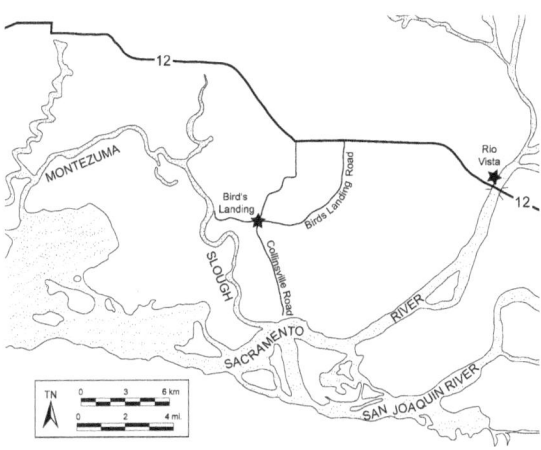

FIGURE 1. Project area, Sacramento Delta Region. (Map by Bryan Much, 2005.)

townsite poised to take advantage of the profits in agricultural production and commerce to be made from the burgeoning population and economic expansion of the Gold Rush boom time in the surrounding region. Each town survived by shifting the way it exploited the river's cheap transportation and access to both local and more distant national and international markets to keep pace with the vicissitudes of the broader regional economy. The two had very different histories as planned settlements. Rio Vista's development illustrates the classic scenario of the capital-intensive, regionally based, highly mobile speculation strategies often exercised by absentee owners that continue to define much of California's modern political and economic land-

scape. Bird's Landing presents a much different picture: longer term, smaller scale development by individuals who tended more commonly to be residents in their project townsite and who developed more situational strategies over time in response to changing local conditions.

Early Delta Land Speculation

The landscape of the delta had been culturally named and known for centuries prior to the arrival of Europeans. The Spanish, Mexicans, and Californians who came in the earliest phases of colonization continued to name places and features, including the Sacramento River itself. What marks the actions of the Americans who followed in the early 1840s is the explicitly speculative and entrepreneurial nature of their claims as well as the maps, charts, and town plats that document their actions. Since it was water access to a cheap, high volume mode of transportation that imparted a significant amount of value to the surrounding land, real estate speculation went hand in hand with charting the rivers and sloughs and with establishing regular, reliable vessel traffic along their courses.

While this speculative boom is most often told as part of the Gold Rush story, the truth is that such ventures began a decade or more before the discovery of gold along the banks of the American River. As a result, 1850s gold seekers traveled upriver to the mines through a landscape that had structure and landmarks remarkably more familiar and comfortable than they would have encountered as passengers on John Sutter's launch heading up the Sacramento from San Francisco Bay even a decade earlier. By 1850, this was a landscape dotted with townsites, ferry crossings, harbors, wharves, and houses. Ephemeral as some of these early speculative ventures turned out to be, the process set in place much of what was to become the landscape of the lower Sacramento River as well as much of the framework for linking the river, adjacent sloughs, and the land itself in patterns that were essentially commercial and cosmopolitan in nature.

In 1850, Admiral Cadwallader Ringgold (1851a) of the U.S. Navy executed a series of navigational charts that were among the earliest physical designations of the waterways of the Sacramento River. Both the date and Ringgold's accompanying notes make it clear that his survey was done explicitly to aid in the movement of miners into the goldfields. Much of how the survey was conducted and the actual charts it produced were the result of contacts he had made in the area some eight years prior to the discovery of gold. Ringgold had been a crewmember aboard the *Vincennes,* the flagship of the U.S. Exploring Expedition, chartered to explore the Pacific for U.S. military and commercial interests between 1838 and 1842. During their stay in California in 1841, Ringgold and a team of surveyors and scientists made it as far up the Sacramento as Sutter's Fort, and from there they continued their initial survey of the river as far upstream as Sutter Buttes, an event recorded in Sutter's own diary (Owens 1994:8).

A more accurate sense of the purposes behind the creation of Ringgold's 1850 charts is to be found literally in the fine print on the principal chart, which states that the work was "executed at the request of the undersigned citizens," who identify themselves as being the "Common Council" for the city of San Francisco (Ringgold 1851b). The list of names that follows includes 53 of the principal merchants, politicians, and most importantly, land speculators then in residence in the city, including men who would later establish town- and city sites from San Francisco Bay to Red Bluff at the head of navigation on the Sacramento River.

Ringgold's charts are themselves a fascinating mix of very reliable navigational data and pure speculative fantasy. The navigational data were apparently meticulously accurate and reliable, such as channel depths, harbor soundings, and painstakingly detailed instructions for finding one's way in the braided and frequently treacherous channels of the Sacramento, complete with accompanying lithographs of the river vistas at key waypoints. The information on Ringgold's charts pertaining to anything on shore, however, was of dubious reality at best, unless the information related directly to navigating the river. For instance, the charts appear to display a series of townsites fully platted along the shores of the Sacramento River. Many of these sites were never developed and several were relocated a number of times. Most did not exist at all as towns at the time the charts were drawn, and

even those that did had only the most tenuous of settlements.

In like manner, the other information contained in the charts is an intriguing mix of data crucial to the successful navigation of a meandering, perilous river channel and the plans and aspirations of individuals who intended to develop its various resources. Most of the names on the sponsor list found their way into the place names Ringgold assigned to islands, sloughs, and bays. A few other names appear that are not found on the official list of sponsors but represent key links among the men operating large-scale commercial outfits in the area at the time. These include sloughs, points, and islands named for P. B. Reading, who had served as Sutter's agent for the decade preceding the Gold Rush, as well as Samuel Hensley, a river captain and ally of Sutter's who would found the first steamship company on the Sacramento within three years of the publication of Ringgold's charts.

Almost none of these self-promoting place names were still in use a decade later. Like the largely fictitious town plats, they were intended for an audience that would read the charts as evidence that enough settlement had occurred and enough prosperity was in evidence to justify investing in the region. The more fictionalized data of Ringgold's charts were no more directed towards the average citizen than were the harder data of channel depths or safe bearings. These were not the pamphlets of hucksters, selling fraudulent California town lots on the docks of Boston and New York. His audience, and that of his sponsors, was to be found among the larger-scale capitalists who could join in the development of the region. Witness the man to whom he inscribed the charts, William H. Aspinwall, the New York founder of the Pacific Mail Steamship Company. In his cover letter to Aspinwall, Ringgold (1851b:4) explains, "your intimate connection with the Pacific steam line, the acknowledged commercial and general advantages which have resulted from its early and successful establishment, and the large and beneficial agency of that line, in the development of the vast resources of California" made Aspinwall the logical choice to receive and, by implication, to bankroll the publication of the charts.

Yet Ringgold's charts covered a territory that even by the mid-1840s had seen the initial identification and early settlement of a series of advantageous landing sites along the river channel. Place names already had become associated with these sites, and individual entrepreneurs were identified as proprietors of resident businesses. By 1848, P. Cordua's California Navigation Company had purchased an advertisement that described its monthly running of "a safe and commodious launch from [New Mecklenburg] to San Francisco, touching at Nicholas Algiers, the Embarcadero of Bear Creek, Mr. Hardy's, mouth of the Feather River, Sutterville, Brazoria, Montezuma, and Benecia City" (*The Californian* 1848).

Rio Vista Town Site

The site of called Brazoria in Cordua's list of riverside stops was to become Rio Vista, the first of the case studies discussed here. Brazoria lay along the western bank of the Sacramento River near the confluence of Cache and Steamboat sloughs with the main channel. The site was located immediately downstream from this navigational waypoint and was strategically positioned to catch the river traffic as it entered and exited the shortcut of Steamboat Slough. By the time of the Gold Rush, this advantageous site was already identified as valuable real estate, and several attempts had been made to claim it. As early as 1845, John Sutter had positioned his agent P. B. Reading at the site (Reading 1845) to supervise the efforts of some of Sutter's hired fur trappers who found the marshes along Cache Slough just east of the site among the most productive areas on the western Sacramento for taking profitable furs (Bancroft 1964:297). The agent was living in an adobe house that had just been constructed on the site to accommodate the outpost. Reading had spent part of an earlier winter on the low-lying plain and had even begun cultivating a few fields there (Bancroft 1964:297). These early fields were among the less fanciful terrestrial data that made it onto Ringgold's charts of the area, appearing as faint stippled hatching just north of the (then) entirely fictitious speculation townsite identified on the chart as "Suisun City" (Figure 2) (Ringgold 1851a).

Sutter did not actually hold the land at Brazoria. The real initiation of speculative development for Rio Vista had begun in 1844 when

John Bidwell was awarded the Los Ulpinos land grant from the Mexican governor of California. The grant, whose *diseño* (surveyed map) had been filed originally in 1840, comprised about 17,000 acres, much of which was low-lying swamp and overflow land. As noted in Sutter's letter to Reading, Bidwell had attempted an initial townsite settlement on his rancho almost immediately and had some plots of cultivated land and a small group of settlers wintering on the property by 1846. That winter proved an extremely difficult one. Food was scarce, crops largely failed, and by spring 1847 this early settlement had been largely abandoned (Fraser 1879:267).

One other piece of historical data gives evidence of the close ties between the individual speculators operating across the region at this

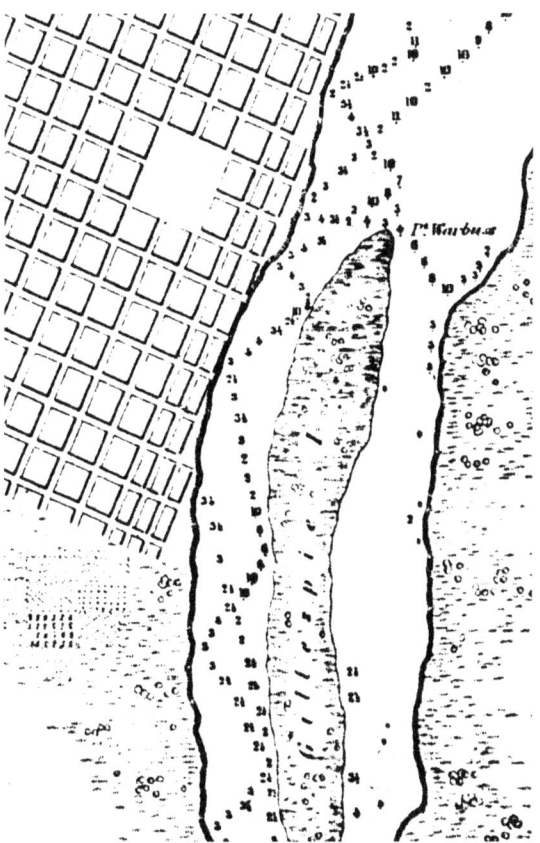

FIGURE 2. Enlargement of portion, Ringgold's 1850 navigational charts, sheet no. 4. Hypothetical "Suisun City" town lots shown above the stippling that indicates early agricultural fields. (California Lands Commission Office, Sacramento, CA.)

time and the way that different components of the emerging settlement system were linked through the personal and business ties among these people. Samuel Hensley was one of the sponsors of Ringgold's charts and would later help create the California Steam Navigation Company in 1854, which would dominate early steam traffic on the river (Bancroft 1964:184). In court testimony supporting Bidwell's land claim, Hensley recounted:

> In the fall of 1844 I took Mr. Bidwell on board of a schooner to the land (Ulpinos or Bidwell grant) with some hands to make a settlement. They remained there and built an adobe house, in which an Englishman, who had charge of the building, remained during the winter. The next season a small part of the land was cultivated, and in the winter of 1845-46 the house was occupied by P.B. Reading and hands (Fraser 1879:267).

By 1848, Hensley had opened a store upriver in Sacramento with Reading as his business partner (Bancroft 1964:184).

The Mexican government of California did not permit outright sales or partitioning of its land grants, so Bidwell attempted to circumvent this impediment to land speculation by selling shares in his investment. With the 1848 U.S. takeover of California, Bidwell was at last free to sell specific parcels of his land, but by that point title for much of the property was hopelessly muddled. His shareholders and former partners sued to recover their losses. As a result, the courts partitioned the entire land grant into 20 large rectangular lots, each fronting along the river and extending inland one league. These lots were then auctioned at the courthouse door in 1855, with the proceeds going to no less than 21 claimants (Fraser 1879:271).

Bidwell's attorney in this case was Nathan H. Davis who proceeded to buy up several of the large lots, including the one that had once held the small settlement. In 1857, Davis began his own town settlement on his property, changing the name Brazoria to Brazos del Rio initially but changing the name again to Rio Vista by 1859 (Hutchings 1860:52). Taking advantage of the site's location at the western mouth of Steamboat Slough, Davis built a small steamboat wharf at the foot of the town's main street in 1858. In late 1859 Davis sold a half-interest in his Brazos del Rio wharf to the California Steam Navigation Company (CSNC).

Headed by old Brazoria hand Samuel Hensley, CSNC immediately expanded the wharf and reoriented the structure to reach deeper water (Solano County 1860:Deed N584; Fraser 1879:273; Swete 1995). The settlement had boomed, becoming a principal stop for all river traffic between Sacramento and San Francisco, with daily stops by the major steamboats of the time. By late 1860, the town boasted two stores, two hotels, a blacksmith shop, butcher shop, drugstore, livery stable, and salmon cannery, as well as a number of residences (Hutchings 1860:52; Fraser 1879:272–273).

This prosperity was to be short lived, however. A tremendous flood during the winter of 1861–1862 wiped the settlement off the map, leaving only scattered piles of brick where chimney stacks had fallen (Fraser 1879:273). The town of Rio Vista was relocated southwest to its current location and continued on to considerable prosperity during the later 19th and early-20th centuries. The original townsite was abandoned to pasturage. Occasional use of the property as an emergency route for releasing excess water from the Yolo Bypass in flood years has helped preserve this relatively low-use function. Although navigational charts from the early 1910s still recorded the presence of "old pilings" along the shoreline at the site, the original location of the site itself was eventually forgotten.

Town Plats and Speculation Strategies

Bidwell apparently never attempted to plat his small settlement, and certainly not at the size or formality suggested by the labeled insets in Ringgold's charts, but Nathan Davis definitely did. His original plat for the town was surveyed in 1857, and the map was filed formally in December 1858, although it is clear that a number of houses, businesses, and Davis's own wharf were already constructed by this time (Figure 3). The plat indicates a conventional grid plan for speculation townsites of the mid-19th century, with the obligatory mid-block alleyways and set-aside blocks for the town's school and church. Davis's wharf lies at the foot of C Street, across a Front Street that is clearly depicted as half-submerged by the river's shoreline. It is possible that part of Front Street was built on piers out over the water,

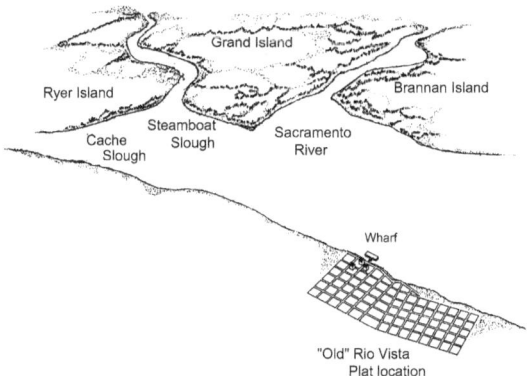

FIGURE 3. Schematic of 1860 Rio Vista townsite location, based on 1995–1998 survey data. (Map by Bryan Much, 2005.)

as occurred in the neighboring contemporary town of Collinsville, a few miles downstream. There, much of the commercial district of the entire town was elevated on piers and flanked a wooden boardwalk that extended inland more than half a mile from the river-fronting wharf to higher ground.

That some pre-existing wharf or docking facility probably anchored the Rio Vista town grid is indicated by the odd row of partial lots that lie along the western boundary of Davis's parcel. Property records that exist for this initial set of town lots indicate that some of the street grid had been in place prior to the official filing of the plat. An 1857 description of the town reads,

> The next building placed upon the town site was a store-house moved from Sidwell's Landing, on Grand Island, and occupied by A.G. Westgate for mercantile purposes. This building stood *on the corner of Front and Main Streets.* This was followed in rapid succession by a butcher-shop by A.J. Bryant, a hotel by W.K. Squires, a blacksmith-shop by Simon Fallman, a salmon cannery by Carter and Son, a store by S.R. Perry, a drug store by James and Thomas Freeman (they also had an hotel) [sic], a livery stable by James Hammel, and several private residences, making in all quite a little village [emphasis added] (Fraser 1879:272).

Those partial lots, however, inspired Davis's western neighbor, Mr. Torode, to file an extension to the Brazos del Rio town plat in 1859, trying to capitalize on the property boom created by the new townsite (California State Lands Commission 1861). Torode's

planned townsite was even more ambitious than Davis's. It consisted of a narrow strip of urban-sized lots along the river's edge abutting and adjoining Davis's own street grid. But the rest of the plat extended the full league's length into the interior of the low plain, with 40- and 60-acre farmsteads flanking a central transportation artery, labeled "Suisun Avenue" (Figure 4). Apparently, Torode's intention was to create a fully self-contained community whose agricultural production could be funneled directly onto his competing wharf and out to local and regional markets. It is unclear whether any of this ambitious plan was ever really implemented, although county deed books do record an official subdivision of Torode's own map in early 1861 (California State Lands Commission 1861).

The block divisions of Davis's plat fell into disuse after the 1861 flood, but many of those marked on Torode's map continue in use today as road rights-of-way and property boundaries. Suisun Avenue in particular remains on current assessor's parcel maps for the area. This convergence allowed archaeologists to resurvey the original town grid during the 1995 and 1996 field seasons and to locate the former positions of the first town wharf, as well as the possible line of a river-fronting street surface, now some 25–30 feet offshore in the river. The resurvey was accomplished by overlaying scanned images of Torode's and Davis's original plats onto cur-

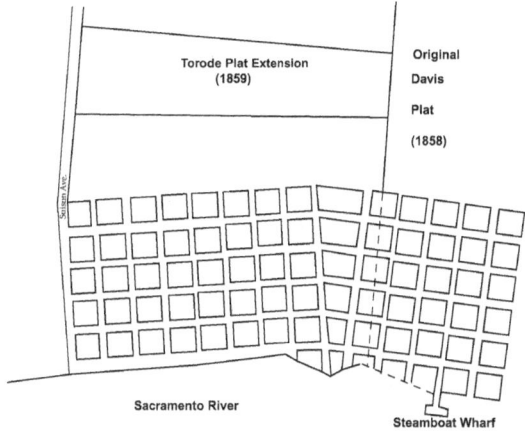

FIGURE 4. Schematic drawn from Torode's extension of the Brasos del Rio plat, 1859. (Map by Bryan Much, 2005.)

rent assessor's parcel maps, a recent aerial photograph, and a USGS topographical quadrant map of the site area. When the route of former Suisun Avenue on the various maps and images was aligned, it was possible to identify an existing property corner that matched a lot corner on Davis's original plat. Accepting the plat dimensions and scale as accurate, the 1995 field school was able to resurvey the southwestern portion of the original townsite, including portions of the town now completely submerged offshore (Figure 5) (Purser and Shaw 1996).

During the 1960s construction of the Sacramento Deep Water Ship Channel just offshore from the site, dredge fill from the channel cut was used to raise and level the property, to help stabilize the topography in the event of overflow flooding from the upstream Yolo Bypass. This fill caps the more inland historical town surface to a depth of several meters in spots. At the same time, an earlier levee was moved inland a distance of some 10 meters or more. This process effectively submerged the remaining site surface between the older and more recent levee locations, thus preserving at least some in situ features below the water line. Shoreline erosion has exposed a layer of mid-19th-century bottle glass, ceramic, brick, and charred wood lying on a compacted clay surface. This surface and associated features are now recorded as a site and flagged for avoidance in further river and shoreline modifications.

Bird's Landing Townsite

Although its initial speculators were long gone, Rio Vista survived both the economic and ecological instability of its early years. Ultimately, the community thrived as an important river town through the later 19th and into the early-20th century, primarily because of its strategic location on the main waterway between the agricultural lands of the northern Central Valley, the state capital of Sacramento to the

FIGURE 5. 1995 field school students recording features of Rio Vista townsite, river side of the levee. (Photo by Margaret Purser, 1995.)

Perspectives from *Historical Archaeology*

east, and the region's premier port of San Francisco to the west. The second case study of the small town of Bird's Landing had a somewhat different history. Bird's Landing illustrates the strategic differences between large-scale land speculators like Bidwell, whose intentions could be grand but who tended to keep their capital relatively mobile and widely spread around a region, and smaller scale town builders whose efforts tended to be more localized, and to be reinvested again and again in one or two local communities, over what could be decades of vicissitudes in markets, climate, and political control.

Rio Vista may have boomed because of its prime location on the main waterway, but for Bird's Landing, the story was different. Montezuma Slough, the navigable waterway used by this town, was always a byway, a route off the main channel and out of the principal traffic of the river. Skirting the flanks of the west-facing Montezuma Hills at the very margin of the delta itself, the eastern mouth of the slough lay just opposite the junction of the two great rivers, the Sacramento and the San Joaquin (Figure 1). As the slough wound inland between the higher ground and the vast, low-lying marshes of Van Sickle, Grizzly, and Joice islands, it opened up access to what would become the interior farmlands of southern Solano County. Although Montezuma Slough was depicted on Ringgold's original charts, only the site across the main channel from the river confluence had seen any development during the mid 1840s, when a ferry service was established at what would become known as Collinsville. By the early 1850s, settlers were drawn to the surrounding area by the potential of this zone of rolling hills and fertile open grasslands to feed the burgeoning Gold Rush populations. They used the slough to route their crops to the new urban markets ringing San Francisco Bay and to support the growth of a series of small rural entrepôts like Bird's Landing. Montezuma's waters flow in either direction, depending on the tides, and today the slough forms part of the boundary where the brackish, sea-flavored waters of the San Francisco and San Pablo bays meet the fresh water of the mountain-fed rivers. In much the same way, the people settled along the banks have long been caught up in the swinging economic currents of the region as well as the

continuing struggle to match agricultural commodity production to both market vicissitudes and environmental shifts in aridity, salinity, and fertility.

Bird's Landing itself was a small crossroads town, not a "landing" at all. Along the eastern margins of Montezuma Slough, a wide belt of marshy and frequently flooded land bordered the slough proper, making easy access from land to water difficult and costly. A slight rise in elevation, however, between half a mile and a mile inland meant significant crops of wheat and other grains could be grown on the narrow tableland. On the rising slopes of the Montezuma Hills just beyond that, grazing for sheep and dairy cattle was substantial. People in the Montezuma Slough area solved the problem by putting their farmsteads and fields inland and building a few elevated roadways to strategically placed, privately owned commercial landing sites along the slough's margins. The townsite designated as Bird's Landing was actually located at an intersection of two of these main roads: one leading west and south along the face of the hills to the ferry landing at the slough's eastern mouth, and one leading from the interior of the hills west to the commercial landing site known as Mein's Landing (Figure 6) (Esser 1999).

John Bird, the owner of yet another slough landing site further south from Mein's, began this crossroads settlement. Bird was a native of Onondaga County, New York, who headed for San Francisco in 1859. His early experience in the region marks him clearly as a farmer.

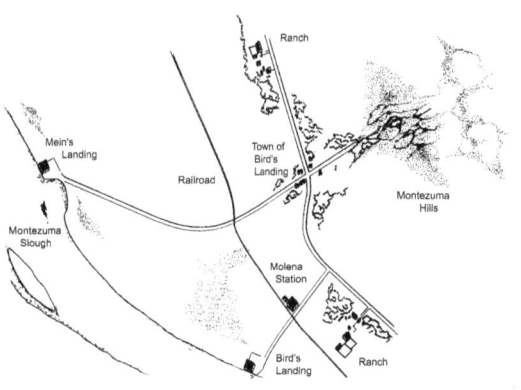

FIGURE 6. Schematic of Bird's Landing settlement system with associated features. (Map by Bryan Much, 2005.)

He worked in Marin County for three years as a farm foreman. In 1862, he moved to Sacramento where he ran his own dairy and stock farm. Finally, in 1865, he purchased 960 acres of land near Montezuma Slough and began to raise grain and dairy cattle (Gregory 1912: 427). Here he joined a growing number of other individual farmers and ranchers who had begun to settle along the higher tablelands just inland from Montezuma Slough and at the foot of the Montezuma hills during the later 1850s and early 1860s (Fraser 1879:482–489).

Four years later, Bird began to diversify his investments. Seeking to control his access to the waterways for his own ranch produce, in 1869 he built his first wharf and warehouse on the eastern bank of Montezuma Slough (Gregory 1912:427). From there, he began shipping butter and grain to San Francisco (Bird 1985). This enterprise was the original "Bird's Landing," and the landing site continued to be a significant component of Bird's business dealings well into the early-20th century. Fire insurance maps from 1885 indicate that a second, even larger, warehouse was built in 1878. This structure was actually a double building with a total capacity of 5,000 tons. It was built on pilings, 4 ft. aboveground, to accommodate the frequent flooding of the area, and fronted onto a wharf that ran approximately 100 ft. along the bank of the slough (Sanborn Map Co. 1885).

The landing site on the marshy slough had no potential for development as a town. Beginning some time in the early- to mid-1870s, Bird began to purchase and develop land located at the crossroads some three miles inland and to the north of his landing site. Here he began to invest in attracting the critical enterprises that formed the core of small-town commercial districts in the later 19th century. By 1871, he had built a blacksmith shop along the slough, credited with being the first one outside Suisun City (Gregory 1912:427). What would ultimately make John Bird a town builder, in addition to a local farmer with a profitable landing site, was his partnership with Moses Dinkelspiel, a German immigrant who had spent time in commercial ventures around New York state in the late 1840s and early 1850s. Dinkelspiel had arrived in the Solano County area a few years earlier than Bird and in 1858 settled in Suisun City, the small inland port town developing at

the other end of Montezuma Slough (Fraser 1879:289; Shine 1976:10). There he began a small mercantile establishment with his uncle, Jacob Frank (Fraser 1879:289). Although John Bird ultimately became the town's namesake, his association with the Dinkelspiel family provided the additional capital and shared risk that gave both men the opportunity to build a town and, in so doing, shape much of the landscape in and around Bird's Landing.

In 1875 and 1876, the partnership of Jacob Frank & Moses Dinkelspiel purchased a plot of land at the crossroads from John Bird and constructed the first general store (Figure 7). The town officially received the name Bird's Landing in 1876 when the post office was established in the store (Shine 1976:10–11; Solano County 1876:92). In the decade that followed, the partnership expanded significantly, and the business interests diversified. Dinkelspiel and his wife, Lena, bought farmland just south and west of the little town, adjacent to Bird's first ranch and lying between the slough and the main north-south road. Property traded hands between the partners; in 1880, Bird purchased the store property back from Dinkelspiel (Gregory 1912: 427). Meanwhile, realizing the potential to capitalize on the business generated by busy landing sites and warehouses, the Dinkelspiels purchased the landing and warehouse from Bird, who continued to operate and manage both for approximately 40 years (Bird 1985).

Bird's Landing as a Settlement System

In terms of the townsite proper, growth was incremental but steady. Intriguingly, Bird never filed a plat map for the townsite, and as late as 1879, a subscription history prepared for the county fails to list Bird's Landing as an official townsite in the Montezuma township (Fraser 1879:311–313). Instead, it was understood that new residents would be attracted to an area that provided an established, stable economy in the form of core commercial businesses and facilities. The economic viability of Bird's Landing would be presented to potential residents through architecture. The result would be that newcomers could purchase land and build new enterprises. The rationale behind this type of town building was that it provided the builders with opportunities to receive returns through their ini-

FIGURE 7. Bird & Dinkelspiel Store, Rio Vista, ca. 1900. (Photo in possession of the authors.)

tial enterprises as well as future income through land purchases and the use of their goods and services by newcomers. Bird's construction of the blacksmith's shop constituted a speculative venture with relatively minimal initial capital outlay yet significant potential for return. His larger commercial intentions for Bird's Landing were realized as new investors settled in the town, purchased land, and constructed the buildings that would eventually form the town's main intersection. Regardless of how well or poorly these new ventures turned out, much of the development ultimately returned profits to Bird and his partners, the Dinkelspiels. According to his son Henry Bird, Jr. (1985),

> W. Cerkel of Suisun built a large two story building in 1875 and the same caught on fire on Sunday night before it was occupied ... They had to work hard

saving the present store that still stands. J.B. Blythe built another store and hall across from the Bird & Dinkelspiel Store. Never stocked, Father (John Bird) got that when he bought the 160 acre ranch where the last home of the Birds burned down. D. Weingartner built the hotel that was known as the Union Hotel. E. Krause built the hotel known as Montezuma Hotel, also the first Meat Market. The first Saloon was run by H.E. Winters. After that there were two more, one in each hotel. Another Blacksmith Shop was added to the town being run by OT. Owens, a Paint Shop run by Mr. Warren, a China Wash House being conducted by a chinaman named Bow Yuen, and other dwellings, so the town was ready for business.

It is the way these business partners articulated their townsite ventures with the surrounding region that constitutes the signature feature of this system of town building. By the early-20th century, the Bird & Dinkelspiel partnership integrated components of all the available commercial and transportation systems of the Montezuma area, including shares in several small scows and schooners, a Montezuma Slough landing and warehouse, a station on the new railroad, a general store in the small crossroads town, and a larger store in a neighboring commercial port. Viewed as components of a system that evolved over time, these investments demonstrate the willingness of both Bird and Dinkelspiel to maintain their long-term commitments to local success and their strategies for sharing risks and mediating loss.

In the town proper, the two men made every effort to make the community as autonomous as possible in terms of available services and to centralize those services in the businesses owned by the Bird & Dinkelspiel partnership, while attempting to minimize the associated risk. The original store formed the heart of these integrative practices. Initially this meant extending the services provided by the enterprise to the full extent of what was possible for a small country store. For example, insurance policies and credit for loans depended on metropolitan bankers. Lacking a local bank, and servicing an agrarian area characterized by only seasonal influxes of cash, Bird & Dinkelspiel sold these items to their customers, secured from the San Francisco's Fireman Fund Insurance in 1883 and The Bradstreet Company in 1890 (Shine 1976: 13). One long-term result of this strategy was the accumulation of additional property, particularly ranch property, when creditees could not pay their loans or when longer term store bills or landing warehouse accounts lapsed.

In a more subtle sense, Bird and Dinkelspiel worked to create a sense of identity between the store as a business and Bird's Landing as a community. For instance, they provided much of the public gathering space available in town, such as the inclusion of the original Odd Fellows Hall in the general store and Bird's later purchase and operation of the adjacent store and hall across the intersection. In an architectural pattern common to many small-town store buildings in the West, the inclusion of an upstairs meeting hall in the store proper allowed the town merchants to encourage a compounding of their commercial ventures with the public identity of the community itself. Over time, residents identified these privately owned commercial structures with the public, civic success of the town.

Similar strategies combining personal prestige and community boosterism built the partners' various avenues for promoting the town in an increasingly competitive county political and administrative arena. The town of Bird's Landing existed as a node of settlement in the county-township system, a territorial form of government control based on geography instead of population. This designation method was successful in pioneer settlements where most of the inhabitants lived on farms scattered throughout the landscape, as was certainly the case along Montezuma Slough (Lingeman 1980:123). Bird's Landing fell under Montezuma Township, as did most of the partners' other business interests, although the Dinkelspiels also retained their interests in commercial properties in the adjacent Suisun Township. The success of their strategies required multiple alliances at a larger but still localized scale, and so Bird and Dinkelspiel furthered their economic interests by becoming community leaders at the township and county levels. Using available political mechanisms, they reinforced their own identities as leading members of their smaller community and that of the community itself as a unified prosperous whole. John Bird in particular involved himself extensively in community matters. According to the 1912 *History of Solano and Napa Counties*,

> For thirty-five years he [Bird] has been a member of the board of school trustees, and has also been clerk of the board during this period. For one term he served as justice of the peace, and under McKinley's administration he served as postmaster of Bird's Landing until he resigned. Politically Mr. Bird is a Republican and is ever ready to assist in everything that has for its object the improvement of the county or community (Gregory 1912:428).

This extended and diversified network of political alliances mirrored the structure of Bird and Dinkelspiel's expansion into other commercial interests over the decades. Their investments in transportation elements perhaps best illustrate the full extent of these strategies. Collectively, these purchases structured a highly articulated but diffuse settlement system whose component parts could be miles apart but that functioned solely to connect the Bird's Landing enterprises to the emerging urban network of San Francisco Bay. The building of the original landing site had launched the partners

Perspectives from *Historical Archaeology*

into the maritime industry that linked the river and sloughs to the larger port facilities inland at Sacramento and to the urban centers of San Francisco and Oakland on the bay. Owning and operating the landing site led Bird, in particular, to expand his investment to include the vessels that carried goods between his landing and the larger ports. But he kept his investments relatively small and widely spread, preferring to own part interest in several vessels, rather than owning any single vessel outright. In his memoirs, Henry Bird, Jr. (1985) writes, "Father was interested in shipping, owned interests in Scow Schooners, first vessel Arab, new vessel to take Arab's place named Lizzie Theresa. Capt. Albert Sims ... owned half interest, John Bird one fourth, J.L. Vermeil and George Wellington one eighth each."

As new opportunities presented themselves, the same strategy was applied, bringing a new transportation node into the partner's existing enterprises and avoiding or diverting competition. When a small regional electric railroad opened in 1912, linking the northern Central Valley town of Chico to the bay, it ran through ranch land the Dinkelspiels already owned and crossed

the road that led out to the Bird & Dinkelspiel landing wharf and warehouse. Here, one of the partnership's final speculative ventures took shape. Moses and Lena Dinkelspiel constructed a station on the new rail line and laid out a small townsite. Platted and filed officially in May 1914, it was named Molena, a combination of their first names. While the townsite itself does not appear to have taken off, it did succeed in attracting investment from new customers when the Taylors, a local ranching family, built a large warehouse at the site. Molena Station, as the site became known, continued in operation until the closure of the railroad in the 1940s (Figure 8).

Fieldwork in Bird's Landing focused on architectural recording of the surviving structures, the use of oral history, and analysis of historic photographs to reconstruct a town settlement plan that the absence of a plat map made difficult to document otherwise. Graduate students from the University of Utah Graduate School of Architecture and the SSU master's in CRM program recorded four surviving residences in town, including one that had been converted from an early town schoolhouse, and the town saloon. Survey teams also relocated the sites

FIGURE 8. Bird's Landing vicinity, taken from site of original Bird's Landing wharf. Taylor warehouse is in the right-hand foreground; town of Bird's Landing is in far left background, in trees. (Photo by Margaret Purser, 1998.)

FIGURE 9. Bird's Store during restoration, summer 1998. (Photo by Margaret Purser, 1998.)

of the original Bird's Landing and warehouse, Molena Station, and the Montezuma Station further south, as well as a number of connecting roads, ditches, and additional slough landing sites (Esser 1999).

Then, in 2000, the Bird Store building was nominated successfully to the National Register of Historic Places (Figure 9). The nomination process provided the opportunity to document this complex network of sites, enterprises, and investment and speculation strategies created by the Bird & Dinkelspiel partnership over the four decades between the initial construction of the store in 1875 and John Bird's death in 1921. More significantly, the store building itself was not nominated merely as an architectural specimen. Its significance was defined in terms of its representation of the entire system of settlement, speculation, and long-term capital

investment—an example of a regional process of town building that had played a critical role in the development of inland maritime California. The success of the nomination on this thematic basis opens the way for further analysis of this kind of physically scattered but economically and socially integrated cosmopolitan landscape along other transportation and commercial corridors in the American West.

Discussion

To return to the initial questions about the nature of urbanization in the West, archaeologists often find themselves dealing with fragmentary, partial, and literally buried relics of urban forms, both planned and realized, vestigial and articulated. There are two scales at which to explore these experimentations with urban

Perspectives from *Historical Archaeology*

form in the 19th-century West. One focuses at the level of the site and looks at the physical basis of the plat maps themselves: the grid, lots, blocks, streets, and alleyways, and the ways that these physical features might or might not linger in either the documentary or archaeological record, as these smaller scale communities developed over time.

The Rio Vista case study points out how complex the relationships between planned space and actual settlement could be. The abstracted grids of Ringgold's early river charts testify to the degree to which urban spatial conventions had become iconic in the legal and cartographic conventions of western land speculation, even by 1850. On the same chart, the tiny stippled lines of P. B. Reading's very real agricultural fields, just beside the entirely speculative Suisun City grid, document that from the very beginning speculative planning did not map uniformly over actual land use patterns. The legal transformation of a Spanish land grant to U.S. property definitions and subsequent gridding of the town at two different scales further complicated matters, as did Davis's platting of what was evidently already an existing town settlement, even in 1858 (cf Church 2002). The original Rio Vista plat retains both its legal and material relevance in the incorporation of Torode's street plan and property boundaries in the current Rio Vista assessor's maps and street grid. This material reality made the relocation and survey of the original townsite possible.

In the case of Bird's Landing proper, any physical manifestation of a true urban grid is simply absent. The only gridded plat that can be associated with the Bird & Dinkelspiel partnership is one of its last endeavors, the tiny townsite of Molena, that seems to have been used only to sell the trackside lot for the Taylor warehouse. Instead, Bird's Landing as a physical site seems to represent an almost vernacular knowledge of the proper dimensions and components of a crossroads town: store, hotel, blacksmith shop, butcher shop, saloon, school. In this regard, Bird's Landing makes sense in a discussion of urban sites only at a larger, regionally comparative scale in conjunction with the other settlements to which it was connected and upon which it was functionally dependent.

Development along the Sacramento Delta initiated along a pattern that urban historian Eric Monkkonen (1988:25) has described as "functionally distinct kinds of cities and villages, all spatially, socially, and economically interrelated." In Monkkonen's model, there are four distinct levels: metropolis, city, town, and village. The center of activity is the metropolis, which offers advantages in communications and specialization in a variety of activities and professions. The city, the second largest development in the model, has a number of specialized functions, maybe even more than the metropolis, but none that can exist independently. Towns, the third level, surround the cities and offer a number of limited services or may exist to support a single economy. The last level in the model, the village, provides only the most basic types of goods and services to a limited area. Described in these terms, there is hardly anything unique about the mechanisms of western urbanization. Early western towns usually developed in locations the initial inhabitants hoped were places with economic futures where individuals could survive and eventually prosper. The early settlements that did survive but failed to develop into full urban centers still had the possibility of becoming trading centers, small country towns, or stops along the railroad, river, or slough.

This larger frame of reference moves archaeologists beyond physical relics specific to individual sites and puts the focus on the more pervasive urban manifestations in the West. The same people who conformed to the legal system of the time and filed the obligatory plat map often held for themselves certain urban-derived assumptions and aspirations about the ways their own enterprises would progress. The exigencies of western settlement itself often reinforced these assumptions. In particular, the potential for significant profit vigorously encouraged land speculation on a massive scale. As the century progressed, the laws structuring speculation increasingly demanded urban-style property definitions and conventions like the grid as a prerequisite to land sales. But the settlement system produced by these strategies often defies categorization in conventional "urban" terms, as components of necessarily fixed typologies, however functional their connections to other places. More importantly, it is vital to avoid assuming any chronological or developmental order in Monkonnen's typological system: in the West, all settlement forms (from cities to villages) developed nearly simultaneously, at dramatically accelerated rates, and often in intense competition with each other.

Instead, these landscapes are best thought of as extended "cosmopolitan" networks that might link component elements across multiple counties. Western archaeologists need to look at linking the various properties and enterprises of town builders who created a system of urbanization that was scattered in its component parts across considerable territories and was linked by networks of kinship, risk, and redundancy to a far greater extent than either capital or property as conventionally defined and perhaps more commonly employed elsewhere. In this regard, the written record for Rio Vista also testifies to enduring personal linkages among individual speculators that spanned development across the entire region and across at least four decades of northern California settlement history. These linkages can be tracked from the self-advertising place names and aspiring grid plans of Ringgold's navigational charts; to the initial settlement attempts linking Bidwell, Sutter, and Reading; to Hensley's partnership with Bidwell's attorney Davis in the building of Rio Vista's first wharf.

But it is the Bird's Landing landscape itself that provides an even more localized, nuanced map of how such partnerships worked to shape space and community over time. Bird's Landing, in Monkkonen's functionalist terms, survived as long as it did only because its principal commercial speculators succeeded in pushing a village to provide services and attract settlers in ways more akin to those of a true town. That success was more than just marketing or even the familiar, pervasive boosterism that characterized so much of 19th-century American expansion. The partners' ultimate success was predicated on their extension of the town's physical resources beyond its initial settlement core to include more remote, specialized sites like landings, wharves, and train stations. Like their central store, Bird & Dinkelspiel operated these facilities in such a way as to blur the distinction between privately owned commercial property intended to create a profit for its owners and some form of public, municipal facility. In the process, they created a landscape that looked rural but functioned as it did only because of its integration into a larger urban sphere. More than mere satellites, places like Bird's Landing created a unique western form of settlement and one on which much more study is needed to understand it in any detail. Most importantly, reading "rural" functions of sites based on current appearances of the landscape risks creating false pasts for these sites and the larger region in which they are located (Francaviglia 2000:47; Howett 2000:197–205). A more appropriate analogy might well come from the future, and the "space colony" settlement scenarios of science fiction: technologically advanced but physically isolated and ecologically challenged nodes articulated through increasingly sophisticated communication and transportation systems. These are also the traits that make the archaeological study of western speculation landscapes powerfully relevant to other later 19th- and early-20th-century contexts of economic expansion and boom-bust economic fluctuations elsewhere on the globe.

In conclusion, in the American West, some "urban" sites can be found in vestigial form in ways that repay careful research and that profoundly structure the archaeological record of these places as sites. Historical archaeologists are only just beginning to understand the complex relationship between the speculative intentions of a plat map and the lived reality of the settlement that the document purports to represent. At a larger scale, even more complex "cosmopolitan" sites may well be scattered, quite literally, all over the map in their various component parts. In these cases, archaeological analysis becomes truly challenging. The physical structure of this fragmented yet articulated landscape and its often uneven or conflicting documentary record bedevil the application of basic concepts like site boundary. Analyses that focus at the level of the townsite proper may fail to include critical features of the town's settlement system that lie at a distance from its residential or commercial core. More importantly, remnant features and structures of these more isolated enterprises can be easily dismissed as insignificant or lacking research potential if their relevance to the larger feature system goes unrecognized. The landscapes created by these unique, multiscalar settlement systems can provide considerable insight into the nature of 19th-century western expansion and the highly diverse social and economic strategies that drove it.

Acknowledgments

A great number of agencies, professionals, and students have contributed time and resources to the project over the course of research. The original impetus for the project grew from a 1995 field school in underwater archaeology in Steamboat Slough directed by personnel from the Los Angeles Maritime Museum (Sheli Smith and Monica Hunter), the California Maritime Academy (Sam Shaw), the California Department of Transportation (Jack Hunter), and the San Francisco Maritime Museum (John Muir), as well as Sonoma State University (Michael Jablonowski). The relocation of the old townsite of Rio Vista could not have been accomplished without the documentary research and fieldwork of freelance underwater archaeologist Richard Swete who discovered the convergence of the old plat map and current tax-assessor parcel data during this phase of the project. William Poe of the History Department, SSU, did the geo-referenced digital overlays of the maps and aerial photos to resurvey the townsite. The California State Lands Commission and the Department of Parks and Recreation, and the U.S. Army Corps of Engineers, San Francisco Office, have also made significant contributions of staff time and materials and have provided invaluable guidance as research has progressed. The River Delta Historical Society, Rio Vista Museum, Solano County Historical Society, Solano County Archives, Clarksburg Museum, Western Railroad Museum and Vacaville Museum have provided documents, photographic materials, and maps, as well as timely suggestions about where to look next for relevant information. Tom Carter directed a field school from the University of Utah Graduate School of Architecture in the project area during summer 1998. Two field classes of SSU anthropology students as well as a number of graduate students from the SSU Master of Arts in Cultural Resources Management program provided critical labor, fieldwork, and analysis over the years. Over the course of the research, the generous people of the Bird's Landing and Collinsville communities opened their homes, ranches, and family archives to SSU faculty and students who were conducting a wide range of material culture research in the surrounding countryside. The project owes a particular debt to Mrs. Shirley Paolini and to John and Leona Benjamin of Birds Landing for their generous support and encouragement.

References

ALANEN, ARNOLD R.
   2000   Considering the Ordinary: Vernacular Landscapes in Small Towns and Rural Areas. In *Preserving Cultural Landscapes in America*, Arnold R. Alanen and Robert Z. Melnick, editors, pp. 112–142. Johns Hopkins University Press, Baltimore, MD.

ALANEN, ARNOLD R., AND ROBERT Z. MELNICK (EDITORS)
   2000   *Preserving Cultural Landscapes in America*. Johns Hopkins University Press, Baltimore, MD.

ASHMORE, WENDY, AND A. BERNARD KNAPP (EDITORS)
   1999   *Archaeologies of Landscape: Contemporary Perspectives*. Basil Blackwell, Oxford, England, UK.

BANCROFT, H. H.
   1964   *California Pioneer Register and Index, 1542–1848. Including Inhabitants of California, 1769–1800, and List of Pioneers*. Regional Publishing Company, Baltimore, MD.

BARTH, GUNTHER PAUL
   1975   *Instant Cities: Urbanization and the Rise of San Francisco and Denver*. Oxford University Press, New York, NY.

BIRD, HENRY, JR.
   1985   Private memoirs. Manuscript, private collection of Shirley Paolini, Bird's Landing, CA.

CALIFORNIA STATE LANDS COMMISSION
   1861   Plan of a Portion of the rancho Los Ulpinos or Bidwell Grant ... surveyed Oct. 1858 and subdivided March 18(6?)1. Plat map, California State Lands Commission, Sacramento, CA.

THE CALIFORNIAN
   1848   Advertisement for P. Cordua. *The Californian* 2(49). San Francisco, CA.

CARTER, THOMAS
   1997   *Images of an American Land: Vernacular Architecture in the Western United States*. University of New Mexico Press, Albuquerque.

CHURCH, MINETTE C.
   2002   The Grant and the Grid: Homestead Landscapes in the Late-Nineteenth-Century Borderlands of Southern Colorado. *Journal of Social Archaeology* 2(2):220–244.

CRONON, WILLIAM
   1991   *Nature's Metropolis: Chicago and the Great West*. W. W. Norton, New York, NY.

ESSER, KIMBERLY S.
1999 Notoriously Swampy and Overflowed: An Inland Maritime Landscape of the California Delta. Master's thesis, Department of Archaeology, Sonoma State University, Rohnert Park, CA.

FRANCAVIGLIA, RICHARD
1991 *Hard Places: Reading the Landscape of America's Historic Mining Districts.* University of Iowa Press, Iowa City.
2000 Selling America's Heritage Landscapes. In *Preserving Cultural Landscapes in America,* Arnold R. Alanen and Robert Z. Melnick, editors, pp. 44–69. Johns Hopkins University Press, Baltimore, MD.

FRASER, J. P. MUNRO
1879 *History of Solano County.* Wood, Alley, and Co., San Francisco, CA. First edition reprinted in 1994 by J. Stevenson Publishers, Fairfield, CA.

GREGORY, TOM
1912 *History of Solano and Napa Counties.* Historic Record Company, Los Angeles, CA.

GROTH, PAUL, AND TODD W. BRESSI
1997 *Understanding Ordinary Landscapes.* Yale University Press, New Haven, CT.

HARDESTY, DONALD L.
1988 *The Archaeology of Mining and Miners: A View from the Silver State.* The Society for Historical Archaeology, Special Publication Series, 6. California, PA.
1991 Toward an Historical Archaeology of the Intermountain West. *Historical Archaeology* 25(3):29–35.

HARDESTY, DONALD L., AND BARBARA J. LITTLE
2000 *Assessing Site Significance: A Guide for Archaeologists and Historians.* AltaMira Press, Walnut Creek, CA.

HEATH, KINGSTON
1997 False-Front Architecture on Montana's Urban Frontier. In *Images of an American Land: Vernacular Architecture in the Western United States,* Tom Carter, editor, pp. 21–39. University of New Mexico Press, Albuquerque.

HOWETT, CATHERINE
2000 Integrity as a Value in Cultural Landscape Preservation. In *Preserving Cultural Landscapes in America,* Arnold R. Alanen and Robert Z. Melnick, editors, pp. 186–208. Johns Hopkins University Press, Baltimore, MD.

HUTCHINGS, JAMES M.
1860 *Hutchings' California Magazine* 4(12):52. Reprinted in 1962 as *Scenes of Wonder and Curiosity from Hutchings' California Magazine, 1856–1861,* R. R. Olmsted, editor, Howell-North, Berkeley, CA.

KAHN, JUDD
1979 *Imperial San Francisco: Politics and Planning in an American City, 1897–1906.* University of Nebraska Press, Lincoln.

KELSO, WILLIAM M., AND RACHEL MOST
1990 *Earth Patterns: Essays in Landscape Archaeology.* University Press of Virginia, Charlottesville.

LIMERICK, PATRICIA NELSON
1987 *The Legacy of Conquest: The Unbroken Past of the American West.* W. W. Norton, New York, NY.
2000 *Something in the Soil: Legacies and Reckonings in the New West.* W. W. Norton, New York, NY.

LINGEMAN, RICHARD R.
1980 *Small Town America : A Narrative History, 1620–the Present.* Houghton Mifflin, Boston, MA.

MONKKONEN, ERIC H.
1988 *America Becomes Urban: The Development of U.S. Cities & Towns 1780–1980.* University of California Press, Berkeley.

OWENS, KENNETH N. (EDITOR)
1994 *John Sutter and the Wider West.* University of Nebraska Press, Lincoln.

PURSER, MARGARET, AND SAMUEL G. SHAW
1996 The Town beneath the Pasture: Rio Vista Rediscovered. *GPS World* 7(4):30–40.

READING, P. B.
1845 P. B. Reading Manuscript Collection. Manuscripts, California State Library, Sacramento, CA.

REPS, JOHN W.
1965 *The Making of Urban America: A History of City Planning in the United States.* Princeton University Press, Princeton, NJ.
1981 *The Forgotten Frontier: Urban Planning in the American West before 1890.* University of Missouri Press, Columbia.

RINGGOLD, CADWALLADER
1851a Chart of the Sacramento River from Suisun City to the American River: California, C.B. Graham, lithographer, Washington, DC. Map Library, University of California, Berkeley.
1851b Correspondence to accompany maps and charts of California, by Commander Cadwalader Ringgold, C.B. Graham, lithographer, Washington, DC. Map Library, University of California, Berkeley.

ROBBINS, WILLIAM
1994 *Colony and Empire: The Capitalist Transformation of the American West.* University Press of Kansas, Lawrence.

SANBORN MAP CO.
1885 *The California Warehouse Book,* revised 1897. Dakin Publishing Co., CA. Reprinted 1983 by Vlad Shkurkin, San Pablo, CA. Fire insurance map, microform, Map Library, University of California, Berkeley.

SELF AND ASSOCIATES, INC.
    2000   Report on the Montezuma Wetlands Restoration
            Project. Report to the U.S. Army Corps of Engineers,
            San Francisco District, San Francisco, CA, from Self
            and Associates, Inc., San Francisco, CA.

SHINE, STEVEN M.
    1976   *The History of Bird's Landing, California.* Victoria
            Books, Concord, CA.

SOLANO COUNTY
    1860   Book of Deeds, N584. County Records Office, Fairfield,
            CA.
    1876   Book of Deeds, Vol. 61. County Records Office,
            Fairfield, CA.

STOREY, NOELLE
    2000   National Register nomination for Bird's Store, Bird's
            Landing, Solano County, CA. Manuscript, Northwest
            Information Center, Sonoma State University, Rohnert
            Park, CA.

SWETE, RICHARD
    1995   Inside the Gate. Paper presented at the Society for
            California Archaeology 29th Annual Meeting, Eureka,
            CA.

WADE, RICHARD C.
    1967   *Urban Frontier: Pioneer Life in Early Pittsburgh,
            Cincinnati, Lexington, Louisville, and St. Louis.*
            University of Chicago Press, Chicago, IL. Originally
            published 1959.

    1995   *The Urban Frontier: The Rise of Western Cities,
            1790–1830.* University of Illinois Press, Urbana.

WHITE, RICHARD
    1991   *"It's Your Misfortune and None of My Own": A History
            of the American West.* University of Oklahoma Press,
            Norman.

YAMIN, REBECCA, AND KAREN BESCHERER METHENY
(EDITORS)
    1996   *Landscape Archaeology: Reading and Interpretation
            of the American Historical Landscape.* University of
            Tennessee Press, Knoxville.

YOUNG, AMY L.
    2000   *Archaeology of Southern Urban Landscapes.* University
            of Alabama Press, Tuscaloosa.

MARGARET PURSER
DEPARTMENT OF ANTHROPOLOGY AND LINGUISTICS
SONOMA STATE UNIVERSITY
1801 E. COTATI AVE.
ROHNERT PARK, CA 94928

NOELLE SHAVER
JONES AND STOKES
42145 LYNDIE LN., SUITE 200
TEMECULA, CA 92591

CHRISTOPHER OHM CLEMENT

Settlement Patterning on the British Caribbean Island of Tobago

ABSTRACT

Sugar planters on Tobago faced a variety of challenges. Foremost among these were creating and maintaining the economic viability of their estates while subjugating a vastly larger enslaved population. As a minority cultural group, however, planters were also faced with the task of reaffirming their own identities as British subjects. These goals were met by constructing a landscape that offered communications, familiarity, and symbolic power. Sugar estate layouts can be interpreted functionally by focusing on the issues of sugar production and control of an enslaved labor force. This paper adds a third dimension by examining the production of sugar and the control of labor from the perspective of the estate house and its relationship to the larger landscape. Additional hypotheses that could account for settlement choices are presented where production and control are insufficient explanation for patterned arrangements.

Introduction

On many Caribbean islands, the manufacture of sugar was the economic goal of the European inhabitants. The settlement patterning that accompanies this endeavor is well documented (e.g., Higman 1988; Armstrong 1990). Sugar factories are located central to cane fields, estate villages are located in positions accessible to both field and factory, and estate houses are built on nearby hilltops. This settlement patterning can be explained with reference to the functional aspects of production. Because the quality and quantity of juice in the cane rapidly decrease after cutting, a location that afforded the shortest travel between field and factory and thus limited the time between cutting and crushing was the most desirable choice for factory siting. To increase worker output, estate villages housing the labor force were located close to both

fields and factory, allowing laborers easy access to their assigned tasks in either locale. Finally, estate houses were sited to take advantage of the healthful benefits of a steady breeze in an environment supporting a host of potentially deadly insect-borne diseases. Added benefits of such a location were managerial: planters obtained an unobstructed view of both ongoing operations at the sugar factory and activities in the estate village.

This paper examines the causality assigned in the above model using documentary and archaeological survey data gathered on the Caribbean island of Tobago. After presenting a discussion of the methods used to locate and identify sites and a description of the patterning revealed by archaeological survey, alternative explanations for the observed patterning are discussed. These explanations are suggested by a broader focus than is the norm in Caribbean plantation archaeology. The data and conclusions presented herein are based on examination of several adjacent estates rather than through focus on an individual plantation. This approach is advocated because it illuminates intersite relationships as well as intrasite relationships. It results in potentially conflicting data that could not otherwise be recognized while supplying the data by which that conflict can be resolved.

The analysis herein indicates that on Tobago the choice of sugar factory location was dependent on water availability for rum production and on factors relating to the transport of sugar, molasses, and rum from plantation to shipping point and that these were the initial concerns of planters when choosing a location for their plantation. The most suitable location for the estate house and estate village were selected after property was acquired and the sugar factory sited. Estate house site selection was based on a variety of implicit and explicit considerations including health, economic and social advantage, and protection from both internal and external threats. On Tobago plantations that enjoyed a higher than normal economic and social status, the estate village was sited and constructed to support that status as well as to provide housing for the plantation labor force.

Archaeological Survey

Tobago is a small island, covering an area of approximately 116 mi., situated at latitude 11°15' N and longitude 60°40' W, the extreme southeastern end of the Lesser Antilles (Figure 1). The island is approximately 26 mi. long and 8 mi. wide at its widest point, and trends from northeast to southwest (Figure 2). It was permanently settled by the British in 1763 after centuries during which various European powers unsuccessfully vied for ownership. Within less than 40 years of settlement Tobago reached the high point of its sugar production, exporting 7,939 U.S. tons in 1799 (Deerr 1949:202). In 1811 the island supported 89 sugar plantations (Young 1812a). Twenty-two were located in St. David's Parish, which was extensively surveyed in 1992 and 1993 for architectural and archaeological remains associated with the sugar industry (Clement 1995). St. David's Parish covers an area of approximately 35 km² and spans the three principle physiographic provinces of the island. These include a mountainous interior, a transitional hills province, and lowlands.

The central geological core of the island rises to elevations of greater than 500 mmsl and is characterized by plunging watercourses, deep, moist valleys, and jagged, abruptly rising hills and ridges. The hills province contains abundant streams of varying sizes and steep, eroded hills grading into gently rolling topography nearer the coast. The lowlands are characterized by flat, arid, savanna-like conditions. St. David's Parish thus contains areas of high relief and areas of little or no relief. It was selected for study because these attributes impose the greatest variety of topographic constraints to structure location, ranging from few in the lowlands to many in the rugged interior. It was therefore expected that St. David's Parish sugar estates would evince the greatest variety in layout. Methodologically, this was an important consideration. From the outset an assumption of the project

FIGURE 1. Tobago and the Lesser Antilles.

was that sugar estate design and layout would be patterned and that patterning would reflect both idealized notions of the way an estate ought to look and constraints imposed on that ideal by the natural environment. Comparing and contrasting a number of estates in a variety of settings would clarify the relationship between the ideal layout and the environment on individual estates. In addition, the broad approach implemented through examination of a study population composed of all estates in an entire parish allowed examination of the relationship between estates as well as within estates.

Survey focused on locating remains associated with sugar estates. The primary mechanical means of locating sites was through pedestrian survey. Few sites would have been located had this method alone been relied on, however, due to the large study area, topographic variation, and dense vegetation. A concerted effort to identify possible sites was undertaken before fieldwork began through the examination of a number of written sources including historic maps, manuscripts and documents, and modern maps and published works. As much of the historic road system on Tobago is still in use today, the modern maps served as a baseline by which descriptions in the literature and graphic representations of past land use were evaluated. Many local informants were also consulted, and several sites were approximately located with their aid.

Survey Results

Remains associated with 20 sugar estates were located during the course of pedestrian survey in St. David's Parish (Figure 3). These include 22 sugar factory complexes utilizing a variety of power sources. Ten windmill towers, 8 water wheels or wheel pits, 5 steam engines, and 1 cattle mill were identified. Domestic components identified were 16 estate houses and four estate villages—a fifth was identified later. In several cases, only a tentative identification of the sugar estate components was made. These components include one probable steam engine, two probable estate houses, and six probable estate villages. Finally, a variety of additional structures were identified, including two coastal warehouses that served as shipping points for

sugar, rum, and molasses from the interior estates, two lime kilns, a residential structure associated with the kilns, and a semaphore station. No remains were found on Dunvegan or Mt. Dillon estates.

Analysis of the located sites occured at both the intersite and intrasite level. Where possible, sketch maps of all factories and estate houses were drawn in the field, with particular focus on layout and aspect in relation to other estate buildings and location. All sites were plotted on modern topographic maps to which superimposed approximate 19th-century estate boundaries derived from available contemporary maps (e.g., Jefferys 1969[1765], 1778, 1794; Byres 1776, 1832) had been transferred.

Of the 22 sugar factories encountered during the survey, 19 are located adjacent to a water source sufficient to provide water for rum production. Significantly, of the three that are not, two were later replaced by new factories located adjacent to streams or canals. The third has a small wind tower that was used to pump water from a nearby river to the factory. This reliance on water for rum-making resulted in the confine-

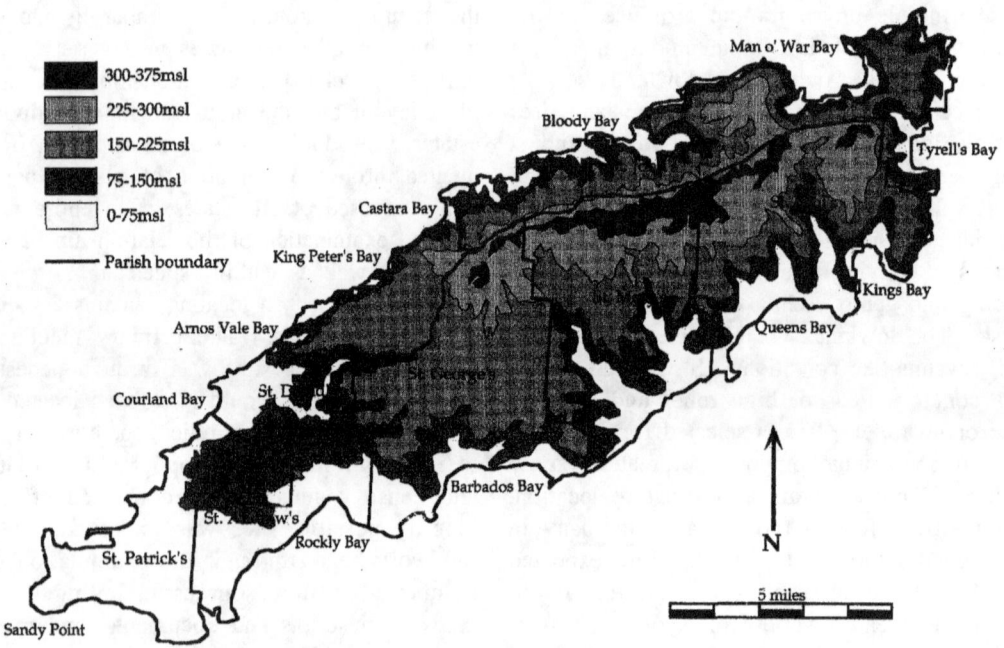

FIGURE 2. Physical features and parishes of Tobago.

Perspectives from *Historical Archaeology*

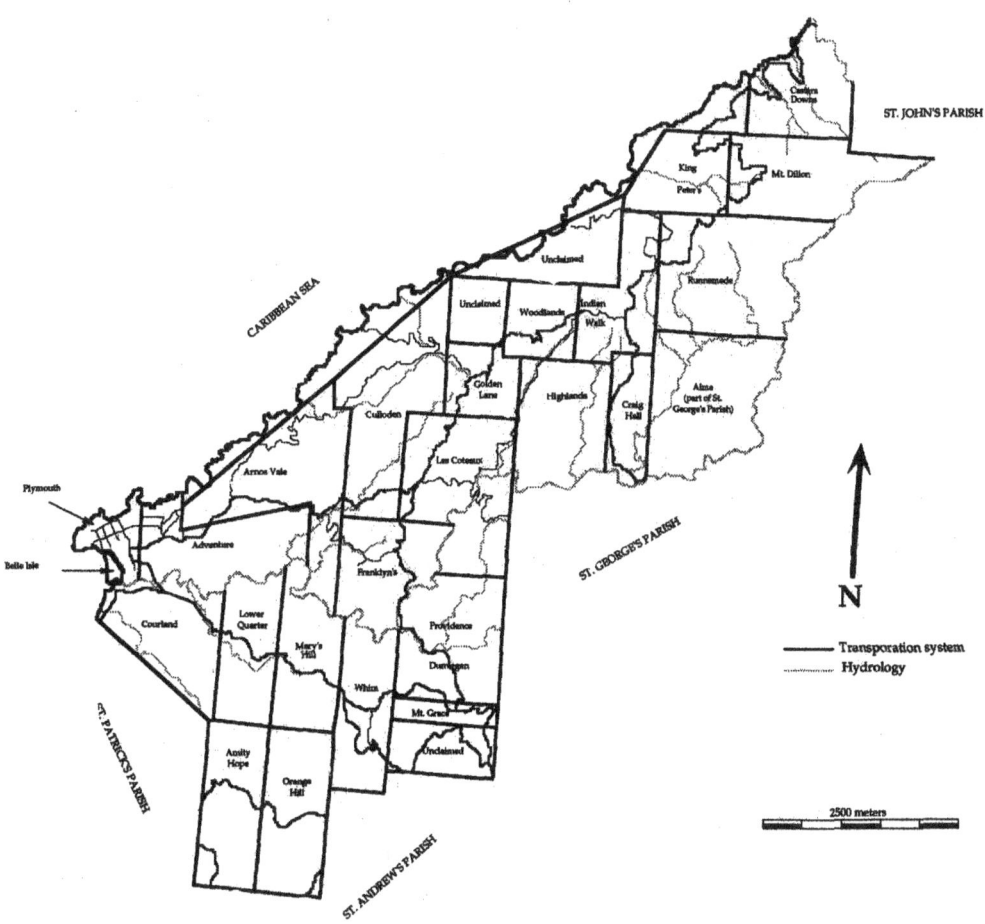

FIGURE 3. St. David's parish estates.

ment of factories to valley bottoms, broad vales, or locations that could be reached by canal in areas of high topographic relief. In addition, all of the sugar factories are located close to a protected bay or near a road with access to shipping points. In the latter case, because sugar, molasses, and rum were hauled in large, heavy quantities, roads were routed so as to minimize climbs between factories and the sea. Whether roads were constructed prior to factories or whether factories were sited in locations with access to suitable routes and the roads built later is unknown, but it seems reasonable to suggest that road-building and factory-siting took place more or less simultaneously.

Layout of the factories varied. Two were constructed in an L form and four in T forms, while three had a linear layout and one was constructed in the shape of a square. The form of the remaining factories could not be determined due to disturbance.

Estate house location is very similar throughout the survey area. All but one are located on elevated landforms, while the exception is low on a hillside overlooking a factory. Elevated locations provided a good view of the sugar estate including the factory, and probably the estate village as well, although too few of the latter were definitively located by the survey to firmly establish this fact. In addition, six estate houses were constructed on elevated piers. Two were not and the remainder could not be determined. Where these piers are extant, they are made from a combination of stone or coral masonry and brick. The brick also served an ornamental purpose in that it was inlaid to create design patterns. These same six estate houses are also identifiable by the presence of arched stairways at the front entrance, and sometimes at the back or side. Brickwork was used in all but one case to highlight these arches. The exception is a house that was built on concrete piers in the post-emancipation period. At all four estate houses where layout could be determined, a T shape was adopted, though one is slightly assymetrical when viewed in plan.

Four slave villages were identified in the survey area during fieldwork and a fifth was identified during a subsequent visit to the island. These are in a variety of locations. Three are adjacent to factories, one is adjacent to an estate house, and one is roughly midway between the factory and the house.

Elements of Factory Location

When British planters first arrived on Tobago they encountered a rugged wilderness; what they saw, however, was a rich and fertile land ripe for colonization. The land was not perfect, however. Steep slopes, dense forestation, shipping access, health concerns, and water availability were factors that added to, or detracted from, the perceived desirability of individual plots of land. Tobago planters selected and bought their chosen lots based on their perceptions of the positive and negative factors affecting their choice.

Land Sales

In all, seven land sales were held on the island between 1765 and 1771 (Archibald 1987:107–123). The rapidity of the land sales reflects the overall attitude among the settlers that sugar could be enormously profitable and that Tobago was well suited for cane cultivation. The distribution of lots sold reflects rapidly changing ideas about where the lands most suitable for cane cultivation and sugar production were located. In the earliest years of settlement these ideas were based on information supplied by word of mouth. Personal observation became

important only during the later period of initial settlement.

Land sales on Tobago occurred initially in the area immediately surrounding the site of the proposed capital town at Barbados Bay (Figure 2), chosen by the government by virtue of its geographic centrality (Young in Archibald 1987:117). The area of Barbados Bay was soon abandoned as a seat of government in favor of a more westerly location, however. The new site, Scarborough on Rockly Bay, was also centrally located, though with reference to population rather than geography. The westward population shift occurred as planters became increasingly familiar with the island. It was initiated by James Simpson, chief surveyor of Tobago and the European most cognizant of the potential of individual land lots.

Simpson bought Lot 1 of St. David's Parish (Courland Estate, Figure 3) prior to the second land sale. Other buyers quickly followed suit, and St. David's Parish lands were the most popular during the 1766 land sales. Sales were confined primarily to the southern and western portions of the parish, however, and included all or part of what would become Amity Hope, Orange Hill, Lower Quarter, Mary's Hill, Whim, Providence, Dunvegan, Les Coteaux, and Franklyn's (Nardin 1969:Plate 4). These are principally the southwesternmost lots in the parish (Figure 3) and are closest to Barbados Bay. Most of them also border the Courland River, which has sufficient flow volume to support water-powered crushing mills.

Attention had shifted away from St. David's Parish by the 1767 land sales. Instead, sales concentrated in St. Patrick's and St. Andrew's parishes to the south. Courland Estate and St. Patrick's and St. Andrew's parishes share two commonalities. Most importantly, they have sufficient surface water to support the rum-making process. Where Courland Estate abuts the Courland River and contains two perennial streams within its boundaries, St. Patrick's and St. Andrew's parishes have many small but reliable springs. Second, Courland Estate shares with St. Patrick's and St. Andrew's parishes a relatively flat topography (Figure 2), the former as a result of Courland River deposition and the latter as a result of emergent coralline formations (Niddrie 1961). Thus, land sales in 1767 focused on areas of low relief that facilitated road construction and maintenance, simplifying problems of transport between field, factory, and shipping point that affect the more rugged portions of the island. Courland Estate and virtually all of the estates of St. Patrick's and St. Andrew's utilized windmills to power their crushing mills (Eubanks 1992). Post-1767 land sales focused on land with access to sheltered bays despite its distance from population centers, indicating that ease of transport outweighed the recognized advantages of access to water power to drive crushing mills (Young 1812a:78).

Power Systems

Possible explanations for the apparent inconsistency between land sales data and the advantages of water power over wind power lie in the relative design complexity of the two power systems, in the materials used in their construction, and in the maintenance required for their upkeep. Water power was acknowledged as the better system:

> On the computation of our most intelligent planters, a "water mill" adds to the value of the plantation one fifth, and one fifth more income from the proceeds of the crop, never being at a stand, or even retarded; from the Negroes never being employed in cutting canes which eventually there may be no wind to grind, and the labours be lost as well as canes; from canes being taken off in their prime, and at the most seasonable and convenient moment, with a certainty of immediate manufacture, and generally from a saving of produce, time, and labour (Young 1812b:78).

While windmill construction was complex, it pales in comparison to the design and engineering skills required for the construction of a water-powered system. Windmills are fairly uniform throughout the island, though some temporal variation in their form is present. The constancy and accessibility of the trade winds meant that the construction of windmills was an uncomplicated operation requiring significantly less labor. While siting to access both wind for power and factory for processing was a critical

consideration, it was a fairly simple task in the relatively flat lands where wind-powered sites are predominant.

In contrast, each water-powered site is unique: variation occurs according to the nature of the water course tapped, the underlying geological formation, and the surrounding topography. In conjunction, these factors effected dam location, canal length, overland entrance and egress, and factory siting. Where high-volume streams required a dam principally designed for diversion, smaller water courses required both diversion and impoundment structures. These were sometimes constructed as a single dam but often also occurred as separate structures. For stability, dams were constructed on bedrock outcrops that constricted the watercourse valley and thus limited the land available for factory siting and constrained road construction. Finally, canals had to be long enough to access factories, usually requiring that they cross smaller drainages, a task accomplished by the construction of small aqueducts. Slope, and thus flow, had to be tightly controlled: too steep, and a canal was subject to damage by erosion; too shallow, and insufficient force was maintained to drive the wheel.

Materials used for windmill construction were also more accessible and easier to work with, given the range of skills available on Tobago. In contrast to water-powered systems where the dam, canal, and wheel pit required stone or brick construction and necessitated skilled masons, windmills were made primarily of wood during the first 50 years of settlement. Though post-1860 windmill towers were tall, circular structures constructed of stone and brick (Anonymous [1870]), as late as 1808 they were primarily wooden structures atop low hexagonal stone and brick bases (Colonial Records Office [CO] 1808; Young 1812a:103).

Both wind- and water-powered systems, of course, were subject to general wear and tear brought about by nearly continuous use during the harvest season. Repair was no doubt a nearly constant task. However, where severe damage to windmills would occur only during tropical storms and rare hurricanes, seasonal rainfall created freshets in Tobago rivers and streams that had the potential significantly to damage water control and delivery systems on an annual basis. Dams, canal inlets, and aqueducts would have been particularly affected, while in severe cases the potential for damage to the water wheel itself was present.

Developing an Estate

The planters who initiated agricultural production on Tobago in the mid-18th century faced not only environmental constraints, but constraints imposed by the government as well. Foremost among these was limited acreage. By the second decade of the 19th century, while not all estates contained the 500 acres or less mandated by parliament (Nardin 1969:296), most did (Young 1812a). The size of Tobago sugar estates averaged slightly more than 400 acres (Young 1812a). They occupied significantly less land than did sugar estates of Jamaica, where the average estate covered just over 1,000 acres (Higman 1988:81). As a result, the layout of Tobago estates was in some ways compacted. For example, where Higman (1988) cites an average area of seven acres for a sugar factory complex on Jamaica, the St. David's Parish sample averaged one to two acres. Whether the distance between the various elements of an estate varies from Higman's model is not known. On Tobago the average distance between the estate house and the sugar factory is 345 m and agrees well with Higman's (1988:81) figure of 357 m for Jamaica. However, three of the five Tobago estate villages were found within 100 m of the sugar factory complex. Though this is in contrast to Higman's figure of 351 m, the majority of activity in the present survey took place within the immediate vicinity of identified sites. As most of those sites were sugar factories, it is readily apparent that sampling bias can account for the apparent differences between the data from Tobago and Jamaica.

The Sugar Factory

Access to water and ease of transport were the principal factors effecting sugar factory location on Tobago; a factory site was chosen only after these requirements were met. In the absence of such a location suitable for water power, windmills, cattle mills, or steam engines were used. In only one instance was a cattle mill used in St. David's Parish. At this site, Golden Lane, hills to the northeast and southwest block prevailing winds, while insufficient water is available in the adjacent stream to support a water-powered mill. There is sufficient water to support rum manufacture, however, and the terrain allowed construction of a road sloping generally downward to a shipping point at Arnos Vale Bay.

The layout of the factory complex itself was determined only after selection of a site. There is a slight preference for a T form on Tobago, and this is probably the most efficient from a production standpoint (Beckford 1790:28). The form is more compact on the landscape and requires less travel time between various areas, reducing transport and enhancing supervision. These should be important concerns in an industry stressing production with forced labor (Wray 1848:285). Had the engineers who designed the factories had such ideas foremost in their minds, all factories would have been constructed with a T-shaped floor plan. Instead, factories were built within the limitations imposed by local topography resulting in the variety of forms encountered by the survey.

The Estate House

By building estate houses on hilltops and on elevated piers, both the view and the breeze were enhanced. Other concerns may have been equally important, however, in both the siting and construction of estate houses. In conceptualizing these concerns, a useful construct is that of internal and external function. This construct was initially formulated by Orser (1988), who used it to differentiate between slaves-as-labor and slaves-as-property: internally, slaves provided labor; externally, they demonstrated the purchasing power of the owner (Padgug 1976:17–18). In more general terms, internal functions contribute to an estate's profit while external functions enhance the status of the planter in the eyes of his peers. These distinctions can also be applied to estate house location.

From an internal perspective, hilltop locations provided enhanced communication, valuable both for security and for economic reasons. In all but one case, the estate houses of St. David's Parish were within view of the established towns of Plymouth and Scarborough or of other estate houses, allowing line-of-sight communication between locations that were distant from one another by road. Also visible from each estate house was at least one semaphore station, maintained by the military for communication between towns and between the two forts and 15 batteries guarding the coast (Young 1809:155). In an extreme case, the station on top of the 244-m-high French Fort hill was visible from the location of an estate house located some eight km distant. The sole exception occurs at Mary's Hill estate, where the planter's residence is located 200 m below the crest of the hill. This hill, however, was occupied by a military semaphore station, and it is likely that the personnel responsible for its operation were housed by the estate.

From the perspective of external function, not only were estate houses visible to one another and to population centers, they also tended to be oriented in those directions. This sometimes compromised the planter's view of the factory. For example, the orientation of the Arnos Vale estate house was to the southwest, affording a panoramic view towards the town of Plymouth and facing estate houses on both Adventure and Courland estates. The village and the factory, however, were to the southeast and would only have been visible from windows in the southeastern facade of the house. At Les Coteaux, while the front of the estate house faces west towards the town of Plymouth, the factory complex is almost due east. A sense of community was thus fostered by the view of a neighboring house in the isolated environment of a Tobago estate. If, in the view of slaves, estate houses garnered an aura of power as the center of estate authority (Armstrong 1990), their siting also engendered a feeling of solidarity on the part of planters (Pulsipher 1992).

Regularity of design was apparent at the estate houses where form could be determined. All but one were symmetrical, and decorative elements such as arched stairways and designs in supporting piers were always present. Symmetry and regularity were attainable aesthetic attributes in estate house design because houses were less bound than factory buildings by functional considerations and topographic variation. In the one case of an asymmetrical layout documented by the survey, the main steps of an estate house were constructed off center to present the appearance of symmetry as the house was approached up the main drive, which was divergent from the main axis of the house. Estate house symmetry operated on an external level. It reflected the Georgian worldview of the planters, who thereby reified their ties with the home country. The grandeur of the estate houses, expressed in their elevated design, gracefully arched main stairways and decorative brickwork on exposed supporting piers, on the other hand, reflects their external function as status symbols, signaling the worth of the owner and his or her association with the aristocracy. That these signals were most apparent from the main approach to the houses indicates that they were directed towards other Europeans rather than towards the slave population, who could be expected to approach the houses, on those rare occasions when they did, by a more direct route between estate house and village.

Otto (1984:127) defines a "showplace plantation" as an estate "where elite travelers could be assured of a hospitable welcome." One estate in St. David's Parish, Courland, fits this description. Its proximity to Plymouth made it accessible while the position and political power of its original owner, James Simpson, made him a well-known figure both on and off the island. At Courland, however, the external "showplace" function may have been complimented by an internal function as a "premier" estate, manufacturing a variety of supplemental products used in sugar production but not readily available otherwise. The craftsworkers—wheelwrights, carpenters, blacksmiths, barrel-makers, etc.—responsible for manufacturing these supplemental products were highly skilled and would have been expensive to buy or train. Because not all estates could afford such an investment, however, only a few supported such supplemental manufacture, making their products available to other estates for a fee. Courland estate house is the only such structure in St. David's Parish that contained a broad variety of ancillary structures in association. Supplemental manufacturing at Courland is a likely explanation for the presence of these structures.

No documentary records exist on Tobago to directly confirm this hypothesis, though support is provided by the fact that only Betsey's Hope estate produced more sugar and rum in 1811 than Courland. Betsey's Hope, in St. Paul's Parish, was owned by Sir William Young, then governor of Tobago and member of a prominent Caribbean family with interests on other islands (Young 1812a). Prominent individuals are here considered more likely to own or build "premier estates." Ancillary structures at the Orange Hill estate house may also have been the sites of supplemental manufacture, though this was not confirmed in the field and they are described as "offices" in the contemporary literature (Anonymous [1870]). The owner of Orange Hill Estate in the late 18th century was William Lindsay, who was appointed Governor of Tobago in 1794. Thus, he conforms to the expected station of a premier estate owner.

Premier estates also existed on Antigua. Betty's Hope was established in ca. 1655 and by 1668 had come into the hands of the Codrington family, eventually becoming their "flagship estate" (Goodwin 1994:100; Pulsipher and Goodwin 1988:1). The Codringtons were on a social par with Sir William Young of Tobago: Young served as the governor of Tobago and the Codrington family of Betty's Hope supplied two governor-generals of the British Leeward Islands in the late 17th and early 18th centuries. The prestige attached to Betty's Hope Estate lasted throughout the 18th century. Its preeminent position in 1897 and the function of a premier estate were described by an Antiguan laborer many years later:

Betty was the largest estate on the island and it would have a good amount of work while the others would have very little—particularly in the dull season—for Betty was responsible to carry out the repairs on the mills and other equipment for some of the other estates. . . . The workshop at Betty was second to none on the island and the best tradesmen of all kinds was there. Blacksmith service was one of the most important things back then and no place could touch Betty's Hope. Coopering and tanning was also important back then and old Betty was very capable in them things too (Smith and Smith 1986:87–88).

The Estate Village

The generally accepted location of the estate village was "in a peripheral but proxemic position to the main complex" (Lange and Handler 1985:18). At Courland, however, the village is adjacent to the estate house, reaffirming Courland's status as both a showplace and a premier estate. In this view, it is significant that one firmly identified domestic structure and one possible domestic structure excavated within the Courland estate village were aligned on nearly the same axis as the majority of the structures in the estate house complex, reinforcing the overall symmetry of the whole.

Orderliness was also an apparent goal of Tobago planters in the construction of estate villages: "The negroes inhabit three streets, near the plantation to which they are attached: their huts are built of stone, and covered with slates" (Lavaysse 1969[1820]:350). The accuracy of this description is borne out by limited surface survey of Golden Grove Estate in St. Patrick's Parish, one of the estates referred to in the above quote. These data indicate that some planters considered orderliness within the estate village to be important. Orderliness can also be viewed from the perspective of internal and external function. Internally, it reinforced the regimented sugar production system and the power of the planter (e.g., Goodwin 1987; Higman 1988; Armstrong 1990; McKee 1992). Externally, it enhanced the overall pattern of estate regularity (e.g., Pulsipher 1992).

A Dynamic Perspective

The model presented above is static. In reality, sugar estates throughout the Caribbean were modified frequently and regularly, with modifications ranging from equipment upgrades (Eubanks 1992) to the relocation of entire estate complexes (Pulsipher and Goodwin 1982). The estates of St. David's Parish provide several examples.

The earliest archaeologically recognizable modification occurred at Adventure Estate when a new sugar factory was built between 1784 and 1807. The old factory is located on a hilltop in the western portion of the estate (Anonymous 1784) where cane was processed with a wind-powered crushing mill. By 1807, however, Young (1809) notes that the mill was water powered. The water wheel he refers to was located at the site of the new sugar factory adjacent to the Courland River. The late 18th century was a boom time on Tobago. As sugar profits steadily rose, more capital became available to Tobago planters. The owner of Adventure responded to increased capital availability and the prospect of greater profits by building a new, more efficient water-powered mill. This necessitated the relocation of the entire factory complex to its new location on the Courland River.

A similar economic argument can be used to explain steam engines at Franklyn's and King Peter's Estates by 1807 (Young 1809) and the fact that 13 estates were put into sugar production after 1786 (Young 1812b). Planters with insufficient capital to immediately initiate sugar production, or with estates located on land that was marginal for sugar production, could fall back on a variety of crops. Land use figures for Tobago indicate that during the period of initial settlement by the British, planters often relied on cash crops other than sugar (Young 1812b:92). Foremost among these was cotton: in 1774, 96,500 lbs were produced on the island (Young 1812b:83). One of the major advantages of cotton is that it does not require extensive capital outlay for processing facilities. Rather, although it is labor intensive, when labor is available cotton is inexpensive to produce. Capital from cotton production, or indigo, coffee, or cocoa, could then be reinvested in sugar processing equipment. Franklyn's and King Peter's estates are poorly suited for wind- or water-powered mills. Steam, though experimental at the time, was seen as a viable means of sugar production in the absence of alternative power sources. The steam engines at Franklyn's and King Peter's estates may have been bought by the owners as funds became available through the production of other crops, and this same mechanism can account for the addition of 13 estates to the ranks of the sugar producers after 1786 (Young 1812b).

From 1807 onwards, the antislavery lobby made sugar production ever more difficult. Despite growing economic and political pressure on the planters, some continued to reinvest capital in sugar production equipment. Eubanks (1992:199-200) argues that reinvestment was a response to declining labor in the period following emancipation. Briefly, machinery upgrades were primarily directed towards increasing juice-yield per cane. Production levels were thus maintained despite the decreasing availability of labor to work the cane fields. At Arnos Vale, a steam engine was installed adjacent to the crushing mill to supplement the power derived from the water wheel, increasing juice-yield per cane from an estimated 61 percent when crushed with a water-powered mill to as much as 81 percent when crushed with a steam-powered mill (Benjamin 1880:839). At Courland Estate, the owner went beyond upgrading equipment. The Courland old estate house was occupied as late as 1837, when Eliza MacDougal was laid to rest in a tomb adjacent to the house. Later in the nineteenth century, however, a new estate house was built adjacent to the sugar factory. By placing his house near the manufacturing process, the planter was able to oversee production more closely, eliminating inefficiency resulting from a poorly supervised work force. Although the date of this move is uncertain, it most likely followed the hurricane of 1847, which destroyed 30 estate houses on the island (Woodcock 1866:107). The Courland old estate house was subsequently replaced by a new structure at the new location.

A factor that Eubanks does not discuss, but which may have contributed to the tendency to reinvest in sugar production despite is decline, was an influx of immigrants, and presumably capital, in the period following emancipation. Between 1832 and 1866, every estate in St. David's Parish changed hands (Woodcock 1866:Appendix 7, Appendix 10). Based on the surnames of the owners, this represents the abandonment of sugar production by the old, established families of Tobago. The enthusiasm of the newcomers is reflected in the remains of sugar estates. All the dated milling equipment encountered during the survey and by an island-wide survey in 1989 (Eubanks 1992) was acquired in the mid-19th century. In addition, six of the 10 identified windmills in St David's Parish utilized post-1808 design plans.

Conclusion

This study has attempted to elucidate the functional aspects of settlement patterning on Tobagonian sugar estates. Since the appearance of Gordon R. Willey's (1953) pioneering "Prehistoric Settlement Patterns of the Virú Valley," settlement pattern studies have been a useful tool in the prehistoric archaeological kit. Historical archaeologists have also used settlement patterns to their advantage (e.g., Paynter 1982; Lewis 1984; Warren and O'Brien 1984; Adams 1990). Despite the utility of settlement pattern studies, however, plantation archaeologists have concentrated on individual sites rather than broader areas (cf. Delle 1994). Only during the analysis stage has comparative data been utilized.

Plantation archaeologists in the southeastern United States have focused primarily on questions of plantation social structure (e.g., Otto 1975, 1977, 1980; Lewis 1985; Orser 1988) and slave lifeways (e.g., Wheaton and Garrow 1985; Brown and Cooper 1990; Jamieson 1995; Wilkie 1995). This focus reflects the statement that historical archaeology can make the greatest contributions through studies of "issues for which there is simply inadequate documentation" (Deagan 1988:9). Thus, slaves and their place in the plantation power structure constitute im-

portant subjects because they are rarely discussed in the historical documents.

Research questions of plantation archaeologists in the Caribbean have primarily focused on issues relating to slaves. The most successful efforts have been those that illuminate African retentions and cultural change in the slave population. For example, Handler and Lange (1978) have closely examined these issues with regard to mortuary patterns on Barbados, while Armstrong (1990) has studied the changes in slave domestic life that occured with emancipation on Jamaica.

In addition to its obvious utility for the study of disenfranchised peoples, however, historical archaeology can contribute to our understanding of well-documented groups in ways that history can not. This paper has focused primarily on estate owners. It has demonstrated that estate layout reflects as much their unstated goals, goals that related to their social standing in the community and to their economic well-being, as it does the goals they made explicit in their writings. Beyond issues of which groups constitute an important focus of study for historical archaeologists is the issue of what questions to ask. If studies of "the complex relationships which bond cultural institutions" are also valid research issues for historical archaeologists (Cleland 1988:14), then the focus on individual plantations that has characterized plantation archaeology should be extended to incorporate groups of plantations. This paper has begun to define the relationship between neighboring estates by focusing on intersite settlement patterns rather than individual sites. This approach suggests that a hierarchy of estates existed on Tobago that can be defined through archaeological techniques in the absence of historic documentation. Though all estate owners participated in an often lucrative economic enterprise by producing sugar, molasses, and rum for export, only a few invested in the infrastructure necessary to produce manufactured goods for local consumption. Estates producing these goods, referred to herein as premier estates, were owned by prominent families or individuals whose enhanced economic status is reflected in the layout of the estate.

Ancillary structures where supplemental manufacture occured are associated with planter residences on premier estates, while estate villages are laid out in patterned arrangements, reinforcing planter control of the labor force (Armstrong 1990) and reifying the status of the estate owner through patterned regularity.

This paper has also examined factors relating to the location of sugar factories. Locational choices were based on a variety of considerations. Though sugar production was a primary goal of planters on Tobago, in the absence of transportation routes this production would have been pointless. Sugar factories were sited with access to routes that made the transportation of the finished product to the market easier. In addition, though rum production was intimately tied to sugar manufacture from a technological perspective, the data presented here also indicate close ties from an economic perspective. Sugar factories that were poorly sited for rum production, defined by the absence of a suitable water source, were abandoned in favor of more advantageous locations, suggesting that the economic viability of an estate rested as much on the production of rum as on sugar.

ACKNOWLEDGMENTS

This research was completed under the auspices of the Tobago Archaeological Program, a joint research effort of the Tobago House of Assembly and the Institute of Archaeology and Paleoenvironmental Studies at the University of Florida Department of Anthropology. The preliminary study was funded by a research grant from the Amoco Foundation, Inc., sponsored by Amoco Trinidad Ltd., while the bulk of the research was performed under a National Science Foundation dissertation improvement grant (#9218780). Finally, the majority of the excavation at the Courland estate village was supported by a second Amoco grant. These were the second and third Amoco grants Program researchers have received; the Tobago Archaeological Program greatly values their continued support. My dissertation committee, Peter R. Schmidt (Chair), Kathleen A. Deagan, Ralph B. Johnson, William F. Keegan, and Michael E. Moseley, commented on the ideas presented in this paper while reviewing my dissertation, and their input is greatly appreciated. Additional comment or aid was received from Thomas Hales Eubanks, David L. Niddrie, and Keith Laurence.

A draft of this paper was thoughtfully reviewed by Paul Farnsworth, David R. Watters and an anonymous reviewer. Permission to work at the Courland estate village was granted by Neal and Massey Corporation, Trinidad. The Departments of Architectural Engineering and Geography, University of Miami, allowed me to use their computers to produce the graphics included in this paper, as did the University of Florida Department of Surveying and Mapping and the University of South Carolina Department of Civil Engineering.

REFERENCES

ADAMS, WILLIAM HAMPTON
1990   Landscape Archaeology, Landscape History, and the American Farmstead. *Historical Archaeology* 24(4):92–101.

ANONYMOUS
[1870]   *Plan of the Orange Hill and Amity Hope Estates in the Parish of St. David, Island of Tobago.* J. King & Co. (Limited), London.
1784   *Carte Militaire de l'Ile de Tabago.* Archives Nationale, France.

ARCHIBALD, DOUGLAS
1987   *Tobago: Melancholy Isle.* Vol. 1, *1498–1771.* Westindiana Ltd., Port of Spain, Trinidad.

ARMSTRONG, DOUGLAS V.
1990   *The Old Village and the Great House: An Archaeological and Historical Examination of Drax Hall Plantation, St. Ann's Bay, Jamaica.* University of Illinois Press, Chicago.

BECKFORD, WILLIAM
1790   *A Descriptive Account of the Island of Jamaica.* T. and J. Egerton, London.

BENJAMIN, PARK (EDITOR)
1880   *Appleton's Cyclopædia of Applied Mechanics: A Dictionary of Mechanical Engineering and the Mechanical Arts,* Vol. 2. D. Appleton and Company, NY.

BROWN, KENNETH L., AND DOREEN C. COOPER
1990   Structural Continuity in an African-American Slave and Tenant Community. *Historical Archaeology* 24(4):7–19.

BYRES, JOHN
1776   *Plan of the Island of Tobago, Laid Down by Actual Survey.* S. Hooper, London.
1832   *Plan of the Island of Tobago, Laid Down by Actual Survey.* New edition. James Wyld, London.

CLELAND, CHARLES E.
1988 Questions of Substance, Questions that Count. *Historical Archaeology* 22(1):13–17.

CLEMENT, CHRISTOPHER OHM
1995 Landscapes and Plantations on Tobago: A Regional Perspective. Unpublished Ph.D. dissertation, Department of Anthropology, University of Florida, Gainesville.

COLONIAL RECORDS OFFICE (CO)
1808 *CO 285/13*. University of the West Indies Library, St. Augustine, Trinidad. Microfilm. Original manuscript on file, Public Records Office, London.

DEAGAN, KATHLEEN
1988 Avenues of Inquiry in Historical Archaeology. *Advances in Archaeological Method and Theory* 5:151–177. Michael B. Schiffer, editor. Academic Press, NY.

DEERR, NOEL
1949 *The History of Sugar*. Two volumes. Chapman and Hall Ltd., London.

DELLE, JAMES A.
1994 The Settlement Pattern of Sugar Plantations on St. Eustatius, Netherlands Antilles. Spatial Patterning in Historical Archaeology: Selected Studies of Settlement, edited by Donald W. Linebaugh and Gary G. Robinson. *Occasional Papers in Archaeology* 2:33–61. Department of Anthropology, William and Mary Center for Archaeological Research, Williamsburg, VA.

EUBANKS, THOMAS HALES
1992 Sugar, Slavery and Emancipation: The Industrial Archaeology of the West Indian Island of Tobago. Unpublished Ph.D. dissertation, Department of Anthropology, University of Florida, Gainesville.

GOODWIN, CONRAD M.
1987 Sugar, Time and Englishmen. Unpublished Ph.D. dissertation, Department of Archaeology, Boston University, Boston, MA.
1994 Betty's Hope Windmill: An Unexpected Problem. *Historical Archaeology* 28(1):99–110.

HANDLER, JEROME S., AND FREDERICK W. LANGE
1978 *Plantation Slavery in Barbados: An Archaeological and Historical Investigation*. Harvard University Press, Cambridge, MA.

HIGMAN, BARRY W.
1988 *Jamaica Surveyed: Plantation Maps and Plans of the Eighteenth and Nineteenth Centuries*. Institute of Jamaica Publications, Ltd., Kingston, Jamaica.

JAMIESON, ROSS W.
1995 Material Culture and Social Death: African-American Burial Practices. *Historical Archaeology* 29(4):39–58.

JEFFERYS, THOMAS
1778 *Tobago from Actual Surveys and Observations*. Robert Sayer, London.
1794 *Tobago from Actual Surveys and Observations*. Laurie and Whittle, London.
1969 Tobago. Reprint of 1765 map. *La Mise en Valeur de l'Ile de Tabago (1763–1783)*, by Jean-Claude Nardin, pp. 88–89. Mouton, Paris.

LANGE, FREDERICK W., AND JEROME S. HANDLER
1985 The Ethnohistorical Approach to Slavery. In *The Archaeology of Slavery and Plantation Life*, edited by Theresa A. Singleton, pp. 15–32. Academic Press, Orlando, FL.

LAVAYSSE, J. J. DAUXION
1969 *Statistical, Commercial, and Political Description of Venezuela, Trinidad, Margarita, and Tobago*. Reprint of 1820 translation. Negro Universities Press/ Greenwood, Westport, CT.

LEWIS, KENNETH E.
1984 *The American Frontier: An Archaeological Study of Settlement Pattern and Process*. Academic Press, Orlando, FL.
1985 Plantation Layout and Function in the South Carolina Lowcountry. In *The Archaeology of Slavery and Plantation Life*, edited by Theresa A. Singleton, pp. 35–65. Academic Press, Orlando, FL.

McKEE, LARRY
1992 The Ideals and Realities Behind the Design and Use of 19th-Century Virginia Slave Cabins. In *The Art and Mystery of Historical Archaeology: Essays in Honor of James Deetz*, edited by Anne Elizabeth Yentsch and Mary C. Beaudry, pp. 195–213. CRC Press, Boca Raton, FL.

NARDIN, JEAN-CLAUDE
1969 *La Mise en Valeur de l'Ile de Tabago (1763–1783)*. Mouton, Paris.

NIDDRIE, DAVID L.
1961 *Land Use and Population in Tobago: An Environmental Study*. Geographical Publications Limited, Bude, Cornwall, England.

ORSER, CHARLES E. JR.
1988 The Archaeological Analysis of Plantation Society: Replacing Status and Caste with Economics and Power. *American Antiquity* 53(4):735–751.

OTTO, JOHN SOLOMON
    1975   Status Differences and the Archaeological Record: A Comparison of Planter, Overseer, and Slave Sites from Cannon's Point Plantation (1774–1861), St. Simons Island, Georgia. Unpublished Ph.D. dissertation, Department of Anthropology, University of Florida, Gainesville.

    1977   Artifacts and Status Differences—A Comparison of Ceramics from Planter, Overseer, and Slave Sites on an Antebellum Plantation. In *Research Strategies in Historical Archaeology*, edited by Stanley South, pp. 91–118. Academic Press, NY.

    1980   Race and Class on Antebellum Plantations. In *Archaeological Perspectives on Ethnicity in America: Afro-American and Asian Culture History*, edited by Robert L. Schuyler, pp. 3–13. Baywood, Farmingdale, NY.

    1984   *Cannon's Point Plantation, 1794–1860: Living Conditions and Status Patterns in the Old South.* Academic Press, Orlando, FL.

PADGUG, R. A.
    1976   Problems in the Theory of Slavery and Slave Society. *Science and Society* 40:3–27.

PAYNTER, ROBERT
    1982   *Models of Spatial Inequality: Settlement Patterns in Historical Archaeology.* Academic Press, Orlando, FL.

PULSIPHER, LYDIA MIHELIC
    1992   Here Where the Old Time People Be: Reconstructing the Landscapes of the Slavery and Post-slavery Era in Montserrat, West Indies. Paper presented at the Conference "The Lesser Antilles in the Age of European Expansion," Hamilton College, Clinton, NY.

PULSIPHER, LYDIA MIHELIC, AND CONRAD M. GOODWIN
    1982   Galways: A Caribbean Sugar Plantation; A Report on the 1981 Field Season. Unpublished manuscript on file with the authors.

    1988   The Betty's Hope Conservation Project, Betty's Hope Estate, Antigua, West Indies. Pilot Study report submitted to Antigua and Barbuda Betty's Hope Committee.

SMITH, KEITHLYN B., AND FERNANDO C. SMITH
    1986   *To Shoot Hard Labor: The Life and Times of an Antiguan Working Man, 1877–1982.* Edan's Publishers, Scarborough, ON.

WARREN, ROBERT E., AND MICHAEL J. O'BRIEN
    1984   A Model of Frontier Settlement. In *Grassland, Forest, and Historical Settlement: An Analysis of Dynamics in Northeast Missouri*, edited by Michael J. O'Brien, pp. 22–57. University of Nebraska Press, Lincoln.

WHEATON, THOMAS R., AND PATRICK H. GARROW
    1985   Acculturation and the Archaeological Record in the South Carolina Low Country. In *The Archaeology of Slavery and Plantation Life*, edited by Theresa A. Singleton, pp. 239–259. Academic Press, Orlando, FL.

WILKIE, LAURIE A.
    1995   Magic and Empowerment on the Plantation: An Archaeological Consideration of African-American World View. *Southeastern Archaeology* 14(2):136–148.

WILLEY, GORDON R.
    1953   Prehistoric Settlement Patterns in the Virú Valley. *Bureau of American Ethnology Bulletin* 155. Washington, DC.

WOODCOCK, HENRY ILES
    1866   *A History of Tobago Reproduced from the Printed Manuscript.* Box and Labels Colour Printers Ltd., Port of Spain, Trinidad.

WRAY, LEONARD
    1848   *The Practical Sugar Planter.* Smith, Elder and Co., London.

YOUNG, SIR WILLIAM
    1809   *An Historical, Statistical, and Descriptive Account of the Island of Tobago.* Microfilm. University of the West Indies Library, St. Augustine, Trinidad. Original manuscript on file, British Library, London.

    1812a *An Historical, Statistical, and Descriptive Account of the Island of Tobago.* Microfilm. University of the West Indies Library, St. Augustine, Trinidad. Original manuscript on file, Windsor Library, Windsor Castle, London.

    1812b An Historical, Statistical, and Descriptive Account of the Island of Tobago. Original manuscript on file, University of the West Indies Library, St. Augustine, Trinidad.

CHRISTOPHER OHM CLEMENT
SOUTH CAROLINA INSTITUTE OF ARCHAEOLOGY AND ANTHROPOLOGY
1321 PENDLETON ST.
COLUMBIA, SC 29208-0071

Mark P. Leone
James M. Harmon
Jessica L. Neuwirth

Perspective and Surveillance in Eighteenth-Century Maryland Gardens, Including William Paca's Garden on Wye Island

ABSTRACT

Since 1981, 18th-century formal gardens and landscapes in Annapolis have been archaeologically explored to demonstrate that they are exercises in using solid geometry to control perspective. Building on this earlier work, William Paca's last garden, built on Wye Island in the late 1700s, is interpreted to explore the methods by which these gardens were constructed and the meanings and uses of the gardens. Scholars have suggested that by the 1720s the genteel in America routinely created gardens as extensions of their homes. The desire to manage the views in gardens is in the application of the laws of geometry to wilderness. It is suggested that these ordered landscapes, as centerpieces of leisure in the midst of the working plantation and as places to display oneself to visitors and workers alike, were also consonant with slaveholder ideology and the ideals of the new republic.

Introduction

Since 1981, 18th-century formal gardens and landscapes in Annapolis have been archaeologically explored to demonstrate that they are exercises in using solid geometry to control perspective. The hypothesis that such landscapes were built to create and manage optical illusions was developed because few American scholars had explored the volumetric quality of 18th-century gardens. Such gardens were built to create a focal point that managed the view and helped to create the illusion that the object in sight was either closer or farther away than the viewer could guess, depending on the way that the space used was structured (Brown 1990; Leone and Shackel 1990; Ernstein 2004:88–121). The ways in which these illusions were constructed on the ground is further examined here through a description of recent archaeological work on William Paca's late-18th-century plantation on Wye Island on the Eastern Shore of the Chesapeake Bay in Maryland (Figure 1).

Some attention will also be given to the reasons why such formal geometric shapes were created as part of the landscape of the 18th-century Chesapeake. Scholars have suggested that many of the genteel in the American colonies, especially those in regions that were closely tied to European markets like much of the Tidewater Chesapeake, routinely created gardens as extensions of their homes by the 1720s. The desire to build geometric shapes into the land and manage the views in gardens lay in the application of the laws of geometry to "wilderness"; that is, gardens represented an application of the laws of God as understood by humans. Gardens, and houses for that matter, built in the baroque fashion demonstrated the owners' abilities to shape land and to change perceptions of the space around them. Gardens also created a stage upon which the genteel performed. The vistas of gardens, like the Chinese porcelain tea set in the house, were designed to instruct, inspire conversation, and display the knowledge of the connoisseur (Bushman 1992:127–133).

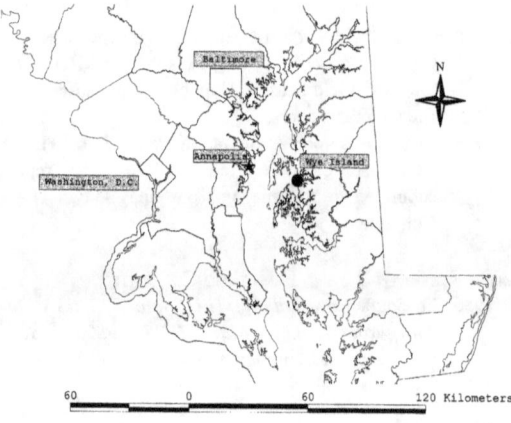

FIGURE 1. Study area location. Data source: ESRI, Redlands, CA. (Drawing by J. Harmon, 2004.)

It is suggested here that formal gardens also played a role in developing and instructing a new nation as to the proper way to organize nature, farm the land, and manage workers, enslaved or free. Scholars have suggested that the majority of formal gardens constructed in the Chesapeake in the 18th century were created for slave- and land-holding gentry. Further, the formal geometry of such gardens, popular long after such conventions were rejected in England for more fluid, naturalistic gardens, reflected a reaction to the expanses of open land, creating the desire for ordered landscapes, not ones that echoed the wilderness that the colonists faced (Sarudy 1998:141). Also consonant with the slaveholder ideology were the ordered landscapes, the hierarchy of movement throughout the gardens, the control over access to the gardens, the use of gardens as places to display oneself to visitors and workers alike, and the emphasis on the great house and garden of leisure in the midst of the larger working plantation. The romantic landscape garden that became fashionable in England in the late-18th and early-19th centuries, which emphasized a turn to more private and personal use of the space, did not answer the slaveholders' needs to engage in rituals of hierarchy and control every day. William Paca's garden on Wye Island offers an interesting case study of the Chesapeake formal garden of the late-18th century, a garden that attempted to incorporate some of the latest garden designs from England while maintaining the geometry and formalism of the new nation.

Three major 18th-century city gardens have been explored in the city of Annapolis by Archaeology in Annapolis since the program began in 1981: the William Paca Garden, built about 1763, the Ridout Garden of about the same period, and the garden designed and built in 1771 by Charles Carroll of Carrollton (Figures 2 and 3). The Paca garden was excavated by three archaeologists between 1968 and 1972, and subsequent analysis focused on the use of rules of perspective in its design (Leone 1984; Paca-Steele and Wright 1987; Brown 1990; Ernstein 2004). The Ridout garden, a largely unaltered site on city lots that were not subdivided over time, remained within one family's ownership. It was mapped topographically in the mid-1980s (Hopkins 1986). The Charles Carroll garden

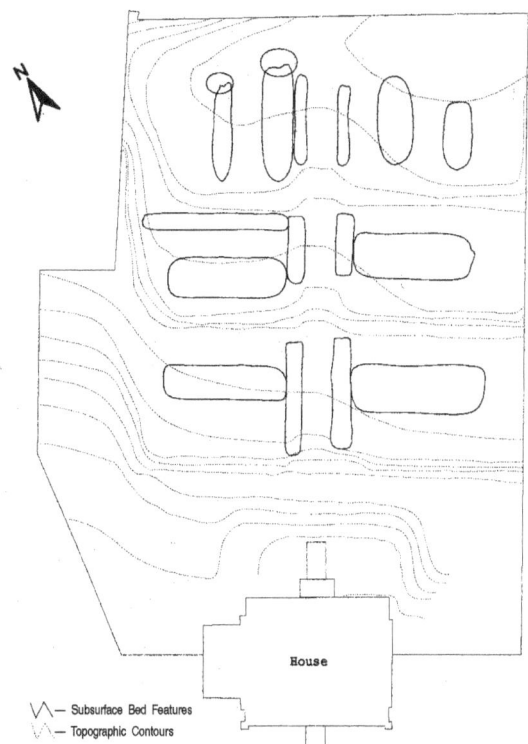

FIGURE 2. Joseph Hopkins topographic map of the Ridout Garden, Annapolis, Maryland (after Hopkins 1986; digitized by Thomas Cuddy, 2004).

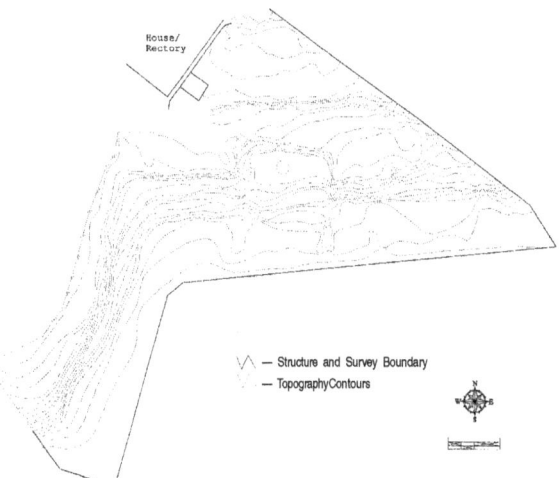

FIGURE 3. Roulette and Williams topographic map of the Charles Carroll Garden, Annapolis, Maryland (after Palus and Kryder-Reid 2002:figure 4.4).

was mapped topographically in the early 1980s. This topographic map was the first to accurately record the terraces and was essential to Paul Shackel's work (Leone and Shackel 1990), which demonstrated that the garden was a perfect 3 x 4 x 5 Pythagorean triangle. A series of soil cores taken from the site at that time indicated that the site was largely intact as well (Palus and Kryder-Reid 2002:4.5–4.12).

These three sites comprise the body of archaeological data that has been used to identify and describe the use of planned volumes to create geometric landscapes and to create the illusions of distance or, alternatively, closeness. An important aspect of the sites that contributed to these analyses is that there was an adequate record of the depositional and structural integrity within each to work out a realistic appraisal of how these gardens must have worked optically. In these gardens, archaeologists were often able to recover the beds through stratigraphic excavation and careful mapping. The presence of distinct patterns of dark organic soil and profiles of cross sections allowed for mapping all three dimensions of the beds as well as the relationship of the beds to each other. There was also little evidence of gullies or slumping to indicate erosion of terrace edges over time. The details of the archaeology of the Paca Garden (Shellenhamer 2004) and of the Carroll Garden (Palus and Kryder-Reid 2002) indicated how these places were constructed and provided a three-dimensional map of how these spaces looked over time. The topographic map of the Ridout Garden (Figure 2) was equally revealing, as documentary evidence indicates that this was an unaltered space, under the control of one family over time. With little change to the lot over time, it appeared fairly certain that the features as mapped represented the 18th-century garden plan.

Eighteenth-century gardens were not built in a vacuum, nor do contemporary archaeologists work in one. The complement to the archaeological evidence for these deliberately shaped spaces of the 18th century was the contemporary books and other literature that provided instruction on how to build formal landscapes in the city or in the countryside. These books, in particular Batty Langley's (1728) *New Principles of Gardening,* Richard Bradley's (1717) *New Improvements of Planting and Gardening,* and Philip Miller's (1731) *The Gardener's Dictionary,* were well known and widely used in the English-speaking world, including Annapolis (Sarudy 1989: 153–159). These books went through many

editions, are recorded in inventories of period libraries, and were used in the same way, by informal and formal practitioners alike, as were contemporary architectural pattern books. This literature contains detailed descriptions of how to build garden features and how to create flower beds, groups of shrubbery, and other plantings (Miller 1755). Miller also details the specific rules and formulas for building *volumes,* or three dimensional spaces made of hedges, according to the laws of perspective, information that has helped archaeologists understand the gardens that the authors have explored archaeololgically. These specific rules are illustrated in garden paintings found throughout Barbara Sarudy's (1989) work.

Early to mid-18th-century prints and descriptions also contain a great deal of information about the appearance and construction of English and American gardens. From all these sources it is apparent that mid-18th-century gardens contained avenues of trees, terraces and falls, lawns, and planting beds in which flowers, vegetables, herbs, and shrubs were grown (Sarudy 1998; Laird 1999). Planting beds were often in geometric shapes, usually enclosed with privet or boxwood, clipped into a regular border to emphasize the geometric form. The plants in beds were usually the first part of the garden to go when the owner, adequate staff, or both were no longer there to direct or carry out maintenance work.

The 18th-century garden literature also details plans that use converging and diverging lines of sight to manipulate the relationship between distance and a focal point. For example, if a garden in an urban space was small and its designer wanted it to appear larger, then the lines of sight on a focal point, such as a gazebo or some other monument, would converge. The sides of a path leading to the focal point would not be parallel but would draw together as they approached the distant object. The sides of the garden beds or the clipped sides of hedges could be shaped so that they converged as they approached the object of view, thus drawing the eye forward while creating an image of distance or length that was not there.

Such constructions or design elements were identified in both the Ridout and Carroll gardens through topographic mapping. There were no surviving design elements that suggested lines of sight in the Paca garden because large portions of the garden were destroyed early in the 20th century when it was removed to build a hotel. William Paca's house in Annapolis still stands and was built in 1763 when he was a young man and recently married for the first time. Paca's Annapolis house has survived to the present initially because in the early-20th century, the house became the frontispiece for a large hotel that served U.S. Naval Academy visitors, legislators, and others and because Annapolis, a famous backwater after independence, became one by being bypassed in the Industrial Revolution. When the hotel was demolished in the 1960s, the house was saved through the efforts of the Historic Annapolis Foundation.

The original 18th-century garden was not as lucky as the house. Only the descending ground planes remained, as evidenced by the sloping foundations of the original and extant garden walls, buried beneath the parking lot of the hotel. The terraces, or *flats*, of the garden descended from the viewer at the top of the garden. They were connected by *falls*, or slopes, built on a 3:1 angle; for every foot of height there was 3 ft. of width (Paca-Steele and Wright 1987; Leone and Shackel 1990). These landscape features were used to create the illusion of distance in Paca's Annapolis garden.

In the Ridout garden, elements of the original beds have survived, and these were useful in understanding how such features were built and used to create perspective (Figure 2). On the terraces, three sets of beds flanked a central ramp as it descended over three *parterres*, or terraces. The front ends of the beds were equidistant and parallel to each other. However, the beds became narrower as they receded from the viewing platform at the top of the garden. While they remained rectangular in actuality, they looked like trapezoids, as the back edges appeared to be converging lines guiding the view down the ramp to the focal point.

Four additional beds on the lowest terrace at the bottom of the Ridout garden also contributed to the creation of perceived distance through control of perspective. The four large beds comprise two pairs or sets that run parallel to the main walk. They are of the same length but are of two different widths. The beds that are situated on the inside, closer to the garden's main axis or central path, are wider

than the outer beds. The outer, narrower, beds are parallel. This arrangement helped build the lines and volumes that created the illusion of distance that was begun on the upper terraces by the three sets of beds there.

The beds in the Ridout garden were discovered by accident. When the garden was mapped, slight depressions were noticed during visual reconnaissance. By systematically exploring and marking the locations of these depressions, it was possible to map the outline of the beds. Although the outlines are accurate, no excavation was done in these areas to determine depth, stratigraphy, or subsurface shape. Given their position on the garden terraces and the lack of extensive modifications to the remainder of the yard space over the last two centuries, they are assumed to be expressions of original beds or at least of original design.

There is no archaeological evidence for beds from Paca's Annapolis garden. However, a large body of historical evidence supports their likely existence, and some archaeological evidence exists for beds from other contemporary Annapolis gardens. Today, in the Paca garden, the beds, planted as parterres, are tightly planted to give the appearance of being woven or sculpted. The beds comprise four large outdoor rooms and are a powerfully evocative reconstruction of what might have been there. Peale mentions the parterres on the terraces of Charles Carroll's garden, but the actual outlines of beds were found only in the Ridout garden.

Early 18th-century efforts at controlling perspective in formal gardens have been relatively well documented in Annapolis. Such controlled perspectives, meant to be experienced by the walking visitor, act on the eye to create the illusion that a garden focal point is either bigger or smaller than it is in fact and to create illusions throughout the garden that place the viewer at the center of shifting perspectives. This set of optical facts, combined with baroque theories of power, makes the viewer the subject of the geometric manipulation of the garden space and reveals rules of perspective and geometry known and used by the master builder. The application of the laws of geometry indicated that the builder understood geometry, understood the laws of nature and of God, and knew how to put them to his or her own use (Bacon 1968). Those in the know, who came to walk in the garden and experience the execution of this knowledge, shared in the appreciation of this skill, witnessed the power the builder had over those he compelled to work for him, and understood that the builder was at the top of the hierarchy, regardless of whether he was a plantation owner, a royal functionary, or a head of state.

Formal, geometric landscapes did not disappear with the initiation of republican government, but they did change. Both Jeremy Bentham (Bowring 1962) and Michel Foucault (1979) pointed out that when the citizen replaced the monarch as the source of power, citizens learned to watch each other so as to enforce the rules for proper civic behavior, another source of power. Such surveillance was internalized to become self-discipline and was institutionalized in the new American republic through many mechanisms (Leone and Shackel 1987; Shackel 1993), such as the adoption of genteel codes of behavior (forms of disciplining speech, dress, manners, and consumerism), the growth of social structures that monitored public behavior (e.g., the poor house), and through the use of panoptic structures such as prisons and state houses (Leone and Hurry 1998). Many American plantations were built with the understanding that the plantation house could serve this panoptic purpose (Epperson 1999). It is suggested here that William Paca used accepted ideas of perspective when designing both his home in Annapolis and his new plantation and garden on Wye Island. William Paca built a house and garden where he could see and be seen and did so to reinforce and teach hierarchy, not equality.

William Paca's Garden at Wye Island

These understandings of perspective and surveillance, and the archaeology of Annapolis' gardens, served as the background for beginning long-term archaeological work on William Paca's second garden, located at Wye Hall Plantation on Wye Island. When Paca retired from active political life in Annapolis, he began to build an elaborate neoclassical house and to develop the surrounding grounds, beginning in about 1792. The garden was one of two designed in the neighborhood of Wye Island by a professional landscape architect, Luke O'Dio, whose correspondence with Thomas

Jefferson about both gardens survives in the Jefferson Correspondence collection in the National Agricultural Library (O'Dio 1802).

By 1798, Paca's holdings on Wye Island included 1,414 acres of land, roughly half of the island. Much of this land came to Paca through marriage to his first wife, Henrietta Maria Lloyd. The tax assessment from that year lists two outbuildings and the main house at Wye Hall (U.S. Bureau of the Census 1790; Federal Tax Assessment 1798). One of these outbuildings presumably was a carriage house that is still extant today, albeit in much modified form, to the southeast of the garden terraces. These same records report holdings of 100 slaves. Like most large plantations on the Eastern Shore, the Wye Hall land was used primarily in the production of wheat and tobacco.

In 1876, Paca's great house on Wye Island burned down along with most of its contents, including, most people suspect, his archive of personal papers, as he is one of the signers of the Declaration of Independence whose papers do not survive. The shell of the house was rebuilt but in a different form by the Paca family who owned the property into the early-20th century. The debris from this fire was used as fill in specific spots in the landscape but was not broadcast wholesale. The rebuilt house was in turn torn down in the 1930s, after the Paca family sold the property, and the present house was built in the late 1930s. The current building sits on or very near the footprint of the original, the proposed plans for which survive (Figure 4).

FIGURE 4. Joseph Clarke's elevation and plan of the 1792 House at Wye Hall Plantation. (Courtesy of the Maryland Historical Society, Baltimore, MD.)

Paca's Wye Island garden is one of a handful of large rural gardens dating to the late-18th or early-19th century that have been excavated archaeologically. This investigation represented an opportunity to examine landscape and garden design in the new republic, to explore the influence of the English landscape-garden tradition in America, and to describe large-scale landscape modifications in plantation settings. In addition, with the extensive work done by Archaeology in Annapolis on urban, earlier 18th-century gardens, there was an opportunity for comparison of garden design style and rationale. The two Paca gardens were built at least 30 years apart. Did the principles used to build them change? This last question contains within it the beginning of an essential exploration of what gardens have in common over time, including an attempt at understanding what purposes they served.

The investigation of Paca's Wye Island garden was framed with two thoughts. First, William Paca was one of Maryland's foremost political figures. He signed the Declaration of Independence, would not support the U.S. Constitution without the Bill of Rights, was the third elected governor of Maryland, was re-elected twice, and was the first federal judge in Maryland. William Paca was a wealthy lawyer and knew and had frequent interaction with the other founders of the country (Stiverson and Jacobsen 1976; Russo 1990). Paca was familiar with the ideas, philosophies, and plans of the Maryland gentry and lived in the active, aggressive, intellectual world they shared. This leads to a first assumption. Such people were not only building a new country with new institutions, but they also set out to build active models in society that would create and re-create the ideas they were working with. They did not just write documents but also built institutions to transform society as they knew it. Houses and plantations were models for this transformation, not simply demonstrations of their owner's wealth or taste. Plantations (and slave ownership)—as the physical embodiments of Euroamerican aspiration—ratified, taught, and extended personal authority and power. Houses and plantations were locales that presented opportunities to generate social interactions that had transformative authority. This understanding of the reflexive nature of the material world provides the underlying assump-

tion for the investigation of Paca's Wye Island plantation reported on here.

Earlier analyses of William Paca's house and garden in Annapolis also served to help frame the study of his later home on Wye Island (Leone 1984, 1987; Leone and Shackel 1990). This work on gardens in Annapolis was aimed to shift the focus away from seeing Paca's garden as a reflection of his personal taste, as unique, and as a flat space. Rather, research has been directed toward demonstrating that Paca's taste was a part of his social politics and that the garden was an active part of the construction of gentility as a form of personal discipline, power, and a particular rationalized world that served the gentry of Maryland. The garden books mentioned earlier show that Paca's Annapolis garden was a product of standard landscape-design practice and would compare with many other contemporary gardens, whether Paca designed it himself or hired someone like O'Dio to do so. Paca's garden was a volumetric space, built according to well-known period formulas, constructed using the principles of perspective, all of which deliberately shaped the land and instructed visitors in hierarchy, authority, and learning. This position also influenced the work on Paca's landscape on Wye Island.

The work on the Wye Island plantation that is discussed here began in the summer of 2000 but was preceded in the 1980s by testing done by Anne E. Yentsch, Karen Bescherer, and Conrad Goodwin (Bescherer and Yentsch 1989). At that time, excavations of several deposits associated with the plantation kitchen wing were carried out, demonstrating that some of the archaeology of the plantation was intact. Further, an excellent and comprehensive topographic map of the great garden terrace was made at the time (Figure 5). This map reveals the essential features of the formal garden that one could recognize without massive excavation.

During the 2000 excavation season, a research strategy designed to survey the landscape that made up the historical period core of the plantation was implemented. The purpose of this work was to document the spatial structure of the working plantation, to look for evidence of the larger design of the garden, and to explore the relationship of the garden to the whole. A systematic shovel test survey was the primary means of recovering this layered

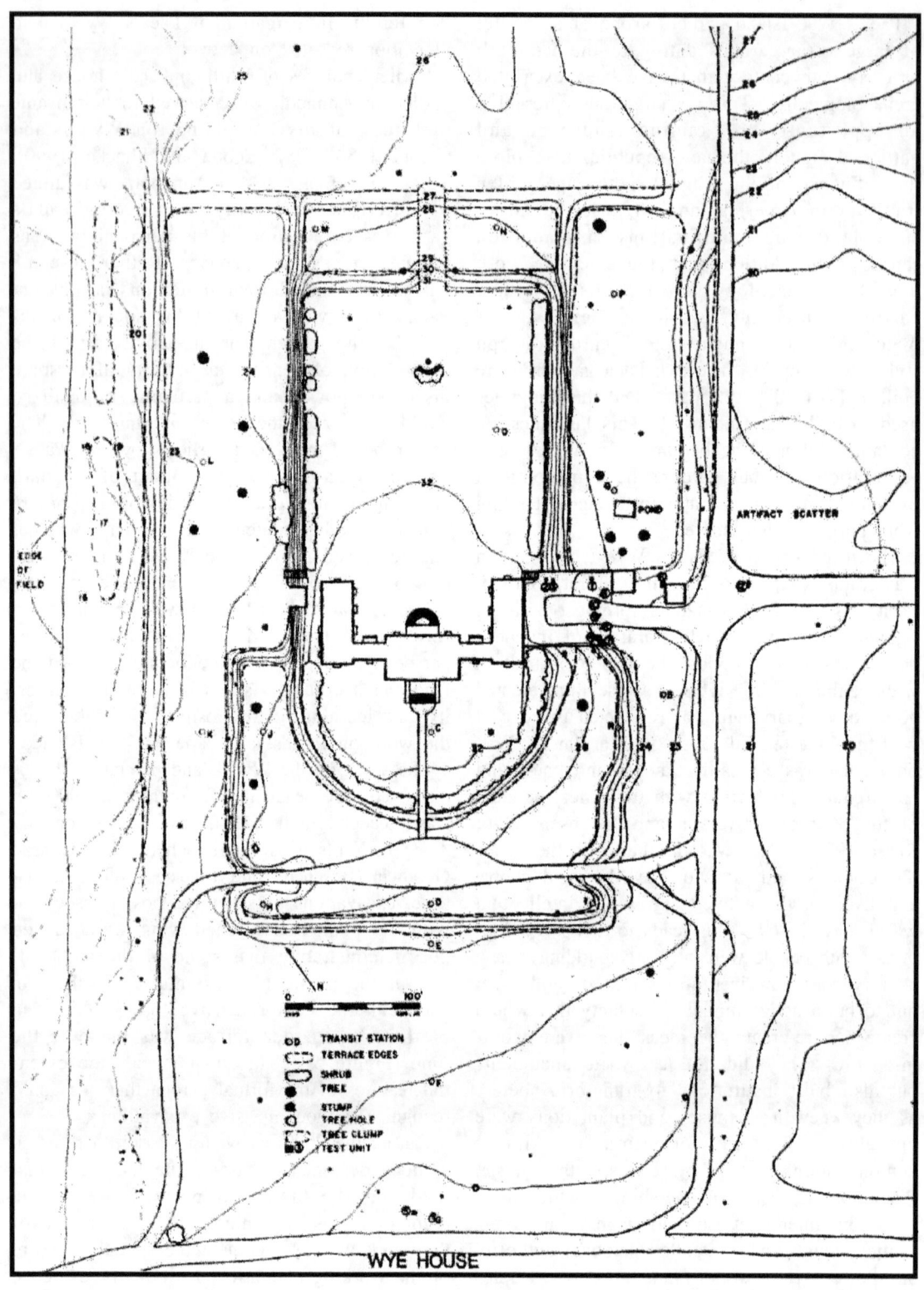

FIGURE 5. Conrad Goodwin map (1989) of Wye Hall's terraces (after Bescherer and Yentsch 1989).

Perspectives from *Historical Archaeology*

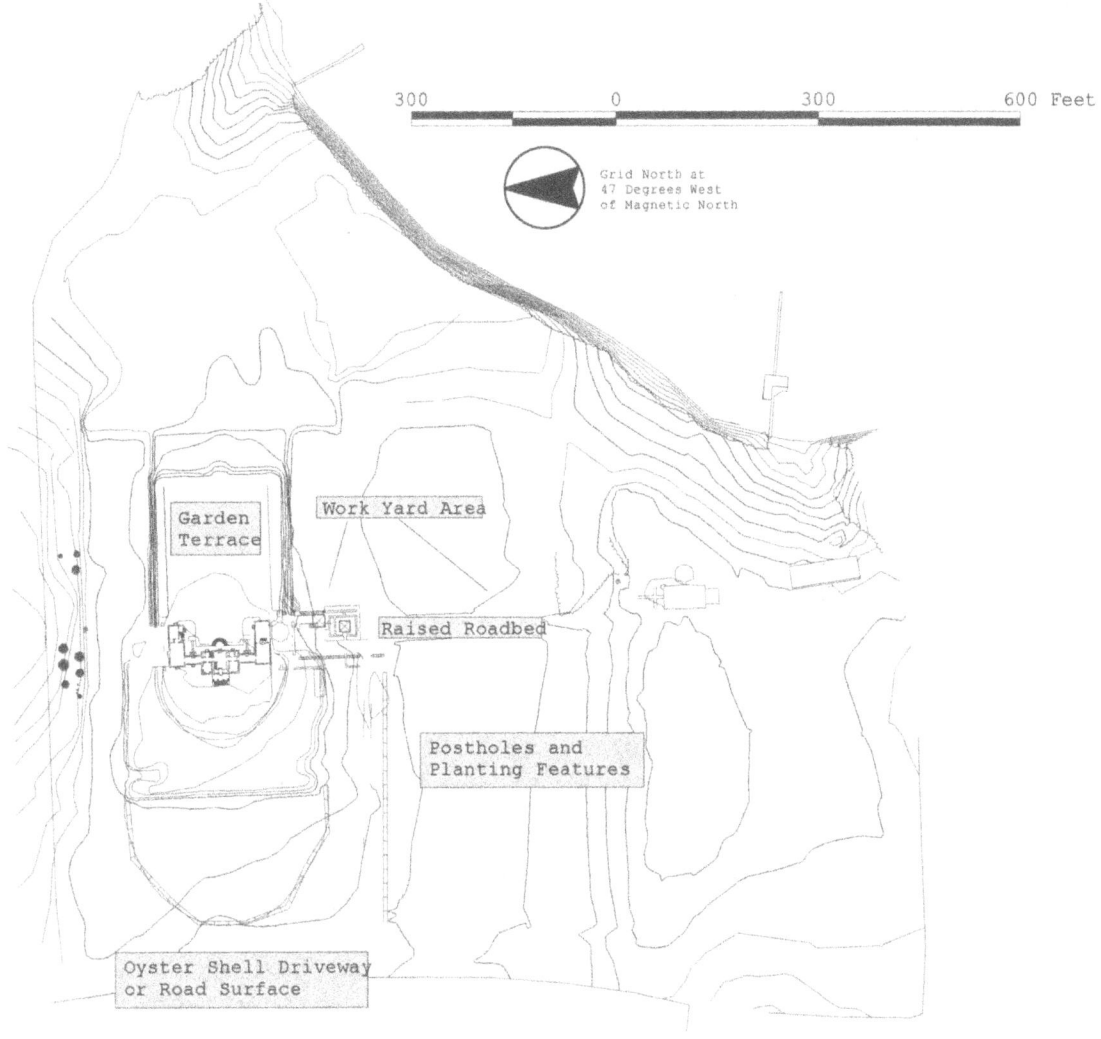

FIGURE 6. Plantation landscape features. (Drawing by J. Harmon, 2004.)

and changing layout. These shovel tests were eventually supplemented by a series of larger excavation units and backhoe trenches. The first, and most significant, of the results of this investigation was the finding that much of the landscape, and much of the archaeology of the late-18th- and early-19th-century occupations, was largely intact (Harmon et al. 2003).

Features were identified in areas near the house and terraces that were helpful in interpreting the layout of the core of the plantation (Figure 6), including evidence of an oyster-shell driveway or road surface in the large yard area west of the house and a series of postholes and planting features adjacent to the access road that parallels the house site. The latter were interpreted as evidence for a fence line, with plantings placed at intervals along its inner edge. Although the date at which they were removed or buried remains uncertain, they do not predate the original Paca house and are most probably evidence for the layout of this part of the yard during the early- to mid-19th century.

The area surrounding a raised roadbed, which connects the house site with the still extant carriage house to the southeast, was also tested during the 2000 fieldwork. This road feature can actually be traced to the far end of the island, reported to be the site of late-17th and early-18th-century occupations. Further, it forms the principal north-south axis around which much of the Paca plantation was organized. Artifacts and features associated with a work yard were concentrated in a zone (approximately 200 x 50 feet) along the side of this road. Evidence for at least one structure was found here, which was present as early as the late-19th century. The function of this area changed through time, although it generally served as a utilitarian work yard in various forms. Use of the area for this purpose persisted until the middle of the 20th century.

During this initial field season, a utility-and-waterline trench (27-ft. long, 5-ft. deep) was excavated across the narrow dimension of the large platform immediately outside the garden door of the house. The profiles of this trench revealed microstratigraphic evidence of dozens of relatively small loads of silty sand soils of local origin that were carried there to make the garden platform. This stratum was about 3 ft. deep and was undisturbed wherever it was found on the terrace. The platform dates to at least the 1790s, as this stratum was overlain by garden beds containing artifacts dating to the construction of the original Paca House. William Paca owned 100 slaves on this plantation at this time, as recorded in the 1798 Federal Tax Assessment, which leads to the suggestion that the labor of enslaved people built the massive earthworks on Wye Island. This interpretation is supported by interviews taken in the late-19th and early-20th centuries that record traditions of slaves using baskets and wheelbarrows to build the garden.

The initial trench showed no evidence of planting beds. However, it was hypothesized (based on period sources as well as the advice of Michel Conan, director of Landscape Studies at Dumbarton Oaks who came to see the garden at the authors' invitation) that the terrace would not have been empty but would have contained extensive flowerbeds, shrubs, and trees to provide shade from the hot Chesapeake sun. All would have been oriented toward the water view. Much of the most recent research on the plantings in English and American gardens of the late-18th and early-19th centuries also suggested that the height of the plants and shrubs would be graduated in size up to the sides of the terraces so as to create a widening funnel of the view to the water.

2001–2002 Investigation of the Terrace Garden Site

A more intensive testing and excavation program oriented toward two specific goals was needed to address this hypothesis regarding the overall structure of the garden on the terrace. First, it was necessary to determine if more intensive testing would indeed reveal evidence of the original garden design. Second, it was necessary to assess the extent to which disturbance and later modification of the terrace may have impacted any preserved features. Although the initial testing had shown that intact areas were on the terrace, it was also clear that some surfaces had been disturbed by construction of the extant house.

Given these goals, relatively large exposures were necessary to identify and examine the garden's structure. The most efficient method was to excavate a series of large but shallow trenches with a backhoe. Once the sod layer and approximately 8–12 in. of surface soils were removed, each trench was shovel-scraped and then troweled to reveal any features present. Eventually, 24 of these trenches were excavated across the terrace (Figure 7).

Shortly after the investigation on the terrace was begun, relatively large and well-preserved features that were associated with the late-18th-century garden were found. After the initial trenches on the north side of the terrace were excavated, two distinct types of features were identified, consisting of actual planting beds and a series of smaller, more isolated soil stains identified as the locations of individual trees or other plantings.

Three major planting bed features were identified. These features were initially identified as large, dark grayish-brown soil stains that were distinct in color from the surrounding yellowish-brown soils that made up the terrace matrix. The terminal ends of the bed features were all rounded. The beds were all located on the northern half of the terrace. One bed was 12 ft. wide; its immediate partner was 6 ft. wide. The narrower bed was located nearer the centerline of the terrace. Based on the one bed fully exposed during excavation, a

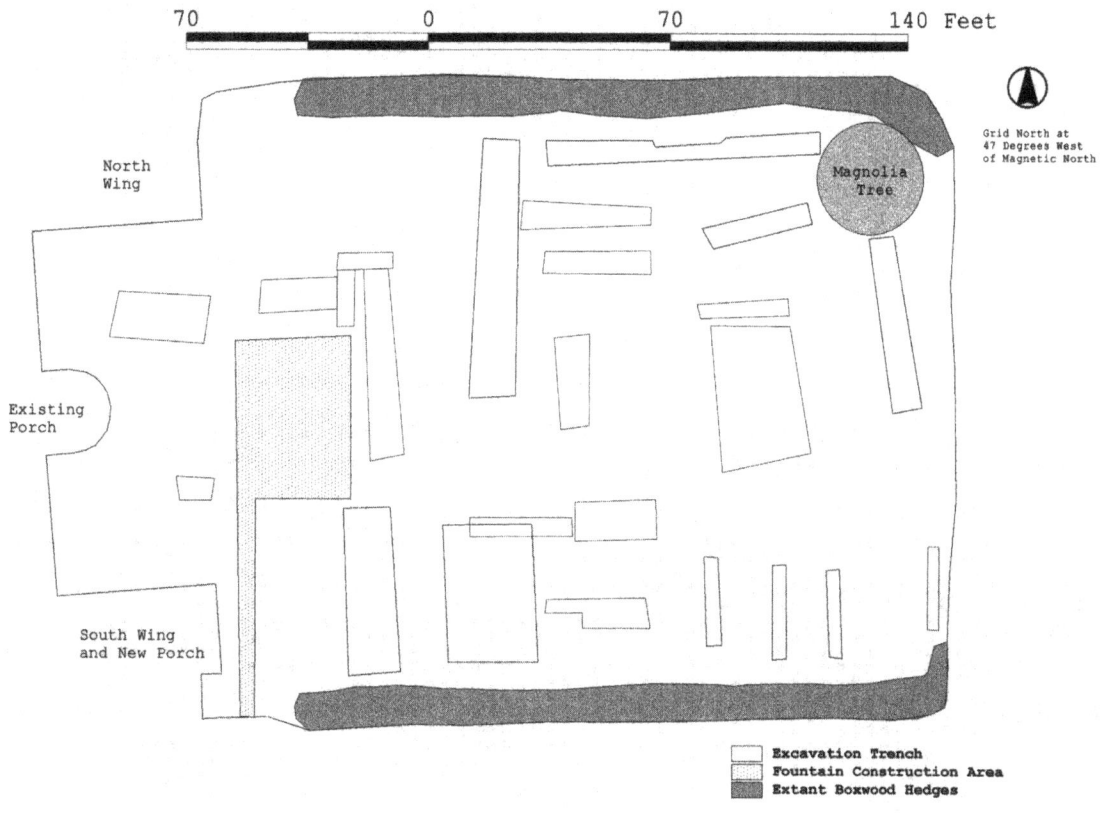

FIGURE 7. Locations of the trenches excavated on the garden terrace, 2000–2002. (Drawing by J. Harmon, 2004.)

projected length for the beds was approximately 60 ft.

The long edges of these beds were scalloped and slightly irregular, particularly along the long axes. In some cases, larger, but shallow, lobe-shaped structures extended from the sides of the beds (Figure 8). These features were created by the use of edging plants, probably of a shallow-rooted variety. Jay Graham, landscape architect for the current reconstruction, suggested that these plantings may have been boxwood on the basis of their depth, size, and form, but no archaeological evidence for a particular type of plant was recovered. Although soil samples were taken, they have not been analyzed to date, and no identifiable seeds or plant remains were recovered during fieldwork.

A much deeper and more regular depression was discovered within the bed section nearest the eastern edge of the terrace. Here, the depression was found to extend 12 in. beneath the base of the bed feature, which was itself about 6 in. thick. The excavation of a section across the depression revealed a pit with relatively straight sides that was 12 in. wide and 12 in. deep (Figure 9). The pit contained the base and portions of the body of a dark olive-green wine bottle of late-18th-century origin. Similar artifacts have been found as "paving" in planting features in roughly contemporary kitchen gardens in Williamsburg, Virginia, where they were interpreted as aids to drainage (Brown and Samford 1990:108–109).

Several features located in a number of the trenches excavated on both the north and south sides of the main terrace were found to be associated with these beds. The features were relatively widely dispersed and were made up of dark brown to yellowish brown soil stains. The shapes of these stains varied, but all were

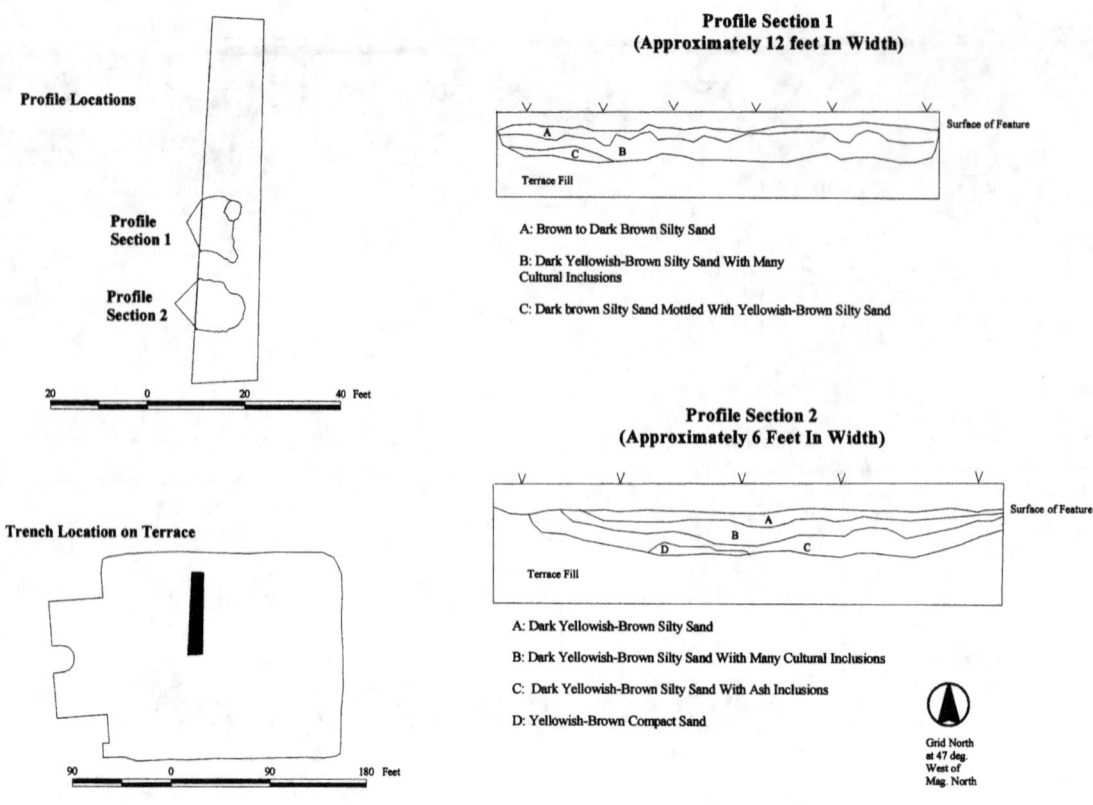

Profile Locations

Profile
Section 1

Profile
Section 2

20   0   20   40 Feet

Trench Location on Terrace

90   0   90   180 Feet

Profile Section 1
(Approximately 12 feet In Width)

Surface of Feature

Terrace Fill

A: Brown to Dark Brown Silty Sand

B: Dark Yellowish-Brown Silty Sand With Many
Cultural Inclusions

C: Dark brown Silty Sand Mottled With Yellowish-Brown Silty Sand

Profile Section 2
(Approximately 6 Feet In Width)

Surface of Feature

Terrace Fill

A: Dark Yellowish-Brown Silty Sand

B: Dark Yellowish-Brown Silty Sand Wiith Many Cultural Inclusions

C: Dark Yellowish-Brown Silty Sand With Ash Inclusions

D: Yellowish-Brown Compact Sand

Grid North
at 47 deg.
West of
Mag. North

FIGURE 8. Garden bed plans and profiles, north-central section of the terrace. (Drawing by J. Harmon, 2004.)

relatively amorphous, oval to round. Sections were excavated from several of the more discrete features on both sides of the terrace. Excavated features were found to be 12–24 in. deep and had rounded bottoms with lobate extensions (Figure 10). This same pattern was echoed within the southeastern quadrant of the terrace. Based on the authors' conversations with two landscape architects, it was hypothesized that these features had been the locations of individual plantings, tall enough to provide shade and larger than those that would have been planted in the beds (Jay Graham and Kevin Campion 2002, pers. comm.).

A wide range of artifacts was recovered from the sections that were excavated from the planting beds. Much of this material was burned oyster shell and brick fragments, but a large amount of glass, many nails and other unidentifiable metal fragments, bone, bottle glass, and ceramics were also found. Several brass and shell buttons were also recovered. The material dates from 1790 to 1820.

The ceramics recovered from the bed features provided some information relevant to determining a date for the beds. Sherds of creamware and Chinese porcelain originating in Canton were recovered from all three of the beds. These wares are usually dated as originating as early as 1780 on Maryland sites, declining in importance after 1820 (Reeves et al. 1991, after Maryland Geological Survey, Division of Archaeology Historic Artifact Chronology). One remarkable artifact that was recovered from the largest of the bed features was a single 18th-century cuff link, probably made of a silver-plated base metal.

Given the O'Dio letter cited above and the presence of the late-18th- and early-19th-century artifacts in the features, it appears that the beds were created around 1792, at or near the time the original house was constructed. Evidence of importation of burned material into the garden

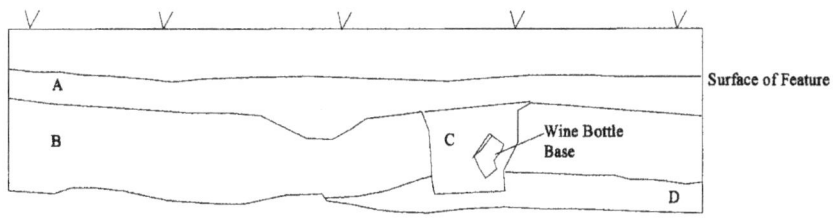

A: Dark Yellowish-Brown Silty Sand (Interior Bed Feature

B: Yellowish-Brown Silty Sand Mottled With Dark Yellowish-Brown Silty Sand (Interior Bed Feature)

C: Yellowish-Brown Silty Sand With Large Bottle Fragment

D: Strong Brown Sandy Clay (Terrace Fill/Subsoil)

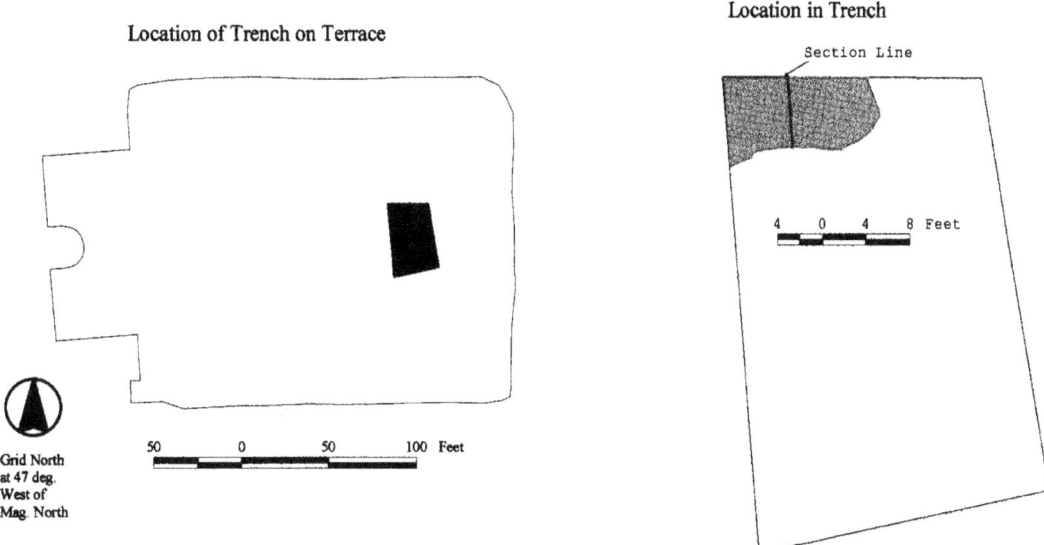

FIGURE 9. Plan and profile of bed feature with bottle base, northeast section of the terrace. (Drawing by J. Harmon, 2004.)

area seems to indicate that the garden beds were abandoned and filled when the original house was destroyed in 1879. This fits well with the known historical chronology for the terrace and house and is not contradicted by any other archaeological or historical evidence. Therefore, it appears that the original Paca and O'Dio design for the garden survived for approximately 80 years.

Figure 11 presents an interpolated layout for the original late-18th-century garden that is derived from the locations of the archaeological features. This reconstruction is based on features indicat-ing that the garden was slightly asymmetrical and assumes that it was roughly a mirror image from one side of the terrace to the other. The dividing line within this mirror image would have been a perpendicular axis running from the center of the central block of the house down the center of the terrace east to the edge of the river.

Interpreting the Results of the Archaeology: Formal Dimensions of the Paca Garden

Excavation and mapping of archaeological features in the Wye Hall garden reveals that a

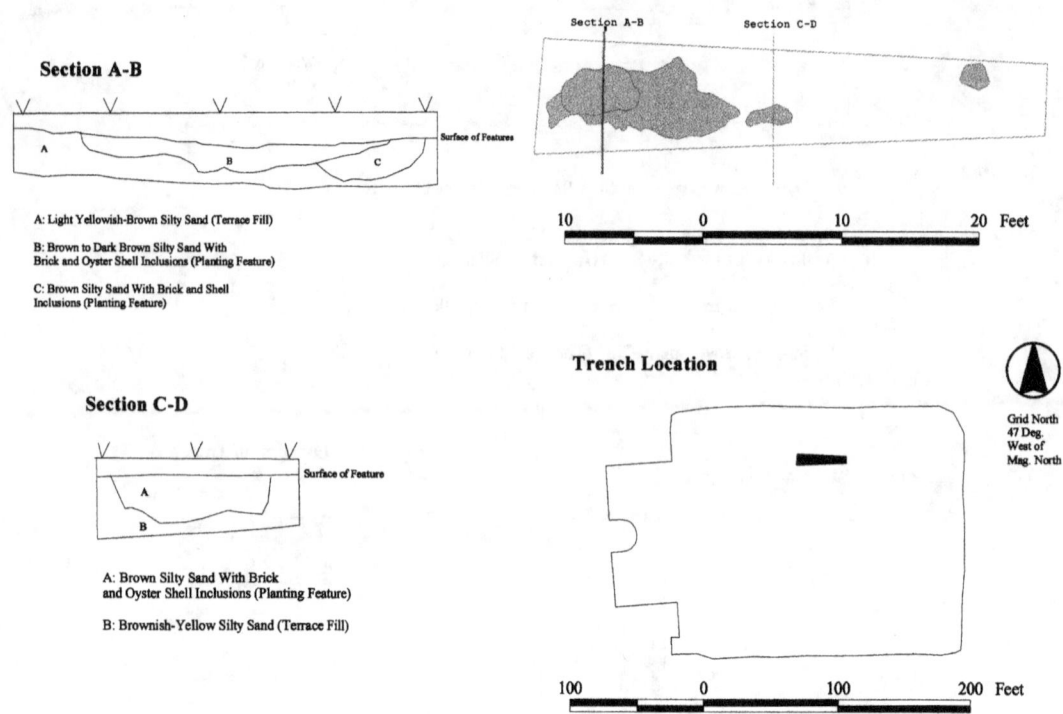

Section Locations

Section A-B

Surface of Features

A: Light Yellowish-Brown Silty Sand (Terrace Fill)

B: Brown to Dark Brown Silty Sand With
Brick and Oyster Shell Inclusions (Planting Feature)

C: Brown Silty Sand With Brick and Shell
Inclusions (Planting Feature)

Section A-B   Section C-D

10   0   10   20   Feet

Section C-D

Surface of Feature

A: Brown Silty Sand With Brick
and Oyster Shell Inclusions (Planting Feature)

B: Brownish-Yellow Silty Sand (Terrace Fill)

Trench Location

Grid North
47 Deg.
West of
Mag. North

100   0   100   200   Feet

FIGURE 10. Representative plan and profile of isolated planting features. (Drawing by J. Harmon, 2004.)

regular geometric pattern underlies the architecture of the garden. The first aspect of this pattern lies within the dimensions of the terrace itself. The highest portion of the terrace is 210 ft. long and 180 ft. wide (Figure 5). If the lower terrace is included, then the total length of the structure is 300 ft. The uppermost terrace's elevation is approximately 6 ft. above the surrounding side yards, and the lower terrace is approximately 3 ft. lower than this surface. All of these dimensions are evenly divisible by a factor of three. In addition, the long dimensions of the terrace parallel the line of sight from the rear of the house to the water and, being divisible by 3, form the "square and a half" geometric form that is the initial basis for the creation of an illusion of perspective distance.

The garden's geometry in relation to the factor of three is continued within the size and layout of the beds. They are 12 and 6 ft. wide respectively, with the narrower bed located nearer to the center of the terrace. The bed that contained the bottle-filled planting feature, farthest east of the house on the main terrace, echoed these dimensions. The total length of the beds, as evidenced by one full exposure, was approximately 60 ft.

In addition to their size, the placement of the beds on the terrace is also governed by the factor of three. The outer edge of the large bed discovered on the northern side of the terrace is approximately 60 ft. from the northern edge of the platform. Although the edges of the beds exposed by the excavation are irregular, they are approximately 6 ft. apart. Finally, if these beds are assumed to be one-half of a mirror image, with similarly placed beds on the south side of the terrace, then the two groups of beds would range between 15 and 30 ft. apart, with the distance increasing farther from the house.

The exact angle at which the beds diverge from the centerline of the terrace is difficult

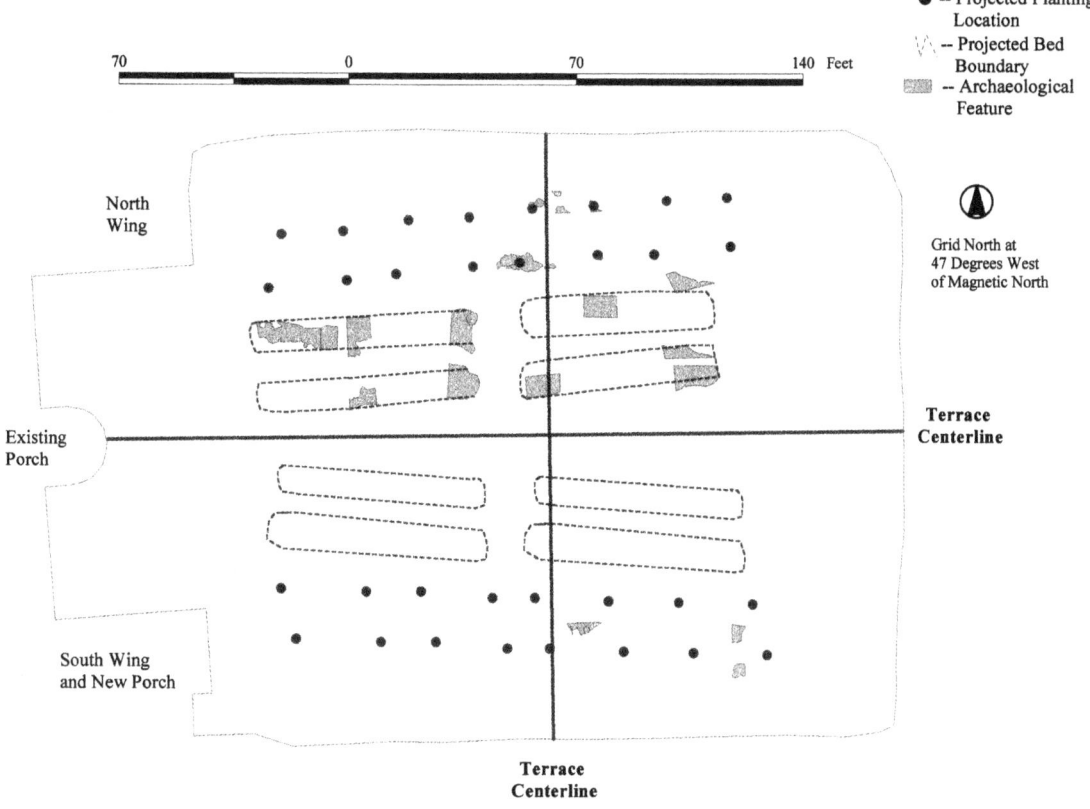

FIGURE 11. Late-18th-century garden layout. (Drawing by J. Harmon, 2004.)

to determine because of the relatively limited exposure afforded by the excavation. It is clear that the beds do diverge with distance from the house. The hypothetical layout indicates that this angle from centerline may be as much as 15° over a distance of approximately 120 ft.

Given the design of Paca's earlier garden in Annapolis (ca. 1760s), these findings are not entirely unexpected. When William Paca built his earlier garden in Annapolis, the ideas that the rules of perspective and diverging lines of sight could be used to manage a garden's focal point and that a sympathetic underlying regularity to the geometric layout of the garden as a whole would further manage the way the garden was viewed were well established.

However, by the late-18th century, rectilinear gardens of the style that Paca had built in Annapolis were no longer popular in England. The rectilinear designs of both beds and layouts had given way to more curvilinear styles. The curved ends of the beds, the lack of rigid symmetry in the layout of the terrace as a whole, and the flanking plantings that would have varied in size and placement provide evidence that the design of this garden was developed in response to changes in England. The demi-lune shape of the terrace in front (west) of the house introduced a curving form to all those who approached the house. Further, the geometrically constructed garden sits within a larger managed landscape that provided the park-like setting more typical of the English landscape garden of the later 18th century.

Great flat terraces surround the geometric raised garden, all of which show little evidence of early cultivation. The soil profiles seem to indicate these areas had been planted in grass, and few structures appear to have been built on these flats. Evidence from the first season of archaeological investigation also suggests that these flats were fenced and that, at least across the front of the yard, no access existed up the flat terrace to the main door of the house. Rather, the fencing lines found seem to indicate that access to the house came by carriage road to the side entrance. Guests entered the garden from inside the house, either to the back main terraces or to the front demi-lune and grassy flats. Such a pattern of access to the garden is well in keeping with the English landscape tradition of using the pleasure gardens surrounding a great house as a park to stroll, converse, and enact the rituals of gentility.

Later Features: The Post-1880 Garden

Some evidence for a later garden on the site was also recovered during this investigation. This evidence is much more fragmentary than that for the earlier garden, and it is impossible to hypothesize a layout for this later design as a whole (Figure 12). Most of the features associated with this phase are located near the western edge of the terrace, in and around the areas of the terrace most intensively impacted by construction. Further, much of the evidence is in the form of dispersed lenses of rounded gravel that formed pathways and lined beds. This construction technique proved to be much less resistant to the vagaries of preservation than the beds and planting features associated with the earlier Paca and O'Dio design.

The first, and most well preserved, of the features associated with this phase of the garden consists of the remnants of a large platform located on the north side of the current porch. This feature was located just a few inches below the ground surface, and within the trench it measured approximately 12 x 6 ft. in area. The northern edge of this feature had been interrupted by a drainage trench excavated when the current house was built (Figure 12).

The platform feature consisted of a very compact mixture of pale yellow sand and shell-tempered mortar. The feature ranged

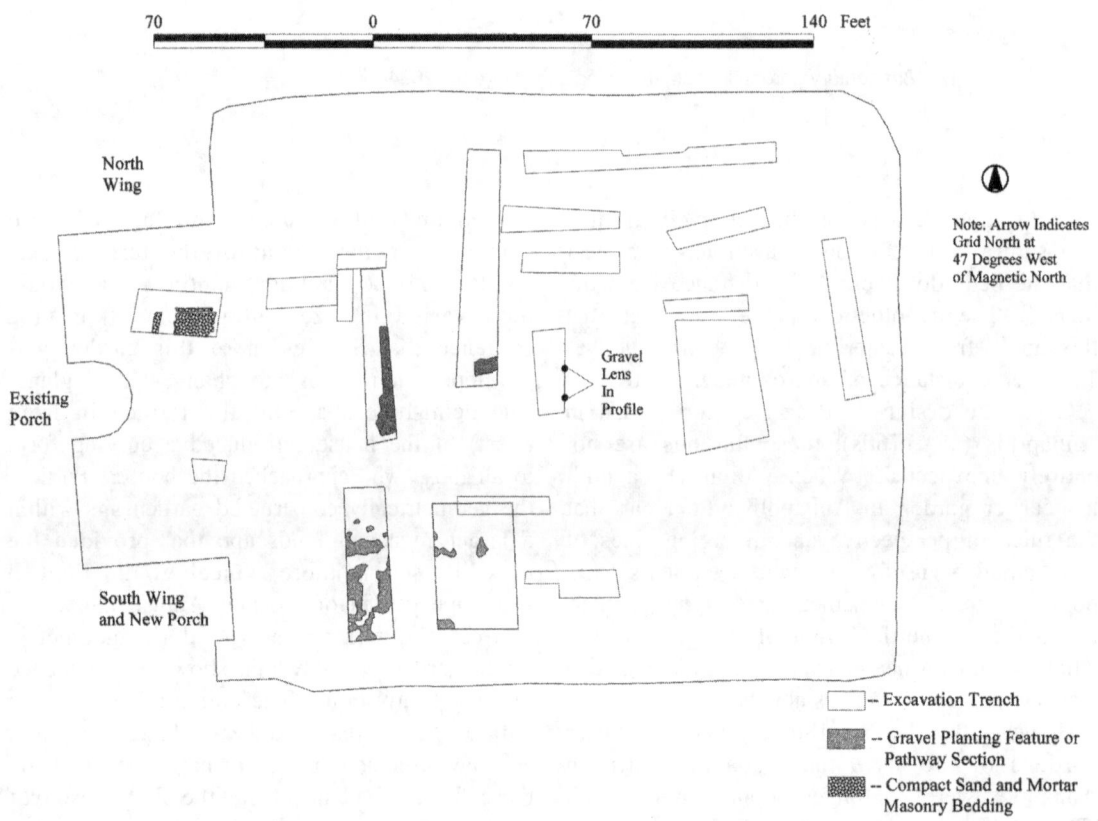

FIGURE 12. Post-1879 garden features. (Drawing by J. Harmon, 2004).

Perspectives from *Historical Archaeology*

between 3 in. and 6 in. in thickness and was the underbedding for a brick pavement from which the bricks have been removed. A few partial bricks were present within the feature, which were probably part of a viewing platform associated with the second house, extant between approximately 1879 and the middle 1930s.

The second set of features associated with this phase of the garden is a series of remnants of gravel pathways that were located immediately beneath the ground surface. Deposits of well-sorted, yellowish brown pea gravel formed paths or walkways on the terrace. The remnants indicate at least one path down the central axis of the terrace and one perpendicular crossing path. There did not appear to have been any excavation done in establishing the paths, and there was no evidence for any edging or other element that would have bounded them. One section of the crossing gravel path contained a small section of dry-laid handmade brick, which formed a small platform (ca. 2 x 4 ft.) on a line immediately down the central east-west axis of the terrace.

The final set of features that were associated with this phase of the garden was located within the southwestern quadrant of the terrace. Here, relatively large gravel beds were discovered that were much more amorphous in form than the deposits identified as pathway remnants. Sections from these features were excavated, and they were found to be of varying depth, ranging between 3 in. and 12 in. in thickness with irregular bottoms. These are apparently the remnants of shallow gravel beds that were placed around the bases of larger plantings, either trees or fairly significant shrubs. The growth of roots out from the centers of these beds pushed the gravel into the forms that were identified when the trenches were excavated. Although it is difficult to make a precise determination, it is probable that the plant species were of a shallow-rooted variety, in that the major direction of this growth appears to be out rather than down.

Based on their stratigraphic position, the features that make up this phase of the garden have been identified as being later in time. All are located just beneath the ground surface, several inches above the earlier beds described in the preceding section. In one case, the gravel and brick pathway features are actually superimposed over the earlier 6-ft.-wide bed described above. The remnant of the viewing platform by the current porch is located at approximately the same elevation.

The historical record relating to the plantation and house suggests that this iteration of the garden may relate to the second house, built between the destruction of the original in 1879 and the construction of the current house in the late 1930s. By ca. 1940 no evidence of these pathways or beds was visible within the aerial photos taken at the time the current house was being built. It is probable that this design existed only for the approximately 50-year period between these two dates. Given the fragmentary nature of the evidence for this phase of the garden, no overall layout can be hypothesized. There were at least two elements to this later phase, the pathways and the gravel beds surrounding larger plantings or trees. This garden probably only occupied a portion of the terrace, insofar as features were located only on the western portion of the terrace, nearer the house. Unfortunately, this area was also subjected to the most disturbance by various modifications of the house and immediately surrounding yard.

Summary and Conclusions: Perspective and Surveillance in the Wye Hall Garden

Three gardens were built on William Paca's Wye Island plantation: one for Paca's original house, one for the rebuilt house, and a third for the colonial revival mansion. The built platforms around the house remain symmetrical, connected to access roads, farm buildings, and fields, but significant parts of the original, large-scale planned landscape have disappeared from view. Nothing is known about the productive landscape or the landscape of the producers, the enslaved African Americans. Censuses show a slave population that grew from 100 in 1790, to 150 in 1860 (Maryland State Archives 1860). For example, slave quarters certainly were on this property, but no information shows how they were planned in relation to the rest of this large systematic effort.

However, the Wye Hall investigation has yielded a number of discoveries about the spatial organization and morphology of the 1790s garden. The original beds were ordered in sets around a central axis. Those beds closer to the central axis were 6 ft. wide; the beds that were farther away, closer to the terrace edge, were 12 ft. wide. These beds are not situated on a perfect perpendicular to the house and were not parallel to the axis but, rather, were on a divergent angle that pointed the beds away from the garden door. The beds served to direct one's view toward the house or away from it toward the Wye Narrows to the east. Each of the beds had rounded ends and was deeper in the middle than at the edge, with deeper depressions punctuating the midlines, suggesting the presence of shrubs within them. Lawn surrounded the beds; there was no evidence of brick or gravel paths. Finally, there was a row of shrubs or small trees on the edge of the terrace beyond the beds. The garden does not appear to have been entirely symmetrical, although absolute confirmation of this was difficult because recently buried utilities limited the area that could be excavated.

Trenches dug into the terraces comprising the center of Paca's late-18th-century landscape revealed that they were built up with thousands of basketfuls of soil. The house stands on what may have been a slight natural rise that was built up through the addition of many feet of fill and rests on a deep cellar, which further elevates the structure above the surrounding landscape. The house, elevated above the surrounding plain, set off by series of geometric shapes that constituted the formal garden, stood like a centerpiece in a well-designed stage setting. Even today, when approaching the house, it is clear that one is encountering a powerful human constructed and ordered landscape.

The current house, which is clearly inspired by the original, has windows in all directions and allows sight in all directions, also like the original. The fields, a river on either side, and most human activity connected with work were and are visible from the house, while much activity within and around the house was also constantly visible. The transparency of Paca's Wye House was aided by the way the beds on the terrace work. From the garden door of the house and from all the windows on the garden side, the lines of the beds diverge, thus creating a powerful optical illusion that draws all objects closer. From the water and surrounding fields, these same beds and plantings focused views toward the house and its occupants, who could easily be seen from backlit windows, and made the house appear bigger and taller than it was.

The authors' hypothesis is that the original house was not built for privacy; nor was it a retreat. It was the active center of the working plantation and a constant, visible reminder of the wealth, style, and social position of its owner. The activities of the homeowner and family would have always been easy to view from the land around the house. Therefore, was the idea behind the house that the owner was to be noticed? Did the refined life of the master of the house serve as an example for all to see? Was the transparency of the house supposed to aid in the surveillance of a slave-based business? Was the labor of the slaves that is embedded in the terraces supposed to be an advertisement for the virtues of a slave economy? Do they work together to show how the management of a post-independence plantation should work?

Chandra Mukerji (1997) argues that Louis XIV built a version and a vision of the territory of the new nation of France at Versailles. The Sun King combined military skills of engineering with French aesthetics and the politics of social life to create a model of how France should work. Landscape was not incidental but was an extension of this model for society; it was ordered, hierarchical, and controlled by men. This powerful, general hypothesis is in accord with the argument that Paca was demonstrating his command of natural law in his Annapolis garden; he could show that he, by manifest example, could be thought of as belonging to the apex of the order that resided in the natural hierarchy among humans. Even though the garden books and themes of garden design most familiar to Paca were English in origin, they drew heavily on French and Italian precedents and shared with the works of Louis XIV a common baroque ideology.

At Wye Hall, Paca had achieved the power he had wished for 35 years earlier as expressed by his Annapolis garden. But his wealth was still based on slavery, the antithesis of the liberty, democracy, and the freedoms that he worked so hard to achieve for many others. Wye Hall is not just an old-fashioned garden that replays the rules used by Paca and his contemporaries in Annapolis in the 1760s and 1770s. Gardens were too dynamic in these societies to be seen that way. Besides, Paca's Wye Island neighbor and peer, John Beale Bordley, was actively experimenting with horticulture and animal husbandry, and he wrote a book on improving farming to encourage other gentlemen farmers to use their land to develop self-sufficiency (Bordley 1799). Paca was not only aware of the early science of farming, but he was also aware of the effort of his Annapolis neighbor, Charles Carroll of Carrollton, also a signer of the Declaration of Independence, to industrialize Baltimore using iron smelting, canals, railroad construction, and other techniques of mass production. Carroll used both free and slave labor and was concerned with the role of wage laborers in the new democracy where they might vote. Just as Paca used natural law in his first garden to demonstrate his control over nature, he employed the same principle at Wye. He created an intimate view in an enormous space. However, because he built a house that could be seen through, in the midst of a theatrical garden that enhanced the view all people had of him, it is hypothesized that he also sought to simultaneously design a surveillance environment for slave management that incorporated ideas of manipulating views by using lines of sight. He used his lifestyle as an example.

While the Wye Island garden is more than a large-scale version of Paca's Annapolis garden, it is very much in the same geometric, formal, late-baroque tradition as the earlier garden. Indeed, many scholars have noted that American gardens, and Chesapeake gardens in particular, embodied the geometric rules of design long after the English had abandoned such formal designs for the curvilinear and naturalistic designs of the landscape garden. Europeans noted this American preference for Italian Renaissance design and the French iteration of this style that was popular in the 18th and 19th centuries. Following the American Revolution, professional gardeners and landscape architects from Europe began to target the newly opened market, selling to the emerging national elite. Favoring the more formal styles of the Continental gardeners, it is not surprising that Paca and Jefferson were interested in hiring Luke O'Dio (Sarudy 1998: 141–144). This suggests that the ideology of slave-holding society found particular resonance with the continued use of the geometric garden and its underlying concepts.

The formalism of the tightly controlled and centralized French nation found an echo in the world of control and surveillance that was slave society. Garden, house, and personal comportment all became outward signs of the appropriate order for society and of the inner psychic comportment necessary to be a model citizen therein. These are well illustrated by George Washington's *Rules of Civility* (Phillips 2003). In slave societies, hegemonic sway extended from these constant rituals of status, to the daily surveillance of the master and overseer, to the violence of punishment and patrollers. The threat of death, or corporal punishment, underlay and gave great power to the image of the master in his house on the hill. William Paca's Wye Island garden thus served to represent, ratify, and extend his power; and it served to create a vehicle for surveillance. The garden also suggested a model of how slaves and poor whites should act in the model society, all while hiding the violence that kept the system running (Faust 1982; Isaac 1982).

William Paca hired Joseph Chase to design his Wye Hall house. Paca had been governor of Maryland close to the time of the design and building of the Maryland State House dome that Chase designed in Annapolis in 1788. The hypothesis about the purpose of using sight for surveillance as a management strategy at Wye follows upon previous research about the Annapolis dome (Leone and Hurry 1998). The new dome was more like a panopticon than it is either a dome or a tower. It is argued here that it is an all-seeing, elevated platform with two functions, just as Jeremy Bentham proposed for his contemporary panopticon or reform house (Bowring 1962). First, from an elevated platform in the middle of a central place from which everybody could be seen, a viewer could look in all directions to see whether his or her charges were behaving. Second, because people who are watched can also imagine themselves to be watched, they, by assumption, will memorize and internalize the rules of proper behavior and develop consciences. Documents at the Maryland State Archives (2004) suggest the effect of 1788 dome on the state house:

> The dome which Clark designed and built for the State House has been the defining landmark of the Annapolis skyline for 208 years. It was also, for many years,

a popular spot from which to observe the city and the Chesapeake Bay beyond. Charles Wilson Peale planned a domestic cyclorama of Annapolis with eight views from the dome and a centerpiece drawing of State Circle from Cornhill Street. Thomas Jefferson spent a most enjoyable three hours in September 1790 on the balcony of the dome with James Madison, Thomas Lee Shippen, and an Annapolis friend who entertained them with the gossip related to each of the houses they could see from their perch above the town.

This quote indicates how a panopticon should work—as a surveillance device. It is proposed here that the state house dome of the 1780s and Wye Hall Plantation of the early 1790s are both panopticons or at least combine many of the elements and effects of a panopticon. Mark Leone and Silas Hurry (1998) also argue that Paca would have known of Bentham's work, which was used by Benjamin Latrobe, architect of Baltimore's cathedral and of the U.S. Capitol building after it was burned by the British. The research at Wye Island indicates that Paca adapted these ideas to American uses at that plantation. William Paca was likely to be aware of this possibility for the dome. It is suggested that he combined use of a panopticon with those of older, hierarchical baroque ideas for building spaces to highlight authority. At Wye, panopticism was achieved by the techniques of the transparency of the house and the optical illusions created by the lines of sight in the garden. Paca combined the rules of perspective and the effects of the panopticon to show an emerging nation how to make a slave-based plantation work by watching. Combined with the ability to enforce his will through whatever physical means necessary, the effects of the panopticon certainly gave great authority to William Paca's plan for surveillance.

ACKNOWLEDGMENTS

The authors are grateful to the owner of Wye Hall, who is the sponsor of the archaeology reported on here, for the opportunity to excavate the property. Jay Graham, the landscape architect for the current reconstruction, suggested the archaeological project and has helped to inform and coordinate it. Jean Russo corrected an earlier version of this essay and provided important parts of the research background. Julie Ernstein discovered the letter from Luke O'Dio to Thomas Jefferson. She made many important suggestions that have improved this essay substantially. Michelle Niedzwiadek conducted most of the archival research associated with this project, under the direction of Jessica Neuwirth. Anna Hill and Kristofer Beadenkopf directed portions of the fieldwork and performed much of the laboratory analysis that supported this work. We are also indebted to Christine Jirikowic for the invitation to participate in the Gunston Hall symposium where this paper was originally presented. We are grateful to the reviewers—Gregory J. Brown, Julie H. Ernstein, and Matthew Johnson—who made many helpful suggestions that greatly improved this work.

REFERENCES

BACON, EDMUND N.
1968   *Design of Cities*. Viking Press, New York, NY.

BESCHERER, KAREN, AND ANNE YENTSCH
1989   Initial Archaeological Testing at Wye House, Wye Island, Maryland. Report to Historic Annapolis, Inc., Annapolis, MD, from Historic Annapolis Foundation, Annapolis, MD.

BORDLEY, JOHN BEALE
1799   *Essays and Notes on Husbandry and Rural Affairs*. Printed by Budd and Bartram for T. Dobson, Philadelphia, PA.

BOWRING, JOHN (EDITOR)
1962   *The Works of Jeremy Bentham*, Vol. 4. Russell and Russell, New York, NY.

BRADLEY, RICHARD
1717   *New Improvements of Planting and Gardening*. W. Mears, London, England.

BROWN, C. ALLAN
1990   Thomas Jefferson's Poplar Forest: The Mathematics of an Ideal Villa. *Journal of Garden History*, 10(2): 117–139.

BROWN, MARLEY R., AND PATRICIA M. SAMFORD
1990   Recent Evidence of Eighteenth Century Gardening in Williamsburg, Virginia. In *Earth Patterns*, William Kelso and Rachel Most, editors, pp. 103–121. University of Virginia Press, Charlottesville.

BUSHMAN, RICHARD L.
1992   *The Refinement of America: Persons, Houses, Cities*. Alfred A. Knopf, New York, NY.

EPPERSON, TERRANCE W.
1999   Constructing Difference: The Social and Spatial Order of the Chesapeake Plantation. In *"I, Too, Am America" Archaeological Studies of African-American Life*, Theresa A. Singleton, editor, pp. 159–172. University of North Carolina Press, Charlottesville.

ERNSTEIN, JULIE H.
2004 *Constructing Context: Historical Archaeology and the Pleasure Garden in Prince George's County, Maryland, 1740–1790*. Doctoral dissertation, Department of Anthropology, Boston University. University Microfilms International, Ann Arbor, MI.

FAUST, DREW GILPIN
1982 James Henry Hammond and the Old South: A Design for Mastery. Louisiana State University Press, Baton Rouge.

FEDERAL TAX ASSESSMENT
1798 Federal Direct Tax 1798. Microfilm, Maryland State Archives, Maryland Hall of Records, Annapolis.

FOUCAULT, MICHEL
1979 *Discipline and Punish*. Random House, New York, NY.

HARMON, JAMES, ANNA HILL, KRISTOFER BEADENKOPF, JESSICA NEUWIRTH, MARK P. LEONE, AND JEAN RUSSO
2003 Archaeological Investigations at Wye Hall Plantation, Wye Island, Queen Annes County, Maryland. Report from Archaeology in Annapolis. Manuscript, Historic Annapolis Foundation, Annapolis, MD, and Department of Anthropology, University of Maryland, College Park.

HOPKINS, JOSEPH W. III
1986 *A Map of the Ridout Garden Annapolis, Maryland*. Historic Annapolis Foundation, Annapolis, MD.

ISAAC, RHYS
1982 *The Transformation of Virginia, 1740–1790*. University of North Carolina Press for the Institute of Early American History and Culture, Chapel Hill.

LAIRD, MARK
1999 *The Flowering of the Landscape Garden: English Pleasure Grounds 1720–1800*. University of Pennsylvania Press, Philadelphia.

LANGLEY, BATTY
1728 *New Principles of Gardening*. A. Bettesworth and J. Batley, London, England.

LEONE, MARK P.
1984 Interpreting Ideology in Historical Archaeology: Using the Rules of Perspective in the William Paca Garden in Annapolis, Maryland. In *Ideology, Representation, and Power in Prehistory*, Christopher Tilley and Daniel Miller, editors, pp. 25–35. Cambridge University Press, Cambridge, United Kingdom.
1987 Rule by Ostentation: The Relationship between Space and Sight in Eighteenth-Century Landscape Architecture in the Chesapeake Region of Maryland. In *Method and Theory for Activity Area Research: An Ethnoarchaeological Approach*, Susan Kent, editor, pp. 604–633. Columbia University Press, New York, NY.

LEONE, MARK P., AND SILAS D. HURRY
1998 Seeing: The Power of Town Planning in the Chesapeake. *Historical Archaeology,* 32(4):34–62.

LEONE, MARK P., AND PAUL A. SHACKEL
1987 Forks, Clocks, and Power. In *Mirror and Metaphor: Material and Social Construction of Reality,* Daniel W. Ingersoll, Jr., and Gordon Bronitsky, editors, pp. 45–61. University Press of America, Lanham, MD.
1990 Plane and Solid Geometry in Colonial Gardens in Annapolis, Maryland. In *Earth Patterns*, William Kelso and Rachel Most, editors, pp. 153–167. University of Virginia Press, Charlottesville.

MARYLAND STATE ARCHIVES
1860 Federal Census 1860, entries specific to William B. Paca. Microfilm M7229-2, Frames 225 and M5167-1. Maryland State Archives, Maryland Hall of Records, Annapolis.
2004 Maryland State House, Annapolis, MD Maryland State Archives, Annapolis. May 2004 <http:www.archives.state.md.us/msa/stager/s1259/121/5847/html/story.html>.

MILLER, PHILIP
1731 *The Gardener's Dictionary*. Philip Miller, London, England.
1755 *Figures of the Most Beautiful, Useful, and Uncommon Plants Described in the Gardener's Dictionary*. Philip Miller, London, England.

MUKERJI, CHANDRA
1997 *Territorial Ambitions and the Gardens of Versailles*. Cambridge University Press, Cambridge, United Kingdom.

O'DIO, LUKE
1802 Letter to Thomas Jefferson, 23 June. Thomas Jefferson Correspondence Collection, Special Collection Division, National Agricultural Library, Beltsville, MD. <nal.usda.gov/speccol/>.

PACA-STEELE, BARBARA, AND ST. CLAIR WRIGHT
1987 The Mathematics of an Eighteenth-Century Wilderness Garden. *Journal of Garden History,* 6(4):299–320.

PALUS, MATHEW M., AND ELIZABETH B. KRYDER-REID
2002 Archaeological Investigations Conducted at the St. Mary's Site (18AP45), 107 Duke of Gloucester Street, Annapolis, Maryland, 1987–1990, Vol. 1, Site History, Results, and Recommendations. Report to Charles Carroll House, Inc., Annapolis, MD, from Historic Annapolis Foundation, Annapolis, MD.

PHILLIPS, JOHN T. II
2003 *George Washington's Rules of Civility*. Goose Creek Productions, Leesburg, VA.

REEVES, STUART, JEAN B. RUSSO, DENNIS J. POGUE, AND JOSEPH M. HERBERT
    1991 Myrtle Point: The Changing Land and People of a Lower Patuxent River Community. *Jefferson Patterson Park and Museum, Occasional Papers, No. 3.* Maryland Historical Trust, Crownsville, MD.

RUSSO, JEAN
    1990 *William Paca House and Garden.* Historic Annapolis Foundation, Annapolis, MD.

SARUDY, BARBARA WELLS
    1989 Eighteenth-Century Gardens of the Chesapeake. *Journal of Garden History,* 9(3):101–159.
    1998 *Gardens and Gardening in the Chesapeake, 1700–1805.* The Johns Hopkins University Press, Baltimore, MD.

SHACKEL, PAUL A.
    1993 *Personal Discipline and Material Culture: An Archaeology of Annapolis, Maryland, 1695–1870.* University of Tennessee Press, Knoxville.

SHELLENHAMER, JASON P.
    2004 The Archaeology and Restoration of the William Paca Garden, Annapolis, Maryland: 1966–1990. University of Maryland <http://www.bsos.umd.edu/anth/arch/pacagarden/index.htm>.

STIVERSON, GREGORY A., AND PHOEBE R. JACOBSEN
    1976 *William Paca: A Biography.* Maryland Historical Society, Baltimore, MD.

U.S. BUREAU OF THE CENSUS
    1790 *Heads of Families at the First Census of the United States Taken in the Year 1790: Maryland.* Reprinted in 1977 by the Genealogical Publishing Company, Baltimore, MD.

MARK P. LEONE
DEPARTMENT OF ANTHROPOLOGY
1111 WOODS HALL
UNIVERSITY OF MARYLAND COLLEGE PARK
COLLEGE PARK, MD 20742

JAMES M. HARMON
NORTHEAST REGION ARCHEOLOGY PROGRAM
NATIONAL PARK SERVICE
15 STATE STREET
BOSTON, MA 02109

JESSICA L. NEUWIRTH
OFFICE OF ACADEMIC PROGRAMS
HISTORIC DEERFIELD, INC.
DEERFIELD, MA 01342

HENRY M. MILLER

Baroque Cities in the Wilderness: Archaeology and Urban Development in the Colonial Chesapeake

ABSTRACT

Historians have long assumed that Maryland's 17th century capital was an unplanned, scattered village with little urban character. In this paper, new archaeological evidence is presented which demonstrates that St. Mary's City was actually an elaborately planned settlement, laid out according to principles of Baroque design. This is the earliest known use of Baroque urban planning in America. Comparison of the St. Mary's layout with that of other colonial cities reveals that these Baroque urban concepts were only employed in the Chesapeake region. Possible reasons for this unusual distribution are presented and the implications of this finding regarding the relationship between society, economy, settlement system and urban form are discussed.

Introduction

Founding cities was an integral element of European expansion into the New World. America offered a superb opportunity to cast aside Roman and Medieval arrangements which had long dominated most European cities and create new communities in a virgin land. The forms and structures of these cities not only tell of the colonists' aspirations but of the realities they encountered in actually settling the wilderness. It is important to learn what types of cities they created, how and why these settlements differed between the colonies and how these new cities evolved with the growth of colonial society. Some answers can be derived from available historical and cartographic evidence. However, this apparent wealth of documentation is incomplete and often biased. Archaeological investigation is therefore essential because the physical remains of cities hold crucial data for illuminating the beginnings and subsequent development of these urban places.

Urban sites research is now a major element of historical archaeology, but little attention has been given to the overall forms or internal structures of cities until quite recently (cf., Leone 1984; Hopkins 1986; Shapiro 1987; Rothschild 1987; Wall 1987). This subject is of significance because cities are built environments which display a systematic arrangement of elements ordered by cultural ideas and needs (Rapoport 1984:56). City form is defined as "the physical arrangement of structures and open spaces, including streets and other pathways, within some defined area" (Agnew, Mercer and Sopher 1984:11). Urban forms express the traditions, economy, social structure and ideology of a given culture.

In this paper, the role of historical archaeology in the study of urban form is explored using data from a vanished 17th century community: St. Mary's City, Maryland. Questions addressed include: What do archaeological remains reveal about the nature and form of this city? Do the findings agree with historians' notions regarding urban development in the Chesapeake colonies? Finally, how does St. Mary's City compare to other cities established in 17th century America?

Town Planning in Colonial America

Before presenting the archaeological data, a brief overview of the city forms used in the New World and their relationship to Old World urban concepts is presented. This provides a context within which the St. Mary's evidence may be evaluated.

The earliest cities founded by European settlers were in Spanish America. While there was some initial variation, a standard city design rapidly evolved and after about 1540, Spanish colonial cities display similar layouts (Reps 1965; Kubler 1978; Markman 1978). This consisted of a grid with a central open space or plaza where the church stood. Major roads led directly into this plaza. In 1573, the Law of the Indies was enacted which required Spanish colonial towns to follow this plan. The law remained in effect and was followed throughout the colonial period (Reps

1965:29). Portuguese and Dutch settlements in South America were either of a grid arrangement or had irregular plans (Hardoy 1978).

Cartographic data reveal that cities in the Dutch, English and French colonies of North America were, despite more diversity, mostly variations on two distinctive themes—the grid or an irregular plan. Of the principal Dutch cities, New Amsterdam had an irregular form while Albany followed a loose grid arrangement (Reps 1965:148–151). In New France, Quebec was of an irregular shape while the streets of Montreal had a linear grid pattern (Trudel 1968).

English colonists used both grids and irregular forms. Variations of the grid were employed in New Haven, Charleston, Philadelphia and other settlements while the irregular city is best exemplified by Boston (Reps 1972). The grid had a long heritage in England, dating from Roman times, and remained popular because it was simple to survey and provided equitable divisions of land (Conzen 1981).

Although the development of cities was much less successful in the Chesapeake, colonists in that area also apparently preferred grid plans. Legislation to create port towns enacted by Maryland and Virginia during the late 17th and early 18th centuries suggests that the lawmakers intended the towns to be of grid form. Surviving plats of communities actually established by these town acts confirm that they were generally laid out in this way; examples include Marlborough, Yorktown and Tappahannock in Virginia and St. Leonard, Upper Marlborough and Oxford in Maryland (Reps 1972). Although the information is very limited, Virginia's 17th century capital of Jamestown apparently had its streets arranged in a loose grid form (Cotter 1958; Reps 1972:48–49). Irregular plans were not absent, however. A plat from the community of Calverton on the Patuxent River in Maryland shows a haphazardly arranged settlement and there is evidence that other such towns existed (Pogue 1985). Historical records imply that Maryland's capital of St. Mary's City also had an irregular form (Carr 1974).

In only two instances are urban designs in colonial America known to differ from the above patterns. Both towns (Annapolis, Maryland and Williamsburg, Virginia) are in the Chesapeake and thought to be the products of one man, Francis Nicholson, who served as royal governor of both colonies. Annapolis was a small settlement dating from the mid-17th century and had apparently been laid out in a grid pattern in compliance with a town act of 1683 (Reps 1972; Hopkins 1986). After becoming Maryland's capital in 1695, Governor Nicholson made significant changes in the Annapolis plan, adding circles and radiating streets (Figure 1). This geometric arrangement is thought to be the first use of sophisticated European concepts of urban design in the New World (Reps 1965:15). It created a city in which two principal buildings—the State House and Anglican Church—were the central foci of the urban environment and the streets radiated outward from these focal points. Such a layout is believed to be a reflection of Italian Renaissance ideas about urban design (Reps 1972).

Four years later, Nicholson was appointed Governor of Virginia and he soon moved the government from Jamestown to the new town of Williamsburg. For the layout of this city, Nicholson employed an axial plan with the principal buildings—the Capital, Church and College—spaced along this axis, and the secondary streets in a grid arrangement. This design was also inspired by Renaissance ideas, but is quite different in style from the geometric, radiating street plan of Annapolis. Both of these cities are thought to represent major innovations in American urban planning (Reps 1972) and they contrast sharply with the simple 17th century towns found along the shores of the Chesapeake and in other colonies.

St. Mary's City: The Historical Perspective

St. Mary's was founded in 1634 by English colonists sent by Cecil Calvert, the second Lord Baltimore. They selected a site near the confluence of the Potomac River and Chesapeake Bay, along a tributary of the Potomac now called the St. Mary's River (Figure 2). This was the first settlement in the colony and became the center of

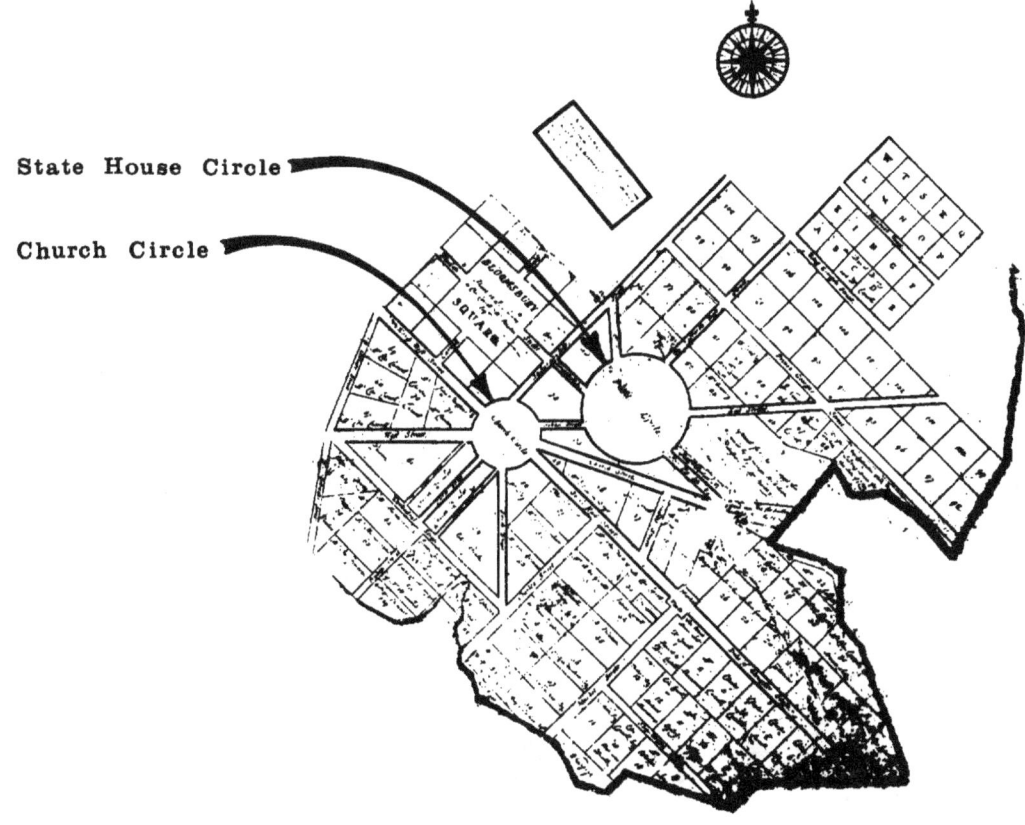

State House Circle

Church Circle

FIGURE 1. Plan of Annapolis, Maryland (c.1718) showing the two circles and radiating street design.

government (Menard and Carr 1982). Due to political problems associated with the English Civil Wars, Maryland grew very slowly during the 1640s and 1650s. Not until the restoration in 1660 of Charles II to the throne of England did conditions stabilize and Maryland experience rapid, sustained growth. In 1667, Lord Baltimore ordered the incorporation of St. Mary's as the first official city in the colony and significant expansion of the capital began (Maryland Archives 51:64). By the 1680s, a maturing settlement had appeared along the St. Mary's River but it did not last. A Protestant revolution in 1689 and rising anti-Catholic feeling resulted in the government being moved to Annapolis in 1695. Without the business of government, St. Mary's had no economic basis and

most of the settlement was abandoned. By the mid-18th century, nearly every trace of the former capital had disappeared.

Unfortunately, Maryland's first city is very poorly documented. No map of the settlement survives. There are no detailed written descriptions and various court house fires have destroyed most of the land records. Despite these serious gaps in historical documentation, the remaining land records, occasional references in other documents and limited evidence about the few known archaeological sites were carefully marshalled to produce a tentative map of the city (Carr 1974). This map (Figure 3) implies that St. Mary's was a widely scattered, haphazardly built community. No reference to any city planning exists in the historical

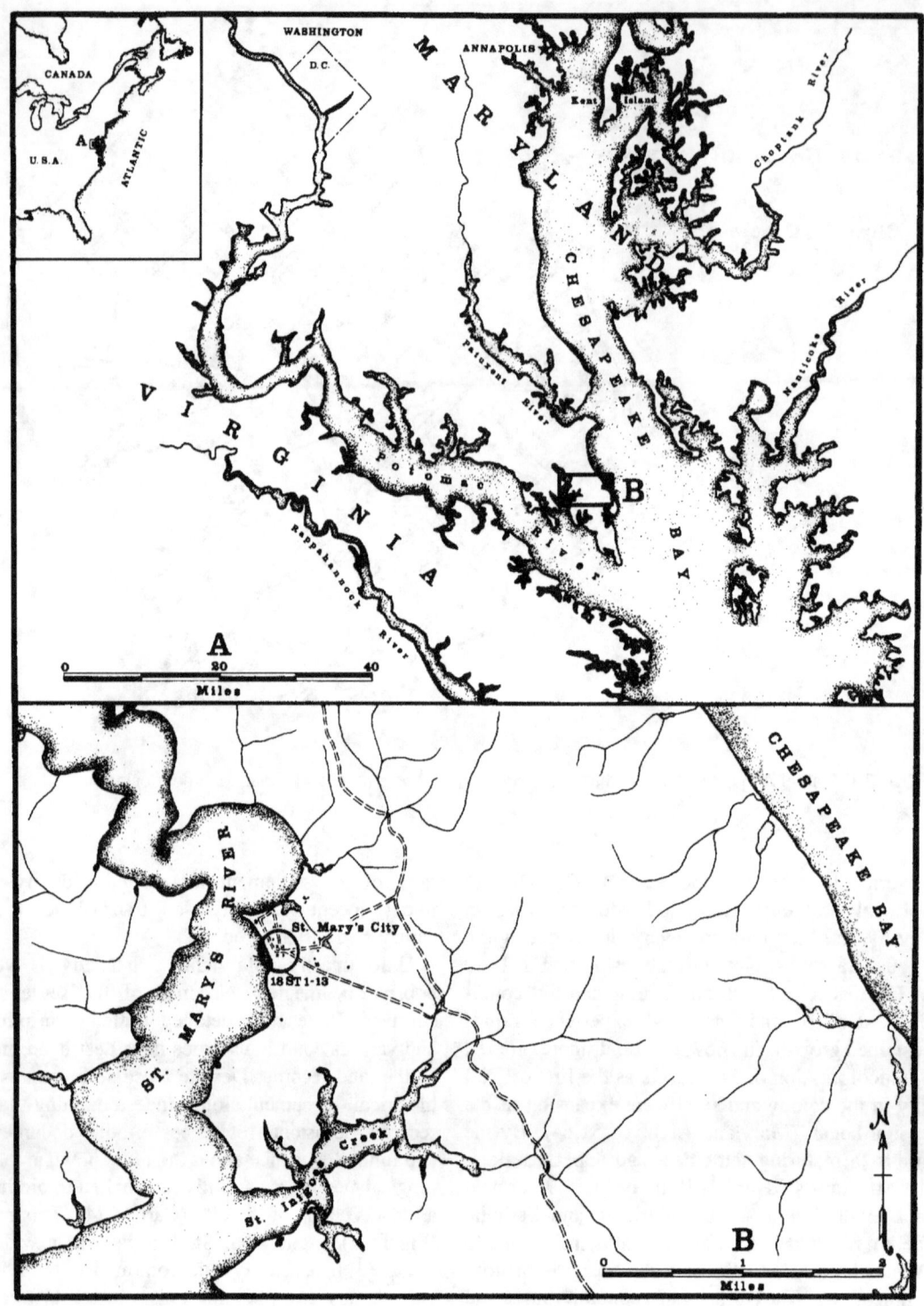

FIGURE 2. The location of St. Mary's City and the Town Center Site (18 ST1-13).

Perspectives from *Historical Archaeology*

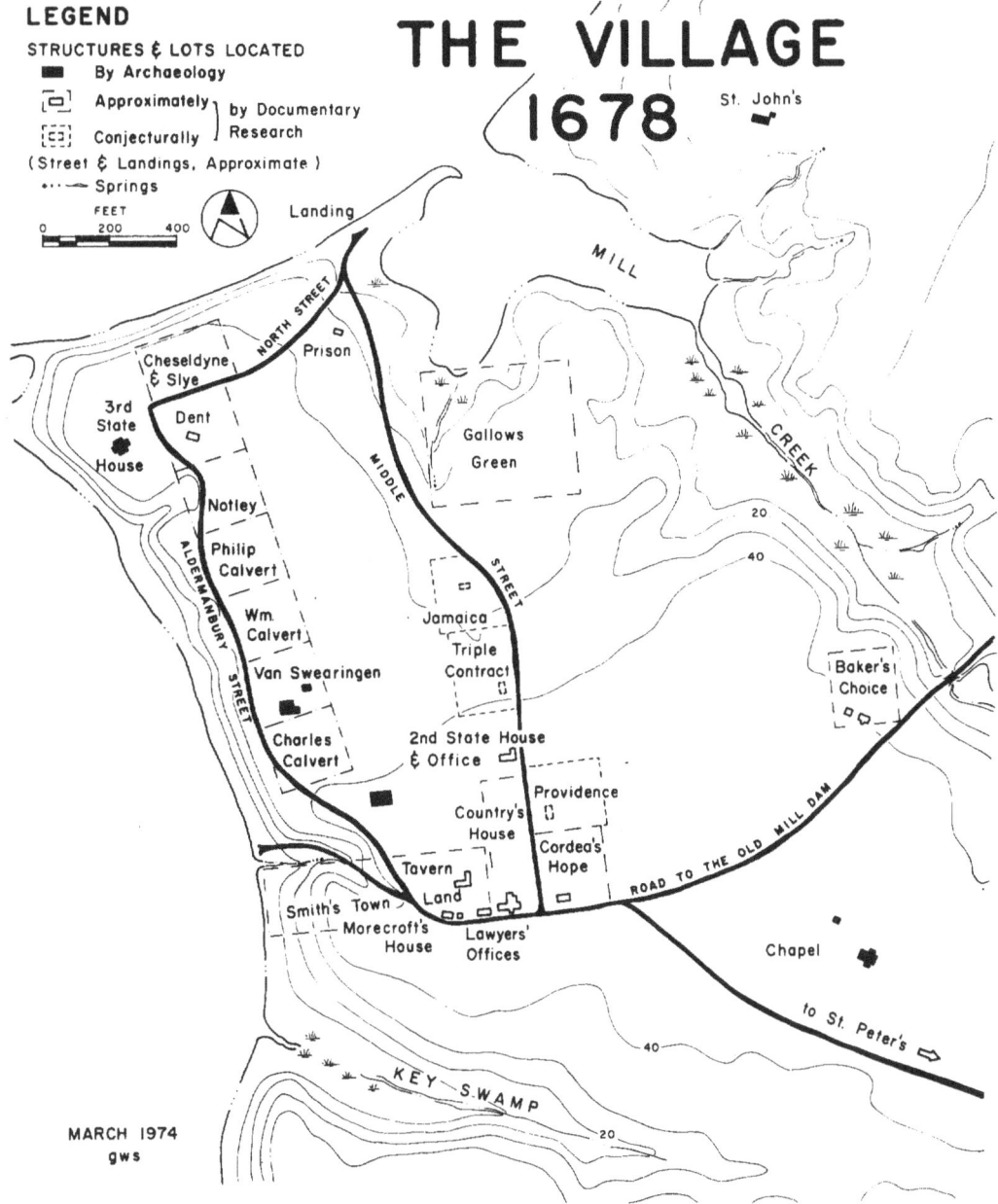

THE VILLAGE
1678   St. John's

Landing

MILL

NORTH STREET

Prison

Cheseldyne & Slye

3rd State House

Dent

Gallows Green

MIDDLE STREET

CREEK

20

40

Notley

Philip Calvert

Wm. Calvert

Jamaica

ALDERMANBURY STREET

Van Swearingen

Triple Contract

Baker's Choice

Charles Calvert

2nd State House & Office

Providence

Country's House

Cordea's Hope

ROAD TO THE OLD MILL DAM

Tavern

Land

Smith's Town

Morecroft's House

Lawyers' Offices

Chapel

to St. Peter's

KEY SWAMP

40

20

MARCH 1974
gws

FIGURE 3. Tentative map of St. Mary's City based upon historical research.

record and such an irregular form suggests organic growth rather than conscious design. An irregular layout is not surprising, given the forms of other known cities from the period. Verification of this document-based map was still necessary, however, and this required archaeology.

St. Mary's City: The Archaeological Perspective

Since St. Mary's was mostly abandoned by 1700, it is essentially a fossilized 17th century city undistorted by later urban development. Most of the townlands have been in agriculture since the early 18th century and remain fields today. Testing of the historical map through archaeology was, therefore, a relatively straightforward matter, but due to lack of access to key parcels of land, this evaluation could not be initiated until 1979. Preliminary survey work in 1979 and 1980 revealed that 17th century materials were actually concentrated to the west of the hypothesized town center location. Guided by this information and supported by a research grant from the National Endowment for the Humanities, archaeologists began a four year project in 1981 to discover the center of the community (Miller 1983, 1986). A program of stratified random sampling followed by more selective excavations identified the town center (18 ST1-13) and major sites within it (Figure 2). Traces of paling fence ditches permitted property lines to be identified and matched with dimensions given in land records. This allowed structures to be tentatively identified and artifactual evidence was then employed to test these identifications. Arrangements of buildings and yard fences also permitted the precise orientations of streets to be determined.

Findings from these excavations reveal that the actual town center was over 500 feet west of the location predicted by the historical map. Archaeological data also show that the chief properties were configured differently than indicated on the document-based map. With this new archaeological evidence, the historical data and information on sites located elsewhere in the city were reinterpreted and a more accurate map of the settlement produced (Figure 4). Initial inspection of this new map does not suggest that the city was significantly different from that depicted on the earlier one.

While the town center location had moved westward and the properties were in a different arrangement, St. Mary's still appears to have been a scattered, irregular settlement. Thorough analysis of the map was essential, however, before this could be confirmed.

Analysis of the City Map

In the study of town plans, urban geographers have identified the key elements for analysis (Conzen 1960, 1978, 1981; Smailes 1966; Goodman 1968). These are: a) the nature of the site, b) the street system, c) open space, d) the lot pattern, e) the building arrangement and, f) building type. Topography and previously existing cultural features are important because they strongly influence the specific form a community can take. Street layout, however, provides the real structure to a settlement. Street plans and the distribution of open spaces are usually culturally determined. Open spaces are sometimes nothing more than a widening of the street for a market, although in many instances they are more formal plazas or circles. Lot patterns and building arrangements generally tend to follow streets.

It is also important to make a clear distinction between the types of buildings. Vernacular architecture as opposed to formal or elite architecture are products of different segments of culture with their own meaning and dynamic. This distinction has relevance because works of formal architecture, such as public buildings, churches and palaces, are more often distributed according to symbolic and design considerations than are vernacular buildings (Clavel 1984:31). One example is the placement of the church and government buildings on the central square in Spanish colonial towns. Thus, public architecture often provides more direct evidence of planning than do domestic structures.

To begin analysis of the St. Mary's plan, it is first necessary to note that the site lies on a high, generally level plain bordering the St. Mary's River (Figure 4). It is actually a peninsula of land formed by the river on the west and north, an

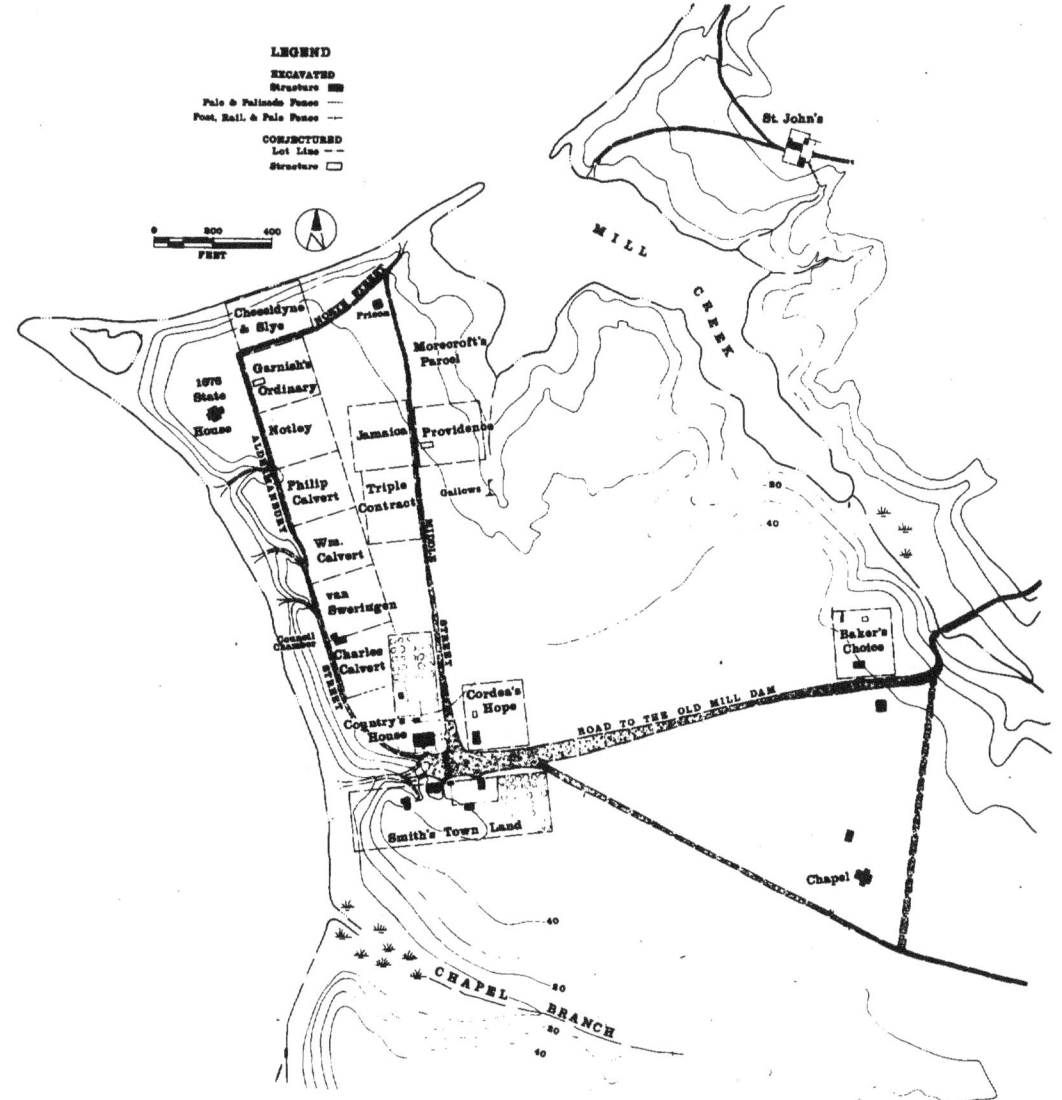

FIGURE 4. Revised map of St. Mary's City based upon archaeological and historical data.

estuarine embayment and creek on the east and small swamp to the southwest. This topography defined the core of the town and clearly influenced its form.

The street pattern, based upon a combination of data from historical and archaeological sources and aerial photography, is in the shape of two rough triangles with the primary streets meeting at the town center. Such a street pattern is quite different from that seen in other colonial cities. To the extent that they are known, the lot patterns also appear to follow this triangular street layout.

The arrangement of buildings in the town center does suggest some planning. At the precise center

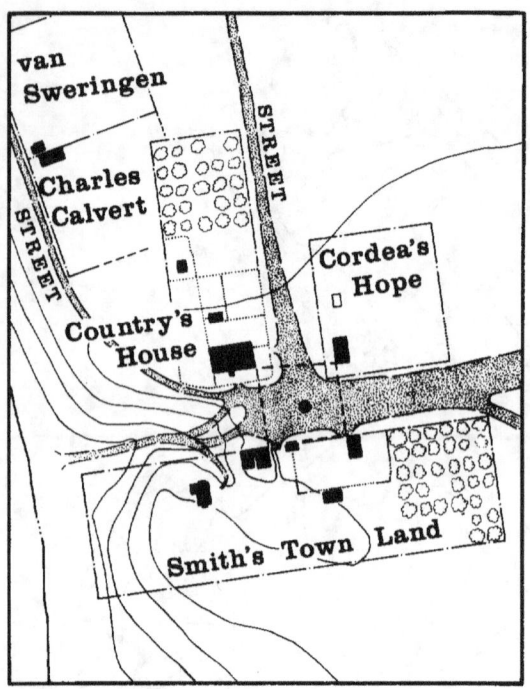

FIGURE 5. Close–Up of the Town Center showing the four principal structures and their square arrangement.

of the settlement were four structures (Figure 5). The Country's House was the home of the first governor, built about 1636. During the 1660s and early 1670s, it served simultaneously as a government meeting place and the largest public inn or ordinary in Maryland. Two of the other structures were also ordinaries and the last was a lawyer's office/lodging. These structures were built between 1667 and 1674. Planning is implied by their arrangement in a square with the corners of these buildings equal distances apart (about 125 feet). They framed the central crossroads of the community and form a large open space, 100 feet wide and over 150 feet long. Local legend suggests that this area served as a market place for the city (Miller 1986:125).

Each of these buildings was constructed of wood and sheathed with clapboard, the typical vernacular architecture of the 17th century Chesapeake. Only four brick structures are known to have stood

in St. Mary's and these were examples of public architecture (another brick building, the private home of Chancellor Philip Calvert (Forman 1938), stood just outside the city). Indeed, the two most monumental public buildings in 17th century Maryland—a State House and Catholic Chapel—stood in St. Mary's. Both of these had cruciform floor plans and were built on physically prominent locations. The State House (Figure 6) stood on a point of land overlooking the river and the Chapel was placed on a small knoll, the highest spot of land in the town. While the location of the State House has long been known, the Chapel's precise placement and orientation was uncertain until 1983 when archaeologists uncovered and mapped a portion of it (Miller and Seagle 1987).

Examination of the map reveals that their entry doors are one-half mile apart. This spatial separation, based upon the English system of measurement used by the colonists, suggests that these monumental structures were not positioned by chance. They were also placed near junctures of the major streets, as if to accentuate the nodes of the road system.

The other major brick structures in the city were the prison for the colony and a "School of the Humanities" run by the Jesuits. Locations of these are not absolutely certain. Folklore and an 18th century map place the prision near the city landing, approximately at the juncture of Middle and North Streets. The presence of modern structures precludes extensive archaeological testing in this area but a surface survey has recovered hand-made bricks in the predicted location. The school's placement is less certain. Recently, however, surface reconnaissance detected evidence of a large, apparently brick structure in an area now known as the Mill Field. There is no historical documentation for a structure in this location but there is a possibility it is the school. The school is thought to have stood in this portion of the town, it is the only other brick building known to have been in the city, and the beginning of site occupation indicated by artifacts matches that of the school. Finally, archaeologists recovered two religious medals on the surface adjacent to the brick concentration. This may be the site of the Catholic school, but

FIGURE 6. The 1676 Statehouse in St. Mary's City, one of the four known brick structures in the town. This 1934 reconstruction is based upon the original builder's contract and archaeological evidence.

regardless of its identity, it is certain that a prominent brick structure stood in this location, near the juncture of two roads. More testing is necessary but available evidence indicates that each corner of the road network was marked by brick structures; three of these and perhaps all four served important social functions.

What is the relationship of these buildings to other major elements of the settlement such as the town square? Measurement from the center point of the town, defined as the middle of the square framed by the four wooden structures, shows that the Chapel door is approximately 1400 feet from this point and the State House door is the same distance. Such similar distances again imply something more than accidental placement. The distance from the center point to the prison and possible school site cannot be determined precisely but both are estimated at between 1400 and 1600 feet.

Another very important element of communities, often demarcated by elaborate gates, are the principal entryways. St. Mary's City had two major access points—one by water and the other by land. Travelers coming by ship entered at the main landing, which was northeast of the State House. Persons coming by horse or on foot used a mill dam as a causeway over Mill Creek. This dam was northeast of the Chapel and its remnants are still visible. Measuring from these places where people entered the town to the center point discloses that they are again similar distances— approximately 1700 feet. It is also notable that the State House is slightly over 800 feet from the boat landing while the Chapel is about the same distance from the chief land entrance.

These findings strongly argue that St. Mary's was actually a planned city, not a haphazardly built settlement. It incorporated a town square, the

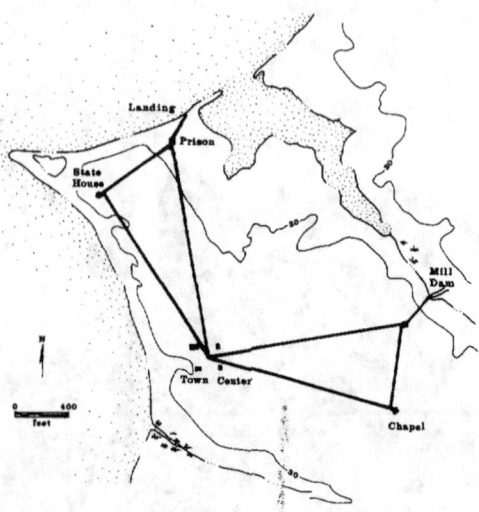

FIGURE 7. Triangular design of the city incorporating the town center, four major brick structures and the principal entryways.

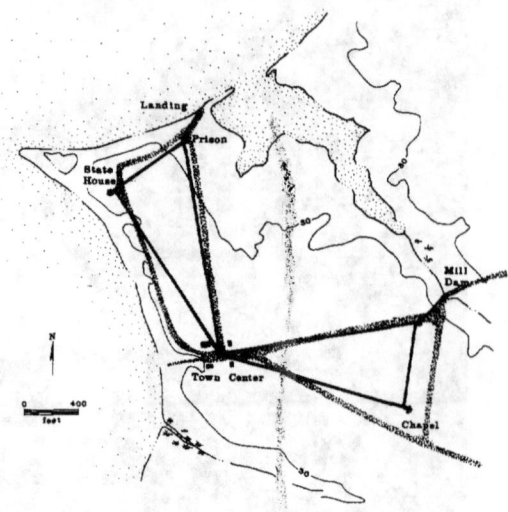

FIGURE 8. The placement of the roadways in relation to the triangular design of St. Mary's City.

principal entryways and the major brick structures within the city into a balanced composition (Figure 7). The design apparently consisted of two symmetrical triangles extending from the town square with the corners of these triangles demarcated by major brick structures. Principal roads followed these triangles closely, although topography and previously existing cultural features (i.e., the Country's House lot) produced some distortion (Figure 8). Lot arrangements also appear to have conformed to this overall design. Due to the lack of historical evidence and the fact that large tracts of land within the city remain unexplored, it is not yet known where secondary streets were placed or how they were oriented. Nevertheless, there is sufficient evidence to support the argument that St. Mary's had a distinctive urban design, despite the total absence of evidence for any planning in the surviving historical record.

Evaluation of the City Plan

These findings reveal that St. Mary's did not follow the grid or irregular layouts of most other colonial cities, so what type of plan is it? Of all the urban designs in use during the 17th century, St. Mary's seems to correspond most closely to the characteristics of the Baroque city. A product of the Italian Renaissance, Baroque ideas were first employed in Rome during the 16th century and rapidly spread to other parts of Europe. They emphasized geometric form, symmetry and proportion as well as the need for spatial integration and openness (Norberg-Schulz 1971:13; Hohenberg and Lees 1985).

The basic formula for laying out a Baroque city consists of the following: "Choose a set of commanding points throughout a terrain and site important symbolic structures at those points. Connect these foci by major streets . . . shaped as visual approaches to the symbolic points, or nodes . . . (then) a more intricate, less controlled pattern of streets and buildings can occupy the interior triangles between these linking arteries" (Lynch 1981:281). Unquestionably, the brick State House and Chapel were of real and symbolic significance in Maryland society. They were also visually distinctive in a land dominated by wooden build-

Perspectives from *Historical Archaeology*

ings covered with weathered clapboard. As previously noted, the State House was placed on a commanding point of land where it was plainly visible to all persons entering the St. Mary's River. The Chapel was built on the highest spot of land in the town and near the principal land entrance. Also of importance was the Prison and possible School. In their spatial distribution, the Prison was linked with the State House, and the School with the Chapel. Finally, each of these buildings was placed near junctures of streets and formed foci of the road system. This evidence strongly suggests that the St. Mary's City plan was based upon European Baroque principles of urban design.

Such a discovery is unexpected given the simple urban layouts found elsewhere in the New World. Until now, the earliest use of these sophisticated Baroque ideas in a colonial city was thought to have been at Annapolis, Maryland in the late 1690's. However, analysis of construction dates of the principal buildings, surveys for roads and other data suggest that these Baroque concepts were first applied in St. Mary's City during the late 1660s, some 30 years before Annapolis. It is perhaps not a coincidence that Lord Baltimore's formal incorporation of St. Mary's as Maryland's first city occurred in 1667.

Baroque Cities on the Chesapeake Frontier

A leading scholar on urban development in America has written that the simple gridiron plans which characterized most colonial Chesapeake towns ". . . symbolize the lack of sophistication of a frontier society . . . which, even if the will had been present, lacked the necessary skills and knowledge to lay out communities on any other patterns than the most obvious" (Reps 1972:116). The new archaeological discoveries at St. Mary's indicates this statement requires modification, for at least some of the colonists did possess this knowledge and skill. Nevertheless, it is surprising that such advanced urban concepts were employed on the Chesapeake frontier because frontier culture is typically much simpler and less sophisticated than that found in the homeland (Thompson 1973).

Baroque urban design was not applied in any major way to English cities until the 18th century, although it was proposed after the Great Fire of London in 1666 (Reps 1965; Rasmussen 1937; Milne 1986). Why then were these Baroque concepts used in St. Mary's City?

Although there is no direct proof, it is almost certain that creation of a Baroque plan for St. Mary's would have been guided by Cecil Calvert, Lord Baltimore. Calvert controlled Maryland as proprietor and long had an interest in town development, beginning with the first expedition in 1634 when he instructed the settlers to build and live in towns (Hall 1910:22). This was unsuccessful because the colonists found it more advantageous to live on plantations and raise tobacco. In addition, political turmoil prevented any urban development during the 1640s and 1650s. After the Restoration, Calvert devoted great effort to developing the colony and personally ordered the incorporation of St. Mary's as the first official city in Maryland (Maryland Archives 51:64). Given the opportunity of creating a new urban settlement, it is not unreasonable to assume that he wanted the capital of his colony to be both impressive and fashionable. Urban scholars have noted that one advantage of the Baroque plan is that it ". . . lays the groundwork for a memorable and monumental city" (Lynch 1981:380).

Calvert may have also been influenced by a catastrophe—the Great Fire of London which consumed much of England's capital in September of 1666. Only a few days after the flames were extinguished, individuals began submitting plans to King Charles for the rebuilding of the city and much discussion about the merits of various urban designs followed (Rasmussen 1937; Milne 1986). Two of these plans, by Christopher Wren and John Evelyn, called for a radical redesign using Baroque urban concepts. Although favorably received by the King, the complexity of the massive land redistribution these plans required and political pressure made them unacceptable (Rasmussen 1937:113–15). Lord Baltimore, who had a residence in London, was probably aware of these proposals since they were well known. While no definite link can be established, due to the destruction of most of Lord Baltimore's personal papers, it is quite possible that the St. Mary's plan was a direct result of the urban design efforts which followed London's Great Fire. Thus, the application of fashionable urban concepts to produce an impressive city helps explain why Baroque design principles were used at St. Mary's.

Both of Maryland's colonial capitals display Baroque layouts and it is possible that St. Mary's influenced Annapolis. Regrettably, the incomplete documentary records for these cities makes evaluation of this possibility difficult but comparison of the two city plans may provide some insight. While it seems probable that Calvert and Nicholson both wished to create impressive urban places, Baroque layouts have other purposes. At the most abstract level, Baroque design serves as ". . . visual embodiment of the structure of the Baroque world" (Norberg-Schulz 1971:16). More specifically, it ". . . lays the groundwork for public symbolism" (Lynch 1981:281). Expression of ideology through symbolism is thus an important function but one which is hard to assess. Did the designers of St. Mary's and Annapolis use these plans to make some symbolic statement or were they unaware of such a function and merely copying a poorly understood but stylish idea?

Examination of the plans of each city reveals some contrasts that could have relevance. One is the use of adjoining circles in Annapolis but less formal and more widely separated open spaces in St. Mary's. Even more distinctive are the spatial distributions of the government and religious structures. In St. Mary's, the State House and Chapel were built on prominent locations at opposite ends of the town, one half mile apart, and symmetrically positioned in relation to the town center and entryways. In Annapolis, on the other hand, these structures were built on the highest land in the center of the settlement and within adjoining circles (Hopkins 1986). Could this difference in the physical arrangement of these structures have been intended to convey meaning? To help answer this, it is worth considering the relationship between religion and government in colonial Maryland.

Religion was a tremendous source of conflict during the 17th century. In Europe, Protestants battled Catholics in a series of wars, while in England, Catholics were oppressed and denied a role in government. Lord Baltimore hoped to avoid this situation and create a new society by implementing an idea novel to the English experience—religious toleration. This was an integral component of Maryland life from 1634, and codified by "An Act Concerning Religion" passed in 1649 (Carr 1984; Fausz 1984). With it, Protestants and Catholics lived together, jointly served in government and did not overtly engage in religious arguments. To make it work, colonists had to separate religion from government, although this was a *de facto* separation not explicitly sanctioned by law. This effort at toleration was successful until 1689 when a group of Protestants revolted and took power from Lord Baltimore (Carr 1984). Their petition to the King for royal control of the colony was approved. Lionel Copley, the first royal governor, died a year after taking office and was replaced by Francis Nicholson in 1693. Copley and Nicholson did away with religious toleration and made the Anglican faith the official Church of Maryland. Catholics were barred from government office and eventually forbidden to worship publicly. Nicholson made the final break with the former government by moving the capital from the center of Catholic population to a Protestant enclave at the site of Annapolis.

This was a major shift in social ideology which had a tremendous impact upon the colony and it is reasonable to assess the town plans of St. Mary's and Annapolis in light of this change. The spatial arrangement of the Church and State House at St. Mary's can be seen as symbolizing the efforts at religious toleration and separation of Church from State. In Annapolis, the side by side arrangement of these buildings can be interpreted as expressing the new, direct relationship between government and a state-supported religion (Hopkins 1986). While there is no direct evidence, this correspondence between city form and prevailing social ideology is striking and suggests that symbolism was indeed a function of these designs. Nicholson may have deliberately employed similar Baroque ideas of city planning, but with a different arrange-

Perspectives from *Historical Archaeology*

ment of elements to form a clear contrast with St. Mary's and symbolize the arrival of a new social and political order.

While fashion and the need for symbolic expression might explain the specific forms of these two cities, they do not adequately answer a broader question. Why, during the colonial period, were principles of Baroque design only applied to cities in the Chesapeake region? St. Mary's, Annapolis and Williamsburg were all of this style. Before the discovery of the St. Mary's plan, the use of these elegant concepts was attributed solely to the presence of Francis Nicholson, but this is no longer a satisfactory explanation. Calvert and Nicholson were certainly men of intellectual refinement but equally sophisticated individuals lived and exercised political power in other colonies and they did not choose to design such cities. Why not in New France, New England or the Middle Colonies?

The explanation for this unusual distribution may lie in the intended functions of these cities. Capitals of the other colonies were both economic and political centers. They supported sizeable populations engaged in trade and industry as well as supplying government services. Although their founders had various concepts of what a city should be, these always combined economic and governmental functions (Fries 1977).

In the Chesapeake, attempts were made to establish cities from the earliest years of settlement. Colonists carried instructions from their financial backers to build cities that would be the foci of industry, trade and population (Morgan 1975). All attempts failed to produce such urban centers. In the late 17th and early 18th centuries, the governments of Maryland and Virginia made repeated efforts to legislate towns into being but these endeavors also met with limited success (Heite 1966; Rainbolt 1972). The difficulty of creating urban centers of any size in the Chesapeake was obvious to the colonists. Maryland governor, Charles Calvert, noted in 1678 that towns in the colony would not form until "it shall please God to encrease the number of People and soe to alter their Trade as to make it necessary to build more close and to Lyve in Townes" (Maryland Archives 5:266). At the turn of the 18th

century, Robert Beverley of Virginia observed that towns were few because of "the Ambition each Man had of being Lord of a vast, tho' unimproved Territory, together with the Advantage of the many Rivers, which afforded a commodious Road for Shipping at every Man's Door" (Beverley 1947: 57).

Historians agree with these contemporary observers and explain this failure as a product of the Chesapeake region's unique physiographic and economic features (Carr 1974, Rainbolt 1972; Morgan 1975). A focus upon tobacco as the cash crop, abundant land, a dispersed settlement pattern of plantations, and the presence of a superb network of navigable rivers and creeks led to a decentralized economy. Merchant ships went to the individual plantations to collect the year's crop and sell manufactured goods from England and Europe. Although there was some effort at establishing tobacco collection points to improve efficiency and a few year-round stores began to appear in the 1730's, this basic system endured for most of the colonial period (Carr 1974). As a result, there was little to support towns and no major commercial centers with sizable populations developed until the late 18th century. For most of the colonial period, only government-related business supported modest urban populations at the respective capitals of the colonies.

It is proposed here that the design of these Chesapeake cities is directly related to an economy and settlement system that would not support commercial towns, such as existed elsewhere in America. However, an administrative center was still required for government and there was a real need in this rural setting for a place in which political and social authority could be expressed. Consequently, cities were designed to serve as centers of political power, not centers of commerce. The available model for this type of city was the Baroque, then being used for the capitals of states and principalities in Europe (Hohenberg and Lees 1985). Baroque design "has always been an elite model: a way of using the city as an expression of central power and a strategy for attaining visual magnificence and control within available means" (Lynch 1981:283). Another student of urban places has noted that "Above all the baroque city is a setting and celebration of authority—secular, spiritual and cultural" (Fries 1977:119). Social and economic features of the "tobacco colonies" did not encourage commercial centers but they did support the development of special places where political and social authority could be exhibited by a rural-oriented planter gentry. Despite the limitations imposed by a frontier setting and a small human population, the cities in the colonial Chesapeake were successful in serving the functions for which they were intended—capitals, not economic central places. In light of this argument, it is notable that when the city of Washington, D.C. was being laid out on Maryland soil in 1791, the planner followed this same "elite" model and used a Baroque design for the new capital of the United States.

The colonists themselves seem to have distinguished between these government communities and other settlements. Colonial legislation to encourage urban development consistently refers to creating "towns" in the region for economic purposes. The word "city" is only employed for the settlements of St. Mary's, Annapolis, Williamsburg, and occasionally, Jamestown.

Summary and Conclusions

Archaeological research has led to the discovery of a previously unsuspected urban design for St. Mary's City which dramatically alters perceptions of Maryland's first capital. Rather than an irregular, haphazardly built settlement, it was apparently the first city in America to employ Baroque concepts of urban design. Such a finding suggests that Maryland's proprietor, Cecil Calvert, was making a more sophisticated effort to develop the capital of his colony than historians have believed. This discovery also provides important new insights regarding the history of urban design in the United States and illustrates the contributions archaeology can make to fields such as urban geography and urban history.

The prevailing historical interpretation of towns in the Chesapeake as failures has been questioned by Pogue (1984). His work with small communities established by the town acts on Maryland's Patuxent River suggests that while these towns never developed large populations, they played important economic roles. Archaeological evidence from St. Mary's expands this view and argues that the Chesapeake settlement system and the subject of urban development in this region should both be reevaluated, not from the perspective of population size or economic power but of the functions these communities served.

The Baroque cities of the 17th century Chesapeake can be seen as a skillful response to the need for expression of ideology and authority in an agrarian society lacking a centralized economy. Even though the role of individuals such as Calvert and Nicholson cannot be discounted, the application of these Baroque concepts seems to be a product of broader cultural and economic forces within the Chesapeake region. Archaeologists are beginning to learn of the effects that different crop economies in plantation agriculture have on settlement patterns, social structure and other aspects of culture (Joseph 1987). Different economic patterns also appear to strongly influence the form and nature of urban settlements because no city can develop independently of its larger social and economic setting. Hence, the explanation for these Baroque cities offered here carries importance beyond the Chesapeake for it helps to reveal the complex relationships between society, economy, settlement system and urban form.

The influence of political and social conditions on material patterns is also illustrated by these findings. Specifically, the strong correspondence between the forms of Maryland's capitals and official status of religion suggests how church-state relations can affect settlement planning. Although the underlying ideology expressed in city design is often difficult for archaeologists to interpret, especially in the absence of written records, these plans nevertheless offer important insights into the beliefs and social structures of past societies and deserve greater attention.

That Baroque ideas were utilized in colonial America should come as no surprise. Renaissance European culture was dominated by a Baroque aesthetic and world view in the 16th and 17th centuries and this influenced England. Baroque concepts were perhaps not easily expressed in 17th century America due to the constraints of frontier life but that does not mean colonists were ignorant of intellectual trends in the homeland. Certainly many of the elite in colonial society were aware of Baroque ideas, as evidenced by the designs of formal gardens and many of the elaborate mansions built in 17th and early 18th century America. These are applications of Baroque concepts deriving from the Italian Renaissance. Archaeologists have made much of the so called "Georgian" world view and numerous comparisons of Medieval versus "Georgian" aesthetics have appeared. However, it is important to remember that this world view developed well before the Georgian era. More research and careful examination of the data may reveal that the Baroque had a greater influence on 17th century America than previously thought.

Finally, this discovery vividly illustrates the value of precise data. Archaeologists have often been criticized by historians for producing only minor details that do not significantly change historical notions of the past. Similar criticism was heard when it was learned that the town center of St. Mary's was actually a few hundred feet west of its hypothesized position. Yet without knowing precisely where the town center was located and exactly how the buildings and properties were arranged, the urban plan of St. Mary's would never have been discovered. With the systematic collection and application of archaeological data, many unexpected insights into early American society will emerge that significantly alter perceptions of that long vanished world.

ACKNOWLEDGEMENTS

Many organizations and persons made these research findings possible. The National Endowment for the Humanities through Grant RO-1244-81 and the State of Maryland provided the funding for the Town Center investigation. The many individuals who served on the field and laboratory crews during this project deserve thanks for their fine efforts. Reviewers of this manuscript, including Julia King, Tim Riordan, Dennis Pogue, Daniel Mouer, Susan Hanna, James Horn and Charles Fithian made many valuable comments. Mark Leone inspired the search for evidence of a town plan. Finally, Lois Green Carr and Garry Wheeler Stone produced the solid foundation of knowledge about St. Mary's City which was essential for discovery of the city plan. The assistance of each of these individuals and organizations is greatly appreciated.

REFERENCES

AGNEW, JOHN, JOHN MERCER AND DAVID SOPHER, EDS.
  1984 *The City In Cultural Context*. Allen and Unwin, Boston.

BEVERLEY, ROBERT
  1947 *The History and Present State of Virginia*, edited by Louis B. Wright. University of North Carolina, Chapel Hill.

BURKE, GERALD
  1971 *Towns in the Making*. Edward Arnold, London.

CARR, LOIS GREEN
  1974 "The Metropolis of Maryland: A Comment on Town Development Along the Tobacco Coast". *Maryland Historical Magazine* 69:124–45.
  1984 "Toleration in Maryland: Why It Ended." *Maryland 350th Anniversary Lectures*, pp. 51–62. Maryland Department of Economic and Community Development, Annapolis.

CLAVEL, PAUL
  1984 "Reflections on the Cultural Georgraphy of the European City". In *The City in Cultural Context*, edited by John Agnew, et al., pp. 31–49. Allen and Unwin, Boston.

CONZEN, M.R.G.
  1960 *Alnwick, Northumberland: A Study in Town-Plan Analysis*. The Institute of British Geographers, Publication No. 27, London.
  1978 "Analytic Approaches to the Urban Landscape". In *Dimensions of Human Geography*, edited by K. W. Butzer. pp. 128–65. Department of Geography, University of Chicago, Chicago.
  1981 "Historical Townscapes in Britain". In *The Urban Landscape: Historical Development and Management*. edited by J.W.R. Whitehand. pp. 55–74. Academic Press, London.

COTTER, JOHN
  1958 *Archaeological Excavations At Jamestown Colonial National Historical Park, Virginia*. National Park Service Archaeological Research Series 4. Washington, D.C.

FAUSZ, J. FREDERICK
  1984 The Secular Context of Religious Toleration in Mary-
       land. *Maryland 350th Anniversary Lectures*, pp. 5–
       22. Maryland Department of Economic and Commu-
       nity Development, Annapolis.

FORMAN, HENRY CHANDLEE
  1938 *Jamestown and St. Mary's: Buried Cities of Romance*.
       The Johns Hopkins Press, Baltimore.

FRIES, SYLVIA DOUGHTY
  1977 *The Urban Idea in Colonial America*. Temple Univer-
       sity Press, Philadelphia.

GOODMAN, WILLIAM I.
  1968 *Principles and Practices of Urban Planning*. Interna-
       tional City Managers Association, Washington, D.C.

HALL, CLAYTON C.
  1910 *Narratives of Early Maryland*. Barnes and Noble,
       Inc., New York.

HARDOY, JORGE E.
  1978 "European Urban Forms in the Fifteenth to Seven-
       teenth Centuries and Their Utilization in Latin Amer-
       ica". In *Urbanization in the Americas From its
       Beginning to the Present*, edited by Richard Schaedel,
       Jorge Hardoy and Nora Kinger, pp. 215–48. Mouton
       Publishers, The Hague.

HEITE, EDWARD F.
  1966 "Markets and Ports." *Virginia Cavalcade* 16 (2):9–
       41.

HOHENBERG, PAUL AND LYNN H. LEES
  1985 *The Making of Urban Europe 1000-1950*. Harvard
       University Press, Cambridge.

HOPKINS, JOSEPH W. III
  1986 Ideology Writ Large: Three Centuries of the Nichol-
       son Plan in Annapolis, Md. Paper presented at the
       51st Annual Meeting of the Society for American
       Archaeology, New Orleans.

JOSEPH, JOSEPH W,
  1987 Highway 17 Revisited: Pattern and Process in Planta-
       tion Economy. Paper presented at the Society for
       Historical Archaeology Annual Meeting, Savannah.

KUBLER, GEORGE
  1978 "Open-Grid Town Plans in Europe and America". In
       *Urbanization in the Americas from its Beginning to
       the Present*, pp. 327–42. Mouton Publishers, The
       Hague.

LEONE, MARK
  1984 "Interpreting Ideology in Historical Archaeology:
       The William Paca Garden in Annapolis". In *Ideology
       Power and Prehistory*, edited by D. Miller and C.
       Tilley. pp. 25–36. Cambridge University Press, Cam-
       bridge.

LYNCH, KEVIN
  1981 *A Theory of Good City Form*. The M.I.T. Press,
       Cambridge, Mass.

MARKMAN, S.D.
  1978 "The Gridiron Town Plan and the Caste System in
       Colonial Central America". In *Urbanization in the
       Americas from its Beginning to the Present*, pp.
       471–90. Mouton Publishers, The Hague.

MARYLAND ARCHIVES
  1883–*The Archives of Maryland*. 72 volumes to date.
       Maryland Historical Society, Baltimore.

MENARD, RUSSELL AND LOIS GREEN CARR
  1982 "The Lords Baltimore and the Colonization of Mary-
       land". In *Early Maryland in a Wider World*, edited
       by David B. Quinn. Wayne State University Press,
       Detroit.

MILLER, HENRY M.
  1983 A Search for the "Citty of Saint Maries": Report on
       the 1981 Excavations in St. Mary's City, Maryland.
       St. Mary's City Archaeology Series No. 1. St. Mary's
       City.
  1986 Discovering Maryland's First City: A Summary Re-
       port on the 1981–1984 Archaeological Excavations in
       St. Mary's City, Maryland. *St. Mary's City Archae-
       ology Series* No. 2. St. Mary's City.

MILLER, HENRY M. AND REBECCA SEAGLE
  1987 The Chapels of St. Mary's: A Report on an Archae-
       ological Survey of the Chapel Field in St. Mary's
       City, Md. *St. Mary's City Research Series* No. 6.

MILNE, GUSTAV
  1986 *The Great Fire of London*. The Museum of London.
       Historical Publications Ltd., New Barnet, Hertshire.

MORGAN, EDMUND S.
  1975 *American Slavery American Freedom: The Ordeal of
       Colonial Virginia*. W.W. Norton and Company, New
       York.

NORBERG-SCHULZ, CHRISTIAN
  1971 *Baroque Architecture*. Harry N. Abrams, Inc, New
       York.

POGUE, DENNIS J.
  1984 Town Rearing on the Maryland Chesapeake Frontier:
       A Reinterpretation. Paper presented at the Society for
       Historical Archaeology Annual Meeting, Williams-
       burg.
  1985 "Calverton, Calvert County, Maryland: 1668–
       1725." *Maryland Historical Magazine* 80:271–76.

RAINBOLT, JOHN C.
  1972 The Absence of Towns in Seventeenth-Century Vir-
       ginia. In *Cities in American History*, edited by Ken-
       neth T. Jackson and Stanley K. Schultz, pp. 50–65.
       Alfred A. Knopf, New York.

RAPOPORT, AMOS
  1984 "Culture and the Urban Order". In *The City in
       Cultural Context*, edited by John Agnew, John Mercer
       and David Sopher, pp. 50–75. Allen and Unwin,
       Boston.

RASMUSSEN, STEEN EILER
   1937 *London: The Unique City.* The M.I.T. Press, Cambridge.

REPS, JOHN W.
   1965 *The Making of Urban America: A History of Town Planning in the United States.* Princeton University Press, Princeton.
   1972 *Tidewater Towns: City Planning in Colonial Virginia and Maryland.* Colonial Williamsburg Foundation, Williamsburg.

ROTHSCHILD, NAN A.
   1987 "On the Existence of Neighborhoods in 18th Century New York: Maps, Markets, and Churches." In *Living In Cities: Current Research In Urban Archaeology,* edited by Edward Staski. Society for Historical Archaeology Special Publication Series, Number 5: 29–37.

SHAPIRO, GARY
   1987 The Anthropology of Town Plan at San Luis. Paper presented at the Society for Historical Archaeology Annual Meeting, Savannah.

SMAILES, ARTHUR E.
   1966 *The Geography of Towns.* Hutchinson University Library, London.

THOMPSON, STEPHEN I.
   1973 *Pioneer Colonization: A Cross-Culture View.* Addison-Wesley Module in Anthropology No. 33.

TRUDEL, MARCEL
   1968 *An Atlas of New France.* Les Presses de l'universite Laval, Quebec.

WALL, DIANA DIZEREGA
   1987 "Settlement System Analysis in Historical Archaeology: An Example from New York City". In Living In Cities: Current Research In Urban Archaeology, edited by Edward Staski. *Society for Historical Archaeology Special Publication Series* No. 5:65–74.

HENRY M. MILLER
DIRECTOR OF RESEARCH
HISTORIC ST. MARY'S CITY
ST. MARY'S CITY, MARYLAND. 20686

MARK P. LEONE
SILAS D. HURRY

Seeing: The Power of Town Planning in the Chesapeake

ABSTRACT

Urban planning in St. Mary's City and Annapolis is argued to be guided by a baroque theory of power. The layouts of both cities use the same principles. Baltimore is argued to be built using a panoptic theory of power. Planning and building in these important Maryland cities was to promote and solidify hierarchy.

Introduction

Our intent is to use material from historical archaeology, as well as from maps, photographs, and documents to compare and analyze the urban designs of three Maryland cities. This approach views these cities as very large artifacts to be studied. The focus of the analysis is quite broad: cities and power. The arguments here are speculative, but offer an interpretation that addresses both change and maintenance of the status quo. All of these arguments rest on the contention that design is used to affect people by manipulating sight so that people see what they are supposed to see. It is not suggested that this is the only way to approach these cities. One of the strengths of modern historical archaeology is the growth and development of multiple perspectives. In comparing the designs of St. Mary's City, Annapolis, and Baltimore, the goal is to demonstrate how each of these cities reflects the status of local and regional governmental authority. It is suggested that St. Mary's City and Annapolis, until the American Revolution, were planned and built using a baroque theory of power. Then, after Independence, Annapolis and Baltimore employed a panoptic theory of power wrapped in neoclassical symbolism.

We have worked in Maryland on issues of urban design and its execution and specifically in situations at St. Mary's City and Annapolis where documentary evidence did not exist on urban design, or where previous interpretations foreclosed understandings subsequently reached by using archaeological information. Hurry works at St. Mary's City through the State of Maryland's Historic St. Mary's City, the State museum at the site of Maryland's first city. Leone works in the Historic District of Annapolis, the current capital of Maryland, through Archaeology in Annapolis. The latter project is administered jointly by the University of Maryland, College Park and Historic Annapolis Foundation, one of Maryland's leading preservation groups. The authors both have longstanding interests in Baltimore, although neither has excavated there. A few of the many reports on Baltimore's archaeology have been reviewed for support of the hypotheses offered here. Baltimore is now Maryland's major city and has been so since early in the 19th century. Annapolis became the capital in 1695 and is presently a city of over 30,000 people. St. Mary's City, founded in 1634, on the other hand, is a museum setting, having been both abandoned and depopulated since early in the 18th century.

The discussion will present each city in chronological order, thus moving forward in time while becoming less reliant upon traditional archaeology. The work in St. Mary's City is firmly grounded in archaeological data and the interpretations are largely based upon archaeological discovery. St. Mary's represents a century when the historical record, while extensive, is not complete enough to provide many details. Little concerning the city's design survives in the records. Annapolis blends a richer documentary record with a large dose of archaeology which anchors the work to the ground and which provides separate evidence for the contention that space was manipulated to reinforce power. Interpretations about Baltimore are based solely on an "archaeological" reading of architectural and historical data and observations of surviving elements of the city. Much of 19th-century Baltimore still exists and that which has not survived is often well documented. The elite buildings and monuments discussed here are particularly well-studied. While the data sets used to construct these arguments are somewhat disparate, St. Mary's City, Annapolis, and Baltimore provide a valuable case study of change and continuity in the use of design and an opportunity to explore some of the meanings behind urban plans in America.

St. Mary's City

Maryland was established at St. Mary's City in March of 1634. It was the fourth permanent English colony in North America and the first to be a successful proprietary colony owned by a single individual, Cecil Calvert, the Lord Baltimore. Perhaps because Maryland had an English Catholic proprietor, the colony had several unusual features. Lord Baltimore's directions to the first settlers in 1633 and his subsequent actions emphasized the highly unfashionable ideas of religious toleration for all Christians and a separation of church from state. He envisioned a society based upon a hierarchical model of social relations with the proprietor having princely powers over the colony and its development. As was true of all other colonization efforts, Lord Baltimore also sought financial rewards from his new colony.

St. Mary's served as the capital of the colony and its principal city until the winter of 1694-1695. Movement of the provincial government to Annapolis at that time led to the abandonment of St. Mary's City. No trace of the original settlement has survived above ground. Since neither map nor detailed descriptions of the town layout survived, it was assumed by historians, based upon the available evidence, that the town was a scattered, randomly arranged settlement that grew haphazardly over the century. Some testing of the building sites was carried out in the 1930s (Forman 1938) with modern archaeological excavations on selected sites beginning in 1971 (Stone 1974). The initial findings from these efforts seemed to support the historical viewpoint. When the first comprehensive survey

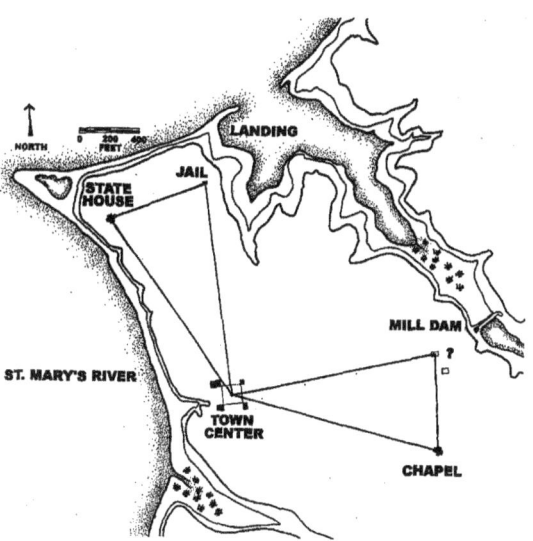

FIGURE 1. Baroque arrangement of principal buildings in St. Mary's City, Maryland.

work was conducted in the late 1970s, additional details regarding site distributions became available. These surveys and the results of 25 years of testing and excavation on dozens of archaeological sites have produced much of the primary data regarding St. Mary's City. There was, however, no reason to entertain the idea that the settlement's layout was notable or as grand as the social and political design that characterized the founding of Maryland.

In the mid 1980s, Miller (1986, 1988) proposed an idea that was contrary to the expectations of historians. Miller suggested that the placement of the principal buildings, constructed in the 1660s and 1670s, was not random but intentional, and that they were linked by axes forming two symmetrical triangles joined at the town center. These axes involved the careful placement of major buildings: the Jesuit chapel, the 1676 statehouse, a brick prison, a possible school, other structures with brick architecture, and commercial buildings in the town center (Figure 1). These created a balanced composition of urban space. A variety of evidence shows that these axes were also the chief streets or thoroughfares of the town. The commercial buildings in the town center were placed precisely to form a square measuring 130 ft. (40 m) on a side and into which the principal streets intersected. The massive Jesuit chapel (ca. 1667) and the brick statehouse (1676) were exactly one half a mile apart and separated from the center of the town square by a distance of approximately 1400 ft. (425 m). Recent archaeology has revealed that the brick prison (1676), located near the boat landing for the city, and structures near the principal land entrance were also placed at this same 1400 foot interval. Miller (1986, 1988) proposed that there was too much evidence of regularity in the archaeological record for the town to have been an unplanned, scattered settlement. Furthermore, he suggested that this was an example of baroque town planning, reflecting continental ideas regarding urban design. The square, for example, was a key feature of the Italian baroque, later widely used throughout Europe and America. The emphasis upon placement of principal buildings at the nodes of the street system, the location of the church and statehouse at opposite ends of the town in topographically prominent locations, and the integration of the key entryways of the city into the plan are all elements of Renaissance and baroque design. Finally, the formal architecture of the chapel and statehouse, along with the use of costly construction materials such as brick, tile, and imported stone for the chapel, statehouse, prison, and other structures is very rare in early Maryland, where nearly every building was of wooden construction. This evidence strongly implies that St. Mary's City possessed a carefully conceived and executed town plan based upon European design principles that were meant to impress.

The idea that baroque principles of design had been used to lay out and build St. Mary's City was not what had been expected. Historical scholarship, coupled with contemporary descriptions of life in the town, had left the impression that St. Mary's was small, primitive, even Late Medieval in appearance. Most of its houses were probably wooden, ephemeral, and placed with no particular plan. An architecture of impermanence and a lifestyle of "rude sufficiency" was suggested. While Lord Baltimore ordered that the settlers create and live together in a town after their arrival in 1634, there is no evidence that this first effort was a success. Due to numerous periods of unrest and outright rebellion during the 1640s and 1650s, it is unlikely that there were any significant efforts to develop St. Mary's City before 1660, when Charles II returned to rule England. Given both what was known historically and initially known through archaeology, St. Mary's did not seem to have the appearance of an early modern capital with a conscious plan behind its uses of landscape.

If the city were intended to be a baroque capital that had major formal structures representing church and state at the terminus of each street, then it was a quite different place. Many authors have discussed the nature of the baroque and its applications to city design (Zucker 1959; Mumford 1961; Lynch 1981). To explore these we use the idea (Zucker 1959:233-235) that late baroque town planning and landscape architecture used lines of sight to direct eyes to points of reference in space that represented hierarchy, and monarchy in particular. This is in contrast to the earlier tradition of the Italian Renaissance in which vistas were deliberately kept open so as to shift sight to infinity. In the later baroque, especially in France, Belgium, Germany, and eventually England, the vistas were foreclosed by being fixed on objects so that no alternatives appeared visually possible. In the European conceptions of baroque planning there is the notion that much of society is made up of persons considered neither as relatives nor as fixed masses—the faithful, renters, farmers, etc.—but as individuals (Rowe 1966:1-20). It is these—individuals—who are defined as the units of society (Deetz 1977:43, 133-136). They are considered worthwhile, and to have wholeness or integrity. It is they who can own things and have rights (Handler and Saxton 1988:242-265). This is the unit that walks through the baroque plan and for whom it was designed and built. There is no crowd here. There are sets of eyes; each set is called to focus on a source of authority. In Maryland that authority was hierarchical and then monarchical. It was wealthy by right of rents and the taxes collected from trade and crops, and thus, the better the colony was run, the wealthier the authorities became.

People who saw themselves as individual owners, with futures, raised crops and could prosper in early Maryland. They could change their social position by work, use of the law, and by taking advantage of opportunity. An occasional woman could think this way too, such as Margaret Brent who became a major landowner and, as such, even asked for the right to vote (Spruill 1934). There was not a peasantry and there is nothing medieval in a social situation with so much flux and built on opportunity and individualism. So it is appropriate to suggest that an early modern social setting with a hierarchy of profit-oriented individuals would benefit from a baroque physical setting. Members of the Maryland political hierarchy were new and needed to affirm their status and create stable conditions. It is suggested that they built for themselves a spatial environment whose unity of design would foster these social elements and produce stable relations. This is in contrast to the view of St. Mary's with which we are usually presented, an unplanned, unimpressive frontier town. It is now thought that the city was designed to be something else.

Who were the personalities behind the application of these baroque concepts? Why do they appear so early in Maryland? Much of the credit must be given to the colonial elite who dominated Maryland in the 17th century. Maryland was founded as an English proprietary colony by the Calvert family, the Roman Catholic Barons of Baltimore. Catholics were disfranchised and persecuted in England during the 17th century, thus members of the Catholic elite in England routinely had to send their children to the Continent to receive a Catholic education in the 17th century. We know that Philip Calvert, the colony's Chancellor and a principal figure in the

development of St. Mary's City, was educated in Portugal. Jerome White, the colony's Surveyor General, was raised and educated in Rome and was even described by the famous English designer John Evelyn as a "very ingenious gentleman" (Bray 1886:72). This European education facilitated the communication of baroque ideas from Europe to Maryland. These members of the colonial Catholic elite were steeped in the innovations of the European baroque which they attempted to translate into an impressive city in the New World.

Equally relevant is the presence of the Jesuits in Maryland. The Society of Jesus was one of the largest investors in the colony and its members were an active force in Maryland throughout the 17th century. They probably built the chapel at St. Mary's City, the first example of massive formal architecture in Maryland, and a key element of the city plan. Jesuits were a powerful and highly educated group who were at the forefront of the Counter Reformation in Europe. They utilized Renaissance and Baroque ideas, architecture, and art to advance the Catholic faith. Among the Jesuits were scholars who served as instructors in the great universities of France, Italy, and the Low Countries. They recognized the need to impress and persuade individuals and acted upon this by designing and building some of the most innovative examples of church architecture during the baroque era. Their church designs employed clear lines of sight to focus attention on the power of God. With the Jesuits, sight was a powerful tool to influence, persuade, and inspire individuals. The presence of these highly educated priests, along with the ruling elite of Maryland who were trained on the Continent, is an important factor in evaluating the influences which shaped this 17th-century colony (Lucas 1990).

To understand better the nature of St. Mary's City, some information about major examples of its architecture is presented. At the apex of one triangle that defines the baroque plan stood the brick chapel constructed by the Jesuits about 1667. This massive, cruciform brick building rose high into the air resting on a foundation that extended into the ground a full five feet. The building was embellished with a tile roof, complex window traceries made with special mullion bricks, an imported stone floor, and apparently used a design informed not by English precedents but instead those of the Continent. This structure was not hidden, but occupied one of the most prominent locations in the city. It spoke loudly that Roman Catholics held power and its use of brick and tile said this was permanent. Such a structure was especially significant in a symbolic and political sense because it was illegal for Roman Catholics to build free standing churches in England at the time.

Another of the major structures was the 1676 statehouse. This building was tall and also had a cross shaped floor plan. Analysis suggests that it possessed certain Continental features including a low roof pitch and ornamental elements on the corners, flourishes designed to impress. Built of brick and roofed with imported Dutch tile, it too speaks to a permanence and formality that was atypical in a society dominated by impermanence and folk design. The statehouse was situated in a prominent location on a high headland that extended into the river. This placement allowed it to be visible to all traveling to the city by water. From the land, it provided a focus for major sight lines along two streets.

Another structure was the jail for the colony. Also built in 1676, it was of brick construction and had an imported Dutch tile roof. Most penal facilities of this period in America were of frame or log construction. Again, the use of brick and tile suggests a serious effort to achieve permanence. Placement of this building at the junction of two major streets and overlooking the main boat landing for the city further demonstrates the effort to make this structure visible and obvious to all. Several other buildings incorporating brick into their architecture are known and two of these flank the major land entrance into the city. There is currently insufficient archaeological work on these structures to provide details regarding their architecture.

The presence of these buildings and their placement within the town implies a sophisticated effort at consciously shaping urban space. The design controlled sight in a manner to affect individuals. This is not to say that Maryland's 17th century capital was more polished than it was. Due to geographic, demographic, and economic forces, urban development was very slow in the Chesapeake region throughout the 1600s and early 1700s (Reps 1972; Carr 1974). Movement of the government to Annapolis effectively killed the city of St. Mary's just as it was beginning to mature as an urban place. Nevertheless, the evidence seems to indicate an effort to create symmetry and order through the application of baroque design principles for the colonial capital. Such an undertaking was no doubt inspired by fashion, and the fact that such a sophisticated urban concept existed, demonstrated refinement. At the same time, the use of baroque urban design was a device for enhancing and displaying power. As two prominent scholars of European urban history have noted about the baroque era, "Rulers were the greatest builders of all, seeing in the new architecture and urban design the means of symbolizing and thus affirming their political dominance as well as their cultural refinement" (Hohenberg and Lees 1985:152). By placing symbolically important structures in visually prominent locations within a street network, the designers of St. Mary's City were ensuring that both visitors and residents were aware of the power of the proprietary government and the Catholic faith of Maryland's ruling elite. Such a finding suggests that Maryland's sophisticated social and legal design was accompanied by an equally sophisticated early modern urban design and architecture.

Annapolis

It seems likely that there was a tie between St. Mary's City and the baroque city planning used for Annapolis by the new royal governor. Francis Nicholson took Anne Arundel Town, which Protestants settled in 1649, and redesigned it in 1696. At the end of the 17th century the town had at most only a couple of hundred people living in it. Nicholson designed and superimposed a baroque plan on the few streets already there. He composed two circles, a series of streets radiating from them, a large square, and placed all these on a set of hills and ridges (Figure 2). He then made a setting for the statehouse, Anglican church, school, and a whole set of houses. He was determined to displace St. Mary's City and certainly knew French and English urban planning. Nicholson borrowed heavily from landscape architecture, from what he had seen in Versailles and from the plans for rebuilding London proposed by Wren and Evelyn (Reps 1972:127). He no doubt knew from personal experience how St. Mary's City was designed,

since he had lived there in 1694. Recent research at Historic St. Mary's City suggests that Nicholson and his milieu may have been more influenced by St. Mary's than previously believed (Riordan, Hurry, and Miller 1995). Both the new statehouse and the Anglican church in Annapolis shared intriguing design elements with the St. Mary's statehouse and the brick chapel. All of these structures used cruciform plans. The use of a cruciform plan for the Anglican church, St. Anne's, is particularly unusual since most contemporary Anglican churches used rectangular plans. Since he was a much traveled, educated, and experienced English civil administrator, he also knew about urban and rural planning, including its use in colonial settings. Most interpretations of Nicholson's work see his accom-

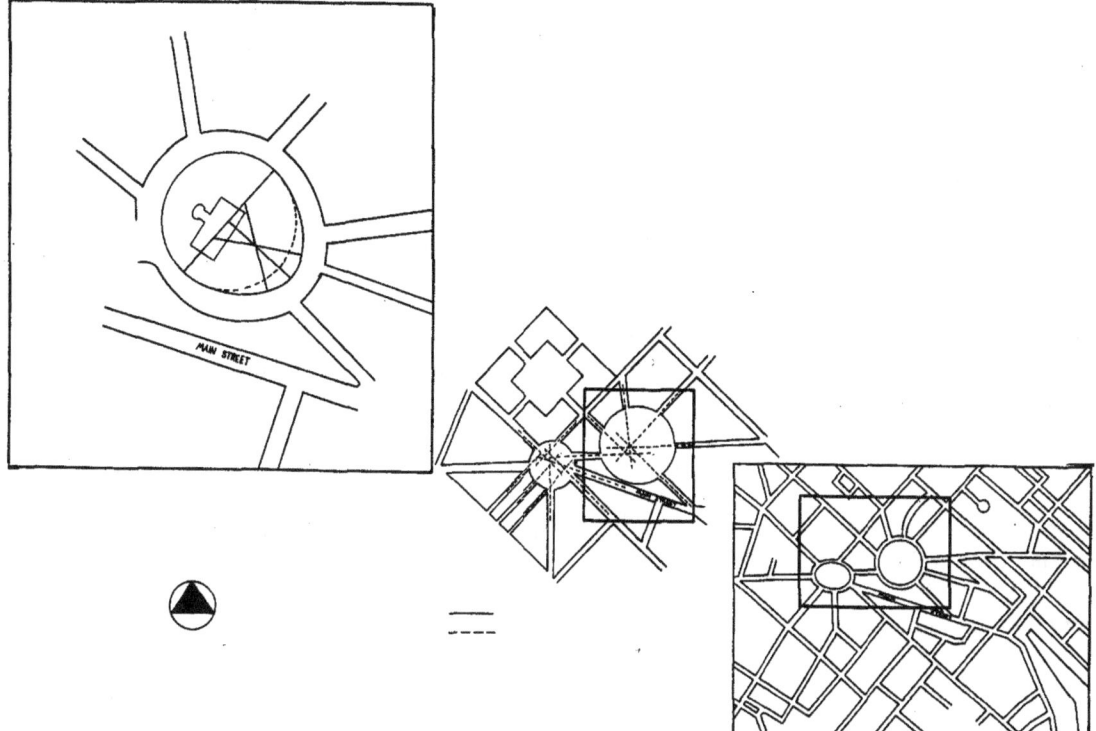

FIGURE 2. The center of Annapolis is State Circle shown here on the left as a geometrical egg. The center lines of the streets intersect on the location of the Maryland State House, in a drawing based on Reps (1972). The city plan dates to 1694, and was in place by 1710. Solid lines are streets and dashed lines are hypothetical. The earliest existing survey of Annapolis is 1718 and all these illustrations are based on it (drawing by Prashant Kaw).

plishment in Annapolis, and later at Williamsburg, which he also designed, as a product of his background as a colonial administrator.

Nicholson's design is treated traditionally in two ways. First, his redesign for Anne Arundel Town, which he renamed Annapolis, for Queen Anne, is usually seen as a baroque plan overlaid on an earlier grid (Baker 1986:191-209). Second, traditional scholarship has not seen baroque design as tied to the ideas behind the condition of monarchical government (Reps 1965, 1972). Rather, it was seen purely as an effort to create a fashionable city. Such treatments are incomplete and inappropriate for understanding the historical circumstances of the founding of Annapolis. We argue that baroque street layout was not to facilitate commercial development or land speculation. The planning was not independent either of the condition of the government nor of the buildings situated in the design.

An analysis of the center of Annapolis using archaeological data challenges parts of this traditional view (Reps 1965, 1972). State Circle is a ring road that forms one of the boundaries of the perimeter around the Maryland Statehouse. The circle was built around an unevenly sloping hill with the Statehouse on the top of the hill and the road circling the whole landscape. From the circular road, eight roads and alleys radiate out into the city. If we flash forward to 1990, the worn-out circle was to be completely rebuilt with all overhead wires, and all underground pipes replaced. A new surface was to be laid. Members of the group, Archaeology in Annapolis, excavated 22 pits at historically significant points around the circle. These excavations (Read 1990) showed that the stratigraphy of about two-thirds of the circle's perimeter was intact, with the earliest levels dating to the 1720s. There was nothing dating to the 17th century and all the stratigraphy was gone on about a third of the circle's western circumference. Archaeology produced about a dozen securely dated points at previous circumference markers which included rows of fence palings, two wells, a walk, and a post for a sign or light. The archaeologists concluded that the circumference of the circle had never been stable, and that the circle had often not been a true circle. With archaeology alone, no one involved could determine an original shape. No one ever thought it was possible that no circle had ever existed.

Between 1990 and 1994, a series of maps of State Circle was used to develop a hunch based on looking at a 1990 map: The circle was in the form of an egg. Geometrically, an egg is four connected arcs drawn from four centers, three of which are arranged as the points of a triangle, with the forth center in the middle of the triangle's base. The fourth center is the point base of a mirror-image right triangle. Using trial and error, an egg drawn this way was fitted on the perimeter of the 1990 circle and it fit almost perfectly. Thus, Leone and others (Leone, Stabler, and Burlaga 1998:291-306) suggested that the circle is actually an egg. For how long, and why, no one could say.

Subsequent analysis of an 1882 map showed the circle to be an egg then and in about the same place and with the same dimensions as the current one. Then, going back further in time, points on the perimeter dating archaeologically from 1800 to 1830 were plotted using AutoCad, which then linked as many points as possible. On this plot a true geometric circle and a true egg, respectively, were superimposed. Neither geometric form fitted well to the shape provided from the dated pits. Then, the same exercise was performed on locales on the circle dating from 1700 to 1800. This plot approximated an egg. The result was also an egg when the original Stoddart Plan of 1718 was plotted digitally and tested against a superimposed egg and a circle (Figure 2). The egg form derived from the 18th-century information is smaller, with the peaked end pointing in a different direction from the one built in the 1880s that still exists today. So, while the circle appears always to have been an egg, it does not always appear to have been the same one.

Landscape design books of the 17th and 18th century (Langley 1971[1728]: vii, 17, 202) show how to build eggs and indicate that they should be used when integrating hill tops and hillsides into a design. The reasons for this are still not fully understood but they do include creating the image of a circle by taking uneven slopes and oddly juxtaposed points on them, which must be seen from every direction, and providing the illusion of uniformity, or circularity, the preferred element of baroque landscape design.

The streets entering the circle is the key to understanding baroque ideas of design in Annapolis. The organization of these shows that Nicholson knew that he was dealing with optical principles in the service of authority. The longest five streets that enter the circle have sides that diverge as they enter, making the statehouse appear closer than it was as one walks up them toward the center of power. One street has parallel sides like those in the rest of the city and the two shortest streets have converging sides that act to create the appearance of distance from their heads. Using converging or diverging sides was a device to enhance the image of the statehouse in a systematic way. It uses optical illusions to make the object of view appear closer and bigger, or more distant and smaller, depending on where the spectator stood, thus using slights of the eye to both impress and fool.

The second circle, Church Circle, also is not circular. Its true geometric shape has not been examined thus how it was designed cannot be said. This circle, too, is entered by a set of streets, some of which have nonparallel sides. Measurements of other streets in Annapolis were taken from current maps and it was discovered that those not forming vistas have parallel sides.

Baroque thought assumed movement through a planned volume or set of volumes. So, both in St. Mary's City and Annapolis, we should suppose that the streets served to guide residents and visitors through the city in such a way that the monuments in the vistas appeared to be connected visually. We do not know whether there were predetermined routes through the city, but the juxtaposition of the statehouse and church in both cities must have been both a frequent route and sight.

Based on the archaeological work on State Circle, and the historic maps that were digitized, the details of the baroque principles used to create the city are beginning to emerge. Lines of sight were laid out and built to focus attention on centers of authority. It is suggested that the precision used by Francis Nicholson to lay out the city has been missed, particularly by Reps (1972:123-124). It is also the case that virtually all local scholars and preservationists have failed to understand that the city was laid out with the management of sight in mind and that Nicholson conceived of it as a volume, not from a bird's eye view, and not like the grids used in New York, Philadelphia, Alexandria, or Savannah.

Perhaps the major lack of understanding that frequently accompanies interpretations of baroque uses of space is the failure to understand that it is associated with a theory of power, particularly monarchical power. Although Zucker (1959) is only one of a number of authors who write on this topic, he summarizes this theory of power when he points out that the French, Dutch, and British baroque traditions of architecture, landscape, and urban planning began with the Italian tradition. The Italian Renaissance fostered this tradition in which space was used to keep the eye moving and focused upon vistas. In the early baroque, monuments, fountains, and other objects became prominent focal points in these vistas. The French, English, and later Italian traditions of baroque design put buildings of authority at the end of the vistas. This fixed the spectator's eyesight and kept it from flight. The point was to capture the attention of individuals repeatedly and to orient them to symbols of authority. This was the aim of much of baroque building and accompanied the consolidation of power at Versailles and urban planning in some British colonies. Annapolis and Williamsburg are important illustrations because Nicholson had to wage a political fight to create both capitals, and in Maryland his task was to replace a Catholic proprietary government with direct rule by the English crown. He was operating in the kind of unstable political condition that was at the heart of baroque political thought (Braudel 1979:489-491). We argue that Annapolis did not simply succeed St. Mary's City based on political considerations alone. Rather, the same Continental theory of power and urban design were available to both the Calverts and to Nicholson. St. Mary's City and Annapolis were designed using the same principles, which constituted one major way European monarchs aggrandized themselves.

Henry M. Miller (1997, pers. comm.) has suggested that, although a number of other towns were ordered laid out during the 17th and early 18th centuries in both Maryland and Virginia, it is significant that none of them appears to have utilized baroque principles to any degree. Legislation was passed by Charles Calvert in 1668 and again in 1671 to create port towns in Maryland. The Maryland legislature ordered many more towns created in 1683. These were to have 100 equal lots of one acre size and it seems likely that the legislators had a grid type of arrangement in mind. A review of the surviving town plats and physical inspection of many of these town sites by Miller shows that most were apparently laid out simply. The earliest surviving town plat in Maryland is of Calverton on the Patuxent River. Created in the 1668 act, the plat dates to 1682 and was discovered by Pogue (1985). It shows 12 structures, including outbuildings, and most of these were arranged in a linear fashion, probably along a street. Among the buildings is a court house, chapel, and prison, all located near each other along the street. There is also a plat, dating to 1706, of St. Leonard's Town in Calvert County. It was created by the 1683 legislation and the later plat seems to reflect the original survey. This settlement was a grid shaped to conform to the topographic setting. It has also been suggested that

the irregular grids of Oxford and Wye on the Eastern Shore reflect the original 17th-century layout of these communities, even though the actual plats are of early 18th-century date (Forman 1956:49-52; Reps 1972:111). The important community of Londontown, created in Anne Arundel County by the 1683 act, also apparently had a basic grid arrangement (Alvin Luckenbach 1996, pers. comm.). During the 18th-century, other towns were created in Maryland and these too seem to have followed the grid plan (Marlborough [1706], Green Hills [1707], Vienna [1706] and Chestertown [resurveyed 1730]). In Virginia, a number of port towns were ordered established by the legislature beginning in 1680 (Heite 1966; Rainbolt 1972; Reps 1972). Among the towns laid out were Tappahannock, Onancoch, Marlborough, Yorktown, and Norfolk. Surviving plats of these communities demonstrate that all followed a grid arrangement, although the actual form varied to fit the local topographic conditions (Reps 1972).

All of these towns in both Maryland and Virginia were intended to concentrate trade, serve as commercial centers, and spur some diversification of the local economy. Since many of them became seats of local jurisdictions, they controlled import and export activities. Thus, revenue collection was a major factor in their creation. As Rainbolt (1972) has argued, the various acts which called for establishment of these towns were far too ambitious for success. He also suggests that there was a conflict between the crown and its supporters and the lower house of Assembly in Virginia over the very purpose of towns. The colonials saw the towns as a way of sponsoring economic development while the affluent English merchants and the crown wanted them to remain "modest" settlements, serving to enhance trade with England (Rainbolt 1972:58). Similarly, Lord Baltimore probably saw the focus of commerce on ports as a way of improving collection of tariffs. Thus, none of the other towns created during the 17th century was intended as a capital, although some did have local govern-

Perspectives from *Historical Archaeology*

ment functions. Based upon the surviving evidence, it seems likely that the use of a simple grid was employed for these port communities. While any could have employed a baroque design in their layout, the fact that they did not serves to emphasize the unusual nature of the plans for the capital cities.

To bolster the argument that baroque town planning is associated with the maintenance of centralized authority we want to move to its last use in Maryland before the Revolution. After Annapolis was redesigned and built by Nicholson in the period 1695 to 1710 using monuments organized along sight lines, another use of these principles occurred in the dozen or more great, formal gardens built as falling landscapes. Annapolis saw these appear in the politically crucial period 1763 to 1790. Leone (1984, 1987) argues that the principles and circumstances of these planned landscapes are related to those used by Nicholson when he redesigned the capital almost a hundred years earlier. They would also be the same principles used in St. Mary's City in the 1660s.

The most famous garden in Annapolis today is William Paca's restored garden, originally constructed in the 1760s. It was rebuilt in the 1960s and early 1970s, and was opened to the public. It was excavated and rebuilt using many strategies to determine historical accuracy. Archaeology and analysis of contemporary garden design books show that it was built according to English gardening principles derived from garden/ dictionary manuals which date to the 1720s. The space is two square adjacent acres, and the design uses a series of terraces and falls to create a falling garden. The garden is largely green, has a focal point, and was constructed with precision in mathematics, optics, hydrology, and horticulture. All this information has been fairly well established (Powell 1966; South 1967; Little 1967-68; Orr and Orr 1975; Leone 1984, 1987; Paca-Steele and Wright 1987).

Historic Annapolis Foundation uses an interpretation of the garden that holds it to be a unique

expression created by the young, newly married Paca. The public tour says he combined his classical education, taste, and wealth to build this extension of his city house. The one or two contemporary visitors whose opinions of the garden remain indicate that Paca had built the best garden in the city and so it was unique. It also looked like the other gardens in the city but neither it nor any of the others remaining in the city had been analytically connected to the baroque plan of Annapolis.

Using historical archaeology in Annapolis over a period of a decade and working with Historic Annapolis Foundation, homeowners in Annapolis, students, and colleagues; archaeologists set out to modify the picture of uniqueness that had accompanied the Paca garden through the 1980s. A topographic map (Hopkins 1984) was made of the Ridout garden, built in the 1760s in the city and never destroyed. A similar map (Roulette and Williams 1986) was made of the Charles Carroll of Carrollton garden, built in the city in the early 1770s and still intact. Visits were made but no mapping was done of the gardens at Upton Scott house, Hammond Harwood house, Chase Lloyd house, Acton Place, Adams Kilty, and Brice houses. A map was also made for the garden of Bordley Randall House (Matthews 1996). Garden fragments survive at all of these houses.

The topographic maps showed that the Carroll and Ridout landscapes were falling gardens made up of flats or terraces alternating with falls or descents, accompanied by ramps and focal points. Examination of the period gardening books showed that Annapolis gardens were designed and built using the sophisticated and precise knowledge of landscape design available in published form in English. Thus, while Paca's garden was the finest, it was in no way unique regarding any aspect of its design.

The research of Leone and his colleagues (Leone 1984, 1987; Leone and Shackel 1990; Kryder-Reid 1991) also showed that falling gardens were constructed as volumes with the management of sight as a foremost aim. Thus, (1) converging or diverging sight lines were built by using the edges of the ramps and the edges of planting beds; (2) shades of green in grass, shrubs, and trees moderated from light to dark; and (3) bottom planes beginning wide and narrowing were used to make a small garden appear larger than it actually was. The reverse of these principles was used to make a big space appear to be smaller. A unit of measure derived from some part of the house, usually the facade, was the base measure for the layout of the garden. All of these aspects of garden design reflect a knowledge of visual manipulation making the viewer "see" that which was intended to be seen. While doing all this work, it became clear that there were thousands of similar gardens built as necessary accompaniments to great houses up and down the East Coast of British North America in the late colonial and early federal eras, as well as in British colonies throughout the world. From about 1750 to 1790 in Tidewater Maryland, such gardens were built using most of the same principles of design.

Once it became clear that the baroque principles used to design a multitude of garden spaces in Annapolis were the same as those used by Nicholson to design Annapolis and by the Calverts for St. Mary's City, then why was consistent use of them not made instead of these episodes? Why were there lapses in the use of these design principles and inconsistency in their application from place to place?

Leone (1987) suggests that this use of baroque principles coincides with attempts to establish hierarchical authority in the face of opposition. The Calverts had to establish, and not merely recite, their power, especially after the period of civil unrest during the 1640s and 1650s. Nicholson had to assert, not just talk about, royal power. Paca, Carroll, Ridout, and the other members of the Maryland landed gentry were under attack when they built their baroque gardens. Lapses in power, or efforts to establish or maintain it, called for the use of baroque plan-

ning and this is what tied St. Mary's design to the design of Annapolis and then to the many gardens built like each other late in the 18th century in the capitol and elsewhere in the colony.

This 18th-century use of baroque principles in gardens to affect and impress others may be seen as a personalization of the power of members of the colonial elite as individuals. These gardens were private constructs which manipulated the landscape to affect the way people saw the seeker of status. Baroque principles were used, not to aggrandize the state this time, but to emphasize the presumed rights of the rising colonial elite. A case in point is the Carroll Garden. As Roman Catholics, the Carrolls were disfranchised and heavily taxed in the 18th century. Their economic position, however, partially obtained through the old proprietary regime, allowed them to survive, flourish, and through the garden, to advertise their hoped for social and economic status. Sight manipulation on the personal level did not require participation in the political machinery. Their ardent support for the American Revolution, however, demonstrated their longstanding desire for full citizenship and real political power.

A Theory of Power for a Republic: The Maryland Panopticon

Once baroque ideas are seen as plausible citations for describing the common design elements of St. Mary's City and Annapolis, there are two other intellectual problems to be faced. One, since such design elements were associated with monarchy, then we ask why was Annapolis not redesigned during the Federal era? Why did Maryland not move its capital at this time as Virginia had? Second, since Maryland's new rising city, Baltimore, did not have a baroque design, but was such an active scene of architectural innovation during the Federal era, how was it designed? Since many wealthy and powerful Marylanders such as both branches of the Carroll family and the Lloyds were responsible for the look of both cities, how could post-revolutionary Annapolis and Baltimore appear to be so different?

The effort to explore these questions is guided by the common ideology of American Independence—an individual is a citizen with rights and is at the center of the new American nation. To continue, a citizen was an individual, who among other things, could own property and vote. While the citizen, like the subject in a monarchy, was to be loyal to the state, the citizen in a republic voted to empower the state, according to American logic. A citizen could see the government as being composed of his representatives. That individual could argue that those who made up the government changed because of the way he voted. A citizen, like any individual, could achieve and acquire, could grow and change. Both the individual subject in a monarchical state and the individual citizen in a republic could walk through an urban landscape and be faced with the power of the state. The individual who was the subject was commanded to pay attention to a state that argued that it pre-existed the individual and obtained its authority from sources other than the individual. It took a different landscape for the citizen to see himself as responsible for the founding and continuation of the state. He was not only subject to the commands that came from the centers of power in an urban political landscape, but he could even suppose that he caused those commands to be made, in one way or another. It is suggested that the changes made in the centers of Annapolis and Baltimore provide part of the solution to understanding what the two cities have in common, based on hypothesizing that the voting citizen was a key element in their urban redesign.

There are several ways of conceptualizing the shift in urban design which occurred with the change in political structure at the end of British domination. Edmund Morgan (1975) and Rhys Isaac (1982) present the idea that the new power brokers of the Revolution put themselves in place after the British top of the pyramid was truncated. To maintain their new political position, members of the economic elite created and enabled institutions which protected their sources of power while investing other groups with a stake in maintaining the status quo. We propose that urban design reflects this balancing act as surely as the elite-protecting mechanisms built into the Constitution guarded the power of the entrenched through legislatively elected senators and the electoral college.

To extend this position, it is of value to consider the views of Jeremy Bentham (Dinwiddy 1989). Bentham was one of the foremost economic and political thinkers of the early 19th century. He was reacting to a changing polity which saw democratic ideas of freedom coming to the forefront at a time when social institutions to temper this freedom were transmuting from the previous hierarchical paradigm. Initially Bentham focused his attention on those in society who appeared to be ill-adapted. Bentham used the panopticon, or inspection institution, for all those citizens who were not well, or who were deviant. Foucault (1979) presents the case that any citizen, by definition, had a potential pathology within and thus all had to be kept under surveillance. This is not what Bentham saw, but it is what those who held traditional political power saw in Bentham and what, we hypothesize, was built in Baltimore.

We borrow the idea of panoptic power from Foucault who derived it directly from Jeremy Bentham. Foucault (1979:195-293) argues that the new republican federal states of the early 19th century, the United States and France, focused their attention on the capacity of the citizen to discipline himself by watching his thoughts, actions, habits, and duties. The self-disciplined, self-watching citizen was self-maintaining by using the norms of society and the laws of the state because each had voted for them, and saw himself and his welfare in them. Thus, the citizen kept himself and others like women, children, slaves, and immigrants in their place. This conception of citizenship, which is a conception of power, was enabled or aided by

FIGURE 3. A front view of the State House at Annapolis the Capital of Maryland from the *Columbian Magazine* (1789).

the use of panoptic or surveillance institutions. It is clear that in some circumstances, women were incorporated and in others they were excluded from citizenship and public life, as then seen. They clearly saw themselves as individuals and, as a result, they could have been subject to panopticism and other ways of absorbing them into subordinate positions (Ryan 1992, 1997; Davidson 1995; Kerber and DeHart 1995; Kerber, Kessler-Harris, and Sklar 1995).

In Annapolis after the Revolution, over a period of almost two decades (Radoff 1972:1-27), a new dome was built on the Maryland Statehouse and the road around it was leveled with the gullies filled in (Figure 3). There may have been other changes planned for the capital, but it is the new dome that occupies our attention and which occupied the capital. The dome was begun as a large version of the temple-like pavilions that form the focal points of so many 18th century formal gardens (Wright 1977:173). The one in the William Paca garden, which is rebuilt based on its image in Charles Willson Peale's portrait of Paca, is a convenient example. Such focal points were usually circular or octagonal and were meant to capture attention and hold it. The Statehouse dome may be a vastly enlarged version. On the other hand, the cupola on Bladen's Folly (Tatum 1977:175), now Macdowell Hall of St. John's College, while a reproduction, has a large octagonal base for a lantern and might also have served as a model for the current late-18th century dome on the

Capitol. The Annapolis dome, when finally executed, did not use the half hemisphere principle like the domes being built or planned for so many new capitol buildings, although one was planned and then modified (Radoff 1972:28). The dome has always been referred to as one. In the years between 1774 and 1798, the roof of the State House and its dome were constantly modified, the result being the placement of a dome on an unusually tall drum that presents the overall appearance of a tower. This is all apparent from both contemporary texts and pictures (Radoff 1972:1-27).

We present the possibility that the dome as built, and as currently seen, is a panopticon. This is a hypothesis based on our understanding of Jeremy Bentham's idea in the late 18th and early 19th century that was widely published and immensely popular. The panopticon was to be an instrument for social reform based on the belief that the individual could reform himself or herself as an isolated individual, when monitored instructions were provided. This principle of inspection was explicitly opposed to the use of violence as a form of control and reform. No literature has been found to suggest that a redesigned Statehouse dome was to serve such a panoptic purpose, so we rely on the dome's odd shape and the popularity of the panopticon as an idea for the plausibility of the hypothesis.

To facilitate the social aspect of reform, Bentham designed an eight-sided building covered by a domed or multi-hipped roof. Since he saw this building first as a jail, he placed the cells for solitary confinement all around the perimeter. These were back lit by windows and the doors all faced into the center where a warden was placed at a high desk that could face in all directions. The inmates were isolated from each other and were not supposed to infect each other with social diseases. In the isolation of the panopticon, each could be seen by the warden, under whose gaze each was to learn both how to behave properly and a task of economic value.

Bentham proposed the panopticon as a watchful institution that could be used for a large

Perspectives from *Historical Archaeology*

range of purposes. It became famous as a prison but was also built as a hospital, school, library, house, and for other diverse purposes. Conventional understandings would have us focus on the interaction between the prisoner who was shorn of his traditional bad company and his new superior who watched and taught.

The core of Bentham's idea was expressed in the 1780s as a "House of Correction" (Figure 4):

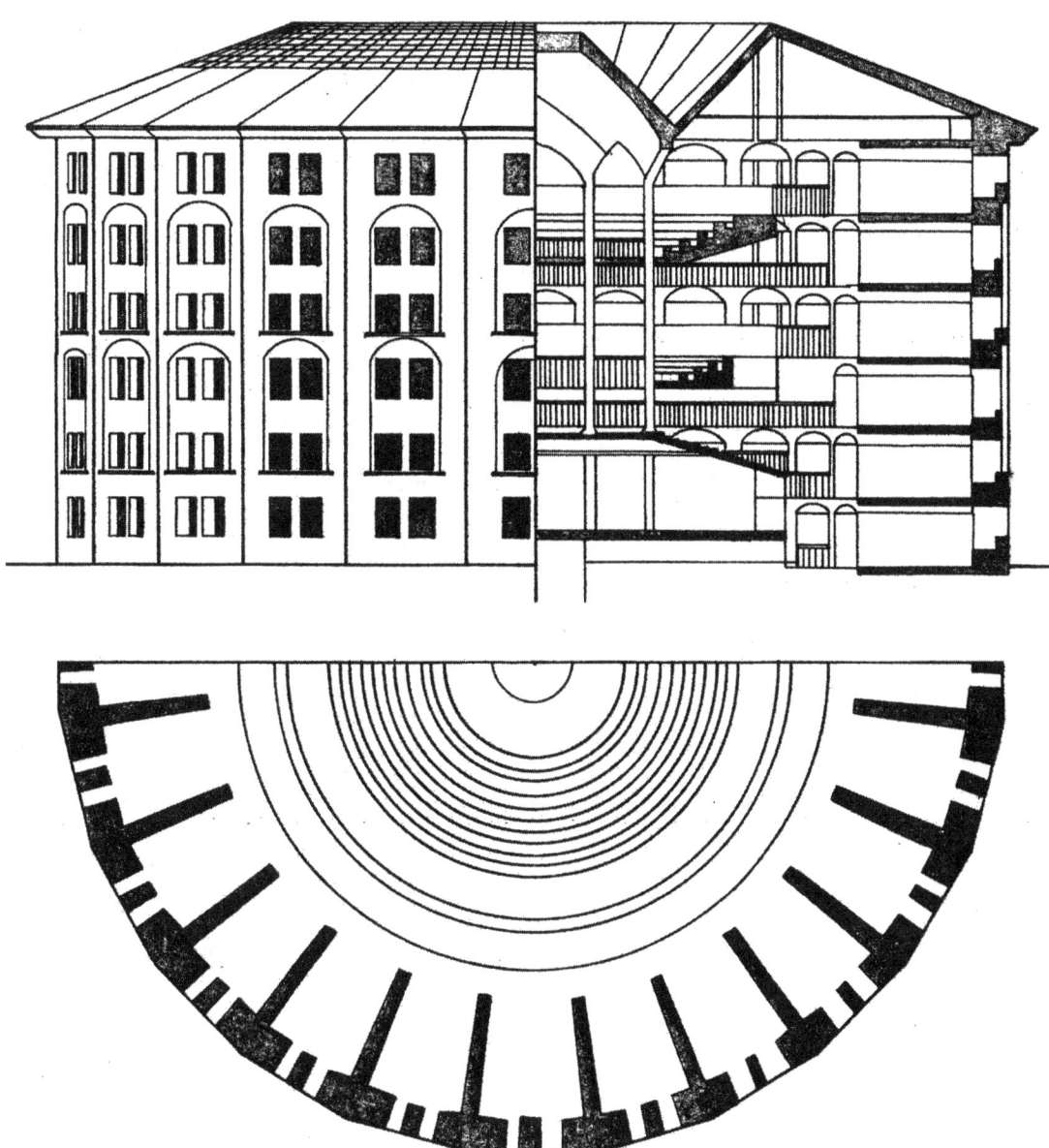

FIGURE 4. Bentham's Panopticon (drawing by Prashant Kaw).

It occurred to me, that the plan of a building, lately contrived by my brother, for purposes in some respects similar, and which, under the name of the Inspection House. . . . I look upon as capable of application of the most extensive nature. . . .

To say in one word, it will be found applicable . . . to all establishments whatsoever, in which, within a space not too large to be covered . . . a number of persons are meant to be kept under inspection. No matter how different, or even opposite the purpose: whether it be that of punishing the incorrigible, guarding the insane, reforming the vicious, confining the suspected, employing the idle, maintaining the helpless, curing the sick, instructing the willing in any branch of industry, or training the rising race in the path of education: in a word, whether it be applied to the purposes of perpetual prisons . . . or workhouses, or manufactories, or mad-houses, or hospitals, or schools.

It is obvious that, in all these instances, the more constantly the persons to be inspected are under the eyes of the persons who should inspect them. . . . Ideal perfection . . . would require that each person should actually be in that predicament, during every instant of time. This being impossible, the next thing to be wished for is, that, at every instant, seeing reason to believe as much, and not being able to satisfy himself to the contrary, he should conceive himself to be so.

Before you look at the plan, take in words the general idea of it. The building is circular. The apartments of the prisoners occupy the circumference. . . .

The cells are divided from one another and the prisoners by that means secluded from all communication with each other. . . . The apartment of the inspector occupies the center . . . the inspector's lodge . . . [has] a vacant space all around [it]. . . . Each cell has in the outward circumference, a window . . . not only to light the cell but . . . the . . . lodge. The inner circumference of the cell is formed by an iron grating, so light as not to screen any part of the cell from the inspector's view. . . . To cut off from each prisoner the view of every other. . . . The windows in the cells . . . should be as large as the strength of the building . . . will permit. To the windows of the lodge there are blinds, as high up as the eyes of the prisoners in their cells can . . . reach . . . small lamps, in the outside of each window of the lodge, backed by a reflector, to throw the light into the corresponding cells, would extend to the night the security of the day. . . . A small tin tube might reach from each cell to the inspector's lodge . . . by means of the implement, the slightest whisper of the one might be heard by the other. . . . And in the case of hospitals, the quiet that may be insured by this little contrivance . . . affords an additional advantage (Bowring 1962:40-41).

Bentham above points out that the relationship between the inmate and monitor is symbolic and imaginary. Necessary for the panopticon to work is the possibility of being watched, not the actual presence of a monitor. He argued that the possibility of being watched was enough for the inmate to observe the rules of behavior and to inculcate a self-watching or self-monitoring frame of mind. He argued that this was the basis for self-discipline among workers in industrial societies. Foucault (1979) makes the point that a citizen who learned self-watching is the base for power in the new republics.

Bentham, as quoted above, and Foucault (1979:195-228) point out that in panoptic institutions the individual is diagnosed as ill, but curable through the use of rational, not violent means. As a result, Foucault (1979:193) says that every healthy adult had within them a potentially criminal, childish, uneducated, or unhealthy element and, simultaneously, a corrigible, undeveloped, incomplete self. When combined, these elements meant that self-watching became preferable for most people, compared to the possibility of the perpetual gaze of the state's agents. Using this argument, a republic did not need an army or a big police force because the citizens policed themselves. They did so willingly, either because they could not stand the gaze and therefore internalized it so as to gain its approval, or because they became convinced that they elected the monitor.

Foucault's (1979) view of the panopticon as harshly manipulative, using raw power to control people, is pessimistic. Bentham's thesis, as quoted, argued for control mechanisms which were to be benevolent and which strove to improve the individual by affecting them to control themselves. Bentham is considered the father of the school of economics known as Utilitarianism. The basic premise of Utilitarians is "the greatest good for the greatest number." Positivism is the watchword of Utilitarians. Positivism and improvement often focus attention on those who are in the weakest and least protected situations, hence the focus on prisons and hospitals.

The Maryland Statehouse was rebuilt after the success of the Revolution. At one point it was both the temporary capitol of the United States and an aspirant to be the permanent United States capitol. The new dome was built under these circumstances and when it was built, no other changes were made to the surrounding street pattern, of which we are aware, except that State Circle was leveled which enhanced its capacity as a viewing platform and amphitheater for public spectacles. The dome/tower has eight sides and four ranks of windows, one above the other. It can be seen over the whole city by using the streets of the old baroque plan. The dome, if it is a panopticon, reversed the focus of attention from the previous form of the state house, and instead of being the focal point, became a mirror for each citizen. The citizen should then see the elected individuals beneath the dome as his representatives and thus as potentially interchangeable with himself. The purpose of the windowed tower was to hold and represent monitors. It was in fact open to the public for decades. The windows can be seen universally. Any citizen is visible from them, especially since the sides of five of the streets and the facades of the houses along them are on lines of sight that open up at the base of State Circle. We suggest that the new dome was an experimental panopticon and was built to watch over the whole city of new citizens. This would be a novel use of the panopticon, one on a grand scale, and we are not sure yet if this hypothesis is correct. It is sure, however, that the men running Maryland at the time were well enough read to have had such an idea.

The suggestion that the new dome on the Maryland Statehouse was a panopticon is offered for several reasons. First, the idea takes a unique and unclassified architectural expression and gives it an important architectural home by making it part of one of the most important social experiments of the revolutionary and Federal eras. Second, members of the Maryland elite were deeply involved with the conceptualization of space in social terms and were familiar with the need to find architectural expressions for the set of ideas they were promoting. Such men were intellectuals and were part of a group of Marylanders and others who were concerned with ways to make a new republic work. Annapolis and the new and fast-growing city of Baltimore were centers of this discussion and it is argued that the spaces they promoted and built were expressions of their social designs.

Baltimore

There are three principal buildings in Baltimore that we believe demonstrate an architectural effort to promote the panoptic design of life in the city in the first two decades of the 19th century. These structures include the first building of the University of Maryland's medical school, known as Davidge Hall, the Baltimore Exchange and

FIGURE 5. Medical College. First Building of the University of Maryland (Maryland Historical Society, Baltimore).

FIGURE 6. Mid 19th century photograph of Baltimore with the Washington Column (courtesy of the Library of Congress, Washington).

Customs House, and the first monument built anywhere to George Washington. The Exchange was demolished at the beginning of the 20th century but Davidge Hall (Figure 5) has been restored and the Washington Monument (Figure 6) stands, largely unchanged.

In parallel with this group of edifices are a number of other dominant buildings in Baltimore that share an architectural idiom with the panoptic buildings but whose panoptic characteristics vary. These buildings include a number of large churches built in a neoclassical style which dominated the skyline of early Baltimore. The Roman Catholic Cathedral of the Assumption, St. Paul's Episcopal Church, the Unitarian Church, and the First Baptist Church all use neoclassical design which focus upon a dome. One additional construction deserves special note. The

Battle Monument, built to commemorate Baltimore's victory over England in the "Second War of Independence," features classical devices in the form of a column made up of Roman fascia. Within this combined set of churches and panoptic buildings, all but the Battle Monument feature rotundas on the model of the pantheon. Most were built before Jefferson executed his design for a new university in Charlottesville.

The Baptist Church was demolished long ago and the interior of the Unitarian Church was also redesigned long ago. St. Paul's burned but the Roman Catholic Cathedral is still there, altered but not substantially harmed. Davidge Hall was built in 1812, the First Baptist Church in 1818, the Unitarian Church in 1817-1818, the Cathedral of the Assumption between 1808 and 1821, the Battle Monument was begun in 1815, and the

Perspectives from *Historical Archaeology*

Washington Monument constructed between 1815 and 1829. While Benjamin Latrobe designed the cathedral, his colleague Maximillian Godefroy was responsible for the Unitarian Church and Battle Monument. Robert Mills, an engineer and Latrobe's student, designed the Baptist Church and the Washington Monument. Robert Cary frequently modeled much of his work on Latrobe and is responsible for Davidge Hall of the University of Maryland Medical School and St. Paul's Episcopal Church (1812). Finally, the Exchange was a joint effort of Latrobe and Godefroy and was built at the end of the second decade of the 19th century.

The social circumstances revolving around the erection of the buildings show that Baltimore in the early 19th century was a rising mercantile center in the new nation's maritime trade. The city was incorporated in 1795, joining three separate communities which had developed in the 18th century. Each of these previous communities, Jonestown, Baltimore, and Fells Point, had focused on the water and navigation. Each had a haphazard plan which, when merged, created a riot of street angles which was only rationalized in the expanding city and not in the oldest cores (Power 1992, 1993). Baltimore's growth in the 19th century was precipitous. By 1820 it was the third largest city in the new nation, having surpassed Boston in population. This growth was driven by Baltimore's location where the fall line and navigable water almost coincide. Drawing on a rich hinterland, Baltimore's water powered mills ground the grain while the harbor was used to ship the products to the world.

Baltimore was a place that was self-conscious of its growing importance in the early national period. The first railroad in the United States ran west from Baltimore. In the 1840s the first telegraph linked Baltimore to Washington, D. C. The city was known as the "Monumental City" for its architectural gems (Beirne 1957:7). This title was bestowed by President John Quincy Adams, who used the phrase in a toast in 1827 (Dorsey and Dilts 1973:xx). There was, however, another side to Baltimore. The melting pot of immigrants from many nations often boiled over, earning Baltimore by 1830 her second sobriquet: "Mobtown" (Greenberg 1995:166). In this context of negotiating relationships between "haves" and "have nots" the panoptic constructs served the "haves"—how effectively we do not know. The city's elite often felt threatened by the consequence of democracy. The twin strains of controlling the rabble and improving the depressed often conflicted but sometimes blended. It is within this setting that the conscious use of neoclassical links to the past and the panopticon must be discussed.

An important aspect of these buildings is not solely who designed them, but for whom they were designed. Instead of promoting governmental power or the power of the individual, these buildings were generally constructed to aggrandize private institutions such as churches or for civic or economic good, as is the case with Davidge Hall and the Exchange, or for civic pride in the case of the monuments. The Roman Catholic cathedral is a case in point. After the Revolution, Catholics regained the franchise. Growing immigration from Europe led to a major increase in the Catholic population. As an institution, the Roman Catholic Church revitalized itself and created a monument in the form of the cathedral. Baltimore was the United States primacy, home of its first bishop, John Carroll, a member of the prominent Maryland family. After suppression under the colonial government, the church made a major architectural statement by placing this monumental structure on the Baltimore skyline. It advertised its commitment to the style associated with democracy.

The exterior of many of these buildings appears more or less the same, with a low Roman dome capping a rotunda which is either encased in a rectangle as with the cathedral and Unitarian Church, or has rounded sides exposed, as with the Baptist Church. There is usually a deep porch, pillared and pedimented. The interiors all have low-domed, circular rooms at the center with rows of seats, sometimes arranged in semicircles, all facing a focal point. From the few surviving interior pictures it is clear that the focal point of these buildings was an altar, pulpit, lectern, or operating table. The dome enables good acoustics, so hearing was easy in these buildings. Lighting was usually from large plain glass windows or indirect from windows around the dome so that reading and seeing were facilitated. These buildings were designed to facilitate communication, both spoken and unspoken, by using clear lines of sight and advanced acoustics.

The buildings mentioned here were sited in specific locations in Baltimore. They were placed because of a conception of the city. A geographer (Olsen 1985:42-43) has described the city:

> Buildings would express meanings and impose order. The most impressive were the great domes—the Catholic Cathedral, the Exchange, the Unitarian Church, Saint Paul's Episcopal Church, First Baptist, and that superb edifice, the Medical College. . . . For siting their monumental structures, the builders developed a new appreciation of the natural topography as a stage. Baltimoreans determined to build on a scale at once to rival and exploit its piedmont setting. The original site for a cathedral . . . was abandoned . . . in order to fix it upon a hill. The Washington Monument . . . was relocated on Howard's Hill. . . . The beautiful domed Medical College, founded by the doctors in the southwest, had a magnificent prospect of the Patapsco River. . . . The charter for the Medical College contained the concept of a state university. . . . Within walking distance was laid out the Lexington Market, also on a hill. Citizens were determined to create symbols in the center of the city as well. . . . Two blocks south and east [of the courthouse, War of 1812 Battle Monument, and the Masonic Hall], toward the waterfront, the merchants decided to build an Exchange, a collective palace that would outclass the country houses of the planter aristocracy. . . . The construction of the exchange was an attempt to create order, symmetry, and mass in the midst of a waterfront all disordered, bustle. . . . Symbolic of the curious mixture of great vision and grudging implementation was the practice of financing all these magnificent structures by lotteries and taking for granted their future operation as self-supporting.

The visual unity of the city was achieved through the strategic location of buildings—usually domed and placed upon natural high points.

They were visible from a distance but were not the focus of the street network in the way a baroque city was designed. Baltimore was a simple grid plan but with an impressive array of highly conspicuous monumental architecture. Its social unity was achieved through the functions of these new buildings. The most famous and most widely used architects, Latrobe, Mills, Godefroy, Cary, and Long, all knew and worked with each other. All were working with a similar architectural idiom based on neoclassical design. All created structures that were designed to be seen as focal points. By far the most famous of these architects was Benjamin Henry Latrobe.

Latrobe is widely considered one of the most significant architects and engineers of the early national period. He was responsible for a number of truly important structures, including a rationalized United States Capitol building. He designed canals, naval yards, and water works throughout the new United States. Latrobe had been trained in Europe and worked in England. There he "had the happiness to inherit from my father the friendship of the great Mr. Howard"(Hamlin 1995). John Howard was the foremost English prison reformer of the third quarter of the 18th century who "erected model cottages on his Cardington estate, provided elementary education for the village children, and encouraged the individual industry of the villagers" (Van Horne and Formwalt 1984:76:note 18). Latrobe specifically referred to his familiarity with John Howard's work as part of the basis for his ability to design a new panoptic prison for Virginia at Richmond (Figures 7-8).

John Howard was one of Bentham's heroes (Mack 1969:197) and Bentham was concerned with the revision of penal codes, prison management, and thus with prison architecture. Bentham's most prolific and influential period was from the 1770s to the 1820s. Latrobe was born and raised in England, educated in Germany where he learned engineering skills, then worked as an architect and engineer in London until he came to the United States in 1795. In Philadel-

FIGURE 7. Latrobe's Virginia Penitentiary, Richmond (Valentine Museum, Richmond, Virginia).

phia, where he lived and worked before coming to Washington and Baltimore, he was familiar with the Walnut Street Prison and its methods of reform (Van Horne 1986:285-290). The building and its methods are parallel to Bentham's and probably are very close to those of John Howard. It is plain from Latrobe's design for the Virginia penitentiary that he knew of all the work on prison reform, including Bentham's.

Prisoners were to make nails, shoes, cloth, barrels, clothes, and to saw marble. The goods supported the prison and were to be made from resources readily available locally and which would have a ready market. Prisoners were to work together under supervision where they could copy each other and compete against each other. With this training, "the great object of the penitentiary system must necessarily be to correct the habits of the prisoners. The man who for seven years or even for one year rises at the same hour, works the same length of time, eats and drinks the same moderate quantity without any variation, must necessarily acquire habits of industry and sobriety" (Van Horne 1986:287-288). This was written by Latrobe to Robert Mills in 1806. It comes from a man who knew Howard's work on English prisons, who knew of the reform prison in Philadelphia, who won the competition to build a new state prison in Richmond in 1797, and who worked in the midst of

Bentham's success (Van Horne 1986:289, note 4). Their unity is formed by the social principle behind the panopticon. Between 1789 and 1812 Bentham's "vision gradually encompassed all of

FIGURE 8. Cell in Latrobe's Prison (Valentine Museum, Richmond, Virginia).

FIGURE 9. Latrobe's Baltimore library; never built (Maryland Historical Society, Baltimore).

taining the status quo vis a vis their own power. Latrobe himself articulated many of these ideas in a letter he (Andrews 1925:672) wrote in 1806:

> Ever since the Revolution the internal state of the United States has been undergoing a regular and gradual change. That deference of rank which, without the existence of titles and nobility, grows out of the habits and prejudices of a people, was bequeathed to the Americans by the English manners and institutions which were established before the Revolution. These manners could not be suddenly altered, nor did the institutions of the country undergo any great or sudden change. After the adoption of the Federal constitution, the extension of the right of suffrage in all the States to the majority of all the adult male citizens, planted a germ which had gradually evolved and has thus spread actual and practical democracy and political equality over the whole union. . . . There is no doubt whatsoever but that this state of things in our country produces the greatest sum of happiness that perhaps any nation has ever enjoyed. Every man is independent.

The architectural idiom used by Latrobe and others to design these panoptic buildings was neoclassical. The emphasis was on democratic Greece and republican Rome. Many of the symbols and ideals derived from classical sources were adopted by the early American democrats. Latrobe himself self-consciously manipulated details to make his classicism more American. He used New World plants and New World images in the design for column capitals and interior decoration that served as New World symbols for the new individuals. The panopticon affected the citizen individual of the new republic through personal self-inspection and improvement because successful democracy required that the individual believe he was the power behind the state and thereby could maintain or change the status quo.

Latrobe and his peers may have translated Bentham's self-discipline through self-watching to a whole new city in a new republic. They clearly saw that the power of inspection was learned by being on display, by being seen (Figures 9-10). Of the buildings being discussed in Baltimore, only the operating theater has semicircular rows of seats which could facilitate mutual observation (Figure 11), although some of

England, then Europe, and the world" (Mack 1969:189).

We think Latrobe, Godefroy, Cary, Mills, and Long were affected by the same set of ideas which led Bentham to articulate his theory of panoptic control of the free individual. Bentham was reacting to a changing environment which saw the evaporation of traditional hierarchical control and the rise of individual rights and privileges. The new American experiment in democracy was the best articulated expression of this shift in power structures and institutions. The earliest internal stresses within the new nation concerned how to deal with power. Those who led the fight to overthrow English domination in the American Revolution included large numbers of individuals who had a vested interest in main-

the churches may also have had them when first built. In the circular operating theater, each student could be a focal point.

The Baltimore Exchange and Custom House had large elements of panoptic design in its conception. The dome was specifically designed to facilitate observation of ships coming into the harbor so that the commercial traders would have the best information about incoming goods. Catwalk promenades allowed easy viewing outward while the dome was visible throughout the main commercial area. Banks, the Federal Customs offices, and private enterprises all shared this space, observing and being observed.

This whole architectural environment helps explain the Washington Monument, built in the center of the new city (Figure 12). The 178 foot pillar, with a dome room at its base, had and has a statue of Washington on top. It was prominent in the 19th century, as opposed to today where it is hedged in on all sides by taller buildings. Washington is presented and invoked as an achieving citizen and founding father. He is above all, but part of all. He was elected because of his public achievements. He was a model, we argue, just as the elected legislators could be models and his monument was the analogue to the statehouse dome in Annapolis. He was meant to attract attention and one reason may have been so that each citizen could monitor himself and be like him. He was not a Roman god, even though he wore a toga; he was ordinary and the ordinary could make themselves like him. They could do this by using centers of learning, business, worship, work, and correction, and by walking under his gaze.

Did this range of panoptic devices work? That is, did the architectural infrastructure actually affect people? Did these structures and their placement actually impress people? A comprehensive answer to these questions is not possible at this time, but contemporary anecdotal sources seem to suggest some success. Frances Trollope wrote "Domestic Manners of the Americans" relating her travels in and impressions of the United States at the beginning of the second quarter of

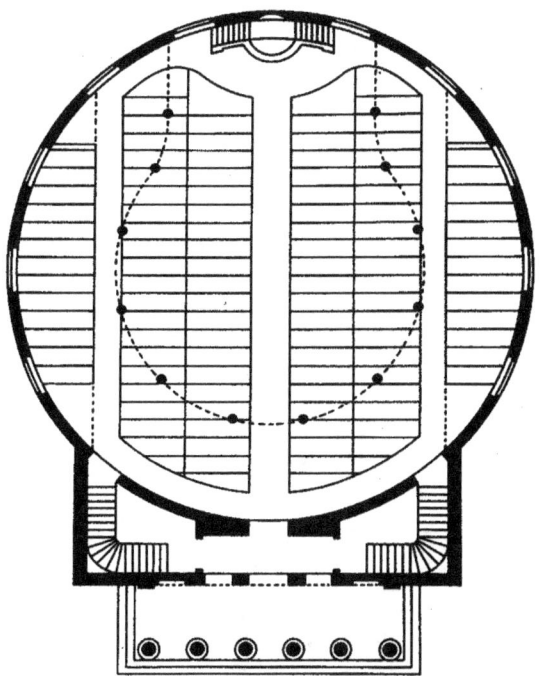

FIGURE 10. Robert Mill's plan of the first Baptist Church. Dotted line is the balcony and the supporting pillars (Maryland Historical Society, Baltimore).

the 19th century when she returned to her native England. Trollope was perhaps one of the greatest critics of the new Americans, describing the national character as "To doubt that talent and mental power of every kind exists in America would be absurd. . . . But in matters of taste and learning they are woefully deficient" (Trollope 1997[1832]:256). Trollope was no friend of these new Americans. Of Baltimore, however, she (Trollope 1997[1832]:155-156) wrote:

> Baltimore is, I think, one of the handsomest cities to approach in the Union. The Nobel column erected to the memory of Washington, and the Catholic Cathedral with its beautiful domes, being built upon a commanding eminence, are seen at a great distance. As you draw nearer, many other domes and towers become visible, and, as you enter Baltimore Street you feel you have arrived in a handsome and prosperous city.

Clearly Ms. Trollope was impressed and historians for years have noted that she was not an easy woman to impress. In her description she virtually inventories the very facets of Baltimore which we see as linked devices with panoptic overtones and notes how seeing these edifices effects the individual with a positive feeling.

If we left Bentham and the uses of him in the early 19th century United States untouched by Foucault, we would see the two men's theories with their architectural expressions as different and even antithetical. Foucault (1979) and, on a different basis, Morgan (1975) and Isaac (1982), see the power relations of the early American republic as little different from the colonial era. The rich who were out of power earlier were now the powerful and a hierarchy still existed but could be seen much less clearly because of the idea of representative government. These authors distinguish between what was said and believed on the one hand, from what was actually done on the other. They all saw a society and a government based on unevenly held wealth and power. Then they asked: How was such inequality kept in place?

Foucault (1979:195-228) argues that panoptic institutions enabled a citizenry to keep itself in its place and that place was subordinate to the locales of actual power. Those locales were factories, churches, schools, hospitals, prisons, commercial exchanges, banks, and legislative bodies. The mirrored gaze from these institutions oper-

FIGURE 11. Interior of Davidage Hall (Lane 1991:109).

ated on their inmates and on ordinary citizens who; because they were said to have, potentially, elements of childishness, criminality, ignorance, and illness within themselves; were no different, potentially, from those subject to more enforced instruction. The hierarchy of the panopticon as planned by Bentham was thus hidden in America by saying that the power of the monitor was derived from those monitored.

Cities and Seeing

Baroque and panoptic theories of power appear to be quite different from each other because the first is associated with monarchy and hierarchy, and the second with republican government. One commanded the subject, the other turned the subject into the citizen. One proclaimed the center to be the source of power, the other proclaimed that power in the center was a reflection of power spread throughout the state. These represent different theories of how the urban environment could be shaped and how vision is called into play to foster different senses of authority.

It can now be hypothesized that the archaeology of baroque town planning reveals non-parallel lines, slopes calculated to hide features, and graded distances. Such management was about illusions and appearances, not about efficiency or ease of recording. It was about building hierarchy when it was weak. Panoptic buildings used by the new republic have different material manifestations from those used in the baroque era. The range of these material manifestations has not been established. These may include clear glass, huge piers for domes, massive similarities in ceramics used to standardize the etiquette of worker citizens, and massive piles of similar pieces of debris from prison workshops and central clock, bell, and watch towers. Certainly the simple grid design was better suited to commercial activities and far more expressive of equality than baroque design.

Several archaeological evaluations on parts of turn-of-the-century Baltimore are available and

FIGURE 12. A bird's eye view of the city in mid-century (Maryland Historical Society, Baltimore).

show two patterns associated with big buildings from the period. Much work has been done on the commercial wharves of the city (Norman 1987) and has been summarized and a pattern established (Stevens 1989). Wharves were the foundations built to hold superstructures and moor ships. They were built on unstable conditions and had to hold enormous weight and also contain great stress. American wharves, however, did not have to withstand the same stress as those in England because the tidal changes were not as abrupt. Similar conditions of weight and stress faced the architects of the large domed buildings discussed above. The cribs for wharves were made of wood or stone, built on pilings, and fixed with tar (Norman 1987:98-117). Norman tells us their quality varied depending on the amount available to be invested, not on the importance or weight of what they were to hold. On the one hand, the wharves show that the technology was available to hold great weight and stress, but the use of the technology was situational, depending on finances. Did these conditions apply to panoptic structures built simultaneously?

The second pattern concerns street layout and parks. There is a good deal of information on the reconfiguration, redesign, and reuse of streets in Baltimore, both their layout and look (Figure 13). There is also information on the redesigns of the enormous landscape of the nearby Charles Carroll, Barrister, mansion (Eastern Team 1987). Street patterns were dynamic. They were extended, widened, closed, enclosed, and constantly rationalized (Weeks 1988:11-21; 1989). No one has yet considered whether that planning and building included panoptic considerations.

The bridging of the baroque and panoptic theories of power relies on the commonality of affecting people by use of sight design. The effects, to aggrandize hierarchy or to co-opt individuals into believing they had a stake in the status quo, were quite different but are both ways of maintaining a stasis in societies that are in flux. Both applications of power come from above and are both aimed at impressing and manipulating. The drive to control evolves down from the absolute government, to individuals, and then to institutions which affected society and its distribution of political and personal power. In-

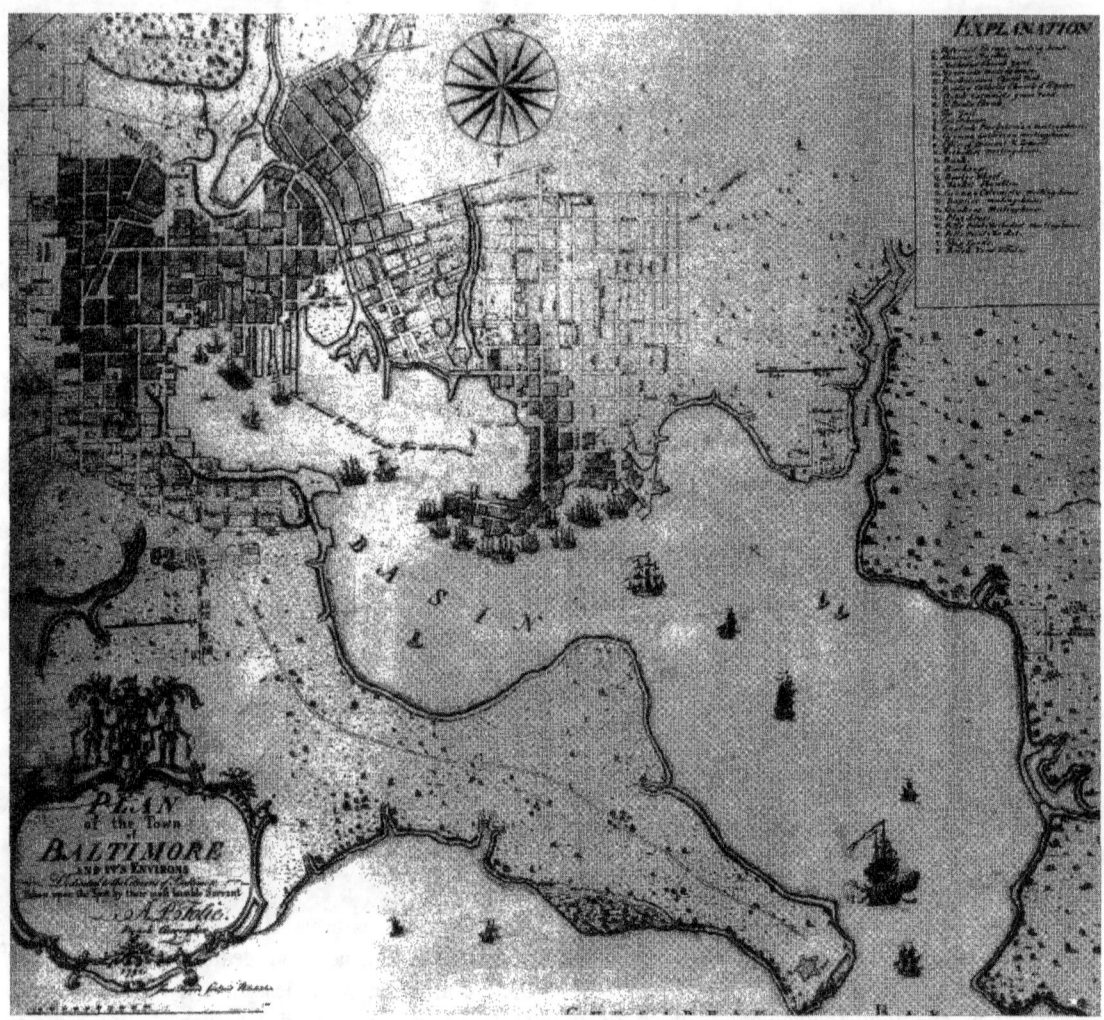

FIGURE 13. Baltimore and its environs in 1792 (Maryland Historical Society, Baltimore).

Perspectives from *Historical Archaeology*

dividuals were constantly being made to look a certain way and focus on a certain thing and thereby see what each was supposed to see.

Cities are among the most complex human creations and can be studied in many different ways. This essay presents one approach whereby the design of the city is linked to concepts of power. It is not the only viewpoint but does represent a means of explaining the differences between Maryland's chief urban settings over a period of more than two centuries of dramatic change. The sense of sight is a key element in this shaping of urban space and it is a tool in the establishment and maintenance of power. By analyzing a city as a large, multifaceted artifact, historical archaeologists can go beyond simple attributions of cultural influence or economic functionalism and gain a more nuanced perspective on cities as dynamic entities that both shape and reify human relations.

ACKNOWLEDGMENTS

Leone developed some of the research presented here regarding Annapolis and Baltimore in the *American Anthropologist* (97:2:251-268, June 1995). Elizabeth Anderson Comer read an earlier version of this piece and suggested an array of site reports and analyses on Baltimore, produced largely through the work of the Baltimore Center for Urban Archaeology. Henry Miller of Historic St. Mary's City was an early contributor to this study and his assistance and insights are greatly appreciated. Linda Konski and Kathryn Schaffer prepared the manuscript. Christopher Gordon organized all of the photgraphs. We also acknowledge help from anonymous reviews on the conditions effecting English and American wharves, the place of movement in baroque urban design, and the place of women in panoptic conditions and definitions of citizenship.

REFERENCES

ANDREWS, MATTHEW PAGE
1925 *Tercentenary History of Maryland.* S. J. Clarke, Chicago.

BAKER, NANCY T.
1986 Annapolis, Maryland 1695-1730. *Maryland Historical Magazine* 81(3):191-206.

BEIRNE, FRANCIS F.
1957 *Baltimore: A Picture History.* Hasting House, New York.

BOWRING, JOHN (EDITOR)
1962 *The Works of Jeremy Bentham,* Vol.4. Russell and Russell, New York.

BRAUDEL, FERNAND
1979 *The Wheels of Commerce: Civilization and Capitalism, 15th-18th Century.* Harber and Row, New York.

BRAY, WILLIAM (EDITOR)
1886 *Diary and Correspondence of John Evelyn, F.R.S.A.* George Bell & Sons, London.

CARR, LOIS GREEN
1974 The Metropolis of Maryland: A Comment on Town Development Along the Tobacco Coast. *Maryland Historical Magazine* 69(2):124-145.

COLUMBIAN MAGAZINE
1789 *Columbian Magazine,* February. MSA SC 194, Maryland State Archives, Annapolis, MO.

DAVIDSON, CATHY N.
1995 *Subjects and Citizens: Nation, Race, and Gender from Oroonoko to Anita Hill.* Duke University Press, Durham, NC.

DEETZ, JAMES
1977 *In Small Things Forgotten: The Archaeology of Early American Life.* Anchor Press/Doubleday, Garden City, NY.

DINWIDDY, JOHN
1989 *Bentham.* Oxford University Press, Oxford, England.

DORSEY, JOHN, AND JAMES D. DILTS
1973 *A Guide to Baltimore Architecture.* Tidewater Publishers, Cambridge, MD.

EASTERN TEAM OF THE DENVER SERVICE CENTER
1987 *Mount Clare Restoration, Master Plan.* Denver Service Center, National Park Service, Washington.

FORMAN, HENRY CHANDLEE
1938 *Jamestown and St. Mary's: Buried Cities of Romance.* Johns Hopkins Press, Baltimore, MD.
1956 *Tidewater Maryland Architecture and Gardens.* Bonanza Books, New York.

FOUCAULT, MICHEL
1979 *Discipline and Punish.* Random House, New York.

GREENBURG, AMY SOPHIA
    1995   Mayhem in Mobtown: Firefighting in Antebellum Baltimore. *Maryland Historical Magazine* 90(2):165-180.

HAMLIN, TALBOT
    1955   *Benjamin Henry Latrobe*. Oxford University Press, Oxford, England.

HANDLER, RICHARD, AND WILLIAM SAXTON
    1988   Dyssimulation: Reflexivity, Narrative, and the Quest for Authenticity in 'Living History.' *Cultural Anthropology* 3:242-265.

HEITE, EDWARD F.
    1966   Markets and Ports. *Virginia Cavalcade* 16(2)9-41.

HOHENBERG, PAUL M., AND LYNN H. LEES
    1985   *The Making of Urban Europe 1000-1950*. Harvard University Press, Cambridge, MA.

HOPKINS, J.W., III
    1984   *A Map of the Ridout Garden, Annapolis, Maryland*. Historic Annapolis Foundation, Annapolis, MD.

ISAAC, RHYS
    1982   *The Transformation of Virginia 1740-1790*. University of North Carolina Press, Chapel Hill.

KERBER, LINDA K., AND JANE SHERRON DeHART (EDITORS)
    1995   *Women's America: Refocussing the Past*. Oxford University Press, Oxford, England.

KERBER, LINDA K., ALICE KESSLER-HARRIS, AND KATHRYN KISH SKLAR (EDITORS)
    1995   *U.S. History as Women's History: New Feminist Essays*. University of North Carolina Press, Chapel Hill.

KRYDER-REID, ELIZABETH
    1991   *Landscape as Myth: The Contextual Archaeology of an Annapolis Landscape*. Ph.D. dissertation, Brown University, Department of Anthropology. University Microfilms International, Ann Arbor.

LANE, MILLS
    1991   *Architecture of the Old South: Maryland*. Abbeyville, New York.

LANGLEY, BATTY
    1726   *New Principles of Gardening*. Bettsworth and Batley, London.

LEONE, MARK P.
    1984   Interpreting Ideology in Historical Archaeology: Using the Rules of Perspective in the William Paca Garden in Annapolis, Maryland. In *Ideology, Representation, and Power in Prehistory*, edited by Christopher Tilley and Daniel Miller, pp. 25-35. Cambridge University Press, Cambridge, England.
    1987   Rule by Ostentation: The Relationship Between Space and Sight in Eighteenth Century Landscape Architecture in the Chesapeake Region of Maryland. In *Method and Theory for Activity Area Research: An Ethnoarchaeological Approach*, edited by Susan Kent, pp. 604-633. Columbia University Press, New York.

LEONE, MARK P., AND PAUL A. SHACKEL
    1990   Plane and Solid Geometry in Colonial Gardens in Annapolis, Maryland. In *Earth Patterns*, edited by William Kelso and Rachel Most, pp. 153-167. University of Virginia Press, Charlottesville.

LEONE, MARK P., JENNIFER STABLER, AND ANNA-MARIE BURLAGA
    1998   A Street Plan for Hierarchy in Annapolis: An Analysis of State Circle a Geometric Form, In *Annapolis Pasts*, edited by Paul Shackel, Paul Mullins, and Mark Warner, pp. 291-306. University of Tennessee Press, Knoxville.

LITTLE, GLEN, II
    1967-   Re: Archaeological Research on Paca Garden.
    1968   8 November 1967, 24 May 1968. Manuscript letters, Historic Annapolis Foundation, Garden Visitors' Center, Annapolis, MD.

LUCAS, THOMAS M. (EDITOR)
    1990   *Saint, Site, and Sacred Srategy: Ignatius, Rome and Jesuit Urbanism: Catalogue of the Exhibition*. Biblioteca Apostolica Vaticana, Rome

LYNCH, KEVIN
    1981   *A Theory of Good City Form*. M.I.T. Press, Cambridge, MA.

MACK, MARY PETER (EDITOR)
    1969   *A Bentham Reader*. Pegasus, New York.

MATTHEWS, CHRISTOPHER
    1996   'It is Quietly Chaotic. It Confuses Time.' *Final Report of Excavations at the Bordley-Randall Site in Annapolis, Maryland, 1993-1995*. Historic Annapolis Foundation, Annapolis, MD.

MILLER, HENRY M.
    1986   Discovering Maryland's First City: A Summary Report on the 1981-1984 Archaeological Excavations in St. Mary's City, Maryland. *St. Mary's City Archaeology Series* No. 2. St. Mary's City, MD.
    1988   Baroque Cities in the Wilderness: Archaeology and Urban Development in the Colonial Chesapeake. *Historical Archaeology* 22(2)57-73.

MORGAN, EDMUND S.
   1975   *American Slavery, American Freedom.* W. W. Norton, New York.

MUMFORD, LEWIS
   1961   *The City in History: Its Origins, Its Transformations and Its Projects.* Harcourt Brace Jovanovich, New York.

NORMAN, JOSEPH GARY
   1987   *Eighteenth-Century Wharf Construction in Baltimore, Maryland.* MA thesis, Department of Anthropology, College of William and Mary, Williamsburg, VA.

OLSEN, SHERRY H.
   1985   *Baltimore, the Building of an American City.* Johns Hopkins University Press, Baltimore, MD.

ORR, KENNETH G., AND RONALD G. ORR
   1975   The Archaeological Situation at the William Paca Garden, Annapolis, Maryland: The Spring House and the Presumed Pavilion House Site. Manuscript, Historic Annapolis Foundation, Garden Visitors' Center, Annapolis, MD.

PACA-STEELE, BARBARA, AND A. ST. CLAIRE WRIGHT
   1987   The Mathematics of an Eighteenth-Century Wilderness Garden. *Journal of Garden History* 6(4)299-320.

POGUE, DENNIS J.
   1985   Calverton, Calvert County, Maryland: 1668-1725. *Maryland Historical Magazine* 80(4):271-276.

POWELL, B. BRUCE
   1966   Archaeological Investigation of the Paca House Garden, Annapolis, Maryland. Manuscript, Historic Annapolis Foundation, Garden Visitors' Center, Annapolis, MD.

POWER, GARRETT
   1992   Parceling Out Land in the Vicinity of Baltimore: 1632-1796, Part 1. *Maryland Historical Magazine* 87(4):453-466.
   1993   Parceling Out Land in the Vicinity of Baltimore: 1632-1796, Part 2. *Maryland Historical Magazine* 88(2):151-180.

RADOFF, MORRIS L.
   1972   The State House at Annapolis. *Publication* No. 17. The Hall of Records Commission, Department of General Services, Annapolis, MD.

RAINBOLT, JOHN C.
   1972   The Absence of Towns in Seventeenth-Century Virginia. In *Cities in American History*, edited by Kenneth T. Jackson and Stanley K. Schultz, pp. 50-65. Alfred A. Knopf, New York.

READ, ESTHER DOYLE
   1990   *Archaeological Investigations Around State Circle in Annapolis, Maryland.* Historic Annapolis Foundation, Annapolis, MD.

REPS, JOHN
   1965   *The Making of Urban America.* Princeton University Press, Princeton, NJ.
   1972   *Tidewater Towns.* Colonial Williamsburg Foundation, Williamsburg, VA.

RIORDAN, TIMOTHY B., SILAS D. HURRY, AND HENRY M. MILLER
   1995   *"A Good Brick Chappell" The Archaeology of the c. 1667 Catholic Chapel at St. Mary's City.* Manuscript, Historic St. Mary's City, St. Mary's City, MD.

ROULETTE, BILLY RAY AND EILEEN WILLIAMS
   1986   *A Topographic Map of the Charles Carroll of Carrollton Garden, 1771.* Historic Annapolis Foundation, Annapolis, MD.

ROWE, JOHN
   1966   The Renaissance Foundations of Anthropology. *American Anthropologist* 67(1)1-20.

RYAN, MARY P.
   1992   *Women in Public: Between Banners and Ballots, 1825-1880.* Johns Hopkins University Press, Baltimore, MD.
   1997   *Civic Wars: Democracy and Public Life in the American City During the Nineteenth Century.* University of California Press, Berkeley.

SOUTH, STANLEY
   1967   *The Paca House, Annapolis, Maryland.* Manuscript, Historic Annapolis Foundation, Annapolis, MD.

SPRUILL, JULIA CHERRY
   1934   Mistress Margaret Brent, Spinster. *Maryland Historical Magazine* 29(4):259-268.

STEVENS, KRISTEN L.
   1989   An Investigation of the Archaeological Resources Associated with the Brown's Wharf Site (18 BC 59) on Thames Street, Baltimore, Maryland. *Baltimore Center for Urban Archaeology, Research Series* No. 28. Baltimore, MD.

STONE, GARRY WHEELER
   1974   St. John's: Archaeological Questions and Answers. *Maryland Historical Magazine* 69(2):146-168.

TATUM, GEORGE B.
   1977   Great Houses from the Golden Age of Annapolis. *Antiques* January and February:174-185.

TROLLOPE, FRANCES
  1997 *Domestic Manners of the Americans.* Reprint of 1832 edition. Penguin Classics, London.

VAN HORNE, JOHN.
  1986 *The Correspondence and Miscellaneous Papers of Benjamin Henry Latrobe*, Volume 2, 1805-1810. Yale University Press, New Haven, CT.

VAN HORNE, JOHN, AND LEE W. FORMWALT (EDITORS)
  1984 *The Correspondence and Miscellaneous Papers of Benjamin Henry Latrobe*, Volume 1, 1784-1804. Yale University Press, New Haven, CT.

WEEKS, BARBARA K.
  1988 An Archival Investigation of the Archaeological Resources Associated with the American National Plaza, Boston and Hudson Streets, Baltimore, Maryland, 18 BC 56. *Baltimore Center for Urban Archaeology, Research Series* No. 27. Baltimore, MD.

  1989 An Investigation of the Archaeological Resources Associated with Sons of Italy/Columbus Plaza Development Project on Eastern Avenue and Jones Falls Boulevard, Baltimore, Maryland. *Baltimore Center for Urban Archaeology, Research Series* No. 31. Baltimore. MD.

WRIGHT, ST. CLAIR
  1977 The Paca House Garden Restored. *Antiques* January and February 172-173.

ZUCKER, PAUL
  1959 *Town and Square.* Columbia University Press, New York.

MARK P. LEONE
DEPARTMENT OF ANTHROPOLOGY
UNIVERSITY OF MARYLAND
COLLEGE PARK, MD 20742-7415

SILAS D. HURRY
HISTORIC ST. MARY'S CITY
ST. MARY'S CITY, MD 20686

Michael Given

Mining Landscapes and Colonial Rule in Early-Twentieth-Century Cyprus

ABSTRACT

In the early 20th century the large-scale copper and asbestos mines of Cyprus were intimately associated with colonial rule, both in their ideologies and in their actual operations. For the Cypriot miners, this represented a major disruption of long-standing values and required a new negotiation of their relationship with their British colonizers. Attempts to control mining landscapes and communities interplayed with a range of actions from submission to everyday resistance to strikes and riots. These dynamics are most clearly seen by examining the entire landscape. Particularly revealing aspects include the naming of mining landscapes, the surveillance of miners, the complex relationship between mining and agriculture, the actual and symbolic manipulation of artifacts, the expression of control and resistance in miners' housing, and shifting concepts of community.

Introduction

On 26 April 1929, a motor lorry driver for the Cyprus Asbestos Company stopped in the village of Kato Amiandos, on his way up to the mine. A woman gave him a bundle of cloth and requested him to take it to her husband, Stylli Hadji Ktori, who worked in the mine. He agreed and continued on his way up the mountain road. At the entrance to the territory controlled by the mining company, he was stopped by a mine official, distinguished by the cloth badge on his arm:

> He asked me if I had bread in my car. I said "no." He said that he would search my car. I said that he could search and when he searched he seized the bundle which was given to me by the wife of Stylli Hji Ktori saying that it contained 3 loaves of bread (Cyprus State Archives SA 1/909/1929, Red 14).

As Stylli Hadji Ktori knew very well, the Cyprus Asbestos Company refused to allow its employees to bring their own bread into the mine. Instead they had to buy the expensive bread made on the premises using flour imported from abroad. As this story shows, the Amiandos asbestos mine (Figure 1) and the other mines of early-20th-century Cyprus formed autonomous territories with their own border points, regulations, and economies. When the British colonial government heard about the bread incident, they were concerned that the mine was becoming an "*imperium in imperio*," and began a series of investigations (SA1/909/1929, Red 4).

"An empire within an empire" is precisely what the mines were. With their carefully regulated and orchestrated activities where each mine worker had a precisely defined role, with their paternalistic institutions such as benevolent societies and model workers' housing and clubhouses, and with their absolute control over a landscape dedicated to their own profit, the mining companies were modeled on colonial rule. They even became "models for" colonial rule, expressing the ideal of a perfectly regulated but paternalistic state. As with major state building projects, where the antlike activity of thousands of workers symbolizes the state's control of society (Paynter and McGuire 1991:9), so here does the mining landscape with its highly controlled processes and social organization reflect the ideal of colonial rule.

The investigation focused on the intimate relationship between the organization of mining landscapes and the mechanics of colonial rule. The open cast and underground copper and asbestos mines of the 1920s and 1930s in Cyprus provide a wealth of material, documentary, and oral information, and the political conditions of the time brought the imperialist organization of the mines into public debate—as Hadji Ktori succeeded in doing following the confiscation of his bread.

Methodology

The main historical sources in this paper consist of government correspondence preserved in the Cyprus State Archives in Nicosia and oral history data from informants in the former mining village of Mitsero and elsewhere.

FIGURE 1. Pano Amiandos Mine from the northeast.

Archaeological data come from the examination of mines and mining structures in Amiandos and Mitsero and from the Sydney Cyprus Survey Project, a multiperiod interdisciplinary archaeological survey project working in the copper ore zone in the Northern Troodos Mountains (Given and Knapp 2003).

The approach to this material is mostly based on historical archaeology and landscape archaeology. Historical archaeology, as practiced in North America and Australia, is a very recent discipline in the Mediterranean context. It undertakes both detailed examination of historical data and a fully contextual analysis of material culture. The history of mining in Cyprus has been discussed from perspectives that are technical (Bear 1963), descriptive (Lavender 1962), or political (Georghallides 1985:327–328). Historical archaeology adds a perspective that does not rely on the rhetoric of government reports or political pamphlets, or on the impersonal statistics of colonial bureaucracies. In particular, the examination of the role of artifacts, structures, and landscapes in social relations throws light on modes of domination and resistance not otherwise apparent (Paynter and McGuire 1991:13–19).

Landscape archaeology examines the organization of human activities in their full landscape context, rather than looking at particular activities or sites in isolation. An important refinement on this perspective is that different social groups have different perceptions of the landscape and different systems of organization within it. Particularly relevant for a study of 20th-century mining is the investigation not only of social and economic landscapes, such as settlement patterns and trade routes, but also of conceptual and ideational landscapes. This last includes communal or political associations that different groups may have with a landscape. With the mining landscapes of early-20th-century Cyprus, as has been recognized for prehistoric landscapes, it is impossible to separate the two categories (Knapp and Ashmore 1999:15). The social, economic, and ideational associations of the mining landscapes of early-20th-century Cyprus became so intense that they often verged on the ideological, carrying a much more explicit and unified set of associations (Knapp and Ashmore 1999:13).

Perspectives from *Historical Archaeology*

Rather than describing and analyzing each mining operation one by one, the actual operation of control and resistance in a mining landscape is highlighted by discussing a series of mechanisms (here italicized). A mining landscape needed to be defined and *named* before it could operate as an entity. Once officially in existence, it had to be organized to allow proper *surveillance*. Because of the long rural tradition of Cyprus and the need to feed so many workers, there was a complex relationship with *agriculture*. Both domination and, more subtly, resistance were often expressed in the actual and symbolic manipulation of *artifacts*. The ideological imposition of control and order—and resistance to it—was often carried out by means of *architecture*. On a broader scale, this was done by means of shaping and manipulating the whole *community*.

Historical Background

Following the Congress of Berlin in 1878 the British took over the administration of Cyprus from the Ottoman Empire. Outright possession was not confirmed until 1914, when Britain formally annexed the island, and 1925, when it

was declared a Crown Colony. Until 1927 this anomalous position included the payment of a heavy "tribute" to the Ottoman Empire raised from local taxes, which left very little to invest in the development of the island (Georghallides 1985:41–52). The economy of Cyprus during this period was very much based on agriculture. At the beginning of British rule six out of seven Cypriots were village dwellers, almost all of them smallholders relying on small-scale agriculture to feed their families, pay taxes (much of which went to the Ottoman "tribute"), and escape the twin evils of drought and debt (Katsiaounis 1996:99–109).

Because of historical records, the existence of copper ore was known from the beginning of British rule, and there were various half-hearted attempts at exploitation during the 1880s, particularly in the northwest of the island (Wood 1887:52; Lavender 1962:50). In 1912 the prospector Godfrey Gunther arrived on the island. Within a year he had bought land at the ancient copper mines of Skouriotissa (Figure 2) and was drilling systematically. The Cyprus Mines Corporation was launched in New York in 1916. After a series of financial difficulties, Gunther committed himself in 1920

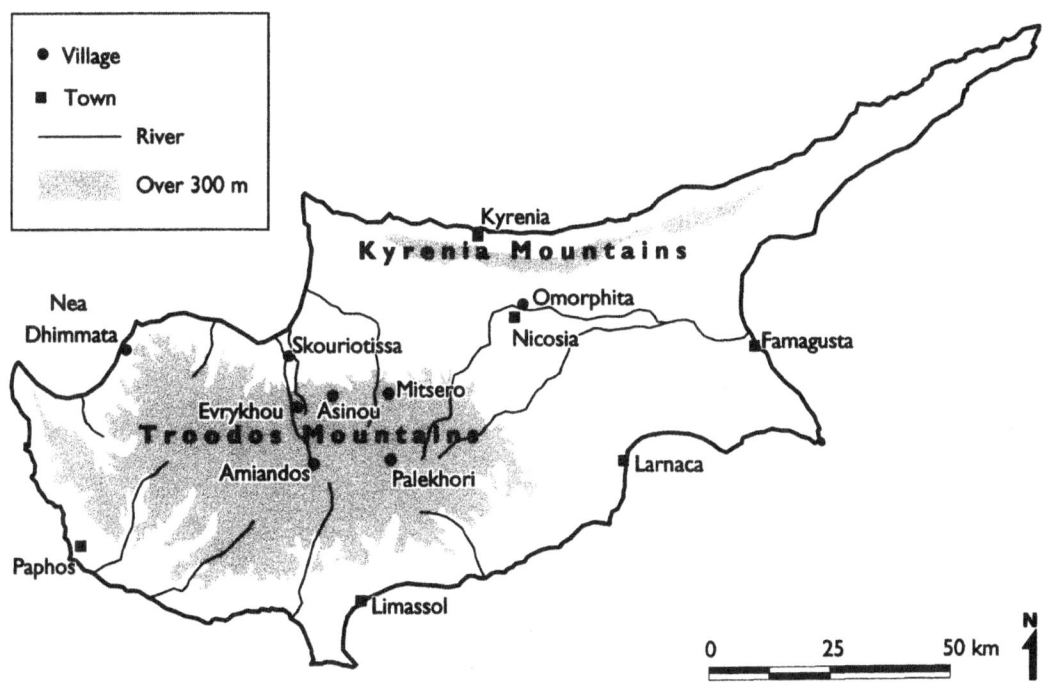

FIGURE 2. Map of Cyprus, with places mentioned in the text.

to producing 10,000 tons of pyrites in the first year of production (Lavender 1962:104,118). Other copper mines took longer to develop. At Mitsero and Agrokipia, for example, prospecting in 1936 was followed by the extraction of gold and silver, and after the foundation of the Hellenic Mining Company in 1948, large-scale pyrites extraction only took place in the 1950s (Bear 1963:30,67,70).

The development of asbestos mining began a little earlier than that of copper but followed essentially the same path. In 1904 a Limassol dentist-cum-entrepreneur named Cesar Trombetta extracted a sample from the deposits above the village of Amiandos, which itself means "asbestos" (SA1/3025/1904). In 1907 the government granted various concessions. In 1908 the Cyprus Mining Company founded an asbestos extraction, crushing, and cleaning establishment at Amiandos (SA1/1766/1907). Production and employment increased at a considerable rate, especially after World War I. In 1922 the company was bought up by the Cyprus Asbestos Company Ltd. By 1927 it owned eight separate crushing mills and 25 miles of light railway, with an aerial cable that took 2 hours 50 minutes to transfer the asbestos to the port at Limassol. The projected annual production for that year was 12,000 tons. In the winter 1,200 workers were employed and 6,000 in summer (SA1/1195/1927, Red 192).

The rise of the copper and asbestos mining industries in the 1910s, with their labor-intensive methods such as crushing ore by hand, coincided with the pressing need of poor or landless peasants to find alternative means of employment. Workforces increased dramatically during the 1920s, peaking in 1929, just before the industry was hit by the depression. This was also a period that saw a considerable increase in British attempts to control the population of Cyprus, using education and ideology as much as political or military means (Given 1997: 69–72; 1998:12–15). The mining landscapes of this critical period were just one component of the new ideological struggle for control over the Cypriot landscape and population.

Naming

By the 1920s Cypriot villages had a long historical tradition behind them. Even though some had been abandoned, particularly in the 17th century, the sites and names of the surviving ones generally went back at least to the 16th century and often before, as can be seen from historical village lists (Grivaud 1998: 445–472) and from the results of archaeological survey (Given and Gregory 2003:292–293). The needs of Ottoman and British administration divided up the entire landscape into districts, subdistricts, and village territories: every part of the landscape was defined and named.

The onset of large-scale mining in the 1910s and 1920s saw a new type of exploitation of the landscape with new divisions and settlements that did not coincide with the old village territories. As with the European colonies of 19th-century Africa, new entities were carved out with boundaries that had no respect for local organization or segmentation. A mining landscape, then, was a colonial creation with its boundaries, name, and identity imposed by the colonizers of the land. In this respect it was a model *of* the colony, as it followed the same system, and also a model *for* the colony because it illustrated the principle clearly in a limited and manageable area.

As Gunther's copper mining landscape developed, with its hut settlements, overseers' houses, workshops, mines, and railway, the colonial government realized that in administrative terms it was an anomaly. In particular, the area of the mining operations fell within the territories of three different villages and a monastery. In 1929, therefore, a characteristically drawn-out process was begun to provide this landscape with a named identity and an official existence. The Commissioner of Nicosia, Charles Hart-Davis, drew attention to policing problems and stressed that it was important to police the entire landscape, not just the settlement:

> The proposal to create a village here was intended primarily to meet police requirements. Disturbances, accidents, & incidents involving police action generally are far more likely to arise in the mines themselves and especially in the workshops than in the hutments. [Another reason was] to have one village authority, Moslem & Christian, responsible for the entire area so that there may be no uncertainty in what authority's area any disturbance, accident or other incident actually occurred (SA1/844/1929, Minute 35).

A further problem was the lack of a name, as Hart-Davis commented: "I am unable to suggest any name by which the area referred to ... was commonly known. I don't think it had any common name" (SA1/844/1929, Minute 35). The first suggestion was to call it Gunther's Village, on the grounds that it was "a name in common use among the villagers, perpetuating the memory of the discoverer of the mine and the founder of the village" (SA1/844/1929, Red 5). When the government realized that it had to provide a name for the whole of the mining landscape, rather than just the settlement as had originally been suggested, they chose Skouriotissa, the name of the local disused monastery that had become the headquarters of the mining operation.

A map was produced with a red line defining the new territory, land was taken from the surrounding villages to give to the new entity, and on 24 February 1931, a proclamation declared Skouriotissa a full village, with three village authorities (SA1/844/1929, Red 16). The mining landscape had been named, defined, and inscribed into the ledgers of imperial control.

Surveillance

One way of interpreting a landscape as experienced by people is as a complex web of lines of sight. When there are relationships between the people in that landscape, especially relationships of unequal power or status, these lines of sight become a medium for the playing out of those relationships. Surveillance is the key to control. Attention is particularly focused at important entrances into the mining landscape, such as the checkpoint where Stylli Hadji Ktori's bread was confiscated. The cloth badge to distinguish the mines official and the systematic searching of private possessions emphasize to all employees that they are very much under surveillance. Watchtowers, peepholes, and security cameras—the means of surveillance—can be as intimidating as the highest of walls.

Surveillance can also be carried out by means of the positioning of structures and activity areas across the landscape. In the coffee plantations of early-19th-century Jamaica, for example, the overseers' houses were carefully located to have views over the slave village and the coffee drying areas. The houses were equipped with verandas and balconies to maximize the field of view (Delle 1999:151–153). A

more extreme example can be seen in Michel Foucault's famous analysis of Bentham's *panoptikon*, where each inmate of an institution is isolated in a cell but overlooked by a watchtower in the center of the ring-shaped building (Foucault 1977:200–204).

This system, albeit not so elaborate, was certainly favored by the colonial government of Cyprus. In the 1910s and 1920s, the government built a series of village police stations according to a standard plan. This plan showed a building that was unusually high in proportion to its ground plan, with an upper story and a prominent balcony. Characteristically these police stations were situated a little outside the village, controlling the main approaches and with a view from their balconies over the surrounding countryside and communications routes. In 1912, for example, the police chief decided that the police station at Evrykhou, 6 kilometers south of Skouriotissa, should be moved to the hillside outside the village, so it would command the main road coming from Nicosia (SA1/1756/1910).

The organization of mining landscapes in 20th-century Cyprus shows this emphasis on surveillance, mostly expressed through the medium of policing. At Amiandos it was decided in 1916 to build a large police station, positioned beside the road coming into the mining concession from Nicosia (SA1/955/1916). During the government's inquiry into the bread confiscation case, it turned out that the company had been privately paying a bonus to policemen based at the mines since 1908, in return for support of their regime, without any authority from the colonial government (SA1/909/1929, Red 22).

The Mitsero-Agrokipia mining landscape of the 1950s, controlled by the Hellenic Mining Company, combines this emphasis on surveillance with a more subtle expression of class and status. The concession was divided across the middle by a high ridge, which formed a natural border between the two villages of Mitsero and Agrokipia (Figure 3). The company, however, had two mines on the Mitsero side and one on the Agrokipia side, regarding the whole area as one unit. To symbolize the new and, to the villagers, artificial unity and to demonstrate their surveillance of each side, the company built its overseers' and foremen's housing on top of the ridge, exactly straddling the boundary between

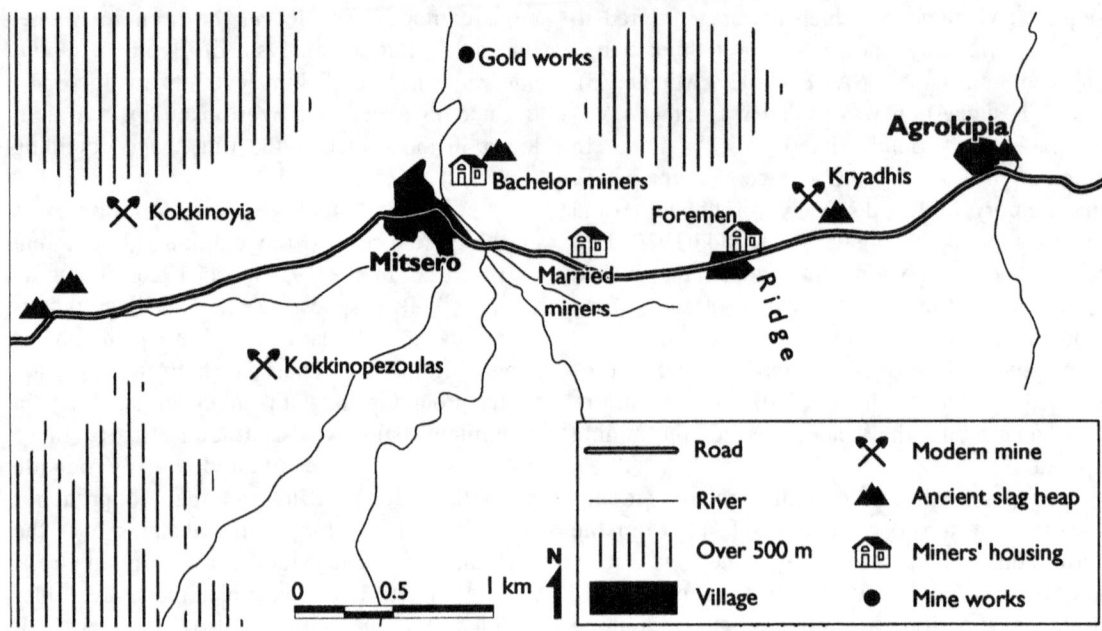

FIGURE 3. Map of the Mitsero-Agrokipia area.

the two village territories. Below them was a block of two-room housing for married miners, and at the bottom of the valley was Mitsero village itself with a large house with space for bachelor miners (Seretis and Diacopoulos 2003: 115–116).

A similar layout, with overseers' and staff houses topographically and symbolically above those of the workers, can be seen at Amiandos and Skouriotissa (Lavender 1962:229). These examples, however, hardly constitute a *panoptikon*. Even if the overseers had cared to venture out of their houses and look, they were too far to see precisely what individuals in the settlements were doing. The location of their houses was more to be seen than to see. They demonstrated visually that workers were part of a controlled and hierarchical mining landscape, rather than being members of different agricultural and kin-based village communities.

Agriculture

Full-time miners require others to produce a considerable agricultural surplus to maintain them. A system of "agricultural support settlements," for example, has been suggested for the copper miners and smelters of Late Bronze

Age Cyprus, based on archaeological survey (Knapp 1997:59). As William Douglass points out, however, there are many more possibilities than a simple increase in local agricultural production (Douglass 1998:105). In early-20th-century Cyprus, two specific factors complicate this relationship: the large number of poor agriculturalists requiring supplementary employment and the workings of colonial rule.

Because of successive droughts, insufficient investment in agriculture by the colonial government, and chronic rural indebtedness, there was a considerable body of poor or landless peasants who required some sort of extra employment for cash (Georghallides 1985:432; Katsiaounis 1996:34–35). The seasonal nature of most of the mining work, especially at the asbestos mine at Amiandos, was ideal. In 1927, for example, 6,000 workers were employed during the summer, of whom 4,800 were laid off for the winter (SA1/1195/1927). Even capital-intensive mining such as this can use seasonal and informal labor (Knapp 1998:4).

This balance between agricultural work and mining work is frequently commented on by elderly Cypriot villagers who once worked as miners—and farmers. In the village of Mitsero, Konstantinos Ttaouxis (interviewed 16

Perspectives from *Historical Archaeology*

June 1998) described a typical summer day and night's work in the 1950s: he would walk in the evening with his donkey to his most distant fields 7 kilometers away, sleep a little, harvest all night on his own, then walk back to the pyrites washing plant, where he would leave his donkey and spend all day breaking up pyrites by hand with a hammer, return home in the afternoon, and in the evening walk back out to his fields. Other similar stories tell of men who married into the village and so owned no land and had to work at the mines. In the remote village of Asinou (now abandoned) the entire male population spent the summer at the asbestos mines of Amiandos, leaving the women and children to see to the crops and the goats.

Such stories and memories emphasize the part-time attitude towards mining, something never felt towards agriculture. Even while on the job, any spare time could be used for some useful task, even if there was no time to return to the fields. In the 1920s and 1930s, women were commonly employed at crushing ore, using hammers and flat stones as anvils, and on sieving, screening, and loading cars; "those not immediately engaged sat on the ground in sociable groups, feeding their babies and working on their beautiful Cypriot lace" (Lavender 1962:138,173).

In spite of such part-time arrangements, a workforce of 10,000 asbestos miners could not be expected to feed itself; a major system of food procurement was required. Rather than stimulating local production, however, which was desperately needed by many of the poorer mountain villages, the mining companies chose to import their food and sell it to their captive workforce. The Cyprus Asbestos Company set up a new company, Cyprus Hygienic Bakeries Limited, which was supposedly independent but in fact a subsidiary company, and forced its workers to buy their bread from it—hence the confiscation of the bread sent up to Hadji Ktori by his wife. Following Hadji Ktori's complaints, the government inquiry received the following justification from the bakery manager for his monopoly and high prices:

> We use for our bread the first quantity [sic] Australian and American flour, the English yeast, which we receive every fortnight from England. ... Presently it is impossible to reduce the price of our bread. According to the sliding Scale of Prices, the price of a 2-lbs. loaf in England is 4-1/2 d. [pence] or 135 Cyprus paras, but the cost of materials is higher here than in England: we pay £1.0.0 custom duty on each ton of flour and nearly double price for the fuel oil (SA1/909/1929, Red 6).

Adding to this a 9% markup on each loaf, the bakery made a handsome profit out of their workers (unless production was so low as to be uneconomical, which the manager claimed was often the case). It also supported farmers and wholesalers in Britain, America, and Australia—but not the poverty-stricken villagers just outside the mining concession.

Artifacts

Artifacts carry many more associations than the dates and functions generally attributed to them by archaeologists. In a colonial situation, thanks to historical archaeology, artifacts can convey important information about modes of domination and, more particularly, modes of resistance, including both implicit everyday resistance and open defiance (Paynter and McGuire 1991:12–13). This is often evident in conflicting traditions of foodways, which are archaeologically visible by means of the pottery used. Plantation slaves in 18th-century South Carolina, for example, used undifferentiated plain wares that emphasized local production and communal organization, in implicit opposition to the hierarchical and individualist ceramic styles used by their Euroamerican oppressors (Ferguson 1991:32).

One set of artifacts from the 20th-century asbestos mine of Amiandos clearly shows a similar conflict. Loaves of bread may not usually be archaeologically visible, but they are certainly artifacts and can take on considerable symbolic value. This particularly applied to the Greek Orthodox miners who were very much in the majority at the Amiandos mines. Each Sunday, loaves of village bread—the "bread of life"—were stamped with a cross and the letters "IΣ-NK" (Jesus Christ is victorious), and at the end of the Eucharist they were blessed and pieces were handed out to the congregation as they left.

This is why the Battle of the Bread at Amiandos became so significant. It was about more than economics or a personal preference for the taste of one's own village bread. The continual smuggling of a few loaves of bread for personal use or distribution to friends was a part of the ongoing resistance to the uniform and alien culture imposed by the foreign company and its servants. It was not uncommon for 45 loaves to be confiscated from a single lorry (SA1/909/1929, Red 12). Ending the bread monopoly became one of the rallying cries of strikers, along with shorter hours and more pay (SA1/1065/1929, Red 11), and was eventually discussed in the island's Legislative Council, though to no effect (Georghallides 1985:327–328).

Police reports reveal another form of ongoing resistance based on artifacts. At the Amiandos mines there was continual pilfering of sacks, rafters, and tools, so much so that whenever a worker was issued a sack, he was given a permit so he could prove it was not stolen (SA1/909/1929, Red 11). More important was the theft of wood, as F. Kukulas, the manager of the mine, told the government inquiry:

> During the course of a year we also expirernced [sic] hundreds of conversions of Company's property most of which are cases of destroying quarry equipment for the purpose of using the wood for burning and for making furniture (SA1/909/1929, Red 20).

In isolation, this seems like petty theft, caused by impoverished villagers making use of whatever resources were available. When viewed in the light of the forestry policy of the colonial government, it becomes more significant in ideological terms. Right from the beginning of colonial rule, the government had imposed restrictions on the collection of fuel and timber from the forests. During the 1920s the government progressively banned goatherds based in mountain villages from pasturing their goats in the forests, as it inhibited regeneration of the pine trees. This caused intense resentment from villagers, whose livelihood depended on pastoralism, producing a series of arson attacks on the forests (Georghallides 1985:449). Stealing wood from the mines provided the necessary fuel for cooking and heating and the material for making furniture, while simultaneously constituting another part of the ongoing resistance to the colonial regime. Similarly, stories are still told in Mitsero of smart operators who managed to outwit the authorities and extract gold from old

workings. The point of the stories is as much the outwitting as the financial profit.

On 25 July 1929 the Battle of the Bread came to a peak, with a major riot and a strike at the Amiandos mine. The police accounts stress a series of recurrent material indicators of the protest and the intimidation of other workers: wagons were upturned, sticks were brandished, stones were thrown, tools were taken away (SA1/1065/1929, Red 11). These were clearly intended as very visible indicators, as the agitators worked their way round the mine, demanding to be allowed to bring in their own bread. There was another material object in action on that day, which became a symbol of the riot to the colonial authorities. It so happened that Reginald Nicholson, the officer administering the government (i.e., the acting governor), was visiting Amiandos and arrived in the middle of the riot:

> The car came under fire & I stood up & signalled to the man on the terrace to stop. As I did so a stone *weighing half a pound came straight at my head from the terrace. I had no time to dodge & had to catch it, & got a cut & a nasty blow on the left hand. *weighed in Nicosia, & enclosed. RN (SA1/1065/1929, Red 8).

The miscreant stone, symbol of insurrection, was duly wrapped up and sent to the chief of police, along with Nicholson's account of what happened. This battle was fought with stones, loaves of bread, and conflicting perceptions of how the mining landscape should be organized.

Architecture

From the medieval period to the 1930s, Cypriot village houses had a very recognizable and familiar structure and layout. They were generally built in stone below and mud brick above, with a flat roof; all materials were local. An enclosed courtyard was entered from the street, and a variety of rooms round it were used for living, storage, and keeping animals (Ionas 1988:43–45). Each house formed a household for one nuclear family, according to the social structure of rural Cyprus and the system whereby parents gave a house as dowry for their daughter (Ionas 1988:11).

The mining companies needed to accommodate large numbers of men and women who were often separated from their families and only present for temporary periods of various lengths. They clearly required a very different solution. Initially these tended to be somewhat ad hoc. In the 1910s the workers' village at what was to be named Skouriotissa consisted of seven mud brick houses, plus a *khan* run by a man "said by local gossip to be a professional murderer" (Lavender 1962:100). A *khan* or *caravanserai* at this period in Cyprus was usually a large hollow square, lined with rooms facing inwards for travelers, merchants, and their animals. It was very much a symbol of impermanence. In 1922 Gunther built two barracks of mud brick tempered with seaweed, one for men and one for women. Additional space was provided by converting a large cave and an old sulphur and devil's mud store (Lavender 1962:168). All of this was not just a symbol of impermanence but was a negation of the strong kin-based values of rural Cypriot society.

The asbestos mines at Amiandos faced similar problems. One scheme of the early 1920s shows the beginnings of the paternalistic colonial desire to create a model settlement, based on their own perceptions of order and sanitation, rather than making it appropriate to the local social structure. The Pano Amiandos mineworkers' housing consists of separate blocks of housing, each block containing six two-room units with their own internal fireplace (Figure 4). They were stone built, with roofs of asbestos sheeting (appropriately enough for workers' housing at an asbestos mine). A small inner courtyard (10 x 6.5 m) contained two latrines, a large central fountain, and an open drain. To the eyes of the British architect who designed it and the mining companies who approved it, this was model housing: clean, visibly well organized, and cheap. To a Cypriot family, however, it provided no private courtyard, and no place to keep animals or engage in the small-scale agricultural activities that defined rural life.

Another attempt in the early 1950s to design modular family housing was a failure before it had even finished. The married workers' housing at Mitsero, halfway between the overseers' houses on the ridgeline and the village in the

FIGURE 4. Worker's housing block at Pano Amiandos.

valley (Figure 3), was designed along the lines of a *khan*, with four wings of two-room units forming a 65-m square. Once again, there was no organic structure appropriate to a kin-based society and none of the private courtyard space that an agricultural or rural outlook requires. With improvements in roads and motor transport in the 1950s, it was decided to abandon the structure when only its foundations had been laid (though one wing was later completed). Daily or weekly commuting by lorry meant that the characteristically part-time miners could still live in their own villages and cultivate their fields and vines as well as work in the mines. This rejection of planned housing is another aspect of the everyday resistance against the uniformity imposed by the mining company.

Community

A mining community is usually regarded as a temporary community—or not as a community at all. This especially applies to the "gold rush" type of mining camps in North America and Australia, which "flared and faded" as individuals shifted from one promising spot to another (Knapp 1998:5). Even this impermanence can allow some sense of community, when miners' shared aims and vocation bring them together in any number of different locations—not to mention friends and family coming out to join the pioneers (Douglass 1998:102,106). Excavation of 19th-century miners' housing at Dolly's Creek, west of Melbourne, shows that the material culture expresses this tension between the temporary and the permanent, the individual and the community. Tents were temporary and widely separated, but their arrangement in the landscape suggests a focused mining community, and the pipe-clayed fireplaces and a few finer possessions gave a sense of pride and belonging (Cheney 1992:39–40; cf. Behrens, this volume).

In the Cypriot context there was a major conflict between traditional perceptions of community and the regulations and organization imposed by the mining companies and the colonial government. The sense of community in a traditional rural village depended on more than the local materials, nuclear households, and agglomerated layout of its houses. Villages usually clustered round a central church or mosque, with other institutions such as coffee houses, fountains, and annual fairs also playing an important role in community life (Ionas 1988:20–39; Given 2000:214–217). An agricultural lifestyle brought communal facilities such as olive presses and water mills as well as a seasonal cycle of labor shared by everyone in the community and a host of metaphors for the workings of everyday life. Conservatism in the architectural styles and icon painting of churches suggests a strong sense of continuity from the Byzantine and Medieval periods, which also appears in folk tales and songs.

The caves, barracks, and converted sulphur stores provided by Gunther at Skouriotissa could hardly be further from this ideal. In the mid 1920s he tried to improve conditions by providing communal facilities: a company hospital; communal bathhouses, with soap and wood for fuel available at cost price; and communal toilets and laundries (Lavender 1962:189). Yet such attempts, which were echoed at Amiandos, failed to address the actual workings of communal life in the rural villages of Cyprus. This failure was demonstrated graphically during the 1929 strike at Amiandos, which was led by miners from the mountain village of Palekhori. So important was this unit of identity that after the riot had been quelled, a rumor went round that the chief foreman would "dismiss all the Palechori people from the work because they were the cause of the trouble in the morning" (SA1/1065/1929, Red 11). Miners from a specific village retained that identity, despite all the company's attempts to foster a new sense of community.

The attempts of the mining companies to create new artificial communities foreshadowed the advent of town planning and model housing after the World War II, which saw a proliferation of such schemes in Cyprus. The colonial Public Works Department drew up designs for a "Subsidized Workers' Housing Scheme" at Omorphita in 1946, referred to disparagingly by its inhabitants as "The Standard" (Schaar et al. 1995:88–90). In the same year the Forestry Department decided to move the villagers of Dhimmata, who lived in houses of "the usual squalid type," to a new "model rural settlement," in order to make them an "example of social uplift in village life"—and incidentally to keep their goats out of the forest (SA1/970/1944/1,

Reds 39,32,44). Whether it was the Public Works Department, the Forestry Department, or a mining company attempting to impose artificial systems of social organization, Cypriot villagers firmly resisted, and continued to evolve their own sense of community.

Conclusions

Ktori was no innocent victim of the Cyprus Asbestos Company's injustice and tyranny. He had worked for two years collecting fees from traders in the company's market place, until it was discovered that he was creaming off some of the payments for himself (SA1/909/1929, Red 20). Even with the bread incident, he knew exactly what he was doing. Three weeks later, he tried to increase the stakes:

> On 14.5.29 I took 100 okes of bread to Amianto and sold to the laborers. I took purposely to see if any bread would be seized but nobody appeared, to remark to me. But Pte 4050 Hari [a policeman] was putting down the names of the laborers who were purchasing bread from me and I heard that all of the were taken before Mr. Kukulas who warned them if they buy again they would be sent away (SA1/909/1929, Red 13).

For all his determination, and in spite of the exhaustive government enquiry, no action was taken. The colonial secretary decided that "Government intervention would only be justified if evidence of harsh or unconscionable treatment were forthcoming," and the officer administering the government—the same one who had fielded the miner's stone—simply said, "I agree," and the matter was dropped (SA1/909/1929, Minutes 7,8).

The story of the confiscation of Ktori's bread, the ensuing strike, and his determined publicizing of the issue constitute much more than one single, aberrant episode. Because of the particular circumstances, including the persistence of one individual, it was investigated and recorded by the colonial government, and so is accessible to historians in the Cyprus State Archives. It was, however, just one critical point in the ongoing conflict between two differing interpretations of a mining landscape.

This conflict was played out using a variety of different weapons, both actual and symbolic. Surveillance, for example, could be countered by smuggling bread or pilfering firewood. Often it was more a matter of maintaining an accustomed lifestyle, in the face of pressure to change. Throughout the whole period of large-scale mining in colonial Cyprus, there was a complex set of dynamics between mining company and colonial government, between overseer and miner, and between miners from different villages. These dynamics were negotiated not only by words but also by the manipulation of artifacts, structures, and landscapes.

ACKNOWLEDGMENTS

Most of the primary historical material for this paper comes from the Cyprus State Archives, and I am very grateful to the director, Effy Parparinou, and to all her staff for their constant help and support during my research there. The copyright of all material from the Cyprus State Archives remains with the Government of Cyprus. I am grateful to the many villagers in Mitsero and Amiandos who have told me about their mining history, especially Andreas Papanastasiou, Konstantinos Ttaouxis and Loïzos Xynaris. Thanks also to the members of the Sydney Cyprus Survey Project. The participants of the SHA 2000 "Landscapes of Industrial Labor" session gave many comments, suggestions, and ideas that were both helpful and stimulating. I would like to thank them and the session organizer Mark Cassell. All photographs and maps are by the author.

REFERENCES

BEAR, L. M.
    1963 The Mineral Resources and Mining Industry of Cyprus. *Cyprus Geological Survey Department, Bulletin*, No. 1, Nicosia.

CHENEY, SUSAN L.
    1992 Uncertain Migrants: The History and Archaeology of a Victorian Goldfield Community. *Australasian Historical Archaeology*, 10:36–42.

CYPRUS STATE ARCHIVES [SA]
    1904–1944 Unpublished government correspondence. Cyprus State Archives, Nicosia. [*Red* refers to the page number of the correspondence in the back of the file; *minute* refers to the number of the minute in the front of the file. Copyright remains with the Republic of Cyprus.]

DELLE, JAMES A.
    1999 The Landscapes of Class Negotiation on Coffee Plantations in the Blue Mountains of Jamaica: 1790– 1850. *Historical Archaeology*, 33(1):136–158.

DOUGLASS, WILLIAM A.
1998 The Mining Camp as Community. In *Social Approaches to an Industrial Past: The Archaeology and Anthropology of Mining*, A. Bernard Knapp, Vincent C. Pigott, and Eugenia W. Herbert, editors, pp. 97–108. Routledge, London, England.

FERGUSON, LELAND
1991 Struggling with Pots in Colonial South Carolina. In *The Archaeology of Inequality*, Randall H. McGuire and Robert Paynter, editors, pp. 28–39. Blackwell, Oxford, England.

FOUCAULT, MICHEL
1977 *Discipline and Punish: The Birth of the Prison*, Alan Sheridan, translator. Penguin Books, Harmondsworth, England.

GEORGHALLIDES, G. S.
1985 Cyprus and the Governorship of Sir Ronald Storrs: The Causes of the 1931 Crisis. *Cyprus Research Centre, Texts, and Studies in the History of Cyprus*, No. 13. Nicosia, Cyprus.

GIVEN, MICHAEL
1997 Star of the Parthenon, Cypriot Mélange: Education and Representation in Colonial Cyprus. *Journal of Mediterranean Studies*, 7(1):59–82.
1998 Inventing the Eteocypriots: Imperialist Archaeology and the Manipulation of Ethnic Identity. *Journal of Mediterranean Archaeology*, 11(1):3–29.
2000 Agriculture, Settlement, and Landscape in Ottoman Cyprus. *Levant*, 32:215–236.

GIVEN, MICHAEL, AND TIMOTHY E. GREGORY
2003 Medieval to Modern Landscapes. In The Sydney Cyprus Survey Project: Social Approaches to Regional Archaeological Survey, Michael Given and A. Bernard Knapp, editors, pp. 284–294. *Monumenta Archaeologica*, No. 21. Cotsen Institute of Archaeology, University of California, Los Angeles.

GIVEN, MICHAEL, AND A. BERNARD KNAPP (EDITORS)
2003 The Sydney Cyprus Survey Project: Social Approaches to Regional Archaeological Survey. *Monumenta Archaeologica*, No. 21. Cotsen Institute of Archaeology, University of California, Los Angeles.

GRIVAUD, GILLES
1998 Villages Désertés à Chypre (Fin XIIe–Fin XIXe Siècle). *Archbishop Makarios III Foundation, Meletai kai Ipomnimata*, No. 3. Nicosia, Cyprus.

IONAS, IOANNIS
1988 *La Maison Rurale de Chypre (XVIIIe–XXe Siècle): Aspects et Techniques de Construction.* Cyprus Research Centre, Nicosia, Cyprus.

KATSIAOUNIS, ROLANDOS
1996 Labour, Society, and Politics in Cyprus during the Second Half of the Nineteenth Century. *Cyprus Research Centre, Texts, and Studies in the History of Cyprus*, No. 24. Nicosia, Cyprus.

KNAPP, A. BERNARD
1997 *The Archaeology of Late Bronze Age Cypriot Society: The Study of Settlement, Survey, and Landscape.* Department of Archaeology, University of Glasgow, Glasgow, Scotland.
1998 Social Approaches to the Archaeology and Anthropology of Mining. In *Social Approaches to an Industrial Past: The Archaeology and Anthropology of Mining*, A. Bernard Knapp, Vincent C. Pigott, and Eugenia W. Herbert, editors, pp. 1–23. Routledge, London, England.

KNAPP, A. BERNARD, AND WENDY ASHMORE
1999 Archaeological Landscapes: Constructed, Conceptualized, Ideational. In *Archaeologies of Landscape: Contemporary Perspectives*, Wendy Ashmore and A. Bernard Knapp, editors, pp. 1–30. Blackwell, Oxford, England.

LAVENDER, DAVID
1962 *The Story of the Cyprus Mines Corporation.* Huntington Library, San Marino, CA.

PAYNTER, ROBERT, AND RANDALL H. MCGUIRE
1991 The Archaeology of Inequality: Material Culture, Domination, and Resistance. In *The Archaeology of Inequality*, Randall H. McGuire and Robert Paynter, editors, pp. 1–27. Blackwell, Oxford, England.

SCHAAR, KENNETH W., MICHAEL GIVEN, AND GEORGE THEOCHAROUS
1995 *Under the Clock: Colonial Architecture and History in Cyprus, 1878–1960.* Bank of Cyprus, Nicosia, Cyprus.

SERETIS, KYLIE, AND LITA DIACOPOULOS
2003 SIA 5: Mitsero Village. In The Sydney Cyprus Survey Project: Social Approaches to Regional Archaeological Survey, Michael Given and A. Bernard Knapp, editors, pp. 109–118. *Monumenta Archaeologica*, No. 21. Cotsen Institute of Archaeology, University of California, Los Angeles.

WOOD, H. TRUEMAN (EDITOR)
1887 *Colonial and Indian Exhibition, London, 1886: Reports on the Colonial Sections of the Exhibition.* William Clowes and Sons, London, England.

MICHAEL GIVEN
DEPARTMENT OF ARCHAEOLOGY
UNIVERSITY OF GLASGOW
GLASGOW G12 8QQ
SCOTLAND

Brooke S. Blades

European Military Sites As Ideological Landscapes

ABSTRACT

The American tradition of devoting substantial quantities of public resources to the acquisition and preservation of battle sites is generally foreign to European nations. Many battlefields in Europe are unmarked or have few monuments. Preservation efforts at most of the remaining sites have concentrated upon relatively small portions such as isolated structures or natural vistas. Cemeteries are at times integral elements of these landscapes. Selected battlefields in Ireland, Scotland, England, France, Belgium, Luxembourg, and the Czech Republic provide varied examples of European landscape preservation and commemoration. It is argued that the often minimal preservation efforts in Europe reflect an ideological landscape of modern political and social concerns.

Introduction

A 53 year-old Serbian resident of Kosovo was quoted during summer 1999 as saying, "This is Serbian holy land. Our churches and our graves are like a stop sign to us. They don't let us leave here" (Erlanger 1999). His comments were made near the Field of the Blackbirds in Kosovo, the site where the Serbs lost a 14th-century battle against the Turks but, so legend holds, found cultural identity. The image of the Field of the Blackbirds was frequently invoked by the former dictator Slobodan Milosevic as a means of promoting national unity.

A military base in northern Germany was renamed in May 2000 for Anton Schmid, an Austrian solider in the army of the Third Reich who saved hundreds of Jewish citizens in Lithuania from capture and murder and who was himself executed in April 1942 for doing so. The base had formerly honored Günther Rüdel, a *Wehrmacht* general during World War II. Rudolph Scharping, the German defense minister, justified the redesignation by stating, "We are not free to choose our history, but we can choose the examples we take from that history" (Cohen 2000).

This article presents an overview of the various perspectives that Europeans bring to the commemoration of landscapes of conflict and military sites within their continent. The study is a subjective one, not conducted in a systematic fashion with regard to either time or place. For example, no review is offered for World War I battlefields in France or Belgium, which have been interpreted in traditional and macabre ways and where the futility and horror of war is a unifying theme. I have chosen to emphasize sites of which I have some direct knowledge—except for those in Scotland—and to place those sites within European historical contexts both national and regional in character. In this sense, therefore, the sites chosen are representative of various time periods for countries in western Europe. Site visits have taken place over a period of 25 years; earlier observations have been updated through reading and correspondence.

Furthermore, the analysis focuses not on the interpretation of excavated data from these battle sites but, rather, on a theoretical foundation for understanding site interpretations that are offered or suggested reasons for not interpreting or preserving sites in the first place. European battle sites have attracted particularistic and even antiquarian excavation attention for decades or centuries. However, I contend that modern needs and concerns have often transformed these sites into the material reflections of nonphysical ideological landscapes, and it is this transformation that holds fundamental anthropological interest and importance.

What follows, then, is an overview of the manner in which battle sites and cemeteries are interpreted—or ignored—in various European countries. In so doing, I will consider two questions: (1) Since so few military sites are actually selected for preservation and interpretation, what are the factors that influence this selection; (2) to what extent does regional or national ideology influence preservation and interpretation?

The concept of ideology utilized herein is derived loosely from that reproduced and discussed by Mark Leone (1984:26). Ideology in the present usage does consist of ideas about people, nature, and causality. Beyond naturalizing and masking social inequality, however, ideology in the commemoration of past or present military sites serves to guard against that which people fear or to protect that which they cherish in the present, as the above quotations from Kosovo and by the German foreign minister suggest. To the extent that ideology is successful in making current social relations or political beliefs seem resident in the past, these modern hopes and fears will be viewed as natural, inevitable, and justified.

Physical and Nonphysical Perspectives on Landscape

Military landscapes may be traditionally categorized within a variety of physically oriented perspectives. A relatively straightforward temporal framework may be summarized as follows:

- *Historical Landscape:* This perspective relates to vestiges of strategic and tactical events related to the military conflict under consideration. Components of the historical landscape, in the restricted usage employed herein, would include the following: archaeological artifact distributions generated during the military event; architectural features such as roads, bridges, buildings, or earthworks constructed prior to or during the conflict; vegetation patterns and topographic features (fields, woods, open meadows, streams, etc.) that closely approximate those at the time of the battle.

- *Memorial Landscape:* This perspective addresses the manner in which original participants and subsequent persons have commemorated and interpreted the events of historic significance. Monuments designed and erected by veterans are elements, as are later concepts of commemoration. The ruins of Battle Abbey near Hastings, erected by William following the 11th-century Norman victory, are obviously historic but would represent elements of the memorial landscape under this definition.

- *Modern Landscape:* The modern landscape serves to define those sites that exist at present with little or no protection from alteration and with minimal interpretative recognition. Whatever topographic, archi-

tectural, and archaeological elements such landscapes possess have survived by accident or perhaps through the efforts of an individual landowner or small local group. These locations have effectively been ignored for the purpose of preservation.

It is possible to place battlefield landscapes or specific elements of battlefields within a given landscape in one of these categories, and references to these perspectives will be made on occasion in this analysis. One will quickly discover, however, that most military sites in Europe, and I strongly suspect in the rest of the world, are modern landscapes with little or no interpretive focus.

The primary concern of this analysis is the identification of circumstances under which sites are ignored or, if preserved as memorial or historical landscapes, the reasons for such preservation. I submit that decisions whether or not to preserve and interpret military sites, and the form of preservation that does occur, may only be comprehended with reference to a nonphysical "ideological" landscape. This perspective considers the meaning of the event in cultural contexts past and present. The ideological landscape represents the philosophical foundation that provides the conscious or unconscious motivations for preserving or ignoring a particular physical site or commemorating an event. These perceptions direct, for example, whether preservation efforts focus upon recreating a stark and violent historic landscape or allow a less threatening park-like memorial setting to emerge.

The use and abuse of historical reality to promote a broader mythology or ideology are primary examples of the ideological landscape. It is particularly important to recognize that several conflicting ideological landscapes may coexist at particular moments in time, and that this nonphysical landscape may be reinvented through time by changing ideological perceptions.

Ireland

The site of the 1690 Battle of the Boyne lies in the Republic of Ireland just north of Dublin. The less well-known Battle of Benburb on the Blackwater River, a 1643 victory for Irish forces over a Scottish army, occurred in the province of Ulster.

It seems apparent that the Irish have been faced with a geographical paradox. Since the site of the Irish victory at Benburb falls within modern Northern Ireland, it is not surprising that the Protestant majority would have little interest in commemorating such a site. Conversely, the Republic of Ireland has until recently virtually ignored the site of the Boyne, a crushing defeat for Catholic Jacobite forces that dashed hopes of an independent Irish state for more than a century.

It is in the north of Ireland where one may see clear consequences of the use of the military past to support the political present. The Protestant victory at the Boyne is celebrated each July; Protestants in the city of Londonderry have an additional parade each August to commemorate the successful defense of the fortified city shortly before the Boyne. The July parade represents a veneration of the event, since they are denied effective access to the site of the battle. However, the past has proven a fertile source of inspiration for both sides. Protestant graffiti celebrate links to William III, the victor at the Boyne, and to Great Britain. Graffiti in Catholic neighborhoods invoke the memory of the 1916 Easter Rebellion in Dublin as a means of legitimizing the IRA campaign in the 1970s.

It should be noted, however, that an expansion of efforts to preserve and interpret Irish battlefields is afoot. Duchas, the Heritage Service in the Republic of Ireland, has begun to acquire portions of the field at the Boyne. The site will eventually become a national monument with interpretive signage (Eugene Keane of Duchas in Nicholas Brannon 2000, pers. comm.). The Environment and Heritage Service in Northern Ireland has recorded battle sites in the Sites and Monuments Record database with the intent of providing a degree of protection from development (Nicholas Brannon 2000, pers. comm.).

Scotland

The Scots and the English fought for more that half a millennium to define a border and eventually determine whether Scotland would remain an independent kingdom. The National Trust for Scotland (NTS) owns large portions of several battle sites, including two with very different consequences for Scotland.

Bannockburn was the site of the June 1314 victory of Robert the Bruce's army over the invading English that affirmed Scottish independence, at least for a time. The memorial landscape today consists of open fields, car park, visitor center, and large 1960s equestrian statue of Robert the Bruce. Approximately 60,000 persons pass through the visitor center each year. One of my correspondents at NTS described the interpretation as being decidedly pro-Scottish.

Culloden, the site of an April 1746 battle, commemorates a very different event. As stated in the NTS publication, "No name in Scottish history evokes more emotion than that of Culloden ..." (National Trust for Scotland 1998). Culloden culminated in a disastrous charge by the Highland clans that had no real hope of success. The consequent defeat of the clans led to the end of the Jacobite rebellion (the "Forty-Five") and the last Scottish military attempt at independence.

For more than a century, expressions of clan identity such as tartans and bagpipes were outlawed, Highland populations were displaced as land use patterns were altered, and much of Gaelic culture was suppressed or eradicated (Prebble 1961; Myra Lawson 1999, pers. comm.; National Trust for Scotland 1999). During the 19th century a roadway was laid out directly through the battlefield, disturbing a number of Scottish burial mounds from the battle.

Modern management of Culloden is more enlightened. The site is a memorial landscape, but attempts to restore the battlefield to "its state on that fateful day" (National Trust for Scotland 1999) reveal a conscious desire to recreate an historic setting. A car park and visitor center greet those who stop: approximately 125,000 persons come through the center alone between February and December. The site itself is marked by burials of both English and Highland Scottish soldiers. This is an important point as it introduces a theme that is encountered repeatedly on European battlefields: the juxtaposition of the military event with the logical consequence of that event—violent and untimely death.

Interpretation at Culloden is subdued and, in the opinion of the NTS, balanced. "Culloden is a very somber place and is virtually a shrine for the Gaels; the Trust is conscious of this ... for example, we have no battlefield re-enactments and the retail outlet sells primarily books" (Myra Lawson 1999, pers. comm.).

This approach reflects a complex blend of regional and national ideologies. Harmony within Great Britain is probably considered a desirable goal at the national level, so preservation and interpretive efforts that offend no one would seem to contribute to that goal. However, it is important to remember that the NTS is a private organization that is clearly conscious of local or regional sensitivities. The spirit of independence has never died in Scotland, particularly in the Highlands, and the impending creation of a Scottish Parliament in the current process of devolution will only serve to augment that spirit. It is also interesting to note that the Scots embrace the "Forty-Five" as a "lost cause" in a manner reminiscent of the American South and the Confederacy. Celeste R. Ray (1998) provides a detailed examination of this last point.

England

The many medieval and Renaissance battle sites are generally marked solely by monuments in the field and notations on Ordnance Survey topographic maps. Sedgemoor in the west of England provides an example of such a modern landscape. This site of an unsuccessful late-17th-century attempt to mount a challenge against the English crown is greatly altered by the installation of drainage ditches on the moor (Smurthwaite 1984) and is of interest chiefly as the location of the last armed conflict on English soil.

Interpretation may be undertaken on a local and fairly informal level. The site of the 1066 Battle of Hastings lies within the grounds of a private school and surrounding farms, although some of the lands have evidently been preserved by a local trust or by English Heritage (Smurthwaite 1984; Myra Lawson 1999, pers. comm.). During the 1970s interpretation at Hastings was provided by a guidebook that could be purchased at local shops (Lemmon 1970). The author indicated that permission for visitors to stop at various spots around the battlefield had been granted by private landowners.

Some sites are owned, probably coincidentally, by the Ministry of Defense and a few others, such as the 15th-century Bosworth Field, are preserved by the local county authority (Myra Lawson 1999, pers. comm.). For the most part, however, English battle sites were offered minimal protection in the mid-1980s (Smurthwaite 1984).

Continental Europe

A fundamental difference between the Continent and the British Isles may be found in the extent to which local populations were active participants in the issues being decided by force of arms. Battles within Britain were insular affairs, usually focusing on issues of royal succession or the ultimate political relationship of neighboring countries with England. As such, local inhabitants were often active combatants. By contrast, the nature of the continental land mass ensured that armies followed certain campaign routes repeatedly over the centuries. As a result, battles were fought on lands occupied by populations who may not have been actively involved in combat, although civilians suffered just the same. As a consequence, a certain detachment from the event, particularly of older battles, may be anticipated.

Czech Republic and
Belgium—Napoleonic Era

Napoleon remains a dominant historical figure from the early-19th century and not only in France. The site of Napoleon's 1805 victory over Russian and Austrian armies at Austerlitz (or Slavkov to local residents) lies in southern Moravia. An excellent map of the field has been produced that outlines important elements of the battle. The field headquarters of Napoleon stood on a "hill" that was, in fact, a burial mound from the 5th and 6th centuries A.D. The hill with a 1930 monument is considered an "extraterritorial region of the French Republic" (Špatný and Grieblerová 1991). It may be relevant to note that the monument was erected during the period between the First and Second World Wars when Moravia was itself part of an earlier Czech Republic after the end of the Austro-Hungarian Empire and prior to the rise of the Soviet Eastern Block. France and the Soviet Union both supported the new republic.

The site of Waterloo south of Brussels was the scene of the final defeat of Napoleon in 1815, but sources suggest that one would scarcely realize that he had in fact lost the battle from visiting the area (Myra Lawson 1999, pers. comm.). Remember, however, that Waterloo lies within the French-speaking southern part of Belgium.

France and World War II

Americans are quite naturally interested in European battlefields of the 20th century, due in no small measure to the substantial role played by American soldiers in those conflicts. The immense scale of these military campaigns precludes the acquisition of large tracts as public lands, even if such a tradition existed in Europe. Commemoration efforts have focused upon preservation of small loci, museums, isolated monumentation, occasional driving tours, and military cemeteries.

The names Normandy and D-Day evoke powerful images for older Americans; the reality of war is never far removed in this region of France. Several sites have been acquired by the Coastal Conservation Trust. The British and Canadian beaches fell in or near resort villages, so only small patches have been obtained. The American landing beaches are located in more rural areas, and larger tracts have been preserved. Point du Hoc is one such site. An attempt to return the point to its appearance in June 1944 has been undertaken. The Comité du Débarquement sign here is particularly daunting as it warns of the potential danger posed by as yet undetected mines in the surrounding fields. Since 1979, this site has been owned by the United States Government and maintained by the American Battle Monuments Commission, which also administers the U.S. military cemeteries, so an American philosophy of landscape presentation is not surprising (American Battle Monuments Commission 1984). Point du Hoc represents an historic landscape as defined herein.

Omaha Beach is clearly a memorial landscape that looks nothing like it did on D-Day. The overlook above the beach at Colleville-sur-Mer reveals a verdant landscape with a curved walkway that, in fact, wraps around the site of a large gun emplacement. However, the formidable nature of the terrain is evident. The earliest American cemeteries were established on the beach. The 1947 Michelin map (Michelin 1947a) indicates a number of cemeteries on and behind Omaha Beach; all of these were subsequently abandoned when the cemetery containing more than 9,000 graves was created on the bluff at Colleville. The 1947 map does not indicate the location of German cemeteries, but modern Michelin maps do, and one

containing more than 21,000 burials may be found at la Cambe.

Military cemeteries, large and small, are defining features of the Normandy landscape. The numbers of graves are staggering (Table 1). Since most burials, except those of the Americans, have remained in their original locations of interment, these cemeteries provide more eloquent testaments to the ferocity of the fighting than any museum exhibits or restored landscapes. Further, no mention has been made of the loss of civilian life or destruction of Norman villages.

TABLE 1
MILITARY BURIALS IN NORMANDY

Nationality	Burials	Cemeteries
American	13,796	2
British	19,736	16
Canadian	5,007	2
Polish	650	1
German	77,966	6

Comité du Débarquement (ca. 1984).

Belgium and Luxembourg—World War II

The *Voie de la Liberté* or Road to Liberty was established in 1946 and 1947, following the route of American troops from Cherbourg in Normandy across France through Luxembourg to Bastogne in Belgium (Michelin 1947b). Small concrete pylons were placed every kilometer along the route and many remain in place. The route leads to the area of the Ardennes campaign more familiarly known as the Battle of the Bulge. As in Normandy, the Ardennes region of Belgium and Luxembourg has deep emotional meaning for Americans and Europeans. As in Normandy, the landscape is marked by museums, monuments, and military cemeteries. Unlike Normandy, however, virtually none of this land has been acquired for conservation.

Bastogne is one of the most well-known places associated with the Ardennes battle; a memorial on Mardasson Hill erected in 1946 honors the sacrifices of American soldiers who defended the town and the country. A nearby modern museum (the Bastogne Historical Center organized by M. Guy Franz Arend and the town of Bastogne) uses a film and multilingual map program to present an interpretation that still pays homage to the American defenders.

An easing of some of the anger and passion on the part of citizens in Belgium and Luxembourg is to be expected with the passing of time. Such passions burned brightly indeed in September 1945 when a plaque referring to *les hordes nazies* was placed on a strategic bridge in Stavelot. The village of la Gleize was virtually destroyed in December 1944; its idyllic appearance today suggests none of the damage sustained by this and many other Ardennes villages. The Musée Décembre 44 is housed in a new brick building and a rebuilt stone one that served as a military hospital. A "souvenir" of the battle—a massive tank abandoned by German troops—dominates the square outside; inside, an extensive collection of photographs labeled in four languages (Dutch, English, French, and German) documents the agony of la Gleize and surrounding villages. Although the interpretation is balanced, background musical recordings of the Andrews Sisters and the Glenn Miller Orchestra are decidedly one-sided.

"Objectivity" in presentation is frequently mentioned in the Ardennes. The Musée National d'Histoire Militaire in the Luxembourg town of Diekirch advertises in its brochure a "balanced and objective historical presentation of the military operations in the Ardennes from the American, German, and civilian points of view." Such an emphasis on objectivity is probably due to the passage of time and the proximity of the Ardennes to Germany. A portion of the Belgian population in this area speaks German; many *Luxembourgeois* are bilingual, having French and German. Tourism from Germany to the military monuments and museums of the Ardennes is commonplace.

Most military sites, however, have no monumentation. The small collection of farmhouses at Erria was the scene of a ferocious battle on the night of 27 December 1944, yet no markers are present or at least obvious. Fields that are placid today may in fact have been the scenes of horrific events. The setting of the Malmédy massacre is a farm pasture; the names of 86 American prisoners who were murdered here are inscribed on a memorial wall at the nearby crossroads.

As in Normandy, the military cemeteries are dominant features. The Luxembourg Cemetery at Hamm contains 5,076 American burials, marked by Latin crosses and Stars of David (American Battle Monuments Commission 1998a). A few kilometers away may be found the German cemetery of Sandweiler, with nearly 11,000 interments, more than half of whom are unknown. The cemetery at Sandweiler was started by the United States Army Burial Service (Volksbund Deutsche Kriegsgräberfüsorge n.d.a).

The differences in design and symbolism between the American and German styles of military commemoration are marked and complex. Consider the grave markers. American headstones reveal the name, state, military unit and rank, and date of death. The American headstones mark individual graves, but references to state and army unit establish a unity of association and purpose.

Gravestones in the German cemeteries mark the graves of several persons, each identified by name, rank, dates of birth and death, but with no mention of army unit. German graves are collective but emphasize the life span of the individual with no reference to membership in a particular army division. Further—and this is somewhat speculative—this emphasis upon the individual may consciously or unconsciously reinforce the view that ultimate responsibility for monstrous military and political acts lay with the Nazi Party and certain fanatical army units. Such apportionment of responsibility would hold that German soldiers were as much victims of fascism as were the Allied soldiers and European citizens who died. These attitudes reflect major philosophical perspectives in post-war Germany (Knischewski and Spittler 1997). Although the cemeteries were transferred to the ownership of the Federal Republic of Germany in the 1950s (Volksbund Deutsche Kriegsgräberfüsorge n.d.a), they are maintained by the Volksbund Deutsche Kriegsgräberfürsorge (German Association for the Provision of War Graves), a group that solicits funds from private donors.

The cemeteries also reflect the degree to which passions have eased through time. As was the case in Normandy, German cemeteries in Luxembourg and Belgium are not shown on the 1947 Michelin commemorative map, which does mark the locations of the American ones at Hamm and north of Bastogne at Foy. However, modern Michelin maps indicate both the German cemetery at Sandweiler and another (Recogne-Bastogne) near Foy. The former American cemetery at Foy, which lay across a narrow road from the German one, was subsequently abandoned as the burials were moved to Hamm or to the Ardennes Cemetery near Liège (American Battle Monuments Commission 1998b).

Conclusion

The World War I battlefields in Belgium and France have not been mentioned. Such places include Ypres, Mons, the Somme, and particularly Verdun, where the horror of war is vividly depicted in the "Trench of the Bayonets" or in the underground ossuary of human bones. Indeed, a pamphlet produced by the Volksbund Deutsche Kriegsgräberfürsorge (n.d.b) describes Belgium as *das Land der toten Soldaten* (land of the dead soldiers). The numbers of war burials in Belgium from two world wars are much higher than those in Normandy, although certainly not for France as a whole (Table 2).

TABLE 2
MILITARY BURIALS IN BELGIUM

Nationality	Burials
American	13,500
Belgian	16,000
British Commonwealth	204,000
German	180,000

Volksbund Deutsche Kriegsgräberfüsorge (n.d.b).

Urban settings as military sites have also not been considered, although many have been battle sites for centuries. Most importantly, I have devoted little attention to the suffering and privations of civilian populations, although their stories are recounted on monuments, in the remains of martyred villages such as Oradour-sur-Glane in France (Keegan 1982:156) and Lidice in the Czech Republic, and at the sites of labor and extermination camps spread across the continent.

What I have examined are the ways in which battle sites have been commemorated and some of the motivations and meanings that underlie those commemorations. The manner and means

of commemoration have changed through time, in concert with changing perceptions of past events and new concerns of the commemorators. As such, it may be argued that the study of military sites in Europe is less a window on the past than a reflection of the present, particularly on a succession of presents.

Two questions were posed at the outset of this paper: why are European sites preserved and what is the impact of ideology upon preservation and interpretation? The prevailing European philosophy towards the preservation of physical remains of the past is not one that embraces the acquisition of large land holdings to commemorate any event. However, battlefields and military events stir the greatest passion and interest *if* the issues being contested by force of arms *then* are perceived as having relevance *now*. The reverence paid to the site of Culloden provides the current desire to establish a separate identity within Great Britain with an apparent pedigree that is centuries old.

The commemoration of Austerlitz, a French defeat of the Austrians and Czarist Russians, when the Czechs were recently liberated from one and soon to be dominated by the other, may also reflect this relationship. The site was celebrated in 1930 by the Czech Republic at a time when alliances with France and the Soviet Union were formed.

The annual revival of memories of the Boyne and the siege of Londonderry by Northern Ireland Protestants are clear expressions of present fears and desires by means designed to exclude Catholic residents. The Serbian resident of Kosovo who was cited in the introduction of this paper was invoking a 700-year-old tradition to sanctify—by use of the term *holy land*—the current struggle to dominate non-Serbian residents.

Military site commemoration reflects a complex interplay of ideological influences, with regional concerns sometimes reinforcing broader national ones but at other times proving to be of greater importance. The Scottish Highland identity with the "Forty-Five" at Culloden within the political sphere of Great Britain indicates the importance of regional ideology.

Regional identity in substantial portions of Luxembourg and Belgium, including the area around Waterloo, has been heavily influenced by French culture. In transitional areas such as the Ardennes, there exists a need to honor Allied liberators while presenting a "balanced" interpretation that recognizes the importance of the military events to modern Germans.

The historical landscape purports to show a visitor how it was; memorial landscape elements attempt to tell one how it should have been, or why it was important. The nonphysical ideological landscape provides the conscious or unconscious motivations for those who memorialize or who strive for historical "accuracy." In the context of the present, what actually happened during a past event—assuming it is possible to acquire that knowledge—is less important than the utility of the event to promote a modern need or ward off a modern evil.

As these needs or evils shift through time, so too does the ideological landscape of modern perceptions. The "objective" interpretations of World War II events in Belgium and Luxembourg and the notation of German military cemeteries on maps in these countries and in France reflect less anger with and more acceptance of Germany as an ally in the modern political and cultural climate of Europe.

The redesignation of a military base in honor of a compassionate Austrian soldier, as discussed in the introduction, is a conscious attempt to provide modern German soldiers with a new example selectively chosen from their history. The displacement of General Rüdel, who had been considered a model soldier following the war, admirably illustrates the shifting ideological landscape. Objections to his displacement from older German soldiers, such as a former base commander (Cohen 2000), reveal that conflicting ideological landscapes compete in the effort to define and redefine the physical presentation of the military past.

European perceptions of war are shaped by the knowledge that armies are extensions of cultural groups and that war always has a devastating impact on soldier and civilian. Cemeteries are unquestionably the most powerful memorial features of battlefield landscapes. Yet such symbolically laden landscapes may be constructed to convey very different messages. Consider, for example, how different a reaction one may have in visiting a well-maintained cemetery, even a huge one, and then gazing upon the piles of human skulls and limb bones visible in the ossuary at Verdun.

It has been argued that the extent and nature of military site commemoration in Europe reflect ideological landscapes oriented to perpetuation of the present. The role of ideology is fundamental to understanding these commemorations as "that knowledge of the past that present society would emphasize in order to reproduce itself as it is now constituted" (Leone 1982:754). As the manner in which a society is "now constituted" changes, so too will the corpus of past events, opinions, and people change that is incorporated into or omitted from the interpretation. Military sites are obviously not the only ones subject to this sort of ideological manipulation, but they are often directly linked to the formulation of a national identity. Given that ideological landscapes may compete across space and change through time, one may conclude that selected military events have not and may never come to an end.

ACKNOWLEDGMENTS

I am most appreciative for the assistance provided by Myra Lawson and Indira Mann of the National Trust for Scotland and by Nick Brannon, director of Built Heritage of the Environment and Heritage Service in Northern Ireland. Nick kindly read and commented upon a draft of this paper. Paul Shackel and three anonymous reviewers provided comments on an earlier draft that improved the quality of this paper. I am indebted to Paul and to Mark Leone for their support during my time as a research associate at Maryland. My understanding of the meaning of past military sites to the present world has been greatly focused by the thoughts and writings of Mark Leone, for which I am very grateful.

REFERENCES

AMERICAN BATTLE MONUMENTS COMMISSION
 1984 *Normandy American Cemetery and Memorial.* Pamphlet. American Battle Monuments Commission for the 40th Anniversary of D-Day. [Available at the cemetery in Colleville-sur-Mer, France.]
 1998a *Luxembourg American Cemetery.* Information sheet. American Battle Monuments Commission. [Available at the cemetery in Hamm, Luxembourg.]
 1998b *Ardennes American Cemetery.* Information sheet. American Battle Monuments Commission. [Available at the cemetery in Neuville-en-Condroz, Belgium.]

COHEN, ROGER
 2000 New Model for Soldiers in Germany. *New York Times,* 9 May:A3.

COMITÉ DU DÉBARQUEMENT

[1984] *The Landing Beaches*. Pamphlet. Comité du Débarquement for 40th Anniversary of D-Day. [Available in Normandy, France, in 1986.]

ERLANGER, STEPHEN

1999 At Site of Serbs' Identity, Fears over the Albanians' Wrath. *New York Times*, 9 June:A1, A4.

KEEGAN, JOHN

1982 *Six Armies in Normandy: From D-Day to the Liberation of Paris*. Reprinted in 1984 by Penguin Books, Ltd, Hammondsworth, England.

KNISCHEWSKI, GERD, AND ULLA SPITTLER

1997 Memories of the Second World War and National Identity in Germany. In *War and Memory in the Twentieth Century*, Martin Evans and Ken Lunn, editors, pp. 239–254. Berg, New York.

LEMMON, CHARLES

1970 *The Field of Hastings*. 4th edition. Budd and Gillatt, St. Leonards-on-Sea, England.

LEONE, MARK

1982 Some Opinions about Recovering Mind. *American Antiquity*, 47:742–760.

1984 Interpreting Ideology in Historical Archaeology: Using the Rules of Perspective in the William Paca Garden in Annapolis, Maryland. In *Ideology, Power, and Prehistory*, D. Miller and C. Tilley, editors, pp. 25–35. Cambridge University Press, Cambridge.

MICHELIN

1947a *Bataille de Normandie, Juin–Août 1944 (Battle of Normandy, June–August 1944)*. 40ᵉ anniversaire du débarquement 6 juin 1944. Réimpression de la carte historique de 1947. Pneu Michelin, Paris.

1947b *Voie de la Liberté, Juin 1944–Janvier 1945 (Road to Liberty, June 1944–January 1945)*. Réimpression de la carte historique de 1947. Pneu Michelin, Paris.

NATIONAL TRUST FOR SCOTLAND

1999 *Visit the National Trust for Scotland 1999*. Pamphlet. Public Affairs Division of the National Trust for Scotland, Edinburgh.

PREBBLE, JOHN

1961 *Culloden*. Penguin Books Ltd, Hammondsworth, England.

RAY, R. CELESTE

1998 Scottish Heritage Southern Style. *Southern Cultures*, 4(2):28–45.

SMURTHWAITE, DAVID

1984 *Battlefields of Britain*. Webb and Bower Ltd., Exeter, England.

ŠPATNÝ, JAN, AND JINDRA GRIEBLEROVÁ

1991 *Slavkov Austerlitz* [map]. Geodézie, Brno, Czech Republic.

VOLKSBUND DEUTSCHE KRIEGSGRÄBERFÜSORGE

n.d.a *Sandweiler*. Pamphlet. Volksbund Deutsche Kriegsgräberfüsorge. [Available at the cemetery in Sandweiler, Luxembourg, in 1999.]

n.d.b *Belgien: Deutsche Kriegsgräberstätten in Belgien (German Military Cemeteries in Belgium)*. Pamphlet. Volksbund Deutsche Kriegsgräberfüsorge. [Available at the cemetery at Recogne-Bastogne, Belgium, in 1999.]

BROOKE S. BLADES
DEPARTMENT OF ANTHROPOLOGY
NEW YORK UNIVERSITY
25 WAVERLY PLACE
NEW YORK, NY 10003

Tracy Ireland

"The Absence of Ghosts": Landscape and Identity in the Archaeology of Australia's Settler Culture

ABSTRACT

This article is a case study investigating archaeology as a practice embedded in a complex web of culturally constructed codes of meaning or discourses. A distinctive form of discourse concerning the landscape and its role in determining national identity characterizes Australian culture. This discourse has been central to the construction of the idea of the nation and its past: in particular, concepts of the land as hostile and empty, of the bush as the essence of Australia, and of the landscape as feminine. The paper considers the ways in which this landscape discourse has operated within historical archaeological research and heritage management and discusses the implications of these discursive relationships for past and future research.

Introduction

> It was the fearful loneliness of the place that most affected her—the absence of ghosts. Till they arrived, no other lives had been lived here. It made the air that much thinner, harder to breathe. She had not understood, till she came to a place where it was lacking, the extent to which her sense of the world had to do with the presence of those who had been here before, leaving signs of their passing and spaces still warm with breath—a threshold worn with the coming and going of feet, hedges between fields that went back a thousand years, and the names even further; most of all, the names on the headstones, which were their names, under which lay the bones that had made their bones and given them breath (Malouf 1994:110).

This discussion of landscape, identity, and Australian historical archaeology considers certain discursive themes within the Australian cultural tradition, which have particular relevance to the way in which archaeologists have studied the historic past in Australia. Representations of landscape in the Australian imagination have constructed a powerful discourse through which the landscape and human behavior within it has, subsequently, been understood. Landscape discourse has, therefore, been central to the narrative construction of the Australian settler nation and its past. In particular, the landscape is seen as a determinant of not only the course of colonial history but also of the distinctive characteristics of national identity. In her comparison of bicentennial commemorations in Australia (1988) and the United States (1976), Lyn Spillman has pointed out how central the landscape was to expressions of national identity in the Australian celebrations. This contrasted markedly with the United States where the land had formed only "a minor part of the symbolic repertoire." She also noted that the Australian land was more important in national iconography in 1988 than it had been in the centennial celebrations of the previous century (Spillman 1997:125).

It is important to clarify that in studies of Australian cultural traditions, the term "landscape" is used often and broadly. It may cover a grab bag of concepts from the biophysical environment, to a natural backdrop in films and literature, or the more specific genre of landscape painting. Generally, the term is used to describe representations of nature. Nature in this context is the opposite to culture, and in the Australian settler context, nature is the enemy of culture and the opponent of civilization (Gibson 1993:212). Tom Griffiths suggests that "the competing realities of geography and history, land and culture, have stood for a fundamental, persistent tension between origins and environment in Australian life" (Griffiths 1997:11). This concept of an environment somehow opposed to the fostering of cultural development is central to colonial narratives of settler history in Australia.

However, concepts of landscape and environment are also elided into metaphors of settler self-representation and the identity of the nation. Australian nationalism of the 20th century is characterized by an escalation of the value and meaning attributed to the special characteristics of the Australian environment: the visual qualities of the landscape and the unique native flora and fauna. Settler identification with landscape is, however, ambiguous and full of contradictions. To the largely urbanized settler population, nature (the Outback or the bush) is the source of the genuine Australian experience, yet it is seen, simultaneously, as the indigenous wilderness from which they are alienated (Morton and Smith 1999:175).

For the purposes of definition however, it is important to note here that *archaeological* understandings of landscape as a cultural palimpsest or, more simply, as a human constructed or influenced environment cannot be overlaid upon concepts of landscape in Australian culture generally. For instance, the idea of *pristine wilderness* (that is, nature unaltered by humans) is so prominent in Australian culture that conservationists and land managers still struggle with the idea that most of the continent is a cultural landscape, shaped by a long history of human occupation. In historical archaeology, understandings of cultural landscape compete with the colonialist construction of the expanding of a frontier that is not simply geographical but also a major ontological disjunction between the beginning of history and the end of prehistory (Rose 1999: 9). The colonial inheritance of the institutional and academic division of history, prehistory, and historical archaeology has left little conceptual territory within which to explore hybrid cultures and landscapes (Colley and Bickford 1996; Murray 1996c).

Hence, there is a complex entanglement of culturally constructed ways of knowing the Australian landscape, landscape-based expressions of national identity, and the historical and archaeological research that is both constructed through these cultural traditions, while also seeking to explain them. This analysis is less concerned with critiquing the basis in reality of these constructions concerning landscape and identity than with understanding the way in which they operate within culture as discourses or self-perpetuating codes of meaning (Foucault 1972; Schaffer 1988).

An important context for this analysis is recent critiques of identity discourse and archaeology, including literature on archaeology, ethnicity, and nationalism (Bond and Gilliam 1995; Kohl and Fawcett 1995; Atkinson et al. 1996; Diaz-Andreu and Champion 1996; Graves-Brown et al. 1996; Jones 1997). These critiques spring from widespread intellectual interest in the social context of knowledge production and, in particular, the use of knowledge about the past in maintaining or subverting power in society. American historical archaeologists have pursued this issue more vigorously in the arena of investigating capitalism, both in the past as well as the way in which it

forms the context for question formulation in the present (Leone and Potter 1999).

Following postcolonial theorists, this paper approaches nationalism as a significant form of cultural identity that may be expressed through and constituted by all kinds of cultural practice (Anderson 1983; Bhabha 1990; Brennan 1990; Parker et al. 1992; Ashcroft et al. 1995). The Australian nation was created through the events of British colonial expansion and through the eventual transferal of colonial control from the founding metropolitan country to the colony itself, where it has been maintained through the unity and complicity of the settler group (McClintock 1994:258). Nationalism and colonialism cannot be considered as two separate or opposing ideologies in Australia; they remain fundamentally intertwined. Australia experienced no war of independence and still maintains the Queen of England as the head of state. The 1992 High Court of Australia's Mabo decision concerning lands rights for indigenous people has been claimed by some to be the most significant disruption of ongoing colonialism in this nation's history (Attwood 1996a:109).

Rather than looking at archaeology as a discipline that may be impacted upon, to greater or lesser degrees, by external influences such as nationalism, this paper seeks to understand traditions of understanding that are embedded within Australian historical archaeology and the subtle, multilayered relationships between archaeology and other cultural discourses. Such analysis necessarily relates to debates concerning disciplinary objectivity, relativism, and academic responsibilities (Kohl and Fawcett 1995; Lampeter Archaeology Workshop 1997). Discourse analysis, as employed here, accepts that all ideas, theories, and explanations are created within and through a complex historic, socio/cultural, and linguistic situation. Further, this analysis is admittedly political in that it addresses current social and ethical concerns about how nationalist/colonialist pasts are used to promote restrictive and oppressive identities in the present.

The quotation at the beginning of this paper comes from David Malouf's novel *Remembering Babylon*, a recent re-examination of what is, perhaps, the most dominant theme in Australian settler art and literature—the question of the land and its role in shaping national identity. Malouf takes the trope of Australia's hostile environment and explores the real effects of this culturally constructed perception in the day-to-day lives of settlers. In this way, he disrupts the familiar colonialist narratives, which center on success or failure in the battle against the environment. In the passage quoted above, Malouf describes how a settler from Scotland feels about her surroundings on a remote Australian farm. He catalogues what is absent from the place: the features of the European landscape that formed her cultural identity and to which her culture gives symbolic meaning. Malouf's settlers *do* see the land as empty and threatening, and this is based on the European perception that property involves improvement and exploitation of resources rather than simply living with the land as the Aborigines are seen to do (Fletcher 1997:177). The novel, in fact, employs a conceit whereby Aborigines become literally invisible to the settlers, as invisible as the ecological balance of the land that they struggle to make more like home. This invisibility was also found in the historical narratives of colonial settlement before the appearance of challenging revisionist histories such as those by Henry Reynolds (1981, 1987). Despite the impact of Aboriginal histories, some sections of the community reject these interpretations of the national past as "black armband" history, a view reinforced by the Australian Prime Minister in a famous 1996 speech (Howard 1996, Birch 1997).

In the phrase "the absence of ghosts," Malouf describes the cultural foundations of the concept of *terra nullius* in the minds of settlers. This concept is central to the understanding of colonialist representations of and responses to Australian land and, therefore, a crucial component of what is called landscape discourse in this paper. *Terra nullius* was the legal description of the concept that the continent of Australia was vacant and wilderness before the possession of the land by the British, based on the belief that Aborigines and Torres Strait Islanders, as hunter-gatherers, did not improve the land and, thus, had no proprietorial rights to it. This legal doctrine was finally overthrown by the High Court's Mabo land rights decision in 1992, which provided the first legal basis for the recognition of prior ownership of Australian land by indigenous people. Malouf's settlers' perception of the Australian landscape as hostile and without a human dimension results in a con-

stant and unhappy emphasis on survival and on the hardships associated with changing or battling the land to conform to their understanding of civilization and progress. It also results in the formation of a group identity based primarily upon fear of their opponents: nature or the environment and Aborigines as nature's strange envoys in human form (Fletcher 1997:176).

The paradigm of *terra nullius* is crucial to the foundational histories and popular understandings of Australia as a nation of settlers rather than conquerors. Although no longer upheld by law, the concept remains deeply embedded within Australian culture, from beliefs about pioneers and settler identity through to understandings of traditional Aboriginal culture, the land, nature, and so-called wilderness (Langton 1995). Recent studies have attempted to understand the significance of *terra nullius* and its subsequent overturning in the Mabo decision to Australian settler culture and national identity through a consideration of how the term has operated within various fields of discourse such as colonial history, science, politics, literature, and Aboriginal archaeology (Attwood 1996b; Murray 1996a; Griffiths and Robin 1997; Gelder and Jacobs 1998). The main aim of this analysis of historical archaeology is to draw out the way in which landscape discourse has operated within and through research and writing. However, the research that is critiqued in this paper should not be considered to be without value because it has perpetuated colonialist constructions of the past. Analysis of the cultural and social context of research, which is not just an interesting subfield of the history of archaeology, enables constructive new readings of research and allows past research to be built upon rather than being simply dismissed as outdated.

Landscape and Identity in the Australian Cultural Tradition

This section briefly reviews key elements of Australian settler history and intellectual traditions that have contributed to understanding the landscape in particular ways. Settling Australia was an imaginary as well as a physical process. The culture of the settlers provided the forms and descriptions through which the landscape was given a meaning and shape that was comprehensible to them. Australian settlers were predominately from Britain and Ireland, more than 160,000 arriving as convicts until transportation finally ceased in 1868. Free immigrants were also predominantly English, Scottish, and Irish, although some Europeans were encouraged, especially Germans, thought to be culturally and racially closest to the British. Chinese immigration, largely associated with the gold rushes of the 1850s and 60s, caused immense social debate in the late-19th century. Consequently, one of the first acts of the newly federated nation in 1901 was to pass legislation that was to become the basis for Australia's notorious White Australia Policy, which persisted until 1966 (Curthoys 1999b: 279). However, despite this predominance of settlers of Anglo-Celtic heritage, it should be remembered that the settler group was still ethnically, religiously, and politically diverse (Melleuish 1998:10). Postwar migration radically changed the ethnic composition of Australian society. Since the late 1940s, there has been a steady widening of the potential countries-of-origin of immigrants, and this has engendered a diverse society, which struggles in a search for appropriate expressions of cultural identity and national unity (Pettman 1992). In the absence of a common cultural legacy, the experience of place has been described as central to identity constructions in settler societies (Ashcroft et al. 1995:152). In Australia, the ideology of colonialism has constructed the land as the prime object of desire, and it is the consequences of this desire that provides the clearest basis for a community identity that is different from the idea of the mother country.

The Land As Empty

A philosophical rationale for the colonization or invasion of Australia in 1788 was in part provided by the Scottish Enlightenment philosophers, such as Adam Smith and Adam Ferguson, who expounded an influential theory of the evolution of human society (Attwood 1996b:ix). This four-phase explanation saw hunter-gatherers as the first stage in a natural evolution that concluded with commerce and empire. Hunter-gatherers, they proposed, had no conception of property and so their lands were deemed desert or waste—*terra nullius*. Interest in cultural evolution was one of the scientific rationales for the

journeys of exploration into the Pacific. "The Moral Philosopher ... who loves to trace the advances of his species ... draws from voyages and travels the facts from which he is to deduce his conclusions respecting the social, intellectual, and moral progress of Man" (Jacques Julien de Labillardiere, 1800, quoted in Dixon 1986:6). These journeys were, therefore, conceived of as travel into the ancient past that could be used to complete knowledge of "the history of man."

Within this framework, Aborigines were thought of as living in a different time from the Europeans: a time before history. Brian Attwood (1996b) has analyzed the implications of the epistemological framework of the European discourse of history for both the act of colonization and the subsequent construction of Australian colonial history. European historical discourse, following enlightenment and evolutionary thinking, aligns time with progress in an inevitable linear progression. This discursive alignment formed part of the mental framework that enabled the British to see the Australian landscape as wilderness and available for possession. Attwood (1996b:viii) therefore claims that "History was not only the discourse of the colonizers; it was also a colonizing one." Colonization and its attendant Christianity, civilization, and progress enabled history, therefore, to begin on a continent where time in European terms had previously been meaningless.

In 1828, Sir Thomas Mitchell was appointed as Surveyor General of New South Wales. A man of great energy, Mitchell saw his mission as translating the tracts of wilderness into intellectually defined objects through a process of survey and naming. At that time, settlement was confined to areas close to Sydney, but the whole of the east coast had been claimed for Britain. Mitchell undertook extensive journeys of exploration in eastern Australia in order to lay the necessary framework for this imperial possession. His exploration diaries detail how each expedition was led by Aboriginal guides who negotiated with the various tribes encountered along the way. Although Mitchell records daily encounters with different groups of Aboriginal people, he was, nevertheless, able to write that he saw "a country which is yet in the same state as it was when formed by its maker ... . A land so inviting, and still without inhabitants" (Lines 1991:71). Mitchell named the lush valleys of

Victoria "Australia Felix" and wrote, "Of this Eden it seemed that I was the only Adam and it was indeed a sort of paradise to me" (Schaffer 1988:60).

The Land As Hostile:
Explorers and Pioneers

Mitchell and the early explorers wrote of Australia in rapturous terms; however, as settlement and exploration progressed, as explorers perished, and farmers experienced drought, the land came to be seen as harsh and threatening. As early as 1849, when Charles Sturt published an account of his failed journey to locate an inland sea in the center of the continent, visions of rapture were replaced with a perception of the continent as inhospitable to civilization (Gibson 1996:92). But the dangerous and threatening character of the land was to be construed as the test of Empire and the test from which Australian manhood would emerge ennobled:

> To successfully plant a young Colony ... seems to require special qualities, physical, moral and intellectual, which are possessed in their highest form by the Anglo-Saxon people. It is a small matter to supplant the Aboriginal inhabitants of a barbarous country and to secure possession of their land ... . It is battling with Nature, conquering the soil, holding on against capricious seasons, fighting with the elements and compelling the earth to yield ... . (William Harcus's 1876 emigration guide, quoted in Schaffer 1988:84).

Sir Keith Hancock's 1930 history *Australia* is seen as a crucial text in establishing and giving academic authority to a nationalist history connecting the land with national character. Hancock's history was centrally concerned with land settlement and the pastoral industry as the instrument of colonial possession. The battle for possession is the battle to establish European agricultural systems in the Australian environment. The enemy in this battle is, therefore, nature, not international trade, economic depression, or the inequities of the colonial administration (Schaffer 1988:87). Failure on the land, through drought, bushfire, and flood, came to be seen as the mythical forge for national character. Pioneers were the free immigrants from Britain and Ireland (as opposed to the non-free convicts) who fought to establish new lives free of Old World class prejudices and poverty. The settler's "failure" in material terms is compensated by the

spiritual benefits of pioneering strength, stoicism, and love of the land, love of the nation.

Anne Curthoys interprets Australia's pioneer legend as an essentially "victimological narrative," which, she argues, resonates meanings derived from Judeo-Christian history and from biblical stories such as the Exodus (Curthoys 1999a:4). The inheritance of these pioneer and land myths, Curthoys claims, underlies the inability of many Australians to deal with a history that paints them as colonial aggressors, rather than as the victims or survivors of a history of struggle.

The Bushman and the Bush
As the "Essence" of Australia

The 1890s have been constructed through later historiography as the decade in which a true national culture was crystallized. By this time, 70% of the settler population was Australian-born, and the six colonies were instigating the process of federation, which led to the creation of the continent nation in 1901 (Byrne 1996). Australian writers, artists, journalists, and politicians began to consciously articulate descriptions of a unique national character at this time, using imagery that, although reinvented, remains current and influential at the start of the 21st century. The results of the settler experience became essentialized in the myth of the "bushman." The bushman was a model of masculinity created by the effects of the Australian landscape, resulting in a typical national character that was defined in Russell Ward's *The Australian Legend* as the antiauthoritarian larrikin, practical and independent, but loyal to his mates (Ward 1958:1–2). The Great War of 1914–1918 saw this same national type heroized as the Digger or the Anzac (White 1981; Lake 1992:313).

Henry Lawson's stories and poems are perhaps the best-known exemplars of the bushman genre. One form of the bush hero beloved by Lawson is the Swagman, an out-of-work man who wandered the roads of rural Australia carrying nothing but his swag, or bedroll. Lawson writes: "The Australian swag was born of Australia and no other land—of the Great Lone Land of magnificent distances and bright heat: the land of Self-reliance and Never give in and Help your mate" (Hodge and Mishra 1990:153). This sentence is a distillation of Lawson's ideology of the bush, clearly articulating how facets of the environment—distance, isolation, and harsh climate—shaped a unique Australian character that was built on egalitarian, masculine mateship.

The main aspect to note about the myth of the bushman is that its most famous exponents were a group of urban writers and the magazine the *Bulletin*, which was a mouthpiece for the urban liberal bourgeois *against* the interests of powerful rural pastoralists. In contrast to the pioneer myths of settlement discussed above, which are more centrally concerned with the process of imperial possession, the bush myths link more strongly with these nationalist, democratic ideologies. The bush or the land is used as an allegory for the masculine freedom that was the political agenda of the writers. However, this allegorical function of the bush within the political context of the 1890s is a largely forgotten aspect of this construction as it was reproduced throughout the 20th century as a key aspect of national identity. This is designed, despite significant critical scholarship that has shown the bush myth and the "The Australian Legend" to be an ideological construct, to reproduce the authority of masculinist, political interest groups (Davison 1978; White 1981; Lake 1986).

The bush myth has also been constituted through and perpetuated by landscape art. In particular, the images of the Heidelburg School of the 1880s and 1890s remain icons in Australian culture today. These landscape images, often employing a heroic figure dwarfed by open surroundings, so dominated Australian art that they led prominent art historian Bernard Smith to state in 1976, "This preoccupation with landscape has been largely responsible for the creation and maintenance of a false consciousness of what it is to be Australian" (Hodge & Mishra 1990:143). The idea that national character is a result of our, or our ancestors', experience of the bush and its hardships still pervades Australian culture today, exemplified in recent films such as *Crocodile Dundee*, *The Man from Snowy River*, and even *Priscilla, Queen of the Desert*. Libby Robin has recently pointed out how the meaning of the bush in national culture has changed since the 1970s. The value of a rural life on the frontier, as conceived of by the *Bulletin* writers, has transmuted into the concept of the spiritually restorative wilderness, required as an escape for suburban Australians from "economy and history" (Robin 1998:123). Of particular interest in Robin's work in this context is her argument

that current meanings of bush and wilderness, associated with the environmental conservation movement, have been developed through the power and meaning of the earlier bush myths, revitalizing in some ways their ongoing centrality in national culture. Further, the texts and representations that created the bush myth, and that were so self-consciously created to express the emergence of a new national culture, are also pervaded by a description of gender relations that continued to resonate in Australian culture in the 20th century (Rowley 1993:186).

The Land As Feminine

If the bushman has represented the nation, then the nation's "other" has been seen as the land or the body of Australia itself. Analysts of cultural nationalism have outlined how the nation develops conceptions of itself in opposition to a perceived other, an object that may be simultaneously both desired and despised. In Australian nationalist traditions, the other can take many forms: it may be Britain, it may be Aborigines or Asians, but frequently the other is the landscape itself. The linguistic signification of Australia as mother and the land as the body of a woman was studied in detail in a groundbreaking analysis published by Kay Schaffer in 1988. In essence, it is the colonialist framework of desire, to possess, master, and tame, which casts the object of this desire, the land, in a feminine role. Historical rhetoric of the 19th and early-20th centuries constantly eroticizes the love/hate relationship between the settlers and the land. The explorers "lift her veils of mystery" and penetrate the vast recesses of the interior. In contrast to the benevolent European construction of Mother Earth, Australia is often personified as a "witch mother," experimenting on her helpless victims.

The consequence of this discourse, which casts the nation as masculine and its other as feminine, is that women as subjects have been almost totally absent from constructions of national identity. In the 1970s, Anne Summers and Miriam Dixson initiated an ongoing analysis into what they considered was an ethos of subtle contempt for women that pervaded the Australian cultural tradition (Summers 1975; Dixson 1976). As has been seen, the bushman is a loner, just a man and the wide-open spaces; freedom is paramount as is loyalty to his mates. The ties of wife and family were construed as the antithesis to this freedom (Lake 1986:118; Lake 1992:312). Significantly, the bush myth casts the battle with the land as establishing the territory of the nation. This creates an inherent tension between the ties of family and nation-building work on the land. As Sue Rowley points out, when women are present in bush literature, their labor is not marked on the land but on their own bodies, which Henry Lawson habitually described as "gaunt" and "haggard": "these women are positioned not as the heroes of the battle, but as its casualties" (Rowley 1993:188).

This construction has since been the subject of much historical explanation. It has led to an overwhelming focus on bush work, mineral prospecting, droving, and pastoralism for instance, as the work that made the nation. Revisionist histories have successfully "discovered" women in the past, included them in popular historical accounts, and even established their contribution to nation building (Margarey et al. 1993; Grimshaw et al. 1994). However, the ongoing power of this discourse, which establishes a relationship between men and the national territory based on patriarchal gender relations, continues to resonate in Australian national life (Reekie 1992:17).

Landscape and Identity As Discourses within Archaeological Interpretation

Landscape discourse is not only a set of ideas about the landscape but also about settler men and women who are constructed in various roles in opposition to it, about history that is seen as a result of it, and about Aborigines who are viewed as part of it. The idea of landscape is so central to the national cultural tradition that research, which takes the settler landscape as its subject, must develop a critical capacity regarding its historical and literary construction. This critique should also be turned back upon the discipline of historical archaeology itself, not only to inform approaches to the historic landscape or the past in general but also in order to understand the cultural context of established research questions and fields of interest.

Historical Archaeology and Heritage

The following review of historical archaeological research suggests that landscape discourse operates within the discipline in a number of ways. First, there is a fundamental and entrenched relationship between the practice of historical archaeology and identity discourse, through the philosophy and institutions of the heritage movement. Historical archaeology, as a practice that studies the physical remains of Australia's history, cannot be considered in isolation from the processes that resulted in the attribution of value to the material remains of the national past. Its emergence as a field of interest in the 1960s and 1970s can be historically located within a national revival of interest in Australian history, literature, art, and material culture (Bennett 1993:236). This, in turn, was linked to local and international conservation and environmental movements and the bolstering of national and regional identities in the face of perceived cultural globalization. The environmental movement, which emerges in Australia in the 1960s, has been described as "a fusion of romanticism, nationalism, and science, but … also an attempt to reject colonialism" (Morton and Smith 1999:172). Although today environmental conservation and settler heritage movements have many tensions and divergent aims, their roots in essentially nationalistic concerns seem to be clear. The idea that landscape and settler identity are linked has been accepted as a fact within environmental and heritage conservation movements—as a taken-for-granted, spiritual association rather than a historically constructed idea. It is also significant that in Australian conservation legislation, heritage is often termed environmental heritage (as in the New South Wales Heritage Act, 1977) and is constituted in legislation as a part of the environment. This implies that heritage, like biodiversity, exists independently of human thought and is not ideologically constructed. Hence cultural resource management has concentrated on developing empirical methodologies to "discover" heritage and organize it into taxonomies of relative value rather than to approach it as culturally constructed or examining the role it plays in community life.

The ethnographic and archaeological interest in Aboriginal cultural heritage has a very different history, which is beyond the scope of this paper. It is important to note however, that this interest developed out of 18th- and 19th-century interest in the natural history of Australia, within Enlightenment concepts of evolution and amateur traditions of collecting and antiquarianism. Historical archaeology, although now linked to Australian prehistory institutionally and methodologically, draws its concepts of value and significance from a process that historicized the settler nation and constructed ideas of national heritage and identity. This is not to say that, as a practice, historical archaeology has not absorbed ways of constructing meaning and attributing value from other fields of discourse; it is obvious that it has. However, the idea that the material remains of the recent past are worth studying at all is one that has been established within the community predominantly through the discourse of national heritage and identity rather than through discourses concerned with the universal value of knowledge, such as history, science, and archaeology in general.

Griffiths (1996:195) and Graeme Davison (1991: 3) argue that what was new about the heritage movement of the 1960s and 1970s was not its nationalistic focus, as heritage and nationalism can be seen as strongly linked in the 19th century, but the redefinition of heritage as a material rather than a spiritual concept. The idea of a material heritage, and its accompanying concepts of collecting, curation, and conservation, gave archaeological methodologies an obvious role in the newly defined heritage movement. Griffiths has shown that an archaeological sense of the past, a belief that scientific methodologies may be used to recover material remnants and decode their meaning, is integral to the nature of the modern preservation movement (Griffiths 1996:196). This linking of materiality with heritage ensured that archaeology as a practice became more deeply involved in the discourse of heritage and, of course, in heritage management work than was the case with the related disciplines of history and anthropology (Byrne 1996:101). Archaeologists, such as Jim Allen, Judy Birmingham, Anne Bickford, Isabel McBryde, Rhys Jones, and John Mulvaney, who were specifically concerned with the potential of the new field of historical archaeology also played a significant role in the formative history of the Australian Heritage Commission, the national body responsible for heritage administration since 1974. Their involvement ensured that historical archaeology defined a strong niche as a discipline responsible for an important component of the nation's heritage (Bonyhady and Griffiths 1996:9).

Historical archaeology in Australia still possesses a limited base in universities and receives relatively little funding from sources that traditionally fund research in Old World archaeology or prehistory (Egloff 1994). Consequently, most historical archaeological work is funded through private clients complying with cultural resource management requirements embodied in legislation, which varies from state to state (Colley 1996; Connah 1998:3). Thus, historical archaeological research must justify itself in terms of its ability to address themes enshrined as important within heritage management frameworks. This in itself need not and, of course, in many cases has not prohibited creative responses to archaeological research issues. However, as some of the examples discussed below will demonstrate, it has tended to link historical archaeological research to a framework of national history, which has traditionally supported dominant identity constructions and which reflects colonialist myths about the nature of the land and men's relationship to it (Ireland 1996:92).

Town and Country

As we have seen, art and literature that valorized men's lives in the bush in the 19th century, for the purpose of allegory supporting a political standpoint, has been taken as evidence of historical experience, as a reflection of reality rather than as a construction for a political purpose. In addition to this, the colonialist history of the "progressive mastery" of the land—peopling it, making it useful through industry and agriculture—has dominated accounts of Australia's national development. This construction of the past can be shown to have constrained and influenced archaeology in a number of ways, but also, significantly, there is some suggestion that the archaeological evidence itself has provided some resistance to it.

"*Of the Hut I Builded*," Graham Connah's 1988 overview of Australian historical archaeology, is an example of how a variety of archaeological research and interpretation may be structured within a framework that tacitly reproduces colonialist and nationalist constructions of the past (Connah 1988, later published under the title *The Archaeology of Australia's History*). The purpose of the following discussion of this text is to analyze its discursive context, not to criticize it for omissions identified with the hindsight of a decade of revisionist history and in the light of a significantly different intellectual climate.

It should be noted that the book was published with assistance from the Australian Bicentennial Authority, a body that funded a host of history and heritage-related projects to mark 200 years of colonization in 1988.

The book mirrors the tendency for historical archaeological research, especially that linked to heritage management projects and funding sources, to follow the popularly understood themes of nationalist history: the centrality of rural expansion in the process of founding the nation, the importance of industrialization, and the hostility of the environment to these processes. The rhetorical style of the text reinforces this thematic structure: for instance, the settlement of Sydney is where the "birth of a new nation can be observed from the archaeological evidence," while convicts are celebrated for their "vital role in the settlement of this nation" (Connah 1988:35,62). The implication of considering the archaeology of early Sydney as a foundation for the nation closes our eyes to the other histories being played out at that time. For instance, the first annexation of Australia clung to the eastern coast, integrating Sydney in a colonial adventure that in the minds of many included the adjacent Pacific islands for as far as Tahiti (Crowley 1974:48). The Australian nation, based on the continental landmass, was not a foregone conclusion in 1788.

The book instantly invokes the mythology of the bush by taking the Henry Lawson poem, *Reedy River*, as its leitmotif. The poem revisits many of Lawson's prominent themes concerning man's insignificance in the Australian landscape, its intractability, and dual status as desired object and hated foe. Three of the book's eight chapters dealing with archaeological evidence are devoted to industry and rural production. Although whaling is discussed briefly in one chapter, maritime industry and trade economies, which account for critical, early transferals of capital into the colony, do not feature as a theme of this land-centered narrative. Evidence from maritime archaeology, covering only the wrecks of Dutch East Indiamen, is confined to a chapter dealing with "pre-colonial contact" and is seen as an interesting prolegomenon to the business of colonization from 1788. However, as Wayne Johnson's paper in this volume shows, the continent of Australia was certainly implicated in European colonial politics from well before this

date. Schuyler has also usefully shown that interaction prior to actual settlement also changes cultural landscapes, and recognition of this interaction allows richer archaeological interpretations than may be achieved within the confines of nationalist history (Schuyler 1991). The evidence of Dutch East India Company shipwrecks is construed by Connah as precolonial because it predates the settlement of Australia by the British. This highlights the understanding of colonization as settlement and nation building rather than as a complex phenomenon including colonial trade, military, and cultural activities.

Although research in urban archaeology and contact archaeology (archaeology of contact between settler and indigenous people) is referred to in the final chapter of the book, much of this research existed in unpublished reports at the time that the text was written. Connah's book also reflects a preference for the analysis of structural and technological remains rather than artifact and material culture analysis, which remains a poorly published issue in Australian historical archaeology (Lawrence 1998b). The incompatibility of the overall themes of land settlement and industry in Connah's text with the social issues addressed by urban archaeology and material culture studies, may be another reason why attempts were not made to address what was then a burgeoning interest in the urban archaeology of the 19th century (Karskens and Thorp 1992; Lydon 1993).

The romance of the bush, then, continues to seduce those seeking the essential qualities of the Australian historical experience. Stephanie Moser has suggested that Australian prehistory sought its disciplinary identity through the rigors of fieldwork in the remote outback, archaeologists themselves reliving Lawson's promise of masculine fulfillment in the arms of the bush (Moser 1995). Historical archaeologists, rather than reliving this tradition, have given much attention to explaining it.

No Place for a Woman

It is in the area of urban archaeology that the realities of the material evidence have drawn archaeologists into directions that challenged the dominant discourses of national development. Historical archaeology's concentration on rural work and industry continued to reconstruct the idea of Australia as "Manzone Country" (Summers 1975). Its focus on pioneer technology and the success or failure of technological processes perpetuated an almost tacit understanding that this was the work that had made the nation, and it was man's work. An analysis of the contents of the *Australian Journal of Historical Archaeology* (now *Australasian Historical Archaeology*) shows how research implicitly reinforced this construction. Since it was first published in 1983, this journal has published 65 case studies on Australian rural or industrial sites or groups of sites, and only eight case studies on urban archaeology (the balance of articles, on other subjects such as conservation and theory, numbers 60).

The alternative thread in historical archaeological research has come from within the heritage management industry rather than from the academy. The creation of legislation protecting historical archaeological relics, particularly in NSW in 1977, has seen a gradual growth in compliance, which has resulted in numerous, large-scale excavations of urban sites and neighborhoods and also in Melbourne (Mayne and Lawrence 1998; Murray and Mayne this volume). Much of this work exists in unpublished reports (but compare Proudfoot et al. 1991; Lydon 1993; Karskens 1999). This paper contends that the explosion in urban archaeology, which began in Sydney in the late 1980s, occurred because of the creation of a solid legislative footing. It also occurred because of the commitment of the cultural resource managers responsible for implementing this legislation and educating the public on the heritage value of historical archaeological material (Temple 1988). However, the debates about the value of these urban excavations suggest that archaeological researchers themselves were struggling for the conceptual and methodological frameworks required to make sense of this kind of archaeology (Birmingham 1990; Karskens and Thorp 1992; Egloff 1994; Mackay 1996; see in particular Thorp quoted in Mackay 1996): "The relics provisions of the NSW Heritage Act allows archaeologists to be lazy. If a relic exists ... it can be the subject of an archaeological excavation. That does not ensure that the site, or object, is significant or worthy of excavation." What this means is that the heritage management infrastructure, through its insistence on the potential value of all archaeological material, forced archaeologists to move in new directions.

Because of the exigencies of the consulting archaeological industry, the lack of full-time researchers, and the fact that these sites produced such huge numbers of artifacts, work from urban sites was slow to be published. Artifact analysis was an overwhelming and expensive proposition, and it took some years for a grounding in analytical skills and an orientation in material culture theory to be established in the professional community (Birmingham 1990; Lawrence 1998b). There are many practical issues that made it difficult for academic and postgraduate researchers to participate in urban archaeological research. The value of inner city land means that it will rarely, if ever, be available for the sort of long-term, planned research that can be scheduled into the university calendar. Rural sites, removed from the pressures of development, suit the academic far better in terms of arranging successive seasons of fieldwork separated by periods of writing and analysis.

However, the material evidence of urban life *has* encouraged consulting archaeologists into productive partnerships with academic archaeologists and social historians in order to interpret and interrogate the material culture (Karskens and Thorp 1992; Mayne and Lawrence 1998; Karskens 1999). The new focus on the domestic sphere has led to a reconsideration of the roles of women as consumers, mothers, homemakers, publicans, and boardinghouse keepers. Growing interest in feminist theory had a major impact in defining the key fields of interest for urban archaeologists (Lydon 1995a; Karskens 1997). Jane Lydon has explained historical archaeology's tardiness in adopting feminist themes in terms of its dominant theoretical approaches, which favored economic and technological explanatory frameworks (Lydon 1995b). The evidence presented here also suggests that nationalist discourse shaped this aspect of practice, reflecting its particular concerns with settling the land, the hostile environment, the bushman as hero, and the absence of women as subjects within this discourse.

The way in which urban archaeology raised issues such as women's lives, ethnicity, and the relationship between identity and material culture, has now provided evidence that reveals the "flatness" of dominant nationalist discourses, the homogenizing effect that narratives of unity and progress have on the heterogeneity of lives and social relationships in the past (Karskens 1999, Lydon 1999). At the same time, Susan Lawrence has chosen to meet the myths head on and has used material culture and archaeological evidence to examine the nature of men's lives in the bush (Lawrence 1998a, 1998b, 1999). Lawrence takes the construction of the lone bushman and shows that the reality is likely to have been far more complicated. She sheds light on the social and sexual tensions of 1890s society by demonstrating the conflicting constructions of masculinity apparent in the context of archaeological and historical evidence. Lawrence's work on various bush sites has also approached industry in its social context, addressing issues raised by revisionist social and feminist historians, as well as aspects of material culture theory, to reveal that "Whalers, miners, and pastoral workers were physically remote from the main stream of society, but they were none the less integrated with it. A habitus that incorporated domestic ideology, and domesticated masculine identity, informed the lives of men, and sometimes women, in the bush" (Lawrence 1998a:5).

Success and Failure

Colonization is underpinned by an understanding of settlement as transformative: wasteland into productive land, nature into culture. As discussed earlier, the construction of the landscape as hostile has its roots in the imagery of the late-19th century and was promulgated through later history writing that emphasized the "battle" against nature as the only battle involved in the process of building the settler nation. Griffiths has shown how successive Australian governments ignored advice on the nature of arid inland environments and continued to promote the spread of settlement on the basis of "national and racial anxiety" (Griffiths and Robin 1997: 11). Nationalistic rhetoric, therefore, construes the Australian environment as hostile, rather than construing the policies of government as wrong headed or as being able to ignore human suffering in order to achieve political ends.

Within historical archaeological interpretation, the idea of the "battle" to settle the land and make it productive has generated a marked tendency to consider sites and landscapes in terms of success or failure. Studies carried out in the 1970s and 1980s aimed to establish a field of

interest for the emerging practice of historical archaeology, and their focus was solidly on the abandoned relics of agricultural and industrial technology (Birmingham et al. 1979, 1983). Further, abandoned rural and industrial sites were under threat from decay, expanding urban settlement, and modern industry, so the recording of such places became established not only as a core interest of the practice but also as a conservation imperative. Abandoned rural and industrial sites now form an important research genre, or field of interest, in Australian historical archaeology, as the number of case studies published in the *Journal of Australian Historical Archaeology* shows. The fact that sites were interpreted within a predominantly economic framework, such as that proposed by Judy Birmingham and Dennis Jeans (1983), also predisposed interpretation towards the success/failure question.

Thus, we see that archaeologists have effectively established a circular and self-perpetuating relationship between the myth of the hostile environment and the battle to establish the nation and the research that seeks to examine it. Abandoned and notionally unsuccessful enterprises are sought out in order to explain their failure. Obviously, research on "successful" sites still in operation is more problematic, and although examples can be found, they are less dominant. Individually these case studies of "failure" often provide insightful analyses. The fact that success/failure becomes a self-evident structuring device in interpretation, however, with the greater weight of evidence falling on the side of failure, means that archaeological research continues to reproduce the idea that the environment in Australia is hostile and the intent of colonization is benign.

The success/failure model has also been employed more broadly: in *Of the Hut I Builded*, Connah devotes a chapter to the archaeology of failed settlements, sites that have held obvious fascination for historical archaeologists, not least as early remains undisturbed by later development. One of the examples reviewed in this chapter is the military outpost of Victoria, Port Essington (in Arnhem Land, northern Australia), which was the subject of a detailed study by Allen in the 1960s and 70s. Allen's interpretation of this site was as a "successful strategic maneuver rather than a failed attempt at colonization" (Allen 1973:44). While Connah refers to Allen's interpretation, he further concludes,

Perspectives from *Historical Archaeology*

"strategic and political considerations were not a sufficient basis on their own for colonial success" (Connah 1988:49). This suggests a moral difference between the motives for establishing a settlement that are purely "strategic" and "political" and motives that are described as a "*genuine* interest in colonization" (Connah 1988:49, emphasis added). As pointed out earlier, in this terminology, "colonization" is synonymous with "nation building," while strategic and political aims appear to be associated more with protecting the selfish interests of remote imperial authorities. Here the success/failure concept invokes not only the idea of battling the hostile environment but also the understanding of colonization as progress towards an outcome of meaning and value, in this case the birth of the nation. This equation is founded in Enlightenment historical discourse and Judeo-Christian narrative structures through which colonization imagines its successful transformation of wilderness into useful, productive land (Rose 1999:8).

Shared Landscapes

The most significant changes in Australian archaeology over recent decades have occurred due to the deconstruction of colonial precepts in Aboriginal prehistory and in the ethics involved in archaeologists working with Aboriginal communities. As part of international interest in the implications of colonialism, there has been a recent spate of papers on how to "decolonize" Australian archaeology (Murray 1992, 1996a, 1996b, 1996c; Pardoe 1992; Byrne 1996; Head 1996, 1998). Historical archaeologists showed an early interest in the issue of contact and in Aboriginal historic sites (Allen 1973 and Birmingham 1992 on the site of Wybalenna investigated between 1969–71). It is only recently, however, that Aboriginal culture since 1788 has begun to be seriously investigated (Murray 1993, 1996c; Colley and Bickford 1996). Sarah Colley and Anne Bickford (1996) have clearly outlined some of the institutional and theoretical barriers that have hindered the development of contact archaeology. These include the fact that settler and Aboriginal heritage are often protected under different legislation. In compliance archaeology, one set of consultants look at Aboriginal cultural heritage, while others are employed to examine settler heritage. Therefore, in day-to-day work,

there have been few arenas in which the cultural landscape of colonialism, the historic period, could be studied in a holistic way. These disciplinary and legislative boundaries are colonial artifacts in themselves, a result of seeing Aborigines as a part of the environment and as a people with no history. Denis Byrne has pointed to the potential power of the historical archaeology of Aboriginal people in countering nationalist constructions of the past and acting for reconciliation (Byrne 1996:102). However, traditional archaeological approaches to studying both prehistoric sites and landscapes and settler landscapes as evidence of agricultural and technological processes have not provided any framework within which to approach what must, in many cases, have been shared Aboriginal and European landscapes. In most contact studies, the point has been to assess the impact of settler culture upon Aboriginal behavior and technology. Traditional archaeological methodologies are not well suited to accommodate attempts to understand complex cultural exchanges and, for instance, impact upon settlers by Aboriginal culture. It is notable that in the history of settler culture, settlers are impacted upon by the environment but rarely by Aboriginal culture. The assumption that colonial activities overwrite and obliterate indigenous cultural landscapes is simplistic—an artifact of a worldview that sees progress and modernity as wiping out all evidence of the past, of the impact of colonialism as fatal and total rather than potentially creative of hybrid forms.

Hybridization of social landscapes requires us to imagine new ways to analyze historical and archaeological data. Nationalist discourse operates to simplify power relations between the colonizers and the colonized in the past. By contrast, Lydon's study of Chinese people living in Sydney, showed how these relationships were "contested and contingent," with the "possibility for shared systems of meaning" (Lydon 1999:174). Lydon contextualizes material culture within an "ethnographic collage" to reveal the way in which Chinese people at the turn of the century could both mimic dominant white cultural practices, while also altering them to accommodate the needs of their traditional cultural forms.

Landscape discourse in the Australian cultural tradition ensured that the Australian landscape was imagined as a purely natural creation: a wilderness without cultural meaning. Ross Gibson's (1993) analysis of recent landscape cinema shows that Australian culture remains fascinated by the idea of the intractability of the Australian landscape; the fact that two hundred years of colonization has made little impact upon "the timeless land." As with Malouf's Scottish settlers, the culture of "others" remains invisible when viewed through the ideology of colonialism, which constructs the land as a commodity, a source of fear and desire. This paper made an argument that the realities of urban archaeology, within the heritage management framework, helped to disrupt a circularity of research within historical archaeology, where research was constructed through landscape discourse while also seeking to explain it. This is not to say that the evidence of the bush should be avoided in future in favor of urban subjects, which are more representative of settler experience. This would imply that urban studies do not have to deal with historical mythologies of their own, when much of this work concerns highly mythologized "slum" sites, characterized as the opposite of the healthy rural lifestyle idolized by Lawson and his fellow writers and artists. While it may be time to go back to the bush and re-examine the communities who lived there, it is also appropriate to reconsider cities and towns as shared spaces of multiple meanings, as advocated by Byrne in this volume and as has been demonstrated by Lydon's study of urban Chinese (Lydon 1999). Contact studies, in both rural and urban Australia, may access a rich array of material, textual, oral, and historical evidence to produce the "ethnographic collage" that is required to retheorize contact (Head and Fullagher 1997; Rose 1999). On the other hand, this may also help to re-examine and to begin to understand the human consequences of colonialism for the settlers who saw only "an absence of ghosts."

Conclusion

This paper demonstrated the discursive relationship between cultural representations of the land and the environment in Australia and the practice of historical archaeology. The ideology of colonialism constructs the land as the object of desire in Australia. In return, archaeological research has contributed to historicizing and

perpetuating this colonial act of possession. The result of this conceptual circularity is that far from revealing any disciplinary objectivity, discursive relationships between archaeology, history, and national identity contrive to actually "create a reality that they appear to describe" (Schaffer 1988:171). However, there is also some evidence that individual practitioners can break out of this conceptual circularity and that archaeological evidence may provide some resistance to erroneous and complicit interpretations.

Deconstruction of colonialist and nationalist discourses has as its central motivation a concern with the ethical implications, in our day-to-day lives, of allowing our own work to promulgate systems of belief and action that oppress and exclude. Lesly Head has recently identified some of the tensions that are felt within Australian archaeology arising from political imperatives and revisionist movements across a range of disciplines. She warns about "… the danger lies in seeing such tensions as differences that need to be resolved, rather than as the problematic from which much of our creativity is springing" (Head 1998:3).

How can this warning to refuse the seduction of comfortable, resolved narratives of the past be heeded? How is it possible to open ourselves to dialogue and risk, when historical archaeology as a practice is so closely defined by the nation, and while the concept of nation itself implies some element of resolved wholeness? In this paper, the response has been to give close attention to the foundational stories of the nation and to the foundations of the way that historical archaeologists think about the Australian past. In doing this, the smooth surface of the road leading back into the past of the settler nation becomes rough and dangerous. Eventually, there is no road at all but a network of crossing paths, leading in all directions, towards untold stories.

ACKNOWLEDGMENTS

A first version of this paper was presented at the University of Glasgow, Department of Archaeology's Seminar Series in December 1998. Thank you to Professor Bernard Knapp for the invitation and to staff and students for discussion and comments. Thank you also to colleagues Wayne Johnson and Matthew Kelly who contributed to some ideas developed here, and to the editors and three anonymous referees who made many useful and challenging suggestions.

REFERENCES

ALLEN, JIM
1973 The Archaeology of Nineteenth-Century British Imperialism: An Australian Case Study. *World Archaeology,* 5(1):44–59.

ANDERSON, BENEDICT
1983 *Imagined Communities: Reflections on the Origin and Spread of Nationalism.* Verso, New York, NY.

ASHCROFT, BILL, GARETH GRIFFITHS, AND HELEN TIFFIN (EDITORS)
1995 *The Post-Colonial Studies Reader.* Routledge, London, England.

ATKINSON, JOHN, IAIN BANKS, AND JERRY O'SULLIVAN (EDITORS)
1996 *Nationalism and Archaeology.* Scottish Archaeological Forum. Cruithne Press, Glasgow, Scotland.

ATTWOOD, BAIN
1996a Mabo, Australia, and the End of History. In *In the Age of Mabo,* Bain Attwood, editor, pp. 100–116. Allen and Unwin, Sydney, NSW, Australia.
1996b Introduction, The Past as Future: Aborigines, Australia and the (Dis)course of History. In *In the Age of Mabo,* Bain Attwood, editor, pp. vii–xxxviii. Allen and Unwin, Sydney, NSW, Australia.

BENNETT, TONY
1993 History on the Rocks. In *Australian Cultural Studies: A Reader.* John Frow and Meaghan Morris, editors, pp. 222–241. Allen and Unwin, Sydney, NSW, Australia.

BHABHA, HOMI K. (EDITOR)
1990 *Nation and Narration.* Routledge, London, England.

BIRCH, TONY
1997 "Black Armbands and White Veils": John Howard's Moral Amnesia. *Melbourne Historical Journal,* 25: 8–16.

BIRMINGHAM, JUDY
1990 A Decade of Digging: Deconstructing Urban Archaeology. *Australian Journal of Historical Archaeology,* 8:13–22.
1992 *Wybalenna: The Archaeology of Cultural Accommodation in Nineteenth-Century Tasmania.* Australian Society for Historical Archaeology, Sydney, NSW.

BIRMINGHAM, JUDY, IAN JACK, AND DENNIS JEANS
1979 *Australian Pioneer Technology: Sites and Relics. Towards an Industrial Archaeology of Australia.* Heinemann, Melbourne, VIC, Australia.
1983 *Industrial Archaeology in Australia: Rural Industry.* Heinemann, Melbourne, VIC, Australia.

BIRMINGHAM, JUDY, AND DENNIS JEANS
1983 The Swiss Family Robinson and the Archaeology of Colonisation. *Australian Journal of Historical Archaeology,* 1:3–14.

BOND, GEORGE CLEMONT, AND ANGELA GILLIAM (EDITORS)
1995 *Social Construction of the Past: Representation as Power.* Routledge, London, England.

BONYHADY, TIM, AND TOM GRIFFITHS
1996 The Making of a Public Intellectual. In *Prehistory to Politics: John Mulvaney, The Humanities and the Public Intellectual,* Tim Bonyhady and Tom Griffiths, editors, pp. 1–19. Melbourne University Press, VIC, Australia.

BRENNAN, TIMOTHY
1990 The National Longing for Form. In *Nation and Narration,* Homi K. Bhabha, editor, pp. 44–70. Routledge, London, England.

BYRNE, DENIS
1996 Deep Nation: Australia's Acquistion of an Indigenous Past. *Aboriginal History,* 20:82–107.

COLLEY, SARAH
1996 Australian Archaeology: Colonialism and Postcolonial Theory. Presented to the Department of Archaeology and Anthropology Seminar Series, Australian National University, Canberra, ACT.

COLLEY, SARAH, AND ANNE BICKFORD
1996 "Real" Aborigines and "Real" Archaeology: Aboriginal Places and Australian Historical Archaeology. *World Archaeological Bulletin,* 7:5–21.

CONNAH, GRAHAM
1988 *"Of the Hut I Builded": The Archaeology of Australia's History.* Cambridge University Press, Cambridge, England.
1998 Pattern and Purpose in Historical Archaeology. *Australasian Historical Archaeology,* 16:3–7.

CROWLEY, FRANK (EDITOR)
1974 *New History of Australia.* Heinemann, Melbourne, VIC, Australia.

CURTHOYS, ANN
1999a Expulsion, Exodus, and Exile in White Australian Historical Mythology. *Journal of Australian Studies,* 61:1–18.
1999b An Uneasy Conversation: Multicultural and Indigenous Discourse. In *The Future of Australian Multiculturalism,* Ghassan Hage and Rowanne Couch, editors, pp. 277–293. Research School for Humanities and Social Sciences, University of Sydney, NSW, Australia.

DAVISON, GRAEME
1978 Sydney and the Bush: An Urban Context for the Australian Legend. *Historical Studies,* 18(71): 191–209.
1991 The Meanings of "Heritage." In *A Heritage Handbook,* Graeme Davison and Chris McConville, editors, pp. 1–13. Allen and Unwin, Sydney, NSW, Australia.

DIAZ-ANDREU, MARGARITA, AND TIMOTHY CHAMPION (EDITORS)
1996 *Nationalism and Archaeology in Europe.* UCL Press, London, England.

DIXON, ROBERT
1986 *The Course of Empire: Neo-Classical Culture in New South Wales 1788–1860.* Oxford University Press, Melbourne, VIC, Australia.

DIXSON, MIRIAM
1976 *The Real Matilda.* Penguin, Ringwood, VIC, Australia.

EGLOFF, BRIAN J.
1994 From the Swiss Family Robinson to Sir Russell Drysdale: Towards Changing the Tone of Historical Archaeology in Australia. *Australian Archaeology,* 39:1–9.

FLETCHER, M. D.
1997 Political Identity in Contemporary Australian Literature: David Malouf and Peter Carey. In *The Politics of Identity in Australia,* Geoffrey Stokes, editor, pp. 175–184. Cambridge University Press, Cambridge, England.

FOUCAULT, MICHEL
1972 *The Archaeology of Knowledge.* Pantheon, New York, NY.

GELDER, KEN, AND JANE M. JACOBS
1998 *Uncanny Australia: Sacredness and Identity in a Postcolonial Nation.* Melbourne University Press, VIC, Australia.

GIBSON, ROSS
1993 Camera Natura: Landscape in Australian Feature Films. In *Australian Cultural Studies: A Reader,* John Frow and Meaghan Morris, editors, pp. 209–221. Allen and Unwin, Sydney, NSW, Australia.
1996 Ocean Settlement. In *Exchanges: Cross-Cultural Encounters in Australia and the Pacific,* Ross Gibson, editor, pp. 89–112. Historic Houses Trust of NSW, Sydney, Australia.

GRAVES BROWN, P., SIAN JONES, AND CLIVE GAMBLE (EDITORS)
1996 *Cultural Identity and Archaeology: The Construction of European Communities.* Routledge, London, England.

GRIFFITHS, TOM
1996 *Hunters and Collectors: The Antiquarian Imagination in Australia.* Cambridge University Press, Cambridge, England.
1997 Ecology and Empire: Towards an Australian History of the World. In *Ecology and Empire,* Tom Griffith and Libby Robin, editors, pp. 1–18. Melbourne University Press, VIC, Australia.

GRIFFITHS, TOM, AND LIBBY ROBIN (EDITORS)
1997 *Ecology and Empire.* Melbourne University Press, VIC, Australia.

GRIMSHAW, PATRICIA, MARILYN LAKE, ANN MCGRATH, AND MARIAN QUARTLY
1994 *Creating a Nation 1788– 1990.* McPhee Gribble, Melbourne, VIC, Australia.

HANCOCK, KEITH
1930 *Australia.* Ernest Benn, London, England.

HEAD, LESLEY
1996 Headlines and Songlines. *Meanjin,* 55(4):736–743.
1998 Risky Representations: The Seduction of Wholeness and the Public Face of Australian Archaeology. *Australian Archaeology,* 46:1–4.

HEAD, LESLEY, AND RICHARD FULLAGAR
1997 Hunter-Gatherer Archaeology and Pastoral Contact: Perspectives from Northwest Northern Territory, Australia. *World Archaeology,* 28(3):418–428.

HODGE, BOB, AND VIJAY MISHRA
1990 *Dark Side of the Dream: Australian Literature and the Postcolonial Mind.* Allen and Unwin, Sydney, NSW, Australia.

HOWARD, JOHN
1996 Confront Our Past, Yes, But Let's Not Be Consumed by It. *The Australian,* 19 November:13.

IRELAND, TRACY
1996 Excavating National Identity. In *Sites: Nailing the Debate: Archaeology and Interpretation in Museums,* pp. 85–106. Historic Houses Trust of NSW, Sydney, Australia.

JONES, SIAN (EDITOR)
1997 *The Archaeology of Ethnicity.* Routledge, London, England.

KARSKENS, GRACE
1996–1997 Crossing Over: Archaeology and History at the Cumberland/Gloucester Street Site, The Rocks 1994–1996. *Public History Review,* 5/6:30–48.
1999 *Inside the Rocks: The Archaeology of a Neighbourhood.* Hale and Iremonger, Sydney, NSW, Australia.

KARSKENS, GRACE, AND WENDY THORP
1992 History and Archaeology in Sydney: Towards Integration and Interpretation. *Journal of the Royal Australian Historical Society,* 78(3/4):52–75.

KOHL, PHILLIP, AND CLARE FAWCETT (EDITORS)
1995 *Nationalism, Politics, and the Practice of Archaeology.* Cambridge University Press, Cambridge, England.

LAKE, MARILYN
1986 The Politics of Respectability: Identifying the Masculinist Context. *Historical Studies,* 22(86): 116–131.
1992 Mission Impossible: How Men Gave Birth to the Australian Nation—Nationalism, Gender, and Other Seminal Acts. *Gender and History,* 4(3):305–322.

LAMPETER ARCHAEOLOGY WORKSHOP
1997 Relativism, Objectivity, and the Politics of the Past. *Archaeological Dialogues,* 2:164–184.

LANGTON, MARCIA
1995 The European Construction of Wilderness. *Wilderness News,* Summer 1995/96:16–17.

LAWRENCE, SUSAN

1998a Becoming Australian: Material Life in the Bush. Paper presented at the Annual Meeting of the Australian Historical Association, Sydney, NSW.

1998b The Role of Material Culture in *Australasian Archaeology*. Australasian Historical Archaeology, 16:8–15.

1999 Approaches to Gender in the Archaeology of Mining. In *Redefining Archaeology: Feminist Perspectives*, Mary Casey, Denise Donlan, Jeanette Hope, and Sharon Wellfare, editors, pp. 126–133. ANH Publications, Research School of Pacific and Asian Studies, Australian National University, Canberra, ACT.

LEONE, MARK, AND PARKER B. POTTER, JR. (EDITORS)

1999 *Historical Archaeologies of Capitalism*. Contributions to Global Historical Archaeology series, Charles E. Orser, Jr., editor. Kluwer Academic/Plenum Publishers, New York, NY.

LINES, WILLIAM J.

1991 *Taming the Great South Land: A History of the Conquest of Nature in Australia*. Allen and Unwin, Sydney, NSW, Australia.

LYDON, JANE

1993 Archaeology in The Rocks, Sydney 1979–1993: From Old Sydney Gaol to Mrs. Lewis' Boarding House. *Australasian Historical Archaeology*, 11:33–44.

1995a Boarding Houses in The Rocks: Mrs. Ann Lewis' Privy, 1865. *Public History Review*, 4:73–88.

1995b Gender in Australian Historical Archaeology. In *Gendered Archaeology: The Second Australian Women in Archaeology Conference*, Jane Balme and Wendy Beck, editors, pp. 72–79. ANH Publications, Research School of Pacific and Asian Studies, Australian National University, Canberra, ACT.

1999 *Many Inventions: The Chinese in The Rocks, Sydney, 1890–1930*. Monash Publications in History, Clayton, Victoria, ACT, Australia.

MACKAY, RICHARD

1996 Political, Pictorial, Physical, and Philosophical Plans — Realising Archaeological Research Potential in Urban Sydney. In *Sites: Nailing the Debate: Archaeology and Interpretation in Museums*, pp. 123–138. Historic Houses Trust of NSW, Sydney, Australia.

MALOUF, DAVID

1994 *Remembering Babylon*. Vintage, London, England.

MARGAREY, SUSAN, SUE ROWLEY, AND SUE SHERIDAN (EDITORS)

1993 *Debutante Nation: Feminism Contests the 1890s*. Allen and Unwin, Sydney, NSW, Australia.

MAYNE, ALAN, AND SUSAN LAWRENCE

1998 An Ethnography of Place: Imagining "Little Lon." *Journal of Australian Studies*, 57:93–107.

McCLINTOCK, ANNE

1994 The Angel of Progress: Pitfalls of the Term "Postcolonialism." In *Colonial Discourse/Postcolonial Theory*, Francis Barker, Peter Hulme, and Margaret Iversen, editors, pp. 253–267. Manchester University Press, England.

MELLEUISH, GREGORY

1998 *The Packaging of Australia: Politics and Culture Wars*. University of New South Wales Press, Sydney, Australia.

MORTON, JOHN, AND NICHOLAS SMITH

1999 Planting Indigenous Species: A Subversion of Australian Eco-Nationalism. In *Quicksands: Foundational Histories in Australia and Aotearoa, New Zealand*, Klaus Neumann, Nicholas Thomas, and Hilary Ericksen, editors, pp. 153–175. University of New South Wales Press, Sydney, Australia.

MOSER, STEPHANIE

1995 Archaeology and Its Disciplinary Culture: The Professionalisation of Australian Prehistoric Archaeology. Doctoral dissertation, Department of Prehistoric and Historical Archaeology, Classics and Ancient History, University of Sydney, NSW, Australia.

MURRAY, TIM

1992 Aboriginal (Pre)History and Australian Archaeology: The Discourse of Australian Prehistoric Archaeology. In *Power, Knowledge, and Aborigines*, Bain Attwood and John Arnold, editors, pp. 1–19. A special edition of the *Journal of Australian Studies*. Latrobe University Press in association with the National Centre for Australian Studies, Bundoora, VIC.

1993 The Childhood of William Lanne: Contact Archaeology and Aboriginality in Tasmania. *Antiquity*, 67:504–519.

1996a Creating a Post-Mabo Archaeology of Australia. In *In the Age of Mabo: History, Aborigines, and Australia*, Bain Attwood, editor, pp. 73–86. Allen and Unwin, Sydney, NSW, Australia.

1996b Aborigines, Archaeology, and Australian Heritage. *Meanjin*, 55(4):725–735.

1996c Contact Archaeology: Shared Histories? Shared Identities? In *Sites: Nailing the Debate: Archaeology and Interpretation in Museums*, pp. 199–216. Historic Houses Trust of NSW, Sydney, Australia.

PARDOE, COLIN

1992 Arches of Radii, Corridors of Power: Reflections on Current Archaeological Practice. In *Power, Knowledge, and Aborigines, Bain Attwood and John Arnold, editors, pp. 132–141. A special edition of the Journal of Australian Studies*. Latrobe University Press in association with the National Centre for Australian Studies, Melbourne, VIC.

PARKER, ANDREW, MARY RUSSO, DORIS SOMMER, AND PATRICIA YAEGER (EDITORS)

1992 *Nationalisms and Sexualities*. Routledge, New York, NY.

PETTMAN, JAN

1992 *Living in the Margins: Racism, Sexism, and Feminism in Australia*. Allen and Unwin, Sydney, NSW, Australia.

PROUDFOOT, HELEN, ANNE BICKFORD, BRIAN EGLOFF, AND
ROBYN STOCKS
    1991 *Australia's First Government House.* The Department
of Planning, New South Wales, and Allen and Unwin,
Sydney, Australia.

REEKIE, GAIL
    1992 Contesting Australia. In *Images of Australia*, Gillian
Whitlock and David Carter, editors, pp. 145–55.
University of Queensland Press, St. Lucia, QLD,
Australia.

REYNOLDS, HENRY
    1981 *The Other Side of the Frontier.* Penguin, Melbourne,
VIC, Australia.
    1987 *Frontier.* Allen and Unwin, Sydney, NSW,
Australia.

ROBIN, LIBBY
    1998 Urbanising the Bush: Environmental Disputes and
Australian National Identity. In *Australian Identities*,
David Day, editor, pp. 116–127. Australian Scholarly
Publishing, Melbourne, VIC, Australia.

ROSE, DEBORAH BIRD
    1999 Hard Times: An Australian Study. In *Quicksands:
Foundational Histories in Australia and Aotearoa,
New Zealand,* Klaush Neumann, Nicholas Thomas,
and Hilary Ericksen, editors, pp. 2–19. University of
New South Wales Press, Sydney, Australia.

ROWLEY, SUE
    1993 Things a Bush Woman Cannot Do. In *Debutante Nation:
Feminism Contests the 1890s*, Susan Margarey, Sue
Rowley, and Sue Sheridan, editors, pp. 185–198. Allen
and Unwin, Sydney, NSW, Australia.

SCHAFFER, KAY
    1988 *Women and the Bush, Forces of Desire in the Australian
Cultural Tradition.* Cambridge University Press,
Cambridge, England.

SCHUYLER, ROBERT L.
    1991 Historical Archaeology in the American West: The
View from Philadelphia. *Historical Archaeology*,
25(3):7–17.

SPILLMAN, LYN
    1997 *Nation and Commemoration: Creating National
Identities in Australia and the United States.* Cambridge
University Press, New York, NY.

SUMMERS, ANNE
    1975 *Damned Whores and God's Police: The Colonisation
of Women in Australia.* Penguin, Melbourne, VIC,
Australia.

TEMPLE, HELEN
    1988 Historical Archaeology and Its Role in the Community.
Master's (honours) thesis, Inter-Departmental
Committee for Historical Archaeology, University of
Sydney, NSW, Australia.

WARD, RUSSELL
    1958 *The Australian Legend.* Oxford University Press,
Melbourne, VIC, Australia.

WHITE, RICHARD
    1981 *Inventing Australia.* Allen and Unwin, Sydney, NSW,
Australia.

TRACY IRELAND
DEPARTMENT OF PREHISTORIC AND HISTORICAL
ARCHAEOLOGY
SCHOOL OF ARCHAEOLOGY
MAIN QUAD A14, UNIVERSITY OF SYDNEY
SIDNEY, NSW 2006 AUSTRALIA

Charles E. Orser, Jr.

Symbolic Violence and Landscape Pedagogy: An Illustration from the Irish Countryside

ABSTRACT

Archaeologists know that landscapes can provide powerful clues about past social interaction. Landscapes are never truly passive because they offer many socially relevant services to the individuals and social groups who inhabit them. Much of what landscapes do is symbolic. Pedagogy can constitute an important function of a landscape, particularly in the hierarchical societies investigated by historical archaeologists. The demesne constitutes an especially evocative pedagogic landscape in an Irish setting. A detailed examination of Coopershill demesne in County Sligo, Ireland, demonstrates the power of landscape pedagogy and the role of symbolic violence in helping to shape it.

Introduction

Archaeologists have long been concerned with understanding the principles involved in the placement and meaning of past human-built features on the landscape. Pioneering research by Gordon Willey (1953) in Peru and O. G. S. Crawford (1953) in England created an interest in the archaeology of landscapes that crystallized in the 1970s (Fowler 2001). Within the past four decades, the archaeological interest in landscapes has dramatically increased, spawning a literature that is far too vast to cite in its entirety (recent works include Ashmore and Knapp 1999; Bender and Winer 2001; Wilkinson 2004). Historical archaeologists have played a significant role in developing the archaeological interpretation of past landscapes, and they have employed a variety of perspectives and approaches in their diverse analyses (recent works include Delle 1998; Perry 1999; Matthews 2002; Rotman and Savulis 2003). From this vast body of research, at least two perspectives have emerged that are pertinent here. First is the concept that landscapes are consciously constructed by the individuals and groups who inhabit them. Landscape analysts are free to decide the characteristics and implications of landscape production as they seek to conceptualize the interlinkages between complex human-human and human-environment networks. Regardless of the exact theoretical position taken, sustained research has clearly demonstrated that constructed landscapes can be manipulated, contested, imagined, and mythologized in numerous, often mutually exclusive, ways (Tuan 1977; Leone 1984; Deetz 1990; Feld and Basso 1996; Orser 1996; Bender 1998; Darby 2000).

A key feature of human-built space is that the created physicality necessarily also incorporates an equally invented sociality. The inseparable connection between society and space thus makes it virtually impossible to disentangle the social relations embodied in the arrangement of rooms, buildings, and landscape features from the social relations that constructed, reconstructed, and maintained them (Hillier and Hanson 1984:2; Delle 1998:37–40; Mitchell 2002). The close association between human society and human space means that any coherent social theory must include physical space as a given from the beginning (Thrift 2002:114). In fact, the structural homology between social space and physical space is so infrangible that a "socio-spatial dialectic"—perceived as a continuous, constantly mutable process—exists in all times and places regardless of the precise characteristics of the sociohistorical context (Soja 1980, 1989:57,81).

Abundant, cross-disciplinary research has demonstrated that a significant feature of the sociospatial dialectic is wholly symbolic in nature. In sociohistorical formations that are described as capitalist, much of the spatial symbolism is authoritarian in design, intended to provide physical reinforcement of the societal power structure (Mitchell 2002). In fact, so embedded is hierarchical power with landscape—and so strong is the sociospatial dialectic—that the word *landscape* can be perceived either as a noun or a verb (Darby 2000:12). Landscapes thus do not simply exist; they are flexible instruments of power that have the ability, when linked with human action, to make things happen. The way a sociospatial process works in practice is uniquely contextual, and its variation does not lend itself to any kind of totalizing interpretation. The principal elements of the process must be teased from the specific sociohistorical milieu under study. One topic for serious examination in capitalist sociohistorical formations—which by definition incorporate a hierarchical sociality rooted in power inequalities—is the question of how social spaces are employed in the reinforcement of power and authority.

The concept of "symbolic violence" provides one insightful way in which to advance this line of research. The meaning of symbolic violence is explored and its utility for the archaeological investigation of human-built landscapes in postmedieval Ireland is considered here as an example, drawing upon research conducted at Coopershill demesne, in County Sligo, Ireland.

Symbolic Violence and Social Pedagogy

Symbolic violence is understood from the critical research of French sociologist Pierre Bourdieu. Like everything in Bourdieu's vast body of work, the concept of symbolic violence is difficult to understand in its entirety. In its simplest terms, Bourdieu's formulation of practice theory presents a model in which individuals and social groups attempt to acquire and control various kinds of capital (Calhoun 1995:141–142). He borrows from Karl Marx the concept of economic capital but, as a critical theorist, argues that classic Marxian theory underestimates the significance of symbolic dimensions of power relations (Swartz 1997:82; Wacquant 2001; but also Bloch 1985:23; Godelier 1988:50–51). Thus, within each sociohistorical formation, individuals and social groups seek to amass various kinds of capital—economic, social, symbolic, and others—that will cement or enhance their social positions. Reminiscent of Marx (1954:42–43), Bourdieu proposes that capital is "accumulated labor" and speaks of capital as being able to produce "profits" and to generate "interest." Human labor thus becomes embodied, largely

in disguise, as economic capital, which can be converted into currency and objectified in property and property rights; cultural capital, which consists of many factors, including educational training that may be converted into economic capital by obtaining a high-paying job; social capital, composed of a network of social relations; and symbolic capital, contextual legitimation (Bourdieu 1986).

A key topic of interest to Bourdieu is how individuals and groups obtain and employ various forms of capital in diverse social situations. The distribution of the different kinds of capital is capable of conferring degrees of power and authority on various individuals within a particular sociohistorical setting (Skeggs 1997:8). This means that Bourdieu's perspective can be identified as a sort of labor theory of value, a staple of Marxian analysis but now greatly expanded (Swartz 1997:74; Beasley-Murray 2000). Since Bourdieu was a sociologist, his interest rested in the creation, manifestation, and practice of various kinds of capital in modern-day society (Bourdieu 1984, 1993). The concept of symbolic capital is also an idea that can be employed to investigate social power in any historical context.

In its essence, symbolic capital represents a situation of dominance whereby the dominators have shifted their power from overt coercion and the threat of physical violence to symbolic manipulation (Swartz 1997:82). Bourdieu believes that any power is guilty of symbolic violence when it has the ability to impose meanings on things and at the same time to legitimate its power by concealing the relations that underlie it (Bourdieu and Passeron 1977: 4). Bourdieu (1990b:126) illustrates the mechanism of symbolic violence with gift giving. A wealthy donor who has the economic capital to endow a hospital wing exercises symbolic violence by the moral obligations and emotional attachments that accompany the gift. Every time patients and visitors to the wing see the donor's name on a brass plaque or above the doorway, they are reminded of the donor's ability to amass capital and to bestow it on those in need. The endowment is usually "misrecognized" as pure altruistic philanthropy when it is really an exercise of lasting power linked to the social capital associated with all aspects of the gift.

The idea of symbolic violence is meaningless without the concomitant conceptualization of social fields. The recognition of the analytical importance of social fields has a long history in anthropological thought (Radcliffe-Brown 1940; Barnes 1954; Lesser 1961), but its greatest refinement outside practice theory has occurred within the "field theory" of social psychology (Lewin 1951). The primary goal of field theory is "to describe the essential here-and-now situation (field) in which a person participates" (De Rivera 1976:3). Social psychologists perceive fields as interpersonal spaces wherein culture is produced and history is made. To think in terms of social fields is to think relationally, to conceptualize networks of social interaction that stretch across time and through space. As Bourdieu phrases it, "In analytical terms, a field may be defined as a network, or a configuration, of objective relations between positions" (Bourdieu and Wacquant 1992:96–97). Fields are multidimensional spaces within which individuals and social groups struggle for legitimation and situationally employ various kinds of capital (Bourdieu 1985:724; also Swartz 1997: 122–129; Orser 2004:137). For Bourdieu (1981: 309–312), the social world—the networks of social fields embedded in the larger networks of the sociohistorical formation—exhibits and projects a double objectivity. On the one hand, following Marx, the distribution of material wealth and power appears objectively arranged among the fields' institutions (Wacquant 1993:131). At the same time, the symbolic representations of these distributions strive to create and sustain tangible social taxonomies and mental classifications. The symbolic structures are thus not simply mystified objectivities that exist only in the minds of social actors. Rather, within limits, "symbolic structures have an altogether extraordinary power of *constitution* [emphasis in original]" but only within the "historical conditions of their genesis" (Bourdieu 1990a: 18). In other words, symbolic structures may not be directly observable, but their outcomes, as constructions, can be seen in the everyday practice of individuals.

An important feature of symbolic power in a particular sociohistorical formation is its ability to be the subject of pedagogic action on the part of the dominating class (Bourdieu and Passeron 1977:5–6). The power of pedagogy is intended to provide the symbolic reification of the imposed power relations by reinforcing that very power. For the pedagogy to operate and be effective all the actors engaged in the social system must accept the underlying structure of society's power relations. The pedagogy is wholly ineffective if the power relations embedded within a social interaction are dissolved or ignored. One must acknowledge the foundational social structure to accept the daily practices of its actors.

Pedagogy, like everything else that involves humans, must occur someplace. Social practice is therefore really sociospatial practice, with the forms of specific practice being relevant only to the sociohistoric formation within which it occurs (Lefebvre 1991). Spatial practice promotes and presupposes space as a dialectical process between actual, physical reality and the ways in which human actors employ, manipulate, and re-create space. A society's spatial practice is revealed through deciphering or decoding its space. For example, the spatial practice of medieval Europe incorporated networks of roads, often Roman built, that connected monasteries, castles, and peasant communities as well as all the other buildings, passageways, and routes used by pilgrims, Crusaders, and everyone else who moved within the social networks that operated in the social structure. Today's urban dwellers re-create their society's space by a complex dialectic of daily routine and individual action. The spaces that are created through such social practice are the "perceived" spaces within which individuals actually move.

A society's spatial practice, exemplified by perceived space, is supplemented by representations of space and representational spaces in an irreducible triad (Lefebvre 1991:38–39). Representations of space are conceptualized spaces imagined by social planners, architects, and designers. These spaces constitute space conceived through subjective knowledge and ideology because they are usually designated by a system of consciously created and situationally relevant signs. Representations of space, though often abstract, still have the ability to establish, reinforce, and reconfigure social relations between people and things. In medieval Europe, representations of space appear in the icons and physical layouts of cathedrals; in today's consumerist society, representations of space appear most obviously in advertising and other forms of manipulative media.

Representational spaces overlay physical space and are directly lived through associated images, symbols, and mythic narratives. Such spaces are frequently comprised of coherent systems of non-verbal signs and symbols. In medieval Europe, representational space determined the focal points of life in accordance with interpretations about important symbolic (religious) beliefs. Shopping malls and department stores are spaces of representation in today's capitalist societies.

Henri Lefebvre (1991:39–40) argues that the three kinds of spaces operate together in a contextually relevant manner. The triad is learned as part of the socialization process, in what Bourdieu famously terms "the habitus." As men and women live spatially, they are largely unaware of the spatial triad's importance because of the illusion that space is irrelevant; it merely "exists" as a given. Space thus appears to pre-exist as a tableau upon which social practice is enacted, rather than as an active agent of social practice itself. The very fact that space is consciously produced and is infinitely mutable (Lefebvre 1979) means that spatial pedagogy is entirely possible for those who control selected elements of a society's spatial practice.

It follows from this formulation that every physical space simultaneously provides portrayals of perceived, conceived, and lived space, with each portrayal being overlaid and yet intertwined with the others in a complex, multifaceted manner. As such, the spatial triad is not a model but rather a concrete feature of lived experience. Representational spaces may appear to be abstract, when in truth they can play a significant role in situationally enacted social practices (Lefebvre 1991:41).

All sociospaces are amenable to analysis as sites of landscape pedagogy, with some instances perhaps offering more transparency than others. Given the inseparable connections between a socially structured hierarchy, the social power it encumbers, and the apportionment of space in that context, spatialization appears as entirely "central to cultural hegemony and dominant ideologies" and as such facilitates spatially "dominant practices" (Shields 1997:189). Agricultural plantations worked by enslaved men and women offer excellent milieus in which to investigate the interplay between symbolic violence and landscape education. In such instances, the social relationships of power, and the concomitant physical spaces, are so prescribed that their creation, manipulation, and re-creation can be profitably examined over time with great insight (Delle 1998). The Irish demesne is another excellent place to attempt to unravel the connection between symbolic violence and the conscious use of landscape to provide memorable lessons about the social order.

Irish Demesnes and Coopershill

Demesnes have a venerable history and thus a range of nuanced meanings. The *Oxford English Dictionary* notes that the word *demesnes* itself is French in origin and provides several meanings—any possessed estate; the exclusive property of the Crown or "royal demesne"; and "ancient demesne," which referred to English lands held by the monarchy at the time of the Norman conquest and recorded in the Doomsday Book of 1086. A common usage is the one adopted here: land owned and controlled by a landlord and carefully restricted for the sole use of his or her family. Demesne land was thus not farmed by rent-paying tenants. Feudal lords in control of demesnes divided them into functional parcels, such as hunting parks. After the ravages of the Black Death, many of them converted these parks into "amenity parks" as a way of seeking peace and comfort as well as providing physical representations of their power and authority (Johnson 1996:145–146). During the 1680s in Ireland, Lord Meath's County Wicklow estate was deemed unique in the three British kingdoms because of its landscape "improvements" that included a deer park (Barnard 2004:188). Beginning in the 18th century, amenity parks became the locus of the English picturesque movement, as the gentry commissioned the construction of statuary, obelisks, ornamental bridges, fountains, romantic temples, and even stone pyramids within their demesnes (Malins and The Knight of Glin 1976; Llewellyn 1989; Hunt 1992, 2002).

The Elizabethan English, as part of their overall colonization scheme, took the concept of the demesne to Ireland. The proposed plan for a Munster seignory in 1586 represents a perfect representation of English colonial space in Lefebvre's terms (Foster 1989:68). In this design, a Protestant church and a mill was to sit in the middle of a 12,000-acre square, surrounded by 1,692 acres of arable land to be divided into allotments ranging in size from 5-1/2 to 400 acres. A gabled mansion for the gentry was to be erected on 1,000 exclusive acres designated the "gentleman's demesne." This highly idealized plan was never possible to effect in its entirety, even in the best circumstances, but most demesnes nonetheless were transformed into small "English islands of rural civility" during the immediate post-Cromwellian era (Canny 2001:160–161) and, during the 17th and 18th centuries, into visual proponents of "Protestant interest, prosperity and civility" (Barnard 2004:191).

English power had destroyed the authority of the Gaelic chieftains by the 18th century, and English control of Ireland was no longer in question by this time. Large Anglo-Irish and mostly Protestant landholders, though no longer entirely consumed with the need for defensive dwellings, nonetheless continued to surround their demesnes with high walls, often complete with corner turrets (Dickson 2000:22). The manicured landscapes within the walls protected its owners from the harsh realities of rural Irish life, a world full of poverty and destitution and a population explosion that dangerously strained the agricultural sustainability of the countryside (Aalen 1989:108). Demesne walls therefore constituted both the tangible evidence for and the symbolic reminders of the sociospatial gulf that separated English and Anglo-Irish (usually Protestant) elites from the native (Catholic) Irish.

At the height of their existence, demesnes covered more than 5% of Ireland (Reeves-Smyth 1997a:549). Many of them were reduced in size following the passage of land reform acts in the late-19th and early-20th centuries. Nonetheless, some owners were able to retain at least some, if not all, of their former estates (Malins and Bowe 1980; Reeves-Smyth 1997b:205). Coopershill is one demesne that has remained both largely intact and owned by the same family since its initial construction.

The Coopershill estate is located in the Barony of Tirerill, in the parish of Kilmacallan in southeastern County Sligo, the Republic of Ireland (Figure 1). Cooper is a prominent name in the county's history. The first known Cooper in the area was Edward Cooper, a cornet with Sir Charles Coote's dragoons (*Coopers of Markree* 1935:2). Like many English officers who served in Ireland, Cooper received land in lieu of payment for his military duty (O'Rorke 1878:152). English families had lived in the county for at least 20 years before Cooper received his land grant, with about 140 families dwelling there in 1641 (O'Dowd 1991:103). The Cooper's main seat of residence was at Markree Castle (also sometimes called Mercury), an expansive tract renowned for its crenelated mansion, its stately trees, and its 19th-century observatory (O'Rorke 1890[1]:17; McTernan 1994:17, 2000:63–64; Watters [n.d.]:12).

The precise familial connection between the Coopers of Markree and the Coopers of Coopershill is unknown (O'Rorke 1890[2]:254–255), but tradition contends that Arthur and Sarah Cooper settled in County Sligo sometime in the early 1650s. Their dwelling, called Tanzyfort House, was the subject of archaeological excavation and architectural examination in 2003 and 2004.

A map drawn by Richard Feely, dated March 1760, indicates that Tanzyfort House was surrounded by a 166.7-acre demesne composed of 31 fields of various sizes and functions. The house itself is depicted in lot 26, "Garden & liberty about the House" (Figure 2).

The Coopers contracted for the construction of a second house—Coopershill House—north of Tanzyfort House, across the Unshin River, beginning around 1755 (Figure 1). County Clare architect Francis Bindon designed this still-inhabited dwelling as a typical Georgian mansion. The house was largely completed in 1774, and its first resident was Arthur and Sarah's son, Arthur Brooke Cooper. Writing in the early-19th century, James McParlan (1802:8) states that Coopershill House was a "superbly fine house." A late-19th-century county historian described the house as built "to last for ever" and compared its size and strength to the pyramids at Cheops (O'Rorke 1890[2]:253).

Sometime during the 18th century, perhaps immediately after the construction of Coopershill House, the Coopers also had another structure built, called the kennel. Located on the grounds of Tanzyfort House, the builders of the kennel intruded it into the north wall of the old house, possibly to reuse a stairway. The

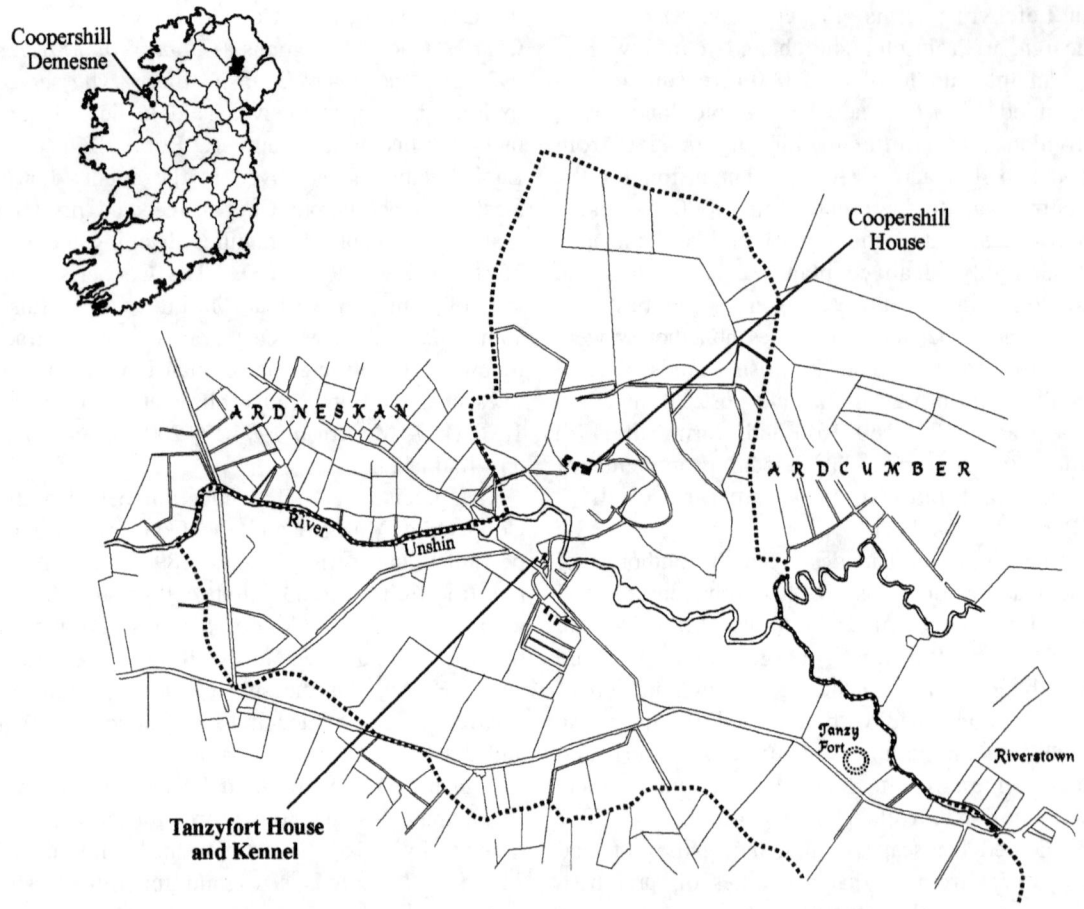

FIGURE 1. Map showing the location of Coopershill Demesne, Tanzyfort House, and Coopershill House. (Drawing by author, 2003.)

estate's hounds keeper lived in the kennel and cared for the hunting dogs that were renowned throughout County Sligo (Wood-Martin 1892: 388).

Arthur Brooke Cooper married Francis O'Hara, and it was their son, Charles William Cooper, who changed his surname in 1860 to O'Hara, his mother's maiden name. The O'Haras were a prominent Sligo Catholic family who converted to Protestantism and "identified completely with the Protestant Ascendancy" (Trench 1997:110). Charles made the change at the request of his uncle, Charles King O'Hara, a bachelor who wished to keep his property at nearby Annaghmore within the family. The eldest son of Charles William Cooper O'Hara, also named Charles, inherited Annaghmore, while another son, Arthur, inherited Coopershill.

Arthur was a bachelor, so the Coopershill estate was inherited by one of his younger brothers, Frank. Frank's sons eventually acquired Coopershill and Annaghmore, and their descendants still own both estates today.

Tanzyfort House was an L-shaped structure, originally containing 2-1/2 stories. Today the building is in ruins and exhibits evidence of massive alteration and reuse since its abandonment as a living space around 1780. Measurements indicate that the building contained 1,675 ft.^{2} on each floor. Preliminary excavation inside the structure revealed the presence of at least two rooms: a front hall, containing 984 ft.^{2}, and a kitchen, containing 690 ft.^{2} (Figure 3). The original hall probably had a flagstone floor, but most of the flooring was either removed or destroyed during the construction of the cobble-

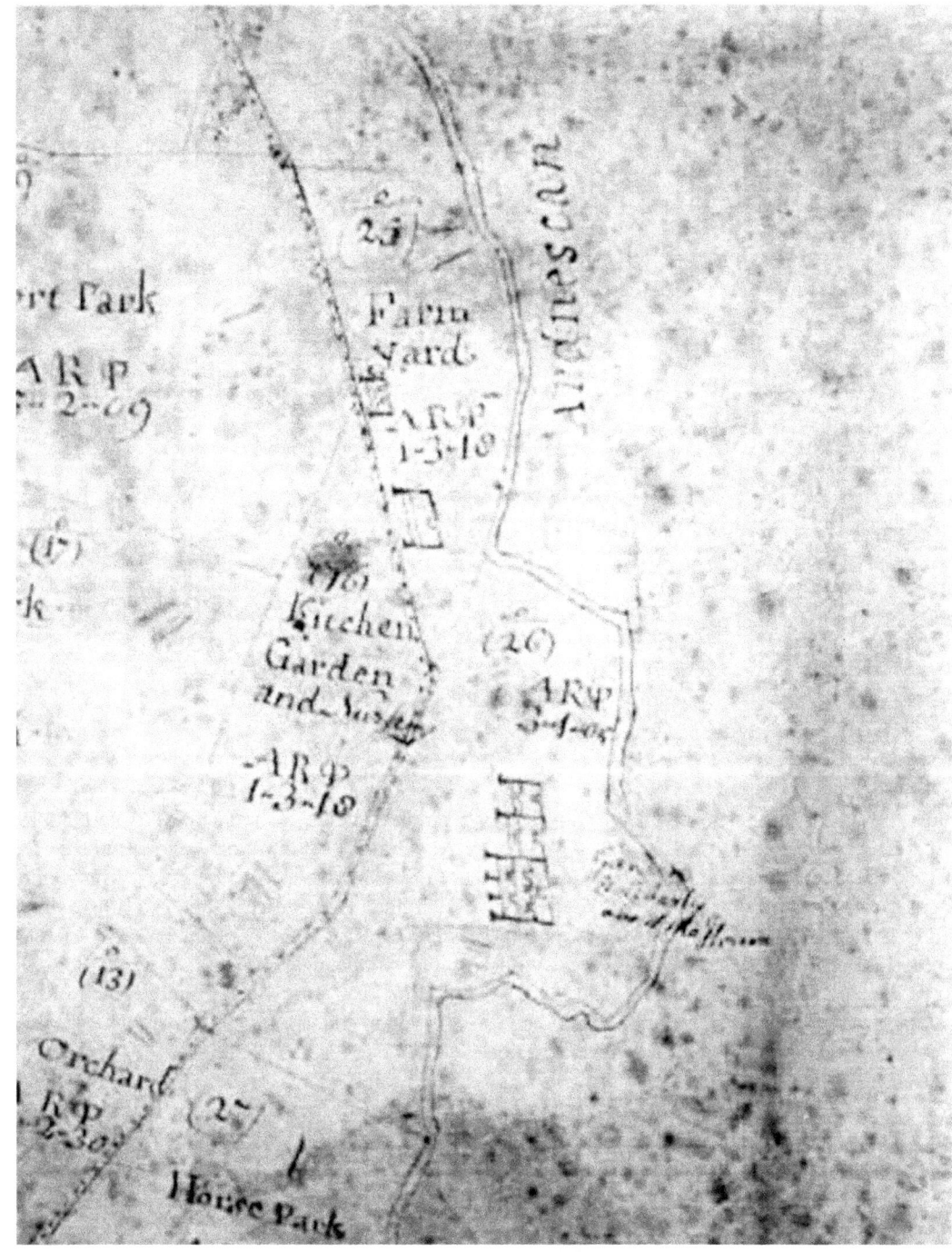

FIGURE 2. Section of Feely's map of 1760 showing Tanzyfort House. North is to the right. (Courtesy of Brian and Lindy O'Hara, Coopershill.)

stone yard built in association with the kennel inside the walls of the old house.

The walls of Tanzyfort House were approximately 3 ft. thick. The outside front wall (on the west side of the ruin) was partly exposed along its northernmost limit where it met the southernmost wall of the kennel. This exposed section of wall indicated that the

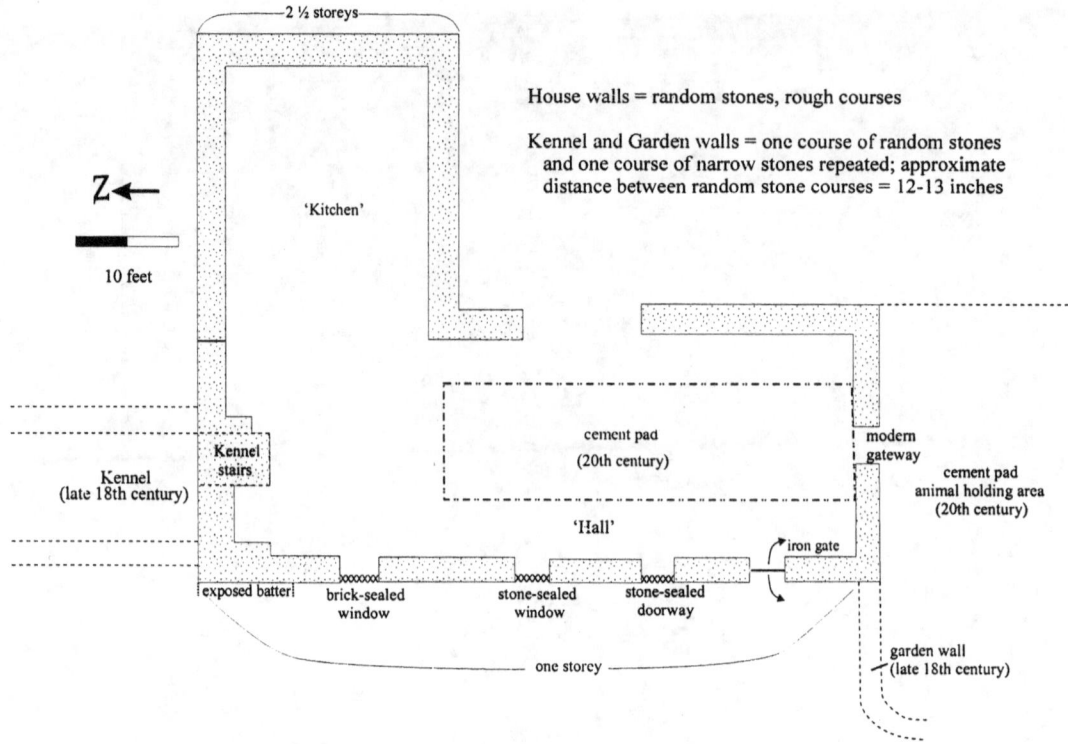

House walls = random stones, rough courses

Kennel and Garden walls = one course of random stones
and one course of narrow stones repeated; approximate
distance between random stone courses = 12-13 inches

FIGURE 3. Floor plan of Tanzyfort House as it appeared in 2003. (Drawing by author.)

structure was built with a sharply angled, short batter.

The west-facing wall of the hall wing contained a doorway and three windows. The wall's face bond was constructed of random rubble that probably was once covered with lime plaster rendering. The door had a cambered arch, but the windows may have been reworked with brick relieving arches. The upper expanse of the house's front wall was dismantled and replaced with vertical stone coping. While inhabited, the house undoubtedly had multiple gables and sturdy chimneys, following the convention of the time (Gailey 1987:91–92). Excavation revealed a possible back entrance almost directly opposite the front doorway, and structural evidence suggests the presence of a fireplace along the north wall of the kitchen and a second-storey fireplace in the building's northeast corner.

In early-17th-century Ireland, L-shaped houses were a common architectural style (Craig 1982:129–133). Castlebaldwin, located just south of the Coopershill estate, constitutes a well-known

example (for the floor plan, see Waterman 1961:273; Craig 1976:56; for a conjectural restoration, see MacLysaght 1969:96). This building is similar in design to Tanzyfort House, but the extending L feature in Castlebaldwin is considerably smaller.

Killincarrig House in County Wicklow bears a stronger likeness to Tanzyfort House (Leask 1961:246). Like Tanzyfort, this building has a front hall and a back kitchen. The two structures are approximately the same overall size (Tanzyfort=1,675 ft.[2]; Killincarrig=1,650 ft.[2]). Like Tanzyfort House, Killincarrig House had a back entrance (the two buildings were even oriented in the same direction) with the short wall of the hall and the long wall of the kitchen facing north.

Landscape Pedagogy and the Social Order

The initial creation of the Coopershill demesne provides a clear example of the enactment of symbolic violence, as almost 167 acres were taken out of agricultural production and reserved strictly for the use of a single Anglo-Irish family. Feely's map of 1760 indicates that the demesne included an orchard, a "kitchen garden," and 14 plots identified with the name "park" among its 31 distinguishable fields. The segregation of a large piece of reserved ground in the midst of Gaelic (and Catholic) Ireland was intended to have clear symbolic content. Not only was the land reserved space, it was also remade in a manner that was distinctively nontraditional in an Irish setting. It was only with the construction of the second Cooper mansion that symbolic capital was applied most concretely to promote the pedagogic action of the refashioned landscape.

Where symbolism is concerned, it is especially intriguing to contemplate the double meaning of the name "Coopershill." The name initially appears to evoke a pure empirical practicality: the owners of the estate were named Cooper, and the second mansion was sited upon a hill. When considered in this straightforward way, the use of the name Coopershill is entirely logical. Equally important may be the poem "Coopers Hill" written by Dublin-born John Denham and first published in 1642. This work, revered by Samuel Johnson, John Dryden, and other literary notables, and imitated by many, including Alexander Pope (a leader in the picturesque movement), was an early topographical poem (Banks 1928:333–350). In this long-remembered work, Denham reflects on the power of nature, the stark contrasts between city and country, and the beauty of the Thames. As Matthew Johnson (1996:92) notes, Denham employs political allegory through his use of perspective (Spencer 1973:58). Most important is that he also foregrounds the evocative power and diverse meanings embedded within well-kept landscapes. Though Denham was writing about the power of Britain's control over its colonies in the "Indies," his lines would have also had symbolic meaning for landowners seeking to create a new landscape in an ancient place (Banks 1928:75,77):

> Finds wealth where 'tis, bestows it where it wants,
> Cities in deserts, woods in cities plants;
> So that to us no thing, no place is strange

Thus, in building Coopershill demesne, the Coopers—educated people who undoubtedly

knew Denham's renowned poem—may have appropriated the name precisely because of its contextual double meaning.

The transformation of the Coopershill demesne was only accomplished with the construction of the bridge over the Unshin River (Figure 4). This bridge, which is still in use today, was at the time a substantial feat of engineering. Local legend holds that its construction was a daunting task. Every time its builders attempted to set its foundation stones, they saw them slowly sink into the marshy bog. After frustrating trial and error, the builders were only able to stabilize the stones by placing sheepskins under them. This account also maintains that the bridge cost as much to build as the mansion. A local historian considers this story to be apocryphal (O'Rorke 1890[2]: 254), but in any case, the construction of the bridge permitted the relocation of the mansion from Tanzyfort House on the lowland adjacent to the river to the heights further north. The repositioning of the mansion clearly had symbolic

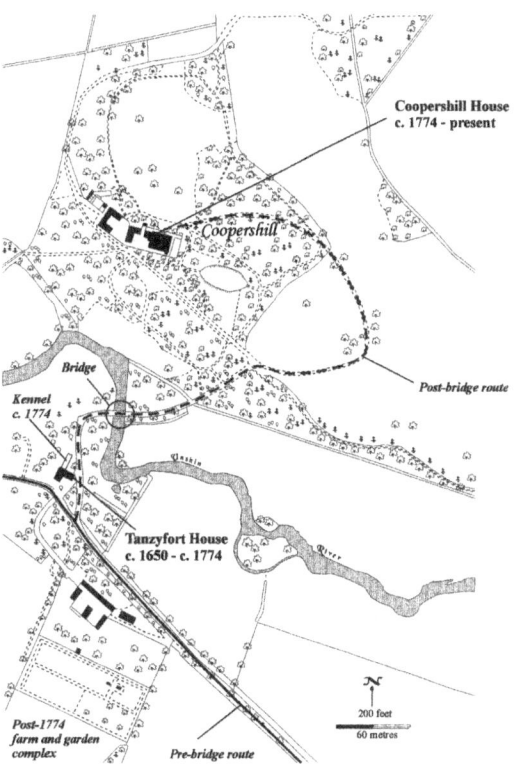

FIGURE 4. Map of residential area of Coopershill Demesne, showing major features. (Drawing adapted by author from 1911 Ordnance Survey map.)

intent and was obviously something the family much desired, or else they would not have expended so much economic capital on construction. The new position of the mansion afforded a better view of the countryside and was consistent with the aesthetics embodied in the growing use of topography to promote "the picturesque" (Hunt 1992, 2002; Howley 1993:6). The site also afforded the hilltop perspective memorialized by Denham. Equally instructive is the realignment of the main demesne road, the subsequent alteration of Tanzyfort House after it was abandoned as a dwelling, and the planting of huge numbers of trees, bushes, and ornamental shrubs.

The Feely map of 1760 indicates that the main road into the demesne originated from the southeast, extended past the southern side of the field in which Tanzyfort House was situated, and then ran further west, roughly parallel to the Unshin River (Figure 4). With the construction of the bridge the main road was repositioned to run in front of Tanzyfort House. The exaggerated loop of this new road, once it passed the bridge, allowed it to skirt the deer

park. Deer parks were a sign of wealth and refinement that extended back in Ireland to at least 1244 (Viney 1997:525–526). Deer still inhabit the Coopershill park today. The road did not have to make the large loop because the bridge could have been located further south and thus have provided a straighter, more direct route to Coopershill House. The construction of the kennel, probably completed sometime immediately after the second mansion was finished, may have provided functional utility to the new road's location, but, in realty, the kennel could have been built anywhere on the estate. In the final analysis, a central feature of the road's new position was that anyone visiting Coopershill House was required, then as now, to pass directly by the ruins of Tanzyfort House.

Tanzyfort House was not allowed to become a ruin naturally. It appears to have been dismantled in a consciously designed manner with the overall intention being to create a romantic, picturesque ruin. When workers removed the upper floor, they installed a vertical stone copping on top of the stonewall (Figure 5).

FIGURE 5. Front wall of Tanzyfort House as it appeared in 2003, facing east. (Photo by author.)

Perspectives from *Historical Archaeology*

The use of this decorative treatment may have been intended to mimic the crenelated battlements of ancient castles, or it may simply have been planned as aesthetic. In either case, the overall intent of the dismantling of Tanzyfort House seems to have been designed to reinforce a sense of history on the demesne property through a conscious use of Lefebvre's tripartite space.

The use of architecture to promote a feeling of nostalgic antiquity on the estates of the English gentry was voiced as early as 1709 by playwright-turned-architect John Vanburgh. In his "Reasons Offer'd for Preserving some Part of the Old Manor" at Blenhiem Palace, Oxfordshire, Vanburgh argued that many houses are revered simply because they provide "more lively and pleasing Reflections (than History without their Aid can do) On the Persons who have Inhabited them; On the Remarkable things which have been transacted in them, Or the extraordinary Occasions of Erecting Them" (Hunt and Willis 1975:120–121). In instances where history "Stands in need of Assistance," it is quite reasonable for the enlightened architect to construct picturesque and historically evocative ruins on the estate. In keeping with this idea, sham ruins became a common sight on the demesnes of the gentry, with the earliest known example in Ireland appearing in 1724 at Castle Ward, County Down (Howley 1993: 106). The importance of ruins on the estates of the wealthy became so widespread and so significant a piece of social capital (denoting antiquity, good breeding, and a host of similar qualities) that adherence to Vanburgh's principles has been termed "the cult of the ruin" (Watkin 1982:45–66). In some places, such as Hamilton's Tower at Glin Castle, County Limerick, the walls of wholly fabricated castles, complete with crenelations, had their windows filled with stones to instill the idea of reuse over a long period and to be pleasing to the eye (Howley 1993:110). This same technique was adopted at Tanzyfort House (Figure 6).

The use of existing towers or the construction of new ones also figured prominently in presenting many demesnes as ancient and picturesque (Howley 1993:48–69). The modifiers of Tanzyfort House were fortunate in this regard because they were not required to construct a new tower. They could simply leave the 2-1/2-story kitchen wing standing and allow nature and time to provide the historic patina, making it appear to represent the remains of a square tower house —a late medieval, defensive structure used well into the postmedieval period (Figure 7). (For more information about Irish tower houses, see Westropp 1899; Leask 1951:75–112; Ó Danachair 1977–79; Cairns 1987; MacCurtain 1988; Barry 1993; Sweetman 1999:137–174.)

In addition to architectural constructions, estate owners could also enhance the visual beauty of their estates and, at the same time, further promote its pedagogic action through the importation and planting of ornamental trees, shrubs, and bushes. Planting, in abundant numbers and of exotic species, was an essential element in the picturesque movement expressed through consciously planned nature. An elite commitment to arboriculture, or dendrology—the "science of the cultivation of trees and shrubs for decorative purposes"

FIGURE 6. Tanzyfort House window with brick relieving arch and enclosed with stones. (Photo by author.)

FIGURE 7. Standing kitchen wing as it appeared in 2003. (Photo by author.)

(Malins and Bowe 1980:62)—grew in tandem with an interest in presenting other visual features on demesnes. Estate owners with the requisite wherewithal are known to have spent considerable amounts on plants for their demesnes. For example, between August 1811 and April 1812, Lord Kenmare at Killarney had more than 1,200,000 trees, seedlings, and shrubs planted on his estate. That some of these were cuttings from English trees further promoted the notion of remaking at least part of the Irish landscape in the vision of England (Malins and The Knight of Glin 1976:190). In another example, Arthur Young (1780:184), in the late 1770s, was so profoundly impressed with the trees planted by the Mahons at Strokestown Park House in County Roscommon that he opined that they constituted "the finest woods I ever saw." A bill dated 23 October 1841 indicates that the Mahons purchased 2,100 trees, shrubs, and seedlings on that day alone (Orser 1996:149).

The science of dendrology was also practiced at Coopershill demesne. In 1802,

when McParlan (1802:8) visited the estate, he commented on the fine "quality of the grounds" when noting the "delightful situation" of the house. Historical accounts confirm the purchase of many plant species for the estate. Receipts for the years 1782–1791 alone show the purchase of seeds of elm, ash, sycamore, oak, pine, fir, beech, yew, and even lime trees. In fact, "along the road from the Corner to the bog at the kennell [sic]"—in the vicinity of Tanzyfort House—the Cooper's planted ash, oak, fir, sycamore, larch, white poplar, and lime (Coopershill Archives).

Conclusion

It may be easy to conclude that no symbolic intent governed the dismantling of Tanzyfort House, and, given the characteristics of Bourdieu's tripartite concept of habitus-capital-field, it is distinctly possible that no conscious motive was in fact intended. Here we may perceive the field in both literal and figurative senses. In re-creating Tanzyfort House within

Perspectives from *Historical Archaeology*

intersecting fields that were in the process of both real and ideological transition, its modifiers demonstrated the "polyvalence of social space" (Lefebvre 1991:85) and bestowed a triple objectivity on the ruin. The Tanzyfort ruin was perceived space (it was the site of social action and interaction), conceived space (conceptualized by architectural and social planners), and lived space (experienced through a complex network of intersecting images and symbols). But the images and symbols represented by the re-created Tanzyfort House were not simply aesthetic; their intent was to naturalize Irish social space—as passively experienced—by offering a pedagogic lesson to everyone in local Irish society: landlord and tenant, English and Gaelic, Protestant and Catholic. The silent pedagogy of Tanzyfort House and the Coopershill demesne demonstrated the antiquity and authority of their owner's family within the sociohistorical realities of 18th-century Ascendancy Ireland. The construction of Coopershill House, and the apparent transformation of Tanzyfort House, occurred at a time when the Anglo-Irish Ascendancy was at the height of its power and authority (McConville 2001:130). As a class, they were able to give their elite social positions expression in numerous ways, including sculpted demesnes. The mere presence of the demesne on the landscape was not enough; its visibility had to be both pleasing to behold and pedagogic in its action. In short, demesnes had to provide lessons about the social order that could be inculcated without much conscious thought or reflection.

The imposition of symbolic analyses on archaeological remains is always contestable. The perception of an analyst may too often be the prime factor in shaping the resultant interpretation. Conceptualized this way, the archaeological analysis of past landscapes offers a potentially powerful window on past social practice, and the close examination of landscapes is particularly relevant to historical archaeology because of the frequent preservation of standing buildings, relict walls, and other meaningful features both above and below the ground. An understanding of Bourdieu's concept of symbolic violence helps to overcome this deficiency in symbolic analysis because it asks researchers to conceptualize both the past and the present in terms of a series of intersecting

networks that embody situationally significant meanings. In the hierarchical societies examined by historical archaeologists, relations of power necessarily impinged on most social interactions. Individuals and groups engaged in diverse practices as they sought to control various forms of capital within the sociohistorical formation within which they lived.

Modern-period Ireland presents an excellent arena for study because of the historical depth of its preserved remains and the sheer abundance of its resources. Postmedieval demesnes were not assembled without conscious intent. Quite the contrary, they were planned as restricted spaces that contained clear messages about English and Anglo-Irish enlightenment and social refinement. They were pedagogic spaces that could instruct and reaffirm. As Coopershill demesne demonstrates, the landscape was free to be altered to meet new pedagogic needs. When the ideas prominent within the field of upper class English and Anglo-Irish life changed, certain landscape alterations were also required. Tanzyfort House, though no longer used as a residence after about 1780, continued to constitute a powerful element of the demesne's pedagogic action. It was an integral element of the landscape that incorporated a massive new house, a looping access road, a carefully engineered bridge, and the abundant decorative plantings.

Acknowledgments

I wish to acknowledge Norman Hammond for giving me the original idea for this paper and Kieran O'Conor for helping me understand the architectural history of Tanzyfort House. I would like to thank Brian and Lindy O'Hara, and the entire O'Hara family, for allowing this research to be conducted and for being helpful in every way possible. Fruitful collaboration with the Sligo Folk Park, Riverstown, County Sligo, also made this research possible, and I wish to thank everyone there for all their gracious assistance, guidance, and support. The excavations at Tanzyfort House were conducted under license 03E0925, administered by the Heritage and Planning Division of the Department of the Environment, Heritage, and Local Government, and the National Museum of Ireland. My interpretation of Coopershill demesne was facilitated by discussions with Katherine Hull, Stephen Brighton, David Ryder, Janice Orser, and Kevin Barton, as well as with everyone mentioned above. I would also like to thank Matthew Johnson and two anonymous reviewers whose challenging, insightful suggestions significantly improved this paper. The responsibility for the final interpretation rests entirely with me.

References

AALEN, FREDERICK
1989 Imprint of the Past. In *The Irish Countryside: Landscape, Wildlife, History, People*, Desmond Gillmor, editor, pp. 83–119. Wolfhound Press, Dublin, Ireland.

ASHMORE, WENDY, AND A. BERNARD KNAPP (EDITORS)
1999 *Archaeologies of Landscape: Contemporary Perspectives*. Blackwell, Oxford, England.

BANKS, THEODORE HOWARD (EDITOR)
1928 *The Poetical Works of Sir John Denham*. Yale University Press, New Haven, CT.

BARNARD, TOBY
2004 *Making the Grand Figure: Lives and Possessions in Ireland, 1641–1770*. Yale University Press, New Haven, CT.

BARNES, JOHN A.
1954 Class and Community in a Norwegian Island Parish. *Human Relations* 7:39–58.

BARRY, TERRY
1993 The Archaeology of the Tower House in Late Medieval Ireland. In *The Study of Medieval Archaeology*, Hans Andersson and Jes Wienberg, editors, pp. 211–217. Almqvist and Wiksell, Stockholm, Sweden.

BEASLEY-MURRAY, JON
2000 Value and Capital in Bourdieu and Marx. In *Pierre Bourdieu: Fieldwork in Culture*, Nicholas Brown and Imre Szeman, editors, pp. 100–119. Rowman and Littlefield, Lanham, MD.

BENDER, BARBARA
1998 *Stonehenge: Making Space*. Berg, Oxford, England.

BENDER, BARBARA, AND MARGOT WINER (EDITORS)
2001 *Contested Landscapes: Movement, Exile, and Place*. Berg, Oxford, England.

BLOCH, MARC
1985 *Marxism and Anthropology: The History of a Relationship*. Oxford University Press, Oxford, England.

BOURDIEU, PIERRE
1981 Men and Machines. In *Advances in Social Theory and Methodology: Toward an Integration of Micro- and Macro-Sociologies*, Karin D. Knorr-Cetina and Aaron V. Cicourel, editors, pp. 304–317. Routledge and Kegan Paul, Boston, MA.
1984 *Distinction: A Social Critique of the Judgement of Taste*, Richard Nice, translator. Harvard University Press, Cambridge, MA.
1985 The Social Space and the Genesis of Groups. *Theory and Society* 14(6):723–744.
1986 The Forms of Capital. In *Handbook of Theory and Research for the Sociology of Education*, John G. Richardson, editor, pp. 241–258. Greenwood, New York, NY.
1990a *In Other Words: Essays Towards a Reflexive Sociology*, Matthew Adamson, translator. Stanford University Press, Stanford, CA.
1990b *The Logic of Practice*, Richard Nice, translator. Stanford University Press, Stanford, CA.
1993 *The Field of Cultural Production: Essays on Art and Literature*, Randal Johnson, editor and translator. Columbia University Press, New York, NY.

BOURDIEU, PIERRE, AND JEAN-CLAUDE PASSERON
1977 *Reproduction in Education, Society, and Culture*, Richard Nice, translator. Sage, London, England.

BOURDIEU, PIERRE, AND LOÏC J. D. WACQUANT
1992 *An Invitation to Reflexive Sociology*. University of Chicago Press, Chicago, IL.

CAIRNS, C. T.
1987 *Irish Tower Houses: A Co. Tipperary Case Study*. Group for the Study of Irish Historic Settlement, Dublin, Ireland.

CALHOUN, CRAIG
1995 *Critical Social Theory: Culture, History, and the Challenge of Difference*. Blackwell, Oxford, England.

CANNY, NICHOLAS
2001 *Making Ireland British: 1580–1650*. Oxford University Press, Oxford, England.

COOPERSHILL ARCHIVES
1782–1791 Coopershill House, D.4031/E/7, Riverstown, County Sligo, Ireland.

COOPERS OF MARKREE
1935 *Coopers of Markree: Sketch of Family History*. NL Mss. Item 230, Sligo Folk Park Library, Riverstown, Ireland.

CRAIG, MAURICE
1976 *Classic Irish Houses of the Middle Size*. Architectural Press, London, England.
1982 *The Architecture of Ireland from the Earliest Times to 1880*. B. T. Batsford, London, England.

CRAWFORD, O. G. S.
  1953 *Archaeology in the Field.* Frederick A. Praeger, New York, NY.

DARBY, WENDY JOY
  2000 *Landscape and Identity: Geographies of Nation and Class in England.* Berg, Oxford, England.

DEETZ, JAMES
  1990 Landscapes as Cultural Statements. In *Earth Patterns: Essays in Landscape Archaeology*, William M. Kelso and Rachel Most, editors, pp. 1–4. University Press of Virginia, Charlottesville.

DELLE, JAMES A.
  1998 *An Archaeology of Social Space: Analyzing Coffee Plantations in Jamaica's Blue Mountains.* Plenum, New York, NY.

DE RIVERA, JOSEPH (EDITOR)
  1976 *Field Theory as Human-Science: Contributions of Lewin's Berlin Group.* Gardner Press, New York, NY.

DICKSON, DAVID
  2000 *New Foundations: Ireland, 1660–1800*, 2nd edition. Irish Academic Press, Dublin, Ireland.

FELD, STEVEN, AND KEITH H. BASSO (EDITORS)
  1996 *Senses of Place.* School of American Research Press, Santa Fe, NM.

FOSTER, ROY F.
  1989 *Modern Ireland: 1600–1972.* Penguin, London, England.

FOWLER, PETER
  2001 Reading the Land. Originally published in *British Archaeology* 62 (Dec.) <http://www.britarch.ac.uk/ba/ba62/ feat2.shtml> 27 February.

GAILEY, ALAN
  1987 Changes in Irish Rural Housing, 1600–1900. In *Rural Ireland, 1600–1900: Modernisation and Change*, Patrick O'Flanagan, Paul Ferguson, and Kevin Whelan, editors, pp. 86–103. Cork University Press, Cork, Ireland.

GODELIER, MAURICE
  1988 *The Mental and the Material: Thought, Economy, and Society*, Martin Thom, translator. Verso, London, England.

HILLIER, BILL, AND JULIENNE HANSON
  1984 *The Social Logic of Space.* Cambridge University Press, Cambridge, England.

HOWLEY, JAMES
  1993 *The Follies and Garden Buildings of Ireland.* Yale University Press, New Haven, CT.

HUNT, JOHN DIXON
  1992 *Gardens and the Picturesque: Studies in the History of Landscape Architecture.* MIT Press, Cambridge, MA.
  2002 *The Picturesque Garden in Europe.* Thames and Hudson, London, England.

HUNT, JOHN DIXON, AND PETER WILLIS (EDITORS)
  1975 *The Genius of the Place: The English Landscape Garden, 1620–1820.* Paul Elek, London, England.

JOHNSON, MATTHEW
  1996 *An Archaeology of Capitalism.* Blackwell, Oxford, England.

LEASK, H. G.
  1951 *Irish Castles and Castellated Houses.* Dundalgan Press, Dundalk, Ireland.
  1961 Early Seventeenth-Century Houses in Ireland. In *Studies in Building History: Essays in Recognition of the Work of B. H. St. J. O'Neil*, E. M. Jope, editor, pp. 243–250. Odhams Press, London, England.

LEFEBVRE, HENRI
  1979 Space: Social Product and Use Value. In *Critical Sociology: European Perspectives*, J. W. Freiberg, editor, pp. 285–295. Irvington, New York, NY.
  1991 *The Production of Space.* Donald Nicholson-Smith, translator. Blackwell, Oxford, England.

LEONE, MARK P.
  1984 Interpreting Ideology in Historical Archaeology: Using the Rules of Perspective in the William Paca Garden, Annapolis, Maryland. In *Ideology, Power, and Prehistory*, Daniel Miller and Christopher Tilley, editors, pp. 25–35. Cambridge University Press, Cambridge, England.

LESSER, ALEXANDER
  1961 Social Fields and the Evolution of Society. *Southwestern Journal of Anthropology* 17:40–48.

LEWIN, KURT
  1951 *Field Theory in Social Science: Selected Theoretical Papers*, Dorwin Cartwright, editor. Harper, New York, NY.

LLEWELLYN, RODDY
  1989 *Ornamental English Gardens*, Robert Holt, editor. Rizzoli, New York, NY.

MacCURTAIN, MARGARET
  1988 A Lost Landscape: The Geraldine Castles and Tower Houses of the Shannon Estuary. In *Settlement and Society in Medieval Ireland: Studies Presented to F. X. Martin*, John Bradley, editor, pp. 429–444. Boethius Press, Kilkenny, Ireland.

MacLYSAGHT, EDWARD
  1969 *Irish Life in the Seventeenth Century*, 2nd edition. Irish University Press, Shannon, Ireland.

MALINS, EDWARD, AND THE KNIGHT OF GLIN
1976 *Lost Demesnes: Irish Landscape Gardening, 1660–1845.* Barrie and Jenkins, London, England.

MALINS, EDWARD, AND PATRICK BOWE
1980 *Irish Gardens and Demesnes from 1830.* Rizzoli, New York, NY.

MARX, KARL
1954 *The Communist Manifesto,* Samuel Moore, translator. Henry Regnery, Chicago, IL.

MATTHEWS, CHRISTOPHER N.
2002 *An Archaeology of History and Tradition: Moments of Danger in the Annapolis Landscape.* Kluwer Academic/Plenum, New York, NY.

MCCONVILLE, MICHAEL
2001 *Ascendancy to Oblivion: The Story of the Anglo-Irish.* Phoenix Press, London, England.

MCPARLAN, JAMES
1802 *Statistical Survey of the County of Sligo with Observations on the Means of Improvement: Drawn up in the Year 1801, for the Consideration, and Under the Direction of the Dublin Society.* Graisberry and Campbell, Dublin, Ireland.

MCTERNAN, JOHN C. (EDITOR)
1994 *Sligo: Sources of Local History,* new edition. Sligo County Library, Sligo, Ireland.
2000 *A Sligo Miscellany: A Chronicle of People, Places, and Events of Other Days.* Avena, Sligo, Ireland.

MITCHELL, W. J. T. (EDITOR)
2002 *Landscape and Power,* 2nd edition. University of Chicago Press, Chicago, IL.

Ó DANACHAIR, CAOIMHÍN
1977–1979 Irish Tower Houses and Their Regional Distribution. *Béaloideas* 45–47:158–163.

O'DOWD, MARY
1991 *Power, Politics, and Land: Early Modern Sligo, 1568–1688.* Institute of Irish Studies, Queen's University, Belfast, Northern Ireland.

O'RORKE, TERENCE
1878 *History, Antiquities, and Present State of the Parishes of Ballysadare and Kilvarnet, in the County of Sligo.* James Duffy and Sons, Dublin, Ireland.
1890 *The History of Sligo: Town and Country,* 2 vols. James Duffy and Sons, Dublin, Ireland.

ORSER, CHARLES E., JR.
1996 *A Historical Archaeology of the Modern World.* Plenum, New York, NY.
2004 *Race and Practice in Archaeological Interpretation.* University of Pennsylvania Press, Philadelphia.

PERRY, WARREN R.
1999 *Landscape Transformations and the Archaeology of Impact: Social Disruption and State Formation in Southern Africa.* Kluwer Academic/Plenum, New York, NY.

RADCLIFFE-BROWN, A. R.
1940 On Social Structure. *Journal of the Royal Anthropological Society of Great Britain and Ireland* 70(1):1–12.

REEVES-SMYTH, TERENCE
1997a The Natural History of Demesnes. In *Nature in Ireland: A Scientific and Cultural History,* John Wilson Foster, editor, pp. 549–572. Lilliput Press, Dublin, Ireland.
1997b Demesnes. In *Atlas of the Irish Rural Landscape,* F. H. A. Aalen, Kevin Whelan, and Matthew Stout, editors, pp. 197–205. Cork University Press, Cork, Ireland.

ROTMAN, DEBORAH L., AND ELLEN-ROSE SAVULIS (EDITORS)
2003 *Shared Spaces and Divided Places: Material Dimensions of Gender Relations and the American Historical Landscape.* University of Tennessee Press, Knoxville.

SHIELDS, ROB
1997 Spatial Stress and Resistance: Social Meanings of Spatialization. In *Space and Social Theory: Interpreting Modernity and Postmodernity.* George Benko and Ulf Strohmayer, editors, pp. 186–202. Blackwell, Oxford, England.

SKEGGS, BEVERLY
1997 *Formations of Class and Gender: Becoming Respectable.* Sage, London, England.

SOJA, EDWARD W.
1980 The Socio-Spatial Dialectic. *Annals of the Association of American Geographers* 70(2):207–225.
1989 *Postmodern Geographies: The Reassertion of Space in Critical Social Theory.* Verso, London, England.

SPENCER, JEFFRY B.
1973 *Heroic Nature: Ideal Landscapes in English Poetry from Marvell to Thomson.* Northwestern University Press, Evanston, IL.

SWARTZ, DAVID
1997 *Culture and Power: The Sociology of Pierre Bourdieu.* University of Chicago Press, Chicago, IL.

SWEETMAN, DAVID
1999 *Medieval Castles of Ireland.* Collins Press, Cork, Ireland.

THRIFT, NIGEL J.
2002 On the Determination of Social Action in Space and Time. In *The Spaces of Postmodernity: Readings in Human Geography,* Michael J. Dear and Steven Flusty, editors, pp. 106–119. Blackwell, Oxford, England.

TRENCH, CHARLES CHENEVIX
    1997 *Grace's Card: Irish Catholic Landlords, 1690–1800.* Mercier, Cork, Ireland.

TUAN, YI-FU
    1977 *Space and Place: The Perspective of Experience.* University of Minnesota Press, Minneapolis, MN.

VINEY, MICHAEL
    1997 Wild Sports and Stone Guns. In *Nature in Ireland: A Scientific and Cultural History,* John Wilson Foster, editor, pp. 524–548. Lilliput Press, Dublin, Ireland.

WACQUANT, LOÏC J. D.
    1993 From Ideology to Symbolic Violence: Culture, Class, and Consciousness in Marx and Bourdieu. *International Journal of Contemporary Sociology* 30(2):125–142.

    2001 Further Notes on Bourdieu's "Marxism." *International Journal of Contemporary Sociology* 38(1):103–109.

WATERMAN, D. M.
    1961 Some Irish Seventeenth-Century Houses and Their Architectural Ancestry. In *Studies in Building History: Essays in Recognition of the Work of B. H. St. J. O'Neil,* E. M. Jope, editor, pp. 251–274. Odhams Press, London, England.

WATKIN, DAVID
    1982 *The English Vision: The Picturesque in Architecture, Landscape, and Garden Design.* Harper and Row, New York, NY.

WATTERS, SIOBHAN
    [n.d.] *The Coopers of Markree.* Manuscript, Sligo County Library, Sligo, Ireland.

WESTROPP, T. J.
    1899 Notes on the Lesser Castles or "Peel Towers" of the County Clare. *Proceedings of the Royal Irish Academy* 5:348–365.

WILKINSON, T. J.
    2004 The Archaeology of Landscape. In *A Companion to Archaeology,* John Bintliff, editor, pp. 334–356. Blackwell, Oxford, England.

WILLEY, GORDON R.
    1953 *Prehistoric Settlement Patterns in the Virú Valley, Perú.* Bureau of American Ethnology Bulletin, No. 155. Smithsonian Institution, Washington, DC.

WOOD-MARTIN, W. G.
    1892 *History of Sligo, County, and Town, from the Close of the Revolution of 1688 to the Present Time, Volume III.* Hodges, Figgis, Dublin, Ireland.

YOUNG, ARTHUR
    1780 *A Tour of Ireland with General Observations on the Present State of that Kingdom made in the Years 1776, 1777, and 1778.* T. Cadell and J. Dodsley, London, England.

CHARLES E. ORSER, JR.
CENTER FOR THE STUDY OF RURAL IRELAND
CAMPUS BOX 4660
ILLINOIS STATE UNIVERSITY
NORMAL, IL 61790-4660

Christopher C. Fennell

Damaging Detours: Routes, Racism, and New Philadelphia

ABSTRACT

The 19th-century impacts of racism and transportation developments on New Philadelphia, Illinois are explored by examining oral history, documentary, and archaeological evidence. This study first addresses the region in which New Philadelphia was located, outlining the contours of a landscape torn by racial strife. Analysis of the history of the construction of a regional railroad that bypassed New Philadelphia is then provided. Evidence shows that the town was bypassed for reasons other than competition from other potential depot towns, engineering concerns with topography, or other rational business reasons. The impacts of aversive racism very likely diverted the railroad route around New Philadelphia, spelling its demise. Finally, the lessons that emerge from these past social, economic, and racial dynamics are considered.

Introduction

New Philadelphia, located in Pike County in western Illinois, was the first town in the United States planned, platted, and legally registered by an African American. Founded in 1836 by Frank McWorter, a formerly enslaved laborer, New Philadelphia developed as a multiracial community through the late 1800s. This town was located in a region that was shaped by racial ideologies and strife, with competing factions of abolitionists and proslavery elements clashing in the surrounding region of western Illinois, and in the nearby slave state of Missouri. Yet, there is no report of racial violence occurring within New Philadelphia during the period that it existed as a town.

Racism very likely impacted this town in a more structural way, however. In 1869, a new railroad was built to connect points on the Illinois and Mississippi rivers, crossing Pike County on an east–west line that should have taken the railroad through New Philadelphia and made the town into a thriving depot facility. Instead, the railroad moved on a straight line from east to west, and then curved northward by several miles before arcing back to the south, thereby bypassing New Philadelphia. The impact of this detour was dramatic, leading to the demise of the town by the late 1880s (Simpson 1981:1; Walker 1983:165–167, 1985:56). Today nothing remains above ground at the town site, which is covered with agricultural fields and prairie grasses.

Such profound effects, resulting from a town's becoming a depot station or of being bypassed by a new railroad, occurred frequently across the Midwest in the 19th century (Conger 1932:285; Jenks 1944:14; Davis 1998:368–370). As historian Theodore Carlson (1951:103) observed: "Every enterprising hamlet had visions of becoming an important commercial city if at least one railroad could be built through the community." Settlements that were known as communities of African American families and businesses were typically bypassed by new railways, however (Cha-Jua 2000:42).

The impact of racism and this important transportation development on New Philadelphia are explored by examining documentary, archaeological, and oral history evidence. A collaborative project of researchers is working to obtain a detailed understanding of the social history of this community, and the many families and businesspeople who resided there in the 19th century. This collaborating group includes archaeologists, African American studies scholars, historians, descendants of families that lived in and around New Philadelphia, and current members of the local communities in the region where the town site is located. The impacts of past and present racism have been among the primary themes and research questions pursued in this project of civic engagement.

The first part of this article addresses the region in which New Philadelphia was located, outlining the contours of a landscape torn by racial strife. Archaeological findings related to potential impacts of racism within the town are also considered. An analysis of the history of the construction of the regional railroad that bypassed New Philadelphia is provided in the second part. Persuasive evidence indicates that the town was bypassed for reasons other than competition from other potential depot towns, engineering concerns with topography, or other rational business reasons that have been known to fuel the decisions of railroad construction companies. Racial prejudices likely diverted the railroad route around New Philadelphia, spelling its demise. The third part of this article considers the lessons that emerge from these past social, economic, and racial dynamics.

A Regional Context of Racial Strife

Frank McWorter's design for New Philadelphia (which was also called Philadelphia) was set out in a plat filed in the Pike County courthouse in 1836. A town covering 42 ac., it was designed to consist of 20 blocks, 144 lots, and several streets and alleyways in a grid pattern. New Philadelphia was located just 25 mi. due east of Hannibal, a small city along the Mississippi River that before the conclusion of the Civil War served as a slave trading market in the slave state of Missouri. The Illinois River was just 15 mi. to the east of New Philadelphia, and the town was platted on a tract of land situated within the "Military Bounty Lands" located between these two river-transport routes. Planned construction of the Illinois and Michigan Canal in the early 1830s, and its anticipated impact on transport flow on the Illinois River to and from Chicago and the Great Lakes, greatly enhanced land values in this region during this time period (Putnam 1909:414; Walker 1985:51).

While many think of the state of Illinois as having developed as a "free" state, famous as the "Land of Lincoln," this region was marked by racial strife and often accommodating views toward the rights of slave owners (Walker 1983:110–111; Davis 1998:19; Shackel 2006:2.4). The land that would be encompassed by the state of Illinois in 1818 was earlier part of the old Northwest Territory, as governed by the Ordinance of 1787. The 1787 provisions generally described this territory as a "free" domain, but were otherwise protective and accommodating to existing claims of property rights in enslaved laborers asserted primarily by French colonial residents (Walker 1983; Davis 1998:94).

Illinois's 1818 state constitution described it as a free state, yet again made a number of concessions to slave ownership claims. Slavery was permitted to continue for 25 years in the southern part of the state, and other slave-ownership claims were converted into legally binding indentured servitude (Savage 1943; Davis 1998:165; Simeone 2000:5). Slavery in Illinois was not effectively outlawed until an 1845 court decision. The state also passed its own version of "Black codes" in the early 1800s, which placed significant constraints on the rights of free African Americans, and attempted to discourage African American families from immigrating into Illinois (Savage 1943:312; Davis 1998:413; Simeone 2000:157).

Illinois and federal laws also provided recognition of the slave-ownership claims of residents in Missouri and other slave states, who often hired bounty hunters to travel through Illinois in search of laborers who were attempting to escape from bondage. These bounty hunters often engaged in kidnapping, enslaving free African Americans by capturing them and destroying the legal documents that proved their free status. Bounty hunters were also known to kidnap enslaved African Americans who did not match the warrants of runaways, so the bounty hunters could profit by unauthorized sales of those laborers in Hannibal and other slave markets (Savage 1943; Davis 1998:289).

Combating these proslavery elements were active contingents of abolitionist groups, and individuals assisting runaway slaves in the networks of the "Underground Railroad." New Philadelphia was located in an area surrounded by abolitionist centers, including Quincy, Alton, and Jacksonville, Illinois (Figure 1). In 1837, Elijah Lovejoy, an ardent abolitionist, was shot dead at his publishing house in Alton by a proslavery crowd that burned the printing press he had used in promoting the cause of freedom (Simon 1994). Abolitionists active in Quincy had frequent clashes with proslavery interests and authorities in Missouri and western Illinois, at times suffering imprisonment and death (*Quincy Herald* 1857b:3; Savage 1943; Turner 2001). Private homes in Jacksonville were active participants in the Underground Railroad (Steiner 1996; Turner 2001). Clashing factions of proslavery and abolitionist advocates faced off in Griggsville, Illinois, in 1838, just 13 mi. to the east of New Philadelphia (Figure 1) (Chapman 1880:516). Frank McWorter and his family, who owned farmsteads in the area surrounding New Philadelphia as well as lots within the town, were reported in oral histories to have helped individuals escaping from slavery (Walker 1983:149; Turner 2001:vii,15).

FIGURE 1. New Philadelphia in regional context. (Image by author, 2008.)

In the midst of this landscape, New Philadelphia grew as a multiracial community of homes and businesses that over time included families raising crops and livestock, merchants, blacksmiths, shoemakers, carpenters, a cabinetmaker, a wheelwright, a wagon maker, a physician, schoolteachers, and a preacher (Shackel 2006:2.12). The town founder, Frank McWorter, had attained the legal rights to found this town in a notably public and visible way. Born into slavery in South Carolina, McWorter had purchased his wife's freedom and then his own while living in Kentucky in the early 1800s. He later purchased a tract of 160 ac. in the Military Bounty Lands of western Illinois, and moved his family there in 1831 (Walker 1985:54). Manumission alone did not provide a free African American with all of the legal rights of someone classified as "white" in the federal census and Illinois state law. Under Illinois law, for example, free African Americans during the antebellum period were unable to give testimony against a white person in court,

and were required to post bonds as evidence of their economic capabilities upon immigrating into the state.

After living in Pike County on his 160 ac. farm for a few years, McWorter obtained support from his neighbors, who were farmers of European American heritage, and he applied to the Illinois legislature to register his name legally and to obtain full legal rights as a free citizen of the state (Chapman 1880:739; Simpson 1981:1; Walker 1983:106–107). These rights would facilitate his plan to plat and found the town of New Philadelphia on a 42 ac. parcel immediately to the south of his farm. An act of the Illinois legislature recorded in 1837 granted him these rights, and publicly recorded his plans to use the proceeds from sales of lots in the newly established town to purchase additional family members from bondage (Illinois State Archives 1837).

His neighbors' support, recorded in an 1837 "certificate of good character," further detailed McWorter's strong reputation, and his intention that New Philadelphia would be a town open for settlement by other free African American families, as well as by European Americans (Walker 1983:107). While there is no direct evidence indicating how McWorter chose the name of "Philadelphia" for this new town, the association of that eastern city with a growing abolitionist movement of free African Americans was well known by the early 1830s (Walker 1983:119–120; Berlin 2003:111; Davis 2006:171). McWorter's accomplishments and plans for the town were sufficiently well known in the following decades to be discussed in local history accounts and public ceremony speeches in 1872, 1876, and 1880 (Ensign 1872:54,100; Grimshaw 1876:31; Chapman 1880:739). Thus, his aspirations and achievements were also very likely known to other residents of this region of western Illinois and Hannibal, Missouri, who may have harbored racial biases against African Americans.

New Philadelphia grew slowly through the 1840s and 1850s, attaining its largest population in the time of the 1865 Illinois census, with approximately 160 residents in 29 households (Shackel 2006:1.2; King 2007). In each of the federal and state census lists compiled from 1840 through 1880, the residents of New Philadelphia were classified as "white," "black," or "mulatto," with approximately two-thirds of the town classified as white, and one-third classified as black or mulatto over the time period in which the town existed (King 2007). The town grew as a community at an agricultural crossroads, with wagon traffic from surrounding farms moving across roads that passed through New Philadelphia on their way to merchant and transport facilities along the nearby Illinois and Mississippi rivers (Walker 1983:167, 1985:55–56).

Daily social and economic events in New Philadelphia, and in other, larger towns nearby were reported in local newspapers in the 19th century. Archival copies of local and regional newspapers provide a rich record of the social history of this multiracial town, with many social and economic events within the town having been reported over the years. Notably, there is no instance of racial violence reported to have occurred within New Philadelphia over the several decades of its existence as a town, even though it was located in a region that was otherwise marked by racial strife, riots, and killings. Archaeological surveys and excavations undertaken in the town site have yielded evidence consistent with such findings from the documentary evidence.

Census lists, tax records, and deed books present researchers with extensive information about the past residents of New Philadelphia. Those documentary sources do not provide detailed maps of the particular locations within the town in which residents over time constructed their homes and businesses, however. Archaeological surveys and excavations can provide that richer detail of the spatial relationships spanning blocks, lots, streets, and the time period of the community's existence. This will be particularly useful data for the social history of New Philadelphia. A newspaper report in 1876 provides an example of frequent instances in which actual lifeways departed from the metes and bounds of official documents: "The village of Philadelphia ... has been readjusting lines, and it is found that most of the people are on other than their own lands. There will have to be some moving of property lines or a general compromise" (*Barry Adage* 1876c:3).

Excavations of several household and merchant locations within the town, dating from the 1850s through the late 1800s, show no evidence

of riots or arson (Shackel 2006). One might speculate that racial tensions within the town would lead to a pattern of segregated housing, with white and black residents occupying different portions of the town's space. Similarly, one might speculate that racial tensions would lead to assemblages of housewares and types of personal property that were distinctive to households of white or black residents. Archaeological surveys and excavations to date, however, show that house and merchant sites associated with both European Americans and African Americans were interspersed with one another, and largely clustered in the north and central part of the town's platted space (Hargrave 2006; Shackel 2006). The types of household belongings recovered from the residences of both whites and blacks, such as ceramic housewares, are also similar (Shackel, this volume).

Differences in, and separations of social activities that correlate with racial categories of white and black were evident in a number of lifeways in the town, however. For example, two cemeteries served the town. African American families typically buried their loved ones in a nearby cemetery where Frank McWorter and members of his family were interred. European American residents primarily used a different graveyard just to the south of town (King, this volume). Up until 1874, the children of African American families within the town were taught within one building, and the European American children learned their lessons in another building nearby. In 1874, a new, integrated schoolhouse was built next to the town's north edge, and accommodated all of the children in the area (Helton, this volume). In addition, archaeological excavations have shown that there may have been differences in the dietary choices made by some of the African American and European American residents in New Philadelphia (Shackel 2006; T. Martin and C. Martin, this volume).

Many instances of the impacts of racism in the United States have occurred in more structural and indirect ways than in overt declarations of prejudice, or in open acts of violence and malevolence (Omi and Winant 1994:56–61; Orser 2001; Leone et al. 2005:576–580). Such structural and indirect forms of racism have been conceptualized as manifestations of "aversive" racism, in which members of a dominant social group channel social and economic activities away from the members of a group targeted by racial prejudices. This aversion to social and economic interactions and opportunities is often detrimental to the targeted group. In contrast to such an indirect and structural impact, "dominant" racism is conceptualized as including direct, overt actions of violence and malevolence against members of a targeted group (Kovel 1970; Gaertner and Dovidio 1986; Kleinpenning and Hagendoorn 1993).

An early example of such a structural impact of racial prejudice can be seen to have occurred in 1840, when business interests of European American residents in the town of Barry lobbied the Illinois legislature to relocate a state road that ran through New Philadelphia on an east to west route between the Illinois and Mississippi rivers (Walker 1983:127–128). The relocation altered the road's course away from the center of New Philadelphia, and to a route that took it through the center of Barry, to the detriment of the town founded by McWorter, and to the benefit of Barry's businesses (Walker 1983:128). This lobbying proved successful, and the roadway changes were implemented in the following decade. As historian Juliet Walker (1983:128) observed, "by 1840 the state legislature was not prepared to give a black town proprietor an economic edge, however indirect, over white town proprietors."

New Philadelphia survived that early setback of 1840, although the pace of its growth was no doubt diminished. The town population continued to grow steadily, and even more land sales occurred at the hands of speculative investors who purchased and sold lots in the town without residing on those parcels. Other roadways passing through the area of New Philadelphia provided the community with regional traffic through the 1850s and 1860s. Entrepreneurs located in the town provided blacksmith, shoemaking, carpentry, wheelwright, and wagon repair services to town residents and to agricultural producers who lived and worked in the surrounding landscape. Another transportation development would have a more profound impact on the town, however. When a new regional railroad was built across the county in 1869, its route bypassed New Philadelphia.

The impact of the railroad's bypassing of New Philadelphia was dramatic, with businesses and residents departing the town over the following years. By 1885, an order was entered into the local court records to vacate the legal status of a large part of the town and to return those parcels to general agricultural use. Local publications attested to the town's demise. For example, the 1872 *Atlas Map of Pike County* observed that the "railroad did not run through the town, which has greatly ruined its trade" (Ensign 1872:10). Charles Chapman's 1880 *History of Pike County* stated of New Philadelphia: "At one time it had great promise, but the railroad passing it a mile distant, and other towns springing up, has killed it. At present there is not even a postoffice at the place" (Chapman 1880:740–741).

There are many reasons that a particular railroad route might take one path rather than another. If a topographic feature such as a high point of elevation or a deep ravine lies along a particular path, a railroad will often be diverted to avoid the expense of traversing that location. The lobbying of existing towns to become depots along a proposed rail route often causes other towns to be bypassed. Yet, none of these typical explanations is persuasive in the case of New Philadelphia.

An Expensive and Damaging Detour

The history of the railroad built across Pike County in 1869 can be studied in detail through surviving corporate records of the companies that funded, surveyed, and constructed the railroad, and the many local newspaper reports published in that period. One needs to read such documents with a critical eye, however, in order to compile data on past events separated from the opinions and biases of the past authors of such records. There is no direct statement in these collections of documentary evidence as to why the railroad bypassed New Philadelphia, whether for sensible business reasons or due to racial biases. Indeed, no reference to the town in those records has been found at all. Upon considering the contextual evidence presented in the following discussion, however, it becomes apparent that the railroad's bypassing of the town was not motivated by rational business choices of minimizing costs and maximizing profits.

In the early 1850s, business interests in Hannibal, Missouri began promoting a plan to create a company that would construct a railroad across Pike County, Illinois, to link Hannibal to the railroad town of Naples, located on the Illinois

River (Figure 2) (*Pittsfield Union* 1853:3; Grant 2004:22). In doing so, these promoters sought to advance Hannibal as a major railroad transport and commercial hub of the region (*Hannibal Daily Courier* 1878:1; Grant 2004:22). Two earlier railroad developments provided the Hannibal interests with this opportunity by creating railroad lines to the east and west of the city (Fishlow 1971:190–191).

To the east, the Northern Cross Railroad had been sponsored by land grants and funding from the federal and Illinois governments (Grant 2004:7–11). Construction began in 1838, and the rail line linked Meredosia on the Illinois River on the west to Jacksonville and Springfield on the east in 1841 (Corliss 1934:19; Grant 2004:7–11). This publicly funded railroad enterprise was later purchased by the privately held Sangamon and Morgan Railroad Company, and by 1849 the line was connected to Naples (*Alton Weekly Courier* 1855:4; Conger 1932:277; Carlson 1951:100; Grant 2004:11–12). Successors of the Northern Cross, including the Sangamon and Morgan and later the Great Western Railroad Company, planned on linking that east–west railroad with the Illinois Central Railroad, which

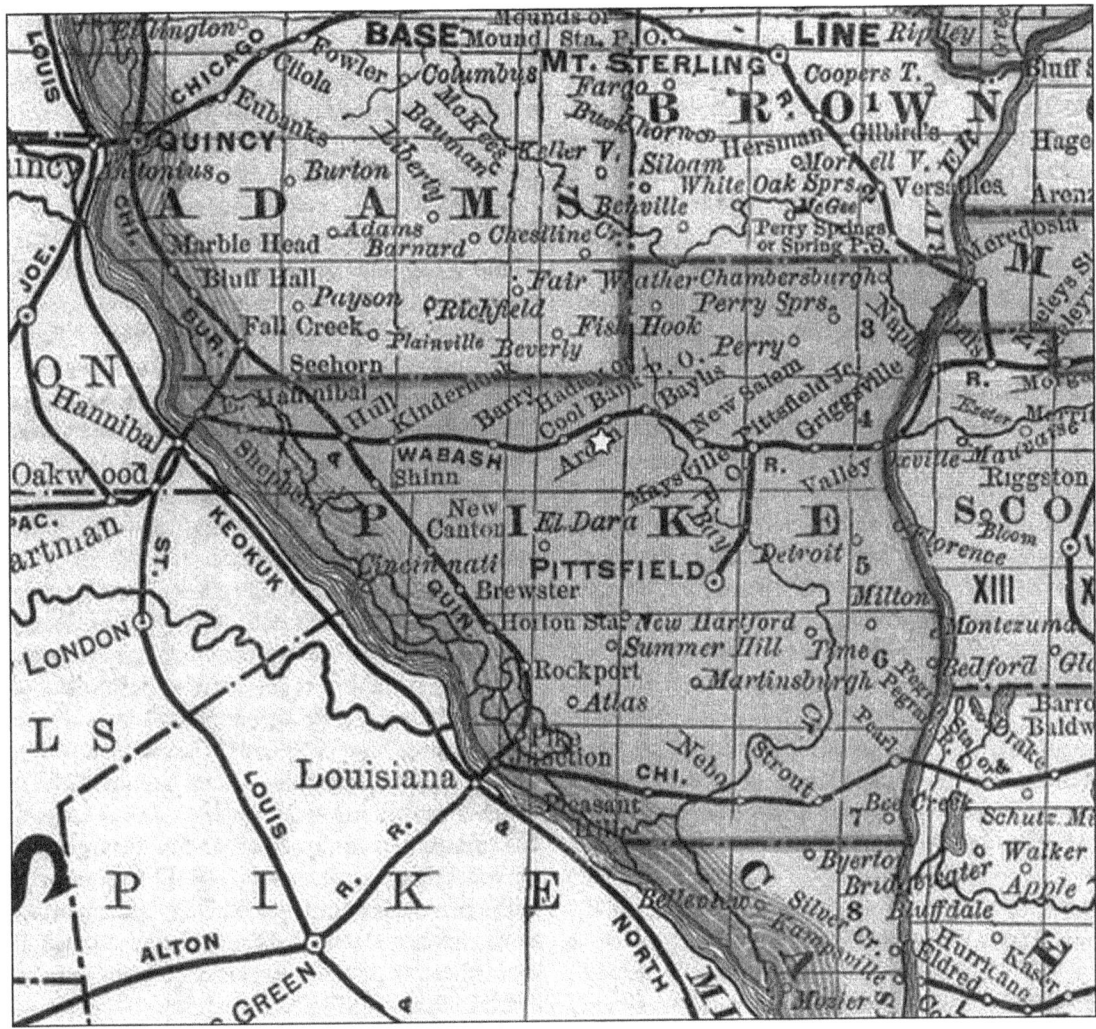

FIGURE 2. An 1895 atlas map showing the region of Pike County, Illinois, and the route of the Hannibal and Naples Railroad, later referred to as the Wabash Railroad (Rand McNally 1895). The location of the New Philadelphia town site is marked by a star. The image is oriented with north at the top; for a sense of the scale, on this map the town of Barry is 17 mi. west of Griggsville.

ran north to Chicago and to further connections with eastern market centers (Corliss 1934:37–38; Grant 2004:13).

In the other direction, the Missouri and federal governments had funded construction of the Hannibal and St. Joseph Railroad in the late 1840s, with a plan to link Hannibal with the town of St. Joseph, located on the western edge of Missouri, and the Missouri River and its transport route to points farther west (*Scientific American* 1848:1; *Alton Telegraph & Democratic Review* 1849:3; Cochran 1950:55–57). The Hannibal and St. Joseph Railroad Company was incorporated in 1847, received land grants and subsidies in the early 1850s, and construction was undertaken in the following years until completion of the line in 1859 (*Hannibal Daily Courier* 1878:1; Million 1894:77–82; Riegel 1923:159). A connecting rail between Naples and Hannibal would link these lines and promote Hannibal on a vibrant east to west flow of freight and passengers in a growing transcontinental system (*Hannibal Daily Courier* 1878:1). The town of Quincy, Illinois, located on the Mississippi River just 30 mi. north of Hannibal, competed to become a similar railroad hub in this interregional network (*Quincy Daily Whig* 1852:3; Carlson 1951:101,104; Davis 1998:375).

The construction of railroads in this midwestern region thus included three prominent projects in the 1840s that were heavily subsidized by state and federal funds, including the Hannibal and St. Joseph Railroad in Missouri, and the Northern Cross and Illinois Central railroads in Illinois (Cochran 1950:55,63; Fishlow 1971:190–191). After experiencing significant challenges in managing finances and in attempting to control both construction and operating expenses in such subsidized railroad projects, representatives of state and federal agencies would later disapprove additional proposals for other subsidized railroad projects (Carlson 1951:100; Davis 1998:230). Instead, other railroads to be built in the region during the 1850s and 1860s were to be constructed by private investment companies funded primarily through local funds and shareholder subscriptions (Riegel 1923:154–156; Fishlow 1971:190–191; Dobbin 1994:23–24,39–41).

To implement a plan for building a new railroad linking Hannibal to Naples, the Pike County Railroad Company (PCRC) was formed in 1857 and received a charter from the Illinois legislature (PCRC Records 1857:14 February). This charter did not involve state subsidies, but rather provided a basic mechanism of state recognition and authorization of a private investment company that might need to request aid of local courts in obtaining rights-of-way in constructing such a railroad. Using a fairly common approach, funds for the PCRC were raised through the sale of stock to investors, and to collectivities of investors in the form of local governments that purchased stock subscriptions later paid for through bond sales (PCRC Records 1857:14 February; Riegel 1923:156). From the outset, this investment company was dominated by business interests based in Hannibal, with the City of Hannibal holding the most voting stock, and the managing board staffed largely by individual investors who operated in that city (PCRC Records 1857:14 February, 1860:4 June, 1862:4 June; Chapman 1880:904–905).

The PCRC accomplished quite a lot in 1857 before a significant economic recession hit the nation and impeded further progress on the railroad project (PCRC Records 1857; Cootner 1963:499; Grant 2004:22). The company optimistically advertised for "sealed proposals for grading and bridging this road" in August of that year (*Quincy Herald* 1857a:1). Grading involves clearing, leveling, excavating, and embanking the roadbed along the designated route for the railroad (PCRC Records 1857:29 December; Vose 1857). The PCRC had hired an engineering firm earlier in the year to survey the best path for the railroad, and progress on the surveying likely motivated the PCRC to start seeking bids for grading the route.

In August, the PCRC also issued a directive to the engineering firm for an additional segment of surveying. A 21 August 1857 stockholders' meeting records an order for "a survey to be made during the fall [of 1857] beginning at some point near the town of New Salem, thence down Keyser Creek to Hannibal, the citizens in that route to pay the expense of such survey" (PCRC Records 1857:21 August). Local newspapers reported on this development as well, observing that "a new impulse has been given to the Pike road, and a new route is spoken of down Keyser creek. The citizens along that route, we are informed, have become aroused to the importance of a rail road to themselves, and with an almost entire unanimity, they propose to subscribe to the road, much more liberally than any other route" (*Quincy Herald* 1857b:3).

Keyser Creek was a relatively shallow streambed that ran from the northeast to the southwest and was located just east of New Philadelphia. The town of New Philadelphia is not mentioned anywhere in the railroad company records of the PCRC or its successor company. This discussion of obtaining a survey of the area "down Keyser Creek" is the only mention of that stream found thus far in the PCRC Records or in newspaper reports about the construction and later operations of the railroad. Another stream, called Hadley Creek, located just to the northwest of the town of Barry, was discussed more frequently in railroad company records and in local newspaper reports about later railway operations, because that creek was prone to flooding (PCRC Records 1857:21 August; *Barry Adage* 1873a:4). Bay Creek, which ran just west of New Salem, is also mentioned in the railroad company records without any reference to flooding concerns. There is no discussion in the railroad company records or in later newspaper reports that would indicate that Keyser Creek was significant as a topographic feature due to its contours, or due to problems of flooding or drainage.

The engineer's survey report to the PCRC was submitted and recorded in December 1857 (PCRC Records 1857:29 December). That report recommended that the railroad route proceed a short distance down the Illinois River from Naples, to a point along the same latitude with the existing towns of Griggsville, New Salem, and Barry. This path down the Illinois River side was viewed as cost effective because of the even grade that could be followed by paralleling the river, and due to a preference for crossing the river at a point level with Griggsville (PCRC Records 1857:29 December). That point for crossing the Illinois River was a location in Pike County originally called Phillips Ferry Landing, and later renamed as Valley City. Phillips Ferry Landing had served as a busy transport stop on the Illinois River, and had facilitated a heavy flow of road traffic across Pike County (Walker 1985:50,63). The engineer's report then recommended that the railroad route should proceed east to west through Griggsville, New

Salem, and Barry, and on to the Mississippi River shoreline just opposite Hannibal (PCRC Records 1857:29 December).

As can be seen in the 1895 map in Figure 2, the route recommended in the 1857 engineer's report was largely followed when the railroad was built in 1869. Notably, that route as described by the engineer should have also taken the railroad on an east–west line through New Philadelphia. The route made perfect sense from a business perspective, as it took the shortest distance between the terminal points of Naples and Hannibal, and thus involved the lowest amount of construction costs in terms of distance traversed by the railroad (PCRC Records 1857: 29 December). That route also would have followed fairly even topography, and would not have incurred extra costs of traversing notably higher or lower points of elevation as the railroad crossed Pike County.

The PCRC continued its work as best it could after the 1857 economic recession. The company completed the surveys for the route of the railroad and began some of the roadbed grading. In 1863, the management of PCRC placed its assets up for sale, and the operation was reorganized under a new company charter, called the Hannibal and Naples Railroad Company (HNRC) (HNRC Records 1863:12 February). The HNRC was made up of the same investors and stockholders, and was again dominated by Hannibal interests (HNRC Records 1863:4 August; Chapman 1880:904–905). A resolution passed by the HNRC management in 1867 clearly expresses this continuing influence of Hannibal and Missouri interests:

> Resolved that the people of Pike County are abundantly able and willing to secure the building and completion of the Hannibal and Naples Railroad and we hereby agree that we will co-operate with the Hannibal and Central Missouri Railroad Company in the construction of both roads as an entire line and we pledge ourselves to the people of Missouri that we will secure such aid as will insure the completion of the Hannibal and Naples Railroad at as early a day as they shall be able to complete their road on the west side of the river (HNRC Records 1867:17 July).

The halting steps of building this railroad across Pike County gained solid momentum in 1868, when a number of interrelated contracts were executed. Utilizing a common strategy, the HNRC focused on constructing the railroad and then leasing it to another company that would operate trains on it (HNRC Records 1868; Jenks 1944:8). On 22 June 1868, the HNRC entered into a contract with the Toledo, Wabash and Western Railway Company (TWWRC) for the latter to lease and operate the new railroad for 99 years (HNRC Records 1868:22 June; Grant 2004:22). The TWWRC also agreed to purchase a majority share of the stocks in the HNRC, and the HNRC agreed to hire a contractor to handle construction of the railroad (HNRC Records 1868:22 June). On 19 August 1868, the HNRC hired J. L. K. Haywood and Company of Hannibal to construct the railroad, using the existing surveys that had been completed by the PCRC (HNRC Records1868:19 August). Such utilization of surveying and earlier groundwork completed in the 1850s when renewing a project after the Civil War, was a fairly commonplace occurrence in such projects (Riegel 1923:153; Cootner 1963:502; Grant 2004:22).

Due to demands made by the TWWRC, the HNRC instructed Haywood that the railroad had to be built using high-quality iron rails, expressed as a greater quantity of iron per yard (HNRC Records 1869:17 March; 1869:1 December). The TWWRC required this quality of iron rails because it was in the business of operating freight and passenger trains over interlinking railroads from the western part of Missouri, through the Midwest, and to Toledo on Lake Erie. The TWWRC therefore demanded higher quality iron rails to withstand traffic, and to lessen its own expense of maintaining the rails over time (HNRC Records 1868:21 August; Grant 2004:21).

Construction of the 52 mi. long Hannibal and Naples Railroad was commenced and completed by Haywood in late 1869, and inspections were conducted by the HNRC in February 1870 (HNRC Records 1869–1870; *Weekly North Missouri Courier* 1869a, 1869b; Grant 2004:22). Haywood transferred the completed railroad to the HNRC in June 1870, and the HNRC ran trains on the railroad for two years thereafter, until the TWWRC's 99-year lease started in 1872 (HNRC Records 1870:8 June; 1872:5 October). The bridge across the Illinois River was open in 1870, and the bridge across the Mississippi River at Hannibal was built in 1871 (Chapman 1880:905–906). The 1895 map shown in Figure 2 depicts the route taken by the completed railroad, which was called the Wabash at the time that map was published.

Why did the railroad bypass New Philadelphia and take a northward arc up and around the town in a way that significantly deviated from the east–west line originally recommended by the engineer's report in December 1857? There is no direct statement in the railroad company records to answer this question. To date, extensive searches through newspaper reports from the relevant region and time period have similarly uncovered no direct statement of the reason. Very persuasive contextual evidence indicates, however, that this bypassing was not motivated by rational business choices.

There are typical business reasons that have motivated other railroads to follow one path rather than another as they traverse their territory. First, the successful lobbying of some existing towns to become depot stations along a planned railroad route often has an effect of pulling the route away from other communities in their area. In addition, topography often explains some parts of a chosen path. It is more costly to build a railroad up to and across high points of elevation, or to cross deep river ravines. Railroad routes are often planned to bypass such significant topographic features (Vose 1857:32; Cootner 1963:484). Do these reasons explain the course of the railroad across Pike County?

New Philadelphia did not lie upon, or next to a significant topographic feature or change in elevation. The town was located at elevation of 732 ft. above sea level. New Salem, to the east, lies at 784 ft. above sea level, and Barry, to the west of New Philadelphia, lies at 712 ft. (United States Geological Survey [USGS] 2007). Kiser Creek (also called Keyser Creek) runs just to the east of New Philadelphia, but is a shallow streambed that was never mentioned in the PCRC or HNRC records as a matter of concern as to its contours, location, or drainage. The primary consideration for keeping construction costs low in building a railroad was to choose a route that involved the least distance between the railroad's end points (Jervis 1861:48; Cleeman 1880:12–13; Webb 1917:3–5). It would have been much less expensive to build the Hannibal and Naples Railroad on a straight line from New Salem through New Philadelphia, and on to Barry and Hannibal, simply because that route involved a smaller linear distance of roadbed and rail than did the route that circled several miles to the north.

The factors of greatest expense in railroad construction were the linear yards of roadbed that had to be graded, excavated, and embanked, and the linear yards of iron rails and ties to be installed (PCRC Records 1857:29 December; Vose 1857:39–40; Cootner 1963:484; Fishlow 1971:118–122). In the 1850s and 1860s, railroad construction projects incurred the expense of obtaining iron rails and related hardware imported from British producers, because American-based producers could not yet meet their volume demands (Jenks 1951:381; Fishlow 1971:138–140). Straight railroad routes were also preferred over curving paths, where possible, because curving routes resulted in extra friction between train wheels and rails, and therefore additional operating, fuel, and maintenance costs (Vose 1857:10,47).

These cost items were particularly relevant for the Hannibal and Naples Railroad, because the TWWRC's 1868 contract with the HNRC required rails with higher weights of iron per yard to be used in the construction of that railroad. In contrast, items such as constructing culverts over stream beds, or even smaller bridges over small rivers, involved significantly lower cost concerns for such a railroad construction project (Cleeman 1880:29–31,44–60). Thus, it was typically less expensive to build a straight railroad route that required a number of culverts across streambeds, than it would have been to build a line that curved extra miles out of the way to avoid construction over those streams. These factors all indicate that there was no business reason to bypass New Philadelphia due to costs related to topography.

Perhaps the effects of lobbying can explain the northward arc of the railroad around New Philadelphia. Looking at the map in Figure 2, one can see a town named Baylis located along the railroad at the northernmost point of the arc. A simple answer to the question could be that the town of Baylis lobbied hard to have the railroad route come up to their location so they could serve as a depot station. This explanation fails, however, because Baylis did not exist before the railroad was built. In fact, no towns existed along that northward path before the railroad was built—it was a circuitous route through undeveloped prairie. Initially named Pineville, the town later renamed as Baylis was platted by William Pine, Jr., in 1869, and grew over the following years as a newly created depot town (Ensign 1872:10; Chapman 1880:641–642).

Another possibility is that one or two influential landowners, such as Pine, were able to lobby the railroad on their own behalf, plying the railroad company with donations to influence the choice of the route (Walker 1985:62). This explanation fails too. The northward arc around New Philadelphia traversed the lands of numerous individuals who each held relatively modest-sized parcels. Similarly, members of the Pine family appear in reports over the following decades as individuals of relatively modest assets, and were by no means Midwest land barons (*Barry Adage* 1876b:3; Chapman 1880:641–642). Nor did the railroad pay for or receive remarkable conveyances of land from those numerous landowners along that line of tracks. Each conveyed a narrow swath of land to the HNRC in 1865 for passage of the railway across his or her parcel in a contingent deed that would become null and void if the railroad were never constructed (Pike County Deed Records 1865:247–248). That was the simple and low-cost method of land acquisition used for most of the pathway of the railroad through the county.

Would there have been a long-term interest in having the new railroad traverse previously undeveloped prairie lands? Such an interest was certainly at play in the construction of the Illinois Central Railroad, which was subsidized by the Illinois legislature and federal land grants. Running north to south from Chicago to Alton, the Illinois Central was purposefully routed through previously undeveloped parts of the state, rather than meandering from one existing town to another along its overall trajectory (Jenks 1944:3; Fishlow 1971:174). This subsidized project was designed to help spur settlement developments and new towns in underdeveloped locations, with the hope of contributing to the state's future economic growth.

Unfortunately, these large-scale, subsidized projects met with considerable time delays, financial strains, and a "consequent waste of millions of dollars [that] was a costly lesson in the evils of inflation and over-optimism"

(Carlson 1951:100; Davis 1998:230). After a subsequent shift to railroad projects being handled by private investment companies, those later private business concerns did not try to play the role of a subsidizing government. Railroad projects managed by private investment companies were designed and managed to keep costs low and profits high.

Railroads built in the 1850s and 1860s, like the Hannibal and Naples Railroad, were designed with a concern for the large-scale interconnections they provided which linked to other regional railroads (Grant 2004:22–23). Such rails were not built simply to connect a hub like Naples with a hub like Hannibal with no concern for the rail traffic in between, however. The local freight and passenger traffic that could be obtained along the extent of such a railroad was also of great concern in order to maximize operating profits (Conger 1932:286; Cochran 1950:56–57; Grant 2004:14). This factor again makes the bypassing of New Philadelphia appear problematic. That town had existed for decades before the Hannibal and Naples Railroad was built, and had grown as an agricultural service community, attracting local traffic of farmers moving their products by wagon to nearby river-based merchant points. No such traffic centers existed along the northward arc that bypassed New Philadelphia; new depot towns had to be built there from scratch after the railroad was constructed, incurring delays in the inflowing traffic available when the freight trains started running in 1870. Here again, no business justification explains the route bypassing New Philadelphia.

Topographic considerations provide another conundrum. The northernmost point of the bypass route, where Baylis would later grow as a depot town, was the highest point of elevation in the region, at 863 ft. above sea level (*Barry Adage* 1876d:2; USGS 2007). This point was sufficiently high that newspaper reports and railroad company records during the 1870s at times called it "Summit Point" or "Summit Station" (HNRC Records 1857:7 October; *Quincy Whig* 1870:4). In addition to requiring greater linear distance to bypass New Philadelphia, this path required even more length of roadbed and rails due to the increasing grade, rising to the highest point in the area. Overall, it was preferable to design a railroad route so "there should be as

little rise and fall as possible" (Vose 1857:32; Webb 1917:3–4).

Such a pathway over a high point of elevation like Baylis did not only cost more in construction outlays. Later operating costs for freight trains were also significantly increased. As one newspaper observed: "Regular outgoing freight trains from Hannibal on the Wabash are drawn by two locomotives as far as Baylis, the highest point on the road between the two rivers" (*Barry Adage* 1876a:3). The primary flow of freight traffic was from Hannibal and Barry eastward to Baylis, and beyond to market centers such as Chicago or Toledo. A freight train had to climb from Barry, at 712 ft. elevation, to Baylis, at 863 ft. elevation. To do so required a helper locomotive for the larger freight trains, and such an extra engine was maintained on the tracks near Hannibal for this purpose. With heavy freight traffic "constantly increasing" on the line, the railroad company soon began considering the possibility of changing the route to reduce this uphill grade (*Barry Adage* 1877:1).

Maintaining and operating a helper locomotive in this manner was an undertaking to be avoided by railroad companies wherever possible, due to manifold expenses (Wellington 1901:601–604). A helper locomotive required extra expenses in wages, fuel, water for steam, and space for maintaining the engine when in use and when waiting for use. Even when waiting, a helper locomotive burned fuel, because its boiler was kept heated so the engine was ready to go as soon as an eastbound freight train was ready to depart. Moreover, there were considerable opportunity costs, with such a locomotive relegated to episodic use on a limited stretch of railway, rather than being employed in a more efficient and continual manner as a sole engine on a long-distance, through-bound freight train (Wellington 1901:601–604).

In the overall operation of a freight train, one can obtain offsetting benefits related to an uphill grade if the train can then roll downslope for a comparable distance, thus conserving some fuel on the downgrade (Vose 1857:37; Wellington 1901:608; Cootner 1963:484). This was not the case for the Hannibal and Naples Railroad, however, as the freight trains incurred a longer and steeper climb from Barry, at an elevation of 712 ft., to Baylis at 863 ft., which was not fully offset by the downhill distance from

Baylis to New Salem at 784 ft. Any benefits of a downslope were similarly overridden by the extra expenses of having to maintain the helper engine (Vose 1857:37; Wellington 1901:608; Cootner 1963:484).

In the 20th century, a succession of railroad acquisitions placed the old Hannibal and Naples Railroad line within the operations of the Wabash Railway Company. Heavy freight train traffic still flowed on these tracks, and the direction of trade remained largely west to east as it did in the 19th century. After incurring the higher operating costs of running freight trains over the high point of Baylis for a number of decades, the Wabash company rebuilt the segment that corresponded to the northward arc that bypassed New Philadelphia in 1869. The Wabash moved the rail route south, away from Baylis, and closer to the town site of New Philadelphia (USGS 2007). The more even grade of elevations achieved in this rerouting lowered the railroad's operating costs from that time forward. Unfortunately, by that time in the 20th century, New Philadelphia existed only as the ruins of a town buried beneath the soil.

Another question of distance and topography can be raised. The PCRC and HNRC planned for the railroad route to pass through the existing towns of New Salem and Barry, and for depots to be located in those two communities. Could New Philadelphia have been bypassed because the railroad company saw no need for additional depot stations on the rail line between New Salem and Barry? The answer is clearly "no," as demonstrated by the fact that two to three additional depot stations were constructed along the rail line that circled to the north around New Philadelphia, linking New Salem and Barry (Figures 2 and 3). The distances between New Salem, New Philadelphia, and Barry fit comfortably in the typical range of distances between the depot stations constructed along this railroad line across Pike County.

Two other subjects concerning the ability of Pike County towns to influence the Hannibal and Naples Railroad route bear attention in this analysis. First, consider the town of Pittsfield, which was the county seat, and one of the larger communities in the area during the time when the railroad path was under consideration. One might expect the citizens of Pittsfield to have been in a confident position to lobby the

HNRC to have the main railway route pass through their community. Pittsfield is located several miles south of the east–west line of the railroad path that was recommended by the engineer's report in 1857, however (Figure 2). Rather than incur the extra expense of diverting the main railroad on a large curve to the south to run through Pittsfield, the HNRC built a separate connecting rail to link Pittsfield to the main line by a shorter distance rail (Figure 2) (HNRC Records 1870:2 June; Ensign 1872:7; Grant 2004:22). The attractiveness of having a county seat and active urban settlement along the main line of the railroad did not outweigh the desire to avoid the expense of building such a meandering route when the HNRC's primary purpose was to link Hannibal to Naples in a cost-efficient manner (Vose 1857:10; HNRC Records 1868). This extra rail line to Pittsfield was also promoted as one with a future potential extension southwest to the town of Louisiana, Missouri (HNRC Records 1868; Grant 2004:23). That additional extension was never built, however (Carlson 1951:104).

Next, one should ask whether the citizens of New Philadelphia attempted to lobby representatives of the PCRC or the HNRC to ensure the town's position along the planned railroad path. Research to date has uncovered no evidence that residents of New Philadelphia or members of the McWorter family attempted to influence the route plan in that way. No evidence has been uncovered that would indicate that the interests of New Philadelphia's residents and businesspeople were represented in the deliberations and decisions concerning the railroad.

Families of both African American and European American heritage resided in New Philadelphia, or lived on adjacent farmsteads and owned extra lots within the town. African American families, including the McWorters and Walkers, were prominent landowners and entrepreneurs with investment interests in and around the town (Ensign 1872:23,54,58; Chapman 1880:752). Frank McWorter, the town's founder, had passed away in 1854. His surviving wife and adult children were also prominent citizens and businesspeople, however. For example, Solomon McWorter was praised in the 1872 *Atlas Map of Pike County*, a publication to which he subscribed, as follows: "He is quite extensively engaged in farming and raising stock, and there are few men in Pike county who are succeeding better than he. ... He is now the owner of five hundred acres of first class land, well stocked with cattle, hogs, horses, and mules. He is a man of good moral habits, and is highly respected by his neighbors" (Ensign 1872:54). Yet, to date no evidence has been found that Solomon McWorter, or others with interests in New Philadelphia worked to lobby representatives of the HNRC to have that town become a depot station on the railroad route.

In 1867, the HNRC appointed a number of local citizens and businesspeople to act as liaisons to the residents of the townships to be traversed by the railroad. John McTucker was listed as liaison to Hadley Township, in which New Philadelphia was located (HNRC Records 1867:17 July). McTucker served as a supervisor and treasurer for Hadley Township at various times (Ensign 1872:100). After construction of the railroad was completed in 1869, a depot named "Hadley Station" was constructed along the railroad's passage through that township (Walker 1983:167). That station was built on a parcel of land owned by John McTucker, located approximately one mile northwest of New Philadelphia (Figure 3) (Ensign 1872:100).

The northward arc of railroad that bypassed New Philadelphia cannot be explained persuasively based on business reasons, or by the lobbying of existing towns. In the absence of those alternative justifications, this dynamic appears to have been the result of the impacts of aversive racism. This was an indirect and structural impact of racial tensions, and not a direct, malevolent act recorded in a dramatic and overt manner. The HNRC was dominated by social and business interests centered in a region that was contorted by racial ideologies and strife for decades leading up to, and following the construction of this railroad.

The same set of circumstances also readily indicates why individuals invested in the community of New Philadelphia and adjacent farms, such as Solomon McWorter, would not be motivated to try to lobby business organizations such as the PCRC and HNRC. The PCRC was dominated by the business interests of Hannibal, and operated while that city contained an active slave market. The HNRC maintained that focus on the interests of Hannibal investors, even declaring in 1867 that the citizens of Pike County, Illinois should "pledge [them]selves to the people of Missouri" and the goals of making Hannibal a primary hub in a growing, transcontinental system of rails (HNRC Records 1867). New Philadelphia suffered a fate seen by other towns bypassed by a new rail, as local roadway traffic was drawn away to new depot towns and stations in their area, and then businesses departed, followed by town residents (Ensign 1872:10; Chapman 1880:740–741; Walker 1983:167). As Mark Leone and his co-authors (2005:579) observe, towns such as New Philadelphia existed in "the midst of racial hostility," and "were subject to antiblack legislation, were sidelined economically, and were then all but forgotten as their inhabitants migrated to cities and larger towns in a quest to maintain their economic viability."

African American residents of the area may have seen some benefits from the placement of Hadley Station on John McTucker's land. The rail route leading from the location of Pineville southwest to a point level with an east–west line to Barry also passed through parcels owned by John Walker and Louisa McWorter, close to the McTucker tract and another neighboring tract owned by Sarah McWorter (Figure 3) (Ensign 1872:100). The railroad company typically paid nothing for such conveyances of a path through individual landowner parcels (Pike County Deed Records 1865:247–248). The fact that John Walker and Louisa McWorter granted such conveyances indicates that those African American land owners did not generally oppose the railroad's arrival in Pike County.

After New Philadelphia was bypassed by the railroad, the lots, blocks, and public streets that made up its configuration as a town were converted into agricultural land over the following decades. Those ensuing changes followed a broader trend in this region of western Illinois. Locations without direct rail line connections in the late 1800s saw more and more acreage placed into agricultural cultivation by farms of increasing size. The expanded transport capacity of interregional railroad networks led to increased demand for livestock and agricultural products, and the lands situated in outlying areas around the railroad stations saw more acreage moved into larger-scale agricultural use (Carlson 1951:111–113). Locations that became railroad depot stations, in contrast, often developed as service

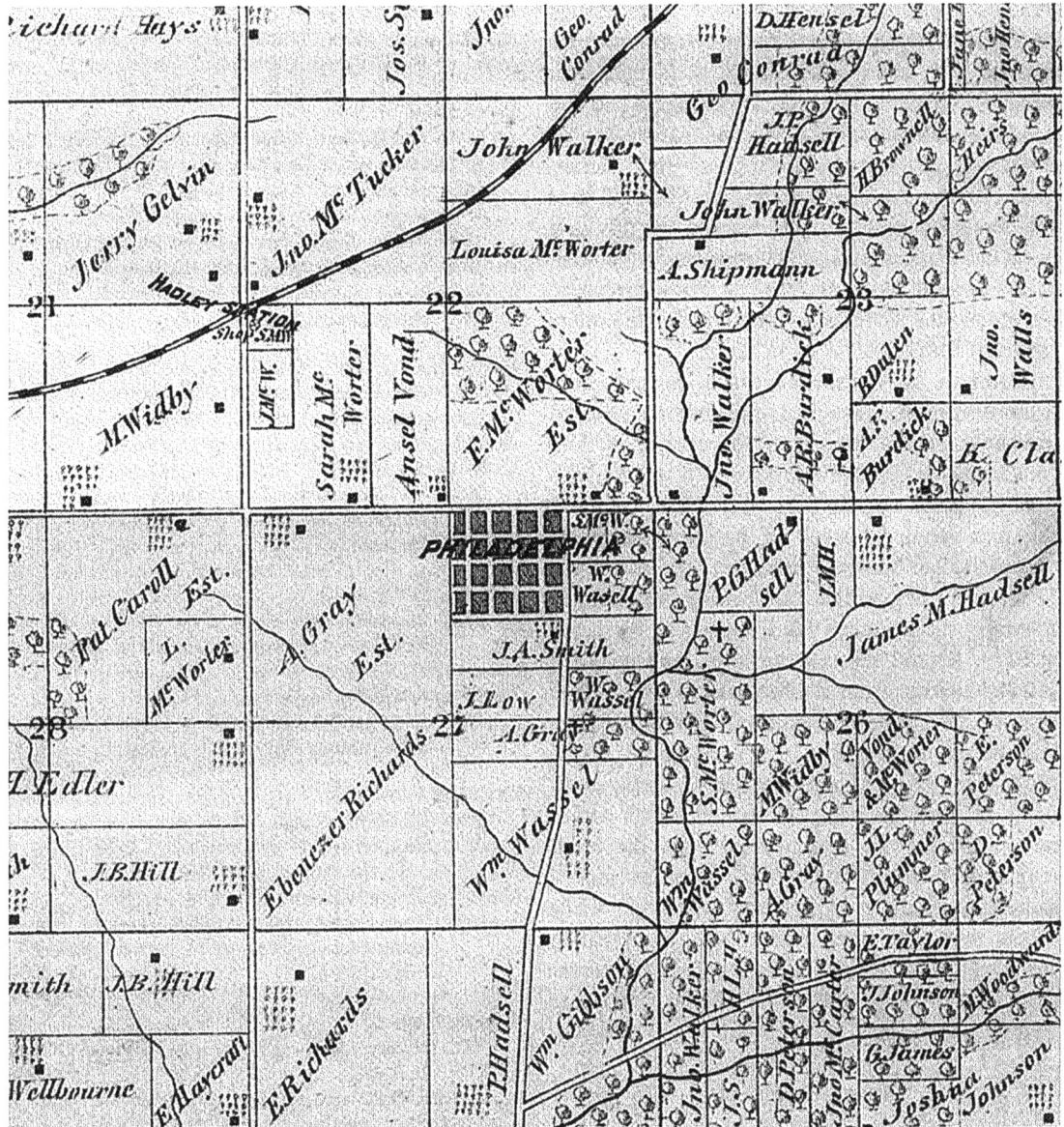

FIGURE 3. An 1872 map of Hadley Township showing Hadley Station on the railroad line crossing land owned by John McTucker, John Walker, and Louisa McWorter, among others (Ensign 1872:100). The map image is oriented with north at the top; for a sense of the scale, the town site of Philadelphia as depicted on this map was approximately 0.25 mi. wide.

centers enjoying an increase in local traffic and merchant trade (Jenks 1944:14; Walker 1985:64; Davis 1998:369–370).

Lessons of Combating Racism and Overcoming Adversity

What lessons are to be learned and communicated about the railroad bypassing New Phila-

delphia? One approach is to focus upon this episode as an example of racist conduct, and to insist that the knowledge and awareness of such past actions should be part of the continuing struggle against racism in the present (Shackel 2003; Leone et al. 2005). Such a message could be articulated by focusing on the racism that shaped the actions of investors and managers of the railroad, and the damage their actions inflicted upon the residents of New Philadelphia, leading to the demise of that community as a town. Yet, some might raise a concern that present condemnations of racism should avoid constantly emphasizing European Americans as those who had choices and agency that victimized African American families. Instead, one can focus on lessons to be learned by this past event by emphasizing the choices made by African American families in New Philadelphia to overcome the adversities that confronted them (Shackel 2003; Leone et al. 2005).

Solomon McWorter provides an excellent example of the ways in which African Americans overcame obstacles and succeeded in their social and business lives. Shortly after the railroad bypassed the town his father had founded, Solomon availed himself of its transport facilities to further his own economic operations. In 1873, according to the *Barry Adage* newspaper, Solomon simply drove his livestock to the depot at Barry several miles to the west, and used the railroad to ship them out for sale. "One hundred head of fat cattle were shipped to Buffalo from this place on Tuesday. They belonged to S. McWorter" (*Barry Adage* 1873b:4). Other residents of New Philadelphia moved on to pursue new opportunities and to deal with the challenges they encountered. Some families moved to nearby cities in Illinois and Missouri, while others moved to more distant locations (Walker 1983:169). The social history of these numerous instances of perseverance should be central to society's reckoning of its past.

Acknowledgments

Archaeological research at the New Philadelphia site has been supported by the National Science Foundation under Grant No. 0353550. Any opinions, findings, conclusions, or recommendations expressed in these materials are those of the author, and do not necessarily reflect the views of the National Science Foundation. I am also very grateful for the generous funding support of the University of Illinois's Research Board.

References

ALTON TELEGRAPH & DEMOCRATIC REVIEW
 1849 No title. *Alton Telegraph & Democratic Review* 30 November:3. Alton, IL.

ALTON WEEKLY COURIER
 1855 Great Western Railroad Opened East to Decatur. *Alton Weekly Courier* 8 February:4. Alton, IL.

BARRY ADAGE
 1873a Jottings. *Barry Adage* 18 January:4. Barry, IL.
 1873b Home Happenings. *Barry Adage* 7 June:4. Barry, IL.
 1875 No title. *Barry Adage* 27 February:8. Barry, IL.
 1876a No title. *Barry Adage* 22 January:3. Barry, IL.
 1876b No title. *Barry Adage* 26 February:3. Barry, IL.
 1876c No title. *Barry Adage* 10 June:3. Barry, IL.
 1876d No title. *Barry Adage* 17 June:2. Barry, IL.
 1877 No title. *Barry Adage* 20 October:1. Barry, IL.

BERLIN, IRA
 2003 *Generations of Captivity: A History of African-American Slaves*. Harvard University Press, Cambridge, MA.

CARLSON, THEODORE L.
 1951 *The Illinois Military Tract: A Study of Land Occupation, Utilization, and Tenure*. University of Illinois Press, Urbana.

CHA-JUA, SUNDIATA KEITA
 2000 *America's First Black Town, Brooklyn, Illinois, 1830–1915*. University of Illinois Press, Urbana.

CHAPMAN, CHARLES C.
 1880 *History of Pike County, Illinois*. Charles C. Chapman & Co., Chicago, IL.

CLEEMAN, THOMAS M.
 1880 *The Railroad Engineer's Practice*. G. H. Frost, New York, NY.

COCHRAN, THOMAS C.
 1950 North American Railroads: Land Grants and Railroad Entrepreneurship. *Journal of Economic History* 10 (Suppl.):53–67.

CONGER, JOHN L.
 1932 *History of the Illinois River Valley*. S. J. Clarke, Chicago, IL.

COOTNER, PAUL H.
 1963 The Role of the Railroads in United States Economic Growth. *Journal of Economic History* 23(4):477–521.

CORLISS, CARLTON J.
 1934 *Trails to Rails: A Story of Transportation Progress in Illinois*. Illinois Central System, Springfield.

DAVIS, DAVID B.
 2006 *Inhuman Bondage: The Rise and Fall of Slavery in the New World*. Oxford University Press, New York, NY.

DAVIS, JAMES E.
 1998 *Frontier Illinois*. Indiana University Press, Bloomington.

DOBBIN, FRANK
    1994   *Forging Industrial Policy: The United States, Britain,
            and France in the Railway Age.* Cambridge University
            Press, Cambridge, U.K.

ENSIGN, D. W.
    1872   *Atlas Map of Pike County, Illinois.* Andreas, Lyter &
            Co., Davenport, IA.

FISHLOW, ALBERT
    1971   *American Railroads and the Transformation of the
            Ante-Bellum Economy.* Harvard University Press,
            Cambridge, MA.

GAERTNER, SAMUEL L., AND JOHN F. DOVIDIO
    1986   The Aversive Form of Racism. In *Prejudice,
            Discrimination, and Racism*, John F. Dovidio and
            Samuel L. Gaertner, editors, pp. 61–89. Academic
            Press, Orlando, FL.

GRANT, H. ROGER
    2004   *Follow the Flag: A History of the Wabash Railroad
            Company.* Northern Illinois University Press,
            DeKalb.

GRIMSHAW, WILLIAM A.
    1876   History of Pike County: A Centennial Address Delivered
            by Hon. William A. Grimshaw at Pittsfield, Pike County,
            Illinois, July 4, 1876. Illinois State Historical Society,
            Springfield.

HANNIBAL AND NAPLES RAILROAD COMPANY (HNRC
RECORDS)
    1863–1876   Hannibal and Naples Railroad Company
            Records, 1863–1876, Norfolk and Western Railway
            Archives, Ms90-096, Special Collections, Virginia
            Polytechnic Institute and State University, Blacksburg.

HANNIBAL DAILY COURIER
    1878   City of Hannibal. *Hannibal Daily Courier* 15 January:1.
            Hannibal, MO.

HARGRAVE, MICHAEL L.
    2006   Geophysical Investigations at the New Philadelphia Site,
            Pike County, Illinois, 2004–2006. U.S. Army Engineer
            Research and Development Center, Construction
            Engineering Research Laboratory, Champaign, IL.
            Department of Anthropology, University of Illinois,
            Urbana-Champaign <http://www.anthro.uiuc.edu/
            faculty/cfennell/NP/Geophys/geophysics.html>.
            Accessed 6 June 2006.

ILLINOIS STATE ARCHIVES
    1837   An Act to Change the Name of Frank McWorter.
            General Assembly Records, Illinois State Archives
            Enrolled Laws No. 2031, HR No. 18, Box 48, Illinois
            State Archives, Springfield.

JENKS, LELAND H.
    1944   Railroads as an Economic Force in American
            Development. *Journal of Economic History* 4(1):1–
            20.

    1951   Capital Movement and Transportation: Britain and
            American Railway Development. *Journal of Economic
            History* 11(4):375–388.

JERVIS, JOHN B.
    1861   *Railway Property: A Treatise on the Construction
            and Management of Railways.* Phinney, Blakeman &
            Mason, New York, NY.

KING, CHARLOTTE
    2007   New Philadelphia Census Data. Center for Heritage
            Resource Studies, University of Maryland, College
            Park <http://www.heritage.umd.edu/CHRSWeb/New
            Philadelphia/censusfiles/CensusDataMenu.htm>.
            Accessed 28 March 2007.

KLEINPENNING, GERALD, AND LOUK HAGENDOORN
    1993   Forms of Racism and the Cumulative Dimension
            of Ethnic Attitudes. *Social Psychology Quarterly*
            56(1):21–26.

KOVEL, JOEL
    1970   *White Racism: A Psychohistory.* Pantheon Books, New
            York, NY.

LEONE, MARK P., CHERYL J. LAROCHE, AND JENNIFER J.
BARBIARZ
    2005   The Archaeology of Black Americans in Recent Times.
            Annual Review of Anthropology 34:575–598.

MILLION, JOHN W.
    1894   State Aid to Railroads in Missouri. *Journal of Political
            Economy* 3(1):73–97.

OMI, MICHAEL, AND HOWARD WINANT
    1994   *Racial Formation in the United States: From the 1960s
            to the 1990s*, 2nd edition. Routledge, New York, NY.

ORSER, CHARLES E., JR.
    2001   Race and the Archaeology of Identity in the Modern
            World. In *Race and the Archaeology of Identity*, Charles
            E. Orser, Jr., editor, pp. 1–13. University of Utah Press,
            Salt Lake City.

PIKE COUNTY DEED RECORDS
    1865   Pike County Deed Records. Pike County Courthouse,
            Pittsfield, IL.

PIKE COUNTY RAILROAD COMPANY RECORDS (PCRC
RECORDS)
    1857–1865   Pike County Railroad Company Records,
            1857–1865, Norfolk and Western Railway Archives,
            Ms90-121, Special Collections, Virginia Polytechnic
            Institute and State University, Blacksburg.

PITTSFIELD UNION
    1853   What Strangers Think of It. *Pittsfield Union* 18 May:3.
            Pittsfield, IL.

PUTNAM, J. W.
    1909   An Economic History of the Illinois and Michigan
            Canal: III. *Journal of Political Economy* 17(7):413–
            433.

QUINCY DAILY WHIG
    1852 No title. *Quincy Daily Whig* 29 June:3. Quincy, IL.

QUINCY HERALD
    1857a Pike County Railroad. *Quincy Herald* 17 August:1.
          Quincy, IL.
    1857b Those Runaway Negroes. *Quincy Herald* 14
          September:3. Quincy, IL.

QUINCY WHIG
    1870 No title. *Quincy Whig* 30 July:4. Quincy, IL.

RAND MCNALLY
    1895 *Atlas Map of the United States.* Rand McNally, New
          York, NY.

RIEGEL, ROBERT E.
    1923 Trans-Mississippi Railroads During the Fifties.
          Mississippi Valley Historical Review 10(2):153–172.

SAVAGE, W. SHERMAN
    1943 The Contest Over Slavery Between Illinois and
          Missouri. *Journal of Negro History* 28(3):311–325.

SCIENTIFIC AMERICAN
    1848 St. Joseph and Hannibal Railroad. *Scientific American*
          3(26):201.

SHACKEL, PAUL A.
    2003 *Memory in Black and White: Race, Commemoration,
          and the Post-Bellum Landscape.* Altamira Press, Walnut
          Creek, CA.

SHACKEL, PAUL A.
    2006 *New Philadelphia Archaeology: Race, Community,
          and the Illinois Frontier.* With contributions by Alison
          Azzarello, Megan Bailey, Caitlin Bauchat, Carrie
          Christman, Kimberly Eppler, Christopher Fennell,
          Michael Hargrave, Emily Helton, Athena Hsieh,
          Jason Jacoby, Charlotte King, Hillary Livingston,
          Terrance Martin, Maria Alejandra Nieves Colon, Eva
          Pajuelo, Marjorie Schroeder, Erin Smith, Andrea
          Torvinen, and Christopher Valvano. Center for Heritage
          Resource Studies, University of Maryland, College
          Park <http://heritage.umd.edu/chrsweb/New%20
          Philadelphia/2006report/2006menu.htm>. Accessed
          6 June 2007.

SIMEONE, JAMES
    2000 *Democracy and Slavery in Frontier Illinois: The
          Bottomland Republic.* Northern Illinois University
          Press, DeKalb.

SIMON, PAUL
    1994 *Freedom's Champion: Elijah Lovejoy.* Southern Illinois
          Press, Carbondale.

SIMPSON, HELEN MCWORTER
    1981 *Makers of History.* Laddie B. Warren, Evansville,
          IN.

STEINER, MARK E. (EDITOR)
    1996 Abolitionists and Escaped Slaves in Jacksonville.
          Illinois Historical Journal 89(Winter):213–232.

TURNER, GLENNETTE T.
    2001 *The Underground Railroad in Illinois.* Newman
          Educational Publishing Co., Glen Ellyn, IL.

UNITED STATES GEOLOGICAL SURVEY (USGS)
    2007 Geographic Names Information System. U.S.
          Department of the Interior, Washington, DC <http://
          geonames.usgs.gov>. Accessed 6 June 2007.

VOSE, GEORGE L.
    1857 *Handbook of Railroad Construction; For the Use of
          American Engineers.* James Munroe and Company,
          Boston, MA.

WALKER, JULIET E. K.
    1983 *Free Frank: A Black Pioneer on the Antebellum Frontier.*
          University Press of Kentucky, Lexington.
    1985 Entrepreneurial Ventures in the Origin of Nineteenth-
          Century Agricultural Towns: Pike County, 1823–1880.
          Illinois Historical Journal 78(1):45–64.

WEBB, WALTER L.
    1917 *Railroad Construction. Theory and Practice,* 6th
          edition. John Wiley & Sons, New York, NY.

WEEKLY NORTH MISSOURI COURIER
    1869a No title. *Weekly North Missouri Courier* 24 June:3.
          Hannibal, MO.
    1869b No title. *Weekly North Missouri Courier* 8 August:3.
          Hannibal, MO.

WELLINGTON, ARTHUR M.
    1901 *The Economic Theory of the Location of Railways.*
          John Wiley & Sons, New York, NY.

CHRISTOPHER C. FENNELL
DEPARTMENT OF ANTHROPOLOGY
UNIVERSITY OF ILLINOIS AT URBANA-CHAMPAIGN
109 DAVENPORT HALL, MC-148
607 S. MATHEWS AVE., URBANA, IL 61801

Jamie C. Brandon
James M. Davidson

The Landscape of
Van Winkle's Mill:
Identity, Myth, and Modernity
in the Ozark Upland South

ABSTRACT

Archaeological investigations at Van Winkle's Mill (3BE413), a mid-to-late-19th century sawmill in the Arkansas Ozarks, were conducted between October 1997 and October 2003. These investigations yielded information that may help clarify the changing social relations and race constructions associated with the end of the antebellum era as expressed via landscape usage. Additionally, the excavations have much to say regarding our stereotypes of both slavery (and by extension the whole African Diaspora) and the inhabitants of the American upland South.

Introduction

In what is now a quiet, overgrown Ozark hollow in a corner of the low mountains and plateaus of northwestern Arkansas was once a bustling community centered around a sawmill known as Van Winkle's Mill. This mill served as a major source of lumber for the region in the mid- to late-19th century and was the dominant provider of the materials for rebuilding after the carnage that marked the American Civil War. Additionally, the narrow hollow now known as "Van Hollow" was home to a good number of men and women—black and white, skilled and unskilled, enslaved and free—who made up the labor force of Van Winkle's Mill.

Like many other regions, this postwar period seemed to mark for northwest Arkansas a passage into a more fully articulated modernity (Harvey 1990:27). The war seems to have served doubly as a catalyst for this change. First, it served as the traumatic moment creating the need for social and infrastructural change (Soja 1989:26–27). The Union armies effectively demolished the Southern way of life—including racial slavery

and its economic infrastructure. Simultaneously, the war's havoc opened up space much like the practice of "creative destruction" did in other contexts (Harvey 1990:19; Boyer 1994:179), and an "explosion of capitol investment in the last two decades of the century" was mobilized to fill that space (Allen 1994:156). Thus the massive social reorganization that occurred on the heels of the war was accompanied by rebuilding the physical landscape.

Landscape-oriented archaeology is, by all accounts, becoming a ubiquitous line of inquiry in historical archaeology (Leone 1984, 1995; Kelso and Most 1990; M. Johnson 1996; Worrell et al. 1996; Yamin and Metheny 1996; Stine et al. 1997; Kealhofer 1999; Epperson 1999b; Delle et al. 2000). By now, it is no longer a novel concept to see social landscapes as intimately connected to social structures (Cosgrove 1984; Soja 1989; Jameson 1991:97–129; Lefebvre 1991). In this vein, archaeology and historical research conducted sporadically at Van Winkle's Mill (3BE413) between 1997 and 2003 presents some interesting perspectives on and poses some important questions about the cultural processes that form cultural memory, stereotypes about the plantation South, the African Diaspora, and the very landscape of the hollow itself.

Some of the entanglements of the landscape and the social realities of Van Winkle's Mill are outlined. Of course it cannot address all of the complex ways in which modernity, concepts of race, the emerging trope of the Ozark "hillbilly," and industrial landscape of Van Winkle's Mill all interacted and changed throughout the 19th and early-20th century. It does, however, hope to focus on more than one of these trends and how it relates to the physical landscape of Van Winkle's Mill.

Peter Van Winkle and Van Winkle's Mill: A Brief Background

Van Winkle's Mill began as a place on the historical cultural landscape in the 1850s when Peter Marselis Van Winkle borrowed money from a local capitalist and purchased the land, equipment, and enslaved labor for his Ozark mill (Easley and McAnelly 1996:156; Brandon and Davidson 2003:8). Peter had been born in 1814 in New York City, the fourth child of a family that had come from Holland in 1619 to be a part of the Dutch New Amsterdam colony (Hicks 1990:3–8). Peter's family had moved west by 1820, and Peter grew up in Franklin and Fulton counties in Illinois (Hicks 1990: 17–18; Easley and McAnelly 1996:156).

Peter Van Winkle first appears in northwest Arkansas in the mid-1830s when he would have been 21 years old (Rothrock 1973:63; Hicks 1990: 15–16). Van Winkle marries his second wife, Temperance "Tempy" Miller, in 1840 and made a living farming, contracting to "break" prairie land, blacksmithing, and making wagons in Washington County, Arkansas, through the 1850s (U.S. Bureau of the Census 1850; Hicks 1990:17; Easley and McAnelly 1996:156). By 1851 he was paying taxes on land in Benton County, Arkansas, and had started lumbering soon thereafter (Hicks 1990:19; Brandon et al. 2000:5). By 1860 Van Winkle had built what has been described as a "plantation style" or "Southern-type" home in Van Hollow (Johnson 1963:33–34; Hicks 1990: 21) where he lived with his wife, eight living children, a tutor from Tennessee, and a young apprentice lathe operator. As early as 1861 he was beginning to acquire the symbols of his newly acquired station: 1,370 acres of land, one saw mill, 34 mules, 1 gold watch, 1 pleasure carriage, and 12 slaves over the age of five (Hicks 1990:21; Brandon et al. 2000:7).

While the first evidence of Van Winkle "owning" slaves was 10 years earlier, coincident with his moving to Van Hollow, by the beginning of the Civil War he enslaved at least 18 human beings (U.S. Bureau of the Census 1860; Hicks 1990:21,51; Brandon et al. 2000: 10). This is not an insubstantial number for northwest Arkansas, where only the largest slaveholders in the region claimed 30 slaves (Smith 1995:42).

Moreover, his sympathies during the war are not hidden in the slightest. Not only did Van Winkle contract with the Confederate government to build barracks and stables for troops stationed in the area (Hicks 1990:21,346–348), he named two of his children after prominent Confederate figures: Jefferson Davis Van Winkle (born 1861) and Robert E. Lee Van Winkle (born 1863; Hicks 1990:175–262). Thus when the tide turned against the Confederate forces in northwest Arkansas, Van Winkle found no quarter. He fled, with his family and slaves, to Bowie County Texas, and his home and mill in Van Hollow were burned to the ground sometime between 1864 and 1866 (Rothrock 1973: 64; Hicks 1990:23; Hughes 2001:35).

Following the war, Van Winkle and company returned to Van Hollow and rebuilt the community along with his two-story house with terraced gardens (Figures 1, 2) and what has been called "the most modern and powerful mill in the west" (Hicks 1990:25; Easley and McAnelly 1996:157). Van Winkle's Mill dominated the regional market in the 1870s and provided the lumber for the postbellum rebuilding of Fayetteville as well as many of the public buildings built following the war (Rothrock 1973:62; Hicks 1990:32,47).

In the larger landscape of the region, Van Winkle's Mill lies in the White River Hills of the Ozark Mountains in the southeastern portion of Benton County (Rafferty 2001:12). This region of the Ozarks is known for its rugged relief and karst topography (Rafferty 2001: 15–16). Historically, it was described as "so broken and uneven that it [was] mostly unfit for cultivation, except in the valleys of the streams" (Goodspeed Pub. Co. 1889:2). Peter Van Winkle was, no doubt, aware that he was building his mill in the southeast corner of the county on "a tract of land, six miles north and south by about eight miles east and west, covered with pine timber, much of which is large enough for lumber and of it there is a seemingly inexhaustible supply" (Goodspeed Pub. Co. 1889:5).

From the perspective of regional settlement patterns, Van Winkle's decision to settle at Van Hollow proved to be "either fortuitous or an act of genius" (Bowers 2003:10). In 1850, when Van Winkle settled in Benton County, only four towns existed near Van Hollow to provide a market for his lumber: Fayetteville, Shiloh (Springdale), Bentonville, and Huntsville. By the time Van Winkle died in 1882, however, Rogers and Eureka Springs had been incorporated and had grown into important places in the northwest Arkansas marketplace—Rogers as a town on the St. Louis and San Francisco Railroad and Eureka Springs as a cosmopoli-

FIGURE 1. Photograph of Van Winkle home ca. 1870. (Photo courtesy of the Shiloh Museum of Ozark History.)

tan tourist attraction and health retreat. Van Hollow is centrally located to these towns on the landscape, providing equal access to northwest Arkansas' largest towns and their markets (Figure 3).

Taking advantage of his central place on the landscape, Van Winkle expanded his lumber concern into a network throughout the 1870s and early 1880s. His "Home Mill" in Van Hollow added door and window manufacturing capabilities; he opened two lumberyards (one in Eureka

Springs and one in Rogers) and began acquisition of timberlands and a portable sawmill in Madison County not far from Eureka Springs (Bowers 2003:50). He had even opened the Van Winkle Hotel, an elegant three-story showplace on the Fayetteville square in 1880 (Brandon et al. 2000:8). By the time of his death he had direct access to markets in Fayetteville, Eureka Springs, and Rogers. Close examination of the Van Winkle probate record reveals that these yards offered plows and other hardware

FIGURE 2. Photograph of raised garden opposite Van Winkle home. (Photo courtesy of the Shiloh Museum of Ozark History.)

in addition to the doors, windows, and lumber manufactured at the Van Winkle's Mill.

Following Van Winkle's death in 1882, Van Winkle's Mill slowly faded into the distance as the 20th century marched on. After a brief time operating in the hands of Van Winkle's relatives, the mill's engine was sold in 1904; the flywheel was blown apart for scrap metal near the end of World War I; and the large, spacious Van Winkle home was finally demolished in 1969, shortly before the Arkansas Department of Parks and Tourism took over the property (Funk 1962; Hicks 1990:47–48; Brandon and Davidson 2003:14; for contrast Brandon et al. 2000:14).

Family history and archival evidence relating to Van Winkle's life emphasize the "modernisms" of this "pioneering" industrialist—his attitudes towards wealth and nature allude to the conscious and unconscious ideologies of knowledge, power, and progress which, when implemented in the proper and rational way, can liberate man from the tyranny of "scarcity, want, and arbitrariness of natural calamity" (Harvey 1990:12; see also Foucault 1970, 1980). His commitment to the Ozarks' modernization is attested to by his stalwart and generous support of projects such as telegraph line expansion and his successful work to coax the Arkansas-Missouri Railroad through the city of Fayetteville (Rothrock 1973:61–62,68–69; Hicks 1990:38–40,389). Additionally, his deft accumulation of symbolic capital (e.g., the gold watch, pleasure carriage, the large home and raised garden) as well as his economic capital (which, of course, also functioned symbolically)

Perspectives from *Historical Archaeology*

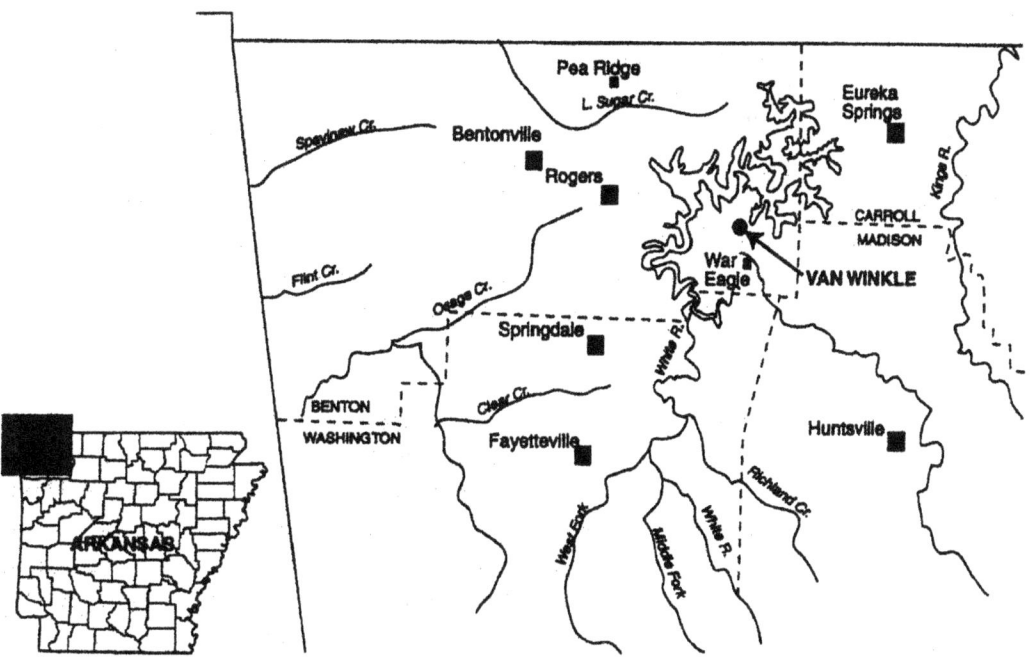

FIGURE 3. Northwest Arkansas area map showing the locations of Van Winkle's Mill (3BE413) and the towns of Fayetteville, Springdale, and Bentonville.

demonstrates his working knowledge of the aesthetic and taste culture of modernity and capitalistic consumption (Bourdieu 1979; Lavine 1988). As we will see later, the landscape of Van Hollow itself reflects these values—emphasizing the need for order, a separation between public and private spheres, the observation/surveillance of labor (Foucault 1977:170–176,195–227, 1980: 146–165), and spatializing and naturalizing social distinctions (Soja 1989; Jameson 1991:154–180; Lefebvre 1991).

Archaeology, Modernity,
and the Landscape
of Van Winkle's Mill

Archaeological investigations have been conducted sporadically at Van Winkle's Mill since 1997, when the Arkansas Archeological Survey conducted an extensive mapping project and limited archaeological testing at the site. Personnel at the developing Hobbs State Park and Conservation Area initiated this project by contacting the State Archaeologist and requesting guidance concerning the documentation and historic interpretation of the mill and related

features (Brandon et al. 2000:2; Brandon and Davidson 2003:15). The original mapping and testing project has been supplemented by a systematic survey of the northern portion of the hollow (Brandon and Davidson 2003:24–33) and a series of small testing and excavation projects.

As no aboveground structural remains have been preserved (aside from a limestone spring house and the steps of the raised garden), specific details about the built environment have been discerned through photographic evidence. Further construction information, as well as temporal data, has been inferred from five testing programs—one at the main house belonging to Peter Van Winkle and family, one at the Feature 9 workers' quarters, one at a possible antebellum slave quarters (Feature 33), one at the blacksmith shop (Feature 31), and one at the location of the sawmill boiler platform (Hilliard 1997; Brandon and Hilliard 1998; Brandon et al. 1999, 2000; Bowers 2003:36–39; Brandon and Davidson 2003).

The natural narrowness of the hollow and its rugged, dissected topography place physical limitations on the construction of the cultural landscape of Van Winkle's Mill (Figure 4). The hollow itself begins in the west, trending southwest northeast, and turns at a slightly more northerly angle where the hollow widens near the former location of Van Winkle's home.

A total of four archaeological loci (features 8, 9, 10, and 33) have been identified in the southwest portion of the hollow. During two brief testing projects (in 1999 and 2000) and the 2001 University of Arkansas field school, the entire footprint of the Feature 9 structure has been uncovered (Figure 5). Feature 9 appears to be a double pen frame structure, perhaps a dogtrot-style building (Brandon et al. 2000:53). The extensive excavations at Feature 9 indicate the structure is domestic in function

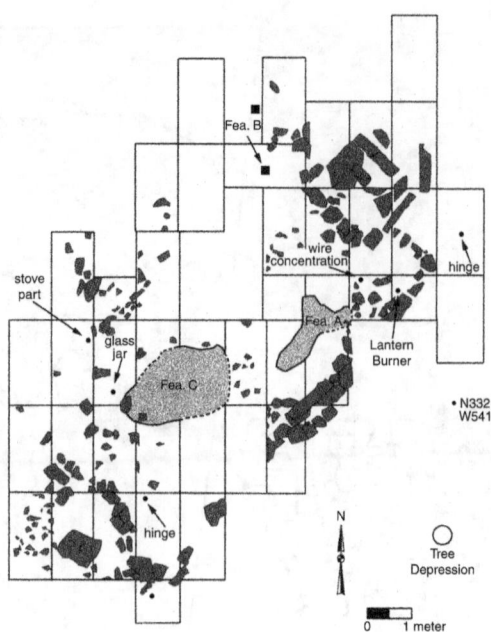

FIGURE 5. Plan view of Feature 9, probable slave/freedmen mill workers' quarters.

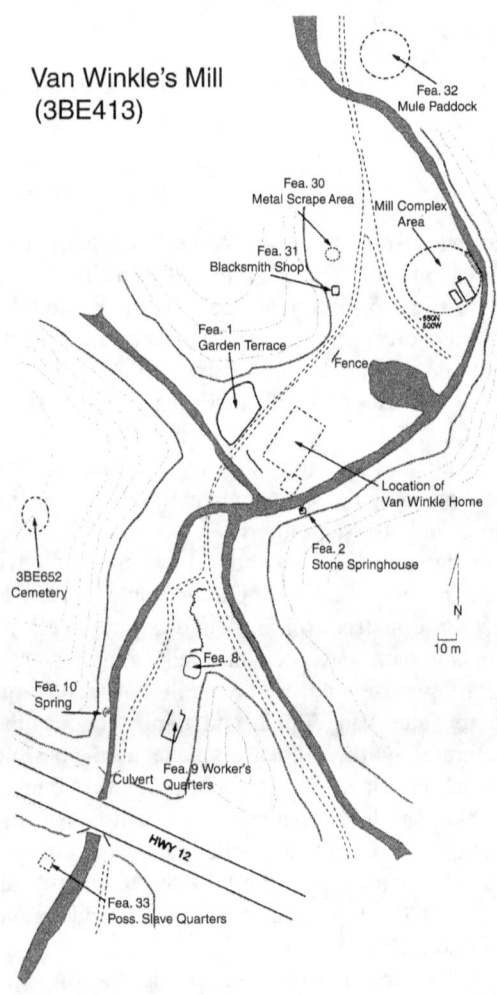

FIGURE 4. Map of Van Winkle's Mill (3BE413), showing cultural features.

and that the major depositional events occurred between 1870–1910 (Brandon et al. 2000: 53–55). Nail and window glass analysis point toward one major and one minor construction period—the major event occurring 1866–1870 and the second, minor event occurring post 1900 (Brandon et al. 2000:38,41–42). Other artifacts recovered from Feature 9 excavations, however, may point toward an ephemeral antebellum (slave?) occupation (Brandon et al. 2000:53; Brandon 2001). The data currently assembled imply that the family of one of the laborers in the mill inhabited the structure.

Eighteen enslaved men and women lived and labored in this place prior to emancipation. After the war, two freedman families returned to Van Hollow to live and work. Of these, the family of Aaron Anderson Van Winkle seems to be the most compelling candidate for the residents of Feature 9 (Brandon et al. 2000:55; Brandon and Davidson 2003:17).

At the age of six, Aaron Anderson Van Winkle (known by some as "Old Rock" or "Uncle Rock") was brought in bondage from Alabama to Arkansas by Colonel Hugh Anderson (*Benton County Democrat* 1904; also see Hilliard 1997 for a discussion of that family and slavery). It is unclear if or when Aaron was sold to Van Winkle, but by the end of the war he is working at the mill as an "engineer" (*Benton County Democrat* 1904; Brandon et al. 2000:14). Family oral history claims, however, that Aaron had a more domestic role in the hollow—"Rock was Peter's 'manservant' and always by his side" (Hicks 1990:52). Whatever Aaron's role at the mill, he managed to garner a great deal of respect from both the black and white communities. When he passed away in 1904, his death was mourned across the racial divide. At least three obituaries in local white papers described his funeral at a black Bentonville church.

Located further up Van Hollow is Feature 33—a probable antebellum slave quarters. Artifacts from the limited testing in 2001 do not support a postbellum occupation. The artifact deposition is thin, and no substantive foundation remains, like those at Feature 9, were encountered. However, multiple geophysical technologies (electrical resistance, magnetometry, electromagnetic conductivity, and magnetic susceptibility) deployed at the Feature 33 location detected a linear data trend with a right angle (Brandon 2001). As this trend roughly matches the extent of the nail rain observed in units excavated at Feature 33, it is thought to represent a wall of the structure. Other features in the southwest portion of Van Hollow include a series of small springs opposite Feature 9 (Feature 10), a cemetery marked with unmodified field stones (3BE652), and a 20th-century structure that does not appear to be residential (Feature 8).

The Van Winkle home—with its raised garden (Feature 1), white picket fence, and massive stone springhouse (Feature 2)—sat just past the bend in the north-south trending portion of the hollow. In 1997, preliminary excavations, including cruciform backhoe trenches, indicate that this is the location of both the original and 1870 Van Winkle homes. The second Van Winkle home was represented by 30–50 cm of highly disturbed midden along with the remains of brick chimneys and limestone supports. The first Van Winkle home, burned during the Civil War, is thought to be represented by a thin (5 cm) anthrosol containing annealed cut nails, melted glass, and charcoal buried by 50–60 cm of sterile soil (Brandon et al. 2000:27–28). This seems to indicate either a burying of the burned remains of the first structure or substantial landscaping of the landform prior to the building of the second Van Winkle home.

Located in the widest portion of Van Hollow is the mill complex itself. The above-ground remains of a large limestone boiler and engine platform, flywheel trench and mounting (Feature 5), and a small, stone-lined cistern-like feature thought to be used in the draining of the boilers (Feature 6) are all that remains of the large two-story grist and sawmill complex. Two separate attempts to locate the foundation lines of the structures that housed these mills using geophysical technologies (electromagnetic conductivity, magnetometry, and electrical resistance) and traditional testing strategies proved unsuccessful (Brandon and Davidson 2003: 36–39,54). Excavations in 2001 have uncovered a portion of the extent of the boiler platform, and partially cleaned out and defined Feature 6 and the flywheel trench (Bowers 2003:36–39; Brandon and Davidson 2003:55–57).

The systematic survey of the northern portion of the hollow has lead to the discovery of several new features of interest to this analysis (Brandon and Davidson 2003:24–33). Located across from the mill is a large blacksmithing shop (Feature 31) and scrap metal storage area (Feature 30). Test excavations and geophysical investigations (magnetometry and electrical resistance) have lead to the excavation of a limestone foundation along the back wall of the blacksmith shop and the eastern half of the forge box (Brandon and Davidson 2003:42–48). Excavations indicate that the forge was probably used throughout the life of the mill and was salvaged sometime in the early-20th century (Brandon and Davidson 2003:53,69). Additionally, the location of a mule paddock (Feature 32, represented only by a large number of mule shoes and large pennyweight nails) and two discreet dumping areas (Features 27 and 28) were also investigated following their discovery during the systematic survey (Brandon and Davidson 2003:25–31,51–53).

These features make up the cultural landscape of Van Winkle's mill and provide us with an opportunity to examine modernity, enslavement, and industrialization in the upland South (Brandon and Hilliard 1998). These phenomena have implications for the relations of groups (both the dominant and the dominated) to the means of production. Moreover, the dynamic transformations that occur during the occupation of Van Hollow (increasingly "efficient" industrialization, the Civil War, and emancipation) offer further insights as to how people actively sought to restructure their worlds in response to changes in these relations.

A few things quickly become evident when you examine the configuration of the Van Hollow landscape. First there seems to be a clearly discernable industrial zone in the northern area of the hollow (Figure 6). Here, in the widest portion of the hollow, were the mills, blacksmith shop, metal scrap areas, lumberyards, and mule paddock. This area was, of course,

a hub of activity and the locus that made Van Winkle's mill "a lively place" (Godspeed Pub. Co. 1889:107) that "resembled a fair as people gathered to trade their produce and wares to each other as well as for the sawmill products" (Hicks 1990:20).

Moreover, the mill's industrial features would have been constituent parts of the whole of the industrial enterprise. All would have variously interacted as nodes in a network designed to produce lumber and sell commodities to the public. For instance, the blacksmith shop would be busy casting and repairing mill parts, reshoeing mules from the paddock, fixing log wagons after delivering their cargo to the mills, and selling goods and services to the general public. Likewise, Robin Bowers (2003:40–51) reconstructs the probable system of interaction of these parts as timber moves from logging and log storage, through the mill and specialty woodworking shops to final distribution. The efficiency of this system of logging and lumber distribution certainly represented an engagement with the modern, industrial mindset of Fordism (Gramsci 1971:277–278; Harvey 1990:125).

The road that passes between Van Winkle's house and his formal garden was no ordinary lane, it was a major thoroughfare that led to a ferry, which he operated on the White River, and to the towns of Rogers, Huntsville, and Eureka Springs. Thus, a constant parade of people would have admired the small world within the hollow that Van Winkle had created. More importantly for Van Winkle, he could see (and be seen by) these passersby quite easily from his second-story balcony or his elevated garden—both conveying Van Winkle's importance and augmenting his already formidable stature. Despite the road's importance and apparent high traffic, it should be noted that at its articulation with the Van Winkle home and raised terrace garden, the roadway bottlenecks to such an extent that someone standing in the bed of a wagon could reach out and touch either Van Winkle's picket fence (demarcating the boundary of the outer yard) or the walls of the family's terraced garden.

The aforementioned narrowness of the Ozark hollow imposed constraints that had to be accommodated, and in many ways, the fact that Van Winkle could have fit all of his landscape into Van Hollow could have been viewed as a

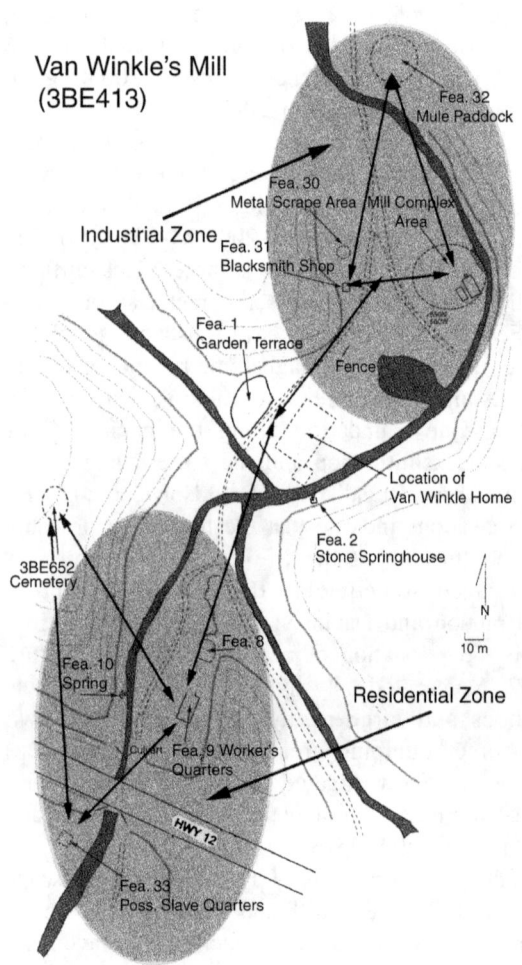

FIGURE 6. Implied landscape zones and interactions between features on the Van Hollow landscape.

Perspectives from *Historical Archaeology*

status symbol in and of itself. Specifically, these modifications to the "natural" Ozark hollow can be seen as a reference to the "man's mastery over nature" theme common to modern thought with its origins in the enlightenment (Foucault 1970:157–162; Leone 1984).

Massive amounts of labor, possibly enslaved, created flat spaces out of slopes when the formal garden was constructed, and again, after the war, a great deal of time was taken to build up the landform on which his first house had stood before the construction of the second structure. This labor, in addition to "capping" the old burned building's remains, widening and flattening the landform, was making more space for the large house and its dependencies.

Meanwhile, in keeping with Victorian ideology of separate public and private spheres, the western arm of Van Hollow is entirely residential and contains at least three, if not four, homes for the enslaved and later free workers in residence. The mill workers were thus both "out of site" (i.e., around the bend) and kept nearby. The landscape creates a north-south line that symbolically delineates a work/home dichotomy. The southern portion of the hollow, where the "domestic" activities of both Van Winkle and the laborers took place, can be contrasted with the northern portion where production, in the formal economic sense, was conducted and managed. The Van Winkle house itself was situated at the center of this narrow, linear world—the mill was situated in the northeastern portion of the complex, Van Winkle's house in the virtual center, and the workers' quarters (Features 9, 33), located past the bend in the hollow in the southwestern portion of the complex (out of sight of the main house for "aesthetic" purposes but close enough to allow labor to be "on call").

Not only did this landscape replicate and legitimate the social hierarchy of the hollow (placing Van Winkle in the center, with all things revolving around him), but this landscape actively sought to remind others of this implied hierarchy. Laborers who lived in the Feature 9 and Feature 33 structures would have been required to walk past Van Winkle's large, impressive home at least twice a day on their way to and from the mill proper—where these "worlds" collide. The mill itself would have been the one place where Van Winkle interacted daily with the entire spectrum of the mill's labor.

Van Winkle's Mill and Settlement Patterns in the Regional Landscape

Widening the scale of analysis slightly, the settlement system immediately surrounding Van Winkle's Mill is examined. Bowers (2003:66–92) examined settlement patterns of six townships surrounding the location of Van Winkle's Mill. Although this analysis is self-described as a "preliminary study of settlement patterns near the mill," (Bowers 2003:69) it does raise interesting questions regarding Van Winkle's Mill and its landscape.

Bowers evaluated the influence Van Winkle's Mill had on general settlement choice following William Langhorne's work on settlement patterns and industrial location in New York State (Langhorne 1976). Plainly stated, Langhorn (and Bowers) hypothesized that certain industries (namely mills) and the services they provide will influence people to settle nearby. Based on land patent data, Bowers found that "the Van Winkle Mill exhibited little influence on settlement of the region" and concluded "that settlers were most influenced by flat, arable land and access to markets" (Bowers 2003:92).

Given the above observations about Van Winkle's Mill and its placement on the regional landscape, this lack of "settlement pull" poses some questions. How is it that the largest, most important mill in the region, one that offered both a saw and grist mill in addition to a blacksmith, did not draw a population that could sustain it as a settlement following Van Winkle's death? How could a place that was listed among the "towns and villages" of Benton County and described as a "very lively place" disappear almost overnight?

One of the answers lies in the relationship between labor and the mill itself. Van Winkle's Mill was not so much a settlement with a mill at its center as it was a fully integrated capitalist enterprise whose "settlement" solely existed to man the mill and its related undertakings. Next, the "socio-spatial dialectic" at work within Van Hollow (Soja 1989:79) and the similarities between the landscape of Van Winkle's Mill and that of a plantation of the lowland South will be examined.

Pines in Place of Magnolias: The Plantation Landscape of Van Winkle's Mill

Interesting light can be thrown on the cultural landscape when it is approached dialectically (Crumley 1997). For instance, several tantalizing strands of information point to the Southern plantation as the model for Van Winkle's mill. First, on a superficial level, Van Winkle's house was described by Mrs. Bertha Blackburn Yeager (quoted in Johnson 1963:33–34) as "Southern-type" and by Marilyn Hicks (1990:21) as "plantation style." This, along with its formal raised garden area, certainly alludes to a style of life that was not common in this mountainous frontier—the life of an affluent planter.

But a deeper look into what is (and is not) *defined* as a plantation may lead researchers to see more than just passing similarities between the characteristics of Van Winkle's Mill and Southern plantations. Landscape geographer Charles Aiken (1998:9) points out that although slavery has been consistently seen as the principle feature of the Southern plantation, it "was not the critical factor that distinguished a plantation." Instead, he outlines what he sees as six characteristics that distinguished plantations from other types of farms.

> First, plantation agriculture requires high capitalization compared with most other types of farming. For new crops and in new regions, the potential profit that can be realized from a planting venture is so large that even speculative capital is invested. Second, plantation agriculture is significantly focused at both the farm and regional scales. Although subsistence crops might be grown to help sustain the labor force, only one commercial crop is emphasized. As in other types of commercial ventures, specialization leads to efficiency. Skills required for planting, harvesting, and processing a crop are competently learned and perfected (Aiken 1998:5–6).

These first two characteristics are broad, and the Van Winkle enterprise certainly falls within their bounds. Van Winkle had expended a great deal of capital into the mill, including venture capital borrowed from local speculative capitalists (Goodspeed Pub. Co. 1889:107–108; Easley and McAnelley 1996:156). Likewise, Van Winkle's Mill focused on a single, specialized form of agriculture—the growth and harvesting of hardwood and pine timber and their manufacture into lumber and finished products for the marketplace.

Aiken's third, fourth, and fifth characteristics regard managerial practices. He insists that both the size of the landholding and the labor force are large enough to achieve economies of scale. He points out "a few intensely farmed plantations of 100 or 200 acres have existed, but most have contained 300 acres or more and have been larger than the legendary American family farm" (Aiken 1998:6). By the time of Van Winkle's death, he owned over 7,000 acres of forestland, including the 3,575 acres surrounding the mill itself (Bowers 2003:13–17). The fact that Van Winkle *owned* all of the land surrounding the mill is undoubtedly the major reason that Van Winkle's Mill was not a "pull" for regional settlement. All of the inhabitants of Van Hollow—his relatives as well as the resident skilled and unskilled labor—were, in effect, tenants of Van Winkle. As only the hollow itself was developed, the vast majority of this acreage was only used for its timber. These were the "fields" of Van Winkle's plantation landscape.

Aiken specifically mentions the fact that "the labor force historically was composed of entire families, not just heads of households." Again, Van Winkle's Mill conforms to this criterion. Not only were whole enslaved and freedmen families involved in the mill's operation and its domestic support (Brandon et al. 2000:10–14), but Van Winkle's own family extended to the skilled labor working in the mills and associated enterprises.

Thus, it seems that the Van Winkle operation would fit into Aiken's first five characteristics of a plantation fairly well. Although it is admittedly odd to think of a timber operation in terms of plantation agriculture, it should be pointed out that Aiken and other researchers (including archaeologists) have noted similarities between some industrial enterprises and plantations. Having established a relative number of structural similarities between Van Winkle's timber enterprise and the Southern plantation model, the analysis returns to the landscape of the mill. Aiken's (1998:7) sixth and final characteristic is of much interest here:

> The sixth characteristic is that a plantation has a unique geographical form that spatially distinguishes

it from other types of farms. A nucleated settlement complex has traditionally been an overt element of the geography. The most important building is the one from which management disseminates. Although the storied big house historically served this purpose on many of the South's plantations, the headquarters often is an office.

As previously mentioned, the narrow Van Hollow is the only developed settlement on the decidedly nucleated Van Winkle landscape, and the "big house" at the center of the hollow's cultural landscape seems an easy fit as the management center for the enterprise.

Furthermore, according to Aiken (1998:7), one of the striking features of settlement complexes on Southern plantations were "a facility to process the crop" before it is shipped to market along with auxiliary structures such as "mule and horse barns." "Houses for workers are also major components of the settlement complex" and these were often situated in a row along one or both sides of a road near the headquarters.

The landscape of Van Winkle's Mill with the its mill complex processing the timber harvested on Van Winkles holdings, its associated mule paddock, blacksmith shop, and workers' housing roughly in a row in the southwestern portion of the complex near the Van Winkle residence seems very much a plantation landscape. Add to this Van Winkle's use of enslaved labor, not common for industrial enterprises, and the plantation picture is nearly complete.

The very fact that Van Winkle, a New York native, *chose* a Southern model for the layout of his operation can be seen as indicating an intricate understanding of the Southern taste culture and a desire to attain a greater standing within its hierarchical structure. Van Winkle had been in Arkansas for at least 15 years before building his first mill in Van Hollow, during this time he was able to learn how the social and economic systems were structured in this corner of the South. It is his Southern social "competence" that is being expressed in this industrial landscape.

The deployment of the plantation model for his timber enterprise, however, seems to have directly contributed to its erasure from the landscape in a concrete way. Following the Civil War, changes in the landscape of Van Hollow can be related to changes in social relations in the hollow. More prominently, changes in the tropes of historical memory, which occur simultaneously with the region's articulation with modernity, serve to effectively erase Van Winkle's Mill. These tropes are tied to changes in conceptualizations of race, class, and the character of the Ozarks themselves. Below, the landscape changes that occurred following the war and the factors that relate to Van Winkle's Mill in the historical memory of the Ozarks is examined.

Mapping Cultural Change in Van Hollow

An added dimension to this landscape analysis is, of course, the temporal aspect. Van Winkle's Mill is advantageous in that it contains both ante- and postbellum components with the two separated by the archaeologically convenient trauma of the Civil War and the accompanied burning of many of the structures in the hollow. This trauma has implications beyond mere chronological significance, as the period is also one of profound reorganization of the social fabric of the region along with the incorporation of new tropes of cultural identity and race (Savage 1999; Birshir 2000).

In the hollow, the very fact that there seems to be a spatially desecrated antebellum slave quarter and postbellum workers' quarter (inhabited by freedmen) seems to point to important changes following emancipation. Conversely, if Van Winkle did effectively reconstruct his 1850s home in 1870 to make the statement "the war will not change me," then the spatial organization of the remainder of his operation undermines that assertion.

Comparisons between the antebellum and postbellum structures may also be instructive. Prior to the March 2000 excavations it was assumed that Feature 9 represented two separate structures—single pen dwellings in a row, perhaps with others obscured beneath the fill of Highway 12. This configuration would, in fact, have been in keeping with examples of labor housing in many of the Southern plantations during both slavery and tenancy (Orser and Nekola 1985; Vlach 1993), as well as housing in industrial wage-labor settings (such as those encountered in mining operations, railroad construction camps, and logging towns). Further excavations, however, revealed a continuous foundation running toward the second chimney fall. It seems likely that both chimneys served the same structure—a large double-pen or dog-trot style dwelling.

There is a clear break that occurs between the pre- and postemancipation occupations of the hollow by the Van Winkle family, with the raising of the landform upon which the first house was built, for the construction of the second house on the site circa 1868. Although not known with certainty, there is archaeological evidence to suggest a similar amount of elaboration and attempt at architectural permanence poured into Feature 9, which experienced a long occupation likely as both an African American slave and later freedman residence.

Feature 33, interpreted as a slave quarters, has an artifact temporal signature suggestive of a pre-emancipation occupation, with little or no occupation after the Civil War and the family's return to the hollow circa 1868. This pre-emancipation residence has the most ephemeral architectural footprint of any structure excavated in Van Hollow to date, with not even undressed stone piers present on the site. In stark contrast to Feature 33, Feature 9 (the residence to the north) has an elaborate continuous stone foundation and impressive twin chimneys composed of dressed stone masonry.

Artifact analysis from Feature 9 narrows the possible dates of construction, inhabitation, and abandonment of the structure—the majority of artifacts recovered from the 1999 and 2000 excavations point toward a primary occupation between 1870 and 1890—in keeping with the hypothesis that this structure served as the postbellum workers' quarters (with a probable antebellum ephemeral occupation). Nail types and frequencies indicate that the structure was framed in the 19th century with some structural repairs and/or modifications occurring after the turn of the century (Brandon et al. 2000:52–55). Flat glass thickness distributions indicate that the first windowpanes installed in the structure were hung around 1870, possibly upon the Van Winkles' return from Texas (Brandon et al. 2000:40–42).

While some of the recovered artifacts have manufacturing ranges that continue into the early-20th century (aqua bottle glass, plain whiteware ceramics, etc.), it would seem clear from an examination of the complete artifact assemblage that the residence was not exten-sively occupied into the 20th century. Chiefly, the assemblage is virtually lacking in common 20th-century temporal markers (mason style glass canning jars, tin cans, etc.; cf. Stewart-Abernathy 1986:156).

While exposing the northern chimney footing of Feature 9 in 2001, whiteware sherds were found directly beneath that portion of the house foundation that skirts or makes a "dog leg" around the chimney's firebox. These ceramic sherds, part of a partially reconstructable shallow bowl, have an impressed maker's mark tentatively dated to the 1820s to 1840s. Although artifacts of pre-emancipation dating had been recovered from Feature 9 previously, the position of these sherds, directly beneath an element of the stone foundation, is strongly suggestive of an occupation on the site prior to the foundation's construction, likely pre-emancipation in dating. If true, this fortuitous discovery suggests a great deal—that the remaking of the landscape of the hollow following the Civil War occurred not only with the home of the elite and white Van Winkle but with the newly emancipated freedmen home as well.

The ephemeral Feature 33, farthest from the white residence, was never occupied again after the war. Rather, it was Feature 9 (the former slave quarters nearest to the home of Peter Van Winkle) that was not only reoccupied after the war but greatly improved in the process, with the laying down of the impressive and permanent continuous stone foundation, double stone chimneys, and glass windows (e.g., the temporal indications derived from the window glass thickness suggests an initial hanging of windows circa 1868).

These physical landscape changes almost certainly reflect changes experienced within the social landscape of the hollow. A geographical distancing and little economic investment in labor's housing before the Civil War alters in the postemancipation years, with a shrinking of the space between black and white, labor and capitalist, and at least some investment in the quality of life and standard of living of the freedman labor.

Certainly material culture recovered from the two structures is indicative of vastly different consumption patterns, reflective of this pre and postemancipation dichotomy. The predominately postbellum Feature 9 was full of mass-produced personal items and "nonessentials" such as the large array of children's toys (Brandon et al. 2000:45–52), while the antebellum Feature 33 assemblage was almost entirely architectural and kitchen related. This change is surely influenced by the newly freed African Americans' desires to assert their humanity and equality through consumption (Mullins 1999:160–170) and the region's quick move toward modernizations following the war, ensuring that a large number of cheap, mass-produced goods were available to consumer markets via mail order catalogs (Harvey 1990:125–140). Finally, the change in geographic placement of the two domestic structures, especially when compared to the nonchanging placement of the Van Winkle's house, may also point toward a exercising of newly acquired freedmen's rights.

Conversely, the second spring serving the predominately postbellum Feature 9 (no spring was observed in association with Feature 33) also seems to anticipate the "separate but equal" metaphor that would come to dominate Southern culture in the Jim Crow era (Hale 1998:23). Since at least the 18th century, the enslaved peoples of the American South were seen as property and perhaps not quite human (Deetz 1997: 246; Epperson 1999b:164), while emancipation required a reworking of the oppressive systems. Now a subtly new, decidedly modern construction of difference emerged along with a whole suite of material expressions. This new modern metaphor was the segregation of the "non-white" (Hale 1998; Mullins 1999:185–190).

It is clear, however, that "when one approaches a problem as important as that of taking inventory of the possibilities for understanding between two different peoples, one should be doubly careful" (Fanon 1967:84). Specifically, one needs to be wary of casting the oppressed as the dupes of the dominant ideology as "oppressed peoples everywhere understand that they are being oppressed" (Franklin 1997:34). Following this assertion, some researchers have stressed that enslaved/free black populations classified the landscape in which they lived in radically different ways than their enslavers and other free persons—thus, looking at multiple possible perceptions of the Van Winkle landscape is also an important area of future research (Kryden-Reid 1994; Epperson 1999b). In this vein it is tempting to look for agency and an

exercise of power in the postbellum relocation of quarters—a move that is not uncommon across the South. Further analysis of Feature 9 and further excavations at Feature 33 may provide a means to understand how enslaved and free African Americans saw Van Hollow's landscapes differently from each other and the other whites working in the hollow.

Cultural Memory in the Arkansas Ozarks: Constructions of the "Ozark Other" and Plantation Slavery

Why does this site, with its modernizing industrialization hand-in-hand with slavery in the Ozark Mountains, seem incongruous with conceptions of history? Finally, another type of terrain must be analyzed in order to understand Van Hollow's unique relationship to the history of the region—the landscape of cultural memory in the Arkansas Ozarks (Shackel 2001).

Needless to say, the Ozarks are known for neither the institution of slavery (Otto 1980) nor their industrial output. Rather an invented tradition that has been elsewhere called the "Ozark Traditional Myth" stresses isolated, rugged, and impoverished yeoman farmers who are the inspirations for such stereotypes as portrayed in the *Snuffy Smith* and *Lil' Abner* cartoons, *The Beverly Hillbillies* television show, and the infamous "folk" song *Arkansas Traveler* (Stewart-Abernathy 1987, 1992, 1999; Brandon et al. 2000:2). Indeed, these mythic conceptions of the upland South begin to be constructed just following the Civil War (contemporary with the mill's operation) through a complex series of popular culture phenomena such as local color writers, popular music, and folklorists (Harkins 1999; Horning 1999, 2001). These tropes served to "legitimize northern middle-class life by presenting the mountain South as the 'other'" and eventually spawning a type of ethnic identity that was both imposed upon and ambivalently adopted by the inhabitants of Appalachia and the Ozarks—characterizing them as backward, antiquated, lazy, and *exclusively* of Anglo-Saxon stock (Horning 1999:121–122; also Harkins 1999:5–6,74–81; Horning 2001:31). In short, the Southern mountaineer was seen as "the illiterate son of illiterate ancestors, cast loose in an immense wilderness without basic mechanical or agricultural skill" and "without refining, comforting and disciplining influence of an organized religious order, in a vast land wholly unrestrained by social organization or effective laws ..." (Caudill 1962:31). They were constructed as a "white other"; however, at the same time they were also seen as a "racially pure" segment of white America descended directly from immigrants from the British Isles (Harkins 1999:74)—a last bastion of hope against an increasingly diverse America "succumbing" to European and Asian immigrations and emancipated blacks.

This characterization may explain the 20th century "erasure" of upland slavery, Van Winkle's Mill, and Peter Van Winkle himself from Arkansas' historical narrative. Van Winkle, despite all of his worldly success and his role in the modernization of northwest Arkansas, is not a well-known historical figure outside a select group of local history scholars and families residing near (or tracing their lineages to) the hollow (Rothrock 1973; Hicks 1990)—no standing buildings, major roads, bridges, or other corporate institutions bear the Van Winkle name in the region.

As Van Winkle did not fit well into the Ozark mythos (Dutch ancestry, industrialist, progressive, modern, slave-holding, etc.), history seems to have favored more recent Ozark entrepreneurs who have "folksy" images more in accord with the myth (Sam Walton of Wal-Mart fame). In fact in the face of this larger "tradition" of recent vintage, Van Winkle's obituaries felt the need to explain his interest in "progress," industrialization, and other non-Ozarkian things as an aspect of his "Dutch blood" (Brandon et al. 2000:23). As already mentioned, Van Winkle's linage stretches back over seven generations to the New Amsterdam colony. Therefore his roots were probably deeper in the American soil than those who felt the need to explain him within the context of the larger naturalized Ozark tradition—he was no more Dutch than they were "Scotch-Irish." Likewise, the labor of Van Winkle's Mill has been erased from the landscape of historical memory, as both industrial enterprise and the enslavement of African Americans run counter to the "hillbilly" trope.

Another problematic set of notions illuminated by the work in Van Hollow has to do specifically with the enslavement of African Americans. Archaeology of the African Diaspora has, by and large, centered on plantation slavery in the lowland American South (Orser 1990; Singleton 1999:12–14). As our knowledge continues to grow regarding enslaved African Americans pressed into service in the agricultural economy of the South, however, attention should be focused on enslavement in other contexts, such as industrial settings, lest we run the risk of stereotyping the systems of enslavement and racialization. Recently, important work "beyond the plantation" has begun to shed light on Maroon settlements (Orser 1996; Deagan and Landers 1999), urban domestic slavery (Yentsch 1994; Herman 1999; Stewart-Abernathy 2004), and postemancipation race constructions (Mullins 1999; Orser 1999). Industrial slavery, however, still remains little studied by either Americanist archaeology or history (but see Dew 1994, and Shackle and Larsen 2000 for exceptions), even though as early as the 1850s, 5% of the enslaved population in the United States was engaged in industrial production—including as much as 20% of those working in bondage in urban areas (Shackel and Larsen 2000:23).

To date, however, most of the historical archaeology conducted in the Arkansas Ozarks has centered on the stereotypical protagonist of the myth—the Anglo-American yeoman farmer (Stewart-Abernathy 1986, 1987, 1992; Cande 1992). Few archaeological studies have centered on African Americans in the Ozarks (Santeford 1980:170–190), and almost none have explored the importance of industrial sites in the development of northwest Arkansas as a region. This stands in stark contrast with the lowland portion of the state where more African American sites in general (Buchner and Childress 1991; Weaver 1991; Buchner 1992; and even an industrial sawmill community that relied on black labor [Stewart-Abernathy 1982]), have been the subjects of archaeological assessments. This is probably due to the more accepted role that African Americans have been accorded in the history of that region. At any rate, this disparity goes a long way toward upholding the stereotype of the Ozark region as backward, nonindustrial, poor, and exclusively white.

Conclusions

Van Winkle's Mill has been examined on a number of levels. Van Winkle's use of a plantation model for the construction of his landscape, the careful separation of public (industrial) and private (domestic) zones in the landscape, and some of the changes that occurred following emancipation and the conclusion of the Civil War, all which have bearing on the implications of this landscape for the laborers who lived and worked in Van Hollow.

Van Winkle sought to create a plantation landscape at his industrial enterprise in the Ozark Mountains. His ideas were decidedly influenced by modernity, although they relied on a model long associated with the agrarian lowland South. This landscape, however, was destroyed by war and its re-creation reflected social changes not entirely of Van Winkle's making. Finally, both Van Winkle and the labor of Van Winkle's Mill were obscured by historical tropes that spring into being through modernity and the pronounced social shift that these actors lived through.

The sense that the South "shifted gears" after the war is by no means a new observation, and in northwest Arkansas the feeling of change (towards the "bigger and better") is evident in local histories. For instance, the Van Winkle hotel took a prominent position as "showplace" in this "new" northwest Arkansas:

> Fayetteville *removed the scars* of Civil War by rapidly replacing the structures destroyed with *larger and better buildings*. By the time the 1870s were coming to a close about 30 buildings had been erected in the town in a six month period. Among these was the Van Winkle Hotel on the north side of Center Street [emphasis added] (Donat 1995).

This shift did not just include the urbanization and industrialization of the South (i.e., its transmogrification into the "New South"), but it also meant a complete reorganization of the concept of race and its spatialization. No longer could the conflation of "black" and "slave" hold as they had since the 18th century (when they replaced the "Christian/non-Christian" trope [Issac 1982; Epperson 1999a]). In its stead stood a broader construction of opposed opposites—white versus nonwhite—that were increasingly seen as immutable and nonfluid (note that terms such as mulatto are present in the 1860 census and disappear in the 1870 census). The monumental *Plessy vs. Fergusson* decision codified in 1896 the post-reconstruction process (signaled in the 1880s and 1890s by laws segregating transportation and public spaces) that already seemed underway in 1870— the spatialization of race and the racialization of space underlying the refusal of larger American society (which was increasingly and self-consciously "white") to consider the possibility of racial mixing (Hale 1998:23).

Almost simultaneously, this larger American society created the "Ozark other," erasing the possibility of this local rupture in a region comprised of its backward, white "contemporary ancestors." To this day the ambivalent figure of the hillbilly complicates the region's relationship to the Civil War, slavery, modernization and any African American heritage.

An analogue can be found in Richard Flores's informed discussion of the Alamo as both reality and myth (Flores 1998, 2002). Flores emphasizes the means wherein the past and the present come together within a "memory-place." Flores concisely pinpoints when and why the Alamo, a crumbling and relatively unimportant building located in San Antonio's old downtown, came to be viewed as sacred ground, literally "The Cradle of Texas Liberty." Although it is stressed by Flores that the Texas Revolution was not fought along simple racial lines but, rather, along class lines and individual political interests, by the late-19th century the dominate Anglo culture in Texas (and the United States as a whole) needed a symbol and an appropriately distorted history to justify a social and economic oppression of Hispanics.

The "Remembering of the Alamo" and the "forgetting" of Peter Van Winkle as an historic figure (and by extension the free and enslaved labor of Van Winkle's Mill) strike similar though opposite resonances; Peter, his accomplishments, and steadfastness to modernity did not mesh with the 20th-century construction of the "Ozark Traditional Myth," which stresses instead isolation and a definite antimodernity; consequently, his very existence is downplayed to the point of erasure from the landscape he helped create.

ACKNOWLEDGMENTS

The authors would like to acknowledge the Arkansas Archeological Survey, the Little Rock District Corps of

Engineers (SWL) and the Arkansas State Department of Parks and Tourism (State Parks) for their support (both monetary and professional). In particular we would like to thank Jerry Hilliard, George Sabo, and Robert Mainfort for their support in time, input, and resources. Thanks to Robin Bowers who took the industrial history of the mill as the subject her master's thesis at the University of Arkansas. Thanks also to the large number of crew, volunteers, and students who made these excavations possible. A great debt is owed to Mark Clippinger, Steve Chryrchel, Christopher Davies, and others at State Parks and the SWL. Thanks are also due to Maria Franklin, Richard Flores, and Samuel Wilson of the University of Texas at Austin who have provided insightful comments from which we have benefited much. Additionally, we would like to thank Kerri Barile for her assistance with the analysis of the architectural photographs from the hollow. Finally, we would also like to thank Marilyn Larner Hicks—great, great, granddaughter of Peter Van Winkle—not only for her excellent work on the Van Winkle family history but also for her kind words and support of the project. Like State Parks and SWL, we hope that our relationship with Ms. Hicks continues in future investigations.

REFERENCES

ALLEN, THEODORE W.
1994 *The Invention of the White Race: Volume One*. Verso Press, London, England.

AIKEN, CHARLES S.
1998 *The Cotton Plantation South since the Civil War*. Johns Hopkins University Press, Baltimore, MD.

BENTON COUNTY DEMOCRAT
1904 No Title. *Benton County Democrat*, 12 May. Bentonville, AR.

BIRSHIR, CATHERINE W.
2000 Landmarks of Power: Building a Southern Past in Raleigh and Wilmington, North Carolina, 1885–1915. In *Where These Memories Grow: History, Memory, and Southern Identity*, W. Fitzhugh Brundage, editor, pp. 139–168. University of North Carolina Press, Chapel Hill.

BOURDIEU, PIERRE
1979 *Distinction: A Social Critique of the Judgment of Taste*, trans. R. Nice. Harvard University Press, Cambridge, MA.

BOWERS, ROBIN F.
2003 Ozark Industry: The Van Winkle Saw Mill, 1857–1890. Master's thesis, Department of Anthropology, University of Arkansas, Fayetteville.

BOYER, M. CHRISTINE
1994 *The City of Collective Memory: Its Historical Imagery and Architectural Entertainments*. MIT Press, Cambridge, MA.

BRANDON, JAMIE C.
2001 Van Winkle's Mill Revisited: A Report on Ongoing Excavations at a Late-Nineteenth-Century Sawmill Community in the Arkansas Ozarks. Paper presented to the 4th annual meeting of the South Central Historical Archaeological Society, Little Rock, AR.

BRANDON, JAMIE C., AND JAMES M. DAVIDSON
2003 Archeological Inventory and Testing of Cultural Resources at Van Winkle's Mill (3BE413) and Little Clifty Creek Shelter (3BE412), Beaver Lake, Benton County, Arkansas. Report to the U.S. Army Corps of Engineers, Little Rock District, Little Rock, from the Arkansas Archeological Survey, Fayetteville, AR.

BRANDON, JAMIE C., JAMES M. DAVIDSON, AND JERRY E. HILLIARD
2000 Preliminary Archeological Investigations at Van Winkle's Mill (3BE413), Beaver Lake State Park, Benton County, Arkansas, 1997–1999. Report to Arkansas Department of Parks and Tourism, Little Rock, from the Arkansas Archeological Survey, Fayetteville, AR.

BRANDON, JAMIE C., AND JERRY HILLIARD
1998 The Van Winkle Mill and the Anderson Slave Cemetery: African-American Related Sites in Northwest Arkansas. *African-American Archaeology*, 22(Fall):1.

BRANDON, JAMIE C., JERRY E. HILLIARD, AND JAMES M. DAVIDSON
1999 Return to Van Hollow: 1999 Excavations at a Nineteenth-Century Mill-Worker's Residence. *Field Notes*, 282(May/June):10–12.

BUCHNER, C. ANDREW
1992 Archaeological Investigations at the Lewis Site (3LE266): A Twentieth-Century Black-Owned Farmstead on the St. Francis Floodway, Lee County, Arkansas. Report to the U.S. Army Corps of Engineers, Memphis, from Garrow and Associates, Inc., Memphis, TN.

BUCHNER, C. ANDREW, AND MITCHELL CHILDRESS
1991 Archaeological Investigations at 3SF332L: An Early Mississippian and Tenant Period Site on Cutoff Bayou, St. Francis County, Arkansas. Report to the U.S. Army Corps of Engineers, Memphis, by Garrow and Associates, Inc., Memphis, TN.

CANDE, KATHLEEN H.
1992 The Ozarks as Destination: Data Recovery Excavations at the Lambert Farmstead, Mountainburg, Arkansas. Paper presented at the annual meeting of the Southeastern Archaeology Conference, Little Rock, AR.

CAUDILL, HARRY M.
1962 *Night Comes to the Cumberlands: A Biography of a Depressed Area*. Atlantic Monthly Press, Boston, MA.

COSGROVE, DENIS
  1984 *Social Formation and Symbolic Landscape*. University of Wisconsin Press, Madison.

CRUMLEY, CAROLE L.
  1997 A Dialectical Approach to Landscape. In *Carolina's Historical Landscapes: Archaeological Perspectives*, Linda F. Stine, Martha Zierden, Lesley M. Druker, and Christopher Judge, editors, pp. 23–33. University of Tennessee Press, Knoxville.

DEAGAN, KATHLEEN, AND JANE LANDERS
  1999 Fort Mose: Earliest Free African-American Town in the United States. In *"I, Too, Am America": Archaeological Studies of African-American Life*, Theresa Singleton, editor, pp. 261–282. University of Virginia Press, Charlottesville.

DEETZ, JAMES
  1997 *In Small Things Forgotten: An Archaeology of Early American Life*. Anchor Press, New York, NY.

DELLE, JAMES A., STEPHEN A. MROZOWSKI, AND ROBERT PAYNTER (EDITORS)
  2000 *Lines That Divide: Historical Archaeologies of Race, Class, and Gender*. University of Tennessee Press, Knoxville.

DEW, CHARLES B.
  1994 *Bond of Iron: Master and Slave at Buffalo Forge*. W.W. Norton and Company, New York, NY.

DONAT, PAT
  1995 The Van Winkle Hotel: A Fayetteville Showplace When It Opened in 1880. *Flashback*, 45(2):9–23.

EASLEY, BARBARA PICKERING, AND VERLA PICKERING MCANELLY (EDITORS)
  1996 *Obituaries of Washington County Arkansas, Volume I: 1841–1892*. Heritage Books, Bowie, MD.

EPPERSON, TERRENCE W.
  1999a The Contested Commons: Archaeologies of Race, Repression, and Resistance in New York City. In *Historical Archaeologies of Capitalism*, Mark Leone and Parker Potter, editors, pp. 81–110. Plenum/Klewer, New York, NY.
  1999b Constructing Difference: The Social and Spatial Order of the Chesapeake Plantation. In *"I, Too, Am America": Archaeological Studies of African-American Life*, Theresa Singleton, editor, pp. 159–172. University of Virginia Press, Charlottesville.

FANON, FRANTZ
  1967 *Black Skin, Black Masks*. Grove Press, New York, NY.

FLORES, RICHARD R.
  1998 Memory-Place, Meaning, and the Alamo. *American Literary History,* 10(3):428–445.
  2002 *Remembering the Alamo: Memory, Modernity, and the Master Symbol*. University of Texas Press, Austin.

FOUCAULT, MICHEL
  1970 *The Order of Things: An Archaeology of the Human Sciences*. Vintage Books, New York, NY.
  1977 *Discipline and Punish: The Birth of the Prison*. Vintage Books, New York, NY.
  1980 *Power/Knowledge*. Pantheon Books, New York, NY.

FRANKLIN, MARIA
  1997 *Out of Site, Out of Mind: The Archaeology of an Enslaved Virginian Household, ca. 1740–1776*. Doctoral dissertation, Department of Anthropology, University of California at Berkley, Berkeley, CA. University Microfilms International, Ann Arbor, MI.

FUNK, ERWIN
  1962 Flywheel of Van Winkle Sawmill Sold to Junk Man. *Benton County Pioneer,* 7(5):7–9. Bentonville, AR.

GOODSPEED PUBLISHING COMPANY
  1889 *Goodspeed's History of Benton, Washington, Carroll, Madison, Crawford, Franklin, and Sebastian Counties, Arkansas*. Goodspeed Publishing Company, Chicago, IL.

GRAMSCI, ANTONIO
  1971 *Selections from the Prison Notebooks*. International Publishers, New York, NY.

HALE, GRACE E.
  1998 *Making Whiteness: The Culture of Segregation in the South, 1890–1940*. Vintage Books, New York, NY.

HARKINS, ANTHONY A. R.
  1999 *The Hillbilly in Twentieth-Century American Culture: The Evolution of a Contested Icon*. Doctoral dissertation, History Department, University of Wisconsin at Madison, WI. University Microfilms International, Ann Arbor, MI.

HARVEY, DAVID
  1990 *The Condition of Postmodernity*. Blackwell Publishers, London, England.

HERMAN, BERNARD L.
  1999 Slave and Servant Housing in Charleston, 1770–1820. *Historical Archaeology,* 33(3):88–101.

HICKS, MARILYN LARNER
  1990 *Peter Marseilles Van Winkle (1814–1882): His Life and Times, His Ancestors Back to the Sixteenth Century and Most of His Descendants*. Henington Publishing, Wolfe City, TX.

HILLIARD, JERRY E.
  1997 A Brief Look at One of Northwest Arkansas' Largest Sawmills: The Van Winkle Site, 3BE413. *Field Notes,* 279(Nov./Dec.):10–12.

HORNING, AUDREY J.

1999 In Search of a "Hollow Ethnicity": Archaeological Explorations of Rural Mountain Settlement. In *Historical Archaeology, Identity Formation, and the Interpretation of Ethnicity*, Maria Franklin and Garrett Fesler, editors, pp. 121–137. Colonial Williamsburg Research Publications, Williamsburg, VA.

2001 Of Saints and Sinners: Mythic Landscapes of the Old and New South. In *Myth, Memory, and the Making of the American Landscape*, Paul Shackel, editor, pp. 21–46. University of Florida Press, Gainsville.

HUGHES, MICHAEL A.

2001 Wartime Gristmill Destruction in Northwest Arkansas and Military Farm Colonies. In *Civil War Arkansas: Beyond Battles and Leaders*, edited by Anne J. Bailey and Daniel E. Sutherland, pp. 31–45. University of Arkansas Press, Fayetteville.

ISAAC, RHYS

1982 *The Transformation of Virginia: 1740–1790*. W.W. Norton & Company, New York, NY.

JAMESON, FREDRIC

1991 *Postmodernism, or the Cultural Logic of Late Capitalism*. Duke University Press, Durham, NC.

JOHNSON, MATTHEW H.

1996 *An Archaeology of Capitalism*. Blackwell Publishers, Cambridge, MA.

JOHNSON, MARTHA SHERWOOD

1963 Bertha Blackburn Yeager Recounts The Van Winkle Home. *Benton County Pioneer*, 8(2):33–34. Bentonville, AR.

KEALHOFER, LISA

1999 Creating Social Identity in the Landscape: Tidewater, Virginia, 1600–1750. In *Archaeologies of Landscape: Contemporary Perspectives*, Wendy Ashmore and A. Bernard Knapp, editors, pp. 58–82. Blackwell Publishers, London, England.

KELSO, WILLIAM, AND RACHEL MOST

1990 *Earth Patterns: Essays in Landscape Archaeology*. University Press of Virginia, Charlottesville.

KRYDER REID, ELIZABETH

1994 "As Is the Gardener, So Is the Garden": The Archaeology of Landscape and Myth. In *Historical Archaeology of the Chesapeake*, Paul Shackel and Barbara Little, editors, pp. 131–148. Smithsonian Institution Press, Washington, DC.

LANGHORNE, WILLIAM T.

1976 Mill Based Settlement Patterns in Schoharie County, New York: A Regional Study. *Historical Archaeology*, 10:73–92.

LEFEBVRE, HENRI

1991 *The Production of Space*. Blackwell Publishers, London, England.

LEONE, MARK P.

1984 Interpreting Ideology in Historical Archaeology: Using the Rules of Perspective in the William Paca Garden in Annapolis, Maryland. In *Ideology, Power, and Prehistory*, Daniel Miller and Christopher Tilley, editors, pp. 25–35. Cambridge University Press, Cambridge, MA.

1995 Historical Archaeology of Capitalism. *American Anthropologist*, 97(2):251–268.

LEVINE, LAWRENCE

1988 *Highbrow/Lowbrow: The Emergence of Cultural Hierarchy in America*. Harvard University Press, Cambridge, MA.

MULLINS, PAUL R.

1999 *Race and Affluence: An Archaeology of African America and Consumer Culture*. Kluwer/Plenum Press, New York, NY.

ORSER, CHARLES E., JR.

1990 Archaeological approaches to New World Plantation Slavery. In *Archaeological Method and Theory, Vol. 2*, Michael Schiffer, editor, pp. 111–154. University of Arizona Press, Tucson.

1996 *A Historical Archaeology of the Modern World*. Plenum Press, New York, NY.

1999 Archaeology and the Challenges of Capitalist Farm Tenancy in America. In *Historical Archaeologies of Capitalism*, Mark Leone and Parker Potter, editors, pp. 143–167. Kluwer Academic Publishers, New York, NY.

ORSER, CHARLES E., AND ANNETTE M. NEKOLA

1985 Plantation Settlement from Slavery to Tenancy: An Example from a Piedmont Plantation in South Carolina. In *The Archaeology of Slavery and Plantation Life*, Theresa Singleton, editor, pp. 67–91. Academic Press, New York, NY.

OTTO, JOHN S.

1980 Slavery in the Mountains: Yell County, Arkansas 1840–1860. *Arkansas Historical Quarterly*, 39(1): 35–52.

RAFFERTY, MILTON D.

2001 *The Ozarks: Land and Life*. University of Arkansas Press, Fayetteville.

ROTHROCK, THOMAS

1973 Peter Manelis Van Winkle. *The Arkansas Historical Quarterly*, 32(1):61–70.

SANTEFORD, LAWRENCE

1980 The Conway Water Supply: An Intensive Archeological and Historical Survey of a Proposed Reservoir Area in Conway County, Arkansas. *Arkansas Archeological Survey Research Report, No. 20*. Arkansas Archeological Survey, Fayetteville.

SAVAGE, KIRK
    1999   *Standing Soldiers, Kneeling Slaves: Race, War, and Monument in Nineteenth-Century America.* University of Princeton Press, Princeton, NJ.

SHACKEL, PAUL A. (EDITOR)
    2001   *Myth, Memory, and the Making of the American Landscape.* University of Florida Press, Gainesville.

SHACKEL, PAUL A., AND DAVID L. LARSEN
    2000   Labor, Racism, and the Built Environment in Early Industrial Harper's Ferry. In *Lines That Divide: Historical Archaeologies of Race, Class, and Gender,* James Delle, Stephen Mrozowski, and Robert Paynter, editors, pp. 22–39. University of Tennessee Press, Knoxville.

SINGLETON, THERESA A.
    1999   An Introduction to African American Archaeology. In *"I, Too, Am America": Archaeological Studies of African-American Life,* Theresa Singleton, editor, pp. 1–17. University of Virginia Press, Charlottesville.

SMITH, TED J.
    1995   Slavery in Washington County, Arkansas, 1828–1860. Master's thesis, Department of History, University of Arkansas, Fayetteville.

SOJA, EDWARD W.
    1989   *Postmodern Geographies: The Reassertion of Space in Critical Social Theory.* Verso Press, London, England.

STEWART-ABERNATHY, LESLIE C.
    1982   The Black Community at Sawdust Hill: Graphic Documentation of the Historic Occupation of the Parkin Site (3CS29). Manuscript, Arkansas Archeological Survey, Fayetteville.
    1986   The Moser Farmstead, Independent but Not Isolated: The Archeology of a Late-Nineteenth-Century Ozark Farmstead. *Arkansas Archeological Survey Research Series No. 26.* Arkansas Archeological Survey, Fayetteville.
    1987   From Memories and from the Ground: Historical Archaeology at the Moser Farmstead in the Arkansas Ozarks. In *Visions and Revisions: Ethnohistoric Perspectives on Southern Cultures,* George Sabo and William M. Schneider, editors, pp. 98–113. University of Georgia Press, Athens.
    1992   Industrial Goods in the Service of Tradition: Consumption and Cognition on an Ozark Farmstead before the Great War. In *The Art and Mystery of Historical Archaeology: Essays in Honor of James Deetz,* Ann Yentsch and Mary Beaudry, editors, pp. 101–126. CRC Press, Boca Raton, FL.
    1999   From Famous Forts to Forgotten Farmsteads: Historical Archaeology in the Mid-South. In *Arkansas Archaeology: Essays in Honor of Dan and Phyllis Morse,* Robert C. Mainfort and Marvin Jeter, editors, pp. 225–244. University of Arkansas Press, Fayetteville.

    2004   Separate Kitchens and Intimate Archaeology: Constructing Urban Slavery on the Antebellum Cotton Frontier in Washington, Arkansas. In *Household Chores, Household Choices: Theorizing the Domestic Sphere in Historical Archaeology,* Kerri Barile and Jamie Brandon, editors, pp. 51–74. University of Alabama Press, Tuscaloosa.

STINE, LINDA F., MARTHA ZIERDEN, LESLEY M. DRUKER, AND CHRISTOPHER JUDGE (EDITORS)
    1997   *Carolina's Historical Landscape: Archaeological Perspectives.* University of Tennessee Press, Knoxville.

UNITED STATES BUREAU OF THE CENSUS
    1850   *United States Manuscript Census: 1850.* Washington, DC.
    1860   *United States Manuscript Census: 1860.* Washington, DC.

VLACH, JOHN M.
    1993   *Back of the Big House: The Architecture of Plantation Slavery.* University of North Carolina Press, Chapel Hill.

WEAVER, GUY
    1991   Analysis and Interpretation of Artifact Collections from Site 3CT271, Randolph Estate Development, Crittenden County, Arkansas. Report to the U.S. Army Corps of Engineers, Memphis, from Garrow and Associates, Inc., Memphis, TN.

WORRELL, JOHN, MYRON O. STACHIW, AND DAVID M. SIMMONS
    1996   Archaeology from the Ground Up. In *Historical Archaeology and the Study of American Culture.* Winterthur/University of Tennessee Press, Knoxville.

YAMIN, REBECCA, AND KAREN BESCHERER METHENY (EDITORS)
    1996   *Landscape Archaeology: Reading and Interpreting the American Historical Landscape.* University of Tennessee Press, Knoxville.

YENTSCH, ANNE E.
    1994   *A Chesapeake Family and Their Slaves: A Study in Historical Archaeology.* Cambridge University Press, Cambridge, MA.

JAMIE C. BRANDON
THE UNIVERSITY OF TEXAS AT AUSTIN
DEPARTMENT OF ANTHROPOLOGY
AUSTIN, TX 78712-1086

JAMES M. DAVIDSON
UNIVERSITY OF FLORIDA
DEPARTMENT OF ANTHROPOLOGY AND
AFRICAN AMERICAN STUDIES
GAINESVILLE, FL 32611-7305

Eric L. Larsen

Integrating Segregated Urban Landscapes of the Late-Nineteenth and Early-Twentieth Centuries

ABSTRACT

The period of legal segregation in the United States is characterized in modern thought as a system of racial separation prevalent in the South around the first half of the 20th century. Separation implies a spatiality that seems to lend itself to a landscape study. In problematizing such a study, it becomes clear that the spatial signs of segregation are markers in a complex system of identity building and maintenance relationships. The association of identity politics with cultural landscape analysis provides a picture of segregation that pushes beyond the bounds of African American neighborhood or residential sites. Examining three turn-of-the-20th-century sites in Annapolis, Maryland, provides an example of how archaeology, in examining urban contexts, has a role in how this period of segregation is perceived.

Introduction

Every little Southern town is a fine stage-set for Southern tradition to use as it teaches its children the twisting turning dance of segregation. Few words are needed for there are signs everywhere. White ... colored ... white ... colored ... over doors of railroads and bus stations, over doors of public toilets, over doors of theaters, over drinking fountains ... And there are the invisible lines that turn and bend and cut the town into segments. Invisible, but electrically charged with taboo. Places you go, places you don't go. White town, colored town; white streets, colored streets; front door, back door. Places you sit. Places you cannot sit ..." (Smith 1994: 95–96).

In the days of segregation ... it did not hit us as a student that much. Well, we learned afterwards, of course. We were happy where we were and the things we did. We weren't aware of the differences in education, in differences in all the kinds of things that were different. That didn't hit us at all. Subsequent to that, of course, we learned (Jopling 1991).

Racism was in the air I breathed in North Carolina. It was not an issue because it didn't ever come up. I was born in a segregated hospital run by the Episcopal Church. There was a black hospital fifteen blocks away... . I went to segregated schools; my church was a segregated church. It never occurred to me that it was any other way than that (Spong 2000).

I was always aware, you always knew that you were black. You could look and see that you were! And certain things you could do and certain things you couldn't do. You were always aware of that. (Jopling 1991).

The racial segregation that developed in the United States in the period following Reconstruction was simultaneously a means of suppressing individual rights and freedoms based on racism, and it was a means of maintaining a [perceived] status quo. Local custom and formal law literalized the metaphor of keeping African Americans "in their place." The use of the term *place* is an apt one as the practice of segregation took on a sense of spatial struggle. The signs posted over doorways and water fountains of public areas not only delineated space but also served as signifiers of black difference and white belonging. This sort of racial bounding extended beyond the liminal areas of the train station and steamship dock and on into the everyday landscapes of many towns and cities of the late-19th and early-20th centuries.

Despite this phenomenon, remembrances, many of them coming from individuals who were children during the later years of segregation, often give a sense of a lack of consciousness to the presence of segregation in people's everyday lives. This is, perhaps, the result of childhood perceptions but may also indicate the degree of segregation's integration into the social landscape—the degree that people were able to "get along" within the social customs of their communities. Realizations of segregation often accompanied episodes of conflict. This may be on a personal level, such as an experience of being denied service at a local restaurant (Jopling 1991), or on a larger, more national level as with the conflicts associated with the Civil Rights Movements of the 1950s and 1960s. These conflicts took place in doorways or at checkout counters. Sometimes conflict took place in the courthouses at the hands of judge and jury; sometimes conflict took place as outdoor "spectacles" (Hale 1998) at the hands of lynch mobs. Outright conflicts may have been sporadic, but, nonetheless, they left the cultural landscape charged.

With the end of formal segregation, the signs have come down. Restaurants and stores no longer overtly discriminate in providing service. Societal norms no longer openly dictate where people can or cannot buy a home. One assumes these broad social changes also affected landscapes. A question arises. What became of the landscapes of segregation? This question's importance builds as urban sites and neighborhoods become topics of historical archaeological inquiry. Where do our responsibilities lie in sorting out these landscapes and what became of them? Archaeology from late-19th and early-20th-century African American sites in Annapolis, Maryland, provides a chance for a preliminary look at these questions.

Multiplicity of Spatialities and Identities

All landscape studies create representations of the spaces under examination, even those critical of the represented norms. In examining the representations of modern urban centers, political economist, Saskia Sassen (1996:183) hoped to establish an "intellectual dialogue on the subject of race and gender ... in the city." In doing so, she examines moments where traditional economic systems of representation intersect with representations associated with identity politics. Some clarification of "identity politics" is probably necessary.

The last 20 years have seen an explosion of literature on identity stemming from many different disciplines. Identity appears as an often used but largely underdeveloped concept. Its use, as of late, is closely associated with elaborations of power relationships and with the forging of a political stance based on one's historical and cultural background (Best and Kellner 1991:203–204). Most of this writing emphasizes the politics of identity through the now well-ensconced academic concepts of race, gender, and class.

Identity politics has, for many, come to take on a particular (and often pejorative) meaning. In this sense it means political activity based upon an often-essentialized identity. It is a largely conscious utilization of identity by individuals, with someone donning an identity for political purposes. This is part (but only part) of the meaning of identity politics used here.

Individuals do make conscious choices in using identity, but identities are also placed upon individuals. Individuals, however, are also bodies that are inscribed with meaning from outside of themselves (Sassen 1996). Katherine Verdery (1994:35), in addressing ethnicity, describes this sort of duel process as being one of self-ascription and ascription. This, she suggests, focuses analytic attention on the possible manipulation of identities and on their "situational" character. There is a multiplicity present in this view that acknowledges that an individual can be active in identity building but cannot escape structure.

Sassen moves toward theorizing presences that are not commonly represented. In her attempt, she finds herself examining moments where traditional economic systems of representation intersect with representations formulated through critical theory in feminism as well as art and architecture. Acceptance and use of multiple representations provides opportunity to look at "analytical moments ... experienced as spaces of silence, of absence" (Sassen 1996:185). Once recognized it becomes necessary to see what happens in those spaces.

Twenty years ago, the business district was a primary focus of successful city centers. Corporate headquarters and successful retail ventures were plums for a city's reputation; they had become the spaces of power. In examining the growing focus on the role of business districts on the urban economy, Sassen (1996:183) notes, "In the last twenty years we have seen the expulsion and continuing exclusion from the center of significant components of the economy and a sharp increase in earnings inequality." She goes on to remind us "many of these components are actually servicing the center."

In thinking of the corporate world of these business districts, we often envision a blue-suited executive working in [most often] his office. These are the common perceptions of the movers and shakers of big city business districts.

> The fact that most of the people working in the corporate city during the day are low-paid secretaries, mostly women, many immigrant or African American women, is not included in the representation of the corporate economy or corporate culture. And the fact that at night a whole other work force installs itself in these spaces, including the offices of the chief executives, and inscribes the space with a wholly different culture (manual labor, often music, lunch breaks at midnight) is an invisible event (Sassen 1996:193).

The significance of these more numerous corporate roles is often downplayed or ignored in representations of urban economic centers. Sassen wishes to valorize these roles by constructing a new narrative about the city. This work provides an interesting framework from which to begin an archaeological examination of landscapes of segregation.

The segregated city landscapes of the late-19th and early-20th centuries might also benefit from this kind of illumination—something that goes beyond marking black and white spaces and the boundaries between them, to examinations of how the two sides articulated. Historical archaeology, in admirable attempts to listen to "the silent men and women of the modern past" (Orser 1996:160–161), has been primarily marking difference by identifying race, ethnicity, gender, etc., in the material record. Much of African American archaeology's success has come from "finding" evidence of enslaved individuals in the archaeological record. This endeavor has been important work. However, because archaeology is an additive discipline, new questions naturally arise. Sassen (1996:192) finds the "lived in city contains a multiplicity of spatialities and identities." Archaeology, now able to identify some of these, needs to question further how they interrelate. Landscape seems to be one avenue for this pursuit.

Landscape archaeology (Kelso and Most 1990; Yamin and Metheny 1996) and identity politics (Best and Kellner 1991) each have their own sets of definitions, rules, boundaries, and narratives. Archaeology is typically grounded at the level of the site, the location of analysis and interpretation, and generally tends to carve up and describe space in analytical units, frozen in time or otherwise essentialized. Identity politics, on the other hand, emphasizes the interplay of multiple identities, both self-described and inscribed from without, and has often focused on analysis of the "body" as the site of this interchange. It would be perhaps useful to blend these somewhat disparate concepts together in an attempt that would introduce movement into examinations of landscape and push the bounds of our analytical units.

Identity and Space

In addressing identity through archaeology, one is confronted with the simultaneity of identities from different levels. Typically these are presented in hierarchical form (from the individual, to household, neighborhood, cities, regions, national identity, etc.) in which the parts (individuals) and wholes (society) are interrelated. Much discussion has occurred over the appropriate level for archaeological study (Beaudry 1984; Schuyler 1988; Orser 1996). The result has largely been the emphasis of one above others. This work, however, hopes to maintain the multiplicity of identities—the messiness of pluralism. Archaeological sites hold the results of the everyday workings of multiple identities; it, therefore, makes sense to attempt including them whenever possible in interpretations.

The last 20 years have also seen a growing recognition of space as culturally produced. This is clearly evident in the body of work coming from geographers (Tuan 1977; Meinig 1979; Daniels and Cosgrove 1988), sociologists (Shields 1991; Zukin 1991), architects (Hillier and Hansen 1984), and anthropologists (Olwig and Hastrup 1997). Events, such as the renaming of Custer Battlefield National Monument to Little Bighorn National Monument (Linenthal 1993) or the disputes erupting from the initial handling of the African Burial Grounds in Manhattan (Harrington 1993; LaRoche and Blakey 1997), show an increasingly conscious merging of identity politics with the politics of space.

Landscape

Landscape has come to mean more than simply visual experience. Landscapes encompass both place and space but also refer to something lived or dwelled in. Recent studies (Ingold 1993; Thomas 1993; Matthews 1998) have used Heidegger's concept of *dwelling*, which infers a casual, unthinking relationship, where the landscape is both product and shaper of human action. Ingold (1993:155) holds,

> a place owes its character to the experiences it affords to those who spend time there—to sights, sounds, and indeed smells that constitute its specific ambience. And these, in turn, depend on the kinds of activities in which its inhabitants engage. It is from this relational context of people's engagement with the world, in the business of dwelling, that each place draws its unique significance.

Through an emphasis on "relational context," landscape has come to be viewed increasingly as process. Seeing the complex daily interplay of these social/spatial relationships is reliant upon a close examination of the particulars of everyday practices. The conversations and silences, meetings and avoidances, even the fences and gates serve as the loci of identity generation and reinforcement.

Examinations of the development of nations and their borders provide examples of this sort of process. Peter Sahlins (1989) provides an account of the development of the boundary between France and Spain and, ultimately, of the making of French and Spanish identities. In noting the gradual and rather flexible demarcations made during the 17th, 18th, and 19th centuries, Sahlins notes that physical boundary itself is of little significance to those in its immediate proximity. The processes—the ever-changing definitions of *us* and *them*—however, have much wider social consequences when one considers the ramifications of taking on the identity of being French or Spanish.

Neighborhood studies provide another example (one relevant to urban landscapes) of this process. An urban neighborhood of the late-19th and early-20th centuries, was a less-imagined community (cf. Anderson 1983). In other words, neighborhoods were delimited settings where one could reasonably expect to see and even know by name others living around them, but the everyday social connections remained unclear.

Neighborhoods are lived-in spaces where inhabitants interact and share daily activities. They are often comprised of people who share some common characteristics such as ethnicity, religion, or class (Rothschild 1987, 1990). Residents as well as outsiders who may be just passing through recognize a sense of neighborhood through perceived associations. This is often more a feeling or reckoning than a list of delineated relationships.

Despite being somewhat familiar entities, neighborhoods remain ambiguous in many urban studies, often presented as a set of material characteristics belonging to a specific area, as having some common economic interest (such as used in many consumer choice and class studies), or as an identity holder/marker (as with studies of ethnic neighborhoods). For all the ability to delineate boundaries, measure demographics, and quantify characteristics, working definitions of neighborhoods have not been able to fully

characterize the dynamic social relationships of these communities. The term *neighborhood* remains vague, though recent work in landscape studies (stemming from a variety of disciplines) sheds some light on this vagueness.

That neighborhoods are spatial in nature is a given. Their spatiality, however, has been interpreted in differing ways. For some, space is purely an object to be measured and defined, something to be filled out as with a boilerplate for a report. Here, space serves merely as a backdrop or scenery in which events take place. For others, there exists more active "mental space[s]" (Lefebvre 1974:3). These are defined largely by the authors of the studies in order make their particular points. Here space can be found in varieties such as economic, demographic, sociological, ecological, political, or national spaces.

Space has also been conceived as the location of practice or dwelling. Geographer Yi-Fu Tuan (1977) provides a helpful move towards this direction. Tuan relates *and* differentiates the terms *space* and *place*. "'Space' is more abstract than 'place.' What begins as undifferentiated space becomes place as we get to know it better and endow it with value. ... if we think of space as that which allows movement, then place is pause; each pause in movement makes it possible for location to be transformed into place" (Tuan 1977:6). Landscapes, through place or spatialities, reflect the multiplicities evident in the identities of the people that inhabit them.

Annapolis, Maryland: A Case Study

There seems to be an idea prevailing among some of our colored citizens that they have not received the proper recognition from our county school authorities that they should have, ... There are 24 public colored schools in this county, and 27 colored teachers. The school levy is predicated upon the entire property of the county, and the distribution of the school fund is made according to the population. The whole amount of school taxes paid by the colored people of this county does not exceed $900.

The state appropriates $6,812.40 for the colored schools of this county, and they receive in all $7,082.15 ... . Under the law, the total amount of taxes paid for school purposes by the colored people not only of this county, but of every county in this State, ... together with any donations that may be made for the purpose, is entirely devoted to the maintenance of the schools for colored children ... . The amount of school taxes paid by the colored people of this county would not pay for the keeping open of three schools. It will thus be seen that the school law of this State is very liberal towards the colored schools, and the amount distributed by the county school authorities is equally so, and instead of our colored people complaining, they should congratulate themselves and our school board over the great facilities that have been granted them (*Evening Capital* 1884:4).

The above newspaper story makes clear that the major concepts of segregation were in place by the 1880s—less than 20 years after the end of the American Civil War and the abolishment of slavery in the United States. Many of the principle arguments that would prevail over the first half of the 20th century are exemplified here. African Americans were noting the inequality of public services and that this was contrary to the spirit of equal treatment under the law. The counter argument outlines a continued paternalism that ignores what had been taken from African Americans for generations and suggests that, in terms of economics, African Americans should be satisfied with the services they receive.

It is clear that segregation was an important ordering principle in the post-Reconstruction South (Hale 1998). Segregation's practice across the South, however, undoubtedly varied (Johnson 1943). Each community must be understood in terms of its specific context.

Annapolis, as part of the upper South, perhaps did not often show the extremes of segregation, but this fact does not suggest that it was not there or that it was not significant. While the state of Maryland never passed legislation limiting voting rights (disenfranchisement that obliquely but purposely targeted African Americans), in 1908 Annapolis tried on the local level and succeeded for a number of years (Callcott 1967). The disenfranchisement plan restricted the vote to males or their descendants entitled to vote prior to 1868, to naturalized citizens and their descendants, or to persons owning more than $500 worth of assessed property (Callcott 1967:225–226). The Annapolis provision was deemed unconstitutional in a Supreme Court decision in 1915. An environment of racism, however, is clearly evident in Annapolis.

It was during this period, around the first decade of the 20th century, that Jim Crow legislation affecting train and steamship travel was first introduced in Maryland. These required all railroads and steamships to provide separate cars or compartments and to segregate the races within such facilities. The laws took effect 1 July 1904 (Callcott 1967:218–219). While other states had lived with segregated transportation facilities since the 1896 Plessy v. Ferguson decision, such provisions were new to Maryland African Americans, and there was resentment at the change. An African American law professor from Howard University, W. H. Hart, when traveling from Pennsylvania to the District of Columbia, refused to change to a segregated car while traveling through Maryland. He was promptly arrested and fined. Upon appeal, however, the Maryland Court of Appeals ruled the statute was an "infringement upon interstate commerce and that only passengers whose journey began and ended in the State of Maryland could legally be segregated by state law" (Callcott 1967:219). This was not the end of the Jim Crow provision but, instead, a reinforcement of localized practices.

Subsequent ordinances followed, further refining the Jim Crow laws. Legislation in 1908 required steamship companies to provide separate toilets and sleeping quarters for white and black passengers. Another act required railroads to provide separate cars, rather than compartmented ones, for use in the heavily African American counties of Prince George's, Charles, St. Mary's, Calvert, and Anne Arundel (where Annapolis is located) counties (Callcott 1967:222). This environment undoubtedly reflected the environment of informal segregation of the races.

Segregation in Annapolis was not without violence either. Several instances of lynchings are evident during the 1870s and 1880s (Mullins 1999:68). The *Evening Capital* (1886:2), a local Annapolis newspaper, suggested, "Judge Lynch is having a busy time of it"—making light of the practice within the region. Later, the hanging of John Snowden by the court system would become a well-known and controversial case. Snowden maintain his innocence throughout but was convicted of rape and murder of a white woman and sentenced to death. Though convicted, 11 members of the jury signed a petition requesting the death sentenced be commuted. Despite such beliefs and petitions, Snowden was hanged in the Calvert Street jail yard on 28 February 1919 (*Evening Capital* 1919a:1). The *Evening Capital* also printed an anonymous letter from the victim's jilted lover, which admitted, "I am sorry you killed Snowden today. He is not a guilty man. I am the man" (*Evening Capital* 1919b:1). All of this suggests that the racial environment of Annapolis, like many Southern urban areas, was charged.

This period undoubtedly spurred the conception of the existence of two Annapolises. Two photo histories of Annapolis were published during the 1990s: *Then Again, Annapolis, 1900–1965* (Warren 1990) and *The Other Annapolis, 1900–1950* (Brown 1994). The first is a mainstream history and photo collection. *The Other Annapolis* is the author's, "attempt, by means of the written word, appropriate pictures and other visual aids, to chronicle and create a picture in the minds of readers of what life was like for the colored segment of the Annapolis population living in racially segregated Annapolis during the first half of the twentieth century" (Brown 1994:7). Philip L. Brown (1994:8) felt it both necessary and important to create a record of the African American community of this time period, "preserving this era of African-American history as a part of the overall history of the city of Annapolis." This community was and continues to be through the mainstream histories, a largely neglected part of Annapolis as a whole.

Archaeology of African Americans in Annapolis

Over the last few decades, considerable effort has gone into examining the history and archaeology of African Americans. Many scholars have worked to establish artifact patterns (Ferguson 1992), diet and nutritional scales (Otto 1984; Reitz, Gibbs, and Rathbun 1985), architecture (Jones 1985), and settlement plans (Lewis 1985; Orser and Nekola 1985) for African American contexts. Much of this archaeology has centered on slavery and plantation contexts.

The nature of this work has changed drastically. A brief look at the historiography provides a stark contrast of how the subject has been approached over the years. African Americans have often been portrayed (most often through neglect) as absorbed into the larger culture, especially in the historic periods following the American Civil War. More recent work, however, acknowledges the maintenance of a distinct and sometimes outwardly resistant identity.

Barbara Fields (1985) for example, describes African Americans making conscious choices regarding their own participation in the capitalist economy. In this type of literature, racial identity is viewed as an adaptive strategy. Other historians, for example Grace Hale (1998), have also written of the strictures placed upon African Americans by white America during this period. This documents a process of creating whiteness through opposing it to the "other"—blackness.

Since 1988, Archaeology in Annapolis has excavated three post-Civil War African American sites (Figure 1). Each excavation recovered a

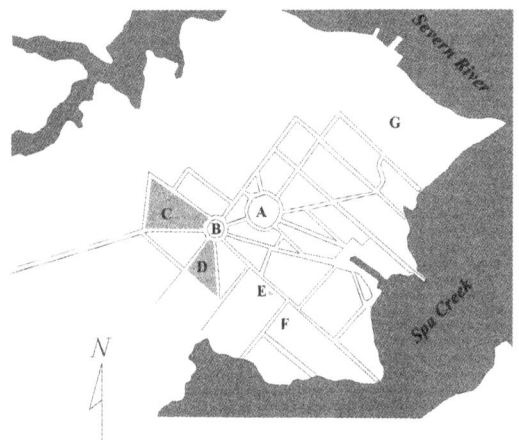

FIGURE 1. Map of Annapolis. (*A*) State Circle, (*B*) Church Circle, (*C*) Gott's Court Site, (*D*) Courthouse Site, (*E*) Maynard-Burgess Site, (*F*) Bryan Alley, (*G*) U.S. Naval Academy.

significant volume of material culture, including ceramics, glass, food remains, and other household refuse acquired, used, and discarded by African Americans.

The first of these sites excavated was Gott's Court (Warner 1992). Gott's Court (Figure 2) was a series of 25 connected, two-story wooden houses built around 1906 and occupied by African American renters until the early 1950s. The Court was located on the interior of a city block within sight of Maryland's State House dome, yet largely invisible from the surrounding streets.

Although archival research for these excavations suggested the area was first surveyed and occupied in the early part of the 18th century, little archaeological evidence could be discerned

FIGURE 2. Map of Gott's Court block, ca. 1913. (*A*) Jail, (*B*) Gott's Court.

dating prior to about 1750–1760. The area was divided into large town lots, and in the last half of the 18th century developed into a mixed residential and commercial/industrial use. During the 19th century, the large lots were subdivided and saw continued mixed commercial and residential use. Around the periphery of the block, long narrow lots took shape, with multifamily houses replacing the larger single-family dwellings of earlier years. This pattern held into the present century. But as undeveloped urban land became scarcer, the interior of the block was also transformed. Just after the turn of the century, the interior was developed into low-rent housing as Gott's court took shape (Warner 1992).

Excavations at Gott's Court provided several insights into African American archaeology.

Perhaps most significant was that excavated artifacts could stimulate dialogue between archaeologists and African American communities. This is exemplified by the identification by an African American informant of a straightening comb made of steel, archaeologists having failed to determine the object's function.

> The archaeologists initially surmised that straightening hair was an effort to assimilate, but this notion was quickly rejected by most African Americans. They instead saw the comb as an artifact which was used merely to give the appearance of assimilation. Indeed, some African Americans saw racism in the archaeologists' initial inability to recognize hair straightening as a conscious social strategy. The archaeologists were forced to acknowledge that this single object and all its associated cultural connotations could have quite different meanings between different contemporary and historical communities (Leone, et. al. 1995:8–9).

The assemblage as a whole suggested that African American consumption strategies are subtle in their differences.

In 1990, Archaeology in Annapolis carried out preliminary investigations of the Courthouse block (Warner and Mullins 1993). Excavations suggested that the area of the Courthouse block was open space during the bulk of the 17th and 18th centuries. Archaeological visibility increased greatly for the 19th- and 20th-century habitation of the block (Figure 3). Assessment records dating to 1860 note 17 houses dispersed between 19 lots on the block. By the turn of the century there were nearly 50 dwellings encircling the block (Larsen 2001). Rich deposits from these periods were uncovered during the 1990 excavations, including house basements, a partial barrel privy, and a dog burial.

Subsequent excavations (Aiello and Seidel 1995) set out to address the potential for 17th-century occupation of the site as well as three areas of interests expressed by members of the local African American community: (1) there was particular interest in learning more about the people living in the six-unit alley dwellings known as Bellis Court (like Gott's Court, Bellis Court was built around the turn of the 20th century and located within the interior spaces of the Courthouse block); (2) there was expressed interest in the archaeology related to Mt. Moriah A.M.E. Church and the associated Parish house located a few doors down the street from the church; and (3) the community wanted to learn

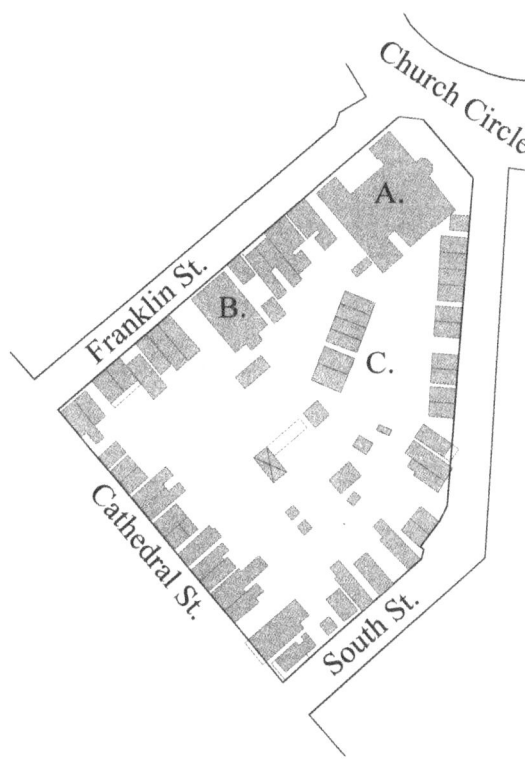

FIGURE 3. Map of Courthouse Site block, ca 1913. (*A*) Anne Arundel County Courthouse building, (*B*) Mt. Moriah A.M.E. Church, (*C*) Bellis Court.

Excavations at the Maynard-Burgess House, an African American owned and occupied household used between 1850 and 1980 (Mullins and Warner 1993), examined the conscious choices made regarding African American relationships with the larger society. Paul Mullins and Mark Warner, using the archaeological record from two household assemblages from the site, looked for similarities to strategies outlined in a 1930s study of African American consumption (Edwards 1932). For example, the number of bottled goods was noted as higher than those found at other comparable sites excavated in Annapolis. Many of these were identified as nationally known products and were interpreted as a possible protection from dependence upon local merchants. Faunal remains note a "preponderance of fish" and suggest the reliance upon resources available from the nearby Chesapeake Bay that may have "promoted a social independence that allowed African Americans to circumvent White Annapolitan merchants or butchers" (Mullins and Warner 1993:125).

This was the beginning of the important detailed studies examining participation of African Americans in the consumer culture, and the racism present in American consumer culture (Mullins 1996, 1999). Mullins holds, that

> All American consumers were racial subjects defined by their distance from, and reproduction of, the ideal, tacitly White consumer, regardless of whether they articulated their identity in purely racial terms. Blacks and Whites occupied opposing ends of the racial spectrum used to resolve and legitimize social and material inequalities through reference to a contrived amalgam of biology, history, culture, and behavioral discipline (Mullins 1999:4).

The stigmatization of racial subjects would bolster the fiction of white racial unity and legitimize White privilege. "Pervasive investment in a racialized America has ensured that the conflicted instability of White identity remains an unexplored and relatively undefined subject" (Mullins 1999:5).

African American Neighborhoods in Annapolis

African Americans have, over most of Annapolis's history, consistently comprised about one-third of the town's population. In 1850, one quarter of Annapolis's entire free population

more about the businesses present on the block during this period (Sanborn Fire Insurance Maps and city directories suggest the presence of several businesses on the block, including small grocery stores, a cobbler, a jeweler, a candy store, and a tailor's shop).

Fieldwork was able to locate Bellis Court. Sampling was done for the backyards of these dwellings, and a substantial privy relating to the court was found and partially excavated. A smaller barrel privy, believed to be associated with the church's parish house was found and excavated. Examination of the businesses on the block was hampered by earlier development. Many of the businesses fronted South Street where residences were torn down in the 1940s to make room for an earlier Courthouse expansion. Fortunately, the 1990 excavations touched on the backyard of the tailor's shop and provided some material related to businesses on the block. Buttons and pins were present, but little else suggested this to be any different from the other residences on the block.

was African American, and before the Civil War, more free African Americans lived in Maryland than in any other state. The appearance of distinct African American neighborhoods, however, did not come about until after the Civil War. During the second half of the 19th century, enclaves or clusters of African American Annapolitans become recognizable—clustering characterized as the product of increasing geographic and social isolations (Ives 1979:130). Upon further examination, however, it becomes clearer that these enclaves were not completely racially exclusive and were further dispersed across the city of Annapolis (despite appearances in Figure 1). While increased isolations based on race are apparent, the reality of this small urban area did not allow for entirely separate lives.

It was through identifying these clusters that archaeologists came to target the sites at Gott's Court and the Courthouse block (Logan 1998). However, these groupings of five or more African American residences (evident from maps, census records, and city directories) seem to defy current beliefs about the segregated South. These were not shantytowns or wrong-side-of-the-tracks places. Indeed, because the clusters were scattered across Annapolis, it is difficult to even speculate as to where the tracks were, let alone figure out which was the wrong side.

James Borchert (1980) described a dispersed pattern of African American residency for Washington, DC. This was a pattern of an outwardly visible social class, living in residences fronting the streets and avenues that literally encompassed and obscured another social group residing within the blocks' interiors. Rather than creating large ghettos, alley communities were hidden behind the homes that lined the streets. Several of Annapolis's African American clusters also include alley dwellings or low-cost housing located in the interiors of city blocks. Gott's Court (Figure 2), Bellis Court (Figure 3), and Bryan Alley (Figure 4) are three examples of this type of housing in Annapolis. While alley dwellings tended to be located within or near black enclaves, they were not characteristic of Annapolis's African American community. Bellis Court, part of the Courthouse block, was surrounded by homes that were occupied not by whites but by other African Americans, including several of Annapolis's African American professionals and business owners (Mullins and

Warner 1993; Aiello and Seidel 1995). The alley communities in Annapolis, unlike the pattern described by Borchert, are perhaps more (and/or additionally) representative of class distinction within the African American community than of racial segregation. They do not fully represent or define the composition of Annapolis's African American community.

In turning to the work lives of Annapolis's African American residents, it too becomes clear that the small urban area did not allow for entirely separate lives. The United States Naval Academy at Annapolis hired many African Americans to work on campus and in other support roles for normal operations (Brown 1994). St. John's College provided jobs similar to those available at the Naval Academy but on a smaller scale. The local restaurants and hotels that served politicians who came to the state capital when the Maryland legislature was in session also depended upon African Americans for labor as maids, waiters, porters, bellhops, and maintenance. While African American contributions were made marginal (made unimportant by being unacknowledged or simply unseen), it is clear that they provided vital services to the very

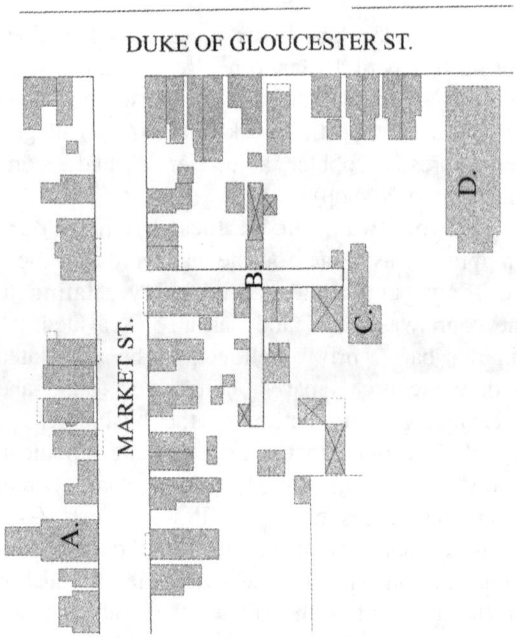

FIGURE 4. Map of Bryan Alley, ca 1913. (A) First Baptist Church (African American), (B) Bryan Alley, (C) "Negro School," (D) St. Mary's School.

institutions that kept Annapolis from becoming a complete backwater community during the 19th and early-20th centuries (Matthews 1998).

It becomes increasingly evident that segregation's practice in Annapolis was not meant to isolate. Instead it appears, like Sassen's (1996) realization that representations of corporate space and power mask the multiplicity of identities in workplaces, segregation was a means of dealing with contested spaces and identities. An appearance of clarity—"African-American space" and "Annapolis space"—is imposed to contain the multiplicity. The result is the [continuing] marginalization of African Americans by creating the appearance that they were unnecessary to the everyday workings of the city.

Conclusions

Landscapes of urban segregation are landscapes of conflict. They may not hold the bloodstained soils of a battlefield, but they are the locations for struggle and pain. There are clearly two established sides to the conflict: those who are among those who belong and those designated as the "other." It is a system rife with inequity. Its goal was to maintain a special status for whiteness, and yet it never reached resolution. The status quo was always under threat, and segregation was always an unfinished product.

The marginalizing of African Americans was meant to create an "other" in an unspoken opposition to whiteness. It always had the potential, however, to backfire. The creation of separateness was perhaps the stated goal. The signs, the neighborhoods, the societal norms of noninteraction are all outward signs of this, but the creation of a black world was not the intent. Black doctors, lawyers, ministers, and businesses threatened the idea of African Americans as marginal "others." It flew in the face of beliefs in racial supremacy (Hale 1998).

Archaeology, through examining the material record from sites attributed to African American occupations, has focused attention on the issue of separation and separate identity building. This has been important work that has led archaeologists to begin to recognize the presence of a black world that had always been present but went largely unseen. It has opened a doorway into a far more complex understanding of the past.

The African American households and communities being studied are clearly products of segregation. If, however, it follows that segregation is not about separation but more about representation, then this very work falls subject to the very racial premises that underlie past practices of segregation.

Some archaeology is beginning to press beyond examining the African American community at home and looking to the vital presences of African Americans in American culture (Mullins 1999). It can now be seen that the frontlines of racial segregation—the immediate landscapes of conflict—take place in the marketplaces, at work, and otherwise around the city.

ACKNOWLEDGMENTS

I wish to thank Paul Shackel, first, for inviting me to contribute to this special volume but, subsequently, for having patience with me as I put aside work to deal with a death in the family. Thanks also for your comments on a very shaky preliminary draft. I am also indebted to the two readers for their time and efforts in slogging through some very murky thoughts. The comments were very helpful—the remaining murkiness is completely my own.

REFERENCES

AIELLO, ELIZABETH A., AND JOHN L. SEIDEL
  1995 Three Hundred Years in Annapolis: Phase III Archaeological Investigations of the Anne Arundel County Courthouse Site (18AP63), Annapolis, Maryland, Vols. I and II. Report prepared by Archaeology in Annapolis, Department of Anthropology, University of Maryland, College Park, MD.

ANDERSON, BENEDICT
  1983 Imagined Communities: Reflections on the Origin and Spread of Nationalism. Verso, New York, NY.

BEAUDRY, MARY C.
  1984 Archaeology and the Historical Household. Man in the Northeast, 28:27–38.

BEST, STEVEN, AND DOUGLAS KELLNER
  1991 Postmodern Theory: Critical Interrogations. The Guilford Press, New York, NY.

BORCHERT, JAMES
  1980 Alley Life in Washington: Family, Community, Religion, and Folklife in the City, 1850–1970. University of Illinois Press, Urbana.

BROWN, PHILIP L.
1994 *The Other Annapolis, 1900–1950*. The Annapolis Publishing Company, Annapolis, MD.

CALLCOTT, MARGARET LAW
1967 The Negro in Maryland Politics, 1870–1912. Doctoral dissertation, University of North Carolina, Chapel Hill.

DANIELS, STEPHEN, AND DENIS COSGROVE
1988 Introduction: Iconography and Landscape. In *The Iconography of Landscape: Essays on the Symbolic Representation, Design, and Use of Past Environments*, S. Daniels and D. Cosgrove, editors. Cambridge University Press, Cambridge, NY.

EDWARDS, PAUL
1932 *The Southern Urban Negro As a Consumer*. Reprinted in 1969 by Negro University Press, New York, NY.

EVENING CAPITAL
1884 Want Better School Facilities. *Evening Capital*, 30 June 1884:4. Annapolis, MD.
1886 Judge Lynch. *Evening Capital*, 1 April 1886:2. Annapolis, MD.
1919a Big Funeral Closes Last Snowden Chapter. *Evening Capital*, 3 March 1919:1. Annapolis, MD.
1919b Anonymous Letter Writer Says He Is Brandon Murderer. *Evening Capital*, 3 March 1919:1. Annapolis, MD.

FERGUSON, LELAND G.
1992 *Uncommon Ground: Archaeology and Early African America, 1650–1800*. Smithsonian Institution Press, Washington, DC.

FIELDS, BARBARA JEANNE
1985 *Slavery and Freedom on the Middle Ground: Maryland during the Nineteenth Century*. Yale University Press, New Haven, CT.

HALE, GRACE ELIZABETH
1998 *Making Whiteness: The Culture of Segregation in the South, 1890–1940*. Vintage Books, New York, NY.

HARRINGTON, SPENCER P. M.
1993 Bones and Bureaucrats: New York's Great Cemetery Imbroglio. *Archaeology*, 16(2):28–38.

HILLIER, BILL, AND JULIENNE HANSON
1984 *The Social Logic of Space*. Cambridge University Press, New York, NY.

INGOLD, TIMOTHY
1993 The Temporality of Landscape. *World Archaeology*, 25:152–174.

IVES, SALLIE M.
1979 Black Community Development in Annapolis, Maryland, 1870–1885. In *Geographical Perspectives on Maryland's Past*, R. D. Mitchell and E. K. Muller, editors, pp. 129–149. Department of Geography, University of Maryland, College Park.

JOHNSON, CHARLES S.
1943 *Patterns of Negro Segregation*. Harpers and Brothers Publishers, New York.

JONES, STEVEN L.
1985 The African American Tradition in Vernacular Architecture. In *The Archaeology of Slavery and Plantation Life*, Theresa A. Singleton, editor, pp. 195–214. Academic Press, New York, NY.

JOPLING, HANNAH
1991 Interview Transcripts from Archaeology in Annapolis African American Archaeological Project. Manuscript, Archaeology in Annapolis, Department of Anthropology, University of Maryland, College Park.

KELSO, WILLIAM, AND RACHEL MOST (EDITORS)
1990 *Earth Patterns: Essays in Landscape Archaeology*. University Press of Virginia, Charlottesville.

LAROCHE, CHERYL J., AND MICHAEL L. BLAKEY
1997 Seizing Intellectual Power: The Dialogue at the New York African Burial Ground. *Historical Archaeology*, 31(3):84–106.

LARSEN, ERIC L.
2001 Phase I/II Report for the Banneker-Douglass Museum Expansion: The Courthouse Site (18AP63), 86–90 Franklin Street, Annapolis, Maryland. Report prepared by Archaeology in Annapolis, Department of Anthropology, University of Maryland, College Park.

LEFEBVRE, HENRI
1974 *The Production of Space*. Translated in 1991 by Donald Nicholson-Smith. Basil Blackwell, Cambridge, MA.

LEONE, MARK P., BARBARA J. LITTLE, MARK S. WARNER, PARKER B. POTTER, JR., PAUL A. SHACKEL, GEORGE C. LOGAN, PAUL R. MULLINS, AND JULIE A. ERNSTEIN
1995 A Plan for the Archaeology of Ethnicity in Annapolis, Maryland. Department of Anthropology, University of Maryland, College Park.

LEWIS, KENNETH E.
1985 Plantation Layout and Function in the South Carolina Lowcountry. In *The Archaeology of Slavery and Plantation Life*, Theresa A. Singleton, editor, pp. 35–66. Academic Press, New York, NY.

LINENTHAL, EDWARD TABOR
1993 *Sacred Ground: Americans and Their Battlefields*. University of Illinois Press, Chicago.

LOGAN, GEORGE C.
1998 Archaeologists, Residents, and Visitors: Creating a Community-Based Program in African American Archaeology. In *Annapolis Pasts: Historical Archaeology in Annapolis, Maryland*, Paul A. Shackel, Paul R. Mullins, and Mark S. Warner, editors, pp. 69–90. University of Tennessee Press, Knoxville.

MATTHEWS, CHRISTOPHER NELSON
1998 Annapolis and the Making of the Modern Landscape: An Archaeology of History and Tradition. Doctoral dissertation, Department of Anthropology, Columbia University, New York, NY.

MEINIG, DONALD W. (EDITOR)
1979 *The Interpretation of Ordinary Landscapes: Geographical Essays.* Oxford University Press, New York.

MULLINS, PAUL R.
1996 The Contradictions of Consumption: An Archaeology of African America and Consumer Culture, 1850–1930. Doctoral dissertation, Department of Anthropology, University of Massachusetts, Amherst.
1999 *Race and Affluence: An Archaeology of African America and Consumer Culture.* Kluwer Academic/Plenum Publishers, New York, NY.

MULLINS, PAUL R., AND MARK WARNER
1993 *Final Archaeological Investigations at the Maynard-Burgess House (18AP64): An 1850–1980 African American Household in Annapolis, Maryland.* Two volumes. Archaeology in Annapolis, Historic Annapolis Foundation, Annapolis, MD.

OLWIG, KAREN FOG, AND KIRSTEN HASTRUP (EDITORS)
1997 *Siting Culture: The Shifting Anthropological Object.* Routledge, New York.

ORSER, CHARLES E., JR.
1996 *A Historical Archaeology of the Modern World.* Plenum Press, New York, NY.

ORSER, CHARLES E., JR., AND ANNETTE M. NEKOLA
1985 Plantation Settlement from Slavery to Tenancy: An Example from a Piedmont Plantation in South Carolina. In *The Archaeology of Slavery and Plantation Life*, Theresa A. Singleton, editor, pp. 67–96. Academic Press, New York, NY.

OTTO, JOHN S.
1984 *Cannon's Point Plantation, 1794–1860: Living Conditions and Status Patterns in the Old South.* Academic Press, Orlando, FL.

REITZ, ELIZABETH J., TYSON GIBBS, AND TED A. RATHBUN
1985 Archaeological Evidence for Subsistence on Coastal Plantations. In *The Archaeology of Slavery and Plantation Life*, Theresa A. Singleton, editor, pp. 163–194. Academic Press, New York, NY.

ROTHSCHILD, NAN A.
1987 On the Existence of Neighborhoods in 18th-Century New York: Maps, Markets, and Churches. In *Living in Cities: Current Research in Urban Archaeology*, Edward Staski, editor. Special Publication Series No. 5: 29–37. Society for Historical Archaeology, California, PA.
1990 *New York City Neighborhoods, the 18th Century.* Academic Press, New York, NY.

SAHLINS, PETER
1989 *Boundaries: The Making of France and Spain in the Pyrenees.* University of California Press, Los Angeles.

SASSEN, SASKIA
1996 Analytic Borderlands: Race, Gender, and Representation in the New City. In *Re-Presenting the City: Ethnicity, Capital, and Culture in the 21st-Century Metropolis*, Anthony D. King, editor, pp. 183–202. New York University Press, New York.

SCHUYLER, ROBERT L.
1988 Archaeological Remains, Documents, and Anthropology: A Call for a New Culture History. *Historical Archaeology*, 22(1): 36–42.

SHIELDS, ROB
1991 *Places on the Margin: Alternative Geographies of Modernity.* Routledge, New York, NY.

SMITH, LILLIAN
1994 *Killers of the Dream.* W.W. Norton and Co., New York, NY.

SPONG, JOHN SHELBY
2000 "Here I Stand." Interview for *The Diane Rehm Show.* National Public Radio, broadcast 24 February.

THOMAS, JULIAN
1993 The Politics of Vision and the Archaeologies of Landscape. In *Landscape Politics and Perspectives*, Barbara Bender, editor, pp. 19–48. Berg Publishers, Ltd., Providence, RI.

TUAN, YI-FU
1977 *Space and Place: The Perspective of Experience.* University of Minnesota Press, Minneapolis.

VERDERY, KATHERINE
1994 Ethnic Groups and Boundaries: Past and Future. In *The Anthropology of Ethnicity: Beyond "Ethnic Groups and Boundaries,"* Hans Vermeulen and Cora Govers, editors, pp. 33–58. Het Spinhuis, Amsterdam, Netherlands.

WARNER, MARK S.
1992 Archaeological Excavations at Gott's Court (18AP52). Department of Anthropology, University of Maryland, College Park.

WARNER, MARK S., AND PAUL R. MULLINS
1993 Phase I-II Archaeological Investigations on the Courthouse Site (18AP63), an Historic African American Neighborhood in Annapolis, Maryland. Archaeology in Annapolis, Historic Annapolis Foundation, Annapolis.

WARREN, MAME
1990 *Then Again: Annapolis, 1900–1965.* Time Exposures Limited, Annapolis, MD.

YAMIN, REBECCA, AND KAREN B. METHENY (EDITORS)

1996 *Landscape Archaeology: Studies in Reading and Interpreting the Historical Landscape.* University of Tennessee Press, Knoxville.

ZUKIN, SHARON

1991 *Landscapes of Power: From Detroit to Disney World.* University of California Press, Berkeley.

ERIC L. LARSEN
DEPARTMENT OF ANTHROPOLOGY
UNIVERSITY OF MARYLAND, COLLEGE PARK
COLLEGE PARK, MD 20742

www.ingramcontent.com/pod-product-compliance
Lightning Source LLC
Chambersburg PA
CBHW080944120626
46546CB00010B/2835

* 9 7 8 1 9 5 7 4 0 2 3 3 8 *